First edition: October 2013   Reprint: **1** (September 2014)

© L.I.L.Y. Publishing

Via Tirso, 8 20141 Milan (Italy)

ISBN: 9788890912214

www.mccartney-recordings.com

e-mail: info@mccartney-recordings.com

Facebook: https://www.facebook.com/paulmccartneyrecordingsessions

Editor: Luca Perasi and Laura Angioni.

Cover Art: Lorenzo Fignon – LGF Grafiche Formazione/Deborah Gatti

Cover photo: © Corbis

Translation: Chuck Rolando and Luca Perasi.

PAUL MCCARTNEY: RECORDING SESSIONS (1969-2013)

A Journey Through Paul McCartney's Songs After The Beatles

Luca Perasi

ACKNOWLEDGMENTS:

Carlos Alomar, Kevin Armstrong, Pete Beachill, Stephanie Bennet, Mark Berry, Robin Black, Brian Blood, Carlos Bonell, John Bradbury, Geoffrey Brand, Adrian Brett, Alan Broadbent, John Lang Brown, Ron Carter, David Clayton, John Clayton, Tony Clark, Tony Coe, Jerry Conway, Carl Davis, Chris "Snake" Davis, Richard Davis, Neil Dorfsman, Pedro Eustache, Frank Farrell, Brent and Clare Fischer, Martyn Ford, Greg Hawkes, Gary Herbig, Richard Hewson, Steve Holley, Gordon Hunt, Laurence Juber, David Juritz, Brian Kay, Gary Kettel, James Kippen, John Leach, John Leckie, Steve Lyon, Wil Malone, Jerry Marotta, Dave Mattacks, Dave Matthews, Bazel Meade, Richard Niles, Leo Nocentelli, Dave O'Donnell, Marty O'Donnell, Alan O'Duffy, Lance Phillips, David Pogson, George Porter jr., Maurizio Ravalico, David Rhodes, Denny Seiwell, Kenneth Sillito, Chris Spedding, Marvin Stamm, Mike Stavrou, Stan Sulzmann, Tim Summerhayes, Joby Talbot, Michael Thompson, Fiachra Trench, Mike Vickers, Graham Ward, Stephen Wick, Ernie Winfrey, Bill Wolfer.

Special thanks to Laura, my parents and family, Chuck Rolando, Steve Lambley, Piero Tarantola, Alessandro Gariazzo, Silvia Drago, Giacomo Polignano, Eva Teichmann, Franco Zanetti, Rolando and Alice Giambelli, Vincenzo Oliva, Roger Stormo, Edward Eikelenboom, Steve Marinucci, Ken Michaels, Joshua Lapin-Bertone, Chaz Lipp, Andre Gardner, James Rosen, Donnie Gentile, Craig Erb, Greg Heet.

Index   pag.

FOREWORD by Tony Clark

Wrote a letter to Abbey Road a long time ago
Got an interview and went with the flow
Met The Beatles, Sir John Barbirolli and
Jacqueline Du Pré
Yet as a young tea boy did not have much to say
But as my journey through time went along
Had a chat with Paul about a song
Then decided at trying to be an engineer
My passion for sound soon became very clear
Made lots of records in a room on the first floor
Cut 'Paperback Writer' to add one more
'Thrillington', Wings and 'Press To Play'
Paul once said "we go back a long way"
It has been my pleasure and good fortune
To be part of his journey for more than one afternoon
So within these pages of Luca Perasi's book
I trust you will try and take a good look
And learn of this great songwriter's gift
That creates within us such an emotional shift

Tony Clark ©   "Have music will travel"

TAKE IT TONY!

Last year, I got in touch with Tony Clark. We agreed to have an initial conversation and I was very excited and honored to speak with the engineer that saw the birth of the first Wings' album, *Wild Life*. He witnessed an historical moment since it was Paul McCartney in the studio with a group, again after The Beatles. I could sense his passion for music as something unique: and we went on and on with further conversations. Something magical has happened: a human relationship was born.

As every human relationship, it has to be fed with sincere gestures and a direct knowledge. I asked him for a brief foreword to my second edition of the Italian book and he responded with great enthusiasm. He surprised me coming up with this poem that you could read above: it sums up his entire career and life in an amazing way. Poetry expresses what it's almost impossible to express in other terms. Then, in March 2013, I invited Tony to participate to a presentation that I held in London, at The Italian Bookshop. He came and had a warm reception from the audience. I asked him my questions and he had the chance to tell a couple of nice stories of his experience in the studio with Paul McCartney.

To have Tony Clark in my book it's not only prestigious, since his great career in music: it derives from a human connection between us. Tony often say, 'dreams come true': he make things happen. His energy, passion and sincerity actually drives me to make the best of my ideas. This book is the biggest of dreams and it came true. (Luca Perasi)

INTRODUCTION "Recording it's a bit like being in a laboratory" (Paul McCartney)

"Compose something more... But let it be short, easy and popular (...) What is slight can still be great, if it's written in a natural, flowing and easy style. Such works are more difficult to compose than all those harmonic progressions which the majority of people cannot fathom": these words – written by Leopold Mozart to his son Wolfgang Amadeus in a letter dated August 13th, 1778 – perfectly encapsulate the essence of Paul McCartney's music.

I preferred to approach one of the most incredible song catalogues in pop music in the simplest way possible. Since I don't like looking at things in hindsight, I chose to name each chapter indicating the year from 1969 to 2013, presenting a flow of events and recordings in the order in which they happened (at least, according to the sources available) instead of relying on the release dates of albums, singles and CDs. In this sense, it is an "historical" book! It seemed to me the best key to following McCartney's solo career and his creative path, without judging too much (but of course, you'll find some of my tastes included...). Facts. As they happened. And when.

Unlike The Beatles – who composed, recorded and issued almost everything in real time (it's no coincidence that the only album issued some time after his recording, *Let It Be*, marked the end of the group) – McCartney's solo career reversed this trend. A lot of recordings, but also a lot of second thoughts, with songs that remained unreleased for decades or that were never released at all. Fragmented publications, and a little bit of schizophrenia.

A virtually never-ending creative flow, that was not organized in order or by McCartney's ability to judge his own material, something that is required to manage such an enormous collection of songs.

To reconstruct the recording studio process, recording dates and studios, musicians involved, I relied upon different sources. Records – official and unofficial – newspaper articles, magazines (with a special mention to Edward Eikelemboom's Dutch fanzine *Maccazine*), interviews given by McCartney or by his collaborators over the years, books (I owe a lot to *Eight Arms to Hold You*, published in 2000 by Chip Madinger and Mark Easter and to Keith Badman's *The Beatles. The Dream Is Over-Off the Record 2* and *The Beatles. After the Break-Up 1970-2000*), Websites (another special mention goes to Chris Brewer's site http://webpages.charter.net/ram71/). Last but not least, I had the opportunity to personally interview many players and other people who were involved in those sessions. Their recollections and memories – although with some comprehensible gaps – allowed me to confront and check a lot of information, in some cases discovering new things, in other cases correcting what I assumed for years to be the case.

That was the only way to try to tell the history of Paul McCartney's recording sessions, specifying where and when the sessions took place, which musicians were involved, playing which instrument.

Gaps, doubts and question marks are still there. I do my best to point out in the clearest way – when it was impossible to discover exactly which studio was used, on which date the song was recorded or who played which particular instrument – if the information is uncertain.

To credit exactly which musicians play on Paul McCartney's records is quite a hard task. Apart from the records where he played all instruments, there's a lack of information on all his Seventies records, from *RAM* to *Back to the Egg*. Even later on, records such as *Pipes of Peace* or *Press to Play* list musicians but without assigning them to a particular track. This is without even considering errors, omissions and other oddities.

Based upon musicians' recollections, arrangers' and engineers' memories, McCartney's interview, articles and – of course – official credits, I tried to build a complete list of musicians for each song. I followed some simple rules.

As a songwriter and composer of popular music, McCartney likes to lay down his songs playing the lead instrument on which he wrote the song. Generally speaking, during the recording of the basic tracks, Paul plays acoustic guitar or piano, leaving any other instruments to the group – if there's one – (e.g lead guitar, bass, tambourine, organ) and overdubbing his bass parts later.

This process of perfecting his bass parts as the final touch of his recording dates back to The Beatles' days. During the *RAM* sessions, guitarist David Spinozza noticed that Paul never played bass while recording with him and drummer Denny Seiwell. Another example comes from the *Driving Rain* sessions: the inner sleeve notes indicate that McCartney overdubbed bass on all the songs.

In some cases – mainly when the song has a straight rock'n'roll structure – McCartney recorded the track as a band number, thus acting as the group bass player: "Hi Hi Hi" or "Give Ireland Back to the Irish" (recording sessions for which were witnessed by engineers John Leckie and Tony Clark, both interviewed in this book) are just two examples.

During his Wings' years, when he was on piano for the recording (such as "My Love", "Let'Em In") he left the bass to Laine or McCulloch: there was no need to have a too complex bass on those songs. He also likes to add a large number of overdubs himself, often without any involvement from others. After he built his own recording studio in Sussex, this process of overdubbing on his own became the rule for McCartney. Even when he's backed by a group, Paul handles a lot of electric guitar parts, including solos: during the *Wild Life* sessions he stated that he fancied playing electric guitar solo parts. He replaced drummers and guitarist quickly, becoming a session-man for himself: he did so for *Band on the Run* or *London Town* when members of the group left.

Paul's records are a showcase for his ability as a multi-instrumentalist, who handled such oddities like ukulele, spinetta, harpsichord, harmonium, clavioline, tambourine, gong, tubular bells, chimes, auto-harp… And the list goes on.

Memory Almost Full could be considered a prime example of the McCartney recording process: although his band (Abe Laboriel Jr., Brian Ray, Rusty Anderson and Wix) received full credit for playing on half of the album, further research shown that in some cases he replaced (almost) all their instrumental contributions. Brian Ray's bass parts were deleted and re-recorded by the man himself! And Brian did this "ghost work" perfectly aware that his role was simply to help McCartney building the basic track.

When he records alone (*McCartney*, *McCartney II*, *Electric Arguments*), Paul usually lays down a drum track first. His recording technique of drums often sees him splitting the parts (bass-drum with snare then cymbals, toms and drum rolls) to different tracks: track sheets included in the *McCartney II* Deluxe Edition prove it, as well as a couple of interviews I've done that you'll find in this book.

Last but not least, I tried to indicate which kind of bass McCartney used during each group of sessions, according to the official information, to photographs and videos appeared over the years: I hope you'll like it.

This book includes all the songs officially released on record and composed by Paul McCartney – written by him or co-written – during his solo career as well as the sessions he took part in as a musician and composer, when he released records under a pseudonym. I'm not dealing with covers: the book is a tribute to one of the most important composers of our era.

Through the 383 song sheets, you'll discover the stories behind each one of them: who (or what) inspired them, how they were initially conceived and then developed in the studio, when and where they were recorded, their harmonic structure, what the lyrics tell, when they were issued (UK release dates were given priority) and when they were performed live.

Comparing the song to a child's growth in the first years of his life, we can say we're going to witness its conception, its birth and development, also explaining its character.

It's a long journey through over 40 years of music, in which McCartney crossed paths with different genres (jazz, black-music, music-hall, classical). Driven by the desire to make his music an encyclopedia of languages, McCartney has shaped them time and again, adapting them to the many styles of popular music. For this, he will clearly be remembered in music history.

This book is mostly translated from the Italian version, first published in February 2012 and then re-issued in a second updated edition in March 2013.

It was a huge success: during an extensive promotional tour through bookstores (including one in London!), Beatles Festivals and Beatles Days, evenings and fairs, everyone suggested I do an English version of it. When I began working on it, I gathered more and more information and so this version has been vastly expanded in comparison to the Italian one.

I wish to thank all the musicians, arrangers and producers that worked with McCartney through the years and who shared their recollections and memories with me: Carlos Alomar, Kevin Armstrong, Pete Beachill, Stephanie Bennet, Robin Black, Brian Blood, Carlos Bonell, John Bradbury, Geoffrey Brand, Adrian Brett, Alan Broadbent, John Lang Brown, David Clayton, John Clayton, Tony Clark, Tony Coe, Carl Davis, Chris "Snake" Davis, Richard Davis, Neil Dorfsman, Pedro Eustache, Frank Farrell, Brent and Clare Fischer, Martyn Ford, Greg Hawkes, Gary Herbig, Richard Hewson, Steve Holley, Gordon Hunt, Laurence Juber, David Juritz, Brian Kay, Gary Kettel, James Kippen, John Leach, John Leckie, Steve Lyon, Wil Malone, Jerry Marotta, Dave Mattacks, Dave Matthews, Bazel Meade, Dr. Richard Niles, Leo Nocentelli, Dave O'Donnell, Marty O'Donnell, Alan O'Duffy, Lance Phillips, David Pogson, George Porter Jr., Maurizio Ravalico, David Rhodes, Denny Seiwell, Kenneth Sillito, Marvin Stamm, Chris Spedding, Mike Stavrou, Stan Sulzmann, Tim Summerhayes, Joby Talbot, Michael Thompson, Fiachra Trench, Graham Ward, Stephen Wick, Ernie Winfrey, Bill Wolfer.

Luca Perasi

1969

Around Christmastime, Paul began recording some songs playing all the instruments himself – just for fun – on his Studer J37 four-track recorder.

Later (January 22nd-February 25th, 1970), he started doing a series of more conventional sessions. Initially, he used the pseudonym Billy Martin – famous second baseman for the New York Yankees – to book Morgan Studios in Willesden. Here, he overdubbed his home-made songs and recorded some new tracks, under Robin Black's technical supervision. Finally, the last recordings and mixing were done at Abbey Road.

The end product of those recordings was Paul's first solo album simply titled *McCartney*. In all, seventeen songs were taped, including three unreleased instrumental tracks: "Cavendish Parade", "Rupert Guitar" – an early version of a song that Paul would record in the following *RAM* sessions, under the title "When the Wind is Blowing" – and "Backwards Guitar Piece".

According to the information included in the press kit sent out with the album at the time, McCartney played Martin acoustic guitar, Fender Telecaster and Epiphone Casino electric guitars, Premier drums and Rickenbacker bass.

1 The Lovely Linda (Paul McCartney)

Recording: December, 1969 **Location:** Cavendish Avenue, London **Release:** April 1970, *McCartney*

The dominant influence on McCartney's solo career was the presence of Linda Eastman. While Linda was not taken seriously by music critics, she has always represented a beacon of reference and a psychological support for Paul; an inexhaustible source of inspiration, she was the muse that allowed McCartney to compose a great many songs.

It is emblematic that the song which would open a new pathway for Paul was dedicated to her; McCartney recorded this acoustic snippet – that was only forty-four seconds long – overdubbing a nice bass and drumming on a book so as to get the percussion effect. "The Lovely Linda" was the track Paul used to sound-test his recorder.

McCartney: "The record is me playing around the house. You hear Linda walking through the living room doorway out to the garden, and the door squeaks at the end of the tape."[1]

The lyrics portray an almost Petrarch-like image of Linda: "She often used to wear flowers in her hair, so it's a direct diary"[2], were Paul's words. It is the portrait of a carefree, happy moment and the hiccupping laugh at the end captures its essence. As Paul said at the time, this recording was an anticipation of the full version of "The Lovely Linda", recorded perhaps shortly thereafter. McCartney tried to complete it with another fragment in Mariachi style and

---

[1] Timothy White, *Paul McCartney On His Not So Silly Love Songs*, in *Billboard*, March 2001.
[2] *Ibid.*

if this recording exists, it remains, to date, unreleased. After the *McCartney* album, the song was included in a string quartet version in *Working Classical* (1999) and in the *Wingspan* collection (2001); for the TV special Paul improvised "The Lovely Linda" on acoustic guitar.

Musicians:

Paul McCartney vocals, acoustic guitar, bass, percussion

2 That Would Be Something (Paul McCartney)

Recording: December, 1969 **Location:** Cavendish Avenue, London **Release:** April 1970, *McCartney*

Rediscovered by a wider audience only in 1991 – when it was dusted off and brought out for an acoustic rendition on the TV show *Unplugged* – "That Would Be Something" is actually one of the *McCartney* tracks that Paul has always liked ("It's very *McCartney*, very me", he declared).

According to Mark Lewisohn's *The Complete Beatles Chronicle*, "That Would Be Something" had been rehearsed with The Beatles during the *Get Back!* sessions in January 1969, but there's no evidence of this performance. The recording included in *McCartney*, done with "only one mike"[3], captures the best features of this track with a folk feel to it that would not have been out of place on the *White Album*.

Despite its hodgepodge structure, "That Would Be Something" is a clear example of McCartney's effectiveness in a recording studio. Mainly, the song is based on a single refrain and the core idea is made interesting thanks to variations on the central theme by means of a "layering" process. The guitar riffs, the tom-toms, the cymbals in syncopation and even Paul's unusual vocals all contribute to the rupestrian simplicity of the track.

The version included in the live album *Unplugged* – and later performed in the *Secret Gigs Tour* (1991) – is arranged with a country flair, with some beautiful slide-guitar by Robbie McIntosh, making it a "minor classic" to be enjoyed. This merely confirms the fact that, "Paul should have disciplined himself to have created less and perfected more."[4] Harrison said: "I think this track is really very good."[5] McCartney played an acoustic version in the *Wingspan* TV special.

Musicians:

Paul McCartney vocals, acoustic and electric guitar, bass, drums

3 Valentine Day (Paul McCartney)

Recording: December, 1969 **Location:** Cavendish Avenue, London **Release:** April 1970, *McCartney*

A tribute to Saint Valentine's Day, it is the first instrumental track recorded during the *McCartney* sessions and was added, as Paul noted, "with more concern for testing the machine

---

[3] Detail taken from: *The McCartney Self-Interview*, 1970.

[4] Bob Woffinden, *The Beatles Apart*, 1981, p.36.

[5] Keith Badman, *The Beatles. The Dream Is Over-Off the Record 2*, 2002, p.9.

than anything else."[6] Not even Paul recalled exactly how the recording went: "Acoustic guitar first, then drums (maybe drums were first)."[7]

Without too many qualms, Paul allowed himself the satisfaction of releasing his homemade recordings on *McCartney*. "Valentine Day" is a short guitar improvisation, composed "as I went along", which ends as soon as it starts, without ever getting to the heart of it.

Musicians:

Paul McCartney acoustic and electric guitar, bass, drums, percussion

4 Momma Miss America (Paul McCartney)

Recording: December, 1969 **Location:** Cavendish Avenue, London **Release:** April 1970, *McCartney*

Another of Paul's homemade recordings, this is a long instrumental, "made up as I went along"[8]: in fact, the track was clearly ad-libbed, if what McCartney says is true, that it was added to the album "on the spot."[9]

"Momma Miss America" – originally titled "Rock'n'Roll Springtime"[10] – is the result of two different tracks stitched together ("First a sequence of chords, then a melody on top"[11]; the join is clear at 1'57"). Nonetheless, it's the most interesting instrumental on the *McCartney* album. It has been commented that "might have made a marvellous soundtrack to a surfing documentary"[12], thanks to its melancholic keyboards and its majestic piano chords, counterbalanced in the second part by the stinging guitar and the deep bass, taking it in turns to play rhythmic and solo parts.

Director Cameron Crowe liked it so much that in 1997 he included "Momma Miss America" – from the *McCartney* album – in the *Jerry MacGuire* film soundtrack.

Musicians:

Paul McCartney bass, Mellotron, piano, acoustic and electric guitar, drums

5 Hot as Sun (Paul McCartney)

Recording: December, 1969 and February, 1970 (overdubs) **Location:** Cavendish Avenue and Morgan Studios (overdubs), London **Release:** April 1970, *McCartney*

Included in the collage of tracks that Paul had recorded on his Studer were some playful pieces dating back to his teenage years. "Hot as Sun" is one of those silly little ditties that everyone has composed, at one time or another, after learning how to play guitar.

---

[6] *The McCartney Self-Interview*, 1970.

[7] *Ibid.*

[8] *Ibid.*

[9] *Ibid.*

[10] You can hear Paul saying these words just before the opening drumbeats to the song.

[11] *The McCartney Self-Interview*, 1970.

[12] Nicholas Schaffner, *The Beatles Forever*, 1979, p.135.

Before *McCartney*, Paul had rehearsed it during the *Get Back!* sessions on January 24th, 1969. He performed the song adding some spoken words to it: "Welcome to the South Sea Islands, where the sound of a wave landing on the sand brings joy to the air."

In specific reference to it, McCartney had admitted, in the self-interview contained in the album: "A song written in about 1958 or 1959 or maybe earlier when it was one of those songs that you play now and then."[13]

"Hot as Sun" is an odd instrumental track for acoustic guitar, so simple and yet so pleasant-sounding with its Latin rhythm; backed by steady drums, the track effectively conjures up the image of the hot Mexican sun beating down on those who have donned their *sombreros* and are intent on catching an afternoon *siesta*.

The excellent percussion and the organ provide the perfect frame for the song. Unexpectedly, McCartney included it in his 1979 *Wings' British Tour*: this version can be found as a bonus-track in the 2011 edition of *McCartney*. Paul also played this track in the 2010 *Up & Coming Tour* soundchecks.

Musicians:

Paul McCartney acoustic and electric guitar, bass, organ, drums, maracas, bongos

6 Junk (Paul McCartney)

Recording: December, 1969 and February, 1970 (overdubs) **Location:** Cavendish Avenue and Morgan Studios (overdubs), London **Release:** April 1970, *McCartney*

The Beatles went to Rishikesh, India in the winter of 1968 for a period of rest and renewal. The Indian sojourn was especially fruitful and productive from the standpoint of musical composition, as well.

There, in the foothills of Himalayas, in their austere cells, each of them found inspiration to write a number of tracks which ended up for the most part on the *White Album*. Of the many songs written by Paul, "Junk" was one of the best.

Upon their return to London, the Beatles recorded "Junk" in an acoustic demo – maybe intending to release it on the *White Album*[14] – but then, the song was not included on that one, nor in the following *Abbey Road*. So, Paul re-recorded it for the *McCartney* album.

It is in this very melancholy ode of such dusky beauty – by now a classic of McCartney's repertoire – that Paul's first solo album reaches one of its highest peaks.

The song incorporates that ascetic and meditative atmosphere that characterized the Beatles' stay with the Maharishi, a feeling which is somehow present in the liquid melodies of the whole of *McCartney*.

---

[13] *The McCartney Self-Interview*, 1970.
[14] This demo was included in *Anthology III*, The Beatles, 1996.

Paul's voice can be heard here and there, almost in hushed under-tones, as he recites an anthology of simple things, of emotions and sentiments tied to an ethereal dimension, to a bucolic environment. McCartney completed the track with crystal clear vocals that included some superb harmonies in the refrain. "Junk" is enhanced by a basic arrangement that is only added to by the soft chimes of the xylophone and brushes, but with a rich bass part.

The instrumental version included in *McCartney* – titled "Singalong Junk" and featuring piano, electric guitar and Mellotron string effects – is the take one of this haunting track. In 1991, Paul performed a graceful instrumental version of "Junk" on the *Unplugged* show and included it in the album with the same title.

Against this background, selected poems by Adrian Mitchell were recited as an *intermezzo* between the acoustic and the electric sets of the 1991 *Secret Gigs Tour*. The song was played again during soundchecks in 1993.

A string quartet version is included in *Working Classical*, whilst the *McCartney* version also appears on *Wingspan*.

Musicians:

Paul McCartney vocals, acoustic guitar, bass, drums, xylophone

7 Oo You (Paul McCartney)

Recording: December, 1969 and February, 1970 (overdubs) **Location:** Cavendish Avenue and Morgan Studios (overdubs), London **Release:** April 1970, *McCartney*

Another *McCartney* track that was added *in extremis*, this song, too, was inspired by Linda.

"Oo You" started out as an instrumental, based on the opening guitar riff; later, Paul added the vocal part and he had fun putting together some verses referring to a female figure. The lyrics are generic, although they seem particularly descriptive of his wife's personality. The song was produced in skiffle style, with sharp electric guitars, percussion, a cowbell and even some aerosol spray; Paul finished it all off with his very gutsy vocals. An all-instrumental version was included in the 2011 edition of *McCartney*.

Musicians:

Paul McCartney vocals, electric guitar, bass, drums, cow-bell, tambourine, aerosol spray

8 Teddy Boy (Paul McCartney)

Recording: December, 1969 and February, 1970 (overdubs) **Location:** Cavendish Avenue and Morgan Studios (overdubs), London **Release:** April 1970, *McCartney*

Another song written by Paul in India in 1968, "Teddy Boy" is one of the best-known tracks on the *McCartney* album, especially since it nearly became a Beatles song.

This track appeared on the list drawn up by Glyn Johns for *Get Back!* but it was taken out at the last minute by Phil Spector who felt that it was not suitable for his production techniques.

"Teddy Boy" was never properly recorded by the Beatles. The version included in *Anthology III* is a bizarre studio rehearsal that is emblematic of the total lack of interest shown by Harrison – who is randomly playing notes on his guitar – and by Lennon, whose drunken vocals amount to an actual sabotage of Paul's offer.

Thus, McCartney found himself with this still unreleased, lovely acoustic song; once in the studio, the arrangement did not overload or modify the song, characterized by the strong guitar chords that open each verse.

In "Teddy Boy", Paul showed off his ability – unfortunately too rarely used – to bring to life an imaginary story inspired by reality.

McCartney very effectively describes the emotional bond between a mother figure and her adolescent son who has had to leave behind his care-free childhood upon losing his father. It is a true-to-life story with a distinct Fifties flavor and which seems to contain a few autobiographical references, although McCartney never explained the meaning of the song.

The lyrics are simple, but effective and the music sums up these feelings. Paul expresses the pain and anger felt by the young boy, emotions tied to the sad memory of the loss of a parent and to the shock of his mother's new love. These feelings are nevertheless attenuated by the awareness of the strength of love.

The production of "Teddy Boy" captures the *naif* tone of the story; Linda's vocal modulation and Paul's drum performance in perfect "Ringo style" contribute to making this one of the most successful tracks on *McCartney*.

Musicians:

Paul McCartney vocals, backing vocals, acoustic guitars, bass, drums • **Linda McCartney** backing vocals

1970

An unceasing composer, McCartney wrote many songs earlier in the year. Some of these – such as "Indeed, I Do" and "Country Dreamer" (see sheet 54) – have turned up in home-demo versions in collectors' circuits.

9 Women Kind (Paul McCartney)

Recording: ? 1970 **Location:** Cavendish Avenue, London **Release:** June 2011, *McCartney* (Deluxe Edition)

Paul himself wasn't able to recall exactly when this recording was made, but he did say that it was probably during the *McCartney* period. The song had already come out in an unofficial recording called *The Piano Tape*, a collection of pieces written by McCartney on his piano at home, most likely dating between 1970 and 1973.

In going back through his old demos, Paul resurrected "Women Kind" and added it as a bonus-track to the 2011 edition of *McCartney*. It is an at-home impromptu in which Paul is playing the piano and singing a crazy whacky rhyme.

Musicians:

Paul McCartney vocals, piano

Paul went to Morgan Studios to complete his homemade December recordings and to tape a new song. Robin Black was one of the sound engineers in the studio and when McCartney arrived, he asked him to work on the sessions.

Black: "It was great seeing Paul play all the instruments. Paul recorded the overdubs fairly straightforward, he knew what he was going to do. Sometimes Paul would describe a particular sound he wanted… Paul made everything seem easy showing what a master of his craft he was!"[15] The sessions were not publicized at all. McCartney told *Rolling Stone* afterwards: "We decided we didn't want to tell anyone what we were doing…That way it gets to be like home at the studio. No one knows about it and there is no one in the studio or dropping by."

10 Kreen-Akrore (Paul McCartney)

Recording: February 12th, 1970 **Location:** Morgan Studios, London **Release:** April 1970, *McCartney*

One day Paul happened to watch a television documentary on the Kreen-Akrore, an Indios tribe that lives in the jungles of Brazil. Seeing scenes of "their lives and how the white man (wa)s trying to change their way of life to his"[16] inspired McCartney to reproduce the tribal

---

[15] Interview courtesy of Robin Black, 13/09/2012.
[16] *The McCartney Self-Interview*, 1970.

sound of the percussion and gave him "get the feeling of their hunt"[17]; so, the very next day he sat down at his drums.

Once he had recorded his long drum solo (with two drum tracks), Paul completed the track, first with two instrumental breaks – brusque electric guitar and organ – then with a few unusual effects produced in the studio with Linda.

It was all in the purest of John-and-Yoko experimentation: animal noises, the sound of an arrow flying (as Paul tells it, "done live with bow and arrow – the bow broke…"[18]) and even the cracking of firewood burning in a fire they had lit in the studio…

Robin Black witnessed that moment: "Paul and Linda went to Harrods to buy a bow, an arrow and a target… We set this up in the studio and recorded the sound of the arrows flying through the air and hitting the target…"[19]

No doubt it was with a smirk on his face that McCartney chose this track to close his eponymous album.

Musicians:

Paul McCartney backing vocals, drums, percussion, bass, electric guitar, organ, piano • **Linda McCartney** backing vocals

On February 21st, McCartney moved over to the familiar – and technically superior – Abbey Road Studio Two for the last batch of recordings, with engineer Phil McDonald assisted by Chris Thomas and John Kurlander. Here, he recorded two of the most acclaimed tracks of his future album in the making.

11-12 Glasses/Suicide (Paul McCartney)

Recording: February 21st-25th, 1970 and December, 1969 **Location:** Abbey Road Studios, London and Cavendish Avenue **Release:** April 1970, *McCartney*

Something done just for fun, "Glasses" is pure ambient noise. Paul started "playing" glasses filled with water and after having "played (them) at random and overdubbed (them) on top of each other"[20], he produced this fifty-second dissonant sequence with shades of ceremonial music.[21]

The fragment testifies to the experimental avant-garde side of McCartney and reveals the influence of Sixties' artist Steve Reich who introduced the theory of "minimalism", a music form in which the creative process and the final result coincide.[22]

---

[17] *Ibid.*

[18] *Ibid.*

[19] Interview courtesy of Robin Black, 13/09/2012.

[20] *Ibid.*

[21] Paul used glasses on a version of "Band on the Run" recorded for the BBC in 2003. During the show, *Chaos and Creation at Abbey Road* (2005), McCartney demonstrated to the audience the process of overdubbing glasses.

[22] Ian Peel, *The Unknown Paul McCartney. McCartney and the Avant-Garde*, 2002, pp.72-73.

Glasses were recorded at Abbey Road Studios. Engineer Phil McDonald: "The title 'Glasses' was fun as we ended up with a huge amount of glasses all filled with water on a big table in Number 3 (Studio). All glasses were meticulously filled with water to the desired pitch of the song." [23]

When Paul decided that it could be put on a record, he also thought of something else. In Cavendish Avenue at his piano, he had recorded the song "Suicide". It has been for decades his most famous unreleased track, as only a snippet of it was included in *McCartney*, crossfaded with "Glasses": a few seconds' worth of piano with his voice in the background.

McCartney had composed this song on the piano at home, more or less around 1958, in a typical Thirties style which he must have heard through his dad, Jim.

At the time of *McCartney*, Paul could still say that "Suicide" was not yet complete and so this track would remain on hold for a few more years. An unreleased version for voice and piano can be heard in the film *One Hand Clapping*, taken from some Wings rehearsals held at Abbey Road in August of 1974. Paul made up his mind to give the song a finished form only in 1977 when he was looking for a singer to perform "Suicide".

Paul finished the song, adding a proper introduction and a refrain[24]: it was nothing more than an enjoyable *divertissement*. McCartney was perhaps a bit too pretentious in offering "Suicide" to no less than Frank Sinatra himself (and after thinking about having Tony Bennett record it)!

Paul explained: "I wrote it in bed at that moment when you're just dropping off and all these things are coming to you (…) I wrote this song called 'Suicide' which was very cabaret (…) Very Sinatra, I thought (…) Years and years later, (Sinatra) rang me at Abbey Road studio, and it was a great moment when one of the engineers said, 'Paul, Sinatra's on the phone' (…) He was asking for a song, so I found the song, made a demo and sent it to him. Apparently he thought it was an almighty piss-take. 'No way!' he's supposed to have said to one of his people. 'Is this guy having me on?' So my career with Sinatra ended in terrible ignominy."[25]

Paul recalled the episode again when he played a fragment of "Suicide", during a BBC interview conducted by Michael Parkinson in 1999.

The complete take of "Suicide" as recorded in 1970 – nothing more than a piano improvisation – was finally included as a bonus-track in the 2011 edition of *McCartney*. In truth, instead of it being a gift to his fans, it confirms the fact that the cut made forty years earlier was not so much advisable, but necessary…

Musicians:

Paul McCartney glasses, piano, vocals

---

[23] *McCartney Deluxe Edition*, in *Paul McCartney Archive Collection*, 2011, p. 44.

[24] The track was broadcast in this complete version on a Boston radio station.

[25] Paul McCartney-Barry Miles, *Many Years from Now*, 1997, pp.144-145.

13 Maybe I'm Amazed (Paul McCartney)

Recording: February 22nd, 1970 **Location:** Abbey Road Studios, London **Release:** April 1970, *McCartney*

The history of the post-Beatles era has never attributed huge importance to Paul's debut album which, because of its at times evanescent quality, was considered more of a *capriccio* than a real musical *exploit*.

Nonetheless, *McCartney* is a priceless part of his discography and much of its reputation and worth, in fact, is due to "Maybe I'm Amazed".

The critics immediately labelled "Maybe I'm Amazed" a "classic" and today, many polls still rate it as the best McCartney's solo song: "Maybe I'm Amazed" ranked 77th in the 'Song of the Century' list drawn up a few years ago by the magazine *Mojo*!

The reasons for this success are quickly explained, for "Maybe I'm Amazed" highlights the most authentic side of Paul McCartney, both from the musical and the human points of view. It reveals an unbridled McCartney who brings together and merges his two souls, both melodic and rock, in the most remarkable song within his body of work as a solo artist.

Paul composed this track "at the piano, in London, probably between 1968 and 1969 with the second verse added slightly later."[26] A brief snippet of the song – in particular its chromatic scale bridge – was performed during the *Get Back!* sessions: then the track evolves into a long jam-session, but this could confirm that it had already been composed at the time. At Abbey Road, "Maybe I'm Amazed" was recorded in a burst of energy. McCartney played all the instruments, shining at performing a brilliant piano part – with its fast chromatic scale between the verses – and a raging electric guitar solo. Preferring the immediacy to the accuracy, Paul even left a minor error in the recording: at 0:44 you can hear the noise of the drumsticks hitting one another.

The piano intro, which features one of McCartney's most typical chord sequences, opens the door to a song performed by Paul with powerful, potent, raging and roaring vocals as he easily and naturally runs the gamut of a wide range of tones.

The honesty and vigor of this song are particularly touching. They are emblematic of the astonishment a man feels in the face of the gift of love and the awareness of the need for a safe harbor at a time of difficulty and confusion.

Some verses of the song could be a reference to the unhappy moments of the late Beatles years and express a sense of uncertainty: Paul doesn't understand what's happening around him and feels lonely.

Lennon certainly appreciated the song, making it clear in this way: during an interview with Yoko in 1972, while talking about the split-up of the Beatles, he sang a verse of it.

---

[26] *The McCartney Self-Interview*, 1970.

For unfathomable reasons, the track was not released as a single from the album[27], an error that Paul tried to correct in February 1977, when "Maybe I'm Amazed" was chosen as a single in a live version taken from *Wings Over America* (#10 in America and #28 in UK).

Since its early live performances, "Maybe I'm Amazed" was lengthened with a coda which McCartney used as a showcase for his screaming vocals. Wings rehearsed the song during the *One Hand Clapping* sessions in 1974 and this version is on the 2011 edition of *McCartney*.

Played by McCartney in all of his tours up to 2005 – with the exception of the 1972 *Wings' University Tour* and the 1993 tour – this track with its vocal virtuosities that are so *black*, would be the ticket to fame for many artists in the years that followed, from Sandie Shaw (1971) to Faces (in 1971 they included a live version in the *Long Player* album) to Carleen Andersson (1998), whose cover reached #26 on the British charts.

The original version of "Maybe I'm Amazed" is on *All the Best!* (1987) and on *Wingspan*; live versions are also featured on *Tripping the Live Fantastic!* (1990), *Back in the US/Back in the World* (2002-2003) and on *McCartney* (2011 edition, which includes the 1979 *Wings' British Tour* performance). The song came up again in some dates of the 2010 *Up & Coming Tour*, the 2011-12 *On the Run Tour* and the 2013/14 *Out There! Tour*.

Musicians:

Paul McCartney vocals, backing vocals, piano, bass, electric guitar, drums, organ • **Linda McCartney** backing vocals

14 Every Night (Paul McCartney)

Recording: February 23rd, 1970 **Location:** Abbey Road Studios, London **Release:** April 1970, *McCartney*

When Paul started the *McCartney* sessions, the majority of the songs had already been composed in the two previous years. "Every Night" was one of those. As Paul said, he had conceived it in 1968 during a holiday in Greece when he jotted down a couple of verses on his notepad, but the song remained in an embryonic form for several months, progressing no further.

Paul played "Every Night" during the *Get Back!* sessions (on January 21st and 24th, 1969), but this snippet could only be said to vaguely resemble the song later released on *McCartney*; Paul is heard singing some lyrics repeating the words of the title but the melody is still rough, without any bridge or refrain.

Once in the studio, Paul was quite hesitant at the final form he would give this track, recording it in two different versions[28], the first of which was taped on February 22nd and remains, to date, unreleased.

---

[27] It's even more surprising considering the fact that the video-clip of this track, a performance of extraordinary historical value, was broadcast during the TV program, *London weekend*, on April 19th, 1970.

At any rate, "Every Night" turned out to be one of the best songs on the *McCartney* album, despite being underestimated for years by both critics and McCartney himself.

The recording is surprisingly clean: the melody is highlighted by the crisp-sounding acoustic guitars and the powerful rhythm section, in addition to McCartney's crystalline vocal performance. The melody of the refrain closely resembles the opening line of The Beatles' "You Never Give Me Your Money".

Phoebe Snow (1950-2011) took it upon herself to show that "Every Night" was, in fact, one of the "nugget(s) hidden in the album"[29]: in 1979 she took the song to #41 on the UK charts.[30]

And shortly thereafter, Paul performed it in his 1979 *Wings' British Tour*. The live version included in *Concerts for the People of Kampuchea* (Various Artists, 1981), taken from concerts organized by McCartney and held in London in December 1979, is a slower, rocking and expanded version featuring a beautiful electric guitar solo by Laurence Juber.

Paul let it rest for a while longer, but in the Nineties he offered-up "Every Night" to his fans, this time in a surprising bluesy rendition that included a memorable *a cappella* section. Arranged this way, the song was captured live on *Unplugged*, then performed again for the 1991 *Secret Gigs Tour* and for the 1993 *New World Tour*.

The original version appears on *Wingspan*. Paul later played the track on his 2002-03 *Drivin' Tour* (this version, only for vocals and guitar, is included in *Back in the US* and *Back in the World*) and for some dates on his 2010 *Up & Coming Tour*.

Musicians:

Paul McCartney vocals, acoustic guitar, bass, drums

15 Man We Was Lonely (Paul McCartney)

Recording: February 25th, 1970 **Location:** Abbey Road Studios, London **Release:** April 1970, *McCartney*

In an embarrassing confession, Paul admitted having composed "Man We Was Lonely", "in bed at home shortly before we finished recording the album"[31], conveying once again a clear idea of just how he approached his first solo album.

As with many of the *McCartney* songs, this one is a Paul-and-Linda duet, of the "alone against the world" variety, which tells of the couple's early years and finds a follow-up in "Some People Never Know" (see sheet 43), issued on *Wild Life* in 1971.

---

[28] Many years later, Paul said he was not completely satisfied of that recording: "When I played the *McCartney* album to Ringo, he said that he preferred my original solo version, when I had first sung it to him"(*Club Sandwich*, n.72, Winter '94, p. 11). In the same interview, Paul stated also that he would like to re-record "Every Night". The lyrics "Every day I lean on a lampost" could be a reference to the famous George Formby's song "Leaning on a Lampost" (see also "Ram On", sheet 35).

[29] B. Woffinden, *cit.*, p.36.

[30] A cover was also released by Richie Havens (1941-2013), who included it in his album *Connections* (1980).

[31] *The McCartney Self-Interview*, 1970.

It also contains references to the Beatles' last period. McCartney: "I think I'm remembering it wasn't that easy when I left the Beatles. I went through a lot of tough times emotionally, so something like 'Man We Was Lonely' reflects that."[32]

Furthermore, just before entering the studio Paul added a middle-eight, obviously written "one lunchtime in a great hurry as we were due to record the song that afternoon."[33]

He did not, however, carry off the bluff; "Man We Was Lonely", a melodic acoustic track cadenced by a jumping bass featuring some steel guitar – Paul achieved that sound by playing his Telecaster with a drum peg – is one of those songs that exposed McCartney to considerable criticism, at that time, regarding his artistic dip.

A new version of "Man We Was Lonely", which remains unreleased, would be later recorded by Paul and Linda during the sessions with Johnny Cash in June 1988. McCartney: "I thought of myself as Johnny Cash on that one."[34] This song also appears on *Wingspan*.

Musicians:

Paul McCartney vocals, backing vocals, acoustic and electric guitar, bass, drums, percussion • **Linda McCartney** vocals, backing vocals

The *McCartney* album, described as "one of the best kept secrets in rock history", was released on April 17th, 1970 by Paul's explicit request. Exactly one week earlier, McCartney had effectively said 'no more' to the artistic endeavor with The Beatles. Lennon had already left, back in September 1969, but he was persuaded not to announce it. McCartney's reaction to the orchestral overdubs added by Phil Spector to "The Long and Winding Road" was raging.

Speaking to the *Evening Standard*, McCartney said: "A few months ago American record producer Phil Spector was called in by John Lennon to tidy up some of the tracks. But a few weeks ago, I was sent a re-mixed version of my song 'The Long and Winding Road', with harps, horns, an orchestra and women's choir added. No one had asked me what I thought. I couldn't believe it. I would never have female voices on a Beatles record."

Promotional copies of *McCartney* were delivered to the press on April 9th along with a self-interview which alluded to the difficult situation The Beatles were facing. Paul was not officially announcing the breakup of the group, but his words left no room for doubt and there seemed to be no hope for the future. A strong argumentative mood surrounded the *McCartney* album. Apple press officer's Derek Taylor submitted some questions to McCartney for the press release, but Paul included additional questions by himself. Taylor: "He was only supposed to write out information explaining how he made his album. Instead he hands us this interview with himself asking questions such as would he miss Ringo. It was entirely gratuitous. Nobody

[32] Timothy White, *Paul McCartney On His Not So Silly Love Songs*, in *Billboard*, March 2001.
[33] *Ibid.*
[34] *Paul McCartney Talks to Guitar World Acoustic*, in *Guitar World Acoustic*, Issue 75, Dec 2004/Jan 2005.

asked him that question. He asked that question himself." Two questions and answers were placed following one another in the self-interview:

"Q. Is your break with The Beatles temporary or permanent, due to personal differences or musical ones?

A. Personal differences, business differences, musical differences, but most of all because I have a better time with my family. Temporary or permanent? I don't really know.

Q. Do you foresee a time when Lennon-McCartney becomes an active songwriting partnership again?

A. No."

This move did not ingratiate him to his colleagues or to the press. *McCartney* obtained some unfavorable barbs from music critics. *Rolling Stone*'s Langdon Winner wrote: "*McCartney* is an album that wants desperately to convince. Its explicit and uniform message is that Paul McCartney, his wife Linda and family have found peace and happiness in a quiet *home* away from the city, and away from the hassles of the music business. This is a beautiful vision and, like most listeners, I wanted very much to believe it was true. On the basis of the music alone I was entirely convinced... My problem is that all of the publicity surrounding the record makes it difficult for me to believe that *McCartney* is what it appears to be... The overall effect of the *McCartney* literature is to turn the package into an undisguised power play.... What this material is saying is that Beatle fans should recognize that the group is totally defunct and now follow the man who was the real genius of the outfit in the first place.... I cannot help but ask if Paul is really as together as the music indicates, how could he have sunk to such bizarre tactics?"

Others, like *Billboard*, found it pleasant: "The future of the Beatles may be in doubt but not that of Paul McCartney. His solo debut as songwriter/singer is a knockout (…) His songs are freewheeling, light hearted, and affectionate and his voice is attuned to his pen. His wife, Linda, joins in at times, but it's Paul's album all the way and he can be proud of it."

The record was a huge success on both sides of the Atlantic, skyrocketing to #1 in the USA (with over 2 million copies sold) and to #2 in the UK.

The legal battles with Apple led McCartney to take the drastic and painful decision to sue his three ex-partners. This happened on December 31st.

While these extra-musical disputes were going on, on October, 4th Paul and Linda set sail for New York, perhaps attracted by John and Yoko's recent adventures in the US. Accompanying them on the luxurious transatlantic liner, the SS France, were their daughters Heather and Mary (Linda became pregnant with Stella the following January). Paul travelled under the alias "Paul (or Billy) Martin".[35]

---

[35] "Paul Martin" according to a NYC newspaper from October, 1970; on May 12th, 1971 Paul is portrayed in Saint Tropez holding a bag with the writing "Billy Martin – Fort Worth, Texas".

As soon as he arrived Stateside – according to some sources, on October, 7th – Paul booked Columbia Studios and started a series of auditions to recruit the musicians to help him with the recordings. Over the previous summer, McCartney had prepared an amazing number of demos, twenty-nine in fact (apparently the tape was unearthed in 2011), a good part of which ended up being developed in the studio for the *RAM* album.

The list included "Tomorrow", "Some People Never Know", "I Am Your Singer" (these three would be recorded later for the *Wild Life* album, see **1971**), "Why Am I Crying?" – an embryonic version of "Fourth of July", a song rehearsed by Paul in 1973 for his *James Paul McCartney* TV Special and recorded in 1974 by John Christie – and "Great Day" (see sheet **260**), released only in 1997 on *Flaming Pie*.

Denny Seiwell was the drummer chosen by McCartney, beating the competition which included expert drummers of the likes of Billy Lavoina.

He vividly remembers the audition. Seiwell: "I went on 45th Street and I didn't know it was an audition. I walked down to this building and it was like a burnt-out building on the west side of town (…) There was a guy sitting at the desk in the lobby and I said, 'Is there a studio there?' He pointed to the basement. I thought, 'I'm going to get mugged here!' I walked down and there was Paul and Linda! Paul asked me to play for him… He had me just go through a few different flavours and styles of rock'n'roll drumming. Later, I got a call from Paul. The plan was to start with me for the first week, Donald McDonald the second week and Herb Lavelle for the third, but after a few days Paul cancelled the other two drummers and booked me for the sessions."[36]

Among the other session-men, Paul contacted guitarists, Hugh McCracken and Dave Spinozza (the latter was one of the most talented musicians on the New York scene) with McCracken taking Spinozza's place after a few days. Two well-known jazz musicians, Ron Carter and Richard Davis, played stand-up bass during some orchestral overdubs. A picture of the two famous players together appears on the *RAM* Deluxe Edition book in 2012.[37]

Spinozza, too, has lots of memories, not all of them positive, of his experience with McCartney. Spinozza's reaction to the phone call he received just before the *RAM* sessions began was really angry. He recalled that Paul contacted him through Linda who introduced herself as his secretary and actually offered him the opportunity to audition.

In the end, Spinozza accepted: "Here I am meeting Paul McCartney and he played these basic rock'n'roll things – ching ching ching. It was embarassing!"[38]

---

[36] Andrew Croft, *Interview with Denny Seiwell*, in Beatology, vol. 3, no.5, 2001, p.13 and *Denny Seiwell Interview*, in *RAM Deluxe Edition Book*, 2012.

[37] Interviews courtesy of Ron Carter and Richard Davis, respectively on 18/09/2012 and 20/09/2012.

[38] Albert Goldman, *Lennon*, 1988, p.453.

Spinozza's statements cast a shadow of doubt over McCartney's harmonic knowledge: "(Paul) had to sing every note or hit it on his guitar, like the three notes of the major seventh. He didn't even know what the chord was called. He called it the 'pretty chord'. The whole album was done in the same format as the *McCartney* album, only we played the parts for him, there was no freedom. We were told exactly what to play."[39] McCartney had often boasted about this musical illiteracy, like many early jazz players did: his was a "calculated primitivism".[40]

Every morning, the recording sessions started with Paul on acoustic guitar or piano, Denny Seiwell on drums and Spinozza (or later McCracken) on electric guitar, rehearsing and trying to lay down the basic tracks. Later, McCartney would work on overdubs for instruments and vocals (along with Linda) most of the time without any involvement from the other musicians.

In January 1971, after the Christmas break, Paul moved over to Phil Ramone's (1934-2013) A&R Studios to continue the recordings and work on the orchestral overdubs. In March, he flew to Santa Monica and went to Los Angeles' Sound Recorders Studios to put the finishing touches, with more overdubs and mixing.

The sessions went on until April of 1971 and were some of McCartney's most prolific, with twenty-five tracks recorded. Three tracks recorded at the time, "Rode All Night", "Sunshine, Sometime" and "Hey Diddle" (overdubbed during the Nashville sessions, see **1974**) went unissued but have recently found place on the 2012 version of *RAM*, whilst another song, "When the Wind Is Blowing" remains unreleased to date (this one and "Sunshine, Sometime" would be reworked for the soundtrack of *Rupert the Bear*, see **1978**)

According to some unofficial sources, Paul came to the first *RAM* recording session only accompanied by Denny Seiwell. To test the recording room, he taped a first version of "Monkberry Moon Delight".

16 Monkberry Moon Delight (Paul and Linda McCartney)

Recording: October? November 5th, 1970 and March-April, 1971 (overdubs) **Location:** Columbia Studios, New York City and Sound Recorders Studios (overdubs), Los Angeles **Release:** May 1971, *RAM*

Still today, "Monkberry Moon Delight" is a jolt like few others in the vast panoply of McCartney's music. Although the inspiration behind it remains unclear, the song represents a *sui generis* moment along Paul's creative pathway; if on the one hand, it is astounding for the sheer force with which he decided to do away with any stylistic point of reference, on the other it is surprising for the expressive vigor and vocal power it releases.

It is as if, drifting away from his typical song style and rejecting any recognizable form, McCartney intended to give vent to the innermost and most hidden part of himself in a lysergic

[39] *Ibid.*
[40] Brian Harker, *Louis Armstrong's Hot Five and Hot Seven Recordings*, 2011, p.75.

journey. For him, it was the search for a *locus amoenus*, but also for a refuge from fear, and an attempt to recover his psychological identity.

Just as Lennon had done a few months earlier with Arthur Janov's *Primal Scream* therapy, McCartney, too, embarked on a journey of self-discovery, to find his inner Ego through a rediscovery of primordial emotions, in particular through the scream and tears.

This is why "Monkberry Moon Delight" – with its lacerating shrieks and obsessive sobs – could be considered as Paul's own *Primal Scream*.

Was McCartney intrigued by Lennon's therapy – which very likely he had heard of – or was he simply trying to mimic *John Lennon/Plastic Ono Band*'s vocal sound (Paul could have added more vocals after listening to John's record)? Although it's not made known, the song is worth listening to even for one only of these reasons.

If *RAM* is McCartney's most emotionally dramatic album, "Monkberry Moon Delight" represents a moment when Paul was feeling most acutely the abyss that he had tumbled into at the time. Although it would be difficult to offer a plausible explanation of the song without stretching its meaning, it is likely that – along with the images obviously owed to acid trips – McCartney was trying to express the terrible moments he went through following the breakup of The Beatles.

In some interviews, McCartney said that he had gotten the idea for the title from his children's baby talk distortion of the word "milk" which had become "monk" and that he thought of "Monkberry Moon Delight" as the name of an imaginary drink (hence, the verse "*sipping* monkberry moon delight"[41]); but he has never really explained the true meaning of the lyrics. And yet, if there is one song which is emblematic of that most desperate emotional side of Paul, it would have to be "Monkberry Moon Delight".

According to some sources, McCartney launched the *RAM* recordings with this very song, laying down the basic track on the piano, in a sort of warm-up session just between him and Seiwell. If this were the case, it would be particularly significant. Paul was foaming at the mouth in anger and he must have felt an urgent need to let it out.

Seiwell: "I remember the lunacy of it all. I still was into crafting the drum part first, so I would listen to the lyrics but I wasn't influenced by them. So my whole concept of making the right drum track came from the music."[42]

And Denny adds: "Paul put great energy into that one... The track came out very funky. It was a quick recording and I played tambourine as an overdub."[43]

---

[41] *Club Sandwich*, n.72, Winter 1994, p.8. Actually, the right verb is "sucking". No one knows if Paul tried to camouflage the acid side of the song of if it is simply an erroneous memory.

[42] Howie Edelson, *Q&A-Denny Seiwell*, in *Beatlefan*, n.169, December 2007, p.26.

[43] Interview courtesy of Denny Seiwell, 12/11/2011.

A confused fog of alcohol, acid or smoke[44], the track presents some sinister images and assorted nonsense. The two opening verses can be considered a key moment in the song, presumably describing the terrible nights spent by McCartney after The Beatles' breakup, when he was overcome by the effects of depression and alcohol.

The track seems to describe a horrible nightmare. In particular, the references to the sobbing and to the pillow (lyrics in the *RAM* songbook say "a *pillow* up my nose" although in the handwritten paper's reproduction inserted in the *RAM* Deluxe edition one could read "a *piano* up my nose" – author's note) that Paul was nearly sinking into, seem to retrace almost word for word the account McCartney gave of what he had gone through after The Beatles' breakup. McCartney: "I was going through a bad time, what I suspect was almost a nervous breakdown. I remember lying awake at nights shaking (...) One night I'd been asleep and awoke and I couldn't lift my head off the pillow. My head was down in the pillow, I thought, 'Jesus, if I don't do this I'll suffocate.'"[45]

All of the anguish and despair felt by McCartney went into his singing performance, the most impressive of his post-Beatles career. McCartney's vocal quality brings to mind the style of the famous singer and actor Screamin' Jay Hawkins (1929-2000), who in 1972 did a great cover of the song. Another fact – if confirmed – would prove the connection: reportedly, in its original demo "Monkberry Moon Delight" was performed by McCartney in a medley with "Frenzy", a 1957 song by Hawkins. With his raucous and aggressive singing, in the "Helter Skelter"[46] style, Paul explores all of his wide vocal range, displaying a large number of vocalizations that were extensively overdubbed. We know McCartney was pleased with the results, because at 4:52 he can be heard shouting "That's nice! Yeah!".

According to the credits in the 2012 Deluxe Edition of *RAM* – which place the recording of the basic track on November 5th – it's possible that the whole take taped with Seiwell was redone from scratch with McCracken on guitar.

Spinozza: "I don't remember recording 'Monkberry Moon Delight'. On subsequent sessions, I recall playing it but I think McCracken is on the final recording."[47]

The structure of "Monkberry Moon Delight" – built on minor chords – would suggest a cleverly masked blues. Another blues connection is McCartney's vocal quality, which resembles African ceremonies, where the singers disguise their voices so to call up ancestors.

---

[44] The final dialog is quite ambiguous and practically unintelligible (from 4:42 to 4:55 circa): "Try some of this, honey (or Sammy?)", "What is it?", "Monkberry moon delight!"

[45] P. McCartney-B. Miles, *cit.*, p.444-445. In an interview published in on *Life* (April 1971), Paul recalls the sensations from the summer before (just after the Beatles' breakup) and phrases it this way: "I stood (all summer) with a knot in my stomach", this being one of the most tension-charged images of "Monkberry Moon Delight".

[46] According to studio assistant Jim Reeves who witnessed it in Studio D, Paul performed 90 vocal takes "to get that raspy sound", as he had done a few years before when recording "Oh! Darlin". See http://reevesaudio.com/vintagesessions.html

[47] Interview by Edward Eikelenboom, in *Maccazine*, vol. 40-41, issues 2-3, p.25.

The song is cadenced by the vehement piano's *staccato* and the powerful bass sound. McCartney's bass is played almost entirely on the first and fifth tone of the root chord: but near the end, Paul lets loose with some scale progressions in pure *Sgt. Peppers'* style.

The climax leading up to the first refrain (at 2:57) is the most dramatic moment and it introduces the coda, with its obsessive refrain and the high-pitched backing vocals sung by Linda and little Heather, in the first of her recurring appearances on her father's records during the Seventies. Here, Paul shows of some refinements, two of which stand out: the vocalization that patterns the underlying bass phrase – the same technique previously used in "I Will" – and the sobbing final sequence.

After *RAM* the song would never again be offered by McCartney. Curiously enough, however, there are two throwbacks to it in his unreleased discography, the first during the rehearsals for the *James Paul McCartney* special (the opening riff, with Linda starting the first verse), the second in the middle of an early take of "Letting Go" (**1974**, see sheet **80**), with a few bars of it played on the electric piano.

An instrumental version was included in *Thrillington* (1977), the album for jazz orchestra and containing all *RAM* tracks that McCartney would commission in the summer of 1971. The song was covered in 1972 by Bahamian musician Exuma (1942-1997).

Musicians:

Paul McCartney vocals, backing vocals, piano, acoustic and electric guitar, mandolin (?), bass • **Linda McCartney** backing vocals • **Hugh McCracken** electric guitar, mandolin (?) • **Denny Seiwell** drums, tambourine • **Heather McCartney** backing vocals

Dave Spinozza came to the studio on October 12th and the trio started recording at top speed. Four of the tracks they recorded would be released officially. At least other three songs ("Monkberry Moon Delight", "Heart of the Country" and "Uncle Albert/Admiral Halsey") would be re-recorded with McCracken in the following weeks. These sessions at Columbia CBS Studio B were engineered by Tim Geelan, assisted by Ted Brosnan.

17 Another Day (Paul and Linda McCartney)

Recording: October 12th, 1970 and January, 1971 (overdubs) **Location:** Columbia Studios and A&R Studios (overdubs), New York City **Release:** February 1971, single

The actual *RAM* sessions began with the recording of "Another Day", as Denny Seiwell remembers: "This was the first tune we did (...) Paul would come in the studio every day with something fresh (…) We had all these incredible tunes to do (…) He'd strap on a guitar or piano and start playing and singing a tune and we'd learn the tune and start recording. We just did a tune a day."[48]

---

[48] A. Croft, *cit.*

But "Another Day" went back at least as far as the *Get Back!* sessions at the Twickenham Studios, when McCartney had played the song on the piano, in a still somewhat rough performance.[49] Some of the lyrics were recognizable, even at that time.

John Lennon, one of the record's most vicious critics, did not mince words (the infamous verses that contain a sort of comparison between "Yesterday" and "Another Day", included in "How Do You Sleep?" from the album *Imagine*, were shooting directly at the mediocrity of McCartney's career), but he probably hadn't even been in the studio or, if he had, he wasn't listening to Paul...

Issued in February 1971 as the first single of McCartney's solo career, "Another Day" is, sadly, best known for the criticism and vicissitudes it faced.

The song immediately achieved enormous success – #2 in the United Kingdom and #5 in America, with over a million copies sold – while, at the same time, kicking up a dust storm of controversy: the songwriting credits were attributed to both Paul and Linda McCartney.

Sir Lew Grade of ATV and Northern Songs – the company which owned Lennon and McCartney songs' copyright – believed it was a clever trickery to guarantee Paul himself 50% of the royalties.

The case actually went to court, but Paul easily won the suit filed against him by Grade. When Linda appeared on the stand, she declared that she was able to compose songs with her husband; there may be some doubt in the particular case at hand, but a collaboration on a piece of popular music is subject to a very special set of rules even though Linda was totally clueless about musical notions ("I knew the chord of C maybe, but I didn't know anything"[50] said Linda).

In the end, on June 1972 a compromise was settled upon whereby Paul agreed to appear on an ATV special (*James Paul McCartney*, produced and broadcast in 1973) in exchange for assigning the songwriting credits to Linda.

All of the controversy aside, "Another Day" had its rightful merits; whilst some critics had, over the years, judged it to be vapid and full of bourgeois values, the song had an air of intimacy and domesticity about it that lent it a homespun attractiveness.[51]

---

[49] The section in ¾ time was still a nebulous idea in Paul's mind: at the time in question (9/1/69, Twickenham Studios) he is proceeding by trial and error to find the right variation of rhythm. This could be a clue that the song had been composed on piano, rather than on guitar, as might have been deduced to the contrary from the official recording. But, on 25/1/69, at Apple Studios, Paul performed the song on acoustic guitar, accompanied by Ringo on drums.

[50] *Linda McCartney: The Lady Looks Hard*, in *Record Mirror*, 27/09/1975.

[51] See Bob Woffinden, *cit.*, p.48: "'Another Day' was slight and simple... But it did have a delicate charm. It's disciplined and it relates to real life. These were positive qualities, the staple of the best popular music; and yet Paul discarded it almost immediately". Woffinden himself, in a flattering comment and drawing an *à propos* parallel, says of the song that it was "closely observed domesticity, a song in the noble tradition of 'Eleanor Rigby', about a lonely woman".

From a musical point of view, the song matches the melancholy vein of the lyrics: in its middle modulated in E minor, Spinozza's guitar underlines the words "sad" and "alone" with a crying tone achieved through the volume fader.

In this portrait of a typical day in the life of a middle-class girl, McCartney reveals a talent for psychological introspection by delving into the topic of loneliness, one of the most recurring themes in his career of over four decades.[52]

The repetitiveness of her daily actions, the boredom of an unsatisfying job – in an office "where the papers grow" – her sense of fatigue and an existence that is full of sadness (which, by the way, the woman is aware of only "sometimes", a detail that accentuates the drama of her life and highlights how mechanical gestures made day in and day out can annihilate any interior conscience) paint a picture of existential meekness that translates into an ineptitude to act: the young woman can only wait "till the man of her dreams comes to break the spell".

When Paul went to the studio and presented the song to his musicians on acoustic guitar, Seiwell sat up on his chair: "I thought, 'Hey, wait a minute! This is not simply another tune… This is 'Eleanor Rigby' in New York!"[53]

Following the same working method used during all of the *RAM* sessions, McCartney and his musicians recorded the basic track following Paul's off-mike guide-vocal.

Seiwell: "We recorded it with Paul on acoustic and Dave on electric guitar… We started out at about ten in the morning and for lunch we had the right take."[54] For the arrangement, McCartney relied on all of his experience and expertise.

Spinozza: "Great song. I remember doing many tracks of overdubbed guitar parts. I thought it was a magical song and production."[55]

The recording of "Another Day" was flawlessly produced, with superb vocals by Paul, who also provides vocal harmonies, including a great low harmony in the last verse. Linda too is featured on backing vocals and vocal harmonies: the modulation of her voice at the end of the second verse is memorable. Seiwell on drums is accurate and he also played fine percussion, on the Manhattan telephone directory![56]

With its middle section in a ¾ Latin-feel beat, the track was embellished with an intricate and ingenious bass part that weaves its way sinuously; it must be counted as one of the most imaginative and richest lines ever created by Paul with this instrument.

---

[52] McCartney had previously dealt with this theme in the epic "Eleanor Rigby" and in the steely "For No-One" (both included in *Revolver*, 1966); later, he would again in "Treat Her Gently/Lonely Old People" (1975, *Venus and Mars*) and in "Average Person" (1983, *Pipes of Peace*).

[53] Peter Aimes Carlin, *Paul McCartney, A Life*, 2010, p.211.

[54] Interview courtesy of Denny Seiwell, 12/11/2011.

[55] Freddie Rodriguez, *Interview. David Spinozza: That Music Legend You Don't Know, But Should!*, 13/08/2012, on www.urblremedy.com

[56] Bruce Spitzer-Allan Steckler, *The Beatles Solo on Apple Records*, 2005, p.124.

There is an interesting anecdote on McCartney's bass. The sound engineer, Dixon Van Winkle – who Paul had just asked to select one track for release as a single – picked "Another Day" and mixed it in a hurry.

Soon, Van Winkle and David Crawford had one hundred copies made to send to the radio stations. But, "the next day, when I heard it on the air, I realized it was a disaster" – the engineer confessed – "We got carried away with the bass part and when it hit the radio station compressor it pumped like crazy. I learned that lesson real quick! But we never remixed the song and Paul never said anything about it."[57]

The song was included in *Wings Greatest* (1978), *All the Best!* and *Wingspan*. Paul would later performed it on his 1993 *New World Tour*, but the poor quality of these renditions made it impossible to include the song in *Paul Is Live!* (1993).[58] "Another Day" was performed again during the 2013/14 *Out There! Tour* with Paul playing 12-string acoustic guitar. At the Boonaroo Music Festival (14/06/2013) the song was dedicated to the memory of Phil Ramone.

Musicians:

Paul McCartney vocals, backing vocals, acoustic and electric guitar, bass, percussion (?), tambourine (?) • **Linda McCartney** backing vocals • **Dave Spinozza** acoustic guitar (?), electric guitar • **Denny Seiwell** drums, percussion, tambourine (?)

18 Three Legs (Paul McCartney)

Recording: October 16th, 1970 and March-April, 1971 (overdubs) **Location:** Columbia Studios, New York City and Sound Recorders Studios (overdubs), Los Angeles **Release:** May 1971, *RAM*

Music critics everywhere have always seen "Three Legs" as one of the harshest moments of the Lennon-McCartney feud of the early Seventies.

Eirik Wangberg – the engineer who did the mixing for *RAM* and who Paul had nicknamed *The Norwegian* – said that the inspiration for the song came to Paul from a picture drawn by his daughter Heather; there is nevertheless the strong temptation to see it as overtly provocative on Paul's part *vis-à-vis* John.

"Three Legs" – originally titled "A Dog Is Here" as reported on Paul's handwritten lyrics, a copy of which was included in the 2012 *RAM* Deluxe Edition – is probably the most sarcastic moment on the *RAM* album. The lyrics present the recurring, sad and unpleasant image of a salty dog, an obvious reference to The Beatles' situation and a warning that the loss of one of its members (Paul himself) would have made it impossible for the remaining three to continue the journey. McCartney has never explained the real meaning of the song, but it's as if the lyrics

---

57 Gary Eskow, *Paul McCartney's Uncle Albert Admiral Halsey*, www.mixonline.com, 01/08/2004.
58 An example of which is the recording of the Charlotte concert (15/6/93), used for the television broadcast of the same event: among the most obvious defects there is the imperfect intonation of Paul's voice and the rough rendition of the backing vocals. Other tapes also show how the group lacked the spirit to perform the song which was perhaps more apt for an *unplugged* style of rendition.

depicted John as the betrayer of the trust that had always been placed in him: Paul thinks that John was a real friend but that – in the end – he let him down. Musically, the track reflects this bitterness in a rough, but nevertheless sinuous, blues where the variety of effects applied on Paul's voice (here, it is sardonic and unpleasant, one of the most Lennon-esque interpretations in his whole career) is paradigmatic of the many nuances offered in *RAM*.

The recording technique was truly unusual. Dave Spinozza: "There's one track, which is a cute thing, a blues tune, which I think it was a unique sound and I had fun doing. 'Three Legs', it's called. Paul likes to double track a lot of things. We both played acoustic on some tracks and then tripled. Sometimes Paul played piano but never played bass while we were there. He overdubbed the bass later. It was a bit weird because bass, drums and guitar would have been more comfortable."[59] The vocal parts were recorded in a special way. Engineer Eirik Wangberg: "I let him have, beside his stereo headset, two small speakers that I placed in front of his face and pointing towards his ears. He would then be surrounded by the sound to sing better, which was what he wanted."[60] A picture taken during the session confirms it.

In 2001 during the *Wingspan* special (radio version), Paul improvised the song on guitar. *Thrillington* includes an instrumental version with a jazz slant.

Musicians:

Paul McCartney vocals, backing vocals, acoustic and electric guitar, bass, tambourine (?) • **Linda McCartney** backing vocals • **Dave Spinozza** acoustic and electric guitar • **Denny Seiwell** drums, tambourine (?)

19 Eat at Home (Paul and Linda McCartney)

Recording: October 16th, 1970 and March-April, 1971 (overdubs) **Location:** Columbia Studios, New York City and Sound Recorders Studios (overdubs), Los Angeles **Release:** May 1971, *RAM*

One of the most conventional tracks on *RAM*, "Eat at Home" is a three-chord song in pure Buddy Holly style,.

Referred to by Paul himself in a 1975 interview as "obscene", it is an ode to the small joys of domesticity (cooking and sex, in this case). Needless to say, musical press unleashed ferocious criticism against these McCartney's muses.

This notwithstanding, "Eat at Home" does contain a remarkable musical part: a typical McCartney guitar riff and excellent vocals by Paul – with high-mixed harmony by Linda – all served up with some steady drumming by Seiwell and a number of guitar solos by Spinozza and McCartney himself. A catchy pop tune, "Eat at Home" was extracted from *RAM* as a single for the European market, hitting #15 on the Italian charts and even getting a fair

---

[59] www.paulmccartneyram.hpg.ig.com.br/entretenimento/17/index_int_4.html

[60] *Claudio Dirani Interview with Eirik Wangberg,* January 2005.

amount of airplay on U.S. radio stations. Using the *RAM* version, the song was tacked on as a bonus track in the Japanese version of *Wingspan*.

The song was used as an opener in some dates of the 1972 *Wings' European Tour*: the Groningen performance has been issued as a digital bonus-track through iTunes in 2012. *Thrillington* contains an instrumental version of the song with a horn arrangement.

Musicians:

Paul McCartney vocals, backing vocals, electric guitar, bass • **Linda McCartney** vocals, backing vocals • **Dave Spinozza** electric guitar • **Denny Seiwell** drums

20 Get on the Right Thing (Paul and Linda McCartney)

Recording: October 12th-16th, 1970 and March-April, 1971 (overdubs) **Location**: Columbia Studios, New York City and Sound Recorders Studio (overdubs), Los Angeles **Release**: May 1973, *Red Rose Speedway*

The fast and stomping "Get on the Right Thing" was a typically light McCartney track.

The song that Paul had Spinozza and Seiwell listen to before the recording was simple, but charming, with lighthearted lyrics. Pulling it off, however, was anything but a walk in the park.

Denny Seiwell: "We recorded the basic track with Paul on piano and Dave on electric guitar, and I covered the drums with tea towels trying to get the Beatles' drum sound from so many recordings, trying to be Ringo! It was an awesome song that took a lot of technique to pull off, and quite complicated as well."[61]

During the take, an unexpected glitch occurred, but it did not stop the recording. Seiwell: "(It happened that) the headphones quit on Paul, but he continued on anyway, and didn't fix that or edit it out."[62] That's what happened: if you listen carefully, at 3:01 one can hear McCartney screaming "My plug came out!"

McCartney's strongly echoed vocals set the tone for this well-crafted pop song, with its easy refrain, flawless backing vocals, excellent bass support and there you have it: a track in which Seiwell's drum rolls show nicely. Paul also recorded some backwards guitar parts, in true *Revolver* fashion. "Get on the Right Thing", though, never made it onto *RAM*, nor did it make the cut as a single, originally planned for an Autumn release in 1971[63]; thus, on the eve of coming out with *Red Rose Speedway* in 1973, Paul came across this track that had been put aside. McCartney was not pleased with it because he had recorded the vocal part at the end of a whole day's work in the studio and hadn't even been able to remember all the words correctly,

---

61 Interview courtesy of Denny Seiwell, 18/11/2011.

62 *Ibid.*

63 At the time the record was released, Tony Barrow from McCartney's press office, said to journalists: "Paul has told me that they want to make another single, probably recorded in a London studio sometime this summer. He and Linda have already written one or two things together which are suitable for a single; but they may decide on something more recent , since they're writing all the time" (*Disc and Music Echo*, May 22nd, 1971).

so he thought it was unusable. It was Denny Laine who convinced him otherwise: "But it's great. I love it. If you change the vocal though, it won't be as strong."[64]

Suddenly this up-tempo song seemed perfect for the melodic rock feel McCartney intended for his new album which he was targeting to a wider audience. The tracks shines thanks to the excellent quality of the original recording, in all likelihood just remixed and perhaps filled out with a couple of overdubs by McCartney.[65] The track would be included in *Red Rose Speedway*.

Musicians:

Paul McCartney vocals, backing vocals, piano, bass, electric guitar • **Linda McCartney** backing vocals • **Dave Spinozza** electric guitar • **Denny Seiwell** drums

After just one week, Spinozza left the sessions. McCartney would have liked him to commit himself full-time, but Spinozza had no intention to give up his other recording sessions.

Denny Seiwell: "Paul asked us to not book any dates (…) He said, 'I want your time for three weeks. Just don't book any sessions, I'd like to hire you from nine to six daily.' Spinozza saw that we'd be sometimes finished by two or three in the afternoon. So he took a date, like a four o'clock session or something. He said to Paul, 'You mind if I take off? I have to do something.' And Paul thought, 'Oh, that's not what we agreed on here.' Paul asked me if there was another guitar player I really liked working with."[66]

At this point the twenty-one-year-old Hugh McCracken (1942-2013) took over on guitar. Later, he would also figure in some recordings for Lennon and for Billy Joel.

21 The Back Seat of My Car (Paul McCartney)

Recording: October 22nd, 1970, January 11th (overdubs part 1) and March-April, 1971 (overdubs part 2)
Location: Columbia Studios, A&R Studios (overdubs part 1), New York City and Sound Recorders Studios (overdubs part 2), Los Angeles **Release:** May 1971, *RAM*

In the interview sheet included in *McCartney* and given to the press, Paul proudly stated that he had "a queue (of songs) waiting to be recorded."[67]

"The Back Seat of My Car" was one of those. During the *Get Back!* sessions on January 14th, 1969 McCartney performed an early version of the song. Paul, on piano, plays the melody without the lyrics, but the song is clearly recognizable.

At that time, the track was still in an embryonic stage, but in the following months, McCartney went back to work on it; by the time he went to New York, "The Back Seat of My Car" had become a rich tune with several different sections, in the style of the *Abbey Road* medley.

---

[64] Interview with Laine published in: Geoffrey Giuliano, *Blackbird*, 1989.

[65] Some new backing vocals and possibly some electric guitar touch-ups might have been added.

[66] Chaz Lipp, *RAM, Wings and Beyond. An Interview with Denny Seiwell*, www.themortonreport.com, 22/05/2012.

[67] *The McCartney Self-Interview*, 1970.

At Columbia Studios, McCartney really got into it. He can be heard in an outtake enthusiastically leading Seiwell and McCracken – whose instrumental parts can be better appreciated here, before the song would be heavily overdubbed – through the recording of the basic track: an amazing take that includes an awesome final jam, with piano and a guitar solo.

The recording was difficult, as Seiwell recalls: "That song took a little longer than any other because of all the movements, and the reprise coda... We celebrated when we got the good take!"[68]

With its fragmented structure, the song is, in fact, one of the most complex compositions written by McCartney and, albeit a little whimsical, one of his best.

Paul was no doubt influenced by listening to classical music which led him to conceive the song as a collage of recurring themes and here again, he was able to demonstrate his skills as a musical arranger and "stitcher" of melodies.

The moving introduction to the song – on a dreamy 9th minor chord played in arpeggio both by piano and electric guitar – leads into the two tuneful opening verses, so typical of McCartney's ballads.

These two verses, which seem to lead up to a smooth slow song, are instead separated by two up-tempo – *quasi* boogie – sections, with a playful superimposition of voices sung by Paul in a curious *gramelot*. McCartney must have had a lot of fun doing it, because in some bits his barely containable laughter is audible.

The original merger of separate fragments peaks in the moving refrain that ends the song (some of the verses were interpreted by Lennon as directed at him), whose dramatic tones are reinforced by the orchestral arrangement, which ranges from brass band to romantic strings.[69]

From a technical point of view, "The Back Seat of My Car" comes across as a masterful show of skill: in it, McCartney pulled out all the stops and flaunted the whole of his vocal range, running the gamut from the lowest and almost cavernous bass notes of his voice all the way to a falsetto, most likely achieved using the Varispeed recording technique. In the last refrain, McCartney probably hits one of the highest notes in his vocal range.

In addition to careful vocal multi-layering, voices were given different roles by McCartney, and they were used both as melodically and as rhythmic support, something it is thought to have been inspired by the techniques used by Brian Wilson.

Considerable overdubbing work was done in Los Angeles under the supervision of Eirik Wangberg, who recalls: "We did lots of overdubbing, such as brand new bass and guitar tracks

---

68 Interview courtesy of Denny Seiwell, 14/11/2011.
69 The New York Philharmonic Orchestra is credited on the *RAM* sleeve notes, but their archives have no record of the sessions. Therefore, also according to Seiwell's recollections (see "Uncle Albert", sheet 28), it is likely that some orchestra's members did participate in the recordings as free-lancers.

(…) Other cool bits were done, such as adding more vocals, such as the improvisation and ad-libs that we superimposed almost syllable by syllable."[70]

Paul proved that he was skilled in recording these instrumental tracks. To the piano and bass parts, McCartney also added the dizzying guitar solo which wraps up the song, just before a brief reprise[71] powerfully introduced by Seiwell's drums. The drum part is acting as a comment and melodic – even more than rhythmic – support. It deserves a Golden Palm for the best percussion performance of all of McCartney's records.

If the meaning behind the title "The Back Seat of My Car" remained unknown for decades (Paul revealed it in 2001, in an interview to *Mojo!* saying: "That's a really teenage song, with the stereotypical parent who doesn't agree, and the two lovers are going to take on the world"), it is not difficult nonetheless to see it as a song about the generation gap. In adolescent code, "the back seat of my car" is the place one goes to make love.

The verses, with the reference to the words "making love is wrong", symbolize the strict rules against sexuality imposed by parents, which young lovers always and everywhere try to escape.

Not a very commercial track, "The Back Seat of My Car" was nevertheless issued in the UK as a single, taken from *RAM*: it was a resounding flop, only making it to #39 on the charts. *Melody Maker*'s critic Chris Welch said: "It's not the most thrilling of songs. So far I have played this seven times in succession. In the final analysis it proves a unmemorable performance." The track was included in the *Wingspan* collection. McCartney rehearsed it for his 2002/03 *Drivin' Tour*, but it was never performed live, even though it was among the band's favorites at that time. The jazz version included in *Thrillington* is beautiful.

Musicians:

Paul McCartney vocals, backing vocals, piano, electric guitar, bass • **Linda McCartney** backing vocals • **Hugh McCracken** electric guitar • **Denny Seiwell** drums • **Marvin Stamm, Mel Davis, Ray Crisara, Snooky Young** brass • **Ron Carter, Richard Davis (?)** double-bass • **David Nadien, Aaron Rosand (?)** violin • **The New York Philharmonic Orchestra** strings, horns

22 Rode All Night (Paul McCartney)

Recording: October 22nd, 1970 **Location:** Columbia Studios, New York City **Release:** May 2012, *RAM* (Deluxe Edition)

After spending so much time and energy recording "The Back Seat of My Car", McCartney & co. decided they had had enough. McCracken took his things and went home until the next session. Seiwell told he was breaking down his drum kit, when Paul strolled back in the studio asking, "What are you doing? I've got something I want to record!"

---

[70] *Claudio Dirani Interview with Eirik Wangberg,* January 2005.

[71] This is the point where McCartney started improvising and where he overdubbed guitar and vocals.

McCartney strapped on his Gibson and led Seiwell into this punchy, semi-improvised and newly written song, significantly called "Rode All Night".

Paul played up in this heavy number, filled with sexual references. Unfortunately, the sound engineer was not so inspired to capture that unforgettable moment; so Paul and Denny launched into another take. This recording, the actual take two that was laid down by the duo, found its place on the bonus cd of *RAM* (2012 edition): "If you think the version you hear is rockin'" – Seiwell later commented – "that first take was balls to the wall rock'n'roll!"[72]

Musicians:

Paul McCartney vocals, electric guitar • **Denny Seiwell** drums

23 A Love for You (Paul McCartney)

Recording: October 26th, 1970, March-April, 1971 (overdubs part 1), January, 1981 (overdubs part 2) and April, 2003 (overdubs part 3) **Location:** Columbia Studios, New York City, Sunset Sound Recorder Studio (overdubs part 1), Los Angeles, Rude Studio (overdubs part 2), Campbeltown and Henson Studios (overdubs part 3), Los Angeles **Release:** May 2003, *The In-Laws Soundtrack*

"A Love for You" was an up-tempo song typical of McCartney's repertoire. In the studio, Paul took up the acoustic guitar and in just a few takes, recorded this fast-paced track with McCracken (electric guitar) and Seiwell, whose drum rolls play the lion's share; the recording of the basic track captures the spontaneity of the cut, with an overdub of the throbbing bass and McCartney's voice off-mike. A real rocker, with Paul's best screaming vocals and a tight ending, unfortunately excluded from the *RAM* track-list. "A Love for You" was resuscitated and given more overdubs in 1981 for the *Cold Cuts* project – with contributions by Wings' members Steve Holley and Laurence Juber – but again, it was nixed.

The right moment came in 2003. McCartney: "I was asked by *The In-Laws* filmmakers if they could use one of my songs that I had lying around for quite a long time (…) I said, 'Yeah, sure. Let me freshen it up a bit and check it and make sure I like it' (…) We remixed it and I saw it on the film and I think it works great!"[73]

Ralph Sall, the film's musical producer, told of a curious coincidence: "I'm a big fan of Paul McCartney, and I tried to figure out what music Michael Douglas' character would listen to. I thought of Paul's unreleased song, 'A Love for You', and I called his office and ran down the concept of the movie. I didn't tell them what song I had in mind, but it turns out that Paul suggested the same song that I wanted!"[74]

[72] http://webpages.charter.net/ram71/mrs.htm
[73] *Entertainment Tonight Interview*, May 2003.
[74] *Billboard*, 10/05/2003.

The track is included in *The In-Laws* soundtrack album (2003). Another version, called 'Van Winkle Mix' is included in the 2012 remastered version of *RAM*. It features other overdubs (a piano, some vocals) probably added by Paul himself in 1986.

Musicians:

Paul McCartney vocals, backing vocals, acoustic and electric guitar, bass, keyboards, percussion • **Linda McCartney** backing vocals, tambourine • **Hugh McCracken** electric guitar • **Denny Seiwell** drums • **Denny Laine** backing vocals • **Steve Holley** backing vocals, percussion • **Laurence Juber** backing vocals, electric guitar

24 Hey Diddle (Paul and Linda McCartney)

Recording: October 26th, 1970 **Location:** Columbia Studios, New York City **Release:** May 2012, *RAM* (Deluxe Edition)

"Hey Diddle" was an unpretentious folk-country tune (its title is a reference to "Hey Diddle Diddle", a famous English nursery rhyme set to music in 1870 by James William Elliott), probably intended for the *Rupert the Bear* project and that McCartney most likely recorded on his own, playing acoustic guitar in his typical fingerpicking style.

A very simple basic track, with bass and some percussion played on a chicken pan pot. Then Paul overdubbed some whistles, to add a bucolic flavor to the song. But the track went unused and this recording saw the light only in 2012, as a bonus track in the *RAM* remastered edition.

McCartney seems to have had an uncanny taste for the track: in 1973 he rehearsed it for the *James Paul McCartney* show and in 1974, while in Nashville, he overdubbed it[75].

"Hey Diddle" found a spot on *Wingspan* in 2001. This is a home recording by the McCartneys, captured *en plein air* in their Scottish farm in June 1971 as they're singing this ditty – together with "Bip Bop" – while the kids hang around and little Mary is giggling in the background.[76]

Musicians:

Paul McCartney vocals, acoustic guitar, bass, percussion, Irish whistle • **Linda McCartney** vocals • **Hugh McCracken (?)** acoustic guitar • **Denny Seiwell (?)** percussion, Irish whistle (?)

25 Long Haired Lady (Paul and Linda McCartney)

Recording: October 27th 1970, January 11th (overdubs part 1) and March-April, 1971 (overdubs part 2) **Location:** Columbia Studios, A&R Studios (overdubs part 1), New York City and Sound Recorders Studios (overdubs part 2), Los Angeles **Release:** May 1971, *RAM*

A huge amount of work was done in the recording studio for *RAM*: in fact, many tracks that McCartney had composed in the previous months were still unfinished or were just fragments of songs that needed to be completed and perfected.

---

[75] Overdubs made on July 8th-9th, 1974: Cate Sisters (violins) and Lloyd Green (pedal steel guitar).
[76] The footage was included on the *Wingspan* video.

This is why Paul had to dust off his arranger's hat and put his best skills to work; he was going to build medleys out of different tunes stitched together, rather than record true songs.

One cannot help but see in his inclination towards musical fragmentation, the deep psycho-emotional malaise that Paul was experiencing at the time.

Certainly, the opinion voiced by Bob Woffinden, who saw in the album some tracks that "change course half-way through or display less glaring signs of schizophrenia"[77], rings true. This syndrome is particularly clear in "Long Haired Lady", a "strangely distended track which has several diverse parts, two of which feature decent tunes trying to get out."[78]

If in *Abbey Road* McCartney had succeeded in merging the essence of pop music with the symphonic language – the *suite* form, where the melodies chase one another, come together, then reappear again separately – *RAM* seems to be lacking the same structure's plan.

In "Long Haired Lady" the main image is referable to Linda; it's a sort of *mini-suite,* but its structure gives the impression of being forced.

McCartney had taped one take without the coda – the long chant "Love Is Long" which he recorded as a separate song – and later he put the two tracks together. An unreleased recording of the basic track shows the song already in this form, with Paul on acoustic guitar – and lead vocals, off-mike – Seiwell on drums and McCracken on electric guitar.

A disjointed track that reveals a chaotic structure: introduction (two verses, sung by Paul and with answering vocals by Linda) – bridge – break – two verses – refrain – two verses – refrain – coda – introduction – bridge – coda.

You can easily lose your way in it. Nevertheless, the dream-like atmosphere of the song does present some lovely folk verses with Paul's voice counterpointed by electric guitar – and by an acoustic instrument, which sounds like a mandolin, maybe played by McCracken – and an ethereal refrain where, once again, McCracken's guitar stands out.

The recording is carefully and masterfully performed; just listen to Paul's exquisite vocal harmonies in the last verse.

The track ends with a long cacophony – conducted by the New York Philharmonic Orchestra horn section – that is reminiscent of the renowned example, "A Day in the Life".

Dixon Van Winkle revealed: "On the track there's a big long trumpet solo. Two players played it. They traded back and forth between phrases, so it sounds like one player playing a long phrase taking no breath, but really it was two guys."[79]

After the recording, Wangberg had McCartney listen to it and he was witness to an exceptional moment: "He rested his arms on my shoulders after hearing it and, as I turned and looked at

[77] B. Woffinden, *cit.*, p.48.
[78] *Ibid.*
[79] *Ram Deluxe Edition* in *Paul McCartney Archive Collection*, 2012, p.59.

his face, tears were rolling down. Paul is a very, very sensitive person! Listening to his vocal work with Linda really got him into it."[80]

A nice episode – occurred during one session held at Columbia Studios – is told by songwriter, producer and sound engineer at Columbia between 1963 and 1996, Don Meehan. Paul was without a guitar pick and borrowed one from him. After the session, McCartney returned the pick to Don, who recalls: "It was only a 25 cent pick, but I sure wish I had thought to have him autograph it."[81]

Paul had played the song again just once, during the rehearsals for *James Paul McCartney* (1973), where he performed a snippet of "Long Haired Lady" on acoustic guitar. This track appears also on *Thrillington*.

Musicians:

Paul McCartney vocals, backing vocals, acoustic and electric guitar, bass, keyboards • **Linda McCartney** vocals, backing vocals • **Hugh McCracken** acoustic and electric guitar, mandolin (?) • **Denny Seiwell** drums • **Marvin Stamm, Mel Davis, Ray Crisara, Snooky Young** brass • **The New York Philharmonic Orchestra** horns

26 Sunshine, Sometime (Paul McCartney)

Recording: October 29th, 1970 **Locaton:** Columbia Studios, New York City **Release:** May 2012, *RAM* (Deluxe Edition)

Its Caribbean flavor suggests that this track could have been written by Paul during one of his exotic holidays. The song was conceived for the *Rupert the Bear* soundtrack, and would be included in the project recorded by Wings in 1978.

For the recording, Paul chose a very basic arrangement: the basic track consisted only of acoustic guitar – and McCartney's guide-vocal, off-mike – electric guitar and an exotic percussion bed, played along with a rhythm-track.

Seiwell: "I kind of remember using some African drums and clicking on the rims with a wooden stick... We built that track as we went, but basically it was done with everyone playing at the same time and then a few overdubs to complete it."[82]

This take, that went unissued for forty-two years, was finally included as a bonus-track on the *RAM* remastered edition in 2012.

Anyway, it's hard to appreciate the track in this still incomplete form, lacking Paul and Linda's vocals and its outstanding walking-bass part. These touches were very likely added later, in July 1978 during the aforementioned sessions with Wings.

Musicians:

---

[80] *Claudio Dirani Interview with Eirik Wangberg*, January 2005.
[81] http://cdbaby.com/cd/donmeehan
[82] Interview courtesy of Denny Seiwell, 02/10/2012.

Paul McCartney acoustic guitar, electric guitar (?) • **Hugh McCracken (?)** electric guitar (?) • **Denny Seiwell** percussion

27 Oh Woman, Oh Why? (Paul McCartney)

Recording: November 3rd, 1970 **Location:** Columbia Studios, New York City **Release:** February 1971, "Another Day" single B-side

During the early *RAM* sessions, Paul launched into several jams, along with his brand-new drummer Denny Seiwell, at the end of the regular recording day.

One of these resulted in the epic "Rode All Night", unreleased at the time[83]: a lengthy, semi-improvised heavy-rock over eight minutes long, in which McCartney's gritty guitar – performing a vast array of remarkable rhythmic patterns – duets with Seiwell's tremendous drumming.

It was probably during that session that Paul came up with the idea for "Oh Woman, Oh Why?", an acid-tinged track that shares a lot with "Rode All Night", especially in its aggressive guitars and its rip-roaring vocals.

However it went, this is the most hard-sounding track taped during the *RAM* sessions: a gutsy recording, with strong drums, heavy distorted guitars and a rolling bass.

Seiwell was enthusiastic about it: "It reminded me of The Beatles... And it remains one of my favorite tracks from that period. The drum sound was amazing, one of the best (we got) from CBS Studios. It was not a jam, Paul brought the tune in and Spinozza played electric (...) Then Paul and I played shakers and percussion."[84]

Seiwell's recollections about Spinozza playing on the track are not supported by the sleeve notes included in the 2012 *RAM* edition: maybe this was among the tracks that had been previously recorded with Spinozza and then re-worked (partially or from scratch) with McCracken.

During the overdub sessions, Paul gave in to his more dangerous instincts and fired off several gun shots, which he added to the track as percussion support. The rustic vocals by Linda completed the background to the rasping vocal performance by McCartney, the truly memorable part of the track. It was issued as the B-side to "Another Day".

Musicians:

Paul McCartney vocals, electric guitar, bass, gun-shots, shaker, percussion • **Linda McCartney** backing vocals • **Hugh McCracken** electric guitar • **Denny Seiwell** drums, shaker, percussion

---

[83] In truth, a few parts were merged together and incorporated in "Giddy", a McCartney track recorded by Roger Daltrey in 1977.
[84] Interview courtesy of Denny Seiwell, 18/11/2011.

28 Uncle Albert/Admiral Halsey (Paul and Linda McCartney)

Recording: November 6th, 1970, January 3rd and 11th (overdubs part 1), March 1st, 9th, 10th, 12th and April 7th, 1971 (overdubs part 2) **Location:** Columbia Studios, A&R Studios (overdubs part 1), New York City and Sound Recorders Studios (overdubs part 2), Los Angeles **Release:** May 1971, *RAM*

McCartney's imagination and creativity as well as his ability to be inspired by real events, places and people were always driving forces behind his composing talent.

The famous "Penny Lane", in which Paul portrayed, in vivid splashes, the Liverpool of his youth is one of the foremost examples.

In this case, McCartney drew on the memories he had of an old uncle of his. Paul: "I did have an uncle, Albert Kendall, who used to quote Bible when he got drunk."[85]

The song, originally titled "We're So Sorry", was conceived by McCartney as an apologize to the older generation of people.

McCartney: "If there was a party, all the uncles and all the older guys would basically just get drunk. That was the way you had fun (…) I had an Uncle Albert, who would get very drunk. Otherwise, in his daily life he was quite a respectable guy (…) I was using him as a symbol of that lifestyle and that way of getting 'out of it'. But we had got into other ways – pot was prevalent at the time. I was imagining that generation looking at us behaving weirdly."[86]

That was enough to inspire McCartney to produce one of his most fascinating and original pieces of work. Once in the recording studio, it turned into a medley; Paul put together "Uncle Albert" and "Admiral Halsey". Paul said the second title was simply a name he liked.[87]

Although some critics considered it to be no more than a re-arrangement of "Yellow Submarine", "Uncle Albert/Admiral Halsey" is a truly memorable track.

Drawing on his ability as an arranger, Paul managed to put together two songs masterfully joined as one. The first part ("Uncle Albert") has a regular cadence and is full of odd and amusing effects, from Paul's voice coming through a telephone to the sound of a thunderstorm: and it is perhaps in this clever gallery of sounds that the only real analogy can be made to "Yellow Submarine".

The second tune was rhythmic and lively. "Admiral Halsey", in grand vaudeville style and opening on a flugelhorn solo, is a very up-tempo song, full of melody changes (at least four), in which McCartney takes full advantage of the breadth of his vocal range (from bass to falsetto) and in which the catchy Paul-Linda two-voice refrain "Hands across the water/Heads across the sky" stands out.

---

[85] Paul Gambaccini, *Paul McCartney in his own words*, 1976, pp.66-67.
[86] *Ram Deluxe Edition* in *Paul McCartney Archive Collection*, 2012, p.42.
[87] These were McCartney's words. In truth, it is the name of a famous American Admiral who commanded a fleet in the Pacific Ocean during WWII.

The effect is comical and it has an ironic self-mocking bent to it that makes it a must for McCartney aficionados. McCartney recently revealed the inspiration behind this patchwork of tunes. Paul: "What I take the influence back to was *The Teenage Opera* by Keith West (…) I think it was just that one record that made you realize that it didn't have to be the same tempo or the same key all the way through, you could cut like a film."[88]

There were a few hiccups in the recording. After a first attempt to lay down the basic track at Columbia Studios with Spinozza, the song was re-recorded with McCracken and then the track was filled out with more overdubs.

Seiwell recalls that about the drum part, too, McCartney's input was decisive in suggesting an accompaniment that was truly original: "If I played a part, like in this song, that was a normal drum part, Paul would say, 'You know what, I'm hearing something a little different in there, can you make something that has more tom-tom, a more of a melodic part? I'm going rough singing something to you.' Paul suggested ideas but he never dictated a part to me."[89]

At the start, the recording was fraught with difficulty. Seiwell: "We did it as one song and it was a difficult one but after a few rundowns with the caliber of musicianship, it was fairly easy (…) We never spent more than one day on any track. Paul really helped with the time changes as he was playing piano along. The 'gypsy' part was interesting because the time turned around, and came back to the beat. It didn't take too much time until we had the right take."[90]

An outtake from those sessions was issued in 2012 on iTunes under the title "Uncle Albert Jam": the recording was a leisure moment for the three musicians. At one point, McCartney started wandering, singing excerpts of "The Back Seat of My Car" and "Cumberland Gap", and old American folk-song from 19th Century made famous by skiffle musician Lonnie Donegan, who took it to #1 on the UK charts in 1957.

A superb arrangement, with an orchestral score written by George Martin (this detail, hidden for nearly 30 years, makes this track the first collaboration between the solo McCartney and Martin, just months after the breakup of The Beatles), a tuba-like bass with alternating fifths and characteristic electric guitar riffs earned "Uncle Albert/Admiral Halsey" a Grammy Award in the Best Arrangement Accompanying Vocalist category for 1971.

Martin came out with an effective orchestral arrangement, working so hard that he had even forgotten the title of the song: the score sheets reproduced on the 2012 Deluxe version of *RAM* reveal that he wrote "Uncle Arthur" instead! Martin: "That was my Freudian slip. I had an Uncle Arthur!"[91] But it could be possible that Martin was thinking of "Uncle Arthur", a song recorded by Bowie in 1967 or that his mind went to the English writer Arthur Maxwell,

[88] *Paul McCartney Discusses His Inspirations, Guitars and RAM with Mansun's Paul Draper*, in http://drownedinsounds.com
[89] A. Croft, *cit.*, p.14.
[90] Interview courtesy of Denny Seiwell, 12/11/2011.
[91] George Martin, in *RAM Deluxe Edition* in *Paul McCartney Archive Collection*, 2012, p.49.

also known as *Uncle Arthur* and who became very famous with his *Bedtime Stories*, a 35 million copies' success worldwide.

Paul himself conducted the orchestra during the A&R Studios sessions, raising some bafflement.

Seiwell: "Paul spent about 45 minutes tuning the New York Philharmonic (…) The musicians were looking at each other. They thought he was only a freaky rich person."[92]

Even Seiwell was shocked: "We were in the studio with the top players… This (wa)s the David Nadien string section that played with the New York Philharmonic. And they're all looking at each other: 'What's this guy doing, tuning us?' He had some very specific ideas on how he wanted the orchestra to sound. And the first playback, half of 'em came into the control room to hear the playback and they said, 'Oh my God, it sounds like the London Symphony.'"[93]

And it's really David Nadien (1926-2014) – the New York Philharmonic Orchestra's first violin between 1966 and 1970 – that appears in a photograph included in the *RAM* Deluxe Edition book.[94] Reportedly, also Aaron Rosand (born 1927) – one of the world's most outstanding violin virtuosos – plays on the record, but the musician has not confirmed his involvement. Ron Carter is also portrayed in the photo, wearing dark glasses, on stand-up bass.

Phil Ramone offers this tale: "Paul had come to the Studio A1 at A&R to record strings overdub (…) After Paul wrote the arrangement, I booked a huge orchestra and I specifically requested an all-star orchestra (…) On the morning of the first session, I discovered that we had no conductor. This could be a problem (…) At the first *RAM* string overdub session, the lack of direction caused by the absentee conductor was telling. 'Why don't you conduct?' I suggested to Paul. 'I'm not trained,' he replied. 'You wrote the song. Who would know better than you how to conduct it? Wave your arms, and you'll be amazed.' So he did and it came out great. The funny thing is about 20% of the orchestra didn't know who he was. They were classical players."[95]

Among the sound engineers present in the studio there were Tim Geelan ("Working on 'Uncle Albert…' was one of the highlights of my career"[96]) and Dixon Van Winkle, who remembers the tricks used to produce the track: "Phil Ramone asked me to work with him on the *RAM* sessions (…) Paul came over to studio 1 to track the orchestra, vocals and some other overdubs with Phil; but he had a scheduling conflict one day and Paul asked me to take over (…) I was a part-time nanny, since Mary would often be crawling around the console (…) Our

[92] Denny Seiwell in the interview with Howie Edelson, *cit.*, p.25.
[93] *Ibid.*
[94] In this photo, maybe taken from the "Uncle Albert" session, the orchestra (16 violins – we can see only 8 of them, but their parts could have been doubled – 4 violas, 4 violoncellos, 1 bass, 1 harp) follows Martin's original score.
[95] Marc Myers, *JazzWax, Phil Ramone Interview, part five*, 13/11/2010: http://www.allaboutjazz.com/php/news.php?id=70287
[96] G. Eskow, *cit.*

usual way of recording horns at A&R was to put a pair of mics either in the front or distant rear of the players. Paul wanted us to stick mics right up in the bell."[97]

The flugelhorn solo was Marvin Stamm's ticket to fame. He recalls: "When Paul decided he wanted a short solo from one of the horn players – me, Snooky Young, Mel Davis, Ray Crisara – someone in the section yelled out, 'Let the kid do it!' Paul must have liked that idea, because he asked me to go ahead with it."[98] Stamm again: "Paul sang the part he wanted and I went on until he liked it."[99]

That recording was absolutely relaxed. Stamm: "By the time this session occurred, I had been in New York for about four years working as a studio recording musician, so I felt very comfortable within the community, although I was only 31 years old at the time. Paul was very relaxed in the studio, he did not try to cause any tension. He was also very open and respectful of everyone. We were going to do the brass for three different songs in three separate sessions, completely apart from the strings overdubs."[100]

Stamm adds: "For 'Admiral Halsey', we listened the backing track, that had a scratch vocal on it and the solo was the last thing we recorded for the track. There was nothing terribly difficult to play. The most difficult thing was to make the music sound the way Paul wanted to sound. It was a challenge. He sat on a chair and sang the part, that he would have like to sound as much as possible close to the old radio days…"[101]

Stamm recalls amused: "I made a joke many times, that at that time I was the most famous unknown horn player in the world, because nobody knew my name!"[102]

McCartney was bursting with ideas. First, he wanted to use a filter to obtain the effect of a voice on the telephone, but something went wrong. Van Winkle: "If you listen carefully, you'll hear Paul gurgling right before the telephone voice comes in (…) McCartney was supposed to give the engineer a cue when he wanted the low pass filter dropped in (…) The engineer made the switch too early and the filter came in on one of the gurgles."[103] And that wasn't the end of it: "I remember Paul telling me that Armin Steiner went out to the edge of a cliff to record that storm and was Paul's idea to add the effect at that point in the track."[104]

For McCracken, too, the recording was one to remember: "This song represented a breakthrough in our musical relationship" – McCracken says – "Paul is a genius. He sees and hears everything he wants, and would give specific instructions to me and the drummer. But he

---

[97] *Ibid.*
[98] "I was in the horn section and I was the youngest at the time" Stamm recalled. Thomas Staudter, *In Person: Outside Vibe, and Verve to Match*, in *New York Times*, May 21st, 2006.
[99] http://www.jazzkc.org/issues/1996-12/q&astamm.html
[100] Interview courtesy of Marvin Stamm, 30/07/2012.
[101] http://www.tumblr.com/tagged/hugh-mccracken
[102] *Ibid.*
[103] G. Eskow, *cit.*
[104] *Ibid.* But Eirik Wangberg reveals: "Is my idea! I suggested it to Paul and he loved it. I used a mono track which I got from Universal Studios." From *Maccazine*, Vol. 40, issue 3 / Vol. 41, issue 1, p.67.

didn't know what he wanted the guitar part to be like on this song. I asked him to trust me and he did. After I came up with the parts, he was very pleased. For the rest of the record, Paul let me try things out before making any suggestions."[105]

Even Lennon admired McCracken's guitar work on the album, as McCracken himself told it: "The first time I met him was for 'Happy Xmas' (…) And he said, 'I heard you were on Paul's album, I really liked your work'. I said, 'Oh, thanks a lot' Then he leaned in and said, 'You know it was just an audition to get to play with me.'"[106]

During the overdub sessions held in April 1971 at Sound Recorders Studios in Los Angeles, engineer Eirik Wangberg called in Paul Beaver (1926-1975), the man who along with Bernie Krause (born 1938) introduced synthesizer in rock music.

Beaver added a synthesizer part, as Wangberg recalls: "He was there to colour the underwater background voices on 'Uncle Albert/Admiral Halsey'."[107]

The market response was sensational and the record exploded in immediate success. Released as the first single from *RAM* in August 1971, "Uncle Albert..." soared to first place on the charts in the US, where it was certified by the R.I.A.A. with a gold record for a million copies sold in the short space of one month's time.

The track was never played live. It was rehearsed for the 1989/90 tour, but Paul wasn't happy with the results and, also due to the fact that the track seemed very difficult to perform, gave up on the idea.

In a recent interview with *Rolling Stone*, McCartney confirmed: "People keep requesting 'Uncle Albert'. It'd be great to do, but it's just a little bit of a challenge to learn, 'cause these are not twelve-bars. But once you get them, and once you do them right, they kind of *feel* like twelve-bars. That's the trick."[108]

It is included in the *Wings Greatest*, *All the Best!* (US version) and *Wingspan* collections. The brass band version included in *Thrillington* is particularly successful. The song was covered by two famous jazz players: trumpeter Freddie Hubbard on his album *First Light* (1971) – featuring Ron Carter on bass, David Nadien on violin and Herbie Hancock on piano – and drummer Buddy Rich on the LP *Stick It!* (1972).

Musicians:

Paul McCartney vocals, backing vocals, acoustic and electric guitar, piano, xylophone (?), bass • **Linda McCartney** backing vocals • **Hugh McCracken** electric guitar, acoustic guitar • **Denny Seiwell** drums **Paul Beaver** synthesizer • **Marvin Stamm, Mel Davis, Ray Crisara, Snooky Young** brass • **David**

---

[105] *Ibid.*

[106] http://www.tumblr.com/tagged/hugh-mccracken

[107] Edward Eikelenboom, in *Maccazine*, Vol. 40, issue 3 / Vol. 41, issue 1, p.65.

[108] Simon Vozic-Levinson, *Q&A: Paul McCartney Looks Back on His Magical Mystery Tour*, in *Rolling Stone*, 25/07/2013.

Nadien, Aaron Rosand (?) violin • **Ron Carter** double-bass • **The New York Philharmonic Orchestra** strings

29 Too Many People (Paul McCartney)

Recording: November 10th, 1970, January (overdubs part 1) and March-April, 1971 (overdubs part 2) **Location:** Columbia Studios, A&R Studios (overdubs part 1), New York City and Sound Recorders Studios (overdubs part 2), Los Angeles **Release:** May 1971, *RAM*

If the image of two beetles mating on the back cover of *RAM* was unanimously interpreted as symbolic of the treatment Paul had received from the other ex-Beatles and in particular, John, it is specifically to Lennon that most of the controversial songs of the album seem to be addressed.

Lennon immediately pricked up his ears when he heard "Too Many People", partly because the song did, in fact, contain allusive verses and partly because he had misunderstood some words.[109]

This is another example of just how far the relationship between John and Paul had deteriorated; the lyrics seem to refer to Lennon's public attitudes at that time and to his decision to break up the Beatles, when the previous year John said he wanted "a divorce", something McCartney called "a mistake" in the song.

It was this very verse that McCartney re-wrote, for initially it had specifically named Yoko Ono ("Yoko took your lucky break"). He then opted for a less direct approach.

Added to the verbal violence, McCartney used aggressive music to make "Too Many People" a strong rocker. The song is introduced by Paul's rending shriek coming after the slash of the acoustic guitar on the first beat: a brilliant opening that foretells the tense atmosphere of the album. The spaced-out guitar riff was achieved by Wangberg, who wanted a "not touchable" sound.[110] Along with the throbbing bass line, the dissonant electric guitar solos are noteworthy: McCracken recalled that McCartney had recorded the blistering central solo in a single take. A funny cacophony of many overdubbed acoustic guitars ends the track.

Seiwell: "For this one, Paul was on acoustic and Hugh on electric. I remember Paul putting on marching... Like boots on an overdub! I played also shaker and a cow-bell."[111] During the overdub sessions in January, Paul added a touch of brass, barely audible in the mix .

The track fits in with the energy and expressive force behind the most part of the music on *RAM*, something McCartney talked about on the eve of the album's release, in a interview for *Life*, presented as a program manifesto: "I'm trying for music that isn't too romantic."[112]

---

[109] Lennon probably misunderstood some of the verses that were not clearly pronounced by Paul, like the opening lines to this song, where McCartney shouts "Piece of cake!" and not "Fuck off yeah!", as Lennon might have misheard. But it's also true that the verse sounds a lot like "Piss off, cake": McCartney confirmed these lyrics, but it might be a case of revisionism.

[110] *Claudio Dirani Interview with Eirik Wangberg,* January 2005.

[111] Interview courtesy of Denny Seiwell, 18/11/2011.

In just a short while, the facts however, would prove otherwise, if we are to believe that one of the most frequent criticisms of McCartney regarded his inclination for overly romantic sentimentalism.

The song appears on *Wingspan* and finally played live during the 2005 *US Tour* and also on some live dates between 2007 and 2008. It is also included in *Thrillington*.

Musicians:

Paul McCartney vocals, backing vocals, acoustic and electric guitar, bass • **Linda McCartney** backing vocals • **Denny Seiwell** drums, percussion, shaker, cow-bell • **Hugh McCracken** acoustic and electric guitar • **Unknown musicians** horns

30 Little Woman Love (Paul and Linda McCartney)

Recording: November 13th and January 20th-21st (overdubs), 1970 **Location:** Columbia Studios and A&R Studios (overdubs), New York City **Release:** May 1972, "Mary Had a Little Lamb" single B-side

Another leftover from the *RAM* sessions, "Little Woman Love" was recorded with a very special guest. Denny Seiwell: "Paul said to me he wanted someone for a slap bass and I suggested Milt Hinton called 'The Judge', 65 years old at the time.[113] We were amazed at the energy he had."[114]

In fact it's true, the elaborate style of Hinton's double-bass is well suited to this lively and remarkable piano performance by McCartney, based on a jazzy riff often used by Paul. It's the same one heard in "Suicide" and in concert during breaks between songs, when McCartney sits down at the piano. Despite the carefree spirit of the recording, the track is enriched by beautiful backing vocals (slightly off-key) and by some excellent bluesy solos.

The exact recording date is uncertain: the 2012 *RAM* Deluxe Edition reports November, 13th on the official credits, while the handwritten date on the studio sheet – included in the same boxset – it reads October 13th.

An accurate reading reveals that the basic track only consisted of piano, bass, three separate drum tracks and a rough vocal by Paul. McCartney himself overdubbed several acoustic and electric guitar parts during the January sessions: each one of them is marked by Paul with notes like "TBE" ("To be erased"), "Check" or "Hold".

Neither Spinozza nor McCracken are listed as musicians, meaning that "Little Woman Love" was probably recorded while the two of them were not available for the session. The November date, though, seems to be the right one, since the song is on the same sheet along with "Heart of the Country" and "Smile Away", both recorded the following days.

---

[112] Interview conducted by Richard Meryman: *Paul McCartney: Break-Up and His New Life*, in *Life*, April 1971.
[113] Hinton, a jazz bass player from Cab Calloway's band for many years, passed away in 2000.
[114] Interview courtesy of Denny Seiwell, 18/11/2011.

According to some sources – although this is not confirmed – "Little Woman Love" was picked up again during the *Wild Life* sessions. It would be only issued in May of 1972 as the B-side to the single "Mary Had a Little Lamb"(see sheet **57**).

"Little Woman Love" was included in the *Wings Over Europe Tour* (1972) and *Wings' British Tour* (1973), as well as on the *James Paul McCartney* TV special and finally, in 1975 during the *Wings Over the World Tour*, always in medley with "C Moon".

Musicians:

Paul McCartney vocals, backing vocals, piano, percussion (?), acoustic and electric guitar • **Linda McCartney** backing vocals • **Denny Seiwell** drums, percussion • **Milt Hinton** double-bass

31 Smile Away (Paul McCartney)

Recording: November 16th, 1970, January 29th (overdubs part 1) and March-April, 1971 (overdubs part 2) **Location:** Columbia Studios, A&R Studios (overdubs part 1), New York City and Sound Recorders Studios (overdubs part 2), Los Angeles **Release:** May 1971, *RAM*

Eirik *The Norwegian* Wangberg: "Editing and mixing work for the *RAM* album was really hard. Paul wanted to record almost everything, 'cause he could have an idea during a session and wanted to have it on tape."[115]

While recording *RAM*, McCartney had shed light on his work method in the studio with some interesting statements.

McCartney: "The best things are often the free bits. I go out into the studio and I know I'm going to ad-lib. If I announce I'm going to ad-lib, I can't ad-lib because I'm no longer ad-libbing. So I've just got to go out there and improvise, and someone's got to be in there in the control room very cleverly thinking, 'He's going to ad-lib now, I'd better tape it.' It's very hard because good things get missed. Last night I was doing a real ad-lib and I was in a great mood and I was exploring what there was to be done – and they missed it. The next time around when they tried the tape, I wasn't exploring any longer."[116]

"Smile Away" is an excellent example of what happened during one of those sessions; at some point Paul started making a strongly distorted bass sound, a kind of unintentional fuzzing, similar to what McCartney had recorded with The Beatles in "Think for Yourself".

Rather than stop, McCartney told them to continue and leave in that sound – which can be clearly heard throughout the finished recording – and reinforcing it by overdubbing an amazing eight different bass tracks. Wangberg: "When we started to record 'Smile Away', I thought the bass track didn't sound good at all. Then I told Paul, 'Should it really be like this?' He

---

[115] This story was told by several acquaintances of the engineer on the Internet group: rec.music.beatles
[116] Richard Meryman, *cit.*

answered, 'Can you give me more of it?' We then both did our best to distort the heck out of the sound."[117]

This sort of plug-and-play rocker was another *RAM* track that the critics and Lennon interpreted as full of unfriendly insinuations: the lyrics are rather generic, but the images they convey certainly give the feeling of having a specific target.

The tasteless references to the betrayal of a friend further embitter this garage-rock, vigorously performed and which reaches its most exciting moment in the climax between 2:46 and 2:53, when Linda's vocal modulation meets Paul's powerful roar. The song is really powerful and raging, one of the best examples of McCartney's aggressive style of the early Seventies.

Unconfirmed reports say that at the end of the tape containing a demo version of "Smile Away" – dating from that Spring-Summer 1970 – Paul would talk to Linda about having Jimi Hendrix and a jazz drummer to record this song (and "Get on the Right Thing"): it never happened, since Hendrix prematurely died soon after, on September 18th.

Because of its simple, three-chord structure, "Smile Away" was performed in 1972 *Wings' University Tour* and in the following *Wings Over Europe Tour*; on some dates the track was used as an opener. The version that appears on *Thrillington* is re-arranged in a humoristic vein.

Musicians:

Paul McCartney vocals, backing vocals, bass, electric guitar • **Linda McCartney** backing vocals • **Hugh McCracken** electric guitar • **Denny Seiwell** drums

32 Heart of the Country (Paul and Linda McCartney)

Recording: November 16th, 1970 **Location:** Columbia Studios, New York City **Release:** May 1971, *RAM*

After years of living in London and following the Beatles' breakup, Paul and Linda moved up to the Scottish countryside, choosing to retreat there for relaxation and for their day to day living.

Thus, Paul started writing many compositions inspired by his new country life and "Heart of the Country", composed by McCartney in Argyll, Scotland is the first example in chronological order.[118] "Heart of the Country" is an acoustic track which did not receive the same overdubbing treatment as other *RAM* songs. The released version was a re-make of the original to which Dave Spinozza had played guitar.

Its simplicity makes it, still, one of the best and yet, least appreciated tracks in McCartney's catalogue.

A bare-bones recording, but performed flawlessly and brilliantly. What are the ingredients? Along with McCartney's walking-bass and McCracken's riffs – which cleverly highlight his

---

[117] *Claudio Dirani Interview with Eirik Wangberg*, January 2005
[118] Other songs that directly sing praise to the country are "I Lie Around" (see sheet 34), "Country Dreamer" (see sheet 54). Sporadic mention is in other tracks like "Tomorrow" (see sheet 45).

guitar's lower tones – Paul's vocals are enhanced by a jazzy scat solo which, according to Eirik Wangberg, "was something Paul wrote while he was recording the song."[119]

Maybe Hinton's visit in the studio for "Little Woman Love" aroused Paul's curiosity, 'cause that was a typical technique of Cab Calloway's style. It is a country-flavored song that Paul has re-worked into his own style.

Even Seiwell was up for it, replacing his drum with a metal garbage can lid that he used to record the sound of his wire brushes.[120]

The text is full of pastoral images about Paul and Linda's bucolic idyll in Scotland; through references to the "holy people", to animals and to a "home in the heart of the country" the lyrics draw a picture of Paul's lifestyle at that time, far away from the spotlight.

"Heart of the Country" was nearly forgotten by McCartney and although Paul had performed a snippet of it for the *James Paul McCartney* show, he never played it live, excluding it at the last minute from the *Unplugged* show as well, although it had been rehearsed. On *Thrillington* there is a version with some very nice vocals.

To compensate for the long period of oblivion, the track was included in *Wingspan*. A snippet of a new version – apparently recorded by McCartney in 2012 – has surfaced on Youtube in January 2013: it features Paul on vocals, acoustic guitar and harmonica.

Musicians:

Paul McCartney vocals, acoustic guitar, bass • **Hugh McCraken** electric guitar • **Denny Seiwell** brushes

33 Little Lamb Dragonfly (Paul and Linda McCartney)

Recording: October-November, 1970, January, 1971? (overdubs part 1) and March, 1972 (overdubs part 2) **Location**: Columbia Studios, A&R Studios? (overdubs part 1), New York City and Trident Studios (overdubs part 2), London **Release**: May 1973, *Red Rose Speedway*

One day, around the start of the year, Paul witnessed the death of one of the lambs on his Scottish farm. On the wave of emotion following the painful event, McCartney wrote this song, one of his most touching and inspired, dedicated to the tender little creature.

McCartney: "It was early in the morning and I had brought my guitar and I thought I couldn't have done nothing for this lamb, so I started singing 'I have no answer for you little lamb'."[121]

At Columbia Studios, McCartney offered up this track to Seiwell and McCracken, originally intended for the *Rupert the Bear* project.

Paul and Hugh recorded the backing track with two acoustic guitars and the support of Seiwell on drums. This recording remained unused, as McCartney thought something was still missing.

[119] *Claudio Dirani Interview with Eirik Wangberg,* January 2005.
[120] B. Spitzer-A. Steckler, *cit.*, p.130.
[121] Interview taken from the magazine *Viva,* January 1974.

"Little Lamb Dragonfly" is a long track (over 6 minutes) with a circular structure that joins together three sections with no connection to one another, in the best Beatles' tradition.

The introduction – embellished by harmonious twelve-string acoustic guitars – is followed by a chorus, repeated in the closing section as a coda. A crescendo leads into the main section of the song, where the instrumentation is enriched by bass, drums, piano, electric guitars – with some delicate arabesques – and orchestra.

Paul's vocal has a depth of emotion rarely heard in his discography. A great crescendo – with the call-and-response vocals – makes the tension rise and peaks in the most touching moment of the song that expresses an agonizing and painful cry: pain is coming back. The lyrics, however, are ambiguous enough as to allow for less naïve interpretations.[122]

The track was put on the shelf until the *Red Rose Speedway* recordings, when it was overdubbed and polished for its release on the album.

Denny Seiwell vividly recalls: "We had recorded the song during *RAM*, and it wasn't finished. One day we were over at Trident Studios, Paul was sitting at the piano and he was saying, 'I never really finished this' and I helped him finish a little bit, but I wouldn't call it co-writing (…) but I wrote some background harmonies."[123]

Jo-Jo Laine, Denny's wife at the time, recalled with real emotion the backing vocals overdub session: "It was the most exciting Wings session I was involved in... The words were so moving.. That I started crying! So, Denny and the others turned to me and the words became *She's crying, the little girl's crying...*"

Musicians:

Paul McCartney vocals, backing vocals, acoustic guitar, bass, piano, electric guitar • **Linda McCartney** backing vocals, dingers • **Hugh McCracken** acoustic and electric guitar • **Denny Seiwell** backing vocals, drums, percussion • **Denny Laine** backing vocals • **Unknown musicians** strings, horns

34 I Lie Around

Recording: October-November, 1970, January, 1971 (overdubs part 1) and November, 1972 (overdubs part 2) **Location**: Columbia Studios, A&R Studios (overdubs part 1), New York City, Abbey Road Studios or Olympic Studios (overdubs part 2), London **Release:** July 1973, "Live and Let Die" single B-side

"I Lie Around" is another episode dedicated to the praise of the country life, so typical of McCartney's early solo period.

This acoustic track is built on a very original arpeggio, with strings played in ascending sequence on guitar: backwards, that is, with respect to the vast majority of songs.

---

[122] According to Manuel Insolera, in *Paul McCartney*, 1979, p. 47. the song should be interpreted as symbolic of drugs' use, as in slang the word "Lamb" means a heroin addict and "Dragonfly" could represent heroin. But McCartney never used heroin; there might be a connection with dream-like images produced by LSD, of which he was was a notorious fan, from the time of *Sgt.Pepper's* .

[123] A. Croft , *cit.*, p.14.

Denny Seiwell: "It was originally recorded for the *RAM* sessions, but finished in the UK. I don't remember if it was at Abbey Road or Olympic Studios. I s(a)ng some backing vocals. Some of the guitar licks sound like Henry McCullough, but I'm not so sure and Paul played a lot of the guitar solos too."[124]

In New York, once the basic track had been recorded, the song was very carefully arranged and filled chock-full of instruments. McCartney finished it off it with strong piano chords, electric guitars and a powerful horn arrangement, probably overdubbed in January.

When the song was finished in London in 1972, McCartney came up with some new ideas. For the opening, Paul used some unusual sound effects that he captured *en plein air*, along with some voices singing the praises of bucolic pleasures (Denny Laines's voice might be recognizable) that culminate in a cathartic plunge into a body of water. For the ending, instead, he used his Mellotron to create additional ambient effects.

Then, more guitar breaks were added, that almost certainly included a contribution by McCullough. McCartney generously allowed Denny Laine to sing it, leaving just a few bars of his original vocal take towards the end of the song.

The song was issued as the B-side to the "Live and Let Die" single (1973).

Musicians:

Paul McCartney vocals, backing vocals, acoustic and electric guitar, bass, piano, Mellotron • **Linda McCartney** backing vocals • **Denny Laine** vocals, backing vocals, acoustic guitar (?) • **Hugh McCracken** electric guitar (?) • **Henry McCullough (?)** backing vocals, electric guitar (?) • **Denny Seiwell** backing vocals, drums • **Unknown musicians** horns

According to Monique Seiwell's personal diary, sessions in New York City lasted until November, 20th.

On October 28th, George Harrison arrived in town to put the finishing touches to his album *All Things Must Pass* with producer Phil Spector. After a few days, Harrison phoned McCartney and they arranged to meet for the first time after the breakup of The Beatles. The meeting quickly becomes unpleasant. The two spoke about Apple and Paul said to George he wanted to get out of the label.

Years later, speaking to Barry Miles, McCartney would recall the conversation he had with George Harrison: "I remember having one classic conversation with him. I swear George said to me, 'You'll stay on the f----- label. Hare Krishna.' That's how it was, that how the times were." Paul and Linda came back to England for Christmas, spending their holidays in the Scottish farm.

They would go back in America in January 1971 to resume the *RAM* recordings.

---

[124] Interview courtesy of Denny Seiwell, 12/11/2011.

1971

The sessions continued between January 11th and February 25th at Phil Ramone's A&R Studios in New York, using the A1 room, with Dixon Van Winkle as a studio set-up man.

Ramone helped McCartney to achieve the deep resonant quality on his Rickenbacker bass. He recalled: "I remember that bass [sound]! We called down to the front desk at the studio and had them round up all the Pultecs they could get their hands on and every EQ in the place; we also got this UREI parametric equalizer. We just rolled up the bass on everything we could, as much as we could get on disc and know that the bass would be heard on radio."

35 Ram On (Paul McCartney)

Recording: February 22nd and March-April (overdubs), 1971 **Location:** A&R Studios, New York City and Sound Recorders Studios (overdubs), Los Angeles **Release:** May 1971, *RAM*

At the time of the Silver Beetles, when each of the band members chose a stage name, Paul had occasionally used Paul Ramon as his.[125] Furthermore, "The Derby Ram" is a traditional comic folk song of Derbyshire, where the animal is so prominent that it became the country's utmost symbol.

These memories are probably what gave McCartney the idea for this track which, in turn, would be the inspiration for the name of his second album. The song, that Paul wrote in the previous months, accompanied McCartney in New York. Paul tells us: "I used to carry one (ukulele) around with me in the back of New York taxis just to always have music with me. They thought I was freak, those taxi drivers."[126]

"Ram On" is one of the most fascinating tracks on *RAM*. The opening is definitely quirky: a warm piano arpeggio – cut and pasted from some other session – bits of a conversation between Paul and Eirik Wangberg ("And me talking and whistling to my dog, sitting next to him in the studio!"[127]), the announcement for take one and a false start follow one another.

Then, the ukulele strumming entirely leads the song, a little jewel with its wistful folk melody. The use of ukulele is further proof of McCartney's ability to draw out the best qualities of the various musical instruments. Paul most certainly remembered George Formby (1904-1961), the English singer and actor who had been an icon of The Beatles' youth.

The insistent percussion – played by McCartney himself as Seiwell was not involved in this recording – the use of Wurlitzer electric piano and the beautiful vocal harmonies by Paul and Linda envelop the song in a mysterious and ethereal atmosphere.

---

[125] This nickname would inspire the name of the band: The Ramones.
[126] Paul Du Noyer, *Alone Again, or*, in *Mojo*, July 2001, p.60 and p.62.
[127] *Claudio Dirani Interview with Eirik Wangberg*, January 2005.

On the track, Paul is heard keeping the time with his foot. The master craftsman behind that unusual sound was Dixon Van Winkle, who recalls: "One day (Paul) was standing around strumming on a ukulele, rocking from side to side, singing 'Ram On'. I ran out and put a mic on the ukulele, one on his face and a pair of mics down by his feet. The tapping you hear comes from the mics on his feet."[128]

McCartney ended the recording with a little surprise. Near the end of the song, Paul suddenly changes tempo, singing a couple of verses that would be used two years later in "Big Barn Bed" (see sheet **49**).

On *RAM*, this final section is presented as a short reprise (0:53) which also works as a sort of introduction to "The Back Seat of My Car". According to Van Winkle, this other song was already complete, and the title "Sleepin' on a Big Barn Bed" appears on the studio sheet included in the *RAM* Deluxe Edition.

There's an anecdote worth telling: while shooting the video-clip for "Hope of Deliverance" (1992), Paul had fun entertaining the audience with a version of "Ram On" played on banjo.

McCartney included "Ram On" in the soundchecks for the 2009 and 2010 tours. The song was finally played live on some of the 2010 *Up & Coming Tour* dates, on the 2011 *On the Run Tour* and on the 2013 *Out There! Tour*. An instrumental version appears on *Thrillington*.

Musicians:

Paul McCartney vocals, backing vocals, piano, Wurlitzer electric piano, ukulele, percussion, drums • **Linda McCartney** backing vocals

36 Now Hear This Song of Mine (Paul and Linda McCartney)

Recording: February 23rd (?) or March-April (?), 1971 **Location:** A&R Studios, New York City **Release:** May 1971, *Brung to Ewe* (promo album)

When *RAM* came out, Paul and Linda McCartney sent a promo disc called *Brung to Ewe* to radio stations. Only one thousand copies were made, making it one of the most coveted collectibles for Paul's fans: a copy is probably worth around 2000 euros.

Not only was the title strange, the content was even stranger: twelve skits played by McCartney, sort of mini-advertisements for *RAM*, with the album's tracks playing in the background and many, many sheep.

To make it, Paul also recorded a piano track. The *RAM* Deluxe Edition Book (2012) reports that this song was taped at A&R Studios, but the engineer Eirik Wangberg recalls that the track was recorded with him at Sound Recorders Studio in Los Angeles during the March-April sessions.

---

[128] G. Eskow, *Dixon Van Winkle*, www.mixoline.com, 2000.

Wangberg: "Paul may have tried recording 'Now Hear This Song of Mine' before coming to me and was not happy. We started from scratch. He went to the piano and I recorded two versions of 'Now Hear This Song of Mine', one bluesy and one up-tempo."[129]

Then, he asked Wangberg to ask bizarre questions to him and Linda. After they've finished, the sound engineer put it all together and McCartney was as pleased as Punch.

To many, it seemed a boring and meaningless idea rather than funny. The only interesting aspect of the *Brung to Ewe* record is the track "Now Hear This Song of Mine", otherwise nowhere to be found in McCartney's production.

It's a awkward song for piano and vocals – with strong percussion – consisting of an endless refrain repeating the words of the title.

The song is featured in the promo disc in a handful of different performances each lasting about thirty seconds, that differ by changes in tempo and arrangement: a rocking one, then a boogie, then one with a gospel feel. The latter version can be considered the most successful.

Musicians:

Paul McCartney vocals, backing vocals, piano, tambourine • **Linda McCartney** vocals, backing vocals

37 Great Cock and Seagull Race (Paul McCartney)

Recording: February 23rd and December 17th (overdubs), 1971 **Location:** A&R Studios, New York City **Release:** May 2012, *RAM* (Deluxe Edition)

This ambiguously named instrumental track was the result of some rock/blues improvisation in the studio that was neither very exciting nor creative.

Probably, McCartney had come up with some riffs and recorded the track on the fly with Seiwell: but since drums are not specifically credited to him, perhaps it means that it was a solo recording by Paul. According to the studio sheet included in the *RAM* Deluxe Edition, McCartney resumed work on the track later in December – maybe when he was in New York with Wings doing some promo interviews for *Wild Life* – adding a few overdubs.

Henry McCullough is listed as guitar player but it's not clear whether his guitar contribution occurred in one of these two sessions – prior to officially join Wings – or whether it was added during 1972-73. The track was aired the same month by radio station WCBS-FM during a Wings' interview, as "Breakfast Blues" (a.k.a. "Rooster") and therefore widely bootlegged. It was finally released as a bonus track in the 2012 Edition of *RAM*.

Musicians:

Paul McCartney piano, bass, electric guitar, piano, drums (?), electric piano (?), percussion (?) • **Denny Seiwell (?)** drums (?) percussion (?) • **Henry McCullough (?)** electric guitar (?) • **Linda McCartney** percussion (?)

---

[129] E. Eikelenboom, *Interview with Eirik Wangberg*, October 2012, in *Maccazine*, Vol. 40, issue 3/Vol.41 issue 1, p.75.

In March, McCartney flew to Santa Monica to complete work on the album. During his stay in Los Angeles, on April 15th, Paul and Linda attended the Grammy Award ceremony, receiving from actor John Wayne the award for *Let It Be* as Best Original Score written for a motion picture. While on stage, Paul simply said, "Thank you" before leaving.

38 Dear Boy (Paul and Linda McCartney)

Recording: March 1st, 9th, 10th, 12th and April 7th, 1971 **Location:** Sound Recorders Studios, Los Angeles **Release:** May 1971, *RAM*

McCartney: "Linda and I mainly doing all the harmonies on *RAM*. God, I tell you I worked her on that album. Because she hadn't done an awful lot, so she was a bit little out of tune. I was not too pleasant to live with, I suppose, then (...) She understood that it had to be good and you couldn't let any shit through. I gave her a hard time, but we were pleased with the results."[130]

It is possible that Paul was thinking specifically about "Dear Boy", the song on *RAM* where the vocal arrangements reach a high level of complexity.

"Dear Boy" was a piano track that McCartney wanted to decorate in a particular way. At Sound Recorders Studios, once the basic track was recorded, the song was completed adding many instrumental parts and all the vocals, with Paul Beaver helping engineer Eirik Wangberg "to do some sound phasing on the vocals."

The effect of Paul and Linda's vocal harmonies in "Dear Boy" highlights the mastery of studio techniques that McCartney had learned during The Beatles' years. Probably inspired by the intertwining vocals of Brian Wilson and the Beach Boys, the track features a rich vocal arrangement. When a few years later Elton John stated that *RAM* contains "the best harmonies (I)'d heard in a long while"[131], it's not hard to imagine he was referring to this song.

The track uses different harmonic techniques – ranging from three-part harmonies, to crescendos, and up to chasing melodic lines – and, by virtue of a stunning mix, McCartney's solo vocals are deliberately overwhelmed by the backing vocals and by the harmony parts.

The result is an unusual kind of song, almost a *suite* in which the intertwining of several vocal parts can puzzle the listener: "Dear Boy" is one of McCartney's "unknown" classics and one of the fullest of feelings and meanings.

Here, Paul's anguish becomes strongly dramatic: the opening in A minor with the descending bass sequence makes the music match the lyrics perfectly.

McCartney said the song was addressed to Linda's former husband: "'Dear Boy' was a song to Linda's ex-husband: 'I guess you never knew what you had missed.' I never told him that,

---

[130] *The Paul McCartney World Tour Booklet*, 1989, p.69.
[131] *Ibid.*

which was lucky, because he's since committed suicide. And it was a comment about him, 'cause I did think, 'Gosh, you know, she's so amazing, I suppose you didn't get it.'"[132]

But it may be that Paul lied purposely. "Dear Boy" could very well be about Lennon, once again, as the lyrics seem to suggest.

The relationship between Paul and John is pictured like one between two lovers who have recently broken up and that scream things like they'll never know what they are going to miss.

It is an emotional abandonment, equaled in *RAM* only by "Monkberry Moon Delight": the sense of loss is well represented by the heartbreaking *climax* that ends the song, in which McCartney's search for a foothold seems to end with a frightening leap into the void.

"Dear Boy" reveals a creative McCartney also from an instrumental point of view. According to Seiwell's recollections, the guitar sound in the fast breaks between verses was the result of a unique kind of teamwork: while Paul changed the pitch of the electric guitar with a bottleneck slide, Denny hit the guitar strings with his drumsticks.[133]

Seiwell: "Jim Guercio was brought in by Paul to help produce the track but it didn't work out too well. Jim was responsible for a few ideas on the track (and sang backing vocals - author's note). The drums were recorded in two passes: the one with only playing toms and cymbals, the other with kick and snare. Difficult, to say the least, but worked out well!"[134]

Guercio's experience with McCartney was a nightmare and he soon decided to leave the sessions: "I think he took offence. I said, 'No, no, this isn't personal, Paul, you don't need me. I can't come in here every day. We've got to finish. I have other obligations. I gave up my damn honeymoon here!'" He adds: "Paul is not an artist you can direct or collaborate with. You kind of have to support his ideas."

Beside Paul Beaver, Philip Davis may also have played synthesizer. He recalls: "On a Tuesday afternoon (could have been on March 9th that was Tuesday – author's note) I was scheduled to do a session at Sunset Sound Recorders Studios in Los Angeles but they wouldn't tell me what it was for. I got there, set up the synthesizer and I sat in the recording engineer chair behind the console. Then this guy walked into the control room and with an intimidating English accent said, 'Who are you and what the hell are you doing here?' It was Paul and I found out I was there to work on the album *RAM* (…) My part on the record was minuscule, but the experience was absolutely monumental."[135]

The version included in *Thrillington*, completely handled by the voices of Mike Sammes Singers, is a fascinating recording.

Musicians:

[132] Paul Du Noyer, *Alone Again, or*, in *Mojo*, July 2001, p.60.
[133] B. Spitzer-A. Steckler, *cit.*, p.130.
[134] Interview courtesy of Denny Seiwell, 18/11/2011.
[135] http://philipmichaeldavis.com/bio.htm

Paul McCartney vocals, backing vocals, piano, electric guitar, bass, percussion • **Linda McCartney** backing vocals • **Denny Seiwell** drums, percussion • **Paul Beaver** synthesizer • **Philip Davis (?)** synthesizer • **Jim Guercio** backing vocals

39 Dear Friend (Paul and Linda McCartney)

Recording: March (?) or August (?) and October (overdubs), 1971 **Location:** Sunset Sound Recorders Studios ? (basic track?), Los Angeles and Abbey Road Studios (basic track? and overdubs), London **Release:** December 1971, *Wild Life*

In the early Seventies, one of the favorite pastimes of reviewers was to find references, barbs, malicious comments and mutual dedications in albums by Lennon and McCartney.

Notably, the resentment between the two had surfaced in their music as early as *John Lennon/Plastic Ono Band* and this bitterness continued with *RAM* and *Imagine*. A succession of tartness, clearly the symptom of some psychological and emotional discomfort for both after breakup of The Beatles.

Whereas for Lennon the end of the group was a sort of artistic and personal release, for McCartney it caused profound distress and resulted in a long period of depression, in which Paul even lost his physical strength[136], while Lennon channeled his renewed energy into peace marches and other – political or musical – activities with Yoko.

In "Dear Friend" Paul set to music a peace gesture towards John. When it was released on *Wild Life* (December 1971), the reviewers focused their attention on the track, interpreting it as McCartney's response to allegations contained in "How Do You Sleep?"

There was never a more inaccurate interpretation in The Beatles' history. Even today, many don't know that "Dear Friend" was written back early 1971 – on the emotional wave of Lennon's interview on *Rolling Stone* – recorded as a home demo and then cut during the *RAM* sessions[137]: therefore, well ahead of the publication of *Imagine*.

Paul confirmed: "After John had slagged me off in public I had to think of a response, and it was either going to be to slag him off in public – and some instinct stopped me, which I'm really glad about – or do something else. So I worked on my attitude and wrote 'Dear Friend', saying, in effect, let's lay the guns down, let's hang up our boxing gloves."[138]

The song, however, didn't make it onto *RAM*. Its tone was very accommodating and maybe Paul was struggling over whether to express this kind of feeling: in the end he put angrier lyrics on the album.

"Dear Friend" is an intensely gloomy song: McCartney chose a dramatic key, C minor, to express the pain of his soul.

---

[136] As Paul recalls: "I didn't get up. Mornings weren't for getting up. I might get up and stay on the bed a bit and not know where to go, and get back into bed. Then if I did get up, I'd have a drink" in P. McCartney-B. Miles, *cit.*, p.443.
[137] Interview courtesy of Denny Seiwell, 11/12/2011.
[138] *Club Sandwich*, n.72, Winter 1994, p.11.

Recording date of this song remains uncertain. Listening to Seiwell's side of the story, it was a very basic recording, with just Paul on piano and him on drums. Seiwell also wielded a trumpet in a few parts, as he recalls: "The track was recorded at Armin Steiner's studios in Los Angeles. I believe that I did play trumpet near the end of the song but they replaced it with a proper horn section when they sweetened it!"[139]

But according to Tony Clark – who engineered the *Wild Life* sessions – the song was recorded (or re-recorded, or overdubbed) later, during the following August (or October): Clark recalls that Denny Laine played bass on the track.[140]

Richard Hewson embellished the track with a magnificent string arrangement, added at Abbey Road probably in October. Its Oriental-ish feeling might be an oblique tribute to John.

Hewson: "Paul gave me absolutely freehand for the arrangement. He just said, 'I want to put some strings on it.' Paul liked the fact that I was different from other string arrangers. Maybe it was the combination of jazz and classical training that produced that particular sound you can hear on the track. I booked some of the best string players in London and we recorded it at Abbey Road Studio Two, that McCartney preferred because it's more intimate than other rooms."[141] Tony Clark: "This was a live take with the band and the orchestra was overdubbed later. There was some discussion about the orchestra being too overpowering but with a phasing effect and subtle level on the mix it seemed to work."[142]

The slow and repetitive pace of the piano accompanies Paul's mourning vocals. McCartney's piano part uses a particular bass pattern, called "lament bass", descending from tonic to the dominant. The orchestral entrance – in a strong crescendo – is one of the most emotional moments of the song.

The lyrics are bare-bones, further evidence that the song was not particularly pondered but rather written in one go: McCartney's anxiety is strong and tangible and he seems to wonder if really "the dream is over", as John had said in "God".

But Paul doesn't seem to believe it: "Is this the borderline?" "Does it mean so much to you?" Are we "really" at the end, dear John? Does it really mean so much to you put an end to Beatles? It is indeed meaningful that the song starts with four unanswered questions, which clearly reveal McCartney's sense of emptiness.

McCartney asks if John is "afraid" or "fool", not understanding what is behind such a violent reaction.

McCartney has often been accused of not being very kind towards the other Beatles (his anger against Ringo, his legal action brought about Apple's financial situation). Paul's dismay is

---

[139] Interview courtesy of Denny Seiwell, 18/11/2011.
[140] Interview courtesy of Tony Clark, 27/11/2012.
[141] Interview courtesy of Richard Hewson, 15/09/2011.
[142] Interview courtesy of Tony Clark, 24/01/2013 and 20/02/2013.

undeniable in this series of questions and amounts to a hand outstretched towards his friend. Paul decided to swallow his pride: this makes "Dear Friend" one of McCartney's most sincere and sorrowful songs.

Musicians:

Paul McCartney vocals, piano, bass (?), vibraphone (?), organ (?) • **Denny Seiwell** drums, trumpet (?) • **Denny Laine (?)** bass (?) • **Unknown musicians** strings, horns

Right after finishing recording *RAM*, the McCartneys returned to England and on May 12th, they took a quick trip to Saint-Tropez for Mick Jagger's wedding. In their happy retreat in Campbeltown, Scotland, Paul and Linda devoted themselves to their family and songwriting.

RAM – preceded in February by the single "Another Day"/"Oh Woman, Oh Why?" – was released on May 17th and credited to Paul and Linda McCartney, sanctioning their artistic partnership after the controversies of "Another Day". The album was an instant commercial success in the United States: the record rose to #2 on the charts – where it spent 37 weeks – and soon went gold for one million copies sold, while in the United Kingdom *RAM* (having got over 100,000 advance orders) took the #1 spot twice, ahead of even *Sticky Fingers* by the Rolling Stones.

However, the album was treated badly by most music reviewers at the time. The reviewers on both sides of the Ocean were for the most part unanimous in their criticism on the record. Jon Landau of *Rolling Stone* was particularly harsh: "*RAM* represents the nadir in the decomposition of '60s rock thus far". The American magazine described *RAM* as "incredibly inconsequential" and "monumentally irrelevant". McCartney didn't forget and got his own back: in 2012 he used the ad "*RAM*, a monumentally relevant record" to promote the re-issued of the album.

Other criticism were addressed to *RAM* from ex-Beatles' members. Ringo Starr told *Melody Maker*: "I feel sad with Paul's albums because I believe he's a great artist, incredibly creative, incredibly clever but he disappoints me on his albums. I don't think there's one tune on the last one *RAM*... I just feel he's wasted his time, it's just the way I feel... He seems to be going strange."

John Lennon was brutally honest: "I thought it was awful! *McCartney* was better because at least there were some tunes on it, like 'Junk'."

Among the few discordant viewpoints, one deserves mention: the English weekly magazine *Disc & Music Echo*, whose reviewer Mike Ledgerwoods called the album "a McCartney master". Notwithstanding the harsh welcome given the album by the majority of the musical press, the song "Uncle Albert/Admiral Halsey" won a Grammy Award for the Best Arrangement Accompanying Vocals of a pop song.

It is worth dwelling on how reviewers commented it over the past decades. During the Seventies, *RAM* was ranked among the weakest efforts in McCartney's discography.

Bob Woffinden's opinion (1981, "The Beatles Apart") makes it clear: "*RAM* is so terrible it's hard to know where to begin (...) There isn't a single consistently effective track on the album. Traces of melody can occasionally be perceived, surfacing for air in the ocean of mediocrity."

Nicholas Schaffner (1979, "The Beatles Forever") described the album a bit less drastically, saying that it boasted "some lovely snatches of melody". But starting in the Nineties *RAM* was re-evaluated by the musical press. In 1997 *Rolling Stone* published a review of McCartney's solo career, where *RAM* was given an excellent treatment; today reviewers are almost unanimous in considering the record as a "must-have" of McCartney's discography.

Paul reacted angrily to the criticism. McCartney told Chris Charlesworth of *Melody Maker*: "I thought I had done a great album (…) I don't see how someone can play it and take in all that stuff and say, 'I don't like it' (…) I thought *McCartney* was quite good (…) It was very down-home, funky, just me... After it got knocked I thought... do just the opposite next time. So *RAM* was with the top people in the top studio. I thought, this is what they want. But again, it was critically panned."[143]

At the same time, he was determined: thinking of immediately "jumping on the road" he asked the musicians who had worked on *RAM* to be part of his new group and to follow him on tour. Denny Seiwell immediately accepted, while Hugh McCracken refused on the grounds that his studio work was more profitable: Paul never lost heart and returned to the idea shortly after.

Not before having booked a three-day recording session at Abbey Road (June 15th-17th, with Tony Clark engineering) to record *Thrillington*, a jazz orchestra version of *RAM*.

The project, released in 1977 under the pseudonym Percy Thrillington, was McCartney's first experimental solo foray. When Paul approached Richard Hewson to work on the project, *RAM* had only recently reached the stores.

Some of the people contacted were greatly embarrassed when they had to admit they had never heard a note of the original album! Paul oversaw it all without getting involved in playing: the band that got together in the studio on June 15th included high level jazz musicians like Vic Flick (guitar), Clem Cattini (drums), Herbie Flowers (bass), Steve Grey (piano), Roger Coulan (organ) and Jim Lawless (percussion).

After recording the backing tracks (all in one day!), the evening was used for overdubs of the orchestra conducted by Richard Hewson and the two following days were dedicated to the vocal parts, performed by the Mike Sammes Singers.

Recorders were played by the Dolmetsch, a well-known family of musicians and instruments' makers that – according to Dr. Brian Blood's memories – added their contribution on one track. Blood: "The recorder players were the same six players – except for my wife Marguerite

[143] Nicholas Schaffner, *The Beatles Forever*, 1979, p.145.

Dolmetsch – who had previously worked with Paul when he produced Mary Hopkin's first album, on the track 'The Game'. On *Thrillington* we played on 'Uncle Albert': Jeanne Dolmetsch (one of Carl's daughters), me and other three members of my family, Christine, Paul and Peter Blood."[144]

The album contains some amazing arrangements, on tracks like "Dear Boy", "Heart of the Country", "Uncle Albert / Admiral Halsey" and "The Back Seat of My Car", which opens with a beautiful jazzy piano part and ends delightfully – upon Tony Clark's suggestion – with the sounds of the water dripping in the toilets at Abbey Road (recorded on four separate tracks so to achieve a stereo effect, of course)!

Then McCartney went back to more concrete projects. On August 3rd, he announced to the press that he was putting together a new group. It only took a few days to decide on the initial line-up: Linda on keyboards[145] (Paul had taught her during the summer), Denny Seiwell on drums and Denny Laine (formerly of the Moody Blues, had recently recorded with Ginger Baker and the Air Force) on guitar. Laine recalled: "Paul called me because he knew I could sing, play and write songs."

Paul and the band spent three days at the farm in Scotland, then moving to Abbey Road to record the songs that would appear on *Wild Life*. According to *Melody Maker*, the first top secret session was held at Abbey Road on Sunday July 25th, with work probably proceeding up to July 27th. The tracks were sweetened and overdubbed during the first half of August.

The approach was bold. McCartney didn't want to overdub too much, preferring a genuine feel to the precision or accuracy that finishing touches could give: the basic tracks were recorded in three days again with Tony Clark engineering, assisted by Alan Parsons.

McCartney took the helm. Alan Parsons noticed that Denny Laine was "very much manipulated by Paul, being told what notes to play. He hadn't got a lot of freedom, musically."[146]

After the recordings, while Linda was in the hospital about to give birth to Stella, one day Paul came up with the expression "wings of an angel" while praying for the good health of this daughter. In a flash Paul had found the solution: after having toyed with the names Dazzlers and Turpentine – and being discouraged by an elderly seventy-nine year old fan! – he named the group Wings.[147] Overdubs and more recordings for the album took place in October, after Stella's birth: Tony Clark recalls that he had to take time off from the sessions for a few days when his wife gave birth to their daughter on the 13th of the same month.

---

144 Interview courtesy of Brian Blood, 28/09/2012.
145 Another reknown example: Louis Armstrong chose his wife Lil as a pianist on his group Hot Five in 1925.
146 Garry McGee, *Band on the Run*, 2003, p.19.
147 Curiously, The Wings was one of the most popular bands in Lagos, Nigeria in the early Seventies.

During the recordings, McCartney as usual handled a lot of instruments, including bass – although pictures or footage from the sessions are not available, McCartney surely played his Rickenbacker again, as he's seen with this bass in stills taken during the summer rehearsals at Rude Studio – piano, acoustic and electric lead guitar: "I'd always fancied myself as a lead guitar"[148] said Paul.

40 Mumbo (Paul and Linda McCartney)

Recording: July 25th-27th, August and October, 1971 **Location:** Abbey Road Studios, London **Release:** December 1971, *Wild Life*

One day, while he was in the studio recording *RAM*, Paul received a visit from Bob Dylan. McCartney: "We met him when he came to New York and we were together awhile. He came to one of my sessions when I was doing *RAM* in New York."[149]

McCartney claimed that the inspiration behind *Wild Life* was Dylan's basic and straightforward recording style: possibly Zimmerman and McCartney talked about it during their meeting.

Some months later, McCartney came up with the idea of a "spontaneous" album, simple and underproduced, a direction and a musical behavior quite different from those of the just-finished *RAM* that was – on the other hand – full of instrumentation and overdubs.

McCartney: "It had been done on that kind of a buzz we'd been hearing about how Dylan had come in and done everything in one take. I think in fact often we never gave the engineer a chance to even set up a balance."[150]

"Mumbo" is an example of this new musical approach. The commanding "Take it Tony!" yelled into the microphone by McCartney ordering the engineer Tony Clark to start the tape in the middle of a jam, perfectly represents the spirit of *Wild Life*.

Seiwell: "We were making this song up at the studio and it was getting good and Tony was just sitting up there drinking his cup of tea!"[151] And he had good reason: Paul's invitation was recorded precisely because Clark had wittily foreseen his intentions.

Clark: "It was really important to capture the moment (...) They were rehearsing that track and you could feel that something was really happening. I turned to Alan Parson and said 'Let's record' so he quickly started the multitrack... In that moment Paul shouted out 'Take it Tony!' I was actually *Take it Tony!* for quite some time with my friends at Abbey Road!"[152]

Clark again: "The whole essence was that whatever was going on, we had to get it as live as we possibly could in the studio. The idea was to get a live feel."[153]

[148] Chris Charlesworth, *Wings Fly*, in *Melody Maker*, 20/11/1971, p.32.
[149] P. Gambaccini, *cit.*, p.60.
[150] *Ibid.*, p.63.
[151] Gillian G.Gaar, *Flight Plan: Wings' 10-Year Journey*, in *Goldmine*, no.555, 2 November 2001, p.15.
[152] Interview courtesy of Tony Clark, 27/11/2012.
[153] Keith Badman, *The Beatles. The Dream Is Over-Off the Record 2*, 2002, p.72.

Linda McCartney: "We were playing it for the first time (…) for five minutes and Paul shouted to the others, 'It's in F!' and in fact you can hear him shouting to the engineer."[154]

Derived from a studio-jam, "Mumbo" is pure rock. And – although McCartney didn't try to find any words besides his personal *gramelot* – his vocal performance came out scratchy and rough. The track is loaded with tons of gritty electric guitar licks and solos, later overdubbed by McCartney and Laine.

A ramshackle garage-rock to be played at high volume and that must be counted among Wings' most exciting takes.

"Mumbo" – that was included as the opening number in the 1972 *Wings Over Europe Tour* – was also added to *Wild Life* as a short instrumental reprise: uncredited in the vinyl edition, it is titled "Mumbo Link" on the CD release: it's nothing more than a brief warm-up, ending with an odd metallic crash. Funnily, the same riff later would become part of the instrumental "Corridor Music", (see sheet **183**) which appears on the *Give My Regards to Broad Street* soundtrack (1984).

Musicians:

Paul McCartney vocals, bass, electric guitar, tambourine (?) • **Linda McCartney** piano, organ • **Denny Laine** electric guitar • **Denny Seiwell** drums, tambourine (?)

41 Bip Bop (Paul and Linda McCartney)

Recording: July 25th-27th, August and October, 1971 **Location:** Abbey Road Studios, London **Release:** December 1971, *Wild Life*

McCartney: "I remember saying to Trevor Horn (see sheet **214**, "Rough Ride") that I really hated songs from that (early Wings') period. And he asks which ones. 'There's a terrible little thing on *Wild Life* called 'Bip Bop' I said, 'It's just nothing'. And he said, 'You're kidding, man, that's one of my favorites!' My son's been playing it recently and I think it's a cracking little track. I'd gone with the current opinion at the time, that it wasn't much good."[155]

It's hard to not agree with that: McCartney had composed this child-like ditty, taking cues from the expression "bip bop", used by daughter Mary, confirming his amazing receptiveness to any source of inspiration and his interest in children's music.[156]

Speaking in 1998 to Chrissie Hynde, Paul recalled: "When James was really little I remember sitting on the sofa with him. He's just a baby and he was sitting with me like we were grown-ups and he was just sort of gaggling and going, 'Ah goo, ah goo.' So I just said, 'Ah goo.' Like

154 *Ibid.*, p.73.
155 *Exclusive Interview with Paul McCartney*, in *Record Collector*, n.214, June 1997.
156 The most famous case is "Yellow Submarine", but Paul's career has many songs and projects for a child audience, written in the early 1970s, the period when Paul became the father of two girls: "Mary Had a Little Lamb", the *Rupert the Bear* project. And later, "We All Stand Together" and "Tropic Island Hum".

agreeing with him in his language. He looked at me like, 'You speak this language?' We're sitting there for hours just 'ah goo.'"[157]

McCartney took the song to the studio without worrying about it too much (who would have told him that it was not appropriate?) and recorded two versions of "Bip Bop".

The first was a short acoustic instrumental piece played by Paul – an "enjoyable Merle Travis style guitar-pickin' hoedown" said critic John Mendelhson – probably his demo: it was not mentioned on the cover of the LP but later listed on the CD as "Bip Bop Link". The second was a band take, with strongly echoed vocals and electric guitars.

Still, the song must have had some relevance for Paul: listening to "Bip Bop" may be disconcerting, but a careful analysis can reveal its meaning.

Putting in music (Paul's favorite means of communication) a kind of regression phenomenon – the track is inspired by a child's first attempts to express itself – maybe McCartney was unconsciously bringing in front of the public eye his drama of orphan of his mother Mary and now of The Beatles? When it was issued on *Wild Life* the song had some success in radio programming in France. McCartney boldly presented "Bip Bop" on the 1972 Wings' tours.

Musicians:

Paul McCartney vocals, bass, electric guitar • **Linda McCartney** vocals, tambourine (?) • **Denny Laine** electric guitar • **Denny Seiwell** drums, tambourine (?)

42 Wild Life (Paul and Linda McCartney)

Recording: July 25th-27th, August and October, 1971 **Location:** Abbey Road Studios, London **Release:** December 1971, *Wild Life*

Paul and Linda shared the love and respect for nature and animals from the beginning of their relationship. "Wild Life", however, is not just another one of the bucolic songs so typical of McCartney's early career but rather anticipates his animal rights and environmental positions of the Nineties.

McCartney had composed "Wild Life" inspired by a sign that he had noticed during his visit in Ambosali, Africa in November 1966 – "The animals have the right of way" – which became a verse of the song.[158]

The recording of the basic track was not a particularly complicated matter. McCartney kept it simple with a stripped down instrumentation: next to his vocals and bass, Laine was on electric guitar, Linda on keyboards – with the sound of an harpsichord – and Seiwell on drums.

In this dramatic blues, an incessant and agonizing howl, McCartney's screaming vocal is reminiscent of the "Monkberry Moon Delight" *tour de force*. Few overdubs were added later: the

---

[157] *Chrissie Hynde's Interview with Paul McCartney*, in *USA Weekend*, 30/10-1/11/1998.
[158] WRKO radio-interview, December 1971.

electric guitar solos (that "were played by Paul"[159] as Denny Seiwell revealed), the short acoustic intro and the backing vocals. The repeated refrain is almost an exhortation full of ancient wisdom, replying to the cry of the great shaman chief: Paul's bass marks the rhythm of the ceremony. The recording is more spontaneous than accurate: you can hear some guitar flaws or even some breathing, along with a few words in the background.

The lyrics evoke bucolic and free feelings: the respect for animal rights is opposed to the intolerance towards the role that Man attributes to himself but that he has no real right to. "And man is the top", says McCartney who, almost stopping to think, adds: "An animal too". Then, he indicates a kind of moral duty to fulfill: the man got to care.

"Wild Life" also contains an anti-establishment statement (with the words "political nonsense in the air"), a bit surprising for McCartney at the time but that anticipated his political statement expressed in "Give Ireland Back to the Irish" (see sheet **46**).

Paul seems to sketch a Utopian society, a state of nature seen as a last hope for mankind, constantly locked up in the cage of the hypocritical social relationships.

The song was released on *Wild Life* and was one of the highlights of Wings' early repertoire. It was performed in 1972 and 1973; although none of these versions has been officially released on record, a great live recording from the 1972 *Wings Over Europe Tour* appears on DVD *The McCartney Years*.

The song was rehearsed for the 1975/76 *Wings Over the World Tour* – a snippet of it can be heard on *One Hand Clapping* – and 1989/90 *Paul McCartney World Tour* but never played live.

Musicians:

Paul McCartney vocals, backing vocals, bass, acoustic and electric guitar • **Linda McCartney** backing vocals, keyboards • **Denny Laine** backing vocals, electric guitar • **Denny Seiwell** backing vocals, drums

43 Some People Never Know (Paul and Linda McCartney)

Recording: July 25th-27th, August and October, 1971 **Location:** Abbey Road Studios, London **Release:** December 1971, *Wild Life*

Meeting and marrying Linda marked the beginning of a new phase in Paul's life: an enchantment that he tried to express in his songs. "Some People Never Know" is one of the couple's most emblematic songs. Paul had written it in the summer of 1969 in the Barbados, on vacation with Linda. A sweet acoustic ballad with a beautiful melody, that Paul wanted to sing as a duet with her. Reportedly, a first version was recorded at home by McCartney with the help of an unknown male singer: it is said to be moving and it's still in the vaults. The recording which ended up on *Wild Life* – although heavily overdubbed – was the take one of the track. Some earlier ideas were thrown out: Seiwell's trumpet solo – present in the rough-mix – was later replaced by two electric guitars played in harmony.

---

[159] Interview courtesy of Denny Seiwell, 11/12/2011.

The final outcome – although penalized by its excessive length (6:35) – is noteworthy, especially thanks to some fine backing vocal parts. The coda features some exotic percussion accompaniment, played on pieces of wood by McCartney and Seiwell. Denny Seiwell also contributed by rotating a plastic cord, bought on the street, to get an odd sound from swirling it around.[160]

Tony Clark confirms: "Paul and Linda had been out to Oxford Street (…) There was that guy selling a long tube, two foot long. And if you span it round, you got that whistling effect. We had no tracks left so we put it on a gap of a vocal track. You can hear that this sound stops suddenly, because it had to drop out before the vocal came in!"[161]

Lyrically, "Some People Never Know" is an ode to Paul's newfound confidence and to the sense of freedom and uniqueness of his relationship with Linda: it's a challenge to the whole world and to its disbelief in the power of love. Maybe some verses are directed to Lennon, but no confirmation from McCartney exists.

"Some People Never Know" – although the song had little in common with the group's rock repertoire – was performed during *Wings' University Tour* in February 1972: the poor quality of the performance is almost embarrassing.[162]

Musicians:

Paul McCartney vocals, backing vocals, acoustic and electric guitar, bass, piano, harmonium (?), maracas, congas, bongos, guiro • **Linda McCartney** vocals, backing vocals, keyboards, harmonium (?) • **Denny Laine** backing vocals, acoustic and electric guitar • **Denny Seiwell** drums, congas, bongos, guiro

44 I Am Your Singer (Paul and Linda McCartney)

Recording: July 25th-27th, August and October, 1971 **Location:** Abbey Road Studios, London **Release:** December 1971, *Wild Life*

After the first vocal partnership in *RAM,* McCartney made room for his wife's vocals also in *Wild Life.* An innocent love song, "I Am Your Singer", nonetheless, deserves a mention for its original harmonic structure and for its sweet Linda and Paul's vocal blending.

In a fitting metaphor, Paul ties himself to the loved one as a singer does with his song, succeeding in effectively describing the magic of his relationship with Linda.

For the recording McCartney used keyboards as the main instrument, creating a very soft and intimate atmosphere. Tony Clark: "We used an electronic keyboard, not the usual Fender Rhodes electric piano."[163] Then, McCartney added a short recorder solo that contributed to the enchanted atmosphere of the song. Paul was not a beginner on recorder. He had played it with

---

[160] Interview courtesy of Denny Seiwell, 11/12/2011.
[161] Interview courtesy of Tony Clark, 27/11/2012.
[162] The amateur tapes of some concerts (Nottingham, February 9th, 1972 and Hull, February 11th, 1972) show how the song was basically improvised on stage: the group had barely learned its structure.
[163] Interview courtesy of Tony Clark, 24/01/2013

the Beatles but in this case it's uncertain if he did take it upon himself. Seiwell: "Paul played that part... He brought in all these Irish flageolets. I played one on the instrumental version of 'Give Ireland Back to the Irish'!"[164]

Clark has a different memory: "The recorders were played by the Dolmetsch Family. And they were overdubbed in Abbey Road Studio One."[165]

Brian Blood from the Dolmetsch: "Listening to the track, it certainly sounds like us! There is a recorder consort involved – not just the top part but all the way down to bass. Apart from the Blood and Dolmetsch families, there were very few working consorts in England at that time. The tone, intonation and rhythmic bite in the top part identifies the Dolmetsch way of playing. I am very confident we are hearing recorders and a whole consort of them."[166]

The Dolmetsch are indeed credited on the *Wild Life* sleeve: but it's not clear if they are listed as performers or as the suppliers of the instruments.

Alan Parsons, *Wild Life* sound engineer along with Clark, recalls a detail: "*Wild Life* was actually the beginning of my career as an engineer, as opposed to an assistant, because every so often (Paul) would disappear with the band, and ask Tony Clark, or myself, to make tapes for him to listen to the next day so he could assess the situation, and decide what he wanted to do next. But one of the songs on the album, I actually mixed myself, as a rough mix, so he could decide what he wanted to do with it. And this was 'I Am Your Singer', which I'm delighted to say ended up being used on the album!"[167]

Scheduled for release as the B-side to the single "Love Is Strange" – a reggae-style cover of Mickey and Sylvia's "Peaches and Herbes" also recorded during the sessions – it was cancelled at the last moment as a result of the disastrous sales of *Wild Life*. Paul included "I Am Your Singer" in the 1972 *Wings Over Europe Tour*: it was one of the few soft moments of the show.

Musicians:

Paul McCartney vocals, electric piano, bass (?), recorder (?) • **Linda McCartney** vocals, organ (?), harmonium (?) • **Denny Laine** electric guitar, bass (?) • **Denny Seiwell** drums, maracas • The Dolmetsch Family: **Brian Blood, Peter Blood, Cristine Blood, Paul Blood, Jeanne Dolmetsch** recorders

45 Tomorrow (Paul and Linda McCartney)

Recording: July 25th-27th, August and October, 1971 **Location:** Abbey Road Studios, London **Release:** December 1971, *Wild Life*

The wandering, ever on-the-road lifestyle, on the quest for authentic sensations, which McCartney expressed with *Wild Life* and with *Wings' University Tour* a few months later, is summed up well in "Tomorrow".

---

164 Interview courtesy of Denny Seiwell, 13/11/2011.
165 Interview courtesy of Tony Clark, 27/11/2012.
166 Interview courtesy of Brian Blood, 28/11/2012.
167 From the cd *The Complete Audio Guide to the Alan Parsons Project*, Arista, 1983.

It's a bluesy song, tinged with melancholy but full of hope: the lyrics combine the philosophy of "day to day" gimmicks that evoked the Beatles' days in Hamburg and the usual, sweet images of love. Paul called it one of the "real big songs (…) that freaks or connoisseurs know"[168] on *Wild Life*. "Tomorrow" is a romantic piano ballad, embellished with marvelous three-part vocal harmonies, reminiscent of *RAM*.

Tony Clark: "Paul, Linda and Denny would work out harmony parts together and sing around the microphone. They were enjoying singing together, working out parts and possibly double-tracking."[169]

The arrangement grants little to stage effects: McCartney played piano, while Laine was on electric guitar (or bass?) and Seiwell took care of the solid drumming part. Then Paul overdubbed some electric guitar parts, most likely with the help of Laine.

Seiwell: "'Tomorrow' may have been written along with the *RAM* songs. We rehearsed this material in Scotland at Paul's farm, and came to London to record it knowing the material pretty well. This track was done fairly quickly, with Paul on piano, Denny on bass and Linda may have played some piano as well."[170]

McCartney delivers a remarkable vocal performance, in a very high key: Linda's father liked the ballad, as Paul recalled, and several times suggested to re-record a "slow, very slow" version of the track. In the lyrics, McCartney put together two elements: nature and the woman he loves. Love, again, is the only solution to overcome the troubles of everyday life, vividly described in the verse which begs his beloved to not to leave him "on Sunday". Paul seems to express a sort of fear.

Paul said that he would like re-record "Tomorrow": actually, in 1975 he recorded an instrumental reggae-style version – which sounds more like a parody – and some sources say that another version has been recorded in 2011 with Diana Krall. Both versions are still unreleased. "Tomorrow" is also included in *Wingspan*.

Musicians:

Paul McCartney vocals, backing vocals, piano, electric guitar, bass (?) • **Linda McCartney** backing vocals • **Denny Laine** backing vocals, electric guitar, bass (?) • **Denny Seiwell** drums

Paul celebrated the release of *Wild Life* and the birth of his new group with a party at the Empire Ballroom on December 8th. Honestly, there wasn't much to celebrate: as soon as the album reached the record shops, the press attacked it furiously, saying that the best track of the album was "Love Is Strange", the only song not written by McCartney.

---

[168] P. Gambaccini, *cit.*, p.60.
[169] Interview courtesy of Tony Clark, 27/11/2012.
[170] Interview courtesy of Denny Seiwell, 12/11/2011.

On January 20th, 1972, *Rolling Stone*'s reviewer John Mendhelson wrote: "*Wild Life* is largely high on sentiment but rather flaccid musically and impotent lyrically, trivial and unaffecting (…) But allow no one to convince you that it's entirely devoid of merit: while it's vacuous, flaccid, impotent, trivial and unaffecting, it's also unpretentious (a humble enough vessel of praise, but one of which neither George Harrison's nor John Lennon's post-Beatles work is worthy), melodically charming in several places, warm, and pleasant. Mostly, it's nicely (but not, as was some of *RAM,* spectacularly) executed pop music, and should be taken or left on that basis alone (…) He's driven by no obsession to demonstrate rock's potential as fine, revolutionary, or religious art, but rather is content to make straightforward pop music, to entertain. 'Some People Never Know' and 'Tomorrow' are archetypal post-Beatles McCartney: banal, self-celebrating lyrics full of many of the most tired rhymes in Western pop; glossy, if unfocused production; pretty, eminently Muzakable melodies."

Despite the criticism, the album reached #8 on the US charts and #11 in England, but quickly dropped into oblivion, getting only certified gold disc for having sold 500,000 copies in America.

Lennon, asked for his opinion about Paul's album by someone in the audience during the Mike Douglas Show in February 1972, graciously said: "I quite enjoyed it. I think (Paul) is going in the right direction."[171]

In December, Paul and Wings flew to New York for a brief radio promotion tour. In an interview on WRKO an embryonic version of "Mary Had a Little Lamb" (see sheet **47**) was aired. To rehearse with the band, Paul built a rudimentary home studio in Scotland, and called it "Rude Studio". He would record his demos there over the next years.

---

[171] http://www.youtube.com/watch?v=4aajk2dKyJY

1972

Paul started off the year with a single idea in mind: to gradually transform Wings into a group capable of tackling the biggest stages in the world. In January, Henry McCullough joined the group as lead guitarist: a blues musician, coming from Joe Cocker's Grease Band. McCullough's melancholy style characterized Wings' concerts: too much studio polishing wasn't to his liking.

Wings first rehearsed in January (17th-28th) at the Scotch of St. James club in London and in February (2nd-7th) at the Institute of Contemporary Arts on the Mall of London theatre. The band performed "Bip Bop", "Wild Life", "Give Ireland Back to the Irish" (see sheet **46**), "The Mess" (see sheet **53**), "My Love" (see sheet **56**), "Seaside Woman" (written by Linda) and the classics "Lucille","Blue Moon of Kentucky" and "Maybellene".[172]

After the recording of "Give Ireland Back to the Irish" – on February 1st – on the 9th Wings set off on a small tour to play in some British universities, showing up unannounced. The first concert was held in Nottingham, Portland Building: six hundred students attended the show.

This was probably inspired by the Dave Brubeck Quartet, which in the Fifties gained popularity among young audiences – more open to new ideas and sounds – touring colleges' campuses. McCartney should have known them well, because years before he borrowed some bars of their famous "Cathy's Waltz" in his "All My Loving".

46 Give Ireland Back to the Irish (Paul and Linda McCartney)

Recording: February 1st and 2nd-4th? (overdubs) 1972 **Location:** Abbey Road Studios and Apple Studios? (overdubs), London **Release:** February 1972, single

When, on January 30th, 1972 the news spread that some Irish civil-rights protesters had been shot by British soldiers in Belfast – an event that went down in history as *Bloody Sunday* – McCartney felt the urge to record a song inspired by those events.

Paul wrote "Give Ireland back to the Irish" in the wake of his emotions over it. McCartney composed the song on his piano in Cavendish Avenue, London: "The morning after I read the newspapers and it just looked wrong to me what the British Army was doing... So I just started on the piano and wrote the song."[173]

The track was recorded at Abbey Road in the Wings' first session with their new guitarist, Henry McCullough on February 1st. Engineer Tony Clark recalls that he had just returned to London from a vacation and he had to run into the studio.

---

[172] Mark Lewisohn, *The ICA Rehearsals*, in *Club Sandwich*, n.74, Summer 1995, pp.12-13.
[173] http://www.youtube.com/watch?v=Q3uD1hZaTXo

Clark: "(My wife said) Paul's in the studio. They've just phoned up; you've got to go in! I actually remember walking down from the Tube station and crossing the zebra crossing and hearing the immense sound coming out of Abbey Road. It was that loud!"[174]

The recording of "Give Ireland Back to the Irish" actually conveys that sense of urgency and spontaneity: McCartney leads the band through the song and his rage stands out. Footage of Wings rehearsing in St. John's Wood shot shortly after the recording (probably in March), testifies to the group's sincere passion in playing the song.

Clark recalled that he was not present at the later sessions, that probably took place at Apple Studios, where the song was mixed by Glyn Johns.

Tony Clark: "I remember that there was a phone at my home on Sunday, asking me to go to the studio urgently. It was rather a tense session but full of energy and Paul chose to finish it with Glyn Johns at another studio."[175]

In an interview issued on February 12th, Paul and Linda seemed to be aware of the controversy that would be raised by the song and they expressed a strong feeling of protest: "It'll have a hard time getting air play", said Linda. While Paul stated: "But it'll get played all the same, even if it's under the table or in dark corners."[176]

The song was released on single in record time on February 25th and an instrumental version – recorded by adding new guitar parts and some Irish whistles to the original rhythm section – became its B-side, with the title "Give Ireland Back to the Irish (version)".

A somewhat disjointed rocker but with a tense ending, as it defended – perhaps a bit rhetorically – Ireland's independence.

Paul was very upset about it, stating in one interview at the time: "I don't now plan to do everything I do as a political thing, you know, but just on this one occasion I think the British Government overstepped their mark and showed themselves to be more of a sort of a repressive regime than I ever believed them to be."[177]

McCartney again: "I was promptly phoned by the Chairman of EMI, Sir Joseph Lockwood, explaining that they wouldn't release it. I told him that I felt strongly about it (…) I knew it wasn't an easy route, but it just seemed to me to be the time."[178]

Promptly as well – on February 10th, even before it was issued – the song got banned by BBC and the single was a complete flop: #16 in the UK and #21 in the United States.

Elsewhere, the reception was better or unexpectedly excellent: it may have been predictable for the song to reach #1 in Ireland, but much less so for Spain. "I don't think Franco could have understood", Paul said.

---

[174] Matt Hurwitz, *Thrillington*, in *Good Day Sunshine*, n.78, 1995.
[175] Interview courtesy of Tony Clark, 07/02/2013.
[176] From *Sounds*, 12/02/1972, p.17.
[177] Interview granted by Paul McCartney to *ABC TV London*'s reporter George Watson.
[178] *Wingspan* book, 2001.

Denny Laine as well was bewildered: "I wasn't happy about the song, although it was heartfelt. I thought it was too political. (…) I'm not criticizing Paul, he did it in all innocence… I don't think he expected that ban."[179]

Paul got a chance to premiere the track during *Wings' University Tour*. "Give Ireland Back to the Irish" was played at the famous Nottingham University gig on February 9th, 1972 thus becoming the first McCartney's solo song to be performed live. The song was played by Wings during their following European tour as well.

In 2001, "Give Ireland Back to the Irish" was at the heart of a curious incident. In an interview, McCartney stated: "I perceived that our soldiers had done something bad in our name, so as a British citizen I wanted to protest about that. I still think that is valid."[180]

Paul himself included the song in *Wingspan*'s initial tracklisting: but, when EMI told him that they didn't want it to be part of the album – due to a terrorist attack in London earlier that year – McCartney was less determined than he had been thirty years before and the song was removed from the record at the last minute.

Musicians:

Paul McCartney vocals, bass, electric guitar (?) • **Linda McCartney** backing vocals, keyboards • **Denny Laine** backing vocals, electric guitar • **Henry McCullough** electric guitar • **Denny Seiwell** drums

The secret *Wings' University Tour* was the real baptism of fire for McCartney. It was a low-key tour. Paul: "The main thing I didn't want to face was the torment of five rows of press people with little pads all looking and saying, 'Oh well, he's not as good as he was.' We decided to go out on that university tour which made me less nervous, because it was less of a big deal."[181]

During Wings' eleven concerts in British Universities between February 9th and 23rd, in addition to their meager repertoire the group performed a handful of McCartney's still unreleased songs, some written by group members and a few classics by Little Richard. Here's the setlist taken from that tour's second concert on February 11th, Hull University:

"Lucille" (Little Richard) – "Give Ireland Back to the Irish" – "Blue Moon of Kentucky" (an old song by Matt Monro, also performed by The Beatles during the *Get Back!* sessions and later played by McCartney in 1991 in his *Unplugged* show) – "Seaside Woman" (sung by Linda McCartney) – "Can't Get You Off My Mind" (written and sung by Denny Laine) – "Some People Never Know" – "The Mess" – "Bip Bop" – "Thank You Darling" – "Smile Away" – "My Love" – "Henry's Blues" (written and sung by Henry McCullough) – "Wild Life" – "Give Ireland Back to the Irish" (encore) – "The Mess" (encore) – "Lucille" (encore). Other tracks were played during the first concert, in Nottingham: "Long Tall Sally" (Little Richard), "Miss

[179] Spencer Leigh, *Paul McCartney and Wings*, in *Record Collector*, n.162, February 1993, pp.16-17.
[180] Patrick Humphries, *The Other Side of Paul McCartney*, 2001.
[181] P. Gambaccini, *cit.*, 1976, p.71.

Ann" (another Little Richard classic, sung by Denny Laine) and "Help Me" (Denny Laine performing a Sonny Boy Williamson's cover).

The reception was triumphant everywhere. Heartened by the experience, McCartney headed back to the studio in record time. During the *Red Rose Speedway* sessions, which began in March, Wings recorded enough songs for a double album.

Some of the tracks Wings recorded during the sessions are still unreleased: "Jazz Street", a long blues-tinged instrumental; "Thank You Darling", a vaudeville-style number (played during *Wings' University Tour*), "1882", a slow blues track, "Tragedy" (a cover of Thomas Wayne's song from 1959) and "Night Out", a hypnotic rocker. "The Mess" was released later in a live version, while Laine's "I Would Only Smile" would appear in his album *Japanese Tears* (1980).

The album sessions were preceded by the recording of "Mary Had a Little Lamb", which was immediately released as a single.

47 Mary Had a Little Lamb (Paul and Linda McCartney)

Recording: March, 1972 **Location:** Olympic Studios, London **Release:** May 1972, single

Unanimously, critics have always considered the release of this nursery rhyme as Paul's sarcastic answer to the criticism received by "Give Ireland Back to the Irish".

There has been talk of McCartney's "total lack of judgment" for releasing such a provocative single at such a crucial time for Wings, just before starting their first European tour.

Paul, however, denied having had any intention to feed the critics with a song like "since these are the things you expect from me, here is the one you will especially enjoy".

McCartney: "I've just got three kids over the last few years, and when I am sitting at home playing at the piano my audience a lot of the time is the kids. I just wrote that one up, the words were already written (…) wrote a little tune up around it, went and recorded it (…) I thought it was all very nice."[182]

Paul decided to record this popular nursery rhyme adding his own music, "just because" – as Denny Seiwell recalled – "these were the first words ever played on a gramophone."[183]

"Mary Had a Little Lamb" had been written by Sarah Josepha Hale and Lowell Mason and published in 1830: on December 6th, 1877 Thomas Edison spoke the first verse of this poem to test his newly invented machine, capable of both recording and playing back sounds.

No more than a bit of fun. But most of all, McCartney wrote it for his daughter Mary, having noticed how much she enjoyed hearing him sing her name.

Denny Laine admitted: "'Mary Had a Little Lamb' was a nice song for kids, but it was wrong for the direction of the band"[184] and even Paul himself had to admit that "it wasn't a great

---

182 P. Gambaccini, *cit.*, p.71.
183 Interview courtesy of Denny Seiwell, 18/11/2011.
184 S. Leigh, *cit.*, p.17.

record… The quote that sums up that song for me is I read Pete Townshend saying that his daughter had to have a copy!"[185]

Actually, McCartney had written the song before "Give Ireland Back to the Irish". A home demo of the track was aired during a *Wild Life* promo interview on radio station WRKO from the MPL New York office, in December 1971.

The first version of "Mary Had a Little Lamb" recorded by Wings was powerful and rocking. Filled with McCartney's aggressive vocals, *à la* "Maybe I'm Amazed", the basic track consisted of strong electric guitars, Seiwell's heavy drums and a wild reprise which unfortunately was dropped from the official version. Denny Seiwell recalled that the session was "musically interesting, we had a lot of fun during the recording and in the coda!"[186]

The song was 4:43 long and can be considered one of McCartney's best alternate takes. Then, Paul rethought it and embellished "Mary Had a Little Lamb" with backing vocals and lighter instrumentation, including xylophone, recorder and percussion.

Musically, Seiwell's opinion can't be disputed. "Mary..." is, indeed, an exquisitely crafted calypso, with a brilliant chord sequence – which becomes particularly intriguing near the end – nice mandolin licks and is childish enough to make you want to hum its chorus all through.

The whole McCartney family, including daughters Mary and Heather, can be heard singing in the chorus and laughing at times in the track.

The single climbed the charts quite well, especially in the United Kingdom, where "Mary Had a Little Lamb" reached #9, while in America the song peaked at #28.

McCartney seemed particularly proud of it: he performed the song during 1972 *Wings Over Europe Tour* and during the *James Paul McCartney* TV special in a newly-recorded version.

Musicians:

Paul McCartney vocals, backing vocals, piano, bass (?), percussion, recorder (?) • **Linda McCartney** vocals, backing vocals, maracas (?), Moog (?) • **Denny Laine** backing vocals, bass (?), electric guitar • **Henry McCullough** backing vocals, electric guitar, mandolin • **Denny Seiwell** backing vocals, drums, xylophone (?), recorder (?) percussion • **Heather McCartney, Mary McCartney** backing vocals

48 Mama's Little Girl (Paul and Linda McCartney)

Recording: March, 1972 and January, 1981 (overdubs) **Location:** Olympic Studios, London and Rude Studio (overdubs), Campbeltown **Release:** January 1990, "Put It There" single B-side

McCartney shifted his attention to family matters in the first years after the breakup of The Beatles. "Mama's Little Girl", one of the most underrated songs of his folksy-pastoral vein, is another example.

---

[185] Keith Badman, *The Beatles After the Break-Up. 1970-2000*, 2000, p.73.
[186] Interview courtesy of Denny Seiwell, 18/11/2011.

Paul wrote this acoustic ballad in 1971, inspired by one of his daughters. The song, which blends childlike innocence and the purity of nature, has a Virgilian idyllic feeling.

Not much is known about the recording. Reportedly, McCartney taped it during a session with just the help of his daughter Heather singing background vocals, and playing some noteworthy fingerpicking on acoustic guitar.

The rest of the instrumentation, with some sketchy drums and a rough electric guitar part, also seems to prove that it was a solo recording, although for sure Seiwell pitched in, adding some African percussion.[187] There's also an uncredited clarinet part.

However, this version was set aside; the song was rehearsed for the *James Paul McCartney* show in 1973, but it was left out at the last minute.

Paul worked on the song for *Hot Hits and Cold Cuts* (see **1981**) when Wings added more instrumentation and backing vocals: but, after the *Cold Cuts* project collapsed, "Mama's Little Girl" remained unreleased.

In the end, McCartney found a place for it as the B-side to the "Put it There" single (1990), in a further overdubbed version, enhanced and produced by Chris Thomas, who in 1987 remixed several tracks for the *All the Best!* collection.

Musicians:

Paul McCartney vocals, backing vocals, acoustic guitar, electric guitar (?), bass (?), tambourine (?), drums, percussion (?) • **Linda McCartney** backing vocals, tambourine (?) • **Denny Laine** backing vocals, bass (?) • **Henry McCullough (?)** electric guitar • **Denny Seiwell** African percussion **Heather McCartney** backing vocals • **Unknown musician** clarinet

At Olympic Studios, Paul called upon as producer Glyn Johns, having formerly helped out in the Beatles' *Get Back!* endeavor.

But things didn't go quite right. Johns recalled that the sessions were difficult: everyone in the studio heavily smoked pot, and that negatively affected the quality of the music. Johns walked out of the sessions after a few weeks. He recalled: "One evening they (Seiwell and Laine – author's note) said, 'We're not happy with you as a producer. You're not taking any interest in what we are doing.' I said, 'If you think that everything you do is a gem of marvelous music, you're wrong. And if you want to sit and play shite and get stoned for a few hours (...) don't expect me to record everything you're doing, because frankly it's a waste of tape and it's a waste of my energy.'"[188]

---

187 *Ibid.*
188 Howard Sounes, *FAB, An Intimate Life of Paul McCartney,* 2010, p.303.

49 Big Barn Bed (Paul and Linda McCartney)

Recording: March (?), 1972 **Location:** Olympic Studios, London **Release:** May 1973, *Red Rose Speedway*

The rate at which McCartney manages to find ideas for new songs is virtually non-stop. But it also means that many of his works remain in an embryonic stage for months before being completed, or lie unreleased for a long time.

"Big Barn Bed" is a good example: Paul had written the song back in 1970 – an excerpt of it is heard in the "Ram On" reprise (see sheet **35**) – and got back to work on it in the following months. By the time McCartney started recording *Red Rose Speedway*, he had finished it up with new verses and a chorus.

Harmonically, "Big Barn Bed" is brilliantly simple: it's all in F Major, and plays on the basic chord triad, overlapping and intertwining several melodies – apart from the introduction, the verses and the refrain all use the same chord progression – driven by McCartney's bass, all syncopated and almost in reggae style.

The song, full of excellent vocals and bright acoustic guitars, flamboyantly proceeds towards a chaotic finale, in which McCartney's piano – mixed higher in an early version – stands out.

Paul chose the song as the opening track of *Red Rose Speedway*, perhaps because of its lively beat. He also included it in the *James Paul McCartney* TV show and on the *Wings' British Tour* in 1973, where it was among the only three songs from *Red Rose Speedway* performed to promote the record. In 2013, McCartney brought out the song during some soundchecks of his *Out There! Tour*, playing it on ukulele.

Musicians:

Paul McCartney vocals, bass, piano • **Linda McCartney** backing vocals • **Denny Laine** acoustic guitar, backing vocals • **Henry McCullough** backing vocals, electric guitar • **Denny Seiwell** drums

50 One More Kiss (Paul and Linda McCartney)

Recording: March (?), 1972 **Location:** Morgan Studios, London **Release:** May 1973, *Red Rose Speedway*

Several tracks on *Red Rose Speedway* show a return to pleasant and innocuous little tunes, full of catchy gimmicks and twinkly effects. Among these, "One More Kiss" stands out as an enjoyable and delicate charmer.

Some will find it hard to recognize Wings in "One More Kiss" as the band-on-the-road of their impromptu and folksy University Tour of the previous February: the group's rock image was perhaps at that time tarnished by these rather predictable melodic songs. But it was a deliberate McCartney choice.

"One More Kiss" has the typical vaudeville-style song structure McCartney likes so much, with the bass jumping around playing alternate fifths. Reportedly, a first take, entirely acoustic, was discarded.

The icing on the cake was Paul's flawless vocals along with Seiwell's brushes and McCullough's country-flavored guitar, making it into a gentle song, that could easily be interpreted as an apology to Linda after a quarrel.

Musicians:

Paul McCartney vocals, acoustic guitar • **Linda McCartney** electric harpsichord • **Denny Laine** bass • **Henry McCullough** electric guitar • **Denny Seiwell** drums

51 Single Pigeon (Paul and Linda McCartney)

Recording: March (?), 1972 **Location:** Olympic Studios, London **Release:** May 1973, *Red Rose Speedway*

Basically a solo for piano and voice, "Single Pigeon" is another variation on the theme of loneliness.

In this song McCartney chose to sing a picture of a London day, as viewed through windows. His quick brushstrokes that portray the sad solitary flight of a dove and a seagull were probably inspired by the dullness of the skies and waters of London, with the evocative image of Regent's Park dominating the scene.

When McCartney recorded the track in the studio, he decided not to weigh it down with too many overdubs.

The instrumentation was stripped down to the bone: along with the piano – the intro sounds a little like "Wrapping Paper" by Cream, 1966 – the track features only a trumpet solo near the end, not credited in the album's liner notes but probably played by Denny Seiwell.[189] A closer listening reveals that a little brass section could have been used.

Seiwell is also listed as the bass player, although in this case his performance isn't that good: "That buzz on the bass… Was definitely me!"[190] This performance – full of inaccuracies and which sounds quite dirty – can be better heard in a rough-mix of the track, that seems to confirm the surprising credit: truly Seiwell could have played bass. A lovely watercolor that opens *Red Rose Speedway* second half (speaking of old LPs').

Musicians:

Paul McCartney vocals, backing vocals, piano • **Linda McCartney** backing vocals • **Denny Laine** bass (?), drums (?) • **Henry McCullough** acoustic guitar • **Denny Seiwell** drums (?), bass (?), trumpet (?) • **Unknown musicians (?)** brass

---

[189] Interview courtesy of Denny Seiwell, 12/11/2011.

[190] *Ibid.*

52 When the Night (Paul and Linda McCartney)

Recording: March (?), 1972 **Location:** Olympic Studios, London **Release:** May 1973, *Red Rose Speedway*

Speaking of *Red Rose Speedway*, *Rolling Stone*'s critic Lenny Kaye comment that "Paul's grandfather would've liked it", was primarily due to tracks such as "When the Night".

Although Kaye liked the track – he said it was his favorite song, containing Paul's best vocal performance of the album – "When the Night" is exactly the kind of song which reveals McCartney's charm as entertainer for the broadest possible audience.

McCartney came up with another melodic and vaguely old-fashioned song, leading the group in the studio on piano in a typical *staccato* Fifties style. Noteworthy, is McCartney's terrific vocal performance especially in the coda, which features some great screaming vocals.

The track is opened by a clear acoustic Latin-flavored intro on layered guitars, played by McCullough and Laine. Paul's scat solo – clearly heard in the rough-mix – is reinforced by electric guitar and (maybe) a kazoo, both not credited. In the end, the lyrics are once again inspired by love-songs' clichés and its harmonic structure is not particularly compelling, but rather a bit boring. The song was enjoyable nevertheless, as testified by some bootlegs of the 1973 *Wings' British Tour*, in which "When the Night" was performed.

Musicians:

Paul McCartney vocals, piano, bass, kazoo (?), Moog (?) • **Linda McCartney** backing vocals, electric piano, Moog (?) • **Denny Laine** backing vocals, acoustic guitar • **Henry McCullough** backing vocals, acoustic guitar, electric guitar • **Denny Seiwell** backing vocals, drums, maracas (?)

The release of "Mary Had a Little Lamb" attracted critics like bees to honey, but despite the blows by the reviewers, Paul spent the spring preparing another tour, this time with all credentials to address a bigger audience and the press ready to accurately report the event.

McCartney chose Europe, skipping the United Kingdom purposely, as he explained to *Melody Maker*: "We will play there sometime or other, but not right now. The audiences are very critical in Britain and we're a new band just starting out. We have to get worked before doing any big shows in Britain or America."

Between July 9th and August 23rd, Wings traveled across France, Germany – Western and Eastern – Holland, Belgium, Switzerland, Sweden, Denmark, Finland and Norway – initial plan also included some gigs in southern Italy – relying now on a broader repertoire although with the occasional *faux pas*. The inclusion of songs like "Bip Bop" or "Mary Had a Little Lamb" can be considered extravagant – to say the least – for McCartney, resolved as he was to regain credibility.

The tour started in Toulon, France, with a performance at the open-air Greek style Chateau Vallon Amphiteatre. James Johnson, *New Musical Express*' critic, wrote: "McCartney could hardly have chosen a more obscure spot to start. Even local taxi drivers had difficulty in finding the Chateau (…) McCartney later admitted that the show hadn't been that good (…) Certain numbers sounded more like something from a local church hall group than a band led by a former Beatle."[191]

Some of the tracks were introduced by McCartney as "taken from the new album" – apparently Paul had a clear idea of the songs that would be included in *Red Rose Speedway* – although many of them would remain on the shelves.

The standard setlist was changed very little throughout the tour. After a few shows "Smile Away" replaced "Eat at Home" as the opening number. Here's the setlist from the Copenhagen concert: "Rock Intro" – "Eat at Home" – "Smile Away" – "Bip Bop" – "Mumbo" – "1882" – "I Would Only Smile" (Denny Laine) – "Give Ireland Back to the Irish" – "Blue Moon of Kentucky" – "The Mess" – "Best Friend" – "Soily" – "I Am Your Singer" – "Seaside Woman" (Linda McCartney) – "Henry's Blues" (Henry McCullough) – "Say You Don't Mind" (Denny Laine) – "My Love" – "Wild Life" – "Mary Had A Little Lamb" – "Maybe I'm Amazed" – "Hi, Hi, Hi" – "Hi, Hi, Hi" (encore) – "Long Tall Sally"

53 The Mess (Paul and Linda McCartney)

Recording: August 21st, 1972 **Location:** The Hague, Amsterdam **Release:** March 1973, "My Love" single B-side

During Wings' first rehearsals, the group worked hard on "The Mess", a powerful rock composition, probably inspired by The Band's "The Shape I'm In" (1970).

The song was developed during rehearsals: "The Mess" was presented during the *Wings' University Tour* and essentially was a guitar showcase for McCullough.[192]

It was a composite track, with many rhythmic variations and full of guitar riffs: a powerful stomper vigorously tackled by Paul's vocals and bass. Recorded during the *Red Rose Speedway* sessions, it was dropped from the album and remains unreleased in its studio version. The recording showed how the track had improved since its first live performances in the *Wings' University Tour*: its structure was disciplined, wisely balancing its irregular rhythm full of breaks with Paul's melodic sense.

"The Mess" would have been a perfect rocking track to counterbalance the many ballads in *Red Rose Speedway*; nevertheless, McCartney decided to leave on the shelves one of the Wings' best recordings.

Fortunately, a rousing live version from the Amsterdam concert during the 1972 *Wings Over Europe Tour* – embellished later with many overdubs and edited down – would be released as the B-side to "My Love". The track would be performed again in 1973 during the *James Paul McCartney* TV show and during the UK tour.

---

191 Keith Badman, *The Beatles. The Dream Is Over-Off The Record 2*, 2002, p.86.
192 *The Mess* seemed to be one of the few well-rehearsed songs on the show.

Musicians:

Paul McCartney vocals, bass, electric guitar (?) • **Linda McCartney** backing vocals, keyboards • **Denny Laine** backing vocals, electric guitar • **Henry McCullough** backing vocals, electric guitar • **Denny Seiwell** drums

During fall, Wings resumed recordings. They completed *Red Rose Speedway* and recorded a handful of songs to be released as the band's next singles. The sessions included two songs that would become major classics: "My Love" and "Live and Let Die".

54 Country Dreamer (Paul and Linda McCartney)

Recording: September 26th, 1972 **Location:** Abbey Road Studios, London **Release:** October 1973, "Helen Wheels" single B-side

As soon as Paul, after having met Linda, moved to the countryside, he also portrayed the country man image in his music, as in "Heart of the Country" (see sheet **32**).

Paul's love for that basic lifestyle, simple and full of forgotten pleasures, is also epitomized by "Country Dreamer", a lovely folk-country song.

McCartney's demo – dating from Spring-Summer 1970 – is surprisingly similar to the final take. According to Denny Seiwell, an early version of this song was attempted by McCartney during the *RAM* recording sessions, but almost certainly it was not recorded. In any case, the song stuck around and Paul picked it up again with Wings.

Seiwell: "'Country Dreamer' was recorded during the *Red Rose Speedway* sessions. Leftover feelings from the McCartneys spending time at their farm in Scotland. Paul played acoustic, Denny was on bass and Henry played a pedal steel guitar.... Never played one before... Not bad, uh?"[193]

The well-crafted recording of the track – later enriched by several overdubs – highlights McCullough's work on lead guitar and McCartney's superb vocal harmonies. Some little flaws were left in the recording, as to emphasize its spontaneity: at 0:02 there is a brief off-mike yelling and at 0:04 a wrong touch by Laine on bass.

The acoustic simplicity of the track is a gallery of the small daily pleasures of country life, the only dimension that – in McCartney's vision – lets one experience long-lost sensations and genuine feelings. Paul sings the delights of taking a bath in a river and of relaxing in a field.

The track was released in October 1973 as the B-side to the "Helen Wheels" single. Surprisingly, the song was supposed to appear – still unreleased – in the *James Paul McCartney* TV special but at the last minute Paul dropped it from the show.

Another recording, *The Backyard* (see **1974**), was the last time Paul performed "Country Dreamer": it's a beautiful acoustic performance, interrupted twice by McCartney himself

---

[193] Interview courtesy of Denny Seiwell, 14/11/2011.

forgetting the words. This version appears on the bonus CD of the deluxe edition of *Band on the Run* (2010).

Musicians:

Paul McCartney vocals, backing vocals, acoustic guitar, piano, percussion (?) • **Linda McCartney** backing vocals • **Denny Laine** backing vocals, bass • **Henry McCullough** slide guitar • **Denny Seiwell** drums, brushes

55 Bridge Over The River Suite (Paul and Linda McCartney)

Recording: September 26th, 1972, November, 1973 (overdubs part 1) and July 11th, 1974 (overdubs part 2)
Location: Abbey Road Studios, London, EMI Studios (overdubs part 1), Paris and Sound Shop Studios (overdubs part 2), Nashville **Release:** October 1974, "Walking in the Park with Eloise" single B-side

During the "Country Dreamer" recording session, McCartney was "getting the feel" for the song and began to improvise on his acoustic guitar going on for five minutes. He recorded this embryonic version of "Bridge Over the River Suite". Alan Parsons did the editing work on the brief instrumental and gave Paul the tape.

McCartney resumed work on the track in November 1973 in Paris, dubbing the rest of the instrumentation over the acoustic guitar backing. The finishing touch was added during the Nashville sessions in 1974 with a horn section, arranged by Tony Dorsey.

McCartney has always been proud of the song, which he thought it was suitable for a film soundtrack. Released in 1974 as the B-side to the single "Walking in the Park with Eloise" – credited to the Country Hams (Wings augmented by Chet Atkins and Floyd Cramer) – the song can't be considered one of the most memorable of McCartney's productions. Nevertheless, it has an intriguing night atmosphere, and good guitar parts by Paul himself.

Musicians:

Paul McCartney acoustic guitar, bass • **Linda McCartney** synthesizer • **Denny Laine** electric guitar • **Jimmy McCulloch** electric guitar • **Davey Lutton** drums • **Bill Puitt** sax • **George Tidwell, Barry McDonald** trumpet • **Norman Ray** baritone sax • **Dale Quillen** trombone • **Thaddeus Richard** sax

56 My Love (Paul and Linda McCartney)

Recording: October, 1972 **Location:** Abbey Road Studios, London **Release:** March 1973, single (from *Red Rose Speedway*)

Written simply "for Linda", this song, released as a single ahead of *Red Rose Speedway*, had been written at least two years before its recording.

Since Paul writes non-stop, that would often happen. It could take many months or even years before getting tracks recorded and released. For "My Love", McCartney said that he had "written it in the early days of my relationship with Linda"[194]: that would date the song, at least in its early stage, somewhere between 1969 and 1970. During the concert at Nottingham

---

[194] White, T., *cit.*

University on February 9th, 1972, "My Love" was almost identical to the officially released version: its structure and lyrics would remain unchanged – except for removing Linda's "answering" vocals – possible meaning that the song had been ready for months.

"My Love" was recorded in a memorable live session at Abbey Road Studios. Richard Hewson, who arranged it and conducted the orchestra, reveals: "Paul sent me a demo of the track and we recorded it live in the studio, because McCartney wanted a certain feeling. It was an experiment... On 'My Love' I got the best jazz musicians I knew... They had this particular warm sound and the record starts with that long note. The session lasted three hours... Everything was done live, even the vocal. But it took 20 takes! The guitar solo was different every time... By the end of the session everybody's got a bit tired and said to Paul, 'We could not play any better!'. I'm not sure which was the actual take they used!"[195]

On this recording, Paul played electric piano, Denny Laine was on bass, Seiwell on drums and Henry McCullough came up with what is probably recognized as his best solo.

Denny Seiwell recalled that Henry had been working on his part for "a couple of days"[196] and, speaking of Henry's solo, McCartney revealed a funny anecdote.

Shortly before the recording session, when the orchestra already set up in the studio, Henry turned to Paul and asked him: "Can I change my solo?". Macca answered: "OK, but not at all!"

This "melodramatic ballad in the same vein as 'The Long and Winding Road'"[197], was flawlessly produced and performed[198]: it was an instant success.

"My Love" made its mark with its smooth F Major chord sequence, Paul's emphatic singing, its sumptuous orchestra and its soft atmosphere.

With four weeks on the top of the US charts (and #9 in the UK) and with over two million copies sold, it became an evergreen of McCartney's repertoire, and was covered by many famous artists in the following years, including Tony Bennet, Nancy Wilson and Cass Elliot.

After the song was premiered during 1972 *Wings' University Tour* and *Wings Over Europe Tour*, Paul also played it on the *James Paul McCartney* TV show – aired simultaneously to the release of the single in the spring 1973 – and in the following *Wings' British Tour*.

In the 1975-76 *Wings Over The World Tour* the song wasn't skipped in any performance, and returned to appear in McCartney's 1993 *New World Tour*, in the 2002-03 *Drivin' Tour* and in several gigs between 2007 and 2013.

Included in *Wings Greatest, All the Best!* and *Wingspan*, "My Love" was also cut in four different live versions, issued on *Wings Over America, Paul Is Live!, Back in the US/Back in the World* and *Good Evening New York City*. An orchestral version is included in *Working Classical*. In 1986,

---

[195] Interview courtesy of Richard Hewson, 15/09/2011.
[196] Gaar, Gillian G. *cit.*
[197] B. Woffinden, *cit.*, p.111.
[198] Careful listening reveals a wrong touch on bass by Laine at 0:03 during the orchestra's opening chord.

when asked about his favorite Wings' track, McCartney said: *"Red Rose Speedway* is a nice memory for me – a romantic period, folks! – and 'My Love' is the song I'd like to choose."[199]

Musicians:

Paul McCartney vocals, electric piano • **Linda McCartney** backing vocals • **Denny Laine** backing vocals, bass • **Henry McCullough** electric guitar • **Denny Seiwell** drums • **Unknown musicians** strings, horns

57 Loup (First Indian on the Moon) (Paul and Linda McCartney)

Recording: October, 1972 **Location**: Olympic Studios, London **Release**: May 1973, *Red Rose Speedway*

In Abbey Road, where Wings were recording during the year, Pink Floyd were working on *The Dark Side of the Moon*.

Maybe speaking to Alan Parsons – who engineered Pink Floyd's album and Wings' *Red Rose Speedway* – Paul may have been inspired to compose "Loup (First Indian on the Moon)".

The atmosphere of song and its harmonic structure are obviously influenced by Waters and Gilmour's band. "Loup..." is, in fact, a particular track in McCartney's discography: an acid instrumental piece in the vein of his experimental productions.

McCartney actually had something else in mind. Seiwell: "Paul said that he crafted that song thinking that, to him, it's what jazz was!"[200]

The lunar atmosphere is recreated with a unique instrumentation: the song, almost entirely driven by McCartney's bass scales, is filled with a tribal-like group chant.

The tribal percussion in the background, McCullough and Laine's shrill guitars, the interweaving of organ, Moog and various effects, reminiscent of certain Beatles-like inventions (there is a gull-like sound in the finale, similar to "Tomorrow Never Knows"), depict the dustiness of lunar craters. The track is on *Red Rose Speedway*.

Musicians:

Paul McCartney backing vocals, bass, acoustic guitar, Moog • **Linda McCartney** backing vocals, organ • **Denny Laine** backing vocals, electric guitar • **Henry McCullough** backing vocals, electric guitar • **Denny Seiwell** backing vocals, drums, percussion

---

[199] *Club Sandwich*, n. 41, Summer 1986, p.14.

[200]   http://www.themortonreport.com/entertainment/music/ram-wings-and-beyond-an-interview-with-denny-seiwell/

58 Live and Let Die (Paul and Linda McCartney)

Recording: October or November 1972 **Location:** AIR Studios, London **Release:** June 1973, single

Through the recording of many soundtracks with the Beatles (*A Hard Day's Night*, *Help!*, *Magical Mystery Tour*, *Let It Be*) and the little-known soundtrack of *The Family Way* (1966) – in which for the first time Paul had experimented with symphonic music – McCartney was well acquainted with this kind of musical language.

When in 1972 Paul was commissioned to write the soundtrack for the upcoming new James Bond film *Live and Let Die*, it wasn't hard for him to come up with a theme song. Curiously, it was the second time that Paul was approached for a Bond film, as in 1971 McCartney was asked to write a track for *Diamond and Dogs*, which failed to materialize.

Paul immediately realized the opportunity in terms of sales and popularity: getting Wings' name and music out through the cinema channel was a unique opportunity to increase fans and give the group high visibility.

Paul often says that good songs never take long to come to light and "Live and Let Die" is a perfect example. Writing and recording the song, which became the greatest success of all the Bond themes, only took a few days. The story goes that after the assignment, McCartney read Fleming's book on Saturday, wrote the tune the next day and recorded it in the studio the following week.

"Live and Let Die" was a real turning point for McCartney: not only it confirmed Wings' recent success but it also marked the return to working with George Martin as producer for the first time since the breakup of The Beatles.

Once again, McCartney had to recognize Martin's talent as producer and arranger: after he wrote the song, Paul sat down at the piano with George, playing the track and giving him suggestions for the arrangement just as in the old days.

As he had done for "Penny Lane", McCartney sang the main theme to Martin and suggested the instruments he wanted, leaving him to score the orchestra.

Wings recorded the track most likely at the end of October or during the first week of November. Paul said in an interview to *New Musical Express* released on November 16th: "We've just done something with George – just the other week. We recorded a track for the next James Bond film called 'Live and Let Die'."

The final take, that took "just a couple of days"[201] was recorded live in studio. Denny Seiwell: "We were at AIR Studios with a 40-piece orchestra. We knew well our parts and had a few rundowns with the orchestra, and it took only a few takes to get the master. I remember

---

[201] P. Gambaccini, *cit*, p.71. The first day they recorded the basic track and the orchestra, the following was dedicated to overdubs.

finishing the track in about three hours. The percussion was done by Ray Cooper, he played the tympani part and also a duck call on the reggae bit.... Great fun!"[202]

Mark Berry, today a well-known producer and working as a tea-boy at the time, recalls: "They had a 63-piece orchestra in there and I felt like I had emptied every ashtray known to man before the end of that one! I set up mikes and I put the charts that George Martin wrote onto the stands of the various musicians and I put the first violin charts where the viola charts were!"[203]

Berry: "Bill Price and Geoff Emerick engineered it. If I remember correctly, McCartney's vocal was done in two or three takes and it was a very fast session... I remember saying, 'Wow, that's it?' 'cause with other musicians it takes hours to do the vocals."[204]

The result was a striking and atmospheric recording, that is considered one of McCartney's most history-making tracks.

Together, McCartney and Martin built the song as two experienced film-makers, mixing pathos, tension and pure action. "Live and Let Die" marches majestically, combining in a three minute pop song an incredible number of tricks, melodic ideas and musical themes.

The opening verse with an intriguing piano chord sequence that accompanies McCartney's voice – backed by Linda and Denny's "ghostly" vocals – makes it a fascinating and timeless classic. Laine may have played bass as in "My Love". Next to the explosive central theme – that goes straight to the heart of Bond's adventures (someone noticed a similarity to a passage from "Belshazzar's Feast" by William Walton, certainly well-known to Martin...)[205] – in the middle section Paul put in a reggae digression (composed by Linda), almost a *divertissement* that softens the song's dramatic and impelling feeling.

A real show of prowess, in which McCartney skillfully combines his different vocal registers, mixing his melodic gift with his screaming voice. After the song was recorded, Martin brought it to the producers and went to great lengths to convince them that what they've heard was the real track and not a demo version: George had insisted – with good reason – to have McCartney both as author and performer of the song.

But it wasn't a whim. In terms of both sales and critical acclaim, "Live and Let Die" was an important success: it went straight to #2 in America – where it was certified Gold, for sales of over one million copies – and #9 in the United Kingdom, and took home a Grammy Award for Best Arrangement Accompanying Vocalists in 1973. Finally, it obtained an Oscar nomination for Best Original Song Written for a Motion Picture.

---

[202] Interview courtesy of Denny Seiwell, 14/11/2011.
[203] Interview courtesy of Mark Berry, 23/02/2013.
[204] *Ibid.*
[205] A recording of "Belshazzar's Feast" won a Grammy in 1973 for Best Choral Performance, Classical.

McCartney premiered the song during the *James Paul McCartney* TV special and he performed it on the 1973 *Wings' British Tour*.

In the following years, "Live and Let Die" became a staple of McCartney's concert repertoire, cleverly enriched by an amazing backdrop of fireworks, strobe lights and other stage magic. The song returned popular when McCartney included it in the 1989-90 *Paul McCartney World Tour*, giving Guns'n'Roses the opportunity to record it as a hit cover, that climbed to #5 on the British charts in 1991.

"Live and Let Die" is included in several albums: the single version can be found in *Wings Greatest*, *All the Best!* and *Wingspan* and there are five different live versions.

The first, on *Wings Over America*, is taken from the 1976 US Tour; the second is included in *Tripping the Live Fantastic!* from the 1989-90 *Paul McCartney World Tour*. The track also appears on *Paul Is Live!* from the 1993 *New World Tour*. The song was also included in the 2002/03 *Drivin' Tour* and then in *Back In The US / Back In The World*, as well as in tour performances in 2007, 2008 and 2009 – another version is in *Good Evening New York City* (2009) – in the 2010 *Up & Coming Tour*, in the 2011-12 *On The Run Tour* and in the 2013/14 *Out There! Tour*.

Musicians:

Paul McCartney vocals, piano, bass (?), electric guitar (?), percussion (?) • **Linda McCartney** backing vocals • **Denny Laine** backing vocals, bass (?), electric guitar (?) • **Henry McCullough** electric guitar • **Denny Seiwell** drums, percussion (?) • **Ray Cooper** tympani, duck-call, percussion (?) • **Unknown musicians** strings, horns

59 C Moon (Paul and Linda McCartney)

Recording: November 1972 **Location:** Morgan Studios, London and Abbey Road Studios (overdubs), London **Release:** December 1972, "Hi, Hi, Hi" single B-side

The reggae style, very successful in Britain in the Seventies, also urged McCartney to explore Jamaican rhythms and Paul became a devotee.[206] Besides, McCartney had already been a pioneer of this revival during the Beatles' period with songs like "Obladì-Obladà".

In December 1971, Paul and Linda had taken a lazy holiday in Jamaica. During this vacation they did not miss the opportunity to browse in little shops overloaded with "no label" 45 rpm to find something interesting; the place was a phenomenal source of inspiration for McCartney, prompting him to compose new songs. Very likely with Jamaica in his mind, Paul made the most of his composer's skills writing "C Moon", a fine example of contamination between reggae and McCartney's catchy pop.

---

[206] During his career Paul recorded several tracks in Jamaican style. His covers of "Love Is Strange" (1971) and "Rudolph the Red-Nosed Reggae" (1979), the middle section of "Live and Let Die" (1973), songs such as "Good Times Coming", "Simple As That" (both from 1986), "How Many People?" (1989), "Don't Break the Promise (1997) and New Moon Over Jamaica (1988) which later Paul recorded with Johnny Cash in a country version. The reggae versions of "Tomorrow" and "Silly Love Songs" remain unreleased. Several other rehearsal recordings with Wings witness how McCartney particularly loved to improvise reggae.

Denny Laine: "Paul was really into reggae and wanted to write something that was really cool. He explained that 'C Moon' was the opposite to 'L7', being a circle instead of being square."[207]

In "C Moon" Paul manages to grasp the essence of Jamaican music, blended with his penchant for simplicity: the song is driven by McCartney's typical piano *staccato* and a bare-bones arrangement makes the track unforgettable.

The song's lyrics are filled with allusions, alliterations and nonsense, with its characters free from stereotypes. Again, it's a song about the generation gap: Paul tells a story of a love beyond social conventions, with two young lovers (Bobby and Patty) that cannot explain their love to the girl's father. A cheerful, light-heartedness recording, in which McCartney even left some mistakes. McCartney: "We left all the little bits that you'd normally clean up for the records. The bit *Is it the intro? I should have been in!* was for real. I missed the intro, and the song has changed because of it!"[208]

Even Paul's doubt about whether or not keep the vocal take was left on purpose on the recording and during the fade-out you can really hear McCartney asking the studio assistants, "Should we do another one?"

The presence in the studio of Paul's daughters – who sang back-up vocals – and a different Wings' line-up – playing unusual instruments for them – boosted its spontaneity.

The basic track consisted of piano (McCartney), bass (Laine), tambourine (Linda), drums (McCullough) and xylophone (Seiwell). During the overdubs, both McCartney and Seiwell added cornets.

Melody Maker magazine reported that Wings had performed "C Moon" in a jam session held on September 3rd with Led Zeppelin drummer John Bonham (see also sheets **91**, **130** and **131**): a performance which unfortunately has never been released.

John Leckie, who engineered some sessions at Abbey Road when Alan Parsons left for one week, recalls: "The first day they'd come from Morgan Studios and had recorded the song (with Mike Bobak engineering – author's note). They had done a mix and didn't really like it: we spent the afternoon doing some kind of remix of the track and overdubbing some handclaps."[209]

Released in December 1972 as the B side to "Hi, Hi, Hi" (see sheet **60**), the song became popular after British radio stations banned "Hi, Hi, Hi" for allusions to sex and drugs: "C Moon" became the A-side reaching #5 on the UK charts.

"C Moon" was released for the first time on LP in 1987 (*All the Best!*) and the song also appears on *Wingspan*. Performed in the *James Paul McCartney* show and in the Wings tours in 1973 and 1975, "C Moon" was also a favorite during soundchecks for the *Paul McCartney World Tour*.

[207] S. Leigh, *cit.*, p.17.
[208] Badman, Keith *The Beatles - After The Break-Up 1970-2000*, p. 85
[209] Interview courtesy of John Leckie, 30/09/2012.

Paul and the band put so much fun and enthusiasm into these rehearsals that one of them became a record: the track, recorded in Milan on October 26th, 1989 again became the B-side to a single ("All My Trials",1990).

This slower version proves how good songs stands the test of time. Paul performed the track live in 1992 (*Ed Sullivan Show*), in the 2002/03 *Drivin' Tour* (including it in the *Back in the US /Back in the World*), in the 2007 *Memory Almost Full Promo Tour* (the June 27th, 2007 concert version is on the 2009 *Amoeba's Secret* EP and in *Live in Los Angeles*, the album released in the UK in 2010 with the *Mail* magazine) and in live gigs in 2008. "C Moon" is often played during soundchecks.

Musicians:

Paul McCartney vocals, piano, cornet • **Linda McCartney** backing vocals, tambourine • **Denny Laine** backing vocals, bass • **Henry McCullough** drums • **Denny Seiwell** xylophone, cornet, shaker (?) • **Heather McCartney, Mary McCartney** backing vocals

At one point during the sessions, Alan Parsons left to do some other job and assistant John Leckie, who previously worked as tape operator for the *McCartney* album, engineered one week of recordings. Leckie: "I remember being scared. I hadn't done many full on sessions and was trying to grab as many engineering jobs I could. Paul would sit at desk with me and go through each instrument and get me to adjust equalization and settings before he was happy. Then he'd run downstairs and play. He'd also nick all our fags! The band were all together but really taking direction from Paul."[210]

60 Hi, Hi, Hi (Paul and Linda McCartney)

Recording: November 1972 **Location:** Abbey Road Studios, London **Release:** December 1972, single

When McCartney went to the studio to record "Hi, Hi, Hi" the track had been tested during the previous tour as its closing number, proving to be quite successful.

The song may not be particularly original: but "Hi, Hi, Hi" was one of those rockers that give the audience one last chance to romp and dance during the concert.

Paul had written the song in Spain in Benidorm in June, just before the starting of the *Wings Over Europe Tour*. He was surely planning to add another number to the group's setlist and soon he decided to release it. The track was recorded at Abbey Road. The session turned out hard and it took about fifty tapes before capturing the right take.[211]

---

[210] *Ibid.*
[211] As told by Henry McCullough in Madinger, C.-Easter, M. *cit.* p. 175.

John Leckie, who was on board recording that track, explains why it was so difficult to get: "'Hi Hi Hi' was written in studio really and no one seemed to know what they were doing except Paul!"[212]

The engineer is probably referring to the structure of the song (number of bars, breaks, solos), typically unpredictable as are many Fifties rock'n'roll numbers.

Leckie: "It took a few days with all the overdubs and most of the vocals. I remember them having lots of goes at it. Paul played rhythm guitar on the track. The session went on 'til 6 or 7 am and they'd come in at 4 pm the next day and tried it again. Paul played the natural Rickenbacker bass but we spent ages getting the sound and even put it through a huge JBL studio monitor. There are lot of guitar parts on the track and some lines from Henry were captured live on backing track and some overdubbed."[213]

Leckie also witnessed the creation of the backing vocals, which McCartney took particular care over: "I think they were done one at a time with Paul in control room."[214]

At the time, McCartney was satisfied with the results ("I think it's the best single we've done as Wings"[215]) but this record could be considered among the less interesting songs of McCartney's first decade after the Beatles. Paul himself admitted in an interview to Terry Staunton and Roy Carr in 1987 that he didn't like the song anymore.

The recording did everything possible to turn this fast and tight rocker into a more easygoing pop song: the track was produced adding a lot of reverb to Paul's vocals rather than giving it a powerful and dirty sound.

Too bad, because this lascivious anthem that McCartney had composed as a tribute to the spirit of the Sixties, contained some rather explicit lyrics to express the "drugs, sex and rock'n'roll" philosophy. The title itself used the term, just as *high*, slang to express feeling exhilarated by drug use, while the lyrics contained verses related to sexual practices (a woman lying on the bed and ready "for my body gun" was the fateful expression). McCartney, taking advantage of the lack of clarity in some parts of the recording, muddied the waters, claiming that the last word was "polygon".

McCartney, under scrutiny after two recent drug arrests and after the political controversy raised by "Give Ireland Back to the Irish", was again in the grip of censorship: so "Hi, Hi, Hi" was immediately banned by BBC radio programming.

Denny Laine: "Paul is a very clever lyricist (…) so he is difficult to censor. He got caught with 'Hi, Hi, Hi' but that's bound to happen once in a while."[216]

---

[212] www.gearslutz.com/board/q-producer-john-eckie/403866-any-paul-mccartney-stories.html
[213] Interview courtesy of John Leckie, 30/09/2012.
[214] *Ibid.*
[215] K. Badman, *The Beatles.The Dream Is Over-Off the Record 2*, 2002, p.94.
[216] S. Leigh, *cit.*, p. 17.

Soon after the BBC ban, Paul changed his version and admitted: "We all thought, you know, (the ban) it might be possible. The story is actually only about sex, not drugs. It's something to sing. I don't care about the lyrics. Not really."[217] BBC replied: "It's just too blatant for us."

A strange sound overdubbed on the track seems to confirm Paul's version: according to some sources, the whirling effect heard at 1:43 was allusive (and in fact comes right after the words "body gun" – or "polygon", if you like it more) and has been made using no less than a vibrator, but John Leckie revealed that "it was the vocal." The conservative attitude of British radio actually benefited McCartney who – by recording such a provocative track – was probably seeking a subtle revenge against the establishment that he felt victimized him. The song climbed to #5 in the UK charts while in America it reached #10, becoming the first Wings top ten overseas. Even Harrison was intrigued: during the *Living in the Material World* sessions he recorded a track, titled "Rolling Over You", featuring Steve Winwood and Pete Townshend. It was a parody of McCartney's song, even mentioning the BBC censored verse.[218] "Hi, Hi, Hi" was included in the 1973 *Wings' British Tour* and in the 1975/76 *Wings Over the World Tour*. The original version is included in *Wings Greatest* and *Wingspan*, while a live version is on *Wings Over America*. The song has been included in the 2013/14 *Out There! Tour*.

Musicians:

Paul McCartney vocals, backing vocals, bass, electric guitar • **Linda McCartney** backing vocals, organ • **Denny Laine** backing vocals, electric guitar • **Henry McCullough** electric guitar • **Denny Seiwell** drums, cow-bell

61 Lazy Dynamite (Paul and Linda McCartney)

Recording: November, 1972 **Location:** Olympic Studios, London **Release:** May 1973, *Red Rose Speedway*

"Lazy Dynamite" was another piano-song written by McCartney. Paul had to come up with some trick to get this track taped: maybe he felt the song wasn't good enough to be recorded on its own and would never have seen the light of day if not included in a medley.

When McCartney thought to add a closing medley to *Red Rose Speedway* is not known. Possibly in December or in January, after EMI refused to release the album as it was intended, Paul went back to work to stitch together something more palatable to a wider audience, taking inspiration from one the cleverest ideas he had come up with during the Beatles period. But Denny Seiwell knows why he did it: "Paul got these songs that he liked but they weren't finished… We recorded the tracks separately and then they were mixed by Glyn Johns."[219] Seiwell's recollection could be wrong and is contradicted by engineer John Leckie.

---

[217] *Hi Times. Paul McCartney Talks to Alan Smith About Lennon, Linda and Courting Controversy*, in *New Musical Express*, 16th November 1972, p.16.

[218] Interview granted by George Harrison to Rob Geurtsen, 1973.

[219] Interview courtesy of Denny Seiwell, 18/11/2011.

Leckie: "I recorded the backing track for the medley, but I think only 'Lazy Dynamite' was used. I remember running through the three songs – 'Hold Me Tight'/'Lazy Dynamite'/'Hands of Love' – and trying to get a take of all three in sequence but it wasn't really happening and we just concentrated on 'Lazy Dynamite'."[220]

McCartney built the recording around a catchy melody, starting from a backing track, with varied and polished instrumentation. Paul added his vocal parts – which he recorded all by himself – a well-studied bass part and Denny Laine contributed a country flavor with his harmonica. It would be used as the second song of the *Red Rose Speedway* medley.

Musicians:

Paul McCartney vocals, backing vocals, piano, bass, Mellotron • **Denny Laine** harmonica • **Henry McCullough** electric guitar • **Denny Seiwell** drums, percussion, tambourine (?)

After the November sessions, *Red Rose Speedway* was conceived by McCartney as a double album. On December 13th, 1972, Paul sent an acetate to EMI, containing the following tracklist: "Country Dreamer" – "Night Out" – "One More Kiss" – "Jazz Street" – "Big Barn Bed" – "My Love" – "When the Night" – "Single Pigeon" – "Tragedy" – "Mama's Little Girl" – "Loup (First Indian on the Moon)" – "I Would Only Smile" – "I Lie Around" – "Little Lamb Dragonfly" – "Get on the Right Thing" – "1882" – "The Mess"

EMI refused it and insisted on a single LP, containing "easy listening" songs, to take advantage of McCartney's name in terms of sales. Paul gave up, in favour of a more commercial style, suitable to his public and critics. But it could have been McCartney's conscious choice. Probably at that point, he went back to his medley idea, and re-recorded some tracks previously attempted with Leckie, while adding a new song to it.

62 Hold Me Tight (Paul and Linda McCartney)

Recording: December (?), 1972 **Location:** Olympic Studios (?), London **Release:** May 1973, *Red Rose Speedway*

Probably back at the Olympic Studios, McCartney put his efforts trying to complete the album. "Hold Me Tight" was a melodic song – whose title was borrowed from an early Beatles' song – that McCartney crafted ingeniously around those three words. Harmonically, its basic triad of major chords is transposed time after time to a different key, resulting in a peculiar "loop" effect. The backing vocals were carefully woven into it and performed by the whole group.

Musicians:

Paul McCartney vocals, backing vocals, piano, bass • **Linda McCartney** backing vocals • **Denny Laine** backing vocals, acoustic (?) and electric guitar • **Henry McCullough** backing vocals, acoustic (?) and electric guitar • **Denny Seiwell** backing vocals, drums

---

[220] Interview courtesy of John Leckie, 30/09/2012.

63 Hands of Love (Paul and Linda McCartney)

Recording: December (?), 1972 **Location:** Olympic Studios (?), London **Release:** May 1973, *Red Rose Speedway*

"Hands of Love", another one of McCartney's lightweight love songs, was also arranged in country style. Paul thought to record it using bright and syncopated acoustic guitars, starting out with sharp chords, reminiscent of the Beatles' "Polythene Pam". Then, he crossfaded it with "Lazy Dynamite", and the song is the third bit of the *Red Rose Speedway* medley. Perhaps the use of teenage love-story lingo is excessive and its melody doesn't seem strong enough to sustain the whole song, in which the chorus is repeated *ad nauseam*.

But the recording was full of gimmicks, as Denny Seiwell recalls: "Paul played ocarina, me played congas… We put some strange effects on drums… It was very funny to record!"[221]

Paul played a few bars of "Hands of Love" on the *James Paul McCartney* rehearsals.

Musicians:

Paul McCartney vocals, acoustic guitar, kazoo • **Linda McCartney** backing vocals • **Denny Laine** electric guitar • **Henry McCullough** percussion • **Denny Seiwell** drums, percussion, congas

64 Power Cut (Paul and Linda McCartney)

Recording: December (?), 1972 **Location:** Olympic Studios (?), London **Release:** May 1973, *Red Rose Speedway*

The frequent power-cuts that happened in Britain at the time inspired this song. During the *Wings' University Tour* – that took place in the weeks following a long strike by English miners, lasting from January 9th to February 25th, 1972 – Wings faced some of these issues. This led Paul to write "Power Cut", the best song of the *Red Rose Speedway* medley.

With McCartney's typical piano *staccato*, "Power Cut" soon leaves his original inspiration to become a classic love song. Its very simple harmonic structure is based on two chords swinging in a fifth interval. Towards the end, all the tracks of the medley slowly emerge and overlap: the intertwining of guitars and vocals take turns, chase each other and join together. A fine example of how well McCartney masters the rules of musical harmony.

Musicians:

Paul McCartney vocals, backing vocals, piano, celeste, Mellotron, bass • **Linda McCartney** backing vocals, electric piano • **Denny Laine** backing vocals, electric guitar • **Henry McCullough** backing vocals, electric guitar • **Denny Seiwell** drums

---

[221] Interview courtesy of Denny Seiwell, 18/11/2011.

1973

After a February holiday in Morocco, in March Wings started recording the *James Paul McCartney* TV special. McCartney had already thought up a show back in the *RAM* period, but for one reason or another, it had been put off until a later date.

Some handwritten papers by Paul – included in the 2012 *RAM* Deluxe Edition – reveal that the show would have included, in addition to the *RAM* tracks, numbers like "Mother Nature's Son" or "I Lie Around".

Finally, this TV special was aired on April 16th in the US and on June 7th in the UK. The show was commissioned to Paul by Sir Lew Grade – the owner of ATV – after their breach over "Another Day" and was ostensibly to be a deeper glimpse into McCartney's personality.

It came off as disappointing from that point of view, as it ended up being just a collage of songs, filmed in different locations. In other words, a great promotional opportunity for McCartney and the *Red Rose Speedway* upcoming album.

The show presented Wings performing some songs recorded on March, 18th at ATV's Boreham Wood Studio D – "The Mess", "Maybe I'm Amazed", "Hi, Hi, Hi" and "Long Tall Sally" – or filmed outdoors: a new recording of "Mary Had a Little Lamb" was accompanied by a clip shot in the open Scottish countryside.

Highlights were the performances of "My Love" and "Live and Let Die" and Paul's acoustic medley with "Blackbird", "Bluebird", "Michelle" and "Heart of the Country".

Another peak moment was the performance of "Yesterday": it was the first time Paul presented a Beatles' song before an audience after the breakup. McCartney rejected "The Long and Winding Road", which was played during rehearsals.

Finally, the show included a quirky scene, with the performance of the controversial "Gotta Sing, Gotta Dance", a Busby Berkeley-style number – unreleased to date – that McCartney had written for the famous model Twiggy.

The piece was performed as a triumphantly kitsch tip-tap dance, with Paul going down a long staircase wearing a pink tailcoat, high heels and a fake moustache.

However, the broadcasting of the *James Paul McCartney* show increased the popularity McCartney was gaining with his band. "My Love" was issued as a single prior to the release of *Red Rose Speedway*: the album was released in May and it immediately jumped to #1 in the US charts and #5 in the UK.

Its inevitable commercial success (a gold disc for one million copies sold in America) was followed by kinder critical reviews than those for previous records, although the reception wasn't triumphant.

According to *Rolling Stone*, "the album is good, competent McCartney, neither his best nor worst, but solidly constructed material".

Others noticed that the album lacked real rockers but the general feeling was that Paul had begun to discipline his musical behavior and *Red Rose Speedway* turned out to be the record with which Wings began to gain respect from the reviewers.

Tony Tyler of *New Musical Express* said: "Well folks, this time Paul has really done it; he's really made a nice record. Certainly *Red Rose Speedway* is lightweight, sure it has no intellectual posture. But, with all the current heaviness and after-me-the-apocalypse brain studs around, I for one am bloody pleased to discover a lightweight record that not only fails to alienate, but actually succeeds in impressing via good melodic structure, excellent playing and fine production. It altogether makes my day".

The EMI marketing department wisely put McCartney's face (with a big red rose in his mouth) on the album cover: years later, this iconic album cover was proudly shown by Oasis in their videoclip for the song "Shakermaker" (1994).

In April, just before his new UK tour, McCartney went to Abbey Road for another odd recording. The following day – on April 26th – he also recorded "Leave It", a song intended for his brother Mike's solo project, *McGear* (see **1974**).

65 Zoo Gang (Paul and Linda McCartney)

Recording: April 25th and November ? (overdubs), 1973 **Location:** Abbey Road Studios, London and EMI Studios? (overdubs), Paris **Release:** June 1974, "Band on the Run" single B-side

The third act of the McCartney-Grade saga: "Zoo Gang" was the title of a British TV serial by Sir Lew Grade's ATV, who asked Paul to write the main theme.

Nobody knows if the questionable result of this track is intentional: McCartney carried out the assignment merely with a short instrumental. And most likely Paul recorded the track completely on his own: despite the credits listed in the 2010 edition of *Band on the Run* (that attribute the performance to Wings), Denny Seiwell does not recall any involvement in that recording.[222] Even electric guitar and drums sound so typical of McCartney's style.

Only the use of an accordion – which, according to some sources, was overdubbed later in Paris – gives a peculiar atmosphere to the song, which could only be appreciated in the context of the tv series, set in Nice, South France. "Zoo Gang" recalls "Kreen–Akrore" for its – vague – ethnic influence. It was issued as the B-side to the single "Band on the Run" in the UK.

Musicians:

Paul McCartney bass, accordion (?), drums (?), keyboards (?) • **Linda McCartney** keyboards (?) • **Denny Laine** electric guitar (?) • **Henry McCullough** electric guitar (?) • **Denny Seiwell** drums (?)

---

[222] Interview courtesy of Denny Seiwell, 18/11/2011.

Without stopping a minute, in May and then in July – after a month-long break – McCartney and Wings launched their UK tour, starting in Bristol.

Strangely, McCartney decided to shorten the show he presented the previous year. The band only performed fifteen songs during the concert. The following setlist – taken from an Apple acetate from the Newcastle concert that took place on July 7th, 1973 – was held about steady for the whole tour: "Soily" – "Big Barn Bed" – "When the Night" – "Seaside Woman" – "Wild Life" – "Little Woman Love/C Moon" – "Maybe I'm Amazed" – "My Love" – "Live and Let Die" – "Go Now" (an old Moody Blues classic, sung by Laine) – "The Mess" – "Hi, Hi, Hi" – "Long Tall Sally"

Laine sometimes also performed his song "Say You Don't Mind". "Live and Let Die" was particularly successful among the younger part of the audience.

Rolling Stone published a favorable review of the New Theatre concert at Oxford on May 12th containing some interviews with the audience. Paul was identified as the front-man of his new band: "We're a little young to remember the Beatles. We've heard of them, but we're here because we're Wings fans."[223] To celebrate the tour's ending, Wings held a special party on May 27th at the Café Royal, in Regent Street, London with Elton John, Neil Sedaka, Rod Stewart, Marc Bolan, Charlie Watts, Keith Richards, Cat Stevens and Cynthia Lennon.

The tour was very successful but right after its completion the tensions within the band came to light. Just weeks before, McCullough had told *Melody Maker*: "I don't suppose we'll be together forever. I'm sure Paul's got more of a tie to The Beatles than to Wings."[224]

The facts proved he was right: when McCartney and the group went back to the farm to rehearse and record the basic tracks for *Band on the Run*, McCullough quarreled with Paul and left the band. McCartney: "Henry came to a head one day when I asked him to play something he didn't really fancy playing. We all got a bit choked about it and he rang up later and said he was leaving."[225] McCullough felt that McCartney's pop style was not what he was searching for. Denny Seiwell asked Paul if they would need another guitar player: McCartney answered that the album would be recorded the same way as *RAM*. That was when Denny felt he was throwing the efforts of the two previous years.

What happened in August is well known: Paul asked EMI for a studio in an exotic place and, among the suggested locations – which also included Rio de Janeiro and Beijing – Lagos looked very appealing to him. But McCartney could have heard about the Lagos musical scene some time before, very likely through Laine's connection with Ginger Baker, who in 1971 also went to Abbey Road to record with Fela Kuti (see "Bluebird", sheet 69) and Nigerian musicians.

---

[223] P. Gambaccini, cit., p.106.
[224] John Blaney, *Paul McCartney: The songs He Was Singing, Vol.I. The Seventies,* 2010, p. 75.
[225] P. Gambaccini, *cit.,* p.74.

McCartney: "We checked on the availability of Lagos and it turned out to be free for the three weeks we wanted to record. So we thought, 'Great – lying on the beach all day, doing nothing. Breeze in the studios and record.'"[226] The very night before the departure, drummer Denny Seiwell also decided to leave the band. The departure date is uncertain: although some sources report August 9th, other accounts refer to August 29th. The latter date is consistent with McCartney's statement above, about the three week period of recording.

Once in Nigeria, Paul, Linda and Denny Laine soon understood they would share not only a musical adventure but also a difficult human experience, sometimes dramatic, and therefore unforgettable. Soon after landing at the airport at Ikeja, Paul realized he wasn't welcome.

During a visit to the city, Paul and Linda were held up at knifepoint and robbed of their cassette-recorder containing demos of some tracks Paul had recently written.

Fela Ranson-Kuti, a well-known local musician and political activist, led a media campaign denouncing McCartney's attempt to steal African music. Even Ginger Baker, Cream's former drummer, didn't make life easy for Paul, insisting that he record the album at his own studio. The equipment was taken directly to Baker's ARC Studios, but at the EMI's insistence, Wings moved to their company's studio, causing friction with Baker. McCartney entered the EMI studio, but unfortunately he had not checked its condition beforehand. When Paul got to Apapa, he found a small and underequipped studio, still being built, with a Studer eight track tape machine and a control desk which worked intermittently. Emerick noticed that apart from two Neumanns, the microphones were "inexpensive models".[227]

Nevertheless, the McCartney-Laine team worked perfectly and the sessions were very productive: the two laid down the basic tracks for seven songs – mainly starting with Denny on electric guitar and Paul on drums – worked hard on overdubs (except for some of Laine's guitar parts here and there and Linda's keyboards, McCartney played everything else) and finished the recordings in three weeks. As noticeable from some photographs, McCartney also used his Fender Jazz bass during the Lagos recordings.

66 Mamunia (Paul and Linda McCartney)

Recording: September 1st-23rd and October (overdubs), 1973 **Location:** EMI Studios, Lagos and AIR Studios (overdubs), London **Release:** November 1973, *Band on the Run*

During Wings' Marrakesh holiday the previous February – some pictures of their vacation are in the *Red Rose Speedway* booklet – the band stayed at the sumptuous Mamounia hotel, one of the most renowned in the world for its luxury and elegance.

The sound of the name was enough to inspire McCartney to write a song. For the lyrics, he was inspired by a sign he saw in a pub in Lagos.

---

[226] *Melody Maker*, 01/12/1973, p.48
[227] Geoff Emerick, *Here, There and Everywhere. My Life Recording the Music of The Beatles*, 2006, p.339.

Once in the studio, "Mamunia" was arranged in a simple way. It was "the first song we recorded in Lagos, in the middle of a tropical rainstorm"[228], as McCartney recalled: led by brilliant acoustic guitars, it celebrates its *joie de vivre* with a radiant chord sequence and with a joyful ending, featuring Linda's Moog solo.

The whole band – joined by an unidentified roadie who played bass-drum – shouts and plays percussion as if they were in the middle of a cheerful ceremony in an African village. Paul can be heard to ebulliently remark, off-mike: "Everywhere I look it's the same old sound, I like it".

McCartney added a prominent bass part that weaves throughout the song, a perfect blend of the flourishing African nature and typically British atmospheres (the 'plastic macs' reference is reminiscent of "Penny Lane"). Final overdubs included some superb three-part vocal harmonies, a real trademark of Wings' sound.

Included in *Band on the Run*, "Mamunia" was originally on the B-side to the "Jet" single in America but it was immediately replaced by "Let Me Roll It".

Reasons are not clear: most likely Paul had considered "Mamunia" for release as a single on its own. This never occurred, although a nice animated video was prepared for the song.

Musicians:
Paul McCartney vocals, backing vocals, acoustic guitar, electric guitar (?), bass, percussion • **Linda McCartney** backing vocals, Moog • **Denny Laine** backing vocals, acoustic guitar, electric guitar (?), percussion • **Unknown musician** bass-drum

67 Helen Wheels (Paul and Linda McCartney)

Recording: September 1st-23rd and October (overdubs), 1973 **Location:** EMI Studios, Lagos and AIR Studios (overdubs), London **Release:** October 1973, single

In McCartney's career, "Helen Wheels" is known for being at the center of a marketing strategy. But the song proved, once again, Paul's art at turning every aspect of his life into music. "Helen Wheels" was the affectionate nickname Paul had given Land Rover, the car that drove him, Linda (and, occasionally, Wings) from his farm in Scotland to London and back.

So McCartney wrote this rolling song, based on the typical rock'n'roll chord sequence, naming the main towns along the route: Glasgow, Carlisle, Kendal, Liverpool and Birmingham, in the most typical road-song style. The title could be a wordplay about "Hell On Wheels" (sung in the chorus), the itinerant collection of gambling houses, saloons and brothels that followed the army of Union Pacific railroad workers in America in 1860s.

In Lagos, it didn't take long to finish the track: Paul laid down his drums while Laine played rhythm guitar. Later, McCartney completed "Helen Wheels" overdubbing bass and lead guitar, before adding his vocal part and the backing vocals with Denny and Linda. A surprisingly unpolished but effective recording.

---

[228] B. Spitzer-A. Steckler, *cit.*, p.174.

Issued as a single on October 26th, 1973, "Helen Wheels" banged on target, hitting the top ten in America but reaching only #12 in UK.

Promptly, before *Band on the Run* was released, Capitol Records put pressure on McCartney in order to include the song in the American edition of the album: to make it more commercial, since at the time Paul decided not to extract any singles from it.

McCartney didn't like to put any formerly released singles in albums: "Another Day" was not included in *RAM*, "Mull of Kintyre" would not be in *London Town* and Paul would also refuse to include "Goodnight Tonight" in *Back to the Egg*, causing friction with Columbia Records.

This time Paul had to yield to Capitol's insistence. McCartney: "I got a call from the company saying we were 'missing a natural marketing opportunity'. I said that the song wasn't written for the album. But finally, reluctantly I said, 'Ok, put it on the album but bury it on side two.'"[229] "Helen Wheels" became the only song in McCartney's career to set a difference between the English and the American editions of his studio albums. Oddly, despite the single's good success, Paul did not include the song neither in his 1975/76 *Wings Over The World Tour* nor in *Wings Greatest*. However, "Helen Wheels" is on the *Wingspan* compilation.

Musicians:

Paul McCartney vocals, backing vocals, bass, electric guitar, drums • **Linda McCartney** backing vocals, Moog • **Denny Laine** backing vocals, electric guitar

68 Band on the Run (Paul and Linda McCartney)

Recording: September 1st-23rd and October, 1973 **Location:** EMI Studios, Lagos and AIR Studios, London **Release:** November 1973, *Band on the Run*

When Paul left for Lagos, he had already written the title-track of his future album. In fact, he had started the song in 1972. It merged McCartney's frustration with drugs prohibition – for which he had paid the price during that year[230] - and his love of assonance.

McCartney: "At the time bands like us and the Eagles were feeling like and being treated like outlaws and desperados. I mean, people were getting busted for pot, that is. And our argument was that we didn't want to be outlaws. We wanted to (...) make our music and live in peace. And that's what the song was about; it was my reaction to the whole scene... It was during the era when everyone was like desperados, people were getting busted left, right and center of things, so the spirit was like 'We're all in this together'. So anything about desperados or 'on the run' kind of united people against the authority. And, you know, we happened to be part of that. So I got this idea of 'Band on the Run'."[231]

[229] *Band on the Run Deluxe Edition*, in *The Paul McCartney Archive Collection*, 2010, p.64.
[230] Paul had been arrested twice: in Gothenburg, during the *Wings Over Europe Tour*, and later in his Scottish farm for marijuana possession.
[231] From *Band on the Run -The Paul McCartney Archive Collection*, 2010, p.10.

The song had been rehearsed with Wings during spring but, when McCartney was robbed of his tapes in Lagos, he had to bring it back from memory.

"Band on the Run" marked a milestone for McCartney's career: the recording of the track masterfully links three different sections. Judging from the pictures of the reel tapes included in the *Band on the Run Deluxe Edition* (2010), only part one and two of the song were taped in Lagos while the final section was recorded in London. As the tapes went through some oxidation that nearly made them unplayable[232], this could be the reason for the guitar sound in the first two sections is affected by noticeable distortion and over-saturation.

The first part serves as an introduction. It has a tense atmosphere: nervous guitars and keyboards are counterpointed by a relaxed rhythm section. The hypnotic vocals speak of the resignation of the prisoners forgotten by society: they are stuck inside a jail and see no hope for the future. A rocking section follows next: aggressive, with an irregular and syncopated rhythm; it replaces the fatalistic mood with an angry roar, charged with rebellion and hope, in the incessant chorus "If I ever get out of here".

The majestic orchestra crescendo leading into the third section – opened by bright acoustic guitar chords – expresses the feeling of escape and freedom, and was not an easy task.

Paul had engaged Tony Visconti to work on the orchestral arrangements for the album. He recalls the issues they ran into for the overdubbing.

Visconti: "I was asked to orchestrate that little interlude between the slow part of 'Band on the Run' and the fast part, and there's no rhythmical relationship between them (…) I remember taking a long time to conduct all of the 50 musicians to play that little phrase (…) It was only five bars long, but it took ages to get right in synch with the track."[233]

The following three minutes – with plenty of little tricks and hooks – make "Band on the Run" a classic Seventies pop song: Paul's slightly sped-up vocals, accompanied by flanged acoustic guitars, tell the story of a band of fugitives.

The track was the second single taken from *Band on the Run* (a 3:55 radio edit was also prepared). Its simple rhymes and the enjoyable guitar licks pushed the song, in April 1974, to #1 on the Billboard Hot 100, and the single reached one million copies sold. "Band on the Run" was released in June in the UK where it reached #3.

Paul's drum performance was praised by Keith Moon, the drummer of Who. McCartney later said it was source of pride for him.

Of course, "Band on the Run" became a song which Paul performed everywhere: from the 1975-76 *Wings Over The World Tour* to the 1979 *Wings' British Tour* (the live version recorded in Glasgow was offered as a digital download from www.paulmccartney.com), through the 1989-

---

[232] Geoff Emerick, *Here, There and Everywhere. My Life Recording the Music of The Beatles,* 2006, p.351.
[233] *Band on the Run-25th Anniversary Edition,* 1999.

90 *Paul McCartney World Tour*, the 1993 *New World Tour*, since his 2002-03 *Drivin' Tour*, 2004 *Summer Tour*, 2005 *US Tour*, 2007 *Memory Almost Full Promo Tour*, 2009 Tour, 2010 Up & Coming Tour, 2011-12 *On The Run Tour*, 2013/14 *Out There! Tour*.

The track was included in three different compilations: *Wings Greatest, All The Best!* and *Wingspan*. Live versions appear on *Wings Over America, Tripping The Live Fantastic!, Back in the US/Back in the World* and *Good Evening New York City*.

The original version is included in the *Give My Regards to Broad Street* soundtrack, but is not present in the album, even though Paul recorded an *ad hoc* version which remains unreleased. The *Band on the Run – 25th Anniversary Edition* (1999) contains an acoustic version (slightly over a minute) recorded by McCartney in December 1998. A new version, arranged with glasses and harmonium, has been presented by McCartney on a BBC Tv programme in 2003 and performed during the *Chaos and Creation at Abbey Road* show in 2005. The 2010 remastered edition also contains the *One Hand Clapping* recording.

Musicians:

Paul McCartney vocals, backing vocals, acoustic guitar, electric guitar, bass, drums, electric piano, synthesizer • **Linda McCartney** backing vocals, Moog • **Denny Laine** backing vocals, acoustic guitar, electric guitar • **Beaux Arts Orchestra** horns, strings

69 Bluebird (Paul and Linda McCartney)

Recording: September 1st-23rd and October (overdubs), 1973 **Location:** EMI Studios, Lagos and AIR Studios (overdubs), London **Release:** November 1973, *Band on the Run*

During his stay in Lagos, one evening Paul popped into the African Shrine, a club whose owner was the Afrobeat local star and political activist, Fela Ransome-Kuti (1938-1997).

The concert of Ransome-Kuti's band was an unforgettable experience for McCartney. As Paul told Mark Lewisohn in 1994: "When Fela and his band eventually began to play, after a long, crazy build-up, I just couldn't stop weeping with joy". Recently, McCartney talked about that night, playing a riff to one Fela's song he remembered: "Why Black Men Dey Suffer?".[234] Ransome-Kuti wasn't quite as happy: after seeing McCartney at the club, he complained on the local radio stations, accusing Paul of trying to steal African music.

Not satisfied, Fela decided to meet Paul face to face: accompanied by his entourage, he arrived to EMI studios, stating his allegations with an intimidating attitude. Paul played the tapes with the tracks to Fela, to prove there was no African music in them, but to not make matters worse, he decided afterwards not to have any Lagos musician to play on the record. A picture of McCartney and Ransome-Kuti together in the studio – included in the *Band on the Run* booklet – proves that the tension was high.

---

[234] *Sir Paul McCartney – Thoughts On Fela* (2013): http://www.youtube.com/watch?v=E4Jnl4iERqE. In this interview, Paul says he was invited to the African Shrine by Fela himself after their argument. A similar percussion rhythm would be used by McCartney for his unreleased "Waterspout" years later.

But, as they say, "If Mohammed will not go to the mountain, the mountain must come to Mohammed". So "Bluebird" was the only track of *Band on the Run* which could boast a Nigerian musician among its ranks, the percussionist Remi Kabaka (from the Ginger Baker entourage): Paul invited him to AIR Studios during the overdub sessions.

Among the *Band on the Run* songs, "Bluebird" was perhaps the oldest one written by Paul, who composed it in Jamaica maybe during his early December 1971 vacation.

It was also, to some extent, already known to McCartney's audience: Paul and Linda had sung it in 1971 during a radio performance in New York[235] and McCartney had also included it in the acoustic medley on the *James Paul McCartney* show.[236]

Lagos seemed the perfect setting to record this exotic-flavored acoustic ballad, whose lyrics deal with the subject of flight and freedom. McCartney used a drum-machine to lay down the rhythm-track and chose a very simple arrangement (acoustic guitar[237] – tuned one step lower – and bass), adding as many percussion instruments as possible: maracas, chimes, triangle and guiro can be heard throughout the song. Some piano notes – not in tune with guitars – are heard between 3:04 and 3:07.[238]

In its final form, "Bluebird" is a fascinating recording: its lazy and relaxed mood, where nature-inspired elements blend with the feeling of freedom, sets the tone for the song.

When overdubbing, McCartney enriched the track by some marvelous three-part harmonies with Linda and Denny: disarmingly simple but very effective.

Then, Howie Casey added his sax solo: soft, enchanting, "nocturnal", it conveys the brightness of the African night and deserves a special place among the best solos in McCartney's records. Casey: "Paul said, 'I've got this nice ballad and I'd like you do play a solo on it.' He played the track and I blew a solo, just coasting through it, looking at the chords. When we came to the end he said, 'That's it. That's fine!' I said, 'Hang on, Paul, I can do better than that'. He said, 'Maybe you can but that what I'm after.' He did let me try a few more times, but he used the first one and hearing it now, I can see he was right."[239] Paul performed it during the 1975-76 *Wings Over the World Tour*: the *Wings Over America* version, featuring an introduction on twelve-string acoustic guitar played by McCartney, is taken from one of these concerts. *Band on the Run – 25th Anniversary Edition* contains an excerpt of "Bluebird" recorded on November 1975 as a "refund" to Japanese fans for the cancellation of their planned tour: the authorities denied McCartney a visa because of his arrest for drug possession in 1972.

---

235 It's a CBS recording. Paul sings strumming acoustic guitar with Linda on harmonies.
236 For ATV's TV show Paul recorded two different versions of a medley in which he played the acoustic guitar while Linda was taking pictures. The unreleased one had "Bluebird/Mama's Little Girl/Michelle/Heart Of The Country"; while the aired one had "Blackbird/Bluebird/Michelle/Heart of the Country".
237 Maybe a 12-string, as Paul is seen playing it in some photos taken from the Lagos sessions.
238 See http://www.11fifty.com/Site_108/Bluebird.html.
239 S. Leigh, *cit.*, p.18.

In its original version "Bluebird" is included in the *Wingspan* collection, whereas the one from *One Hand Clapping* appears on the bonus cd to the 2010 edition of *Band on the Run*. A version played at Cow Palace in S.Francisco (June 1976) is included in the 2013 Boxset Edition of *Wings Over America*. McCartney played "Bluebird" during his 2010 *Up & Coming Tour* in South America and the song is regularly performed at soundchecks.

Musicians:

Paul McCartney vocals, backing vocals, acoustic guitar, bass, percussion (?), chimes (?), guiro (?), triangle (?), maracas (?), piano (?) • **Linda McCartney** backing vocals, chimes (?) • **Denny Laine** backing vocals, acoustic guitar • **Howie Casey** sax • **Remi Kabaka** percussion, drums

70 Mrs. Vandebilt (Paul and Linda McCartney)

Recording: September 1st-23rd and October (overdubs), 1973 **Location:** EMI Studios, Lagos and AIR Studios (overdubs), London **Release:** November 1973, *Band on the Run*

When *Band on the Run* was released, many music critics noted that freedom was one of the most explored themes. Almost with anguish, McCartney was shouting his solution to the problems of everyday life: escape. And in "Mrs. Vandebilt" Paul paints his utopian society, and suggests a return to nature, where man could find his authenticity.

From the conceptual point of view, "Mrs. Vandebilt" is therefore one of the key tracks of *Band on the Run*. McCartney's lyrics draw an idyllic place, unbound from social ties and where people feel free: concerns are swept away, in a dimension which belittles everyday things, as in the jungle neither money nor time have any particular meaning to people. A metaphor to express in which way man can really be free.

The opening lines were another Paul's tribute to music-hall, as they were adapted from a catchphrase used by English comedian Charlie Chester ("Down in the jungle, livin' in a tent, better than a bungalow, no rent").[240]

Interestingly, the verse "What's the use of worrying" could be a derivation from "Pack Up Your Troubles in Your Old Kit-Bag and Smile, Smile, Smile" an old World War I marching song, written by George Henry Powell and published in 1915: the song became very popular between British troops and it contains the same words mentioned above. McCartney could have been familiar with the song through the 1932 Laurel and Hardy film *Pack Up Your Troubles*.

The name of the character was a misspelling of the Vanderbilt family, and specifically of Gloria Vanderbilt. McCartney admitted: "I didn't know anything about her but I just knew she was like... a rich person."[241]

---

[240] http://www.openwriting.com/archives/2004/06/i_pinched_charl.php
[241] Mark Lewisohn, *Wingspan*, 2001, p.70.

When recording the track, Paul chose a particular and simple arrangement. During the overdub sessions in London some external effects – the laughter at the end, partly recorded in Africa – were added. McCartney: "The laughing? It started off in Africa. We were doing sort of daft laughs at the end. When we got back we eventually overdubbed this crowd of people who were laughing. It was great listening to the tapes, trying to select the little bit of laughter that we would use. Most of it was us, but we need a little bit to cushion it up. It was great listening to a roomful of people laughing in stereo. They were getting into all these laughing bits, and we were on the floor."[242]

The arrangement captures the spirit of the song: Paul's incredible bass swings along strong and agile like a gorilla on a creeper through the tangled jungle of wooden acoustic guitars. But everything didn't go smoothly during the recording: there was a black-out and they had to rely on the studio's power generator![243]

The dramatic ascending refrain, reinforced by Howie Casey's sax solo – this melody was repeated exactly in "Mine for Me", the song that Paul would give to Rod Stewart in May 1974 – makes this song particularly catchy.

It was issued as a single in some countries: in Italy and New Zealand the song charted respectively at #15 and #10.

At the October 2008 concert in Kiev, to celebrate Ukraine's independence, McCartney first performed "Mrs. Vandebilt". Three hundred thousand people wildly cheered the performance. The song had been requested by the Beatles.ru fan club through a petition: "Strange as it may seem" – the letter reads – "It happened historically that 'Mrs. Vandebilt' was one of most famous and favorite songs of yours among the soviet people. The "iron curtain" prevented us from hearing much of the rock'n'roll music. But 'Mrs Vandebilt' was the song that everybody knew and loved. The lyrics in the refrain "Ho Hey Ho" could be heard at parties as well as at communist demonstrations, and they were repeated by people of all ages (…) Another reason why we are so particular about this song is that the words in the refrain sound very much like the Ukrainian interjection «Гоп» [hop], so the song has a kind of national coloring!"

The song was performed between 2008 and 2013. A live version is on *Good Evening New York City*.

Musicians:

Paul McCartney vocals, backing vocals, bass, drums, acoustic and electric guitar, electric piano, percussion (?) • **Linda McCartney** backing vocals, keyboards • **Denny Laine** backing vocals, acoustic guitar, electric guitar (?), percussion (?) • **Howie Casey** sax

---

[242] P. Gambaccini, cit., p.80.
[243] B. Spitzer-A. Steckler *cit.*, p.174.

71 Let Me Roll It (Paul and Linda McCartney)

Recording: September 1st-23rd and October (overdubs), 1973 **Location:** EMI Studios, Lagos and AIR Studios (overdubs), London **Release:** November 1973, *Band on the Run*

As soon as *Band on the Run* was released, "Let Me Roll It" was unanimously hailed by music critics as one of the most representative tracks of the album.

It's as if in "Let Me Roll It" McCartney poured out his whole self, trying to launch an indirect and conciliatory message to Lennon, entrusting to the music – more than to the words – the task of building a bridge for communication.

Consciously or not, McCartney addressed a sort of stylistic homage to his friend: several elements of the recording resemble Lennon's productions with Spector, such as the use of the tape echo on vocals (Lennon's trademark, found in songs like "Instant Karma!" or "Mind Games") or the Oriental style guitar riff, so clearly a parody that even Lennon was amused, borrowing it in his "Beef Jerky" on *Walls and Bridges*.

McCartney: "I wrote that up in Scotland one day... I was just sitting outside, plunking my guitar and I got this idea. We took it off to Lagos and put down a backing track with Linda playing organ, me playing drums and Denny playing guitar. Then we overdubbed the big guitars you can hear right the way through it, going through a PA amp, not a guitar amp, but a vocal amp, which was a big powerful one."[244]

But McCartney played the guitar riff entirely by himself, as Geoff Emerick recalls: "The lead guitar part is phenomenal, and it's even more amazing considering that it was double tracked. Paul played that and he did an excellent job of doubling the part with exactly the same phrasing and attitude. The guitar sound is a little reminiscent of John's ultra-distorted guitar in 'Revolution'. More eerily, there's a bad edit after the last chorus that adds an extra beat, just has happened on 'Revolution'..."[245]

The result was surprising. Thanks to a sensational vocal performance, with which Paul was able to recreate Lennon's vocal style (in particular, the screaming vocal modulation towards the end of the song reproduces John's nasal timbre and his Primal Scream), "Let Me Roll It" seems to come directly from *John Lennon/Plastic Ono Band*.

A blues/rock track with a basic arrangement and a bare instrumental simplicity which make McCartney's vocals almost entirely support the song.

McCartney – reluctant to look backward or maybe a skilful dissembler – didn't agree with the interpretation of the song: "It was not really a Lennon pastiche, although my use of tape echo did sound more like John than me. But tape echo was not John's exclusive territory!"[246] In fact, Paul wrote the song thinking of the rite of rolling a reefer with friends – a daily habit at that

[244] K. Badman, *cit.*, p.114.
[245] Geoff Emerick, *Here, There and Everywhere. My Life Recording the Music of The Beatles*, 2006, p.352.
[246] *Club Sandwich*, n.72, Winter 1994, p.11.

time – but he could reveal it only much later. In 2010, during a promotional interview to *Clash* magazine for the new edition of *Band on the Run*, Paul explained: "To tell you the truth, that was more [about] rolling a joint. That was the double meaning there: 'Let me roll it to you.' That was more at the back of mind than anything else." [247]

The song would become a stage-favorite: "Let Me Roll It" was, in fact, one of the most cheered songs during the 1975/76 *Wings Over The World Tour* and the live version is on *Wings Over America*.

Paul included the track in the 1993 *New World Tour* (this live version is on *Paul Is Live!*), in the 2002-03 *Drivin' Tour* (the live version is on *Back in the US / Back in the World*), in the 2005 *US Tour*, on the 2009 Tour (version issued in *Good Evening New York City*), in the 2010 *Up &Coming Tour*, in the 2011-12 *On the Run Tour* and in the 2013/14 *Out There! Tour*. A version recorded during pre-tour rehearsals in Cardington (February 5th, 1993) has been included in *Band on the Run – 25th Anniversary Edition* while the original version is featured on *Wingspan*. The *Band on the Run* 2010 edition contains a version of "Let Me Roll It" taken from *One Hand Clapping*. Elvis Costello played the track during some dates of his *Revolver Tour* in 2011.

Musicians:

Paul McCartney vocals, backing vocals, bass, drums, electric guitar • **Linda McCartney** backing vocals, organ • **Denny Laine** backing vocals, electric guitar

72 Picasso's Last Words (Drink to Me) (Paul and Linda McCartney)

Recording: September 1st-23rd and October (overdubs), 1973 **Location:** ARC Studios, Lagos and AIR Studios (overdubs), London **Release:** November 1973, *Band on the Run*

"Picasso's Last Words" is one of the most popular examples of Paul's songwriting method, often based on the transformation of cues taken from the surrounding world. The birth of "Picasso's Last Words" had an exceptional witness, actor Dustin Hoffman.

In the spring 1973 Paul was at Hoffmann's house in Jamaica, where the actor was shooting *Papillon* with Steve McQueen, when suddenly Dustin asked: "Can you just write (songs) about anything?" Paul answered that he could and Hoffmann handed him a copy of *Time* with an article titled *Pablo Picasso's Last Days and Final Journey*, which was about Picasso's death, that happened on April 8th.

McCartney: "I strummed a couple of chords I knew I couldn't go wrong and started singing, 'Drink to me, drink to my health/You know I can't drink anymore…' They were Picasso's last words." [248] Hoffmann leaped out of his chair, shouting at his wife unbelieving: "Annie! Annie! He's doing it! He's writing it! It's coming out!", saying later that it had been one of the greatest

---

[247] Simon Harper, *The Making of Paul McCartney. The Story of Band on the Run*, in *Clash*, 12/10/2010. http://www.clashmusic.com/feature/the-making-of-paul-mccartney
[248] P. Gambaccini, *cit.*, p.79.

events of his life, "right under childbirth". A tape apparently recorded that very night has surfaced in late 2013 on Youtube, with Paul playing also "Hands of Love" and "Getting Closer" (see sheet **132**). The song was written in the days immediately following April 23rd, the date of the *Time* article about Picasso. Paul got a chance to talk about the song on May 12th, when he sang an extract of the tune during an interview for the *David Symonds Show*.

Interestingly, it was not McCartney's first song inspired by the great Spanish painter: a few years earlier, in the hospital after Linda had given birth to Mary, McCartney noticed a Picasso painting of a old man playing a guitar – actually called *The Old Guitarist* and painted by Picasso in 1903 during his Blue Period – on a wall.

McCartney told Michael Parkinson in 1999, introducing the unreleased song "When the Wind Is Blowing" (see **1969**, **1970** and **1978**): "I looked at it all week and thought, 'What chord's he playing?' I noticed it had just two fingers and I tried to see what chord it (wa)s and if it sound(ed) any good! I tried it as an inspiration and tried to write a song that only had used two fingers." McCartney came back to "Picasso's Last Words" in Lagos and brought it to Ginger Baker's studios when Wings went there to record for one day as a peace gesture: it was the only *Band on the Run* track taped at ARC. The song became one of McCartney's most extravagant and eccentric productions.

During the session, the former Cream drummer also took part in the recording, shaking cans full of gravel, as if they were maracas. McCartney: "Then we got Ginger and a couple of people from around the studio and we got little tin cans and filled them with gravel from outside the studio, and used them as shakers, so at the end you hear this [makes shaking gravel noise], and that's Ginger and a big mob of us."[249]

Thanks to its catchy refrain, McCartney decided to embellish "Picasso's Last Words" with some massive production work, under Tony Visconti's supervision at AIR Studios in London.

He asked the arranger to do something special. Visconti: "For this song, he said, 'Just do your thing, but in the style of Motown strings.'"[250] Visconti added his score, saying that he had been inspired by the style of the famous composer Jack Nietzsche.

Visconti: "Paul came up with this wacky little pastiche of French music that might have been played on the radio around Picasso's time. But he was obsessed with getting the bassoon part right and he kept asking the bassoonist to play more *plummy*!"[251]

So "Picasso's…" became a kind of collage which included orchestral passages, a bass solo and references to some tracks of *Band on the Run*.

McCartney: "(I) thought, Picasso was kind of far out in his pictures, he'd done all these different kinds of things, fragmented, cubism (…) I thought it would be nice to get a track a bit

[249] P. Gambaccini, *cit.*, p.79.
[250] Tony Visconti, *Bowie, Bolan and the Brooklyn Boy*, 2007, p.204.
[251] Tony Visconti, *Band on the Run Deluxe Edition*, in *The Paul McCartney Archive Collection*, 2010, p.41.

like that, put it through different moods, cut it up, edit it, mess around with it – like he used to do with his pictures."[252] This collection of fragments – which included "Jet" and "Mrs. Vandebilt" – was punctuated by external effects: during the instrumental interlude some French words taken from the BBC programme "Le Flash Touristique" were added.[253]

They were spoken by Pierre Denis Le Séve, who died in 2009: apparently he had trouble getting paid for his contribution and finally got a check for around £5!

Unfortunately, the results of this sound collage – totally unrelated to McCartney's music style – were boring to many people and music writer Bob Woffinden called the song "as flatulent an exercise as McCartney had ever concocted."[254] The track was played during the 1975-76 *Wings Over The World Tour* and this live version is on *Wings Over America*.

Musicians:

Paul McCartney vocals, backing vocals, acoustic and electric guitar, bass, electric piano, shaker • **Linda McCartney** backing vocals, shaker • **Denny Laine** vocals, backing vocals, acoustic and electric guitar, shaker • **Ginger Baker** shaker • **Beaux Arts Orchestra** strings, horns • **Unknown musicians** shaker

Back in London (not before having experienced a difficult flight back from Africa), McCartney went to AIR Studios to record new songs and add instrumental overdubs, backing vocals and orchestra, that was arranged and conducted by Tony Visconti.

Visconti: "I was thrilled to be doing this for one of my idols, but not so thrilled when he told me he needed all arrangements by (three days)."[255]

For Visconti the best was yet to come: when *Band on the Run* came out, he did not get any credit, except for a generic 'thanks'. In 1999, when the 25th anniversary edition of *Band on the Run* was issued, Paul acknowledged him and sent him a letter: "You got your credit."[256]

73 Jet (Paul and Linda McCartney)

Recording: October, 1973 **Location:** AIR Studios, London **Release:** November 1973, *Band on the Run*

Just as years earlier, Paul had been inspired by the name of his dog, Martha, for one of his most appreciated Beatles' tunes ("Martha My Dear"), the same happened with "Jet", a song whose title came from the name of his new Labrador puppy.

McCartney: "We've got a Labrador puppy who is a runt, the runt of a litter (...) She was a bit of a wild dog, a wild girl who wouldn't stay in (...) She came back one day pregnant. She

---

252 P. Gambaccini, *cit.*, p.79.
253 1:34 to 1:54: "Ce que je souhaite, c'est que grâce à la campagne publicitaire de nombreux français en decouvre les charmes. Je vous rappelle, notre service d'aide touristique est à votre entière disposition, vous savez nous envoyons gratuitement toute une série de guide, de listes d'adresses très utiles."
254 Bob Woffinden, *cit.*, p.63.
255 Tony Visconti, *Bowie, Bolan and the Brooklyn Boy*, 2007, p.204.
256 *Ibid.* p.206.

proceeded to walk into the garage and have this litter. Seven little black puppies. So *Jet* is one of the puppies."[257]

"Jet" wasn't definitely a song about a dog. As always, Paul filled the lyrics with images containing the most different and elusive links and the track, written by McCartney in a summer day in Scotland, was full of imaginative references: a "sergeant Major", a ride in the sky and a suffragette.

As reported by *Melody Maker* in 1973, Paul had composed a track called "Suffragette", very likely an early title of "Jet". McCartney said: "'Suffragette' was crazy enough to work. It sounded silly, so I liked it."[258] It could be a citation of "Suffragette City", Bowie's track included in his 1972 album *The Rise and the Fall of Ziggy Stardust*. By a strange coincidence, some year later Bowie himself put some vocals, echoing "Jet", on his song "Sons of the Silent Age".

The song was fast and galloping. Paul filled it with some clever tricks, combining bass – which during the verses simply holds a single root note – with a buzzing Moog: it almost sounds like a real hard-rock performance. Tony Visconti added the last touch, reinforcing the main riff with a powerful horn section which also included Howie Casey.

Visconti: "At the end of 'Jet', there's a saxophone phrase that because of the awkward key, the key of A, couldn't be played on the tenor sax. Luckily, the baritone player brought his alto sax and he could play those top notes but he couldn't play the bottom ones. So at the end you hear a great deception. You actually hear two sax player, I don't know at which point the alto saxophonist stopped playing and Howie Casey began, but that's how it happened."[259] The result was this remarkably commercial pop song, which changed the fate of *Band on the Run*.

Capitol's plugger, Al Coury, was the first to realize that "Jet" would work well as a single. Coury: "Shortly after we released the album, we started to get some heavy response from pop radio on the track 'Jet' (…) and they started to edit the song."[260]

Coury also insisted on getting a three minute edit of the song: "I realized that we had to do our own edit! But I had to commit to him that I would put out the edited track backed with the full-length version." McCartney himself later admitted that Coury played a key role in making *Band on the Run* such a success.

In America, the single was released in February 1974, it climbed to #7 in the charts (reaching the same position in the UK), exceeding one million copies sold. It pushed *Band on the Run* to #1 in the charts, for the first of three occasions, a record that is still unequalled today. "Jet" was included in all of McCartney's tours, except for the 1979 *Wings' British Tour*. Four different

---

[257] P. Gambaccini, *cit.*, p.80. During the promotional interviews for the release of the *Band On The Run Deluxe Edition* (2010) Paul said "Jet" was the name of a pony. He may have got mixed up.
[258] *Ibid.* Suffragettes were members of women's organization for right to vote in late 19th and early 20th century. On June 4th, 1913 the activist Emily Davison stepped in front of King George V's horse at the Epsom Derby: she was hit and died four days later.
[259] T. Visconti, *Band on the Run Deluxe Edition*, in *The Paul McCartney Archive collection*, 2010, p.41.
[260] *Band on the Run-25th Anniversary Edition*, 1999.

live versions were released: on *Wings Over America*, *Tripping The Live Fantastic!*, *Back In The US/Back In The World* and *Good Evening New York City*.

A version from the Berlin soundcheck (September 3rd, 1993) is on the *Band on the Run-25th Anniversary Edition*, whereas the one from *One Hand Clapping* is included in the *Band on the Run* 2010 edition. In its original version, "Jet" is included in *Wings Greatest*, *All the Best!* and *Wingspan*.

Musicians:

Paul McCartney vocals, backing vocals, bass, drums, electric guitar, Moog (?), piano (?) • **Linda McCartney** backing vocals, keyboards, Moog (?) • **Denny Laine** backing vocals, electric guitar, piano (?) • **Howie Casey** sax • **Unknown musicians** horns • **Beaux Arts Orchestra** strings

74 No Words (Paul McCartney-Denny Laine)

Recording: October, 1973 **Location:** AIR Studios, London **Release:** November 1973, *Band on the Run*

Since Denny Laine wasn't so prolific a songwriter, Paul encouraged him to compose more and more during the Wings' years, so "to take some of the focus off of him" as Laine said.

"No Words" – Laine's first issued composition with Wings and his first collaboration with Paul – was a song Denny had written earlier in the year. In Lagos, McCartney had helped him finish the track, adding a melodic middle eight and some verses.

McCartney's contribution to the lyrics is obscure, but significantly autobiographical. The lines "It's only me/I love you" refer to some episodes that really happened between him and John Lennon. McCartney: "We were once having a right slagging session and I remember how he took off his granny glasses. I can still see him. He put them down and said, 'It's only me, Paul.' Then he put them back on again, and we continued slagging... That phrase keeps coming back to me all the time. 'It's only me.' It's became a mantra in my mind."[261]

Paul added: "Whatever bad things John said about me, he would also slip his glasses down to the end of his nose and tell me 'I love you'. That's really what I hold on to."[262]

An interesting song, even if perhaps one of the most underrated of *Band on the Run*: a melodic track, with Denny and Paul tightly harmonizing. Paul's solo vocal contribution in the middle section is remarkable for its falsetto. "No Words" is marked by an electric guitar crescendo and a nice closing section featuring some guitar solos by Paul and Denny. Two Wings roadies, Trevor Jones and Ian Horne also added backing vocals, although barely audible.

To help Paul and Denny keeping the time, a rhythm-box is featured on the track, very likely the same one that can be heard in other *Band on the Run* tracks like "Bluebird" and "Picasso's Last Words". Nevertheless, Paul missed the beat: the drum part is totally absent between 1:00

---

[261] McCartney and Hunter Davis phone conversation, happened on May 3rd, 1981. http://www.lastfm.it/group/Sir+James+Paul+McCartney/forum/217824/ /667947
[262] http://www.3news.co.nz/McCartney-bla...8/Default.aspx

and 1:04! In London, Visconti worked on this track too, overdubbing a string quartet to emphasize the main riff. The track wasn't played during the 1975/76 *Wings Over the World Tour* but "No Words" was performed in the 1979 *Wings' British Tour*.

This live version has been officially released as a digital download to the fans that bought *Band on the Run* 2010 through Paul McCartney's website.

Musicians:

Paul McCartney vocals, backing vocals, bass, drums, electric guitar, synthesizer (?), shaker (?) • **Linda McCartney** backing vocals, keyboards, shaker (?) • **Denny Laine** vocals, backing vocals, electric guitar • **Trevor Jones, Ian Horne** backing vocals • **Beaux Arts Orchestra** strings

75 1985 (Paul and Linda McCartney)

Recording: October, 1973 **Location:** AIR Studios, London **Release:** November 1973, *Band on the Run*

The epic majesty of "1985" must be credited simply to Paul's endless lexical imagination. When the song was released on *Band on the Run* many reviewers, attracted by the verse "No one ever left alive/In Nineteen Hundred and Eighty-Five", were tempted to read literary references (the novel *1984* by Orwell) or apocalyptic settings.

Actually, McCartney admitted that the main inspiration was related to a simple rhyme: "All I had of that song for months was the first verse, 'No one ever left alive/In Nineteen Hundred and Eighty-Five'. 'Nineteen Hundred and Eighty-Six' it wouldn't have worked."[263]

McCartney wrote this song starting from the dramatic piano intro. The track was recorded at AIR Studios (the presence of the piano, absent in all the recordings he had done in Africa, proves it), where also Tony Visconti's magnificent orchestral score was overdubbed.

In the studio, McCartney even completed the lyrics the same day of the recording, and then came up with a very strong vocal performance. Following McCartney's statement in an interview to *Melody Maker* ("Denny sometimes doubles on bass"[264]), Laine could have handled bass on the track.

The "1985" ending climax is one of the highlights of the album: a long guitar solo, supported by some inflamed drumming and by a powerful orchestral arrangement, closes the song overwhelmingly. A brief reprise of "Band on the Run" ends the song. Thus, the album comes full circle, reinforcing the idea of a concept album like *Sgt. Pepper's*... although McCartney denied any idea behind it, saying: "It's a collection of songs... There is a thread, but it's not a concept album."[265] The song was performed live for the first time in 2010 *Up & Coming Tour* and it was also included in the 2011-12 *On the Run Tour* and in the 2013/14 *Out There! Tour*.

Musicians:

---

263 P. Gambaccini, *cit.*, p.83.
264 *Melody Maker*, 01/12/1973, p.48.
265 *Ibid.*

Paul McCartney vocals, backing vocals, piano, bass (?), drums, electric guitar, keyboards, synthesizer, shaker (?) • **Linda McCartney** backing vocals, organ, shaker (?) • **Denny Laine** backing vocals, electric guitar, bass (?) • **Beaux Arts Orchestra** strings, horns

Shortly after completing *Band on the Run*, Paul, Linda and Denny went to Paris. At the EMI Studios they taped some quirky tracks with Jimmy McCulloch on electric guitar (he would officially join Wings in 1974) and Davey Lutton on drums.

The group recorded "Luxi" and two tracks intended for a Linda's solo project, "I Got Up" and "Wide Prairie" (the latter will be worked on again during the 1974 Nashville sessions).

Band on the Run was issued in November 30th. After a slow start, in 1974 the record reached #1 in the charts in the USA and the UK, becoming the most popular album in McCartney's career. *Band on the Run* stayed on the Billboard charts for one-hundred and sixteen weeks, selling over six million copies in the United States. The album also won a Grammy Award for Best Pop Vocal Performance by a Duo, Group or Chorus.

Rolling Stone's Jon Landau wrote: "Up until now, the critical assumption has been that McCartney's lyrics mean little if anything, that he is a mere stylist, playing games with words and sounds. And it is of course possible that the words on *Band on the Run* don't mean (or weren't intended to mean) as much as I think they do. But I'll take a chance, and say that *Band on the Run* is an album about the search for freedom and the flight from restrictions on his and Linda's personal happiness. It is about the pursuit of freedom from his past as a Beatle, freedom from the consequences of the drug busts that have kept him from the United States and forced him into thinking of himself as an outlaw (witness the album cover, as well as the title). It is also about two people becoming what they want to be, trying to decide what they want to do, and asking to be accepted for what they are now rather than what they were then. *Band on the Run* is a carefully composed, intricately designed personal statement that will make it impossible for anyone to classify Paul McCartney as a mere stylist again. With the possible exception of *John Lennon/Plastic Ono Band*, (this is) the finest record yet released by any of the four musicians who were once called the Beatles."

The iconic cover of the album – which depicts Wings and six celebrities (John Conteh, Michael Parkinson, Kenny Lynch, James Coburn, Clement Freud, Christopher Lee) as escaping prisoners – has been referenced in the poster of the animated film *Madagascar* (2005).

1974

Between January and February, McCartney reunited his band at Strawberry Studios in Stockport to help his brother Michael record *McGear, pretty much a Wings record in disguise. Paul left the lead vocals to Michael but he co-wrote – or even wrote – almost all the tracks, playing several instruments and singing backing vocals. It seems that the studio unfortunately lost the original tracks with Paul's guide vocals. Three tracks, "Leave It", "Rainbow Lady" and the evocative "The Man Who Found God on the Moon" make the album priceless.

Jimmy McCulloch played guitar, while Gerry Conway played drums. He recalls: "There were no demos beforehand and Paul continually worked on Mike's songs in the studio. He could hear the finished track in his head so he would direct us all towards that goal. Generally all the tracks were recorded quickly with a very positive vibe. On the first take I was feeling very nervous, hoping that he would like what I was doing. We were getting to the outro and I thought it was going OK. I was amazed when he suddenly stood up and started to rock out. From that moment on it was all smiles! It took me a little while to get a relaxed feel on 'The Man Who Found God on the Moon' but Paul was always patient. Nobody used clicks in those days!"[266]

Conway had to turn down Paul's offer to join Wings as an official member: "Paul gave me a copy of *Band on the Run* during the sessions and asked me afterwards if I would like to join but I was committed to a Cat Stevens world tour that I couldn't reasonably turn down at short notice."[267] During the sessions, Paul probably also recorded "I'll Give You a Ring".

76 I'll Give You a Ring (Paul McCartney)

Recording: January-February, 1974 (?) and May-December, 1981 (overdubs) **Location:** Strawberry Studios (?), Stockport and AIR Studios (overdubs), London **Release:** June 1982, "Take It Away" single B-side

McCartney always enjoyed writing songs in vaudeville style. Earlier, with the Beatles, he had already shown his passion for the music-hall style ("When I'm Sixty-Four", "Honey Pie").

In these cases, his composing style is based on a very simple pattern, fingering the root chords with bass playing octaves or alternating fifths. "I'll Give You a Ring" is a typical example of this technique.

McCartney had recorded the song a few years earlier in a demo, and it was actually quite similar to the final version. Paul probably recorded a complete version of "I'll Give You a Ring" on his own, during a break in the *McGear sessions. His performance captures the simplicity of the

---

[266] Interview courtesy of Gerry Conway, 05/02/2013.
[267] *Ibid.*

song marked by the deep bass, the fluttering clarinet and a brilliant, powerful and amused vocal performance.

Actually not even Tony Coe's clarinet performance can help date the recording of the basic track undoubtedly back to January-February 1974, when the musician had added a clarinet part in "Leave It". Coe: "I remember I played in two sessions, one with Wings and another with Paul solo (...) but I cannot remember in which dates! Usually you come into the studio, do your solo, they pay and you go out (...) On 'I'll Give You a Ring' I recorded my clarinet part, that was improvised by me directly in studio."[268]

Obviously fresh in Paul's mind, "I'll Give You a Ring" was included in *One Hand Clapping*, in which McCartney played a piano-only version. Paul shelved the song and only got back to it seven years later adding on some overdubs – the three-part harmonies and maybe some guitar, too – at AIR Studios during the *Tug of War* sessions in 1981. The song was released in 1982 as the B-side to the "Take It Away" single.

Musicians:

Paul McCartney vocals, backing vocals, piano, bass, electric guitar, drums • **Tony Coe** clarinet • **Linda McCartney, Eric Stewart** backing vocals

McCartney spent March and April in America. He met Lennon in Los Angeles and on March 28th, they had their only musical session together during their post-Beatles careers. Lennon (piano) and McCartney (drums) delved into jams and covers of old classics, featuring Stevie Wonder (keyboards), Harry Nilsson (vocals), Bobby Keys (sax), Jesse Ed Davis (electric guitar). Back in London, starting on April 26th Paul held a series of auditions to recruit a new drummer for Wings: Geoff Britton, a karate teacher, beat the competition which included Mitch Mitchell (formerly with Jimi Hendrix Experience) and Roger Pope.

Having formed the new line-up, Paul and Wings arrived in Nashville on June 6th for a six week holiday, that lasted until July 18th. Even there, McCartney couldn't stay away from studios, producing a series of useful sessions, that included the recording of several tracks ("Sally G", "Junior's Farm", "Bridge Over The River Suite", "Walking In the Park With Eloise" – a tune by Jim McCartney – "Send Me the Heart" – written by Paul with Denny Laine – and "Wide Prairie", a track written by Linda), as well as some overdubbing work (the band completed "Hey Diddle" with the addition of Cates Sisters' fiddles).

Ernie Winfrey, who engineered the sessions at Sound Shop Studio in Nashville, recalls: "We were in the studio for about two weeks in July (...) Eveybody was in awe of him... Johnny Gimble asked him an autograph for his grand-daughter!"[269]

---

[268] Interview courtesy of Tony Coe, 27/08/2011.
[269] Interview courtesy of Ernie Winfrey, 11/02/2013.

McCartney met some of the most famous country players in Nashville, like Chet Atkins, Floyd Cramer (both played on the "Walking In The Park With Eloise", later issued as a single and credited to The Country Hams) and Lloyd Green, who joined in on "Sally G" (see sheet **77**).

Later, McCartney invited Green to join him on his upcoming World Tour. He recalls: "Paul told me he wanted to do a 15-minute part of each show with a four-piece band featuring me and him playing country music."[270] Green declined the offer: "It's the most regrettable decision of my professional life."[271]

77 Sally G (Paul and Linda McCartney)

Recording: July 9th, 1974 **Location:** Soundshop Recording Studios, Nashville **Release:** October 1974, "Junior's Farm" single B-side

As soon as he set up in Nashville, McCartney got to know the typical hangouts where country music was born. One night Paul went down town get a few drinks and listen to music in some Nashville joints: McCartney ended up at *Skull's Rainbow Room*, the most famous club of the Printer's Alley district, where singer Diane Gaffney used to perform.

According to Skull Schullman, the owner of the club, Paul had had a few too many that night. Nevertheless, McCartney didn't lose his inspiration even that night.

In fact, McCartney slipped into the back of the club, found a piano and wrote "Sally G" in one go, initially calling it "Diane", from the name of the country singer Paul had just listened to. Later, fearing a law suit, he decided not to use that name.[272] Most likely, McCartney thought of the famous song "Sally", taken from the movie *Sally In Our Alley* (1931): he would include a snippet of this track, from a soundcheck performance, in his live album *Tripping the Live Fantastic!* (1990)

While recording "Sally G", McCartney wanted to keep the atmosphere that had inspired him and he arranged the song in a clever way: adding a country music flavour to his gift for catchy pop, he produced one of the smartest songs of his career.

In the studio, Paul completely transformed the song: first of all, he chose acoustic instruments and a guitar became McCartney's main instrument (Paul had used the piano so not to forget the song[273]). Later, he decided to recruit some local violinists and Lloyd Green, one of Nashville's country guitar pros, whose distinctive touch added vividness to the song, with his never affected licks.

Studio sheets provided by engineer Ernie Winfrey help to reconstruct the musicians' line-up and their instruments. The track was recorded on July 9th in a 6pm-midnight session, with

---

[270] Rick Kienzle, *Lloyd Green. From the A Team to Americana*, 03/05/2010. http://www.vintageguitar.com/3683/lloyd-green
[271] *Ibid.*
[272] The singer had sued a magazine for having written her name in an article.
[273] A recently found clip shows Paul in Nashville rehearsing this track on the piano with Linda.

McCartney on acoustic guitar (and overdubbed bass), Britton on drums, McCulloch on acoustic guitar, Green on pedal steel guitar and overdubbed dobro. There's also a Melodium, a sort of American harmonium. Vocal parts were added by Paul, Linda and Denny Laine.

Winfrey: "Buddy Killen, president of Tree Publishing, acted like host and guide for Paul and Linda. He did get fiddler Johnny Gimble and steel player Lloyd Green for this song and they were both thrilled, needless to say. McCartney was very open for suggestions. Lloyd came up with this idea of using the dobro and he played it on the bridge section of the song."[274]

McCartney masterfully sings the catchy melody: the narrative score is built around the idea of a love affair and musical story between the narrator (Paul himself) and the singer (Sally G). It's made even more enjoyable by its semi-autobiographical inspiration, puns and typical McCartney's nonsense lyrics.

When "Sally G" was released in October 1974 as the B-side to the "Junior's Farm" single, the track seemed wasted, but American radio stations immediately started playing it and it became a great success on the country music charts.

This drove McCartney to release "Sally G" as the A-side in February 1975: but it was too late and the song only reached #17 on the *Billboard* charts.

Musicians:

Paul McCartney vocals, backing vocals, acoustic guitar, bass • **Linda McCartney** backing vocals, melodium (?) • **Denny Laine** backing vocals • **Geoff Britton** drums • **Lloyd Green** pedal steel guitar, dobro • **Bob Wills, Johnny Gimble** violin • **Jimmy McCulloch** acoustic guitar

78 Junior's Farm (Paul and Linda McCartney)

Recording: July 16th-18th, 1974 **Location:** Soundshop Recording Studios, Nashville **Release:** October 1974, single

In Nashville McCartney stayed at the farm of Norbert "Curly" Putman Jr. (a local session-man). It was a quiet place in the countryside in Tennessee: Paul rented it for the whole holiday, thinking he would enjoy a few moments of freedom with his family in its vast garden.

Paul, Linda and the band arrived after a long day of travelling, as Putman recalls: "They were pretty wore out. But they came and we had a little cocktail party to welcome them (...) They just seemed to enjoy being out in the country. They rode horses. Paul was very likable, personable. He just seemed like one of us."[275]

Even that peaceful oasis couldn't stop McCartney's imagination and inspiration; he used the farm as a starting point for a new song.

Apparently, Paul had written the song before his stay: the previous spring, he taped a couple of demos, "Arab Nights" and "Little Bass Man", which contained some good ideas for the track,

274 Interview courtesy of Ernie Winfrey, 11/02/2013.
275 http://www.americansongwriter.com/2011/02/behind-the-lyric-juniors-farm-paul-mccartney/

and developed them. While in Nashville, he was inspired by Bob Dylan's famous "Maggie's Farm" from 1965[276] and called the track "Junior's Farm". It was a tribute to McCartney's temporary home, albeit only in the title. As usual, Paul thought the lyrics had enough musicality and he simply built the song around them.

McCartney: "I wasn't trying to say anything... It has silly words and basically all it means is, 'Let's get out of the city. Let's go out to 'Junior's Farm' or 'Strawberry Fields' or whatever."[277]

Wings quickly rehearsed and recorded the track in the studio. Some outtakes show "Junior's Farm" already well-structured, with just minor flaws. Winfrey: "They rehearsed it at the farm before they came in. Once they got into the studio, they worked on hard again."[278]

"Everything was very calm, laid back" – Ernie Winfrey recalls – "Nobody was in a hurry to do much, because Paul wanted to take his time and do it right."[279]

The band resolutely got into the beat of this intense rocking track in which the contrast of its dramatic E minor ending particularly stands out. For the coda, Paul recorded his bass with the tape at double speed, so that the instrument would sound an octave lower.[280]

Winfrey again: "We ran his bass directly to the console... He used his Rickenbacker, one of the cleanest basses I've ever recorded, from top to bottom and dynamically."[281]

Described by some critics "Wings' 'Get Back!'", the song is a typical McCartney's rocker: sustained by a powerful bass line, "Junior's Farm" runs quickly, punctuated by McCulloch's stinging solos.

Later, McCartney praised Britton's performance, at the same time explaining why – from his point of view – he would leave the group in January 1975: "Geoff was great for that... He was just an ace rock'n'roll drummer... Really brilliant for all the rock'n'roll stuff. But we suddenly would have stuff that probably we'll never even play again. Just that year, we had songs with crazy time signatures and tempos... All weird... With 7/8 coming in from nowhere! That's just not easy for rock'n'roll drummers. That was really probably the basic reason why Geoff left."[282] "Junior's Farm" belongs in the category of songs "on a single note", which had always been one of Paul's passions (see "The Word" on *Rubber Soul*); the song uses a very few chords, as it's almost entirely in G Major.

Ernie Winfrey: "This was actually the last track we recorded. Paul essentially showed everyone what he thought they should be playing but everyone seemed to take it a notch higher. Jimmy McCulloch really got to shine on this song. He, Linda and Denny all overdubbed harmony

[276] Madinger, C.–Easter, M. *cit.*, p. 194.
[277] K.Badman, *The Beatles. The Dream Is Over-Off the Record 2*, 2002, p.142.
[278] Interview courtesy of Ernie Winfrey, 11/02/2013.
[279] Mark Bellinger, *McCartney's Nashville Concert: Memories of Junior's Farm*, 28/07/2010, http://www.newschannel5.com/global/story.asp?s=12884240.
[280] Interview courtesy of Ernie Winfrey, 11/02/2013.
[281] *Ibid.*
[282] *Paul McCartney 1984 Interview*, http://www.mygoldmusic.co.uk/article.asp?id=587762

vocals. Denny was also playing some really nice electric rhythm guitar. The breath on the end is Paul's of course."[283]

McCartney's vocals were later given some treatment: "I didn't put any kind of effects on the voices while we're recording" – says Winfrey – "Maybe Geoff Emerick added something. It's either a phaser or possibly he double-tracked the voice."[284]

The whimsical lyrics contain McCartney's surrealistic fascination and combine Oliver Hardy and the British Parliament. Released as a single, "Junior's Farm" was another overnight success in the United States, where it reached #3 on the charts. Despite a good promotion – including Wings' performance in *Top of the Pops* on November 21st, 1974 – it wasn't much of a success in the UK (#16), where perhaps the audience thought it sounded too American.

McCartney rehearsed the song during the following August session (there's an unreleased version on *One Hand Clapping*) and "Junior's Farm" was included in 1975 *Wings' Australian Tour*, only to disappear for no apparent reason soon after. Probably Paul changed his mind due to the group's disappointing performances, as testified by some recordings from the Australian concerts in September 1975: thus, the song was excluded from the setlist and is not present on *Wings Over America*. "Junior's Farm" had been released on the US versions of *Wings Greatest* and *All the Best!* A DJ edit version that clocks 3:02 appears on *Wingspan*.

Between 2011 and 2013, the track was included in Paul's *On The Run* and *Out There! Tour*.

Musicians:

Paul McCartney vocals, backing vocals, bass • **Linda McCartney** backing vocals, keyboards • **Denny Laine** backing vocals, electric guitar • **Jimmy McCulloch** backing vocals, electric guitar • **Geoff Britton** drums

Back in London, McCartney put the new Wings line-up through the mill with some rehearsals to get prepared for the upcoming tour through America. Filmed and recorded in Abbey Road Studio 2 in late August 1974, they were used for the *One Hand Clapping* documentary.

Only recently released with the remastered version of *Band on the Run* (2010), this project had been shelved for decades. For a long time wrongly considered evidence of the Nashville recordings[285], it soon began to circulate among collectors.

This nearly forty minutes long documentary simply shows Wings performing a selection of tracks McCartney would play during the upcoming worldwide tour: "Band on the Run", "Jet", "My Love", "Let Me Roll It", "Bluebird", "Junior's Farm", "Soily", "Little Woman Love/C Moon", "Hi, Hi, Hi", "Maybe I'm Amazed". The recording seems to be slightly sped-up.

[283] Interview courtesy of Ernie Winfrey, 11/02/2013.
[284] *Ibid.*
[285] McCartney himself said that *One Hand Clapping* was filmed in Nashville. See P. Gambaccini, *cit.*, p.83.

The "Live and Let Die" session was recorded with a full orchestra, conducted by Del Newman: "Paul asked me to conduct the orchestra, and I was required to wear an evening dress suit with tails for a photo session after the performance. We used Abbey Road Studio Two, Paul's favorite, and, as the film had already been released and there wasn't a vocalist present, I assumed that the recording was for his own personal library. Paul was always calm when he was working, and I never saw him raise his voice one decibel. He mingled with the orchestral players during the coffee break, bantering as if it were a picnic on the lawn."[286]

One Hand Clapping also features some footage with Paul playing some songs on the piano: this section includes "Suicide", "I'll Give You a Ring", "Baby Face" – featuring the Tuxedo Brass Band (added in New Orleans in 1975) – "Let's Love", a song Paul had given to Peggy Lee, performed in a medley with "Sitting at the Piano" and "All of You".

In the meantime, McCartney thought up a little supplement to this documentary. On August 24th, sitting in the backyard of EMI Studios in London, he improvised on his acoustic guitar some old rock classics and some of his own songs for twenty minutes. Known to fans as *The Backyard*, most of this short footage is still unreleased. It features the following songs: "Blackbird", "Blackpool" (a clip is on the DVD *The McCartney Years*), "Country Dreamer" (audio included in 2010 as a bonus on the *Band on the Run* remastered edition), "Twenty Flight Rock", "Peggy Sue", "I'm Gonna Love You Too" (this clip also is on the DVD *The McCartney Years*), "Sweet Little Sixteen", "Loving You", and "We're Gonna Move".

In November, back in Abbey Road, Wings recorded three songs for their future album *Venus and Mars*. One of them ("Medicine Jar") was written by Jimmy McCulloch and Colin Allen.

79 Love in Song (Paul and Linda McCartney)

Recording: November 1974, January 16th-February 24th (overdubs part 1) and March 10th, 1975 (overdubs part 2) **Location:** Abbey Road Studios, London, Sea Saint Studios (overdubs part 1), New Orleans and Wally Heider Studios (overdubs part 2), Los Angeles **Release:** May 1975, "Listen to What the Man Said" single B-side (from *Venus and Mars*)

McCartney, who had composed "Love in Song" in August, recalled how the song came out: "I had my 12-string guitar and I started to write this thing. I thought, 'That's a nice opening, *My heart cries out for love…* I said to Linda, 'How do you like that?' And that was it…"[287]

When McCartney gathered Wings at Abbey Road for the new recording sessions, he wanted to cut the song immediately. For this ballad Paul chose a simple arrangement, with a slight exotic touch: McCartney's acoustic guitar playing – with half-tone intervals – gives the song its Oriental-style atmosphere. An epic, evocative and melancholic refrain is emphasized by keyboards and strings, the latter overdubbed in Los Angeles the following March. A distinctive

286 Del Newman, *A Touch From God. It's Only Rock&Roll*, 2010, p.37.
287 K. Badman, *The Beatles-The Dream Is Over. Off the Record 2*, 2002, p.165.

harp part is featured in the song, most likely played by Gayle Levant (see "Listen to What the Man Said", sheet **88**).

McCartney's passionate singing is the real highlight. He also played Bill Black's double-bass, used on the Elvis Presley film *Heartbreak Hotel*, a present from Linda for his 32th birthday.

A funny episode happened probably during the recording of "Love in Song", judging by the sounds heard in the song. Geoff Britton: "I was playing the drum part, and afterwards they had kept the tape running, I'd been fooling about on milk bottles. Paul thought it was great!"[288]

Alan O'Duffy, who worked as sound engineer during the January-February 1975 sessions in New Orleans, recalls: "'Love in Song' was recorded in London with Geoff Emerick and its backing track was really basic: acoustic guitar, bass and some percussion, as far as I remember. Paul brought out from England a leather box with some hand-bells in (…) They were like church bells but very small and all with different rings. They had the sort of sound you might have heard in the Fifties in the school... We overdubbed the bells on this track... It was really a lovely idea!"[289] A bell-like sound is featured in the song but it's clearly heard in "Rock Show" (see sheet **83**): maybe the engineer confused the two tracks.

McCartney's lyrics – "Happiness in the homeland" – are so typical of his world view and express one of the main themes of his discography: discovering the world may be a beautiful adventure, but happiness is in your living room. "Love in Song" is on *Venus and Mars* and was used as the B-side to the single "Listen to What the Man Said".

Musicians:

Paul McCartney vocals, piano (?), double-bass, acoustic guitar, dingers (?) • **Linda McCartney** backing vocals, keyboards • **Denny Laine** backing vocals, acoustic guitar (?), piano (?) • **Jimmy McCulloch** acoustic guitar (?), electric guitar • **Geoff Britton** drums, milk bottles • **Gayle Levant** harp • **Unknown musicians** strings

80 Letting Go (Paul and Linda McCartney)

Recording: November 5th, 1974 and January 16th-February 24th (overdubs), 1975 **Location:** Abbey Road Studios, London and Sea Saint Studios (overdubs), New Orleans **Release:** May 1975, *Venus and Mars*

Paul McCartney is a very prolific songwriter and he has written tons of songs; yet, as he said, the way he composes is mainly based on instinct and immediacy rather than on the traditional rules of music writing. Not knowing score notation, McCartney's first necessity is to roughly accompany the melody he has just written with only the root chords, so as to not to forget it.

"Letting Go" gives us the opportunity to closely follow the typical development of most of McCartney's compositions. Paul had written the song during 1972-73. His home-recorded piano demo shows the song in its early stage: Paul is singing a still shaky melody, with a rough

---

[288] Geoff Britton, in *Wings Official Fun Club*, n.3, 1974.
[289] Interview courtesy of Alan O'Duffy, 24/01/2012.

accompaniment simply insisting on root chords. Paul worked on it and the track was taped at Abbey Road. This first attempt was very different from its final recording and is probably one of Wings' most fascinating alternate takes. It lasts 5:50 and has a more relaxed feel, with a bluesy touch not present in its final version – without any effects, except for a slight reverb on Paul's vocals. The basic track consisted of electric piano, organ, bass, drums and electric guitar and sounds unfinished, with keyboards running out of time especially in the coda.

However, Paul had something different in mind and – perhaps thinking of the upcoming tour – he changed "Letting Go" into a heavy number during the New Orleans sessions. The version later issued on *Venus and Mars*, while containing some instrumental parts of the rough-mix, turned into a mighty rock song, full of echo on vocals and instrumentation.

A heavy number, thanks to McCulloch's guitar riffs and solos and to the addition of a strong horn arrangement. McCartney's deep and pulsating Rickenbacker bass is particularly noteworthy. Paul seemed particularly proud of it: "I think it's a nice track. It's a nice tune and kids sing it all the time. It's my favourite track."[290]

Issued in September 1975 as the second single from *Venus and Mars*, the song didn't attract many buyers: the track was so different from McCartney's recent easy-listening productions. "Letting Go" did not perform very well in the charts, reaching only #39 in the US and #41 in the UK, thus interrupting a series of nine singles in the top ten of the American and/or British charts.[291]

The single version (also appearing on the *Venus and Mars* Deluxe Edition in 2014) is different from the one released on *Venus and Mars*. The edit prepared by Alan Parsons has a more prominent organ glissando at the beginning and a different drum part, featuring Joe English, who would replace Geoff Britton in January 1975. During live performances, "Letting Go" was extended with a coda to give free rein to McCartney's vocals: this version is on *Wings Over America*. "Letting Go" was also included in the *Up & Coming Tour* in 2010.

Musicians:

Paul McCartney vocals, bass, electric piano (?), electric guitar (?) • **Linda McCartney** backing vocals, organ • **Denny Laine** backing vocals, electric guitar, electric piano (?) • **Jimmy McCulloch** electric guitar • **Geoff Britton** drums • **Unknown musicians** horns

---

[290] K. Badman, *The Beatles. The Dream Is Over-Off the Record 2*, 2002, p.165.

[291] The series had started with "Mary Had A Little Lamb" and ended with "Listen To What The Man Said". But also "C Moon" could be counted, since it was A-side in the UK.

1975

For the recording of the new album, McCartney sought something musically exotic and chose New Orleans, Louisiana, where he booked Allen Toussaint's Sea Saint Studios.

After just a few days, Geoff Britton quit the group. Paul quickly replaced him with Joe English, recommended to him by trombonist Tony Dorsey and who had been recording with Bonnie Bramlett.

English: "I was right in the middle of rehearsing when I got a phone call from New Orleans asking me if I'd help record the *Venus and Mars* album, so I found a replacement for Bonnie and left. I recorded the album during February."[292]

About working in the studio with McCartney, English recalled: "It was a completely different style what I'd been used to. I'd been used to jazz, soul and progressive stuff and I wasn't accustomed to working within the kind of limits that the Wings material presented. The most difficult thing to accept was the discipline which that kind of music demands."[293]

At Sea Saint Studios, the band recorded a dozen new songs and was augmented in a couple of tracks by a local horn section, possibly including sax player Amadee Castenell. One track from the sessions, "Crawl Of The Wild" – recorded with David Mason on guitar – remains unreleased, while "New Orleans" – featuring Linda on lead vocals – was issued in 1998 on her album *Wide Prairie*. The group also taped the instrumental "Crossroads" (written by Tony Hatch), the theme from a British soap opera. McCartney could again have played his Fender Jazz bass, as it appears from several shots taken during the recordings by Sidney Smith.

After completing the recording of the basic tracks, in March Wings moved to Los Angeles for string overdubs and the album's final mixing.

Paul's statements about the album were enthusiastic: "In New Orleans, I just thought we'd do a new LP. I had these songs on my scroll and I thought it would be better than *Band on the Run* and I think it *is* better."[294]

81 Lunch Box/Odd Sox (Paul and Linda McCartney)

Recording: January 16th-February 24th, 1975 **Location:** Sea Saint Studios, New Orleans **Release:** April 1980, "Coming Up" single B-side

According to Paul, "Lunch Box/Odd Sox" was Wings' first recording in New Orleans. Perhaps McCartney improvised it in the studio sitting at the piano, since the track only has a few chords and a couple of riffs, one of which recalls the "Rock Show" coda, that would be recorded over the following days. At 3:28 Britton's comment ("That was a good one") can be

---

[292] *Listening to What the Man Said*, in *Record Mirror*, 31/5/1975.
[293] *Joe English: The Unknown Quantity*, in *Record Mirror*, 4/10/1975.
[294] K. Badman, *The Beatles. The Dream Is Over-Off the Record 2*, 2002, p.155.

heard. The outcome was a boring two-part instrumental track, probably the result of a warm-up session, featuring trombone-player Tony Dorsey on bass! McCartney put it on the shelves for a long time. The track finally got released in 1980, as the B-side to the single "Coming Up".

Musicians:

Paul McCartney piano • **Linda McCartney** Moog • **Denny Laine** electric guitar • **Tony Dorsey** bass • **Geoff Britton** drums

82 Venus and Mars (Paul and Linda McCartney)

Recording: January 16th-February 24th, 1975 **Location:** Sea Saint Studios, New Orleans **Release:** May 1975, *Venus and Mars*

Following in the footstep of other musicians (David Bowie – "Space Oddity" – Elton John – "Rocket Man" – and Pink Floyd –*The Dark Side of the Moon*), McCartney too wrote a song somewhat inspired by outer space. When *Venus and Mars* was released, some critics speculated that the two planets in the record's name referred to Paul and Linda.

But McCartney denied it, ruling out any hidden meaning or autobiographical reference in the title: "When we had a party in the States to celebrate having finished the album" – McCartney recalled – "Someone came up to us and said, 'Hello Venus, hello Mars'. I thought, 'Oh no!' When I write songs, I'm not necessarily talking about me, although psychoanalysts would say, 'Yes you are, mate.' But as far as I'm concerned, I'm not."[295]

Paul explained how the song came to life: "The song is about an imaginary friend who's got a girlfriend who's into astrology, the kind of person who asks you what your sign is before they say hello. But the first verse, 'A good friend of mine follows the stars' it could be ambiguous, (could be) a groupie or an astrologer."[296]

"I didn't even know that they were neighboring planets" – McCartney confessed – "I just thought of naming any two planets… Venus and Mars… That's great! I didn't know they were the gods of love and war, either, and I wasn't thinking about the Botticelli's picture someone (George Melly) asked about."[297]

The track seemed the perfect main theme to build an album around. That's why Paul decided not only to use the title "Venus and Mars" for the whole record, but also to tape two different versions of the song.

The first version, only 1:20 long, serves as an intro to "Rock Show": its spacey acoustic guitar chords introduce Paul's voice, like a child singing a sweet nursery rhyme. The song leads directly into "Rock Show" and "Venus and Mars" was chosen by McCartney as the opening song of *Wings Over The World Tour* 1975/76 (the live version is included in *Wings Over America*).

---

[295] P. Gambaccini, *cit.*, p.90.
[296] *Ibid.*
[297] *Ibid.*

Wings also recorded a reprise – actually cut first – as the opening song of the B-side of the album. Here, McCartney's voice and the whole instrumentation are soaked in reverb and the unusual effects in the finale – typical of sci-fi movie soundtracks – enclose the song in a sort of starry gloss and soft night light. A lot of high-pitched harmony vocals were added to the track, including a contribution from engineer Alan O'Duffy. A harp is heard at 1:04.

The single "Venus and Mars/Rock Show" (edited version) was released in October 1975, to increase the sales of the *Venus and Mars* album. The 45 reached #12 on the *Billboard* charts and this edit is included in the *Wingspan* collection.

Surprisingly, after a thirty-five years hiatus, the song was used again as a concert opening number during some dates on the 2010 *Up & Coming Tour*.

Musicians:

Paul McCartney vocals, acoustic guitar, bass (?), piano (?) • **Linda McCartney** Moog • **Denny Laine** acoustic guitar, bass (?) • **Jimmy McCulloch** electric guitar • **Joe English** drums

83 Rock Show (Paul and Linda McCartney)

Recording: January 16th-February 24th, 1975 **Location:** Sea Saint Studios, New Orleans **Release:** May 1975, *Venus and Mars*

Paul wrote most of the *Venus And Mars* tracks for the upcoming tour. He conceived "Rock Show" as the opening act for the concerts: a song to get the crowd on its feet. This track wasn't – as many people thought – a showcase of intentional references to McCartney's past or future.

According to McCartney, the quotes from the Hollywood Bowl (Beatles' concert, 1964), the Concert Gebauw in Amsterdam (Wings' show, 1972) and the Madison Square Garden (Paul would have played there during the American tour in 1976) were just words that rhymed perfectly.

McCartney: "That just happens to coincide. I start(ed) off with an idea... 'Rock show', 'ConcertGebouw' came into my mind (...) so I rhymed it with 'Rock show' in an English pronunciation (...) 'Long hair' well, what else? 'Madison Square'. I could see how you might think, well, he's doing this... But for me it's just writing a song."[298]

In a session at Abbey Road on November 1st, 1974 Wings had recorded a first version of the song, officially released on the *Venus and Mars* Deluxe Edition in 2014. The track was still in progress, with a more relaxed feel and a *monstre* length of 6:55. The structure was hesitant and incomplete, but the very prominent bass kept the energy alive. McCartney – maybe unhappy with Britton's drumming (see "Junior's Farm", sheet 78) – thought the song wasn't working, as

[298] *Ibid.* p.93.

he told *Melody Maker*: "It's an attempt at a kind of rocking thing. The type that you've got to get right." [299]

So, the recording was wiped and re-made in New Orleans. Wings worked hard and "Rock Show" underwent several changes before the final take. The result was a multi-faceted track alternating verses, instrumental breaks and rhythmic variations.

It was supported by McCulloch and Laine's virtuoso performance – full of scales and guitar solos – and features on piano Allen Toussaint, brought in to add his talent to the Wings line-up. A piano-driven coda – maybe taken from a different session – ends the track.

The final version loses the power of the early take – in particular Paul's vocals get a bit lost – but its garage-sound perfectly expresses the playful tone of the recording.

It seems that even Alan O'Duffy ventured on playing in the track. O'Duffy: "Encouraged by Linda, I sang harmonies on a couple of tracks and I played percussion on a rocking track, even if I can't recall exactly the song!"[300] In fact, a percussion part – very likely a cow-bell – can be heard all through the song. Also credited on congas is Kenneth "Afro" Williams, member of New Orleans' famed funk group the Chocolate Milk Band, that became Allen Toussaint's regular studio band.

The song immediately turned out to be one of the highlights of Wings' concerts: an enthralling live version is on *Wings Over America*. The single edit – that peaked at #12 in the US in medley with "Venus and Mars" – appears on *Wingspan*. "Rock Show" had been included in the 2010 *Up & Coming Tour*, in a shortened version.

Musicians:

Paul McCartney vocals, backing vocals, bass, Moog (?), electric guitar (?), percussion (?), dingers (?) • **Linda McCartney** backing vocals, Moog (?) • **Denny Laine** backing vocals, electric guitar • **Jimmy McCulloch** backing vocals, electric guitar • **Joe English** drums • **Allen Toussaint** piano • **Kenneth "Afro" Williams** congas • **Alan O'Duffy (?)** cow-bell

84 You Gave Me the Answer (Paul and Linda McCartney)

Recording: January 16th-February 24th and March (overdubs), 1975 **Location:** Sea Saint Studios, New Orleans and Wally Heider Studios (overdubs), Los Angeles **Release:** May 1975, *Venus and Mars*

Jim McCartney's interest in music and the presence of a piano in McCartney's house, had let Paul familiarize himself with the music of the '20s, which had inspired him in his first vaudeville or music-hall songs.[301] Even later on, McCartney didn't give up the pleasure of writing Fred Astaire-style divertissements, creating pastiches of this kind of music.

[299] John Blaney, *The Songs He Was Singing- Vol. 1 The Seventies*, 2010, p.108.
[300] Interview courtesy of Alan O' Duffy, 24/01/2012.
[301] Paul wrote *When I'm Sixty-Four* and *Suicide* when he was sixteen. Other songs in the same vein are *Your Mother Should Know*, *Honey Pie*, *Baby's Request*, *I'll Give You A Ring*, *Goodnight Princess*.

One night, McCartney watched a movie starring Fred Astaire on TV and wrote "You Gave Me the Answer". His home-made demo most likely dates back to 1972-73. Later, he decided to include the song in *Venus and Mars*: "It's sort of a rock'n'roll album but there's other things I like that aren't necessarily rock'n'roll" – McCartney said – "On this LP I thought I'd like to get some of that in… It's my impression of the Fred Astaire era."[302]

The recording, where probably – apart from Paul's piano and English's drums – McCulloch played the guitar chords that can be heard in the background and Laine handled bass, is made fascinating by the effects on McCartney's voice, that make it sound like an old gramophone.[303] The result is an irresistible, old fashioned-sounding piano piece, enriched by period strings and woodwind: a prominent clarinet solo gives the song the fragrance and the atmosphere of *Old England*, piping hot cups of tea on the table and aristocratic living rooms filled with Victorian Age furniture.

Careful listening reveals an interesting detail: just before the beginning, Paul clears his throat, coughing. As engineer Alan O' Duffy revealed, it wasn't the result of a careless mistake during editing, but was left on the record on purpose.[304]

"You Gave Me the Answer" – included in *Venus and Mars* and later used as the B-side to the single "Letting Go" – was one of the most charming tracks on the 1975/76 *Wings Over The World Tour*. McCartney usually dedicated it to Fred Astaire and occasionally to Gene Autry and Little Richard. A live version is on *Wings Over America*.

Musicians:

Paul McCartney vocals, piano, bass (?), percussion (?) • **Denny Laine (?)** bass (?) • **Jimmy McCulloch (?)** electric guitar (?) • **Joe English** drums, percussion (?) • **Unknown musicians** woodwinds, strings

85 Magneto and Titanium Man (Paul and Linda McCartney)

Recording: January 16th-February 24th, 1975 **Location:** Sea Saint Studios, New Orleans **Release:** May 1975, *Venus and Mars*

Paul had re-discovered comics during one of his visits to Jamaica. McCartney: "When Linda and me were on holiday there, we'd go into the supermarket every Saturday, when they got a new stock of comics coming in. I didn't use to read comics from eleven onwards, I thought I'd grown out of them, but I came back to them a couple of years ago."[305]

Paul was intrigued by the drawings (McCartney has a passion for drawing and paintings and in 1999 in Siegen, he exhibited his works for the first time) and by the names of the characters created by Jack Kirby (1917-1994) and Stan Lee (born 1922): that was the inspiration behind "Magneto and Titanium Man".

[302] P. Gambaccini, *cit.*, p.93.
[303] A rough-mix contains no effects on Paul's voice.
[304] Interview courtesy of Alan O'Duffy, 24/01/2012
[305] P. Gambaccini, *cit.*, p.94.

McCartney conceived it as a song in narrative form, with its own plot and Paul acting like a narrator: the track, with its peculiar structure, tells of the fantastic adventures of Magneto, Titanium Man and Crimson Dynamo, involved in organizing a robbery.

It's a rocking song in A major, led by McCartney's electric piano and overdubbed bass. Paul's vocal performance – with brilliantly orchestrated backing vocals – is excellent, especially during the middle eight.

The whole band took part enthusiastically in the recording and McCulloch performed superbly on electric guitar. The track, included in *Venus and Mars* and issued as the B-side to the single "Venus and Mars/Rock Show", was a success during concerts, with Marvel comics projected in the background. The live version is on *Wings Over America*.

Musicians:

Paul McCartney vocals, backing vocals, bass, electric piano • **Linda McCartney** backing vocals, keyboards • **Denny Laine** backing vocals, electric guitar • **Jimmy McCulloch** electric guitar • **Joe English** drums

86 Spirits of Ancient Egypt (Paul and Linda McCartney)

Recording: January 16th-February 24th, 1975 **Location:** Sea Saint Studios, New Orleans **Release:** May 1975, *Venus and Mars*

Inspired by a book on Egypt that Chet Atkins had recommended at a dinner in Nashville, McCartney went back home and wrote "Spirits of Ancient Egypt".

Most likely Paul created it by sticking together two different songs. Its verses are a bit sloppy – the awkward lyrics give the impression that Paul wrote them on the spot – and they were probably added to the Oriental-style refrain that he had written after reading the book: the song is a well-disguised throwaway, used to patch up *Venus and Mars*.

Paul decided to have the track mostly sung by Denny Laine, maybe with the intention of giving Wings a stronger identity, at least on the surface. Denny's smoothest vocal contribution can be found in a rough-mix of the song, where Paul's vocal harmonies are more prominent.

The final version once again relied on an excellent and clever production, with its elaborate guitar and keyboard arabesques depicting desert dunes, an insistent bass riff and deep percussion. In any case, the best part is Paul's refrain – where ancient Rome and the Spain of the *Conquistadores* come into play – counterpointed by Laine's peculiar vocal modulation.

The song turned into an effective scene act: during the 1975/76 *Wings Over The World Tour* and Joe English could show off with a long drum solo. A live version is on *Wings Over America*.

Musicians:

Paul McCartney vocals, backing vocals, bass, synthesizer (?), gong (?) • **Linda McCartney** backing vocals, keyboards • **Denny Laine** vocals, electric guitar • **Jimmy McCulloch** electric guitar • **Joe English** drums, gong (?)

87 Call Me Back Again (Paul and Linda McCartney)

Recording: January 16th-February 24th, 1975 **Location:** Sea Saint Studios, New Orleans **Release:** May 1975, *Venus and Mars*

Venus and Mars was probably conceived by Paul with more concern to seduce the American market than anything else: this can also be heard in tracks like "Call Me Back Again", a blues-drenched song which Paul had written the previous year.

The song is one of McCartney's many examples of Fifties' revival style, in the wake of tracks like "When the Night": nevertheless, here the track is enhanced by an arrangement that tries to convey the colours of the place.

In November 1974, Paul stayed at the Beverly Hills Hotel in Los Angeles: there he met Lennon and the two even ended up at the studio for a jam session. Soon after that, McCartney wrote the track on electric piano: reportedly he intended it like an invocation to his friend and at first he even thought to make that clear in the lyrics. During the recordings, Paul apparently changed his mind, but rumours say that he mentioned John's name in some of the takes.

In New Orleans, Paul worked hard on "Call Me Back Again", a bluesy track performed using his typical staccato on piano and a raspy vocal. Also buried in the mix, there's a flute-sounding Mellotron part. A powerful horn section, arranged by Tony Dorsey – who probably also played trombone in the recording – fattened up the track along with McCulloch guitar's solos and an excellent bass part by Paul himself.

O'Duffy: "On some tracks Tony helped Paul with the horn arrangement, based on McCartney's ideas. Overdubs were done at Sea Saint Studios and we used some session-men brought in by Allen Toussaint."[306] "Call Me Back Again" was included in the *Wings Over The World Tour*. A live version is on *Wings Over America* while the original one appears on *Wingspan*.

Musicians:

Paul McCartney vocals, backing vocals, piano, bass, Mellotron • **Linda McCartney** backing vocals, keyboards • **Denny Laine** backing vocals, electric guitar • **Jimmy McCulloch** electric guitar • **Joe English** drums • **Unknown musicians** horns

88 Listen to What the Man Said (Paul and Linda McCartney)

Recording: January 16th-February 24th and March 8th (overdubs), 1975 **Location:** Sea Saint Studios, New Orleans and Wally Heider Studios (overdubs), Los Angeles **Release:** May 1975, single (from *Venus and Mars*)

New Orleans is a town full of colours, sounds and music. While Paul was there, he had the opportunity to take part in the famous *Mardi Gras*, the main event of the Carnival, admiring the great number of street musicians and enjoying its feisty atmosphere.

---

306 Interview courtesy of Alan O'Duffy, 24/01/2012.

This stimulated McCartney's imagination, inspiring the track "My Carnival" (see sheet **90**) and the atmosphere of "Listen to What the Man Said", a song "which had an authentically smoky New Orleans flavor."[307]

Even in its early version, "Listen to What the Man Said" had a distinctive upbeat rhythm with a brilliant riff that walks throughout the song. At first, the track was recorded with a very rough arrangement: only vocals, electric piano, rhythm guitar, bass and drums.

In some photos taken by Sidney Smith, McCartney is seen embracing a Fender Jazz bass upside-down: maybe he took it from someone (Laine?) and decided to cut the track that way...

During the overdub sessions, synthesizer, percussion instruments and some great backing vocals by Paul, Linda and Denny were added. Then McCartney spent some time stroking his chin, looking for something different and decided to bring in some local musicians.

Dave Mason, Traffic guitarist, came in and played some guitar, but his contribution for a solo was rejected 'cause it did not capture the feel of Paul's original demo. The cherry on the pie was Tom Scott's saxophone, with his joyful solos and phrases that seem to come right off the streets of New Orleans. That's what made the song a big hit and made "Listen to What The Man Said" one of McCartney's most memorable songs.

McCartney: "It was one of those songs we'd gone in with high hopes for. Whenever I would play it on the piano, people would say, 'Oh, I like that one!' But when we did the backing track, we thought we didn't get it together at all. Dave Mason came in and we did a little bit of overdubbing guitars, and when we wondered what we could do for a solo. We thought it would be great to have a very technical musician and do a great lyrical solo. Someone said, 'Tom Scott lives near here', (I said), 'Yeah, give him a ring', and he turned up within half an hour! He sat down in the studio with his sax, playing through. The engineer were recording it. We kept all the notes he was playing casually. He came in and I said, 'I think that's it.' He said, 'Did you record that?' I said yes and we listened to it back. No one couldn't believe it, so he went out and tried a few more but (the takes) weren't as good. He'd had all the feel on this early take, the first take!"[308] While recording the vocals, McCartney added the playful intro ("Allright, ok. Here we go down to New Orleans. Here we, yeah, yeah!"), doing his impersonation of Leo Nocentelli, the Meters guitarist he met at some point in New Orleans.

Another oddity of the recording was the smack of a kiss, a sound that can be heard right after Paul's verse "Soldier boy kisses girl". Engineer Alan O'Duffy recalls: "I do remember exactly that it was Linda who did the kiss on a microphone during one of the backing vocal takes. I made a point of making sure it was audible in the mix later at Wally Heider studio in LA."[309]

---

[307] B. Woffinden, *cit.*, p.136
[308] P. Gambaccini, *cit.*, p.87.
[309] Interview courtesy of Alan O'Duffy, 25/08/2013.

During the overdub sessions in March, Gayle Levant, one of the best-known harpists in Hollywood, added her parts on "Listen to What the Man Said", as well as on "Treat Her Gently/Lonely Old People" (see sheet **89**) and "Venus and Mars (reprise)".[310]

"Listen to What the Man Said" preceded the release of *Venus and Mars* and was a great hit in America, where it topped #1 on the *Billboard* charts and won a gold disc for one million copies sold. In the UK, the single was successful too, climbing up to #6 in the charts.

A live version was included in *Wings Over America*. Unexpectedly excluded from *Wings Greatest*, the song appears on the *All the Best!* and *Wingspan* collections. The song was brought back into the live setlist for the 2013/14 *Out There! Tour*.

Musicians:

Paul McCartney vocals, backing vocals, electric piano, bass, Mellotron, synthesizer (?), percussion (?) • **Linda McCartney** backing vocals, keyboards (?) • **Denny Laine** backing vocals, electric guitar • **Jimmy McCulloch** electric guitar • **Joe English** drums, percussion (?) • **Dave Mason** electric guitar • **Tom Scott** sax • **Gayle Levant** harp • **Unknown musicians** strings

89 Treat Her Gently/Lonely Old People (Paul and Linda McCartney)

Recording: January 16th-February 24th and March 10th (overdubs), 1975 **Location:** Sea Saint Studios, New Orleans and Wally Heider Studios (overdubs), Los Angeles **Release:** May 1975, *Venus and Mars*

Despite its title, "Treat Her Gently/Lonely Old People" wasn't another of McCartney's medleys, real recording studio surgeries and usually made up of tracks that had nothing to do with each other. Rather, it was the derivation of one song from another: in fact, McCartney wrote "Lonely Old People" while he was rehearsing "Treat Her Gently", which he had written on the piano two or three years earlier.[311]

The studio recording of this mournful ballad didn't drift away too much from the original idea: the basic track had only McCartney on vocals and piano, Laine on bass, English on drums and McCulloch's electric guitar.

After the basic track was recorded, McCartney was ready to get down the backing vocals. Alan O'Duffy recalls: "During the recording, McCartney put a live vocal track. Then he came in the control room, he sat beside me and listened to the track. Then Paul started to sing harmony too. I have the gift of harmony myself and I sang a harmony with him. He quite liked it and asked me to teach that part to Denny Laine, who then sang my part!"[312]

The final touch was a lush string arrangement (played by a 23-piece orchestra), overdubbed in Los Angeles under Sid Sharp's supervision..

McCartney chose to end *Venus and Mars* with an unusually low-key track: it's his hand held out to lonely people, already depicted in songs such as "Eleanor Rigby" and "Another Day".

---

[310] Interview courtesy of Alan O'Duffy, 24/01/2012.
[311] Paul's home demo shows the song still without the "Lonely Old People" part.
[312] Interview courtesy of Alan O'Duffy, 16/01/2012.

The theme of loneliness here is linked to that of old age. Although the song is laden with sadness and melancholy, its comforting verses express compassion. The final invitation is the pursuit of love: to express one's inner feelings it's the only way to make things easy in life.

Musicians:

Paul McCartney vocals, backing vocals, piano • **Linda McCartney** backing vocals, organ • **Denny Laine** backing vocals, bass • **Jimmy McCulloch** electric guitar • **Joe English** drums • **Gayle Levant** harp • **Unknown musicians** strings

90 My Carnival (Paul and Linda McCartney)

Recording: February 12th, 1975 **Location:** Sea Saint Studios, New Orleans **Release:** November 1985, "Spies Like Us" single B-side

New Orleans' vitality gave McCartney the opportunity to meet several famous personalities of that rich music scene, including one of Paul's idols, the blues-jazz pianist Henry Byrd (1918-1980), better known as Professor Longhair.

Influenced by listening to some of the pianist's tracks (like "Tipitina") and by his visit to the *Mardi Gras* the day before, McCartney improvised a typical blues song in the studio. It started off as a variation on "New Orleans", another popular piece by Professor Longhair, taped by Wings during the sessions with Linda on lead vocals.

An early version of "My Carnival", recorded in January and titled "Going to New Orleans" (issued in 2014 as a bonus-track on the *Venus and Mars* Deluxe Edition), proves that the track was a derivation of that song. It's a rough take, with Paul on piano and Britton on drums.

Once in the studio, Paul changed that verse in "Well it's my Carnival/It's a lovely day", but didn't add much more to a song that likely was intended just as a tribute to Bird.

It's hard to say exactly who played what during the recording of the basic track: some footage taken from the session shows Denny Laine on stand-up bass and Linda playing tambourine. Leo Nocentelli and George Porter from the Meters funk band and a brass arrangement added a bit of colour to the track.

Leo Nocentelli, the Meters' guitar player, recalls: "I did play guitar on that session. It was a great honor for me. After the album was completed, we played on the Queen Mary for the party that was held… It was fantastic to see people like Fred Astaire, Tony Curtis, the Jackson Five dancing to my songs! During the years Paul and I became close friends. He even asked me to join in on tour but I couldn't make it because I had other dates to do with the band."[313]

George Porter: "It was a jam-session… I played a cow-bell. They took me up from my house and drove me to the studio where Paul was recording. Linda immediately recognized me and

---

[313] Interview courtesy of Leo Nocentelli, 28/08/2012.

she was very nice... she put my hand on a scanner. Then she said to Paul, 'Guess who's hands are these!' He was very happy to meet me!"[314]

That funny and crazy recording session (the famous R&B singer Benny Spellman was in the studio, too) was set aside and "My Carnival" was finally released in November 1985, as the B-side to the single "Spies Like Us": this is a remixed version, with more overdubbed instrumentation. A second version, called *Party Mix*, can be found in the mix and it's different from the 45 rpm for a series of effects and because of its extended length (6:00).

Musicians:

Paul McCartney vocals, piano (?), electric guitar (?) • **Linda McCartney** tambourine • **Denny Laine** double-bass • **Jimmy McCulloch** electric guitar • **Joe English** drums • **Unknown musicians** brass • **Leo Nocentelli** electric guitar • **George Porter Jr.** cow-bell • **Benny Spellman** vocals

The completion of *Venus and Mars* was celebrated by McCartney with a party on the *Queen Mary*, attended by celebrities from the rock world (Elton John, George Harrison, Michael Jackson, Bob Dylan). The album was released on May 30th and it was a huge success around the world: it went immediately to #1 both in the UK and in the US (77 weeks on the charts), where the advance orders reached one and a half million copies. According to McCartney's official site, the record sold ten million copies.

Critic Robert Cristgau wrote: "Superficially, which counts for a lot with McCartney, his New Orleans venture is his most appealing post-Beatles album (...) His whimsical juxtapositions – robots on Main Street, Rudy Vallee cheek by jowl with Allen Toussaint – sound like they might make some sense. Don't get me wrong – they probably don't – because McCartney's a convinced fool. But when the music is coherent it doesn't matter so much."

McCartney made his own review: "There's a couple of tunes we've got brass on and it's New Orleans brass. But the album doesn't sound very New Orleansy to me. We just wanted to record in America and find a musical city. "[315]

Back in the UK, McCartney entered his Rude Studio and cut demos for "Où Est Le Soleil?" (sheet 217), "Famous Groupies" (sheet 110) and "How High the Swallow", an unreleased Latin-style piece.

After a series of rehearsals between August and September – at the Ealing Cinema in Rye (an old Thirties theatre) and then at Elstree Film Studios – Wings embarked in their world tour, starting off in the UK (September 6th-23rd) and then coming to Australia (November 1st-14th).

To help Linda, Paul asked Fiachra Trench, Irish arranger and composer, to give her some lessons. He says: "I did coach Linda in learning to play some of the McCartney/Wings parts on

[314] Interview courtesy of George Porter, 05/09/2012.
[315] John Blaney, *The Songs He Was Singing- Vol. I The Seventies*, 2010, p.108.

the Mellotron. These lessons commenced in June 1975 at Paul and Linda's house in St. John's Wood, London. They were regular lessons, one or two per week." [316]

Again in London, after the end of their British Tour, Wings recorded some tracks for a new album. Probably the only studio versions of "Soily" (see sheet 100) and "Richard Cory" (a song by Paul Simon) were recorded around this time, and both were included in the setlist of the upcoming world tour. Photos from the sessions show McCartney with his Rickenbacker.

91 Beware My Love (Paul and Linda McCartney)

Recording: August, 1975 (?) and/or January-February, 1976 **Location:** Olyimpic Studios (?) and/or Abbey Road Studios, London **Release:** March 1976, *Wings at the Speed of Sound*

It seems unlikely, and in any case uncertain, that the song's lyrics, quite obscure but about a shaky love affair, were inspired by an autobiographical episode. But when Paul wrote "Beware My Love", he must have felt really psyched up, since he wrote one of his most powerful and aggressive songs. This outstanding rocking track, built on an harmonic structure in crescendo (A – B flat – C – D minor) was probably recorded in two parts. On August 28th, at Olympic Studios, Wings recorded it (the track surfaced in 2014 on the *Wings at the Speed of Sound* Deluxe Edition) with Paul on piano, Linda on Moog, Laine on electric guitar, McCulloch on bass and drums by John Bonham (English probably went back home in the US, see sheet 92) . It was probably re-recorded in winter 1976 at Abbey Road, adding an acoustic introduction – with three-part vocals by Paul, Linda and Denny – and further overdubs. The thundering chord that opens the song, played in unison by electric guitar, piano and bass, sets the track on fire.

McCartney sang at the top his voice giving a powerful performance resembling "I'm Down" and led the song with a fastest bass line, pumped beyond all limits. The rest of the band energetically render the track's dramatic vibe, thanks mostly to McCulloch's guitar.

When it was released on *Wings at the Speed of Sound* in 1976, "Beware My Love" was the only rocker on an album that mainly consisted of gentle and sweet ballads.

Paul had perhaps neglected a proper balance of styles and genres, but this one was a well-aimed blow. It was one of McCartney's best heavy rock numbers, later included in the 1976 *Wings Over America Tour*: a powerful rendition is on *Wings Over America*.

Musicians:

Paul McCartney vocals, acoustic guitar (?), bass, harmonium (?) • **Linda McCartney** vocals, backing vocals, Moog • **Denny Laine** backing vocals, piano, acoustic guitar (?) • **Jimmy McCulloch** electric guitar, acoustic guitar (?) • **Joe English** drums

---

[316] Interview courtesy of Fiachra Trench, 11/10/2012.

92 The Note You Never Wrote (Paul and Linda McCartney)

Recording: October 17th-24th, 1975 and February 13th, 1976 (overdubs)? **Location:** Abbey Road Studios, London **Release:** March 1976, *Wings at the Speed of Sound*

"The Note You Never Wrote" was the outcome of one of the first recording sessions for *Wings at the Speed of Sound*, just weeks before the beginning of Wings' World Tour.[317]

Joe English: "'The Note You Never Wrote' was recorded after I'd just flown in from the States. I just came in and we did the tune.... I like it, it's one of my favorites."[318] McCartney wrote this acoustic ballad in ¾ time and took his demo to the band: once in the studio, he gave the song to Denny Laine. It was a well-chosen decision: Laine's melancholic voice enriches this song all in a minor key, with a harrowing and aching atmosphere, unusual in McCartney's production. In the studio, "The Note You Never Wrote" was carefully produced, with electric piano and acoustic guitar as main instruments, most likely played by McCartney and Laine. During the overdubs, the track was refined with some flute parts – maybe Paul and Denny once again – and a restrained string arrangement, probably added on February 13th.

Fiachra Trench was asked to work on the orchestral arrangement. He recalls: "I scored the strings on it, but not the flutes. I think they were probably played on a Mellotron or a synthesizer (...) It has a wonderful opening line, 'Later on, the story goes, a bottle floated out to sea', it's as if we have come into the middle of the story!" [319]

The string section included some special guest, as unveiled again by Trench: "They were members of the Gabrieli String Quartet (later used by McCartney on the albums *Tug of War* and *Give My Regards to Broad Street* – author's note) and they would have played the solo string passages near the beginning and at the end of the track." [320]

An evocative introduction opens the song: Laine's passionate singing and McCulloch's intense performance on electric guitar effectively portray the soft atmosphere of this song about loneliness and abandonment. The track is on *Wings at the Speed of Sound*.

Musicians:

Paul McCartney backing vocals, electric piano (?), bass, flute (?), Mellotron (?), shaker (?) • **Linda McCartney** backing vocals, keyboards, tambourine (?) • **Denny Laine** vocals, backing vocals, acoustic guitar (?), flute (?) • **Jimmy McCulloch** electric guitar • **Joe English** drums, percussion, tambourine (?) • **Unknown musicians** strings

---

[317] *Wings at the Speed of Sound* recording dates are taken from *Maccazine*, Vol. 38, Issue 3, pp. 4-6.
[318] *Circus*, 17/06/1976.
[319] Interview courtesy of Fiachra Trench, 11/10/2012.
[320] *Ibid.*

1976

Between January and February, during a break in the *Wings Over The World Tour*, Wings recorded *Wings at the Speed of Sound* at Abbey Road. These sessions were shorter than McCartney's usual ones, but the arrangements were polished in detail: McCartney added a horn section – Tony Dorsey, Howie Casey, Thaddeus Richard and Steve Howard – which had been well-tested during the tour and some orchestral arrangements, two of which by Fiachra Trench. Also recorded were "Time to Hide" (by Denny Laine) and "Wino Junko" (McCulloch-Allen). Peter Henderson, hired as sound engineer (assisted by Tony Clark and Mark Vigars), recalls: "I remember one of my first engineering jobs, working with Paul McCartney on *Wings at the Speed of Sound*. He'd do two vocal takes and ask, 'Which is the better one?' And when he played guitar, he'd really lean into it and give it everything he got."[321]

93 Must Do Something About It (Paul and Linda McCartney)

Recording: January 5th and February (overdubs), 1976 **Location:** Abbey Road Studios, London **Release:** March 1976, *Wings at the Speed of Sound*

"Must Do Something About It" – the first track taped by Wings during these recordings – was a song that McCartney had topped off with melancholy lyrics about a lonely man's sad day.

In a first version – released on the *Wings at the Speed of Sound* Deluxe Edition in 2014 – McCartney handled vocals as usual, while the band provided a mostly acoustic arrangement which gave the song a bluesy atmosphere. The track ended with a coda – probably derived from a jam – where Paul let himself go to some improvisation.

Then McCartney had an unusual idea: once the basic track was completed, he thought the song would be well suited to Joe English's voice. Therefore, during the overdub sessions in February, the drummer went to the mike for his only performance as lead vocalist in a Wings record: "We were playing it back" – said English – "And I kept singing it, so Paul said, 'Go ahead and do it!'"[322]

It was a great idea: the song is melodically loose and English's vocal performance, in a higher register than the one sung by Paul in the original version, suits its relaxed feeling well. "Must Do Something About It" appears on *Wings at the Speed of Sound*.

Musicians:

Paul McCartney backing vocals, bass, acoustic guitar (?), shaker (?), harmonium (?) • **Linda McCartney** tambourine (?) • **Denny Laine** acoustic guitar (?) • **Jimmy McCulloch** electric guitar • **Joe English** vocals, drums, percussion (?), shaker (?)

---

[321] http://www.soundonsound.com/sos/jul05/articles/classictracks.htm
[322] From *Circus*, 17/06/1976.

94 She's My Baby (Paul and Linda McCartney)

Recording: January-February, 1976 **Location:** Abbey Road Studios, London **Release:** March 1976, *Wings at the Speed of Sound*

For Paul, the next two years after The Beatles' breakup were not just a time of freedom, but also a period of great creativity and inspiration.

His new family life and the presence of Linda inspired McCartney's songwriting. Footage taken from soundchecks in Australia in 1975, shows McCartney singing a few lines of "She's My Baby". Paul returned to the song for the *Speed Of Sound* sessions, although he had written the song shortly following the Beatles' breakup.

"She's My Baby" dates back to 1970-71 and it was written by Paul at the piano late one night in London. McCartney: "The song is essentially a series of little enigmatic statements, snatches from a diary that seemed to sum up our relationship at that time."[323]

In the studio, Paul probably played electric piano as the guide instrument, supported by English on drums: it's not clear if Paul also handled all the instrumental parts, as electric guitar and bass (melodic and galloping, similar to the one heard in "Silly Love Songs", see sheet **95**) are suspiciously close to his style; on the other hand Laine is reported as the bass player in an article appearing at the time on *Circus* magazine.[324] The session resulted in this candid and light song, stylistically somewhere between a jumpy vaudeville and a delicate love ballad. "She's My Baby" rattles off moments of everyday intimacy, with its tender morning awakenings, little surprises and sweet nicknames. In addition to the *Speed of Sound* version, *Working Classical* has a nice arrangement for a string quartet.

Musicians:

Paul McCartney vocals, backing vocals, electric piano, bass (?), keyboards, electric guitar (?) • **Linda McCartney** backing vocals • **Denny Laine** backing vocals, bass (?) • **Jimmy McCulloch** electric guitar (?) • **Joe English** drums

95 Silly Love Songs (Paul and Linda McCartney)

Recording: January 16th and February 13th?(overdubs), 1976 **Location:** Abbey Road Studios, London **Release:** March 1976, *Wings at the Speed of Sound*

If the American fans had to choose a song to represent Paul McCartney in the Seventies, it would undoubtedly be "Silly Love Songs".

As the lead single from *Wings at the Speed of Sound*, the song was released when McCartney's success in the Seventies had reached its peak, with the *Wings Over America Tour*. "Silly Love Songs" became one of the most successful singles in McCartney's career, helping to renew his

[323] *Working Classical* booklet, 1999.
[324] *Circus*, 17/06/1976.

popularity. On the other hand, it consolidated the image of McCartney as the king of catchy but meaningless pop music among the critics.

Paradoxically, however. It was actually the criticism about insisting in his lyrics on a trite theme – love – that prompted Paul to write the song: "I had been accused around that time of singing too much about love" – McCartney explained – "I said, 'Hey, wait a minute! It's the best thing!'"

Paul recalls: "I wrote it out on holiday in Hawaii; I just had piano and chords, and I then wanted to have a melody on bass. We really pushed the bass and drums right out front (…) We wanted to make something you could dance to, so you *had* to."[325]

No doubt, "Silly Love Songs" owes much of its commercial success to a bass line that's technically simple but so original, melodic and straight to be mentioned among the best examples of McCartney as pioneer of the melodic bass.

Musically, the song is a clear example of McCartney's ability to follow the simple rule of harmony, "if-you-find-a-good-sequence-of-chords-exploit-it-till-the-end": "Silly Love Songs" is skilfully built around a simple chord progression in C major, on which Paul elaborates three different melodies, combining them in a very effective polyphonic layering.

It was a carefree recording: listening to the basic track – still without overdubs – it appears to be the work of a trio, probably composed of McCartney (bass), Laine (piano), and English (drums). In the studio McCartney had fun and you can hear him saying "Latin!" referring to a passage of the track where percussion instruments are prominent.

But McCartney could have played piano during the backing track, overdubbing bass later. An interesting account done by American reporter Barbara Charone gives us a unique insight into one of the sessions and seems to confirm the latter assumption: "McCartney sits at the piano, leans into the microphone (…) Coaching English on several takes, McCartney joyously shouts encouraging instructions to his drummer over a practice vocal. 'Latin beat in four bars', McCartney energetically instructs. 'Now bring it down, keep that up.' (…) As the song begins to blossom, Denny and Linda add imaginary harmonies to the tune. In just over an hour, the song has changed considerably."[326]

The result was a pop song resembling disco-music, but that arrangement came out by chance: "Silly Love Songs" was first attempted in a reggae version. It was only during the tour rehearsals, at Elstree Studios, that the horn section worked on the parts and pulled out another trump card from the deck.

During the intro, one can hear a strange effect, similar to a steam locomotive preparing to leave: tape-loops? Mellotron? Effects cleverly re-produced in the recording studio? No

---

[325] Interview by Tom Mulhern, in *Guitar Magazine*, July 1990.
[326] Barbara Charone, *Linda McCartney: Silly Love Songs*, in *Sounds*, 03/04/1976.

information has surfaced about it, but the sound recalls the cash registrator used on Pink Floyd's "Money".

The final touch was the addition of a flowing string arrangement, with a charming disco flavor. It echoes to the influence of Al Green and his "Sha La La" – a big hit on the US charts in 1974 – a song which probably inspired McCartney for "Silly Love Songs". That's clear not only in some string passages, but also in the structure of the song and in some melodic parts that inspired Paul's bass.

In the spring of 1976, America found itself catapulted into a Beatlemania revival: "Silly Love Songs" – where the word "love" is mentioned so many times that it seems fiercely ironic – stayed in the life of the average American man for three months. Over the airwaves, "Silly Love Songs" came out of car radios and home windows with the lightness of its genuine message.

"Silly Love Songs" got lots of airplay, quickly reaching the top of the *Billboard* charts, and amazingly staying there for 15 weeks. It was given a Gold Disc by R.I.A.A. for one million copies sold in the United States.

While "Silly Love Songs" was all the rage in the American charts (in the UK it reached #2), Wings had just landed overseas for their first tour in the United States where, during the shows, the song "g(o)t the same amuck reception as 'Yesterday' or any of the other five Beatles tunes McCartney performs during the course of the evening. Sometimes even bigger."[327]

One of these live performances is featured on *Wings Over America* and the song was also included in the *Wings Greatest* collection.

A new version of "Silly Love Songs" would be recorded in 1983 and released on the album *Give My Regards to Broad Street*, where Paul's bass line is revisited by Louis Johnson and also features a slap-style solo. The original version can also be found on *All The Best!* and on *Wingspan*.

Recently, "Silly Love Songs" was praised by Bruce Springsteen. Paul recalled: "I remember Bruce Springsteen at one of the Rock and Roll Hall of Fame things saying to me, 'Silly Love Songs', man! I really didn't get it when you put that out – but I get it now! I've got kids!"[328]

Musicians:

Paul McCartney vocals, backing vocals, bass, piano (?), percussion (?), Mellotron (?) • **Linda McCartney** backing vocals, tambourine (?) • **Denny Laine** backing vocals, piano (?) • **Jimmy McCulloch (?)** electric guitar (?) • **Joe English** drums, percussion (?) • **Tony Dorsey, Howie Casey, Thaddeus Richard, Steve Howard** horns • **Unknown musicians** strings

327 *McCartney Comes Back*, in *Time Magazine*, 31/05/1976.
328 Stephen Dalton, *Check His Machine: McCartney Interviewed on McCartney II*, 14/06/2011.

96 Warm and Beautiful (Paul and Linda McCartney)

Recording: February 2nd (basic track) and 13th? (overdubs), 1976 **Location:** Abbey Road Studios, London **Release:** March 1976, *Wings at the Speed of Sound*

McCartney had written "Warm and Beautiful" for Linda. In McCartney's words, the song has a very deep meaning: "That one really does get to me. It captures some of my innermost feelings for Linda."[329]

One day McCartney arrived at the studio early in the morning with the song. He had other two Wings' members listen to it and over a quarter of an hour he completed the recording. Shortly after, they overdubbed strings and McCulloch's slide solo, probably double-tracked.[330]

Harmonically, the song features some typical elements of McCartney's piano songwriting: the opening combines a descending bass line with ascending chords, which can also be found in "Maybe I'm Amazed".

This pretty Victorian-style romantic picture hits the mark with its clear melody. Its understated arrangement – with a string quartet by the Maggini Quartet, according to Dutch fanzine *Maccazine* – was enough to complete the song without weighing it down.

Although Paul said in one interview at the time of the album's release that they used two euphoniums on the song, arranger Fiachra Trench explains: "I was pleased to have the idea of using a string quartet and two tenor horns. The tenor horn was an unusual choice: it's typically found in brass bands."[331]

Snubbed by music critics for decades, "Warm and Beautiful" closes the exuberant *Wings at the Speed of Sound* on an intimate note.

The crisp elegance of this exquisite ballad, that McCartney considered as the opening single from *Speed of Sound*, makes it a "minor" classic of McCartney's production. A string quartet version – included in *Working Classical* – highlights the romanticism of the song.

Musicians:

Paul McCartney vocals, piano • **Jimmy McCulloch** slide guitar • **Maggini Quartet (?)** strings • **Unknown musicians** tenor horns

97 Let'Em In (Paul and Linda McCartney)

Recording: February, 1976 **Location:** Abbey Road Studios, London **Release:** March 1976, *Wings at the Speed of Sound*

One of the most frequent criticisms towards McCartney's music was his unwillingness to write autobiographical songs and his liking for lightweight lyrics. In *Wings at the Speed of Sound*, Paul reacted to those statements in two ways: on the one hand by addressing the criticisms ("Silly

---

[329] *Working Classical* booklet, 1999.
[330] *Circus, cit.*
[331] Interview courtesy of Fiachra Trench, 11/10/2012.

Love Songs"), on the other by releasing "Let 'Em In", one of his most intimate and emotionally honest songs.

Paul pays tribute to his dearest affection: the gallery of characters includes several members of McCartney's family (his brother Michael, his aunt Jin), some fantasy names ("Sister Suzy" could be a reference to Linda and her pseudonym later used on some recordings, see **1977**) and some friends of his are also clearly mentioned (Phil and Don Everly).

Paul did not forget "brother John": although he said "that could be whoever you want", it's not hard to see it as a dedication to Lennon, significant of the affection that still tied the two.

In the studio at Abbey Road, McCartney superbly arranged this piano ballad, marked by a thumping bass line (played by McCulloch). Paul used brass, flutes and even some military drum, reminiscent of the passion for the band tradition he has inherited from his father Jim. Then he packaged it all up with a series of effects and noises recreating the cosy atmosphere of home: the bell at the beginning, suggested by Joe English – probably echoing "Three O'Clock in the Morning", a song recorded in 1921 by Paul Whiteman, which has the same opening melody – or the creak of the opening and closing door. Those original tricks earned "Let'Em In" a Grammy Award nomination in the Best Arrangement of the Year category.

And to think that McCartney had actually written the song for Ringo: "It was half-written with Ringo in mind", Paul said.[332] Luckily he changed his mind, in the end giving him the less inspired "Pure Gold", included in *Ringo's Rotogravure* in 1976. Ringo wasn't disappointed: in 2003 he parodied "Let'Em In" by quoting it in his song "English Garden".

McCartney included the song in the *Wings Over America* tour, where "Let'Em In" was a high-impact stage number and where Denny Laine with his drums got the lion's share. Released in July 1976 as a single from *Speed Of Sound*, in the wake of the album's big success, "Let'Em In" was also a great sales hit: #3 in the States – and gold disc for one million copies sold – and #2 in the UK.

"Let'Em In" was included in *Wings Over America* and capitalizing on its popularity, Billy Paul took "Let'Em In" in the American charts with a cover version in 1977.

McCartney also performed the song during the *Paul McCartney World Tour* starting from February 1990: a live version is included in the CD single "Birthday" from the Tokyo concert on March 5th. A third live version is on *Back in the World*, taken from the 2003 European tour. In the following years – from 2007 to 2010 – "Let'Em In" was performed in many concerts. "Let'Em In" also appears on the collections *Wings Greatest, All the Best!* and *Wingspan*.

Musicians:

332 *StreetLife* interview, 03/04/1976.

Paul McCartney vocals, backing vocals, piano • **Linda McCartney** backing vocals • **Denny Laine** backing vocals, military drum (?) • **Jimmy McCulloch** bass • **Joe English** drums • **Tony Dorsey, Howie Casey, Steve Howard, Thaddeus Richard** horns, flutes

98 San Ferry Anne (Paul and Linda McCartney)

Recording: February, 1976 **Location:** Abbey Road Studios, London **Release:** March 1976, *Wings at the Speed of Sound*

The title "San Ferry Anne" could easily be just a figment of McCartney's imagination. But it could also take a cue from a phrase used by the U.S. military during World War I, a malapropism of the French "ça ne fait rien" – the English translation is "it doesn't matter" – whose pronunciation is very similar to San Ferry Anne. The term "San Fairy Ann" is also used in the monologue *The Burghers of Calais*, written by Scottish poet Marriott Edgar in the Thirties.

It seems that McCartney has heard these words on the Ferry boat with Linda from Calais, on their way to record in Paris in November 1973. Paul may also have recalled *San Ferry Ann*, a comedy from 1965, which was about a group of elderly British on a trip to France.

Moreover, McCartney can be heard pronouncing the words "San Ferry Ann" during some dialogues on the *Get Back!* sessions back in January 1969.

However, even this unpretentious song should be counted among McCartney's "minor" classics. "San Ferry Anne" was recorded without frills: a pair of acoustic guitars and a swinging bass, typical of the folk ballads McCartney likes so much. Paul himself performed a heartfelt vocal, expressing its yearning melody. Also noteworthy is English's jazz-style drum performance, played with brushes. Completed by a warm horn arrangement, which suddenly fades rather than adequately developing, the song is the example of the most typical evil afflicting Paul: laziness. The song is included in *Wings at the Speed of Sound*.

Musicians:

Paul McCartney vocals, acoustic guitar, bass • **Denny Laine** acoustic guitar • **Jimmy McCulloch** electric guitar • **Joe English** drums • **Tony Dorsey, Howie Casey, Thaddeus Richard, Steve Howard** horns, flutes

99 Cook of the House (Paul and Linda McCartney)

Recording: February 4th and ? (overdubs), 1976 **Location:** Abbey Road Studios and Cavendish Avenue (overdubs), London **Release:** March 1976, *Wings at the Speed of Sound*

To give equal prominence to each member of Wings – and maybe wanting them to appear more a group than a backing band for himself – Paul yielded the spotlight also to Linda, giving her a chance to perform as a lead vocalist in one track on *Speed of Sound* .

Many comments, often inappropriately, have been made on Linda Eastman's musical skills. Anyway, Paul has to be credited with having created a peculiar and high impact vocal blending with Linda, taking advantage of her graceful singing: which made the vocal harmonies one of the most charming elements of McCartney's records. Linda had less convincing results as lead vocalist: Paul simply wrote this rocker for her as an ode to her cooking skills.

McCartney revealed the origin of the song: "We were in Adelaide and rented a house to stay at rather than a hotel. After the gig each night, Linda and I would get dropped off and sit up in the kitchen and have a late night bite. They had these pots of sage and onions, all the condiments… I took everything I saw and tried to work into a song. Every line in the song was actually in the kitchen."[333]

A nice and self-mocking exercise, completed with a brass arrangement and even with frying effects recorded directly in the kitchen of McCartney's house in London, as Paul explains: "We went round to our house with the mobile unit and get cooking sound recorded. The mobile was outside the house and we just ran wires into the kitchen. There are chips at the end, which is great because it sounds like applause."[334] Paul also played his "Heartbreak Hotel"'s stand-up bass. Looking back, the song makes us smile affectionately. "Cook of the House" was also issued as the B-side to the single "Silly Love Songs" (April 1976) and was performed during 1979 *Wings' British Tour*: some recordings show that Linda sang the track confidently.

Musicians:

Paul McCartney backing vocals, double-bass, piano, Mellotron • **Linda McCartney** vocals • **Denny Laine** backing vocals, electric guitar • **Joe English** drums • **Tony Dorsey, Howie Casey, Thaddeus Richard, Steve Howard** horns

Wings at the Speed of Sound was released in record time, in spring, with the beginning of the *Wings Over America* tour, preceded by a short European tour with five concerts (Denmark, Germany and France) between March 20th and 26th.

The album, one of the most successful records in McCartney's career, achieved remarkable results, reaching #1 in the USA (the fourth in a row for Paul) and #2 in the UK charts. Yet, reviewers have always emphasized two aspects of *Wings at the Speed of Sound*: first, as it may be regarded as the first (and only) album in which Wings look like a real band, cohesive and united, whose collective work emerged in a project.

Secondly, *Wings at the Speed of Sound* would be nothing more than an interlude within the world tour. That said, it's hard to consider it as a real group effort. This LP reflected only partially a conscious decision by Paul to transform Wings into more than a simple supporting band: the unusually fast recording of the album – surprising, considering McCartney's standards – and its release in an appropriate time both from a commercial point of view and to establish an image of Paul as much as possible tied to his current band, complete the series of clues.

[333] K. Badman, *The Beatles After the Breakup. 1970-2000*, 2000, p.178.
[334] *Ibid.*, pp.178-179.

From the creative point of view, everything remained in McCartney's hands, since only two of the eleven songs hadn't been written by him. A well-studied marketing move, then? The record's title, which tries to paint the band as united and strong and the back cover – a clever reference to *A Hard Day's Night* – cast more than a doubt. *Rolling Stone* considered the album "spectacularly well-arranged and recorded" but also described it like a "mysterious, somewhat defensive oddity by a great pop producer who used to be a great pop writer."

And yet the album, though discontinuous, confirmed McCartney's prolific songwriting and contains a quartet of memorable songs, that are a real must in Paul's catalogue.

With the release of this record, in the middle of the *Wings Over America* tour, McCartney changed the concert setlist, including four tracks from *Wings at the Speed of Sound* and cutting the medley "Little Woman Love"/"C Moon" as well as "Junior's Farm"; a surprising choice, since the latter had been an American hit just over a year and a half before. The American tour was one of the biggest musical events of the Seventies: an organizational machine without smudging that revived echoes of Beatlemania, as proved by the two videos produced in the following years, the documentary *Wings Over The World* and the film *Rock Show*, re-issued on DVD in May 2013. Here's the setlist of the Seattle concert: "Venus and Mars/Rock Show/Jet" – "Let Me Roll It" – "Spirits of Acient Egypt" (sung by Laine and McCartney) – "Medicine Jar" (written with Colin Allen by McCulloch, who sang lead) – "Maybe I'm Amazed" – "Call Me Back Again" – "Lady Madonna" – "The Long and Winding Road" – "Live and Let Die" – "Picasso's Last Words" (sung by Laine and McCartney) – "Richard Cory" (a Paul Simon cover, sung by Laine) – "Bluebird" – "I've Just Seen a Face" – "Blackbird" – "Yesterday" – "You Gave Me the Answer" – "Magneto and Titanium Man" – "Go Now (sung by Laine) – "My Love" – "Listen to What the Man Said" – "Let'em In" – "Time to Hide" (written and sung by Laine) – "Beware My Love" – "Silly Love Songs" – "Letting Go" – "Band on the Run" – "Hi Hi Hi" – "Soily"

The tour itinerary included thirty-one shows in twenty-one cities and six hundred thousand people attended the concerts. The record was set in Seattle on June 10th with a crowd of 67,053 spectators and the tour ended triumphantly with three concerts at the Forum in Los Angeles (June, 21st, 22nd and 23rd). All the shows were recorded on a 24-track machine.

100 Soily (Paul and Linda McCartney)

Recording: June 7th, 1976 **Location:** McNichols Sports Arena, Denver **Release:** December 1976, *Wings Over America*

At the time of the *Wings' University Tour*, the material available to the new band was really limited. Moreover, with the exception of a few, they hadn't rehearsed the songs very much.

Thus, between the unconventional *Wings' University Tour* and the *Wings Over Europe Tour*, Paul had been writing a series of songs that worked mainly as stage tracks, given the urgent need to flesh out the repertoire.

"Soily" was one of these tracks, consisting mainly of some hard guitar riffs, that Paul had knocked out hoping to perfect them over time: some unofficial recordings of the 1972 concerts show how "Soily" would undergo through significant changes in the years to come.

"Soily" is a rock-pastiche full of obscure references and characters coming right out of McCartney's imagination: the title was built upon one of the characters of Bruce McMouse Show, a cartoon movie that Paul had created.

As performed on the *Wings Over Europe Tour*, "Soily" was still in progress: the rhythm was slower than its final version and the track still lacked its most distinctive riffs.

Wings recorded the track in the autumn 1972, during the *Red Rose Speedway* sessions, but this studio version remains unreleased.

Wings worked on "Soily" afterwards and, as can be heard in *One Hand Clapping*, the song turned into a heavy number, with the addition of a powerful bass line by McCartney.

"Soily" was further polished for its inclusion in the 1975/76 *Wings Over The World Tour*, with the addition of a powerful ending in crescendo, that Paul though would be good as the show closing number. Finally, "Soily" was released on *Wings Over America* in a live version taken from the Denver concert on June 7th, 1976. This can be considered the most heavy recording in McCartney's solo repertoire: Paul's vocal performance and his bass, with the horn arrangement and the swirling guitar riffs by McCulloch and Laine, make it a hard rock song in perfect Kiss style.

Musicians:

Paul McCartney vocals, bass • **Linda McCartney** backing vocals • **Denny Laine** backing vocals, electric guitar • **Jimmy McCulloch** electric guitar • **Joe English** drums • **Howie Casey, Tony Dorsey, Thaddeus Richard, Steve Howard** horns

The *Wings Over The World Tour* ended with four European concerts, including the famous charity show on behalf of UNESCO in San Marco square in Venice, in front of thirty thousand people and followed by endless controversy for the alleged damage caused by the organisers' trucks to the pavement of the square.

After the inevitable encores at Wembley, November was release time for the triple live *Wings Over America*.

The album, one of the essential records of McCartney's discography (re-released in May 2013 in a Deluxe packaging which won a Grammy Award in 2014 in the Best Boxed Package Category), has suffered over the decades the negative reputation of being heavily retouched in the studio. Although overdubs were certainly required – mainly on some backing vocals – a comparison between the original concerts tapes and the record, has proven how the performances were exciting and tight.

Paul and Wings listened to 90 hours of tape and chose the best performances from the US tour. Then, at Dea Lane Lea Studios in Wembley, some overdubs were recorded. Engineer Phil MacDonald says: "We overdubbed the bits Paul wanted to redo, that were maybe not as good as he wanted. We redid 'Bluebird' with Denny, Linda and Paul."

This time, McCartney approached the tour with a clear mind and the band was well-rehearsed: "We used to rehearse a little. Everyone hates rehearsing... But the thing is, when you get on the stage, you're in trouble, if don't know the songs. And you've got to improvise a lot... But this time we preferred to learn what's going on and we feel more secure."[335]

Laine recalled: "The main thing about any live album is the feel. While everybody's parts were spot on musically – maybe not the harmonies, maybe not every note was exactly right – but the general feel was pretty good. But I had the feeling it could have been a better feeling, a fuller sound, so I double-tracked the guitars, just to fill it out. Added little bits when you get an obvious mistake. We kept most of the solos and most of the bass parts as it was."[336]

According to a sheet included in the Deluxe Edition of the album in 2013, a number of songs were rehearsed – or simply considered for inclusion in the set-list – but finally left out: we can see Wings and McCartney's solo tracks like "Mamunia", "Mrs.Vandebilt", "No Words", "1985", "Uncle Albert/Admiral Halsey", "Love In Song", "Treat Her Gently" and Beatles' classics like "Here, There and Everywhere", "Got to Get You Into My Life", "Hey Jude" and "Fool on the Hill".

Wings Over America continued the series of American #1 hit records by McCartney and in the US it sold nearly four million copies, driven also by the release of the single "Maybe I'm Amazed", which reached #10 on the *Billboard* charts. In 2013, the album re-entered the US *Billboard 200* chart at #22, with 17.000 copies sold in its first week. In the UK the album peaked at #8. The LP got a Grammy Award nomination on the Best Package Category.

The previous summer, Paul had retreated in his Rude Studio and produced a handful of demos: "Dervish Crazy Moog", "Fishy Matters Underwater", "Hey Man", "Soul Song", "Cards up on the table", "With a Little Luck" (see sheet **109**), "Norfolk Broads", "All it Needs it's a Darn Good Song", "Intro American Whirl", "Don't You Wanna Dance", "Old Siam, Sir" (see sheet **121**) , "How Do You Like the Lyrics?", "Fuzz", "E Moog Melody" and "Second (Soul Song)".

[335] Interview with Dutch television, March 1976. http://www.youtube.com/watch?v=_soXIYkOKnA
[336] Howie Edelson, *Winging It With Denny Laine. Macca's Longtime Bandmate at Long Tells His Side of the Story*, in *Beatlefan*, 2006, p.30.

1977

The recording routine resumed at the beginning of the new year: over a month and a half, Paul and the band worked on five tracks for the upcoming *London Town*, only three of which actually made it onto the album. "Girls' School" would be released in November, as the B-side to the "Mull of Kintyre" single, while "B Side to Seaside" (a reference to the music-hall song "I Do Like to Be Beside the Seaside", written in 1907 by John Glover-Kind) – that Paul wrote for Linda – was issued on the Suzy And The Red Stripes single "Seaside Woman" in May.

In April, McCartney finally released the LP *Thrillington* – the orchestral version of *RAM*, recorded six years before – under the pseudonym Percy Thrillington: its sales were disappointing. Paul admitted that he was behind the Thrillington character in a press conference in 1989, answering to a question by journalist Peter Palmiere.

101 Name and Address (Paul McCartney)

Recording: February 7th-March 31st, 1977 **Location:** Abbey Road Studios, London **Release:** March 1978, *London Town*

According to some sources, the *London Town* sessions started off with the recording of "Name and Address". A rock-pastiche, that probably came out of a jam session.

McCartney: "It's a song I wrote in London and it was an affectionate half-tribute to Elvis Presley, but I hadn't completed it before he died."[337]

Actually the song was left unfinished, as the piece ends abruptly: this makes one think that it was more a rehearsal than a real recording.

It's a straightforward, three-chord rock'n'roll track, where McCartney does his vocal impression of Elvis and plays some guitar solo parts[338]: Paul overdubbed them or Laine may have replaced him on bass.

During the recording session, Hank Marvin of the Shadows came in "for a word". Perhaps McCartney had strong feelings about "Name and Address", leading him to add it to *London Town* at the last minute and exactly as it was, as a tribute to Elvis, who died on August 16th, 1977.

Despite the recording's faithful reproduction of the Fifties flavour ("It's done in the style Elvis used to do back in the old *Sun* days"[339]), the track isn't anything special, with its specious lyrics about a weekend love affair ("Our love affair was over on the second day/You packed a bag and like a birdie flew away").

Musicians:

---

337 K. Badman, *The Beatles. The Dream Is Over-Off the Record 2*, 2002, p.224.
338 P. Gambaccini, *London Town Interview with Paul McCartney and Denny Laine*, BBC Radio 1, 1978.
339 K. Badman, *The Beatles. The Dream Is Over-Off the Record 2*, 2002, p.224.

Paul McCartney vocals, electric guitar, percussion, bass (?) • **Linda McCartney** backing vocals, organ • **Denny Laine** backing vocals, bass (?), electric guitar (?) • **Jimmy McCulloch** electric guitar • **Joe English** drums

102 London Town (Paul McCartney-Denny Laine)

Recording: February 7th-March 31st and August (overdubs), 1977 **Location:** Abbey Road Studios, London and Spirit of Ranachan Studio (overdubs), Campbeltown **Release:** March 1978, *London Town*

London's typical greyness inspired Paul for this song, the title track for Wings' seventh album: and "London Town" perfectly expresses the intimate atmosphere of the whole record.

The song was started in 1975 with Linda while in Perth for the *Wings Over The World Tour* and finished up later with the help of Denny Laine, in Scotland and Mexico.

McCartney: "Linda and I were sitting in the hotel in Perth, which is a big Sheraton hotel... And we came up with the opening lyrics. I hang around for a little while, I just had that first bit. Then I got together with Denny in summer 1976 in Scotland: we sat up, we finished it all and arranged it up a little bit."[340]

At Abbey Road, Wings immediately began working on this laboured composition, actually the result of two unfinished songs, "Purple Afternoon" and "London Town".

Footage taken during an interview of McCartney for the Australian music program *Countdown* on February 10th, shows the whole band working on the backing track: Paul is on piano, Laine on electric piano, while McCulloch rehearses some electric guitar licks. Reportedly, an alternate version was recorded before choosing the released one.

Harmonically and lyrically, "London Town" is rich and well structured. Right from its delicate electric piano intro, the song feels wrapped in the damp air of a rainy day in London and its soft melody accompanies glimpses of everyday life, typical examples of McCartney's skill in putting to music this kind of scenes: some characters (e.g. the street flute player) seem to have been caught live on the spot and that's probably what happened to Paul walking down the streets.

Once again, Paul's lyrics deal with ordinary people, focusing on their strife to reach normality, a dimension that is considered necessary for their existence (common people are, in fact, "impossible to meet"). It's almost a lifeline against alienation and lack of communication.

The instrumental break between 3:04 and 3:47 is really noteworthy: after a slide-guitar solo (McCulloch?), accompanied by Paul, Linda and Denny's backing vocals, there's an excellent electric guitar call and response.[341]

---

[340] P. Gambaccini, *London Town Interview with Paul McCartney and Denny Laine*, BBC Radio 1, 1978.
[341] See "Goodnight Tonight".

Some guitar overdubs could have been added by McCartney himself, during the August sessions, when the track was worked prior to the recording of "Mull of Kintyre" (see sheet **113**), according to sound engineer Tim Summerhayes.[342]

Issued as the third single from the album, "London Town" was poorly received, reaching only #42 on *Billboard* charts and #60 in the UK.

Musicians:

Paul McCartney vocals, bass, piano, acoustic guitar (?), electric guitar (?), synthesizer • **Linda McCartney** backing vocals, keyboards • **Denny Laine** backing vocals, electric piano, electric and acoustic guitar • **Jimmy McCulloch** electric guitar, slide guitar • **Joe English** drums

103 Girls' School (Paul McCartney)

Recording: February 7th-March 31st and August (overdubs), 1977 **Location:** Abbey Road Studios, London and Spirit of Ranachan Studio (overdubs), Campbeltown **Release:** November 1977, single

While in Hawaii in November 1975, Paul got the idea for this song, checking pornographic films' ads in newspapers. He wrote it the same week in which he penned "Silly Love Songs", and originally called it "Love School".

McCartney put imaginary female characters in his representation of the goings-on in a brothel: the lyrics, full of allusions and sex-related double entendres, give the listener the feeling of peeping through a keyhole.

Yuki "the oriental princess", Sister Scala "the Spanish doll" and Roxanne "the trainer" are the figures of this multi-ethnic cat-house where film screenings and special massages mingle.

McCartney blended it all into a very aggressive song: "Girls' School" is one of his best hard rocking tracks.

Its opening – with a mischievous choir singing "Hip, hip, hooray!" – flows into the tense main riff, built on a mighty wall of heavily distorted electric guitars, played by Laine and McCulloch (very likely with some help by McCartney himself).

"Girls' School" is a catchy commercial song, with McCartney's double-tracked vocals and some perfectly executed backing vocals.

Some months later, McCartney would have an argument with Bob Mercer on whether to launch the song as the A-side of a single: Paul knew that "Girls' School", musically powerful and lyrically suggestive, would be better accepted by reviewers after the spread of the punk movement and it wouldn't clash with the new context.

The compromise (a double A-side) didn't work in favour of "Girls' School", and in Great Britain the song was immediately removed from radio broadcasting, replaced by "Mull of Kintyre". The pairing wasn't lucky in America, either, where the track reached only #33 on the charts.

---

[342] Interview courtesy of Tim Summerhayes, 26/09/2012.

"Girls' School" can be considered one of McCartney's most underrated songs: the track was included in the 1987 CD release of *London Town* – whose English edition includes the American promo, an edit lasting 3:15.

It's a shame Paul didn't even consider "Girls' School" for live performances in the 1979 Wings' UK Tour, whose setlist was filled with many rockers. Its single version (4:34) appears on the 1993 remastered edition of *London Town*.

Musicians:

Paul McCartney vocals, bass, electric guitar (?) • **Linda McCartney** backing vocals, piano (?) • **Denny Laine** backing vocals, piano (?), electric guitar • **Jimmy McCulloch** electric guitar • **Joe English** drums

104 Children, Children (Paul McCartney-Denny Laine)

Recording: February 7th-March 31st, 1977 **Location:** Abbey Road Studios, London **Release:** March 1978, *London Town*

The birth of two children had positive effects on Denny Laine's love life, as well as on his songwriting, which became strongly influenced by family matters.

The atmosphere of enchanted innocence of this folk-country nursery rhyme conveys genuine feelings. Wings recorded this song – originally titled "Laine and Heidi" – using soft childish instruments, with shades of traditional Irish music. Relying on violins, flutes, harmonicas, autoharps and acoustic guitars, the song is wrapped in an ethereal aura.

McCartney: "We thought we should do it like a fairy-tale kind of thing: it's like a children song. So we tried to do it as if it was like the soundtrack to a cartoon. You imagine lots of little fairies and elves down in the dingley dell, playing on their flutes or little autoharps and stuff."[343]

Laine's whispered vocals are surrounded by some fine backing vocals. Possibly Joe English (moreover credited as vocalist in the *London Town*'s album notes) may have joined in for one verse. The theme of a utopian, fairy-tale world – as if suspended in make believe – is recurring in many McCartney's songs and it's probably Paul's contribution to the track which, apart from that, is typical of Laine's folk style. "Children, Children" is on *London Town*.

Musicians:

Paul McCartney backing vocals, bass, acoustic guitar (?), violin, flute, autoharp (?) • **Linda McCartney** backing vocals, keyboards, autoharp (?) • **Denny Laine** vocals, backing vocals, acoustic guitar, flute • **Jimmy McCulloch** acoustic guitar (?) • **Joe English** vocals (?), drums, harmonica

In an unexpected move, McCartney decided to give a new exotic setting to his recordings, choosing the Caribbean Sea. So the group rented some yachts off the Virgin Islands, on one of which, the *Fair Carol*, a complete recording studio was installed.

---

[343] P. Gambaccini, *London Town Interview with Paul McCartney and Denny Laine*, BBC Radio 1, 1978.

It was another one of McCartney's "working holidays". Wings spent May on board their boats, recording tracks for *London Town* on a 24-track desk, courtesy of recording studio Record Plant West from Los Angeles.

Not only music: everybody could relax swimming, water skiing, sunbathing (Denny Laine got sunstroke) and enjoying the delicacies cooked by Tony Garton, captain and master chef.

And on May 21st everybody watched the FA Cup final, Liverpool vs Manchester United (won 2-1 by the "Devils"), thanks to a videotape a band assistant had brought aboard.

During the sessions, eight tracks for the album were recorded, as well as the usual number of outtakes: "El Toro Passing" – an instrumental track whose title was inspired by the name of one of the boats, just as would happen some time later for "Wanderlust" (see sheet **160**) – "Running Round the Room", "Standing Very Still" and Laine's "Find a Way Somehow" (already recorded for his 1973 solo album *Aah Laine!*) McCartney is seen embracing both Rickenbacker and Fender Jazz basses on pictures taken during these sessions.

The songs were very likely recorded in the order below, the same running order of a tape – containing rough mixes of the tracks – that hit the bootleg market years some years ago.

Some known recording dates – officially released at the time on *Club Sandwich* or taken from other sources – are consistent with this speculation.

105 Cafe on the Left Bank (Paul McCartney)

Recording: May 2nd and November (overdubs), 1977 **Location:** Mobile Studio Fair Carol, Virgin Islands and Abbey Road Studios (overdubs), London **Release:** March 1978, *London Town*

Paul may have written "Cafe on the Left Bank" during, or immediately after, his stay in Paris in March 1976, when the *Wings Over The World Tour* stopped in the French capital and reminded him what he had seen years before with the Beatles.

The mobile studio had just been finished, when McCartney suggested to Wings this song full of references to the famous *Rive Gauche*, which must have tickled his admiration, with its extravagant and original artists flocking to it daily.

However, the subject was developed more through hints than by telling a story, although the line "watching Charles De Gaulle make a speech" may be real.

An early take of "Cafe on the Left Bank" – appeared on a rough-mix tape from these sessions – is already well structured and very similar to the version later released on *London Town*: only a few tweaks were needed to get the final one.

The song was finished at Abbey Road in November. McCartney: "To get the atmosphere down at Abbey Road, we had the whole place done out with potted plants, and little café umbrellas, little stripes… To make it look like a café!"[344]

344 *Ibid.*

A tight rocking track in D minor, characterized by McCulloch's excellent guitar licks and phrasing: McCartney's vocal performance is surrounded by some effective backing vocals and probably the whole band – according to the *London Town* liner notes – took part playing different kinds of percussion instruments.

Musicians:

Paul McCartney vocals, bass, percussion (?) • **Linda McCartney** backing vocals, keyboards, percussion (?) • **Denny Laine** backing vocals, electric guitar, percussion (?) • **Jimmy McCulloch** electric guitar, percussion (?) • **Joe English** drums, percussion (?)

106 I'm Carrying (Paul McCartney)

Recording: May 5th and December 3rd-14th (overdubs), 1977 **Location:** Mobile Studio Fair Carol, Virgin Islands and AIR Studios (overdubs), London **Release:** March 1978, *London Town*

"I'm Carrying" is a typical McCartney melodic song, where the boundary between sugary sentimentalism and refined gracefulness is blurred.

Lyrically, "I'm Carrying" is the kind of song that asks the loved one forgiveness after the storm: a slight guitar plucking supports Paul's sincere voice, as he sings flawlessly this gentle floral lullaby.

"I'm Carrying" was the second track recorded for *London Town* in the Virgin Islands. Paul taped it while the waves were rocking the studio-boat.

McCartney: "I was on the back deck of a boat, just myself and a guitar. And with the lovely blue water and blue sky, I just recorded the backing guitar and vocal and later we finished it by putting on strings and a thing called Gizmo, an attachment you can have on a guitar."[345] While McCartney was recording, a dolphin came out from the water and followed the boat for a few minutes. Apparently, it was not the only song taped outside, as McCartney and Laine (both in swimsuits) were portrayed in a picture while recording some vocals outdoors.

The track was produced in a very original way: a strong echo highlights the squeaking noise of Paul's fingers on the acoustic guitar fret board while changing the chords.

"I'm Carrying" is sustained by a backdrop of strings and synthesizer, used with a symphonic function that Paul would further explore two years later for *McCartney II*.

McCartney: "I like the squeaks on the fingers. When we recorded it, there was some thought, 'Should we get rid of those squeaks or is it nice to leave it in?' I preferred to leave it in, really. It's something you know what the noise is… It makes it somehow a bit more immediate."[346]

Harrison chose it as his favourite track on *London Town*: "I thought it was sensational" he said.[347] In August 1978, the song was also issued as the B-side to the single "London Town".

Musicians:

---

[345] K. Badman, *The Beatles. The Dream is Over-Off the Record 2*, 2002, p.223.
[346] P. Gambaccini, *London Town Interview with Paul McCartney and Denny Laine*, BBC Radio 1, 1978.
[347] Mick Brown, *An Interview with George Harrison*, in *Rolling Stone*, 19/04/1979.

Paul McCartney vocals, acoustic guitar, synthesizer, electric guitar (with Gizmo) • **Unknown musicians** strings

107 Deliver Your Children (Paul McCartney-Denny Laine)

Recording: May 1st-31st and November (overdubs), 1977 **Location:** Mobile Studio Fair Carol, Virgin Islands and Abbey Road Studios (overdubs), London **Release:** March 1978, *London Town*

"Deliver Your Children", the second track sung by Denny Laine included in *London Town*, was another expression of love for his children.

Denny had written "Deliver Your Children" in Los Angeles during the *Venus and Mars* sessions. The song, a prayer which invokes protection and hope for his children, is the most authentic Laine/McCartney collaboration, as well as one of the best tracks of the album.

Their partnership had become closer during the previous year, as McCartney explained: "Denny and I have written together on previous albums but never more than one tune. Then, in summer '76, we sat down and wrote a bunch together (…) To tell you the truth, we've been helping arrange each other's' songs."[348]

Although in this case the main inspiration is clearly Denny's, McCartney's contribution during the recording was no less important.

This acoustic-driven folksy song contains some fine Spanish guitar solos – played by Laine, who had taken lessons in Spain in 1970 – and features a great counterpoint in McCartney's tight and high harmonies. The result is a duet with the vocal technique used by Paul and John in the early Beatles, featuring a remarkable key change for the last two verses.

Among the most representative tracks of the acoustic soul of *London Town*, "Deliver Your Children" was also issued as the B-side to the "I've Had Enough" single.

Musicians:

Paul McCartney vocals, bass, acoustic guitar • **Denny Laine** vocals, backing vocals, acoustic guitar, Spanish guitar • **Linda McCartney** backing vocals • **Jimmy McCulloch** acoustic guitar (?) • **Joe English** drums

108 I've Had Enough (Paul McCartney)

Recording: May 1st-31st and November 24th (overdubs), 1977 **Location:** Mobile Studio Fair Carol, Virgin Islands and Abbey Road Studios (overdubs), London **Release:** March 1978, *London Town*

After the release of *London Town*, many critics remarked that the album lacked powerful and rocking tracks. "I've Had Enough" was the only heavy song on the record. It was another typical rock'n'roll track written by Paul, a real master at combining this three-chord structure with his original ideas. The song uses the same opening riff as Buddy Holly's "Think It Over".

---

348 Chris Welch, *Goodbye to Yesterday*, in *Melody Maker*, 19/11/1977, p.8.

McCartney: "I was sitting in the studio one day, just working on some chords and I didn't have any words to it. I just had the chorus, 'I've had enough/I can't put up with anymore'..."[349]

The song was first recorded during the Virgin Islands sessions, but left unfinished. In an early take, at a certain point, you can hear Paul shout "drum solo!" to introduce an instrumental section that initially was filled only with English's powerful drums.

Later, McCartney wrote some lyrics and Wings completed the song at Abbey Road on November 24th.[350] Paul added a great vocal performance, and almost certainly along with Laine overdubbed the harmonizing electric guitar parts.

It was perhaps in response to criticism from the media that McCartney chose it as the second single from *London Town* in June 1978. However, the audience greeted this idea wearily (#42 in the UK and #25 in the US), despite some good radio programming.

The number would have worked better on stage: in fact "I've Had Enough" was the only *London Town* track performed during the 1979 *Wings' British Tour*.

Musicians:

Paul McCartney vocals, backing vocals, bass, electric guitar (?), tambourine (?) • **Linda McCartney** backing vocals, keyboards, tambourine (?) • **Denny Laine** backing vocals, electric guitar • **Jimmy McCulloch** electric guitar • **Joe English** drums

109 With a Little Luck (Paul McCartney)

Recording: May 10th and 12th and November (overdubs), 1977 **Location:** Mobile Studio Fair Carol, Virgin Islands and Abbey Road Studios (overdubs) , London **Release:** March 1978, single (from *London Town*)

Another of McCartney's major hits of the Seventies, "With a Little Luck" is a prime example of Paul's ability as a songwriter and producer.

It would be unfair to label this song as merely a pop production: if on the one hand "With a Little Luck" presents an easy and infectious melody, as well as several tricks typical of commercial songs (e.g. the massive use of backing vocals), on the other side the track emphasizes McCartney's talent to assimilate different musical styles.

Built around an incessant refrain, the song is packed with soul influences, with its verses and their very R&B-ish harmonic structure.

"With a Little Luck" is worth considering due to its original arrangement, based exclusively on keyboards and synthesizer and probably inspired by Stevie Wonder's style.

McCartney had written "With a Little Luck" the previous summer and a rough mix reveals that Paul had already conceived its structure. McCartney: "This was a song we started on the boat in Watermelon Bay (...). We just had the backing track, a very rough version."[351]

---

[349] K. Badman, *The Beatles. The Dream Is Over-Off the Record 2*, 2002, p.224.
[350] Dave Gelly, *Wings Work*, in *Club Sandwich*, n.6, November 1977.

The recording may not have required the involvement of the rest of the band, whose members at one point or another were unavailable to record due to various issues: Paul recorded the basic track only with electric piano and a drum-machine – with some real drum fills, that owe something to Paul's style – taking him some time to add his bass part, on May 10th and 12th.[352] Later, during the overdub sessions in London, McCartney realized the sales potential of the song, and enriched it by backing vocals and more keyboards and synthesizer.

McCartney said in 2001: "I enjoyed the chords in that… I have good memories of that song and its belief that things will work out. I'm playing the synth solo there."

"With a Little Luck" is a rather complex and lengthy episode (5:45), in which the bouncy bass is the true leader of the track. Also featured is a delicate, charming and classical-influenced instrumental section, overlapping melodies with synth and keyboards.

Released as a single from *London Town*, "With a Little Luck" became Paul's seventh #1 on the American charts (and reached #5 in the UK), although in a less charming edited version (3:15).

Some unofficial video recordings show that "With a Little Luck" was rehearsed for the January 1980 *Wings' Japanese Tour*: but it would have been difficult to properly reproduce the synth-based sound of the track.

"With a Little Luck" can also be found on *Wings Greatest*, *All the Best!* and *Wingspan* compilations: the full version appears only on *Wings Greatest*, whereas *All the Best!* (US version) and *Wingspan* include the 45rpm edit.

Musicians:

Paul McCartney vocals, backing vocals, electric piano, synthesizer, bass, drums (?) • **Linda McCartney** backing vocals, keyboards (?) • **Denny Laine** backing vocals, synthesizer (?) • **Joe English (?)** drums (?)

110 Famous Groupies (Paul McCartney)

Recording: May 13th and November (overdubs), 1977 **Location:** Mobile Studio Fair Carol, Virgin Islands and Abbey Road Studios (overdubs), London **Release:** March 1978, *London Town*

Harrison had paid tribute to the scruffs – the girls who were always in front of the Apple Corps offices – in "Apple Scruffs" (1970, *All Things Must Pass*). In this case McCartney dedicated "Famous Groupies" to the fanatical girls who follow their singers everywhere during tours: the so-called groupies.

Paul surely well remembered what used to happen with his fans in third category hotel rooms during the Beatles days: thus, "Famous Groupies" is his tribute to that era.

Linda didn't take it amiss: she had started off stalking famous musicians, too. Paul himself joked about it: "'Famous Groupies' it's about anyone who had ever been in a rock'n'roll band,

[351] K. Badman, *The Beatles. The Dream Is Over-Off the Record 2*, 2002, p.225.
[352] Trevor Jones diary. On May 10th, Jones notes: "Paul to do bass on 'Luck'. Took a long time". On May 12th, he writes: "Paul put the bass on 'Luck'. Took the morning getting it right".

and they'll know about groupies, and one or two of them have made themselves pretty famous…"[353]

Paul had prepared a demo of the song in the summer of 1975. Initially, McCartney imagined a screaming rocker – a punk-style version – but the key was too high and Paul discarded the idea. A rough-mix of the backing track, recorded on May 13th in the Virgin Islands[354] featured a very bare arrangement. Beside an acoustic guitar (Laine?), McCartney played (or overdubbed) an already pleasant bass part, while in the background only drums, some electric guitar touches and Mellotron.

At this stage, the track had turned into an acoustic folk song with a dark atmosphere: a grotesque and ironic gallery of characters, with frequent sexual innuendos.

Paul's lyrics played on double entendres and saucy situations (a guitarist from Epping Forest – a woodland in south-east England, mentioned also by Genesis in their song "The Battle of Epping Forest" in 1973 – who did not lose his "rhythm" even when in girls' company).

McCartney made the song interesting with his usual skill on bass and with a fun range of vocal effects. And the way the instruments underline the story is ingenious.

"Famous Groupies" ends with some animal noises, that recall a flock of seagulls, probably caught on the spot while recording on Virgin Islands. The track is on *London Town*.

Musicians:

Paul McCartney vocals, bass, acoustic and electric guitar (?), slide guitar (?), percussion, Mellotron • **Linda McCartney** backing vocals • **Denny Laine** backing vocals, acoustic and electric guitar (?) • **Jimmy McCulloch** electric guitar, slide guitar (?) • **Joe English** drums

111 Morse Moose and the Grey Goose (Paul McCartney-Denny Laine)

Recording: May 1st-31st, November (overdubs part 1) and December 3rd-14th (overdubs part 2), 1977 **Location:** Mobile Studio Fair Carol, Virgin Islands, Abbey Road Studios (overdubs part 1) and AIR Studios (overdubs part 2), London **Release:** March 1978, *London Town*

One of the most bizarre songs in McCartney's catalogue, "Morse Moose and the Grey Goose" was written by Paul and Denny Laine right on board the mobile recording studio in the Caribbean.

The boat's communication system inspired the song, dotted by the effect that reproduces the characteristic cawing of a transceiver.

Paul had the idea in the middle of an evening jam, playing some chords on electric piano. Then Laine accompanied him on piano and the two went on for several minutes.

McCartney: "We were on the boat and the electric piano was set up through a couple of gadgets and it has those weird sounds on it and I started hitting it… I was doing sort of a

[353] K. Badman, *The Beatles. The Dream Is Over-Off the Record 2*, 2002, p.224.
[354] Trevor Jones diary.

morse beat to it… Denny was just leaping over to the piano… We had this five-minute thing that sounded like a morse code… It seems like a germ of an idea! And one night back in London, we wrote another little bit." [355]

Later, Paul found the bass groove and McCulloch added some strident guitar parts, but the song was left unfinished and the vocals were recorded only in the following months.

In the final version, this long track (a good 6:36) alternated between two sections. The first is a fast rocker with a swirling bass line and some wild vocals by Paul, relentlessly shouting an SOS message. The second part – not present in the rough-mix and recorded by Paul and Denny during the November sessions, with the addition of acoustic guitars and a Mellotron – is the chant of a seafaring crew (someone pointed out a similarity with the traditional Irish song "Follow Me Down to Carlow"), full of obscure references to the adventures of a mysterious ship called The Grey Goose.[356] The lyrics "Davy Jones is calling me" contain a reference to Davy Jones's Locker, an idiom for the bottom of the sea.

"Morse Moose…" was finally completed at AIR Studios in London with other overdubs, including an orchestral contribution.

Wil Malone was recruited to score strings and brass. He recalls: "Paul called me up and I went to his house in St. John's Wood and he ran over the song on the piano. When I wrote the first draft of the arrangement for him he said, 'The trouble is this is *your* vibe. We want *my* vibe'. I had no clear idea of what I was supposed to be doing!" [357]

Malone: "Most sessions are kind of happy things, but as fas as I remember this one wasn't particularly happy… Everyone seemed to be a bit miserable. Denny Laine said nothing, Paul wasn't laughing so much… The backing track was recorded on a yacth… It was before computers, there was no click-track and the rhythm track wasn't at all steady! I chose the orchestra, they were all session players and they were led by Gavyn Wright." [358]

The result is a finale in grand style, ending *London Town* strikingly, as McCartney often likes doing on his records.[359] When *London Town* was released, McCartney tried to explain why he filled the album with extravagant songs like this one: "I'd like to make an adventurous album (…) No formula style… I'd welcome the change."[360]

Musicians:

[355] P. Gambaccini, *London Town Interview with Paul McCartney and Denny Laine*, BBC Radio 1, 1978.
[356] Oddly, "The Grey Goose" is the title of an African-American prison ballad, recorded also by William Leadbetter (aka Leadbelly), an American singer and guitarist. In 1934 he cut "Midnight Special", a traditional song rehearsed by The Beatles during the *Get Back!* sessions and recorded by McCartney in 1991. On his 1972 *Wings Over Europe Tour*, Paul performed "Cottonfields", another track from Leadbelly's repertoire.
[357] Interview courtesy of Wil Malone, 14/01/2013.
[358] *Ibid.*
[359] See "Nineteen Hundred and Eighty Five" (1973, *Band on the Run*), "Through Our Love" (1983, *Pipes of Peace*), "However Absurd" (1986, *Press to Play*) or "C'mon People" (1993, *Off the Ground*).
[360] John Blaney, *Paul McCartney. The Songs He Was Singing-Vol.1 The Seventies*, 2010, p.159.

Paul McCartney vocals, bass, acoustic guitar, electric piano, Mellotron • **Linda McCartney** backing vocals, keyboards • **Denny Laine** backing vocals, acoustic guitar, piano • **Jimmy McCulloch** electric guitar • **Joe English** drums • **Gavin Wright** violin • **Unknown musicians** strings, horns

112 Don't Let It Bring You Down (Paul McCartney-Denny Laine)

Recording: May 25th and November 24th (overdubs), 1977 **Location:** Mobile Studio Fair Carol, Virgin Islands and Abbey Road Studios, London (overdubs) **Release:** March 1978, *London Town*

"Don't Let It Bring You Down" deserves a place of honour among the folk-inspired songs that filled the *London Town* sessions. It's a thoughtful acoustic track written by Paul and Denny Laine and the last song recorded in the Virgin Islands.

McCartney had started writing it on his 12-string acoustic guitar in Aberdeen on September 22nd, 1975 during the Scottish leg of the *Wings' World Tour*.

McCartney: "I (was) sitting in our hotel bedroom just before we were going to turn in for the night and I had my 12-string guitar with me (…) I started plonking out a little tune and it became 'Don't Let it Bring You Down'."[361]

Paul brought his demo – recorded at home in St John's Wood – to the Virgin Islands, still incomplete and he played it to the group. Denny helped with some ideas and McCartney suggested that Joe English use brushes in order to get a gentler effect.[362] At that point, the song was committed to tape.

The music of "Don't Let It Bring You Down" fits well with the lyrics, as they philosophize on the ups and downs of life and on how good it is to not to lose hope even in the worst moments.

The lazy navigation of the Fair Carol in the Caribbean sun must have contributed to the relaxed atmosphere of the recording; a rough-mix of the song reveals its acoustic nature, intimate and peaceful, with a beautiful guitar bed.

The track was embellished at Abbey Road on November 24th with several overdubs:[363] Paul and Denny added some Irish tin whistles to make the song softer. Then, they put vocal harmonies with Linda. The trio struggled to get it right. At one point, Emerick stopped the tape: "What's up?" asks Paul. 'Tuning.' 'Oh – our old friend again. Right. Once more." [364]

McCartney sang it masterfully – with a gorgeous alternation of falsetto and bass – and also added the dramatic electric guitar solo that closes the song. Paul revealed: "I play the little bit of lead guitar you can hear."[365] The track is on *London Town*.

Musicians:

[361] K. Badman, *The Beatles. The Dream Is Over-Off the Record 2*, 2002, p.224.
[362] *Water Wings*, on *Sounds*, August, 20th 1977.
[363] Dave Gelly, *cit.*
[364] *Ibid.*
[365] K. Badman, *The Beatles. The Dream Is Over-Off the Record 2*, 2002, p.224.

Paul McCartney vocals, backing vocals, acoustic guitar, bass, electric guitar, Irish tin whistle • **Linda McCartney** backing vocals • **Denny Laine** backing vocals, acoustic guitar, Irish tin whistle • **Jimmy McCulloch** acoustic guitar (?) • **Joe English** drums, brushes

Back from the Virgin Islands, McCartney spent the summer in the Scottish farm, where he began to record about twenty demos in his Rude Studio. Among these, the unreleased "Waterspout", "Agoo Mr. Didi", "Firebird Drama" and "Jamaican Hilite". Paul also recorded a first version of "Mull of Kintyre", which was properly recorded immediately after.

In Campbeltown, Wings recorded some overdubs on "Girls' School" and "London Town", using a 24-track mobile unit, owned by London's RAK Studios.

113 Mull of Kintyre (Paul McCartney-Denny Laine)

Recording: August 9th and October (overdubs), 1977 **Location:** Spirit of Ranachan Studio, Campbeltown and Abbey Road Studios (overdubs), London **Release:** November 1977, single

"Mull of Kintyre" is certainly the most traditional song recorded by McCartney during his career, as well as his most commercially successful single.

The desire to reawaken the Scottish song tradition gave Paul the idea that he could personally contribute to its revival.

It was probably around 1973 that McCartney had began to write a song inspired by this concept, dedicating it to the Kintyre promontory, where his refuge was.

During the summer of 1976, Denny Laine helped Paul finish the song, which became their only successful fifty-fifty collaboration.

Nevertheless, Laine recalled with some bitterness what happened on that occasion: "We sat outside with a bottle of whiskey one afternoon in the hills of Kintyre and wrote the song. Paul had written the chorus. But we wrote the rest of it together, and most of the lyrics were mine. It was number one for sixteen weeks and sold millions of copies. But I personally got very little out of it. When I asked Paul for a special deal on the tune his answer was virtually, 'Look, I'm Paul McCartney, and anyone who writes with me is privileged.'"[366]

Dante's *contrapasso* also held true in this case: Denny Laine was not the only one to complain about financial issues related to a Scottish song!

In August 1977 – after he committed to tape a couple of demos with Denny – McCartney decided to record the track, adding the distinctive touch of bagpipes. So, he recruited fourteen members of the Campbeltown Pipe Band, who were paid the minimum wage. Their names and faces were captured in a valuable vintage photo.[367]

---

[366] G. Giuliano, *cit.*
[367] http://www.campbeltownloch.com/photogallery.php?photo_id=123

Ian McKerrals, today a barber and at that time a very young piper, recalls: "The late pipe major Tony Wilson came to the band hall to say he'd been approached by Paul McCartney to do this song. We thought he was winding us up. Tony had met them and Linda had played the melody of the song on the keyboard."[368]

When Tony Wilson heard the song, he immediately told Paul to re-write the track in the musical key of bagpipes. He showed the notes the instrument could produce and McCartney changed the key. A comparison between McCartney's original piano demo from around 1973 and the final version proves that the key was changed from C to A.

After a month of rehearsals, the Campbeltown Pipe Band went into the studio area in Paul's farm. McKerrals recalls that McCartney, "was very relaxed, wearing jeans, a waistcoat and checked shirt… It took an hour to record the song. We then had something to eat – sandwiches and beer for the boys – and we had a party. But we couldn't stay long because we had school in the morning…"[369]

For the recording, Tony Wilson took with him fourteen band members, seven pipers and seven drummers. The recording happened outdoors, just outside the Campbeltown estate on August 9th. A drawing made by McCartney himself to celebrate the sessions, recently surfaced on the Internet, is dated August 13th.[370]

Tim Summerhays was one of the engineers who assisted Geoff Emerick on the session: "We took the mobile studio to the farm a few days ahead of the sessions and spent time in preparing the control room and recording area. We decanted the truck's equipment to a makeshift control room supervised by Geoff."[371]

Recording outside was not an uncommon practice at the time, but it required some tricks. Summerhayes: "The recording of Paul's vocals and acoustic guitar was done outside of the barn. There was a little bit of wind noise and nobody had a pop filter for the microphone… So we put one of John Hammel's (McCartney's personal assistant – author's note) socks on it!"[372]

Then it was time for overdubbing: "After we got the track down, we overdubbed the bagpipes" – tells Summerhayes – "So we set up about ten microphones in the barn area… We spent the whole day and half of the evening overdubbing and we did several takes."[373]

A funny mishap threatened to undermine the recording. Summerhayes: "We were pulling the tape back and we said, 'What is that?' It looked like oil slick, like a big grey's mark on the

[368] *The Paul McCartney Story*, in *The Scottish Daily*, 06/08/2002.
[369] *Ibid.*
[370] Interview courtesy of John Lang Brown, 05/12/2012. The piper, who took part in the recording, recalled: "I remember it was mid-week". The same date is on: Howard Sounes, *FAB, An Intimate Life of Paul McCartney*, p.339. http://www.stevehoffman.tv/forums/showthread.php?t=297026&highlight=
[371] Interview courtesy of Tim Summerhays, 26/09/2012. This recollection is confirmed by a picture taken during the recording.
[372] *Ibid.*
[373] *Ibid.*

tape… It was evening and dark… The moths that were everywhere in the room – with big wingspan, maybe 3-4 inches with body of 1-1,5 inch – were attracted to the tape's lamp… In the middle they were just squashed and they exploded across the tape! Then we carefully cleaned the tape and I think it's actually stored somewhere at Abbey Road!"[374]

At Abbey Road, McCartney refined the recording, overdubbing more acoustic guitars and backing vocals, which featured no less than Ian Bairnson and Dave Paton, Alan Parsons Project's guitar and bass players, who were next door recording the *I, Robot* album.[375]

In the weeks following the recording, McCartney had terrible doubts about the launch of the song on the singles market: the punk wave had been spreading through England and Paul was uncertain about the reception a similar track would obtain.

Therefore, he asked Bob Mercer of EMI for help and advice. Bob had to work hard to convince McCartney of the commercial potential of "Mull of Kintyre", of which Paul "didn't think it would sell a copy."[376] Paul's solution, despite Mercer's favourable opinion, was to not take the risk: the song was launched as double A-side single with "Girl's School".

Paul admitted, putting it in a very naïf way: "I nearly didn't put it out… At that time everything was punk. But I checked it with a lotta young kids and they liked it, so we went on with it." [377]

But England is a country which loves tradition: the majestic Wings' Scottish song, released on November 11th, 1977, went straight to the top of the charts in the UK, where it remained for nine weeks, selling two and a half million copies by the end of January 1978. It became the best-selling single of all time in England, surpassing The Beatles' "She Loves You" (the record will be broken in 1984 by Band Aid's "Do They Know It's Christmas Time?"). Worldwide sales were around ten million copies, although the song reached only #33 in the US. After the single's huge success, the Campbeltown Pipe Band started complaining through local newspapers and claimed that their contribution was essential in creating the song's distinctive sound. Paul then sent them an extra two hundred pounds each.

The big success of the song was undoubtedly due to McCartney's great skill in coming up with "the kind of family favourite that is as seasonal as Christmas pudding in the U.K."[378] McCartney blended Scottish folk, the Christmas atmosphere and an anthem-like structure, making "Mull of Kintyre" a British music classic. Still today, the tune sometimes pops up in British stadiums during football matches. With its slow three quarters beat marked by acoustic guitars, "Mull of Kintyre" is a march to sing around the fire, so suited to English families. Once again, McCartney's ability to effectively paint places in music was rewarded.

---

[374] *Ibid.*
[375] http://eltonjohnallsongslist.blogspot.com/2009/04/please-eltonites-get-up-stand-up-to.html
[376] B. Woffinden, *cit.*, p.184.
[377] K. Badman, *The Beatles After the Breakup, 1970-2000*, 2000, p.217.
[378] B. Woffinden, *cit.*, p.185.

"Mull Of Kintyre" is included in *Wings Greatest*, *All The Best!* and *Wingspan* and was performed live during *Wings' British Tour* in 1979. In the subsequent tours Paul performed the song in some selected concerts, typically in Scotland or Canada and Australia, where large Scottish communities live. The June 30th, 1990 performance in Glasgow appears on the "All My Trials" 12" single: the performance captures the choral essence of the song and all the warmth of the Scottish audience, driven by the energy of a McCartney at his best.

Musicians:

Paul McCartney vocals, backing vocals, acoustic guitar, bass • **Linda McCartney** backing vocals • **Denny Laine** vocals, backing vocals, acoustic guitar • **Joe English** drums • **Ian Bairnson, David Paton** backing vocals • The Campbeltown Pipe Band: **Tony Wilson, Ian McKerral, David McIvor, John Lang Brown, Archie Coffield, John McGeachy, Dougie Lang** bagpipe • **Jimmy McGeachy, David Hastie, Campbell Maloney, Ian Campbell, Tommy Blue, John MacCallum, Ian MacKenzie** drums

During autumn, both Jimmy McCulloch and Joe English left Wings. McCartney boldly commented the guitarist's departure: "It's a pity that Jimmy is leaving, but problems have been building up for quite a while, and we're happy to carry on without him."[379]

McCartney, with Wings down to a trio, completed *London Town* between October 25th and December 1st, recording at Abbey Road four more tracks, including the unreleased "One Woman". Overdubbing included more work on "Waterspout": this track would be intended for release on *All the Best!* in 1987, but was rejected at the last minute: the song's title is listed on the cover of early copies of the album. The famous "Did We Meet Somewhere Before?" belongs to a separate session. The song, written for the soundtrack of *Heaven Can Wait*, the film starring Warren Beatty and Julie Christie, was rejected and replaced by Dave Grusin's score. The song was a dreamy and ethereal ballad: it would have been another sure hit for McCartney. The punk band Ramones took advantage of the situation, including a snippet of the song in the film *Rock'n'Roll High School* (1979): "Did We Meet Somewhere Before" however, was included in the film but not in the official soundtrack. Between December 3rd and 14th, some *London Town* tracks were enhanced with orchestral overdubs.

114 Backwards Traveller (Paul McCartney)

Recording: October 25th-December 1st, 1977 **Location:** Abbey Road Studios, London **Release:** March 1978, "With a Little Luck" single B-side (from *London Town*)

McCartney's habit of recording fragments of songs, which was particularly noticeable in his début album, emerged in *London Town* too.

---

[379] From *New Musical Express*, 07/09/1977.

Sometimes McCartney seems more interested in including too many ideas in his records – perhaps worrying about the stylistic diversity of his songs – rather than developing them properly.

Initially, Paul thought this track as a kind of suite with "Name and Address" – for which it would work as a prologue – inserting it immediately after it.

For this leap into the past Paul completed the lyrics with a reference to the famous traditional Scottish song "Auld Lang Syne". Then McCartney realized that it was not working and changed his mind, using "Backwards Traveller" just as a filler.

"Backwards Traveller" is an example of this "unfinished work syndrome". Paul had written the song just back from the Virgin Islands recording a three-minute demo, but once in the studio he drastically shortened the song.

The released version only lasts 1:09 and it works on *London Town* just as a simple bridge between the acoustic "I'm Carrying" and the instrumental "Cuff Link".

Too bad, as "Backwards Traveller" is an interesting song. It's a nice melodic rocker in a minor key with a powerful vocal performance by McCartney. It would have deserved more studio work: a couple of verses more, maybe a guitar solo and a horn arrangement would have made it a perfect stage-song in "Jet" style.

Paul himself played drums. McCartney: "Joe had left us, so I decided I had better drum myself and I had a bit of fun on this one!"[380]

Musicians:

Paul McCartney vocals, bass, acoustic and electric guitar, synthesizer, drums • **Linda McCartney** backing vocals, keyboards • **Denny Laine** backing vocals, acoustic and electric guitar

115 Cuff Link (Paul McCartney)

Recording: October 25th-December 1st, 1977 **Location:** Abbey Road Studios, London **Release:** March 1978, "With a Little Luck" single B-side (from *London Town*)

Although Paul's boldest experiments with synthesizer would find their dazzling results in 1980 with *McCartney II*, some tracks in *London Town* testify that McCartney's interest in electronic sounds had been alive for some time.

"Cuff Link" is, along with and "I'm Carrying" (see sheet 106) and "With a Little Luck" (see sheet 109), the best example of the avant-garde side of the album, which balances the folk-tinged tracks, that are the true trademark of *London Town*.

Taken from a jam between Paul – who later overdubbed drums – and Denny Laine, it's a short and uninspired instrumental track, completely synth-based.

The result of interweaving *quasi*-prog keyboards, however, it is dull and makes one think that the track was included in the album not having anything else at hand.

---

[380] K. Badman, *The Beatles. The Dream Is Over-Off the Record 2*, 2002, p.223.

Musicians:

Paul McCartney synthesizer, bass (?), drums • **Linda McCartney** keyboards (?) • **Denny Laine** synthesizer, bass (?)

116 Girlfriend (Paul McCartney)

Recording: October 25th-December 1st, 1977 **Location:** Abbey Road Studios, London **Release:** March 1978, *London Town*

If it is true it only takes a spark to get a fire going, "Girlfriend" proves it. Paul could never have imagined what would happen a decade after composing this song: in fact, "Girlfriend" started the McCartney-Michael Jackson saga, with all that their encounter and collaboration entailed, unfortunately for Paul.

Paul wrote "Girlfriend" at the piano in Switzerland probably between 1972 and 1973, as confirmed by some tapes. The song was specially penned for Michael, as clearly shown by the falsetto part by Paul, already present in this demo version.

McCartney: "Linda and I were gone to a place in Switzerland for a bit of skiing. One evening in the hotel I started doing that song and I thought of it as like something one day I might give to the Jackson Five. It's a souly-type track." [381]

In 1975, in fact, Paul had met Jackson at the party held on the Queen Mary to celebrate the release of *Venus and Mars*: there, he played the song to Michael and asked if he wanted to record it, but it failed to materialize. Meanwhile, Paul picked up "Girlfriend" and eventually recorded it for *London Town*.

It's a light and infectious pop song, marked by McCartney's soulful falsetto in perfect Jackson style, some carefully perfected high-pitched vocal harmonies, a gorgeous bass line – full of glissandos and little riffs – a coda with multi-layered melodies and a dramatic instrumental break, a real *coup de foudre* in perfect *Abbey Road* style.

McCartney played everything (nearly) flawlessly (once again, nearly: the drum part, artfully buried in the mix, is pretty rough and seems to fit with his drumming style).

The song was recorded at Abbey Road, relying on better recording conditions than those in the Virgin Islands: so it's strange to hear a bad glitch, exactly at 2:23.

In some parts, the arrangement of the song is reminiscent of "Hangin' On" (1974) by Al Green. Mike Vickers, once member of the British band Manfred Mann – who conducted the orchestra for the live recording of The Beatles' "All You Need Is Love" and worked on "Step Inside Love", the song written by Paul for Cilla Black – arranged the track.

Vickers: "The track was already done except for the vocals. Paul asked me to add an orchestral arrangement. At one point I went to his house in London to hear the track. I worked at home on the arrangement, as I always did. We recorded it at Abbey Road. My part was quite limited,

---

[381] P. Gambaccini, *London Town Interview with Paul McCartney and Denny Laine*, BBC Radio 1, 1978.

'cause Paul did not want to add so much to the song. We had strings – ten or even less players – clarinet players and flutes."[382]

Shortly after the release of *London Town*, Quincy Jones, Jackson's producer, had the opportunity to listen to the song and raced over to Michael: "I've just heard a song that's perfect for you!" Jackson, of course, already knew it: within a few months, the song was recorded and released on his album *Off the Wall* (1979) and later issued as a single.

Jackson's version had moderate success, reaching #41 in the U.S. charts. Even Paul admired his cover, saying it was better than the *London Town* version.

The praise started a chain reaction: Michael called Paul to thank him, then invited him to a session, Paul returned the favour... You all know how it ended. "Girlfriend" is included in the *Wingspan* collection.

Musicians:

Paul McCartney vocals, backing vocals, bass, acoustic and electric guitar, drums, synthesizer, piano (?), electric piano • **Linda McCartney** backing vocals, keyboards • **Denny Laine** backing vocals, acoustic and electric guitar, piano (?) • **Unknown musicians** strings, flutes

[382] Interview courtesy of Mike Vickers, 13/11/2012.

1978

In January, Paul returned to Abbey Road, overdubbing songs for *London Town*. During the same period, McCartney recorded the backing track of "Goodnight Tonight", one of his most famous and successful songs of the Seventies. Soon later, Wings were back to a quintet: Paul replaced Joe English and Jimmy McCulloch with drummer Steve Holley – who previously worked on some solo recordings by Laine – and guitarist Laurence Juber.

117 Goodnight Tonight (Paul McCartney)

Recording: January 4th-23rd, 1978 and January-February, 1979 (overdubs) **Location:** Rude Studio, Campbeltown and MPL Replica Studio (overdubs), London **Release:** March 1979, single

Among McCartney's greatest hits, "Goodnight Tonight" holds a special place: apart from being one of his most famous songs, its release caused a big dispute between McCartney and his label.

In this case, McCartney got the idea of the song after an evening at the disco. Struck by the rhythms and the sound of disco-music – raging at the time from singers like Gloria Gaynor and Diana Ross – Paul immediately ran into the studio.

McCartney began the piece by building the tempo and, with the help of his drum-machine, he laid down a first, simple track of "Goodnight Tonight".

When the *London Town* sessions resumed, Paul decided to work properly on the song, recording a seven-minute take and playing everything.

Then, on February 1979 the track was enhanced with backing vocals, Laurence Juber's flamenco style guitar overdubbing and other minor embellishments. Those sessions gave birth to one of the most original tracks McCartney's imagination has ever produced.

Through a very clever arrangement, McCartney managed to go beyond a simple disco re-interpretation of his style. Rather, he blended several influences into "Goodnight Tonight", with an explosive mixture of sounds and styles, the reason behind the song's success.

To the Latin-flavored acoustic opening, McCartney added a powerful and punchy bass line: with its octave jumps and its deep penetrating beat, it's a great example of how inventiveness is more important than virtuosity.

In itself, "Goodnight Tonight" relies on an catchy pop melody and has McCartney DNA all over the place. Paul's exuberant ideas enrich the song: the instrumentation blends contemporary sounds – drum-machine and vocoder – with typical pop/rock flavors (e.g. the attractive sequence of electric guitar call and response licks).

Laurence Juber recalls how the group worked on McCartney's basic track: "Paul's recording was unfinished, so we did some work on it in January 1979 at Replica Studio in the basement of the MPL Soho office in London. Denny and I did some electric parts echoing Paul's existing lead guitar. I don't remember who suggested the acoustic lead break, but the Spanish flavor was an obvious choice. I didn't have an acoustic guitar with me so I used Denny's Ovation Adamas guitar – it was very quick, a one-take flamenco flourish!"[383]

Steve Holley offered an ingenious contribution: "I had just spent some time in Morocco and brought some clay hand drums back with me. I added those to Paul's drum track and drum-machine percussion. I believe we all sang the chorus as well."[384]

When the record was released, some reviewers held their noses, on the grounds that McCartney had succumbed to the charm of the current fashion; but the single was a success everywhere, reaching #5 both in England and America, where "Goodnight Tonight" was certified gold by the R.I.A.A. for one million copies sold.

At the same time, the song was a source of controversy between McCartney and his record company: the same disagreement occurred two years before with "Mull Of Kintyre" (see sheet **113**). Paul said he did not feel the track fitted with the style of *Back to the Egg* – the album that Wings will be recording in the subsequent months – and he refused to include it in the LP. He put his intellectual rigor before his sense of business. Bob Mercer recalled the argument: "He sent a test pressing to me because apparently there's been considerable discussion among his own associates about whether or not the song would be a hit (…) I'd learned by this time there was no point in being dishonest with him, because he was just going to do what he wanted anyway. So I listened to it and told him I didn't think it was very good (…) I have seen Paul frequently refer to the fact that the guy at the record company had told him that the song wouldn't be a hit and this was Paul's way of demonstrating that you shouldn't listen to record company advice. But I haven't seen him refer anywhere to 'Mull of Kintyre'."[385]

"Goodnight Tonight" was issued on a 12" single in its full version (7:14) and would be shortened for the release on the 7" single, which clocks at 4:23.

The 7" single version appears on *All the Best!* and *Wingspan*. "Goodnight Tonight" was played live in the 1979 *Wings' British Tour*. On September 8th, 2012, McCartney performed the song in London's Granary Square, joining on stage the group Africa Express.

Musicians:

Paul McCartney vocals, backing vocals, bass, tambourine, vocoder, acoustic and electric guitar, synthesizer, drums, percussion • **Linda McCartney** backing vocals • **Denny Laine** backing vocals, electric guitar • **Laurence Juber** backing vocals, acoustic and electric guitar • **Steve Holley** backing vocals, percussion, clay-hand drums

[383] Interview courtesy of Laurence Juber, 18/09/2011.
[384] Interview courtesy of Steve Holly, 19/09/2012.
[385] B. Woffinden, *cit.*, pp.184-185.

On March 22nd it was *London Town*'s turn. The album was launched with a press conference on a boat along River Thames.

Helped by sales of "With a Little Luck", the album was a huge success on the charts (#2 in the US and #4 in UK), despite some critics' remarks about the lacking of rocking and powerful music to the benefit of an acoustic and mellow style.

Janet Maslin of *Rolling Stone* wrote: "*London Town* is so lighthearted that the album's feeling of familial strength and affection is virtually the only thing that binds it to earth. Paul, Linda and Denny Laine flit blithely from fairy tale to fairy tale, with virtually no notion that there's a real world out there, let alone a real audience. Even the best songs here sound as if Wings were only half trying. As the genial effortlessness of *London Town* demonstrates, Paul McCartney has a lot more talent than he knows, or cares, what to do with."

Melody Maker said: "*London Town* is a fine album, with McCartney producing odd flashes of his undoubted genius."

McCartney, with the new Wings line-up in place, returned to the studio in May. Their first recording together was "Same Time, Next Year".

118 Same Time, Next Year (Paul McCartney)

Recording: May 5th and May 6th (overdubs), 1978 **Location:** RAK Studios and Abbey Road Studios (overdubs), London **Release:** January 1990, "Put It There" 12" single

Weeks before sessions for *Back to the Egg* started, Wings went to RAK Studios in London to record "Same Time, Next Year", a song intended for the soundtrack of a movie with the same title, starring Alan Alda and Ellen Burstyn.

McCartney came out with a soft piano ballad, which dealt with the subject of love as a timeless entity, not affected by the time passing by.

The basic track was recorded on May 5th by McCartney (piano), Laine (bass), Steve Holley (drums) and Juber (electric guitar).

Juber recalls about the session: "I played electric guitar, and I don't remember Linda contributing with any instrument."[386] Finishing touches included acoustic guitars and a tambourine.

Steve Holley: "I don't remember any specific instruction from Paul as to what to play. He did have a very complete arrangement, we definitely were not fishing for parts. I did play the tambourine."[387]

Once the basic track was completed, a sumptuous orchestra – following the arrangement of Paul and Fiachra Trench – was overdubbed the next day at Abbey Road Studios.

---

[386] Interview courtesy of Laurence Juber, 12/11/2011.
[387] Interview courtesy of Steve Holley, 19/09/2012.

Fiachra Trench: "Unlike our work on the *Wings at the Speed of Sound* tracks where I was given a free hand, on this occasion Paul handed me his draft of a string arrangement – all written out with the names of each note to be played (because he didn't write or read musical notation) and said, 'Now you go and make it better!'"[388]

A very large orchestra was used. Trench: "For the orchestral overdubs we had 69 strings (18 1st violins, 16 2nd violins, 14 violas, 12 cellos and 9 basses), plus a quartet of clarinets, a quartet of recorders and a cimbalom (a hammered dulcimer, commonly found in Hungary and in the Central-Eastern Europe – author's note). I may have suggested the clarinets and recorders; I'm fairly certain the cimbalom was Paul's idea." [389]

It was not easy to find someone to play such an uncommon instrument: "The player was John Leach" – Trench recalls – "who is a composer as well as a player of the zither, the cimbalom and other ethnic instruments. He was and still is the only such player I know of in England."[390] McCartney had met Leach some time earlier.

Leach: "I played in a session with the Dolmetsch Family for an 'experimental' album (most likely it was for "Uncle Albert/Admiral Halsey" on *Thrillington* – author's note) and also I played on the soundtrack for *Live and Let Die* with George Martin. In this case there was a part already written for my instrument."[391]

Maybe his name was suggested by Laurence Juber, who could have met Leach in 1975 during sessions for Alan Parson's Project album *Tales of Mystery and Imagination: Edgar Allan Poe* for which they both played on the track "Pavane".

As reported on *Club Sandwich* magazine at the time, The Dolmetsch Family played recorders on the track.

The recording of the orchestra was helped by the studio's acoustic, as Trench points: "There was a passage for 12 strings (4 violins, 4 violas, 4 cellos), which we recorded after the main session. I do remember that the recording engineer didn't have to move the microphones closer for a chamber music sound: Abbey Road Studio 1 had (and still has) such a wonderful natural acoustic."[392]

Reportedly, the producers thought that McCartney "gave away too much of the plot" and the song was not used as the film soundtrack. It was replaced by the marvelous Marvin Hamlisch's "The Last Time I Felt Like This". It's easy to see why: the story of the film is about two persons that have a clandestine love affair, as they're both married. They agree to meet just once a year to celebrate their first encounter. It could have been too hard for Paul to convey such sentiments in a song. At the most, it's a tune that could work as a Christmas release.

---

[388] Interview courtesy of Fiachra Trench, 11/10/2012.
[389] *Ibid.*
[390] *Ibid.*
[391] Interview courtesy of John Leach, 28/01/2013.
[392] Interview courtesy of Fiachra Trench, 11/10/2012.

In 1981, the song was remixed for the inclusion in *Hot Hits and Cold Cuts*. Once the project went up in smoke, Paul came back to work on "Same Time, Next Year" at AIR Studios in the summer 1987. He completed some old songs – between them "Waterspout" – for a likely releasing on *All the Best!*

With Chris Thomas producing, Paul added some vocal harmonies to the track, which was left out from this compilation too.

Finally, "Same Time, Next Year" found its place on the B-side of the "Put it There" 12" vinyl single (1990) in the version worked with Thomas.

Musicians:

Paul McCartney vocals, backing vocals, piano, acoustic guitar (?) • **Linda McCartney** backing vocals • **Denny Laine** backing vocals, bass, acoustic guitar (?) • **Laurence Juber** electric guitar • **Steve Holley** drums, tambourine • **John Leach** cimbalom • **Unknown musicians** strings, recorders, clarinets

As usual during the summer period, McCartney lived secluded for a while and put together a large amount of tracks, which he recorded as demo versions, including "Butterflies", "Boil Crisis", "Give Us a Chord, Roy", "Seattle Build Up", "Take Me to the Garden", "S.M.A.", "Cage", "Praying Mantis Heart" and "Rupert Song".

Between June and July, Wings spent a whole month recording at the Spirit of Ranachan Studio – next to McCartney's Scottish estate – that officially started the *Back to the Egg* sessions. Wings taped six tracks, including some of the most hard-rocking numbers of the album. One of them was Laine's "Again and Again and Again", a song about Denny's sentimental situation, which was actually the combination of two separate songs, as Paul suggested.

As it may seem from clips and shots taken during *Back to the Egg* sessions, McCartney used both Rickenbacker and Yamaha bass for the recordings.

The long session on July 5th, is quite another story, one that has a special place when talking about McCartney's recordings.

On that day Wings recorded all of the songs for the soundtrack of the cartoon *Rupert The Bear*, known thanks to an acetate belonging to drummer Steve Holley.

The album *Rupert the Bear*, which mostly included a series of tracks McCartney had written over a decade – linked together by Paul's narration, based on a script he created with Linda – could be considered one of the most interesting unreleased works in McCartney's career.

The imaginative stories of Rupert Bear were interpreted not only through little musical interludes but also through real songs.

This record is perhaps the best example of McCartney's skill in writing music for children. The soundtrack opens and closes with the main theme of the cartoon, "The Rupert Song", a nursery rhyme with twelve-string acoustic guitars featured in two different versions (the second in reggae style), that frames the story Paul wrote about the innocent atmosphere of Rupert's world.

Then, interspersed with light and ethereal instrumental breaks – often short waltzes or child marches, such as "Tippi, Tippi Toes" or "Nutwood Scene" – McCartney offers some unreleased gems of his repertoire. The two acoustic ballads "Sunshine, Sometime" (see sheet 26) and the mysterious "When the Wind Is Blowing" are noteworthy, as well as the fun medley "Sea/Cornish Wafer" and the dreamy gentleness of "Walking In The Meadow".

Finally, Paul inserted scattered fragments in the record, which made sense within the project: the threatening "The Castle of the King of the Birds", a piano piece that McCartney had presented during the *Get Back!* sessions in 1969 and "Sea Melody", a classical-influenced short piano melody which Paul had played for years to his children and reused in the symphony *Standing Stone* (see **1997**).

119 To You (Paul McCartney)

Recording: June 29th, 1978 **Location:** Spirit of Ranachan Studio, Campbeltown **Release:** June 1979, *Back to the Egg*

McCartney started the sessions promisingly with the powerful "To You". Built around the simple opening guitar riff (Paul's Martin D28, as recalled by Juber in his book *Guitar With Wings*), the track is a very tight stomper. "To You" was recorded in a single session, and had a particular treatment for the recording of Laurence Juber's solo. The effect was completed in only twenty minutes, thanks to the synergy between Juber's guitar and the harmonizer Paul was manipulating from the control room: another proof of McCartney's skill in the recording studio, which becomes brilliant when not an end in itself.

McCartney did not spare even one of his vocal cords: "To You" is one of the best songs of *Back to the Egg*. Unexpectedly it was not performed during the 1979 *Wings' British Tour*.

Musicians:

Paul McCartney vocals, bass, acoustic guitar • **Linda McCartney** organ • **Denny Laine** electric guitar • **Laurence Juber** electric guitar • **Steve Holley** drums

120 Arrow Through Me (Paul McCartney)

Recording: June 29th-July, 27th and October-December (overdubs), 1978 **Location:** Spirit of Ranachan Studio, Campbeltown and Abbey Road Studios (overdubs), London **Release:** June 1979, *Back to the Egg*

Always striving for stylistic variety, McCartney did not disdain to venture into the most different musical territories, even within the context of a mainly rock album like *Back to the Egg*. "Arrow Through Me" is actually McCartney's homage to soul music. Almost an update of "With a Little Luck" (see sheet 109), it's a tribute McCartney offers to his idol Stevie Wonder.

The atmosphere of "Arrow Through Me" smells of Wonder's albums like *Fullfillingness First Finale* or *Music of My Mind*: the insistent synthesizer riff is reminiscent of Wonder's distinctive electronic productions. For the recording, Paul came up with an unusual arrangement, replacing stringed instruments with synthesizer and keyboards.

McCartney's Fender Rhodes effectively replaced his bass, as Laurence Juber recalled: "I remember Paul Simon listening to a playback of it and just being wide-eyed at the sound that we got with this."[393]

The recording featured only two musicians. Steve Holley: "The track was recorded one morning with just Paul and I. Piano, guide vocals and drums. I added a second snare drum part, which Chris Thomas suggested, recorded at half speed, which when played back at normal speed creates the percolating percussion effect. I also added a Flexatone (a percussion instrument invented in England in 1922, used at the time by small circus and jazz orchestras. It consists of a small flexible metal sheet suspended in a wire frame ending in a handle – author's note), which can be heard at the beginning of the song and sporadically throughout."[394]

A rough-mix shows "Arrow Through Me" still unpolished: a simple arrangement with just McCartney on electric piano. His vocal performance also included a part in scat-singing style.

The final touch was the addition of a powerful horn section, another soul-derived feature which makes "Arrow Through Me" a song not to miss in *Back to the Egg*.

Chosen as the second single for the US market in August 1979, the song was unsuccessful, reaching only a disappointing #27 on the charts.

"Arrow Through Me" was played on the 1979 *Wings' British Tour*. As can be heard in the Glasgow concert recording, this difficult track was performed flawlessly. The song was covered by Richie Havens, who included it in his album *Simple Things* (1987).

Musicians:

Paul McCartney vocals, electric piano, synthesizer • **Steve Holley** drums, Flexatone • **Thaddeus Richard, Tony Dorsey, Howie Casey, Steve Howard** horns

121 Old Siam, Sir (Paul McCartney)

Recording: June 29th-July 27th and October (overdubs), 1978 **Location:** Spirit of Ranachan Studio, Campbeltown and Abbey Road Studios (overdubs), London **Release:** June 1979, single (from *Back to the Egg*)

When *Back To The Egg* was released, Paul immediately bet on "Old Siam, Sir". And it was a good move: it was one of the most powerful rockers McCartney had written lately and could perfectly represent the beginning of a new course.

---

[393] I. Peel, *cit.*, p.100.
[394] Interview courtesy of Steve Holley, 19/09/2012.

"Old Siam, Sir" started in 1976. Wings had recorded a demo, called "Super Big Heatwave": simply based on the guitar riff and on the melody written by Linda on keyboards, it was still a kind of odd experiment.

The song was a group effort, even though uncredited. Juber: "We'd be jamming along and then all of a sudden a song would come out. 'Old Siam, Sir' was from a jam session: Steve was playing piano, Linda drums, Paul guitar and Denny bass."[395]

During the recording, the song was completely transformed and only the intro part was retained: Paul recorded his powerful, raw and raging vocals and the group added a middle section filled with a guitar riff, based on a chord sequence by Holley.

In his book, *Guitar With Wings* Juber recalls: "Paul and I doubled up the guitar riff. It was not unusual to find him wielding his Epiphone Casino, as he did on this track, with a dark, growling tone. I played a Les Paul custom, adding a brighter harmony part."

An almost heavy-metal riff is the distinctive mark of the track. Released as a single for the UK market, it wasn't very successful: "Old Siam, Sir" was a disaster and reached only #35 in the charts, the worst result up to that time for McCartney among his lead singles. The song was one of the most powerful numbers in the 1979 *Wings' British Tour.*[396]

Musicians:

Paul McCartney vocals, bass, electric guitar • **Linda McCartney** keyboards • **Denny Laine** electric guitar **Laurence Juber** • electric guitar • **Steve Holley** drums

122 Winter Rose (Paul McCartney)

Recording: July 12th-17th, 1978 **Location:** Spirit of Ranachan Studio, Campbeltown **Release:** June 1979, *Back to the Egg*

"Winter Rose" was a delicate song that Wings recorded with the utmost care: a beautiful backdrop of acoustic guitars, piano and harpsichord were chosen for an arrangement which evokes snow-covered landscapes.

Laurence Juber: "I played the picked arpeggio parts on an Ovation nylon-strung classical recorded direct in stereo. Paul played bass – it sounds like the Rickenbacker. I don't remember doing any overdubs, but it's possible I played some electric too."[397]

But for some reason Paul was not completely satisfied. So he resorted to his tried and tested medley format: when McCartney chose the sequence of songs to include in *Back to the Egg*, he linked it to "Love Awake" (see sheet 128). And actually his idea fits well with this fascinating soft song: the spring awakening atmosphere of "Love Awake" is the perfect counterbalance to the lethargy and the slow paced winter depicted in "Winter Rose".

Musicians:

[395] S. Leigh, *cit.*, p.23.
[396] As witnessed by some concerts' recordings (Glasgow, 17/12/79, Hammersmith Odeon, 29/12/79).
[397] Interview courtesy of Laurence Juber, 18/09/2011.

Paul McCartney vocals, bass, piano, harpsichord (?) • **Linda McCartney** backing vocals, keyboards • **Denny Laine** backing vocals, acoustic guitar (?) • **Laurence Juber** acoustic guitar, electric guitar (?) • **Steve Holley** drums, percussion

123 Spin it On (Paul McCartney)

Recording: July 23rd, 1978 **Location:** Spirit of Ranachan Studio, Campbeltown **Release:** June 1979, "Old Siam, Sir" single B-side (from *Back to the Egg*)

The impact of new-wave on the British public opinion encouraged McCartney to explore new musical styles; in an attempt to give Wings new energy, in some cases Paul drew directly from punk as a source of inspiration. The fast-tempo "Spin it On" was born from an original idea.

Steve Holley: "I remember Paul walking in one morning with the idea, and it just exploded. It was a simple part, just two notes, like a police siren."[398] A closer listening reveals a resemblance to The Stooges' track "I Feel Allright" (1970).

McCartney embellished his dizzying punk hymn with lines suggesting sex, in a relentlessly vocal performance. The track was completed with Juber's swirling guitar solos and Steve Holley's tumbling waterfalls of toms. Holley: "I did one live performance and two drum overdubs. I had a pile of toms on one stand with a snare drum, and I hit that every now and again, which gave it a great back drive."[399]

The song is one of the wildest rockers McCartney ever produced. It was included in the 1979 *Wings' British Tour*: during the breathtaking performances the audience was invited to "pogo". The track is on *Back to the Egg*. It was sometimes played in soundchecks in 1990.

Musicians:

Paul McCartney vocals, bass • **Linda McCartney** keyboards • **Denny Laine** electric guitar • **Laurence Juber** electric guitar • **Steve Holley** drums

In September, Wings rent the Medieval Lympne Castle in Kent to carry on with the *Back to the Egg* sessions. Seven tracks were recorded in this manor: one of them, "Cage", is still unreleased.

124 Reception (Paul McCartney)

Recording: September 11th-29th, 1978 **Location:** Lympne Castle **Release:** June 1979, *Back to the Egg*

At Lympne Castle, Wings went in for some recordings with an unusual atmosphere. The band settled in the large hall of the castle – with Steve Holley's drums placed near the fireplace! – and began the recordings relying on the RAK Mobile Studio.

Presumably born during rehearsals, "Reception" was a powerful rocking track that Wings recorded live in the studio: an instrumental led by an insistent bass line.

---

[398] S. Leigh, *cit.*, p.23.
[399] *Ibid.*

Later, Paul got the idea to use the song's groove for a special *ouverture*: he decided for a sort of introduction on the album, and then tune into the first real song just as you do when you change the radio station. He put together pieces of radio broadcasts, among which *The Lutheran Hour*, a Norwegian program on Norea Radio hosted by the announcer Ølivind Andersen. In the end, "Reception" was chosen as the opening song of *Back to the Egg* in a drastically shortened version compared to the rough mix. An eccentric opening which drew much criticism for the album.

Musicians:

Paul McCartney bass, electric guitar (?) • **Linda McCartney** keyboards • **Denny Laine** electric guitar • **Laurence Juber** electric guitar • **Steve Holley** drums

125 We're Open Tonight (Paul McCartney)

Recording: September 11th-29th, 1978 **Location:** Lympne Castle **Release:** June 1979, *Back to the Egg*

While *Back to the Egg* was being assembled, "We're Open Tonight" was considered as the album's title. "We're Open Tonight" was a delicate acoustic song originally intended to serve as an introduction to the whole record. Based on a simple arpeggio, the track has a similar feel to "Venus and Mars", with its lullaby-song atmosphere and its percussive effects.

Steve Holley was the one who created that particular sound: "What you are hearing are Remo Roto-Toms" – says Holley – "I had acquired them a year or so earlier and thought the sound would be interesting."[400]

That recording was another oddity of those sessions. Juber: "My 12-string acoustic guitar part was actually recorded in the spiral staircase using natural echo."[401]

Juber again: "I took the guitar out of its case and it wasn't tuned properly – the individual pair of strings, instead of being tuned in unison or in octave, were actually tuned in different intervals. I didn't mess with it, I just started playing and it fitted perfectly."[402]

McCartney's suggestive lyrics maybe went unnoticed, but the reference to the brothels' typical invitations (a hint to the Hamburg days?) seems clear.

Before changing his mind, McCartney cherished the idea of a concept-album for *Back to the Egg*. For this purpose Wings recorded a reprise of "We're Open Tonight" which was placed after "So Glad to See You Here", with a similar effect to the one used in *Band on the Run*.[403]

Musicians:

Paul McCartney vocals, backing vocals, acoustic guitar, bass (?) • **Linda McCartney** backing vocals, dingers (?) • **Denny Laine** backing vocals, electric guitar (?), bass (?) • **Laurence Juber** electric guitar, 12-string acoustic guitar • **Steve Holley** percussion

---

[400] Interview courtesy of Steve Holley, 19/09/2012.
[401] Gillian G.Gaar, *cit.*, p.19.
[402] I. Peel, *cit.*, p. 97.
[403] "So Glad to See You Here" was the closing number to the album's rough-mix.

126 After the Ball (Paul McCartney)

Recording: September 11th-29th, 1978 **Location:** Lympne Castle **Release:** June 1979, *Back to the Egg*

It may have been the strange setting of the Lympne Castle that provided inspiration for "After the Ball" to McCartney. It was an evocative three-quarters piano ballad, with a medieval feeling to it, still another twist in Paul's discography.

It could be a tribute to the well-known song "After the Ball", written by American composer Charles K. Harris in 1891, whose sheet music sold in excess of five million copies, making it the most successful Tin Pan Alley song.

On the recording, McCartney's rasping vocals were drenched in reverb: making it sound like the love affair is set in a ballroom that recalls the medieval courtly literature.

To make it work, the song was linked to "Million Miles": Laurence Juber mixed the guitar parts that himself, Paul and Denny had recorded for this other medley included in *Back to the Egg*.

Musicians:

Paul McCartney vocals, piano, bass, electric guitar • **Linda McCartney** backing vocals, organ, tambourine (?) • **Denny Laine** electric guitar • **Laurence Juber** acoustic and electric guitar • **Steve Holley** drums, tambourine (?)

127 Million Miles (Paul McCartney)

Recording: September 11th-29th, 1978 **Location:** Lympne Castle **Release:** June 1979, *Back to the Egg*

McCartney wrote "Million Miles" at least as early as 1973 at the piano, as heard in his home demo. At Lympne Castle, the song became one of his most characteristic recordings. For the occasion, Paul recorded "Million Miles" on a balcony of the fortress, with its wonderful view on the English Channel, and played the concertina, a sort of mini-accordion.[404] McCartney's heart-felt vocal performance blends the feelings of suffering and hope of the believer straining towards his communion with God.

A short track, included in *Back to the Egg*, which reveals an unusual McCartney, acting as a pilgrim-minstrel, while praying the Lord to find the strength to reach the holy place.

Musicians:

Paul McCartney vocals, concertina

128 Love Awake (Paul McCartney)

Recording: September 11th-29th, 1978 and April 1st, 1979 (overdubs) **Location:** Lympne Castle and Abbey Road Studios (overdubs), London **Release:** June 1979, *Back to the Egg*

During these sessions Paul decided to work on a remake of "Love Awake", a song he had demoed in 1976 and already recorded in the previous summer in Scotland.

---

[404] A picture of McCartney while recording the track has surfaced on Juber's book, *Guitar With Wings*.

A comparison between the two versions shows significant differences. The original version was simple and kept the acoustic nature of the piece: the early take of "Love Awake", lasting more than five minutes, was opened only by McCartney and his acoustic guitar. Then the song was enriched by the band instrumentation and Denny Laine's harmonica gave it a genuine country touch. Then McCartney completely changed his mind about the arrangement of "Love Awake".

Thus, it became a more elaborate track, with a pompous brass arrangement that McCartney entrusted to the Black Dyke Mills Band, an idea he had held since the Beatles period: he had written "Thingumybob" for them – the song was also recorded by Paul in a different version, called "Etcetera", still unreleased – which in 1968 was one of the first four singles of the newborn Apple Corps.[405]

Laurence Juber: "I was playing bass when we did (the first version) and when we came to the final take, I was expecting Paul to do it, but he said, 'I like what you did on the demo, so why don't you do it?' He knelt on the floor and he gave a lesson in playing bass, so I adopted his technique and played his part under his direction."[406]

It's one of McCartney's brightest and most hopeful songs: the radiant atmosphere of "Love Awake" would have stood out with a bare arrangement.

On *Back to the Egg*, the song was linked to "Winter Rose" and perfected with Juber's acoustic guitar embellishments and a brass section, overdubbed in a separate session at Abbey Road, seven months later on April 1st, 1979.

McCartney assigned Martyn Ford, a famous English orchestra conductor – whose orchestra, created in 1971, quickly became one of Britain's best-known and which played on the *Live and Let Die* movie soundtrack – to the brass arrangement.

Ford: "It was a strange job. Paul rang me up two days before the session… He said, 'I have booked the Black Dyke Mills Band, can you write some music for them?' They are the most famous brass band in the world, and to be asked to conduct them was an extraordinary privilege but very odd because brass bands are completely different from orchestras! I have had never written for brass bands before! I had to do some homework very quickly to find out what the instrumentation was… It was very challenging… If I was given the job now, I'd write much better music!"[407]

---

[405] Geoffrey Brand, the band's conductor at the time, remembers when McCartney called him to work on "Thingumybob": "I do vividly recall I received a telephone call from Paul McCartney to me, wishing to talk about a new programme to be shortly launched on *London Television Weekend*, called *Thingumybob*, with the comedian Stanley Holloway, who played Bob, the main character. The next day I went to see him in a large office in Mayfair…Paul grabbed a guitar and sang me the tune…and I said 'Ok, sing it more'. He said 'Oh no, that's it!'". Interview courtesy of Geoffrey Brand, 07/09/2012.

[406] S. Leigh, *cit.*, p.24.

[407] Interview courtesy of Martyn Ford, 29/10/2011.

At Abbey Road Studio Two, everything turned out for the best anyway. Ford reveals: "It was an easy session, 2-3 hours... Paul seemed to like it. We did an overdub also for the song 'Winter Rose'. Black Dyke Mills Band so enjoyed working with Paul that they invited me to arrange and to conduct a full album of McCartney and Wings songs by them... I think it's awful, but it's the best-selling album Black Dyke ever had!"[408]

David Pogson, who played flugelhorn, remembers that the session went through some issue: "We performed a concert in North Wales on the Saturday night and traveled down to London, staying in an hotel overnight. On the Sunday morning (and April 1st of that year was actually on Sunday – author's note) we went to the Abbey Road Studios for the recording where we were met by Linda and Paul. Quite a few adjustments to the arrangement were made during the recording session, Paul being such a perfectionist... And the recording lasted most of the day!"[409]

"Love Awake" is a bright manifesto of McCartney's beliefs, with his unspoilt trust in love's power of renewal and in its recurring. Love is a synonym for the McCartney "do it now" philosophy and leaves no room for regrets: love always comes out at the end, as an incredible force.

Something few people know: a reggae version of "Love Awake" was played during the *Back to the Egg* launch party held at Abbey Road Studio Two on June 11th, 1979.

Musicians:

Paul McCartney vocals, backing vocals, acoustic guitar • **Linda McCartney** backing vocals, keyboards • **Denny Laine** backing vocals, acoustic guitar • **Laurence Juber** bass, acoustic guitar • **Steve Holley** drums, percussion • The Black Dyke Mills Band: **David Hirst** soprano cornet • **David Pogson** flugelhorn • **Neil Jowett, Fred Ellis, Christopher Bacon, Peter Moorcroft, Jack Brooke, Phillip McCann, Ken Macdonald, Malcolm Turton, David Carter** cornet • **John Clough, Stuart Derrick, John Slinger, Brian Broadbent** euphonium, baritone • **Kevin Wadsworth, David Essex, Stephen Brooke** tenor horn • **Frank Berry, Dennis Essex, Ian Copeland** trombone • **George Morgan, Alan Holdsworth, Derek Jackson** bass • **Philip Gee, Richard Clough** percussion

129 The Broadcast (Paul McCartney)

Recording: September 11th-29th, 1978 **Location:** Lympne Castle **Release:** June 1979, *Back to the Egg*

To put McCartney in the Lympne Castle was, in a sense, like opening up Pandora's box: the result was the flourishing of the most eccentric ideas Paul ever produced.

"The Broadcast" was inspired by the medieval castle's atmosphere: McCartney added the voice of the castle's owner, Mr. Margary, to a classic piano background, with excerpts from ancient readings from his library, *The Sport of Kings* by Ian Hay and *The Little Man* by John Galsworthy. Margary's reading was recorded in the kitchen of the castle.

---

[408] *Ibid.* The brass contribution on "Winter Rose" was not used.
[409] Interview courtesy of David Pogson, 20/09/2012.

The pleasant piano arpeggio (David Bowie chose the song as his favorite, suggesting even to release it as a single!) is full of effects obtained with Mellotron and Paul's Gitzmotron applied to his Telecaster, according to some Robert Ellis photos shot during the sessions. "The Broadcast" is on *Back to the Egg*.

Musicians:

Paul McCartney piano, Mellotron, electric guitar (with Gizmo) • **Diedre Margary** narration

October 3rd was an intense day of recording at Abbey Road, where Paul summoned a crowd of musicians, chosen among the best of the British rock scene, to bring to life his old idea...

130 Rockestra Theme (Paul McCartney)

Recording: October 3rd-4th, 1978 **Location:** Abbey Road Studios, London **Release:** June 1979, *Back to the Egg*

The idea of forming a rock super-group was a project McCartney had been thinking of for a long time. *Back to the Egg*, Paul's return to rock'n'roll musical primitivism, seemed a perfect stage to make it happen. Paul wrote this song starting from a simple melody that he had written on the piano several years before: a sneaky home recording shows McCartney dealing with a still incomplete song. McCartney decided to bring together the best of the heavy-rock musicians of the Seventies to accompany Wings: the song would be rightly rewarded with the much sought-after Grammy Award in the category Best Instrumental Track of the Year 1979.

Wings had recorded a demo of "Rockestra Theme" and brought it to Abbey Road for the epic session that was held there on October 3rd, 1978. The recording featured musicians such as Pete Townshend, David Gilmour, John Bonham, John Paul Jones, Gary Brooker, Hank Marvin and Ray Cooper.

Holley remembers how the track was built: "We'd been experimenting in Lympne Castle with an EMI 24-track tape and did the song once. Then we did it again and double-tracked ourselves, and then did it a third time. It was a monstrous rock'n'roll orchestra effect, and Paul thought it would be fun to do something in a studio with all these great people."[410]

Extraordinary unreleased footage – only a few minutes has been released in 2001 on the *Wingspan* DVD – lets us follow the super-band throughout the different steps.

Playing piano, McCartney explained his idea to the musicians, accepting their suggestions: in particular, after trying different endings, Paul opted for Townshend's solution.

Steve Holley: "It was daunting. For my part, I'm sitting between John Bonham and Kenney Jones! I basically let them do all the work, sat down, and enjoyed the ride."[411]

---

[410] S. Leigh, *cit.*, p.24.
[411] Interview courtesy of Steve Holley, 19/09/2012.

Bruce Thomas: "I told McCartney, 'I should be paying you royalties-all the stuff I've stolen from you.' He said, 'I've nicked a couple of things from you, too,' and picked up his bass and started playing 'Chelsea.'"[412] The result was a majestic rocker with a granitic sound.

Performed during the Concert for Kampuchea on December 29th, 1979, this version appears on the concert's double LP. The track is on *Back to the Egg* and had been included in *Wingspan*.

Musicians:

Paul McCartney vocals, bass, piano • **Linda McCartney** backing vocals, keyboards • **Denny Laine, Laurence Juber, David Gilmour, Hank Marvin, Pete Townshend** electric guitar • **Steve Holley, John Bonham, Kenney Jones** drums • **John Paul Jones** bass, piano • **Ronnie Lane, Bruce Thomas** bass • **Tony Ashton** keyboards • **Gary Brooker** piano • **Speedy Acquaye, Tony Carr, Ray Cooper, Morris Pert** percussion • **Howie Casey, Tony Dorsey, Steve Howard, Thaddeus Richard** horns

131 So Glad to See You Here (Paul McCartney)

Recording: October 3rd-4th, 1978 and January-February, 1979 (overdubs) **Location:** Abbey Road Studios and Replica Studios (overdubs), London **Release:** June 1979, *Back to the Egg*

The second song that McCartney presented during this session was also conceived on piano. The "Rockestra" sessions clip again shows Paul playing the track on the keyboard. After McCartney's demonstration, the band began recording the basic track: the monumental arrangement, with its energetic chords, make "So Glad To See You Here" an aggressive song, also thanks to Paul's stunning vocal performance, overdubbed the following day.

The song was initially intended to be the closing number of *Back to the Egg*. Wings also added a reggae-style reprise of "We're Open Tonight" that was recorded during the 1979 January-February overdub sessions.

Issued on *Back to the Egg*, the song also drew attention for its lyrics, with explicit references to how to prepare special cigarettes, then a daily ritual of McCartney and his entourage.

Musicians:

Paul McCartney vocals, bass, piano • **Linda McCartney** backing vocals, keyboards • **Denny Laine, Laurence Juber, David Gilmour, Hank Marvin, Pete Townshend** electric guitar • **Steve Holley, John Bonham, Kenney Jones** drums • **John Paul Jones** bass, piano • **Ronnie Lane, Bruce Thomas** bass • **Tony Ashton** keyboards • **Gary Brooker** piano • **Speedy Acquaye, Tony Carr, Ray Cooper, Morris Pert** percussion • **Howie Casey, Tony Dorsey, Steve Howard, Thaddeus Richard** horns

The last batch of recordings for *Back to the Egg* took place around mid-October at Abbey Road Studio Two, where Wings cut two tracks.

---

[412] Dan Forte, *Bruce Thomas Pumps It Up with Elvis Costello*, in *Guitar Magazine*, March 1987.

132 Getting Closer (Paul McCartney)

Recording: October, 1978 and March, 1979 (overdubs) **Location:** Abbey Road Studios, London
Release: June 1979, *Back to the Egg*

McCartney had written "Getting Closer" probably around 1972-73 (Paul played it during his visit to Hoffman's house in Jamaica, see sheet **72**): on his rough piano demo we could recognize the melody and some of the lyrics used later. At Abbey Road, Wings recorded this tough song, originally a Laine-McCartney duet, as shown in a rough-mix.

Paul changed his mind at the last moment and during the following March sessions modified the song: McCartney re-recorded the vocals removing Denny's part, added some overdubs and chose a fade-out instead of the original full ending.

Paul's great vocal performance supports this fast pop/rock, which features a powerful coda, with a majestic riff played in unison by electric guitars and Mellotron.

Laurence Juber: "Paul drove me to be inventive. But where it didn't work, where I was hopeful to get some of that in was the whole end section of 'Getting Closer'. I actually spent the weekend – I had a cassette of the track – I played through every possible kind of cool permutation of bluesy licks, just to be ready to do it. And we walked in and we did it for a while, and Paul said, 'Y' know, what I really want for this is… I want to compose something.' So he came out with that whole riff which was appropriate."[413]

An unusual technique was used for this track, where, "the guitar strings were hit with a drum stick instead of a plectrum to achieve the right sound."[414]

One of the catchiest songs in *Back to the Egg*, "Getting Closer" was the first US single from the album and got better results than the others 45 extracted from the LP, even though reaching #20 on the *Billboard* chart meant a big step backwards if compared to the resounding success of "Goodnight Tonight". As regards the lyrics, "Getting Closer" was surprisingly explicit, with verses describing the technique of "making a joint".

Maybe the less restrictive atmosphere of recent times prevented the song from being censored in Great Britain, when "Getting Closer" was released there as a single.

Or it was simply due to the fact that almost nobody listened to the song, which only reached #60 on the charts. It was among the most liked tracks during the 1979 *Wings' British Tour*.

Interviewed at the 54th Grammy Award MusiCares (2012), Elvis Costello chose "Getting Closer" as one of his favorite Wings' tracks.

Musicians:

Paul McCartney vocals, backing vocals, bass, Mellotron, electric guitar • **Linda McCartney** backing vocals, keyboards • **Denny Laine** backing vocals, electric guitar • **Laurence Juber** electric guitar • **Steve Holley** drums

---

[413] H. Edelson, *Q&A with Laurence Juber: Memories of Recording Last Wings Album*, in *Beatlefan*, n. 189, pp.24-25.
[414] www.paulmccartney.com

133 Baby's Request (Paul McCartney)

Recording: October, 1978 **Location:** Abbey Road Studios, London **Release:** June 1979, *Back to the Egg*

"Baby's Request", another one of Paul's frequent homages to jazz and music hall, was released almost by accident. McCartney wrote the song during the summer. Paul was in the South of France and grasped the opportunity to hop over for a show by the Mills Brothers.[415]

McCartney: "I went to see them backstage and one of them said, 'Hey Paul how's about writing us a song?' So I went back to the hotel and spent the next day writing a song for them."[416]

When the band refused to record the song without being paid for it, McCartney released his own version. Initially, the piece was excluded from the track-list of *Back to the Egg*, preferring "Cage" to it. But at the very last minute, "Cage" was dropped, as it's rumored that Paul was not satisfied with the results.

Thus McCartney decided upon this ballad: an enjoyable 1940s-style number, enhanced by some guitar glissando and a trombone created by McCartney with the use of a synthesizer.

Laurence Juber: "We needed a trombone sound. Don Lusher, who is the greatest trombone player ever, was next door. But Paul said, 'I've got this new synthesizer and I'd rather do it myself.' He preferred the challenge."[417]

The song was recorded at the well-known Abbey Road Studio Two, as Laurence Juber confirms: "It was recorded as a demo for the Mills Brothers, but they didn't end up recording it, so we kept it as a Wings track. I remember everything, except for the Moog solo, being played at once: Paul on stand-up bass, Denny on piano and Steve on drums. I played an old Gibson ES 335, I don't remember the amplifier I used it might have been a Hiwatt – not an obvious choice for a jazz sound, but suitably clean."[418]

Steve Holley: "Since the song was recorded as a demo rather than a contender for the album, therefore the session was perhaps a little more relaxed. I played brushes on a timbale (single headed drums invented in Cuba – author's note) instead of a snare drum because it had a new coated head that sounded crisp."[419]

A little gem with alluring images and the old times atmosphere of a small night club, which was issued also as a 45, unfortunately with embarrassing results: in the UK the song was promoted as a double A-side with "Getting Closer" and reached only #60 on the charts.

---

[415] American vocal group originally composed of four brothers, that started to record during the Twenties. Before their show announcers commonly explained to listeners that the only instrument was a guitar, as the vocal effects made many listeners think they were hearing a muted trumpet, saxophone, and string bass or tuba.
[416] K. Badman, *cit.*, p.247.
[417] S. Leigh, *cit.*, p.23.
[418] Interview courtesy of Laurence Juber, 18/09/2011.
[419] Interview courtesy of Steve Holley, 19/09/2012.

George Harrison, who in April 1979 visited McCartney in the studio[420] – probably Paul had him listen to *Back to the Egg* as it was being finished up – fell in love with this song: "He likes mellow stuff"[421], Paul said.

The song was supposed to be included in the 1980 *Wings' Japanese Tour*. Paul didn't like the idea, but he had decided to include it to make his little son James happy.

McCartney re-recorded the song in 2011, including it as a bonus-track in the *Kisses on the Bottom* Deluxe Edition.

Musicians:

Paul McCartney vocals, vocal harmonies, double-bass, Moog • **Linda McCartney** backing vocals • **Denny Laine** backing vocals, piano • **Laurence Juber** electric guitar • **Steve Holley** brushes

The year ended with the release of *Wings Greatest*. Weakened by a sloppy selection of hits, the record was only partially successful: #5 in the UK and #29 in the US, where it interrupted a string of nine consecutive McCartney albums reaching Top Ten.

[420] Mick Brown, *An Interview with George Harrison*, in *Rolling Stone*, 19/04/1979.
[421] Chip Madinger-Mark Easter, *Eight Arms to Hold You*, 2000, p.245.

1979

After the Christmas break, Paul discovered that Abbey Road Studio Two had been booked by Cliff Richard for many months. So he decided to have an exact copy of the legendary studio built in record time at MPL's headquarters in Soho Square, London.

134 Daytime Nighttime Suffering (Paul McCartney)

Recording: January-February, 1979 **Location:** MPL Replica Studio, London **Release:** March 1979, "Goodnight Tonight" single B-side

Over the decades, one of the harshest criticism directed towards McCartney concerned his alleged tyrannical behaviour towards his collaborators.

Going back in time, Paul had been accused of firing, in order: Stuart Sutcliffe (ineffective), Pete Best (too handsome), Ringo Starr (during the *White Album* sessions) and George Harrison (during the *Get Back!* sessions, he tried to teach him how to play the riff of "I've Got a Feelin'").

An ego problem that occurred even more with Wings: McCartney's band has been considered by many only a relief valve for his creativity, where he would impose his songs and his arrangements, without scruples, limiting contribution of the band members. It resulted in rather complicated and frustrating interpersonal relationships.

During the Seventies, music critics have therefore seen McCartney as a sort of musical despot, contemptuous of any rule: paraphrasing the rules of politics, one might say that he did not bother to agree with the Parliament (the band), because he himself set the laws and passed them (he wrote all the songs and decided to record them). At best, some amendments were allowed (a song by Denny Laine occasionally).

"Daytime Nighttime Suffering" is a prime example of how, sometimes Paul was able to stimulate competition and creativity within Wings.

Steve Holley recalled the episode that occurred in January 1979, while the band was still recording *Back to the Egg*. Wings were working hard trying to come up with a new single, when suddenly Paul said that the band would record – for release on the B-side – the best song any of them could write over the weekend.

So, Holley on his old piano, Laine, Juber and even Linda, all worked hard to write the winning song. On Monday, back at the studio, McCartney put an end to the competition offering "Daytime Nighttime Suffering".

For the recording, McCartney's attitude immediately became less easy going as Laurence Juber confirmed: "They weren't too many times when Paul gave me specific things to play. There's a little guitar lick on 'Daytime…' that he had me because he wrote the song with that lick. But most of the time I was free to do my own thing."[422]

One of McCartney's most significant but underestimated songs as a solo artist, "Daytime Nighttime Suffering" was a melodic rocker, recorded in a few takes live in the studio[423], with a very basic arrangement: sharp electric guitars (in the same *Back to the Egg* vein), a great walking bass part – probably played by McCartney on hih Yamaha according to some photographs of the sessions – and a strong vocal performance by Paul. The message of the song is an ode to the strength of women who can withstand all the abuses: McCartney seems sincere as never before, especially in the middle-eight in C minor.

It's a forceful feminist protest, "a pro-women song", in McCartney's words. He compares woman's strength to that of water: she can redeem herself from suffering, outgrowing her age of illusions and childhood. On this occasion, McCartney proves to be a good lyricist. "Daytime Nighttime Suffering" is a memorable song filled with many pop tricks at which McCartney is a master: the multi-layered vocal harmonies – with Paul's vocal bass part – introducing the three explosive final choruses[424] are a prime example of Paul's unequalled skills as a pop producer.

McCartney chose it as his favourite solo song, but unfortunately he has never been able to give it its proper importance.

In fact, the song was left out of *Back to the Egg* and only used as the B-side to the single "Goodnight Tonight" in May 1979. In 2001, "Daytime Nighttime Suffering" was deservedly included in the *Wingspan* collection.

Musicians:

Paul McCartney vocals, backing vocals, bass, synthesizer (?), tambourine (?) • **Linda McCartney** backing vocals, organ, autoharp (?) • **Denny Laine** backing vocals, electric guitar • **Laurence Juber** electric guitar • **Steve Holley** drums, tambourine (?)

Between May and June Wings went back to Lympne Castle to shoot some promos for the forthcoming *Back to the Egg*. There was also time to record something original, the unreleased "Robber's Ball", an operetta-style track, later considered for inclusion in *Cold Cuts*. *Back to the Egg* was released in June, but, despite McCartney's efforts to give Wings a harsher sound, both critics and audience gave the album a lukewarm reception: in America it only hit #8 (but got a platinum disk for a million copies sold), while in the UK it reached #6, quickly slipping down afterwards. With his typical humour, McCartney gave titles to both sides of the album: "Sunny Side Up" – which was also the title of a famous 1929 musical with Charles Farrell – and "Over Easy", the two most popular ways of cooking eggs.

---

[422] Gillian G.Gaar, *cit.*, p.19.
[423] A small detail proves it: the brief but clear crying of a child (James, a year and four months old at the time) in the break at 2:04.
[424] It's the same structure McCartney used in "Once Upon a Long Ago…"

Rolling Stone was not amused and savaged it: "It is just about the sorriest grab bag of dreck in recent memory. Paul McCartney has been plagiarizing his own material for years now, and he's finally run out of recycled ideas." McCartney didn't worry about it too much: in the seclusion of his farm and his Scottish retreat, he planned to spend much of the summer recording something unusual.

Over a period of six weeks between June and July, McCartney recorded nineteen songs, working alone, as he had done ten years before for the *McCartney* album.

The recordings were inspired by the idea of experimenting a bit with synthesizers sounds, but not to create anything for an audience: "I wasn't trying to do an album. It was just for my own satisfaction. But in the end I got a few tracks and I played it to a couple of people and they said, 'Oh, I see, that's your next album.' So then I got a bit serious on it, trying to make it into an album", Paul said.

McCartney was very keen on using synthesizers at the time: "Synthesizers are amazing things. Instead of spending hours scoring strings sections, you can just sit down at this machine a get a very similar sound immediately."[425]

As seen in some of photos of the *McCartney II* sessions, synthesizers and keyboards played by McCartney included Roland Jupiter 4, Mellotron, Mini Moog, Yamaha CS80 and ARP Pro-Soloist, while Paul played both Yamaha and Fender Jazz bass.

Every day McCartney would start creating a song by simply recording a drum track (or in some cases using his rhythm box) and overdubbing instruments on it: at the end of the day, he would decide whether to keep it or erase it all.

Eddie Klein was the engineer on the recordings. He recalls: "One day I received a call asking me to meet up with Paul to discuss a recording project he had in mind. Paul explained to me that he wanted to do some recordings in the same way he'd done with the *McCartney* album. This entailed simply plugging the microphones into the tape machine inputs and completely bypassing the recording console (...) I don't know of anyone else who has recorded in this way, it seemed so basic and pioneering but the very idea appealed to me. I went away thinking that all I needed to do was to supply a Studer A80 16-track machine with an assortment of microphones and that would be it (...) Delivering the equipment and setting it up for recording was all that was required of me. In fact, I rarely saw Paul. He truly recorded anything on his own."[426]

McCartney recorded a full eighty minutes of music into his sixteen track machine, including five tracks that were not released at the time, but finally would be issued in the 2011 edition of *McCartney II*, part of the "Paul McCartney Archive Collection": "Mr. H Atom", "Bogey

---

[425] *The McCartney Interview. Paul Gambaccini Talks with Paul McCartney About McCartney II*, 1980.
[426] *McCartney II Deluxe Edition*, in *Paul McCartney Archive Collection*, 2011, pp.34-36.

Wobble", "Blue Sway", "All You Horseriders" and "You Know I'll Get You Babe". Judging from the four numbered tape boxes seen in the book accompanying the 2011 version of *McCartney II*, the songs were recorded in the order below.

135 Front Parlour (Paul McCartney)

Recording: June-July, 1979 **Location:** Home Studio, Peasmarsh and Spirit of Ranachan Studio, Campbeltown **Release:** May 1980, *McCartney II*

Paul started his summer experiments on his Studer 16-track with this instrumental piece. "Front Parlour" was the first recording of *McCartney II*: Paul put the drums in the kitchen, to have a natural echo and started recording the basic track.

McCartney: "That song was the first thing I did on the album and it was done in the front parlour of an old farmhouse. It was empty at the time so we just brought the recording machinery in and used the kitchen as an echo chamber."[427]

Then, McCartney overdubbed a lot of synthesizer parts, ad-libbing in the studio after creating bizarre and original sounds, in an atmosphere similar to the following instrumental track "Frozen Jap" (see sheet 136).

The song was included in *McCartney II* actually without much post-production work, apart from one minute editing compared to the rough-mix.

Musicians:

Paul McCartney synthesizer, keyboards, bass, electric guitars, drums

136 Frozen Jap (Paul McCartney)

Recording: June-July, 1979 **Location:** Home Studio, Peasmarsh and Spirit of Ranachan Studio, Campbeltown **Release:** May 1980, *McCartney II*

The second track of the sessions, "Frozen Jap" was another heavily electronic track: the album – as Paul acknowledged – was Talking Heads-influenced.

McCartney laid down the rhythm section playing a robust drum part. Drums were recorded through the usual McCartney process of laying down one part at a time. Track sheet in the 2011 *McCartney II* edition reveals that four different drum tracks were recorded: one for bass drum, one for snare, one for toms while another track – named "B/D snare" – was not used.

Then Paul moved on to the synthesizer, giving the track a chilly oriental atmosphere, probably inspired by the Japanese tour, scheduled for the forthcoming January.

Having to find a title for the song, Paul initially thought of the snow-capped peaks of Mount Fuji ("Frozen Chrystalline Mount Fuji"), but couldn't come up with anything good. Then he thought of "Frozen Jap", using the shortened form only as a matter of space so it could be written on the tape box.

---

[427] *The McCartney Interview. Paul Gambaccini Talks with Paul McCartney About McCartney II*, 1980.

But the *samurai* atmosphere is the only interesting element of this boring instrumental piece which drowns in the hypnotic synthesizer textures.

The song is on *McCartney II*. A curious fact: on the Japanese copies of *McCartney II* the original title of the song (using the informal term *Jap*) was changed to a neutral "Frozen Japanese". "I heard people in Japan didn't like it, so I changed it", Paul said.

Musicians:

Paul McCartney keyboards, synthesizer, drums, bass

137 Summer's Day Song (Paul McCartney)

Recording: June-July and October (overdubs), 1979 **Location:** Home Studio, Peasmarsh, Spirit of Ranachan Studio, Campbeltown and Replica Studio (overdubs), London **Release:** May 1980, *McCartney II*

"Summer's Day Song" was also meant to be an instrumental track, as it was in the original version of *McCartney II*. McCartney wanted to exploit the potential of synthesizer in a symphonic manner and – with only the help of a rhythm-box in the background – he recorded this track, characterized by a sleepy melody.

McCartney: "I had heard a piece of music that I liked, which was a very classical sounding piece (it could be Brian Eno's *Spider and I* from 1977 – author's note). So, that day, when I went into the studio, I thought it would be a nice change if I tried something, sort of, classical. I built it up, wrote a couple of words, and put a few vocals over the top, so it does sound like something classical-cum-something else."[428]

For the occasion, Paul also used his old Mellotron, relying on the flute sounds used by The Beatles in "Strawberry Fields Forever". Only at the last moment – during the mixing sessions for the album, in October – McCartney added his vocals, noteworthy especially in the double-tracked harmony part.

Eddie Klein: "Paul decided that the instrumental called 'Summer's Day Song' should have some lyrics and so we added a vocal and harmony vocal at Replica Studio. This vocal recording was the only thing I did on the album, and Paul mixed it that same afternoon."[429]

Musicians:

Paul McCartney vocals, keyboards, synthesizer, Mellotron

138 You Know I'll Get You Babe (Paul McCartney)

Recording: June-July, 1979 **Location:** Home Studio, Peasmarsh and Spirit of Ranachan Studio, Campbeltown **Release:** June 2011, *McCartney II* (Deluxe Edition)

Similar in atmosphere, rhythm and structure to "All You Horseriders" (sheet 139), also "You Know I'll Get You Babe" came out while McCartney's was improvising in the studio.

---

[428] *Ibid.*
[429] *McCartney II Deluxe Edition*, in *Paul McCartney Archive Collection*, 2011, pp.36-37.

Again, Paul created a simple and monotonous background played by synthesizer, electronic drums and some real percussion instruments as a chance for overdubbing his coarse vocals, going on forever with the title. This song was not included in *McCartney II* , but dug out for its remaster in 2011.

Musicians:

Paul McCartney vocals, bass, drums, keyboards, synthesizer, percussion

139 All You Horseriders (Paul McCartney)

Recording: June-July, 1979 **Location:** Home Studio, Peasmarsh and Spirit of Ranachan Studio, Campbeltown **Release:** June 2011, *McCartney II* (Deluxe Edition)

Since Linda was very fond of horses, Paul decided to put in music a sort of tribute to her passion. During another unusual session, McCartney toyed with a bizarre idea: using synthesizer, he achieved a strange sound similar to the trotting of a horse's hooves: that was enough to inspire him for "All You Horseriders".

At that point, Paul added drums, bass and electric guitar, finishing up the recording with his ad-libbed vocals, treated with Vari-Speed: a series of instructions howled into the microphone and intended for jockeys. As for the previous songs, this one didn't make it onto *McCartney II*, either. It was included only in the 2011 edition of the album.

Musicians:

Paul McCartney vocals, bass, drums, keyboards, synthesizer, electric guitar, percussion

140 Blue Sway (Paul McCartney)

Recording: June-July, 1979 **Location:** Home Studio, Peasmarsh and Spirit of Ranachan Studio, Campbeltown **Release:** June 2011, *McCartney II* (Deluxe Edition)

"Blue Sway" was another song McCartney created directly in the studio. This time Paul laid down a funky guitar part and soon started to record this instrumental track.

The song was built step by step around a single chord: first, a good bass line, then some bluesy guitar solos and some backing vocals. Finally, Paul introduced a rhythm change near the end. Then he filed it away and moved on to another song.

Actually, McCartney must have been particularly satisfied, if in September-October 1986 he had none other than Richard Niles add a great orchestral arrangement, for the release of the song on *Cold Cuts*, that actually never happened.

Niles: "McCartney played me each one of the tracks and he asked me, 'What do you think it needs?' I said, 'Well, this one needs a new drum track, a new rhythm section, this one could be done with strings... At one point I said, 'Of course, you want to re-do the vocals here'. He turned to me as if I had just assassinated his entire family... Then he laughed! I learned right away that he got a great sense of humor!"[430]

"Blue Sway" was one of those suggested by Niles. Paul re-recorded the vocal part and Niles came up with a string arrangement.

"That track was something very special" – Niles said – "and I'm so glad it had finally been released! The sax part was overdubbed by Dick Morrissey."[431] Both versions have been included in the 2011 edition of *McCartney II*.

Musicians:

Paul McCartney vocals, bass, drums, keyboards, synthesizer, electric guitars, percussion, shaker

141 Temporary Secretary (Paul McCartney)

Recording: June-July, 1979 **Location:** Home Studio, Peasmarsh and Spirit of Ranachan Studio, Campbeltown **Release:** May 1980, *McCartney II*

"Temporary Secretary" is one of the most atypical tracks in McCartney's discography: a song which "you love or hate".

When he composed it, Paul imagined writing a letter to an employment bureau for a temporary secretary. McCartney's lyrics refer to Mr. Marks, which was actually the owner of the Alfred Marks Agency, a UK recruitment company. He based the background music on the typewriter-like rhythmic effects of a synthesizer – actually an ARP sequencer Paul rented for the sessions – adding his almost atonal vocal lines.

It's one of the most experimental tracks of the *McCartney II* sessions. Paul said he was a little influenced by Ian Dury, to which he would pay tribute in 2001 recording a cover of "I'm Partial to Your Abracadabra".

McCartney's nasal voice and its repetitive refrain – sprinkled with funny vocal effects – are pleasantly annoying, and are counterpointed by a powerful pulsating bass.

A banjo track was also recorded but not used: Paul himself wrote "don't use" on the recording sheet. After the release of *McCartney II*, Paul had a weird idea and chose "Temporary Secretary" as the third single from the album.

In September 1980 the song was issued in the UK as a limited edition 12" single and therefore it did not enter the charts.

This record – whose 25.000 copies sold out in just sixteen hours – today is one of the most sought after McCartney collectors' items.

Musicians:

Paul McCartney vocals, acoustic guitar, bass, synthesizer, sequencer, keyboards, drums

---

[430] Interview courtesy of Richard Niles, 07/10/2011.
[431] *Ibid.*

142 On the Way (Paul McCartney)

Recording: June-July, 1979 **Location:** Home Studio, Peasmarsh and Spirit of Ranachan Studio, Campbeltown **Release:** May 1980, *McCartney II*

McCartney initially recorded the bluesy "On the Way" almost for fun. In his home studio, Paul laid it down as an instrumental track, with drums and bass.

Then in July, by chance Paul watched a television program, *The Devil's Music*, anchored by bluesman Alexis Korner.[432]

McCartney: "I put down a drum track and some bass and that was that and it sat around for a month or so. The day before going back to it, I had seen Alexis Korner on a TV programme about the blues, and I thought, 'Oh, I've got to do something like that because it's the kind of music I like.' So that's how that one came about."[433]

It was enough to inspire McCartney to finish up the song, adding vocals and some good guitar licks: but he did not care to re-cut his sloppy bass part, full of inaccuracies (e.g. a bad note at 1:16). Only six tracks were used for the recording: bass drum on track 1, "top kit" on track 2, bass on track 3, vocal on track 4 and electric guitars on tracks 5 and 6. The result was this simple but effective 12 bar-blues, recorded with strong echo on McCartney's vocals. The track is on *McCartney II*.

Musicians:

Paul McCartney vocals, bass, electric guitars, drums

143 Mr. H Atom (Paul McCartney)

Recording: June-July, 1979 **Location:** Home Studio, Peasmarsh and Spirit of Ranachan Studio, Campbeltown **Release:** June 2011, *McCartney II* (Deluxe Edition)

If Linda's contribution to the *McCartney II* recordings was limited to only a few harmonies, for this bizarre and surreal punk-style song, she is featured as the lead vocalist.

Paul recorded the fast-paced basic track with drums, bass, synthesizer and flanged electric guitar, while Linda sang the only verse of the song.

Paul acted as a counterpart to her with his recitation, which is dedicated to the number of hydrogen atoms it takes to determine the genetic difference between male and female.

Included in the original double version of *McCartney II*, "Mr. H Atom" was perhaps considered to be an extreme proposal. The song was dug out for the 2011 edition of *McCartney II*. The mix, however, is different from the original: it takes away some guitar tracks leaving more space to synthesizer.

Musicians:

Paul McCartney vocals, bass, drums, keyboards, synthesizer, electric guitar • **Linda McCartney** vocals

---

[432] In December 1970, Paul gave him a phone interview on BBC Radio One discussing the death of Jimi Hendrix.
[433] *The McCartney Interview. Paul Gambaccini Talks with Paul McCartney About McCartney II*, 1980.

144 Bogey Wobble (Paul McCartney)

Recording: June-July, 1979 **Location:** Home Studio, Peasmarsh and Spirit of Ranachan Studio, Campbeltown **Release:** May 1980, *McCartney II* (Deluxe Edition)

"Bogey Wobble" was produced during a session of pure experimentation with synthesizer. Some eccentric sounds attracted the attention of McCartney in this case: the song, entirely instrumental, was built on similar sounds to those you can hear when water is brought to the boiling point!

Then Paul added drums and bass, filling the track with some chords on synthesizer. But when it was time to release *McCartney II*, he decided to hide the song somewhere. "Bogey Wobble" was included in the 2011 edition of *McCartney II* in a slightly shortened version compared to the original.

Musicians:

Paul McCartney bass, drums, keyboards, synthesizer, percussion

145 Wonderful Christmastime (Paul McCartney)

Recording: June-July, 1979 **Location:** Home Studio, Peasmarsh and Spirit of Ranachan Studio, Campbeltown **Release:** November 1979, single

In their eight year career, The Beatles always recorded Christmas albums containing funny skits, greetings and carols for their fans: a tradition McCartney resumed by often recording Christmas related songs.[434]

"Wonderful Christmastime" was certainly not a lavish and sophisticated production. It's reminiscent of The Beatles' style, quirky and full of humour. Paul had written it "on a hottest day in July" and recorded it soon after, during the sessions in Scotland.

Initially, it was only an instrumental backing track, but then Paul added some vocals. The song shares the same atmosphere and spirit of the *McCartney II* sessions: simple, sparse, with a prominent use of synthesizer. A Mellotron sax solo is also featured at 2:43. "Wonderful Christmastime" is a cheerful but awkward Christmas singalong, to play over and over in the frenzy of the end of the year.

The marketing strategy to launch the single was a bit mixed up: the 45, with McCartney on the cover dressed up as Santa Claus – a reference to the popular *White Christmas* cover by Bing Crosby – was credited to Paul McCartney, but the promotion was entrusted to Wings.

In fact, the clip of the song contained footage of the group, including some shots from the 1979 *Wings' British Tour* in which "Wonderful Christmastime" was played.

When the song was performed live, they recreated the Christmas atmosphere on stage, with artificial snowflakes coming down from above.

---

[434] See "Mull of Kintyre" (1977), "Pipes of Peace" (1983) and "Once Upon a Long Ago..." (1987).

At first, the commercial results were barely satisfactory. "Wonderful Christmastime" reached #6 in the UK charts (it did not chart in America), allowing McCartney back in the top ten, a result that none of the singles from *Back to the Egg* had managed to achieve.

Today the song is unfailingly played by radio stations each season: "Wonderful Christmastime" is on the list of the twenty-five most broadcast Christmas songs of all time and has earned McCartney fifteen million dollars in royalties. The song re-entered the British charts also in 2007 (#44) and in 2011 (#72).

McCartney performed the song live thirty years later, during some concerts of the 2009 European tour. It was performed again during the *Up & Coming Tour* in 2010 and during the *On The Run Tour* in 2011.

Musicians:

Paul McCartney vocals, backing vocals, electric guitar, drums, synthesizer, keyboards, Mellotron, tambourine (?), sleigh bells

146 Darkroom (Paul McCartney)

Recording: June-July, 1979 **Location:** Home Studio, Peasmarsh and Spirit of Ranachan Studio, Campbeltown **Release:** May 1980, *McCartney II*

Different ideas were in McCartney's head when he composed "Darkroom", which is among the less interesting songs of the sessions. A reference to the darkened rooms located in the American nightclubs or sexclubs? To the darkroom as a room made completely dark to allow the printing of photographs? All or nothing, as Paul nicely revealed: "A fellow saying to a girl 'Come to my dark room' is a bit like a 'Come, let me take you to the Casbah' kind of thing. So I thought of this double meaning." [435]

Paul recorded the basic track with drums and a deep sounding bass, then completed it with some bizarre overdubs. In addition to the vocals – including crazy parts in falsetto and various imitations – McCartney overdubbed some electric guitar and synthesizer, used here to recreate sounds like birds chirping and singing.

Track sheets reproduced in the 2011 *McCartney II* edition show the following 16 tracks: 4 vocal tracks, 2 drum tracks (double speed and snare), 2 maracas tracks (one high speed, one normal), 4 synthesizer tracks (one of which was not used), toms and tea cup, bass, electric guitar and "swanee whistle".

Paul obviously liked it, but when deciding to put it on the album, he hesitated. "Darkroom" had to be drastically edited down (it is said that a 11 minute alternate take also exists) before being judged worthy to be included in *McCartney II*.

Musicians:

Paul McCartney vocals, bass, electric guitar, drums, synthesizer, maracas, tea cup

---

[435] *The McCartney Interview. Paul Gambaccini Talks with Paul McCartney About McCartney II*, 1980.

147 One of These Days (Paul McCartney)

Recording: June-July, 1979 **Location:** Home Studio, Peasmarsh and Spirit of Ranachan Studio, Campbeltown **Release:** May 1980, *McCartney II*

A song in line with the typical McCartney songwriting style, "One of These Days" is also one of the most poignant tracks in *McCartney II*.

Inspired by the Hare Krishna philosophy, "One of These Days" (initially titled "Breathe Fresh Air") was recorded in absolute simplicity: only vocals, acoustic guitar (two tracks, with some more in the middle) and some tapping on the guitar body. A disarming but effective bareness, which amplifies its reflective and pensive atmosphere.

McCartney: "'One Of These Days' all happened when a Hare Krishna bloke came round to see me. He was a nice fellow, very sort of gentle. After he left, I went to the studio and the vibe carried through a bit. I started writing something a bit more gentle that particular day."[436]

The production, with McCartney's gentle and heavily echoed voice, manages to recreate an atmosphere halfway between a dream and awareness, between an intra-uterine condition and real life, which is the heart of the song. The unforgettable closing track of *McCartney II*.

Musicians:

Paul McCartney vocals, acoustic guitar

148 Secret Friend (Paul McCartney)

Recording: June-July, 1979 **Location:** Home Studio, Peasmarsh and Spirit of Ranachan Studio, Campbeltown **Release:** September 1980, "Temporary Secretary" 12" single B-side

This lengthy track sums up the spirit of the *McCartney II* sessions. Having abandoned any typical pop song format, Paul decided to exceed all limits: with his 10:30 "Secret Friend" is one of the longest tracks in McCartney's repertoire and the most extreme song he ever released.

Extreme, since "Secret Friend" is actually a single verse ("Here are we, where we are" was a refrain often repeated in his family), almost a mantra: many features make the track similar to "Check My Machine" (see sheet **150**), with the high-pitched vocals and its background full of electronic instrumentation.

The song was not included in *McCartney II* due to its excessive length. But Paul released it shortly later, as the B-side to the "Temporary Secretary" 12" single.

Musicians:

Paul McCartney vocals, bass, drums, synthesizer, Mellotron, electric guitar, shaker, percussion

---

[436] *Ibid.*

149 Bogey Music (Paul McCartney)

Recording: June-July, 1979 **Location:** Home Studio, Peasmarsh and Spirit of Ranachan Studio, Campbeltown **Release:** May 1980, *McCartney II*

For this song, McCartney was inspired by *Fungus The Bogeyman*, a children's novel by Raymond Briggs (born 1934), published in 1977. The adventures of Briggs' Bogey-Men tell of creatures who live in dark dripping tunnels underground, hate music and wear dirty, wet clothes: but their young people rebel against this lifestyle, get into rock'n'roll and actually take baths (!) Paul wrote "Bogey Music" based on the story. It's a grotesque twelve-bars boogie, a sort of manifesto of the young generation of Bogey-Men: a clever rock'n'roll era analogy.

Included in *McCartney II*, "Bogey Music" is an odd song: McCartney's vocal tracks, achieved through a Vari-Speed, were heavily slowed down to make funny sounds.

Musicians:

Paul McCartney vocals, electric guitars, bass, drums, synthesizer, Mellotron, tambourine

150 Check My Machine (Paul McCartney)

Recording: June-July, 1979 **Location:** Home Studio, Peasmarsh and Spirit of Ranachan Studio, Campbeltown **Release:** June 1980, "Waterfalls" single B-side

The bare-bones recording technique Paul chose for *McCartney II*, with no mixer and just the Studer recorder – the same approach that he had already used for his first solo album – was the inspiration for this song, taped just to test the recording equipment, probably when McCartney moved to Scotland to go on with the sessions.

It's one of the most unconventional tracks of these sessions. Paul toyed with Varispeed, significantly increasing the pitch of his vocals. The track is introduced by two voices repeating, "Hi George! Morning Terry!"; they are taken from a Tweety and Sylvester cartoon called *Tweet Zoo*. This is the hook of the song, which also features a captivating bass line: the rest is a McCartney's nerve-racking domestic madness exercise, including amused chatting and extravagant instrumentation. Not included in *McCartney II*, the song was released as the B-side to the "Waterfalls" single.

Musicians:

Paul McCartney vocals, bass, drums, electric guitar, keyboards, synthesizer, shaker, percussion, banjo

151 Waterfalls (Paul McCartney)

Recording: June-July, 1979 **Location:** Home Studio, Peasmarsh and Spirit of Ranachan Studio, Campbeltown **Release:** May 1980, *McCartney II*

Originally called "I Need Love", this was the only track already written before McCartney began the *McCartney II* sessions.[437]

---

[437] K. Badman, *The Beatles After the Breakup. 1970-2000*, 2000, p.234.

McCartney had recorded a demo of it in May: "Halfway through the album I got a bit bored. I thought I would do something different. So I decided to do a track left over from the last Wings album (…) The original lyrics were just working lyrics, just spewed out. I thought I'd have to get serious and change them (…) But in time, I got to like them and I thought I should add electric piano and a distant string synthesizer like a mad Swiss orchestra on a mountaintop. And it worked! A lot of people have rung up and said that it's their favourite."[438]

Paul revealed that "Waterfalls" is his "favourite song of the album": it could be actually considered the most representative song of *McCartney II*.

"Waterfalls" is an open door to McCartney's inner world: a simple ballad with the liquid atmosphere of a dreamy and ethereal world, but also an emotional admission of weakness.

The song, with its evocative melody, is a fine example of simplicity and intimacy: lyrics are an invitation by Paul to sit safe, away from risk. Love is safety and a protective screen from the worries of everyday life.

McCartney: "The song 'Waterfalls' is basically saying 'Don't go doing all the dangerous stuff, 'cause I need you'. It's a more mature thought, that I wouldn't have been able to do 20 years ago."[439]

The video-clip, shot in the *Waterfalls* estate, is revealing: McCartney is shut up in the room writing at the piano, then he leaves for a walk around the greenery of his estate and ends his brief excursion with a reassuring return to home, to finish the song. All this takes place within the Paul's safe reality, minimizing unforeseen dangers.

The final version of "Waterfalls" sounds somewhat like a demo. Paul played electric piano (doubled), then overdubbed a short acoustic guitar solo, his vocals and – of course – synthesizer, with six different tracks. McCartney stated that "Waterfalls" is one of the songs he would re-record[440] – and actually in July 1980 he had Fiachra Trench preparing an orchestral score for it, maybe recorded but never used – but a lot of the piece's charm is in its barely fleshed out arrangement, typical of many *McCartney II* tracks.

His fans liked it and "Waterfalls" – although not a very commercial song – was a hit in the UK charts, reaching #9. The song did definitely worse in America, where it did not chart, only bubbling under Billboard Hot 100 singles charts and reaching #109.[441]

The clip-version has a special feature: it contains an electric piano introduction that is not in the album.

438 K. Badman, *The Beatles. The Dream Is Over-Off the Record 2*, 2002, p.265
439 From the album *The McCartney Interview*, 1981.
440 Perhaps also because of a bad cut at 2'55" (edit version)
441 McCartney was thinking of this result, when he mentioned, in an interview published in *Club Sandwich* (n. 72, Winter '94, p. 10), the fact that "Waterfalls" was one of his most overlooked songs. This was confirmed by the surprise with which Paul found out, during an interview (*Record Collector*, n. 214, June 1997, p.21) that the song had been released as a single and it was among the British *top ten*.

A different version (called *Dj edit*, lasting 3:22) was distributed to radio stations when the single was released: this is the version included in *Wingspan*.

Musicians:

Paul McCartney vocals, electric piano, synthesizer, acoustic guitar

152 Nobody Knows (Paul McCartney)

Recording: June-July, 1979 **Location:** Home Studio, Peasmarsh and Spirit of Ranachan Studio, Campbeltown **Release:** May 1980, *McCartney II*

"Nobody Knows", a typical rock'n'roll standard, is one of the less innovative tracks of *McCartney II*. McCartney: "One of the funny things for me is that in blues you'll get what is supposed to be a 12-bars blues, and then you get odd timings come in. On many blues records, they're never exact so, on this track, I do the same thing."[442] Paul arranged this simple song in an almost Country and Western style, overdubbing many bizarre vocal parts – distant and sometimes even unintelligible – and some powerful drums, with the bass drum mixed very high.

Track sheet from the 2011 *McCartney II* edition shows that the drum part was a particularly complicated matter and six different drum tracks were laid down: foot stomp, hi-hat, bass drum, snare and two tracks named "composite drums", one of which was finally not used.

Musicians:

Paul McCartney vocals, bass, electric guitar, drums

153 Coming Up (Paul McCartney)

Recording: June-July, 1979 **Location:** Home Studio, Peasmarsh and Spirit of Ranachan Studio, Campbeltown **Release:** April 1980, single (from *McCartney II*)

"Coming Up" is one of the most remarkable achievements of McCartney's post-Beatles career. Here Paul succeeds in reaching the aim of these recordings: to combine extreme experimentation and his gift for melody.

Over The Beatles' years, McCartney learned many recording techniques and "Coming Up" is a fine example of his skills and inventiveness: the use of studio tricks shows his ability to be a pioneer for future sounds and musical trends.

Paul looked forward with an eye to the past and was able to exploit the potential of the Vari-Speed, an old weird contraption of The Beatles era. The "wound-up" and doubled vocals are the trade-mark of the track, an unequalled blend of funky rhythms and sampled sounds.

Thanks to the track sheets included in the *McCartney II* Deluxe Edition in 2011, we know that the recording process went as follows: McCartney put a rhythm box on track 1, then overdubbed bass-drum and snare on tracks 2 and 3, adding electric guitars on track 4 and 5. He

---

[442] K. Badman, *The Beatles. After the Break-Up, 1970-2000*, 2000, p.266.

then put a synth and recorded four vocal tracks with handclaps, finishing with bass (track 11) and more synthesizers (tracks 12-16), using some space on track 14 to add a tambourine.

The guitar riff that runs throughout the track is the real winning hook and earned McCartney praise from Lennon, who said that "Coming Up" was "a good piece of work".

Synthesizers are employed here to create a horn section, with the dizzying ascending and descending scales. The result was a perfect mixture of Sixties pop and modern *quasi* dance music.

After recording the track – lasting 5:51, it was initially intended to end the *McCartney II* original version and was finally issued on the 2011 edition of the album – Paul realized that the song could also work as a single and edited it down. When it was released as a 45 – on April 1980 it was launched as a premiere of *McCartney II* and reached #2 in the UK charts – "Coming Up" was already known to McCartney's audience.

In fact, Paul had re-arranged "Coming Up" for live performances: the song became a rocker, complete with a horn section and it was included in the 1979 *Wings' British Tour*.

The quality of these performances and the audience reaction were excellent and Wings' live version – recorded in Glasgow during the last concert of the tour on December 17th, 1979 – was released as the B-side to the single.[443]

The song, in that powerful performance, with an elaborate bass line and McCartney's strong vocals, got considerable airplay in America.

"Coming Up (Live at Glasgow)" broke a small record: replacing "Coming Up" (McCartney's solo version), it was the first and only track which reached the top of the Billboard charts in two different versions, following one another.

The track was Wings' last no.1, it was given the R.I.A.A. certification for sales of over one million copies and also got a Grammy Award nomination in the Best Rock Vocal Performance – Male category. This version is in the American editions of *All The Best!* and *Wingspan*.

A funky arrangement of "Coming Up" was performed live starting with the 1989/90 *Paul McCartney World Tour*: two of those performances were included respectively in *Tripping The Live Fantastic!* and in *Live in Knebworth* (Various Artists, 1990). The song was performed during the 1991 *Secret Gigs Tour*, the 1993 *New World Tour*, the 2002/03 *Drivin' Tour* – from which the version released on *Back in The US/Back in the World* is taken – and during the 2007 *Memory Almost Full Promo Tour*. The original version has been included in *All The Best!* and *Wingspan*.

To support the single, McCartney also shot a memorable clip, which he co-directed with Keith MacMillan. In a homage to the famous Buster Keaton's silent movie *The Playhouse* (1921), Paul played ten different roles in the video (with Linda playing two vocalists), pretending they're

---

[443] A different live version, recorded during the special concert for Cambodia on December 29th, 1979, is included in the double album *Concerts For The People Of Kampuchea*.

musicians of a band called The Plastic Macs (a nod to Lennon's Plastic Ono Band, as Paul admitted). McCartney imitates various rock stars, including guitarist Hank Marvin from the Shadows, keyboard player Ron Mael from Sparks, as well as... Beatle Paul, wearing vintage collarless jacket and embracing vintage Hofner bass. A clever and light-hearted way to look back at the Beatles' legacy.

Musicians:

Paul McCartney vocals, backing vocals, bass, electric guitars, electric piano, synthesizer, Mellotron, drums, percussion, tambourine

After the *McCartney II* sessions, Paul returned to Wings. In September, the band met in McCartney's Scottish studio and then in an Eastbourne hall to rehearse songs for the tour due to start soon. It was supposed to be a world tour, which after Great Britain would have reached Japan, Australia and America, but McCartney's arrest in Tokyo the following January interrupted it immediately.

The show included the most original song selection ever chosen by McCartney. With a trend that will be later reversed, McCartney performed only a few songs from The Beatles' repertoire, focusing on Wings and solo material, with some odd choices.

Wings' British Tour (November 23rd-December 17th) was held in theaters and little places; simultaneously, the single "Wonderful Christmastime" was released. The setlist was as follows: "Got to Get You Into My Life" – "Getting Closer" – "Every Night" – "Again and Again and Again" – "I've Had Enough" – "No Words" – "Cook of the House" – "Old Siam, Sir" – "Maybe I'm Amazed" – "The Fool on the Hill" – "Let It Be" – "Hot as Sun" – "Spin It On" – "Twenty Flight Rock" – "Go Now" – "Arrow Through Me" – "Wonderful Christmastime" – "Coming Up" – "Goodnight Tonight" – "Yesterday" – "Mull of Kintyre" – "Band on the Run"

Shortly after, on December 29th Wings sealed with their presence the project of the Secretary of ONU, Kurt Waldheim, who for some months had been personally working to organize a charity concert in favour of the refugees fleeing from Cambodia, and he would have liked to have the Beatles on the stage. Wings' performance is to be remembered: during the encores the band was joined onstage by the Rockestra – in a different line-up compared to that of *Back to the Egg*, without David Gilmour – to play "Rockestra Theme", "Lucille" and "Let It Be", ending with a second rendition of "Rockestra Theme". It was Wings' last concert.

1980

On January 16th, McCartney and Wings arrived at Tokyo's Narita Airport, after a stopover in New York, for their eleven-date Japanese tour. Regrettably, as soon as McCartney landed, his bag inspection resulted in the discovery of 219 grams of cannabis.

Paul was immediately handcuffed. Footage taken from vintage tv news, displays a ridiculous situation: McCartney was smiling and waving to the crowd of fans – who didn't understand what happened – as he was taken to jail, where he would be imprisoned for nine days.

"We were about to fly to Japan and I knew I wouldn't be able to get anything to smoke over there" – McCartney said in 2004 – "This stuff was too good to flush down the toilet, so I thought I'd take it with me."

The Japanese tour was immediately cancelled – many fans did not return their tickets for refund, keeping them as collectors' items – as were the planned Chinese and American dates. Wings had been rehearsing some songs that weren't included in the previous British Tour, like "With a Little Luck", "Another Day", "Baby's Request" and "Eleanor Rigby".

The album *McCartney II* was released on May 16th. Stephen Holden of *Rolling Stone* wrote a quite positive review: "*McCartney II* is an album of aural doodles designed for the amusement of very young children. Most of the songs are merely sound effects... *McCartney II* is passable. Its catchiest numbers make the singer's voice sound like a cross between an insect and a windup toy. Even if you hate it, it's liable to stick to your mind like chewing gum to the bottom of a shoe." The album could have been a turning point in McCartney's artistic path toward an experimental/avant-garde direction. In truth, Paul moved away from the original plan, that had been conceived as a double-album with eighteen tracks – for the most part including instrumental or avant-garde music – and cut it down to a single record, putting aside the most experimental side of the project.

McCartney chose the most commercial tracks, drifting away from the original structure and concept of the record: thus, the final product was disappointing and lacking. Furthermore, releasing a record dating prior to the jail experience, it seemed that Paul wanted to wipe away any emotion, anguish and fear related to those difficult days.

McCartney II was another commercial success. The album reached #1 in the UK and #3 in the US, where after three weeks had sold 450.000 copies. It was later awarded with a gold disc for selling over a million copies. Many years later McCartney himself would disown it: "Listening to it again" – Paul said in 1986 to Richard Skinner – "I might have done something different: synthesizers are cold and thin, they don't sound like real instruments sometimes."

While many considered *McCartney II* as an evidence that something wasn't working with Wings, the album was intended only as a break for Paul: the band was still alive and kicking.

Many projects were brewing for McCartney when the group gathered into the studio in July. First, Wings started rehearsing songs for a new album at the Finchden Manor in Tenterden, Kent. The group resumed rehearsals in October at Pugin's Hall, again in Tenterten.

Some tapes from these rehearsals show that Wings were working on songs that Paul already demoed in August, including "Ebony and Ivory", "Ballroom Dancing, "Take it Away", "Average Person" and "Keep Under Cover". Other demos prepared at Rude Studio by McCartney included "Wanderlust", "Unbelievable Experience", "Sweetest Little Show", "Dress Me Up as a Robber", "Seems Like Old Times", "Give Us a Chord Roy", and "Stop, You Don't Know Where She Came From".

Not long after, Wings recorded another batch of tracks never released to date: "Rock'n'Roll Rodeo", "Ecology of the World" and "Good Morning Song".

In Autumn, Paul got back together in the studio with George Martin. McCartney wanted to release something related to *Rupert the Bear* and started the recordings at AIR Studios with "We All Stand Together". Later, he taped more songs with the help of Laine, apparently with no involvement from any other musician. Two tracks recorded there, "All the Love Is There" and "In My Darkest Hour" are still unreleased. Some time this year, Paul was approached by film-producer Lee Kramer to score the movie *Silver Surfer*, but the project didn't materialize.

154 We All Stand Together (Paul McCartney)

Recording: October 31st, November 3rd, 10th, 15th and 17th, 1980 and 1984? (overdubs) **Location:** AIR Studios, London and Hog Hill Studio (overdubs), Icklesham **Release:** November 1984, single

A few days after the Beatles' breakup, McCartney – who accepted Lee Eastman's suggestion to invest in publishing – went back to his childhood and through his recently founded company *McCartney Productions,* acquired the rights to the cartoon *Rupert the Bear,* whose comic strips he had been fond of since he was a kid.

This bear character was created by Mary Tourtel and dates back to 1920. Its first strip, *The Story of a Little Bear Lost,* appeared on November 8th in the *Daily Express.* When Mary Tourtel retired in 1935 after her eyesight deteriorated and the strip was assigned to Alfred Bestall, Rupert's character was anthropomorphized and transformed into this white bear – wearing a red jacket and yellow checked trousers with matching yellow scarf – which Paul was familiar with.

Although McCartney started writing songs for a Rupert project and recorded a complete soundtrack for an animated film (see **1978**), then things stopped. In 1980, McCartney got back to his animated film idea, not without some controversy.

Alfred Bestall had suggested Paul work on a script based on two stories that he had created, *Rupert's Queer Path* (1949) and *Rupert and the Whistlefish* (1959): McCartney's only answer was to write his own script with the help of other cartoonists.

Meanwhile, McCartney had sketched "We All Stand Together" – a little waltzy song – taping a demo at his Rude Studio in 1980. It's a fascinating recording, which displays Paul's ability to sing all the vocals, combining different registers and parts. A brilliant idea, even before its studio recording.

During October and November, the track was recorded at AIR Studios with a big chorus and an orchestra, arranged by George Martin and led by Kenneth Sillito: it resulted in a somewhat overblown production that would be heavily criticized over the years.

For the choral parts, many special guests were recruited, including the King's Singers, a vocal group that Martin had produced before on several LP's.

Brian Kay, the group's vocal bass, recalls: "I don't remember hearing a demo before the session. In the studio were the usual six singers: me, Nigel Perrin and Alastair Hume (countertenors), Bill Ives (tenore), Anthony Holt and Simon Carrington (baritones). Paul had already put down a vocal track for himself and we operated as a backing group. We just sang the music from the vocal score which had been prepared for us."[444]

The recording, of course, was an unforgettable moment for everyone: "The thrill of the session was simply being in the studio with Paul (...) We knew he'd bought the rights for *Rupert the Bear*, so there wasn't any need to 'explain' the song! The only funny thing about the song was me having to start the whole thing off with a low note, intentionally badly sung to avoid sounding too well bred! The sounds we made were all part of the funny opening to the song!"[445]

Other vocal parts were sung by the London Gospel Community Choir, in their first session for McCartney. Bazel Meade, the choir's director, recalls: "I'm from Montserrat, where there's George Martin AIR Studios and he has a house. And it was him that invited me. He wanted the sound that we created as a gospel choir. I took about 20 singers into the studio. Paul made suggestions and we tried whatever he suggested. It didn't go quickly, because it was in a different style for us, so it took some time to achieve what he wanted. We also recorded another song, but I can't remember which one it was."[446]

Famous flute player Elena Duràn was also invited to perform. The track would receive further treatment in the following years. Trombone player Pete Beachill recalls: "It was in Hastings at his farm. Four of us, Robin Williams on violin, myself, John Barclay on trumpet and Pete Swinfield on flute went down to his farm to do some overdubs. I played euphonium on that one. I remember we had to leave at six o'clock in the morning... For a 10.00 am start."[447]

---

[444] Interview courtesy of Brian Kay, 26/10/2011.
[445] *Ibid.*
[446] Interview courtesy of Bazel Meade, 26/11/2011.
[447] Interview courtesy of Pete Beachill, 29/01/2013.

Beachill's recollections seem to place these overdubs around 1984, as McCartney's own studio was set up at that time. The song wasn't released until Christmas 1984: McCartney included "We All Stand Together" in *Rupert and the Frog Song*, a twenty-minute animated film. In the most important scene the song is sung by a group of multicolored frogs, while Rupert watches their performance from a corner.

The featurette was screened as an opener to the movie *Give My Regards to Broad Street* (see **1982**). Released as a home-video in February 1985, it was a great success in the UK, selling 130.000 copies and was surpassed only by Michael Jackson's *Thriller*.

The single "We All Stand Together" also hit the market. The song, thanks to its Christmas waltzing little tune, climbed to the top of the UK charts (#3) with sales in excess of half a million copies and soon became a classic children's song. It was re-issued as a single the following Christmas and once more entered the charts, reaching #32.

"We All Stand Together" (its B-side was a "humming version", featuring Paul backed by the Frog Chorus, that was the St. Paul's Boys Choir) was included in *All the Best!* (UK version) and as the B-side to the single "Tropic Island Hum" (2004).

Musicians:

Paul McCartney vocals, backing vocals, acoustic guitar (?) • **Eric Stewart** backing vocals • The King's Singers: **Nigel Perrin, Alastair Hume, Bill Ives, Anthony Holt, Simon Carrington, Brian Kay** vocals • **The London Gospel Community Choir** vocals • **Pete Beachill** euphonium • **Robin Williams** violin • **Pete Swinfield, Elena Durán** flute • **John Barclay** trumpet • **Gary Kettel** tympani • **Unknown musicians** strings

155 Ballroom Dancing (Paul McCartney)

Recording: December 7th and 14th, 1980 and March 17th, 1981 (overdubs) **Location:** AIR Studios, London **Release:** April 1982, *Tug of War*

McCartney wrote "Ballroom Dancing", recalling the dance halls of his teenage years. The song was an up-tempo rock'n'roll number: the perfect backdrop to those memories.

McCartney: "I've got memories that go back to when I was a teenager, like when George Harrison and I used to go to the local dance and neither of us would ever dare to ask a girl to dance until the last waltz… We'd always try and grab someone for that last dance. But most of the time we'd get refused."[448]

Paul presented the track to Wings during the July rehearsals: the lyrics were unfinished and the arrangement was only rough-sketched, as witnessed by an underdeveloped bass line, keeping straight on the root notes. In August, McCartney worked again on "Ballroom Dancing" and taped a demo containing a rollicking piano and a jumping bass, similar to the one heard in the final version. This was given to George Martin and the track was recorded at AIR Studios.

[448] K. Badman, *The Beatles. The Dream Is Over-Off the Record 2*, pp.303-304.

A Hollywood-style, well-crafted production, was the result of very careful studio work, as usual: McCartney took the lion's share, playing almost all the instruments, except for some guitar parts (by Denny Laine and Eric Stewart, although the latter is not credited in the liner notes on the *Tug of War* album) and for the overdub of a sparkling horn arrangement, whose strong presence makes "Ballroom Dancing" one of the most pleasant moments on *Tug of War*.

Finally, two prestigious cameos were added, featuring two post-WWII celebrities: a clarinet glissando by Jack Brymer, the Royal Philharmonic Orchestra first clarinet between 1947 and 1963 (an old acquaintance: he participated in the session of "A Day in the Life") and a brief appearance by Peter Marshall, a popular American television and radio personality from the Fifties, Sixties and thereafter, featuring one of his typical announcements.[449] Furthermore, the track could have been hinting at *Come Dancing*, the tv program hosted by Marshall for several seasons, whose participants were amateurs dancers.

A catchy pop song, which at some point was considered for the third single from *Tug of War* before it was turned down in favor of the title-track. "Ballroom Dancing" would be discarded again two years later when the *Broad Street* remake version was to be released as a single and got cancelled at the last minute.

This recording, nearly identical to the original version – except for an extra-verse added to the lyrics – features the following line-up: Paul (vocals and piano, with Linda), Ringo Starr (drums), John Paul Jones (bass), Dave Edmunds and Chris Spedding (electric guitars) and a horn section including Jack Armstrong, John Barclay, Alan Donney, Henry MacKenzie, Dougie Robinson, Tommy Whittle, Ray Swinfield and David Willis.

Musicians:

Paul McCartney vocals, backing vocals, electric guitar, bass, drums, piano, percussion • **Linda McCartney** backing vocals • **Denny Laine** electric guitar • **Eric Stewart** electric guitar, backing vocals • **Jack Brymer** clarinet • **Peter Marshall** narration • **Unknown musicians** horns

156 Keep Under Cover (Paul McCartney)

Recording: December 7th-8th, 1980, February 11th (overdubs part 1) and March 23rd (overdubs part 2), 1981 **Location:** AIR Studios, London (basic track and overdubs part 2) and AIR Studios, Montserrat (overdubs part 1) **Release:** October 1983, *Pipes of Peace*

Written by Paul at the beginning of the year, "Keep Under Cover" was another track that Wings rehearsed in October. McCartney had already recorded a demo in August in his Rude Studio: it was a mid-tempo blues-tinged song, featuring electric piano and a walking bass.

While rehearsing, Wings experimented with different arrangements of "Keep Under Cover". First they attempted a reggae version and subsequently the group tried for a rock-blues one,

---

[449] The narration says: "Well, I can tell you the band is ready. We're starting with the first of five dances in this competition: that's the cha-cha-cha!".

emphasized by Juber's guitar. Nevertheless, McCartney was not convinced and so he completely re-worked it during the sessions with Martin. The track was slowed down and the arrangement was radically changed. They opted for a melancholic piano-based intro, later adding a large amount of echo on Paul's vocals. Probably, McCartney recorded the basic track with Laine, and judging from the sound, also used a drum-machine.

Later, during sessions in Montserrat in February 1981, Stanley Clarke added a bass part, that features some of his characteristic slapping.

Further overdubs followed during the March-December sessions: strings were added, thus making it a glittering Electric Light Orchestra kind-of number.

Still, it was a missed opportunity: a simpler arrangement could have highlighted McCartney's lyrics about the calm epicurean lifestyle as a protective shield against one's daily woes. Paul suggests staying out of the battle and to wait until things are ok.[450] Rejected from *Tug of War*, (McCartney said that it did not fit with the mood of the LP), the track is on *Pipes of Peace*.

Musicians:

Paul McCartney vocals, backing vocals, piano, acoustic and electric guitar, drums (?) • **Linda McCartney** backing vocals, tambourine (?) • **Denny Laine** acoustic guitar (?), electric guitar (?) • **Stanley Clarke** bass • **Eric Stewart** backing vocals • **Unknown musicians** strings

157 Rainclouds (Paul McCartney-Denny Laine)

Recording: December 8th-9th, 1980 and May-December, 1981 (overdubs) **Location:** AIR Studios, London
Release: March 1982, "Ebony and Ivory" single B-side

On the morning of December 9th, when Paul arrived at AIR Studios for the recording session, George Martin asked him if he wanted to cancel it.

McCartney had been informed by phone that John Lennon had been murdered, shot four times outside his New York apartment: Paul was devastated but he decided to go on with the recordings.

That day Paul put the finishing touches to "Rainclouds", a track he co-wrote with Denny Laine. Wings had rehearsed the song in October. The group tried several arrangements: on the tape, you can hear McCartney teaching the chords to the band, and Denny Laine giving suggestions about the song structure. Then, Wings recorded different takes of "Rainclouds" in a country style. But when McCartney got back into the studio in December, he had completely changed his mind about the arrangement.

In that sad session, Paul and Denny were working on "Rainclouds" and they completed this Gaelic-flavored track, featuring some heavy strumming on 12-string acoustic guitars. On this occasion, The Chieftains' Paddy Moloney was invited to the session to play Uillean pipes. He recalled: "Paul looked stunned. He said it was tragic and useless (…). I don't think at the end

---

450 See "Waterfalls".

of the session that it had really penetrated either, that John was dead, gone forever. I'm sure it took a few days before that finally sank in."[451] Moloney: "Paul came in and he was in an awful state. He said that the press had been outside his house since 5:00 am (...) We just sat around talking about John. I remember Linda came in at one point and she had been crying. It was very very emotional." [452]

Geoff Emerick was in the studio that day: "By the time I arrived at AIR, the building was surrounded by hordes of screaming reporters and television crews (...) After a while a grim George Martin arrived. 'What a tragedy' was all he could bring himself to say. Beneath his veneer of British reserve, I could sense that he was shaken to the core (...) A short while later Paul himself walked in, subdued, pensive and deep in thought (...) For a few moments, the three of us stood there numbly, reminiscing about the impact John Winston Ono Lennon had had on our lives..."[453]

Then it was time to go on with the session: "After a while our recollections petered out to an uncomfortable silence. The only thing to do, it seemed, was try to submerge our pain in the work at hand (...) Paddy laid down his parts quickly and efficiently, then, giving Paul an awkward hug, departed for the airport."[454] Emerick adds: "Paul was more than just in a state of shock. He seemed utterly lost and bewildered." [455]

The song is in the key of E major and its dark mood perfectly represents the rainy clouds depicted in the lyrics: they seem a sad premonition of what was bound to happen. The backing vocals on "Rainclouds" are classic Wings, although the song's release – as the B-side to "Ebony and Ivory" (1982) – would happen a year after the group officially disbanded.

Musicians:

Paul McCartney vocals, backing vocals, 12-string acoustic guitar, bass drum • **Linda McCartney, Eric Stewart** backing vocals • **Denny Laine** vocal harmonies, 12-string acoustic guitar (?) • **Paddy Moloney** Uilleann pipes

158 Ode to a Koala Bear (Paul McCartney)

Recording: December 8th, 1980 and March-December, 1981 (overdubs) **Location:** AIR Studios, London
Release: October 1983, "Say Say Say" single B-side

Probably written in November 1975 in Australia during the *Wings Over the World Tour,* "Ode to a Koala Bear" was inspired by the little animal, that McCartney could have seen there. A photograph taken in Australia at the time, shows McCartney hugging a koala. In an interview on the *Saturday Night Live* (May 17th, 1980), McCartney said koala was his favorite animal. Paul

---

[451] G. McGee, *cit.,* p.142.
[452] John Glatt, *The Chieftains,* 1997, p.173.
[453] Geoff Emerick, *Here, There and Everywhere. My Life Recording the Music of The Beatles,* 2006, p.358.
[454] *Ibid.,* p.359.
[455] *Ibid.*

brought out the song during these sessions, maybe having nothing better to work on: it's a pleasant but harmless pop track, featuring a piano *continuum* in Fifties style.

The recording is marked out by heavy reverb on the instrumentation and on McCartney's vocals. No details on the session are available: very likely Paul played most of the instruments, backed by Laine, and the song was overdubbed later with Linda and Eric Stewart's backing vocals. "Ode to a Koala Bear" would have to wait some time before its release: it would find its spot in 1983 as the B-side to the single "Say, Say, Say".

Musicians:

Paul McCartney vocals, backing vocals, piano, bass (?), electric guitar (?), drums (?) • **Denny Laine** electric guitar (?), bass (?) • **Linda McCartney, Eric Stewart** backing vocals

159 Tug of War (Paul McCartney)

Recording: December 16th and 18th, 1980 and March-December, 1981 (overdubs) **Location:** AIR Studios, London **Release:** April 1982, *Tug of War*

Tug of War – along with *Band on the Run* – is the best example that sums-up McCartney's world vision. His approach to anti-racism and pacifistic themes is sometimes oversimplified on the LP but this is balanced out by the liberating force of the meaningful topics: the essence of absence, freedom, the struggle of opposites, the unpredictability of events and the uselessness of anxiety. In McCartney's comedy of life there's always room for a positive solution to contradictions. With its epic majesty, "Tug Of War" sets the tone for the whole project. McCartney said: "I had the title and I wanted to do the whole album around that theme. The idea was conflict – that everything is a tug of war."[456]

McCartney and Martin came up with a very straight and effective arrangement for this track. The song's opening sound effects are taken from an actual tug of war contest, recorded by Eddie Klein in Huddersfield during the *Tug Of War Association* championship.

Paul recorded the first section – a sort of intro to the song – only with acoustic guitar and vocals, with some subtle orchestra in the background. By contrast, the second part was tough and powerful: after the chorus, three thundering electric guitars (Paul, Denny Laine and Eric Stewart, the latter overdubbed during the March-December 1981 sessions[457]) crash in and sustain the hopeful meaning of the lyrics. The lyrics are some of McCartney's best – dealing with subjects such as life's ups and downs, its confrontations and the hope that one can push forward to restore humanity. The song is a sort of hymn to joy, to regain a lost Eden as expressed in the most basic of human emotions: McCartney trusts in the rhythm of a different music, aware of the deepest meaning of life. The lyrics are emphasized by the use of a military

---

[456] Jim Miller, *Paul McCartney Looks Back*, in *Newsweek*, 03/05/1983.
[457] Stewart recalled: "I played my guitar bit at AIR Studios; Denny Laine had already left Paul's band by then". Interview by Ken Sharp, *McCartney's 2nd "Second Banana". A conversation with Eric Stewart*, in *Beatlefan*, n.140, p.18

snare, played by Campbell Maloney, an old McCartney's acquaintance: the major drummer of the Campbeltown Pipe Band, he took part in the recording of "Mull of Kintyre".

For the orchestral arrangement McCartney and Martin called Kenneth Sillito to lead the thirty-piece ensemble. The recording was quite difficult. McCartney: "On the orchestra, we were quite happy with it but we just weren't *over the top* happy with it. So we decided to do it again. With George it was, 'Oh, come on, let's really get it right' and that attitude really made the album enjoyable."[458]

The track, issued as a single in September 1982, did not hit the target, like "Ebony and Ivory" and "Take it Away", stalling at #53 both in the UK and in the US charts. It was also included in *Wingspan*. A reprise, recorded at AIR in March 1981, is still unreleased.

Musicians:

Paul McCartney vocals, backing vocals, acoustic and electric guitar, bass, drums, synthesizer • **Linda McCartney** backing vocals • **Eric Stewart** backing vocals, electric guitar • **Denny Laine** electric guitar • **Campbell Maloney** military snares • **Kenneth Sillito** violin • **Unknown musicians** strings, horns

160 Wanderlust (Paul McCartney)

Recording: December, 1980 and March-December, 1981 (overdubs) **Location:** Genetic Studios (?), Goring (basic track) and AIR Studios, London **Release:** April 1982, *Tug of War*

During the *London Town* sessions, the captain of one of the boats where Wings were recording, immediately smelled out marijuana. He warned McCartney that he would have the place searched if he suspected any further drug use.

Caught red-handed, Paul moved himself and family to a smaller yacht called *Wanderlust*. The event had a noticeable effect on McCartney who sometime later recalling the incident, would write the song, borrowing the name of the boat for its title.

McCartney: "It's actually a personal experience. The captain of the boat that we were on was a little, sort of, heavier than the other captains. We had a sort of argument with him and we wanted to get off onto this other boat, called 'Wanderlust', so it became like a symbol of freedom to me, this catamaran. We only actually stayed one night on it, but this boat was like freedom." [459]

Soon after composing the track, Paul recorded a demo. The arrangement of "Wanderlust" was largely incomplete – only electric piano, drums, bass and acoustic guitar – and the song was still lacking its countermelody, but structure was nearly identical to the officially released version.

In December, McCartney recorded the backing track with Laine – whose dull bass part would later be doubled by McCartney himself – and Adrian Sheppard, who played drums and percussion. Then he sharpened his wits searching for something to enrich the song: the

[458] K. Badman, *The Beatles. The dream Is Over-Off the Record 2*, p.303.
[459] *Maccazine*, Vol. 34, issue 3, p.13.

recording of "Wanderlust" could have been made epic with George Harrison's participation. In fact, Paul intended to have George record a guitar part. Paul, Linda and Denny Laine went to Harrison's house on Henley-on-Thames. Once they got there, as Paul recalled, "(George) said: 'First I've got this track that I'd like you to sing harmonies on ("All Those Years Ago" – author's note)'. We did our bit but then, what with one thing or another, he never got to do the guitar overdub in 'Wanderlust'."[460]

Paul got back home disheartened. But during the overdub sessions, the Philip Jones Brass Ensemble, one of the most famous English brass bands, recorded their overdub: it was an inspired choice. McCartney: "George Martin knew Philip Jones and he brought in the cassettes and this kind of thing. I had the idea for the sound, you know, sort of like Christmassy brass, sort of Pickwick Dickensian sort of feel to it all... Well that sounds to me like old Phil, so I got onto the blower." "Wanderlust" is a touching piano-ballad, enriched by a shimmering brass arrangement and bright acoustic guitars, and embellished by one of Paul's best melodies.

The lyrics convey a great sense of freedom but Paul's controlled vocal seems to hide his deep anguish. The desire to take to the sea, the fear of the dark and a call for help, reveal a plea for peace and quiet. The counter-melody's questions express uncertainty. What am I guilty of? Where have I gone wrong? Paul feels the weight of responsibility and "Wanderlust" is his only foothold. The song represents McCartney's desperate request to be free.

McCartney must have a weakness for "Wanderlust": after *Tug of War*, he re-recorded the song for the *Give My Regards to Broad Street*. This version has a simpler arrangement than the *Tug of War* one: Paul on piano, Ringo Starr on drums and the Philip Jones Brass Ensemble on brass.

Musicians:

Paul McCartney vocals, backing vocals, piano, bass, acoustic guitars • **Linda McCartney, Eric Stewart** backing vocals • **Denny Laine** bass • **Adrian Sheppard** drums, percussion • **The Philip Jones Brass Ensemble** brass

On December 4th, Columbia unexpectedly released the LP *The McCartney Interview*, which contained no music but only one hour interview with Vic Garbarini. Pressed in a limited edition (60.000 copies), it immediately went sold out in a few days, entering the *Billboard* charts at #158 and reaching #34 in the UK.

The LP got a Grammy Award nomimation. Journalist Vic Garbarini recalled: "A few months later a radio station called me to ask how I felt about being nominated for a Grammy with Paul McCartney. I thought it was a practical joke. But it seems there was indeed a Grammy category for Best Spoken Word!"

[460] *Club Sandwich*, n.72, Winter '94, p.7.

1981

At the beginning of the year, Paul returned to his old project *Hot Hits and Cold Cuts*, a collection of some of the best unreleased tracks recorded between 1971 and 1979 by McCartney alone or by Wings. The group gathered at Abbey Road in January to put the finishing touches and overdubs on a group of twelve songs, part of which still remains unissued. In any case, the album has been available to collectors for many years.

This was the tracklist: "A Love for You" – "My Carnival" – "Waterspout" – "Mama's Little Girl" – "Night Out" – "Robber's Ball" – "Cage" – "Did We Meet Somewhere Before?" – "Hey Diddle" – "Tragedy" – "Best Friend (live)" – "Same Time, Next Year"

After the sessions, Paul accepted George Martin's invitation and flew with Linda, his family and Denny Laine to AIR Studios in Montserrat, Caribbean, for a month of recordings. At this point, McCartney and Martin decided not to involve Wings but session musicians instead.

161 Dress Me up as a Robber (Paul McCartney)

Recording: February 3rd and March 23rd (overdubs), 1981 **Location:** AIR Studios, Montserrat and AIR Studios, London (overdubs) **Release:** April 1982, *Tug of War*

McCartney had prepared a demo of "Dress Me up as a Robber" in his Rude Studio in 1977. Actually, it was made-up of three separate demos, thus demonstrating how McCartney's discontinous inspiration could produce good results by joining different ideas into one package thanks to the use of studio tricks. A cut-and-paste technique that worked brilliantly in this case. When Paul got into the studio he had only a guitar riff and another very up-tempo piece, containing drum-machine, some flamenco-flavored acoustic guitars and high pitched vocals.

Most of these elements were retained in the final version, recorded by McCartney and Laine, along with Dave Mattacks on drums and percussion ("It was a very quick one!"[461]) and George Martin on electric piano.

"Dress Me up as a Robber" is the only hard-rocking track on *Tug of War*: it features a powerful riff, played in unison by electric guitar (Paul) and synthesizer (Laine).

The track has two different parts and melodies: the verses – featuring a brilliant falsetto vocal – and a melodic bridge, so typical of McCartney's style. Both are underlined by a floating bass by Paul himself, who does his best playing some intricate parts on Spanish guitar (maybe sped-up). McCartney played the song live on September 25th, 2013 at the Simply Shakespeare benefit reading of *The Two Gentlemen of Verona*, held at the Broad Stage in Santa Monica, LA.

Musicians:

---

[461] Interview courtesy of Dave Mattacks, 25/09/2011.

Paul McCartney vocals, backing vocals, bass, acoustic and electric guitar • **Linda McCartney** backing vocals • **Denny Laine** synthesizer, electric guitar • **Dave Mattacks** drums, percussion • **George Martin** electric piano

162 The Pound Is Sinking (Paul McCartney)

Recording: February 3rd, 4th and 10th, 1981 **Location:** AIR Studios, Montserrat **Release:** April 1982, *Tug of War*

"The Pound Is Sinking" was a song inspired by the monetary crisis and the fluctuating markets that McCartney had read about in the papers. Again, it was the fusion of two separate tracks.

One of these was called indeed "The Pound Is Sinking", which Paul wrote in 1977, while the other was "Hear Me Lover", a melodic love-song.

McCartney: "I see these pictures of all the hundreds of people on the phones saying, 'Did it go up? Did it go down?' But I'm not a big stocks and shares man. The song laughs at how everyone gets so serious about it."[462]

As usual, Paul had prepared demo versions of both songs in his Rude Studio. They are fascinating to listen to and to compare to the final version. On the one hand, they confirm McCartney and Martin's skills as arrangers, on the other they reveal the quality of Paul's songs even without any studio embellishment.

McCartney first recorded the tracks as separate entities during two different sessions with Laine and Dave Mattacks on February 3rd and 4th.

A week later, Paul had clearly thought about it and found the winning move: joining together the two tracks. "Hear Me Lover" would be glued to "The Pound Is Sinking", which served as the main theme.

The track was recorded with Stanley Clarke on bass and Denny Laine on acoustic guitar, while McCartney himself took charge of all the other overdubs, including the fast electric guitar breaks and apparently also drums. Although drums are not officially credited in the album liner notes, this detail was revealed by Martin to a fan outside Abbey Road Studios: maybe Paul re-did the drum part that was cut the previous week by Mattacks.

Mike Stavrou was one of the assistant engineers to Geoff Emerick and George Martin in Montserrat. He reveals an anecdote probably related to the recording of "The Pound Is Sinking": "We did one song one day and it was a fast tempo song (...) and then the next day we did a slow song and then we pulled up the multi-track of the fast song and George conducted a point that we marked. We put a razor blade through the multi-track tape and then inserted from one of the beats of the slow song into that spot several bars of the slow song and joined all back up. It was a seamless edit and it went suddenly from one tempo to another. Then they went an overdub stuff across which made it even more seamless and invisible (...). But I could

462 K. Badman, *The Beatles. The Dream Is Over-Off the Record 2*, 2002, p.304.

never figure out which song it was! It was a very cool and surprising technique, it was *very* George Martin. It worked brilliantly!"[463]

Stavrou was surprised to see that McCartney was aware of that original and perfectly functional approach: "A normal band would practice and practice the tempo change (...) take after take. But this team knew that the best way is to just totally get into the groove of one of the tempos and play this song until it plays itself (...) and then they got into the groove and the mindset of the slower one."[464]

What resulted in this way, was a typical McCartney cut-and-paste song, *à la* "Uncle Albert/Admiral Halsey" (see sheet **28**). The song begins with an acoustic intro – embellished later with odd sound effects like rolling coins, also used in the outro – that leads to the chorus, accompanied by powerful guitar chords.

McCartney did not find any verses for the song: therefore, he inserted an extravagant section, using the bass tones of his voice – almost with a comical effect. He produced a sort of medieval poet's tongue twister, counterpointed by some nervous electric guitar breaks. The 3/4 waltz-time change served as a link with the "Hear Me Lover" section and made the finale truly memorable. Also to be noted are the interplay of backing vocals and one of McCartney's best ever high-register vocal performances since *RAM*. The track is on *Tug of War*.

Musicians:

Paul McCartney vocals, backing vocals, acoustic and electric guitar, keyboards, synthesizer, drums • **Stanley Clarke** bass • **Denny Laine** backing vocals, acoustic guitar • **Linda McCartney, Eric Stewart** backing vocals

The sessions proceeded with bass player Stanley Clarke and drummer Steve Gadd.

163 Somebody Who Cares (Paul McCartney)

Recording: February 9th and March-December (overdubs), 1981 **Location:** AIR Studios, Montserrat and AIR Studios, London (overdubs) **Release:** April 1982, *Tug of War*

The weekend before Clarke and Gadd's arrival in Montserrat, McCartney took a break from studio work: "On this Sunday afternoon, I sat outside and I just got my guitar and went off into a corner (…) I knew that Steve and Stanley were coming in the next day (…) I thought that it would be really nice if I wrote something fresh and I'd play it fresh to them."[465]

The next day, McCartney brought into the studio his freshly-made "Somebody Who Cares".[466] It was a Latin-flavored acoustic ballad, probably written on Spanish guitar, but Paul thought the song was still lacking a middle section.

[463] Interview courtesy of Mike Stavrou, 08/01/2012.
[464] *Ibid.*
[465] K. Badman, *The Beatles. The dream Is Over-Off the Record 2*, 2002, p.303.
[466] To some sources, the *Tug of War* inner sleeve photo show McCartney while writing the song.

So, he told Gadd and Clarke to take a tea-break and wait for him, to see if he would come up with something in the meantime.

McCartney: "I said, 'Give me about an hour.' So I sat around for an hour, got that middle bit and went back into the studio."[467]

McCartney may have composed the major-key chorus, in stark contrast to the pensive nature of the song. The recording highlights the gentle feel of this Latin-American tinged song that Paul composed with Lennon in mind.[468] The lyrics have a comforting meaning, with their search for a helping hand in difficult times.

The intro is played by McCartney's acoustic guitar, underscored by Clarke's distinctive bass phrases and Laine's synth guitar: then "Somebody Who Cares" was given its Andean evocative tone thanks to a terrific Spanish guitar solo by McCartney, a background of percussion and some Pan flute embellishments by Adrian Brett, overdubbed later in London where backing vocals by Linda and Eric Stewart were also added.

Brett gives us a unique insight into that session: "I was called by George Hamer, who booked the musicians for all of Paul McCartney's recording sessions, and asked to go along to AIR Studios in Oxford Street, London for an afternoon session. I was quite excited as Paul McCartney was an artist for whom I had great respect but for whom I had never played and had heard from other musicians he could be quite demanding. I was somewhat apprehensive also as I knew that he could not read music and usually made suggestions to a player without any theoretical music direction but always knowing when something was played which he liked (...) I entered the studio and Paul was sat at the control desk with George Martin, who I had worked for many times in the past and who introduced me to Paul (...) I was the only flute-player in London who played the panpipes and my abilities were somewhat limited (...) I was relieved there was no difficult written-out music!"[469]

Then Paul gave the musician a hard time. Brett: "The track was played to me and as it was playing, Paul told me where he wanted me to play.... But not what he wanted! I must have looked either worried or perplexed for after a few moments Paul turned to me and apologized for not being able to read music and to explain in more detail what he wanted (...) The first thing I had to do was to identify the key of the song which to my relief was C/A minor... And I had panpipes which could play in this key (...) We worked for a while and I made a few suggestions which Paul liked and a few which he did not and the working method (which I had long known about) of playing several solos until he really liked something produced the end

[467] K. Badman, cit., p.303.
[468] Jim Miller, Paul McCartney Looks Back, in Newsweek, 03/05/1983. McCartney said: "I remember being aware of John's death while writing it".
[469] Interview courtesy of Adrian Brett, 26/09/2011.

result used on the track... Including an overdubbed '2nd panpipe' towards the end of the song."[470] The track is on *Tug of War*.

Musicians:

Paul McCartney vocals, backing vocals, acoustic and Spanish guitar • **Stanley Clarke** bass • **Steve Gadd** drums, percussion • **Denny Laine** synth guitar • **Adrian Brett** Pan flute • **Linda McCartney, Eric Stewart** backing vocals

164 Hey, Hey (Paul McCartney-Stanley Clarke)

Recording: February 10th, 1981 **Location:** AIR Studios, Montserrat **Release:** October 1983, *Pipes of Peace*

The day after the recording of "Somebody Who Cares", McCartney began to get to know Stanley Clarke, bass virtuoso and leading figure of the jazz-fusion musical scene during the Seventies and Eighties.

"Hey, Hey" resulted from a studio jam, as Clarke himself recalled: "I had the honor of being contacted by Paul through George Martin to play. Paul was very nice. He asked me to show him how to slap. During this track we got a groove going in a studio jam, and it ended up as 'Hey Hey'. He graciously gave me a co-writing credit, and it's still a thrill to see my name next to his above the music in the song book. Paul definitely had an influence on my bass playing, not so much technically, but more with his philosophy of melodic bass lines."[471]

Mike Stavrou: "Paul and Stanley had a good time together showing each other stuff and playing little riffs and things all the time."[472]

The song is indeed the recording of that jam as performed by McCartney, Clarke and Gadd (and probably Laine). It's an unremarkable rock-fusion instrumental, uncharacteristic of the style of McCartney's records.

Dry guitar riffs run throughout the song in counterpoint to Gadd's busy drums and Clarke's unmistakable bass, that stands out in the slow mid-section, characterized by an ethereal and liquid sound. The song was removed from the final *Tug of War* track-list but turned out to be useful later as a filler on *Pipes of Peace*.

Musicians:

Paul McCartney backing vocals, electric guitar, keyboards (?), synthesizer (?) • **Stanley Clarke** bass • **Steve Gadd** drums • **Denny Laine** electric guitar (?)

165 Take it Away (Paul McCartney)

Recording: February 16th-18th and March 23rd (overdubs), 1981 **Location:** AIR Studios, Montserrat and AIR Studios, London (overdubs) **Release:** April 1982, *Tug of War*

---

[470] *Ibid.*
[471] Stanley Clarke in *Bass Player*, n. 5, July-August 1995, p.22.
[472] Interview courtesy of Mike Stavrou, 08/01/2012.

After several years from their last collaboration, Paul got back in the studio with Ringo. The previous Summer, they got together at the Super Bear Studio in France: McCartney wanted to help Ringo for his upcoming album, offering two brand new songs ("Attention" and "Private Property") for which he had prepared demos.

During a two-week period (July 11th- 21st, 1980) in Les Alpes – a small village in the South of France, between Nice and Monaco – Paul, Linda and Ringo, along with Laurence Juber, Howie Casey and Lloyd Green, recorded five tracks: in addition to the songs composed by McCartney, the group recorded "Sure to Fall (in Love With You)" – a Carl Perkins' cover – "Love's Full Glory" – a song by Linda – and a jam called "Can't Fight Lightning".

Paul was inspired by the meeting and Ringo repaid the favour when McCartney invited him to Montserrat to record. Paul had the idea to have Ringo and Steve Gadd play a duet: he let the two drummers hear "Take It Away", one of his classic dynamic and energetic songs that he had demoed a few months earlier.

This early recording was very different to the definitive version released on *Tug of War*: the demo was lacking the bridge and the arrangement was rough-sketched, featuring only a bed of acoustic guitars.

Paul was keen on the idea, thinking that the song could work, so he presented it to Wings during the October rehearsals.

There is a tape where McCartney can be heard singing the song as he accompanies himself on electric piano explaining the chords: "It's two bits, the chorus is pretty simple, three chords, Buddy Holly style."

Then Juber tries to build an accompaniment but the recording fades out and it isn't clear if Wings made anything of it. However it went, Paul knew his mind and brought the song into the studio in Montserrat.

Paul completed the song and "Take it Away" became a bouncy pop tune with a cool reggae bass riff: a fine balance between the fast changing chords, the catchy hook and the relaxed verses.

With Ringo and Steve Gadd to provide a bed of percussion, the basic track was recorded with George Martin on electric piano. The song was finished adding a sparkling horn arrangement (two trumpets, two saxes and a trombone) overdubbed on March 23rd at AIR Studios.

Mike Stavrou: "I can still see the two of them set up next to each other and playing together (...) So we had Steve Gadd as you were looking through the studio glass on the left and Ringo right next to him to the right. I don't even know if we had any screen separating (...) The studio was great, there weren't any isolation problems."[473]

---

[473] *Ibid.*

A monitor-mix appeared in collectors' circuits shows that the track – which on the record fades out – ended jokingly with a marching tempo. Paul's lyrics include some very intense verses, dealing with the flow of life's events and with the sense of their completion: flowers are "waiting", something that is usually associated with human beings.

Released as the second single from *Tug of War*, "Take it Away" did not miss the mark, reaching #10 in the US charts and #15 in the UK. The single version (later included in *Wingspan*) has a clean intro with more percussion not heard on the album edit, which is crossfaded with "Tug Of War".

The video shoot is worth mentioning. It marks the only performance in front of an audience held by McCartney between 1979 and 1985: six-hundred fans were gathered at EMI Elstree Studios on June 23rd, 1982 to watch this impromptu concert with a band featuring Paul, Linda, Ringo, George Martin, Eric Stewart, Steve Gadd and the Q-Tips horn section.

They launched into Paul's favorite rock'n'roll repertoire, playing "Lucille", "Twenty Flight Rock", "Send Me Some Lovin'", "Cut Across Shorty" and an improvised "Elstree Blues".

Musicians:

Paul McCartney vocals, backing vocals, piano, bass, acoustic guitar • **George Martin** electric piano • **Ringo Starr, Steve Gadd** drums • **Linda McCartney, Eric Stewart** backing vocals • **Unknown musicians** horns

166 Average Person (Paul McCartney)

Recording: February 16th-18th and March? (overdubs), 1981 **Location:** AIR Studios, Montserrat and AIR Studios?, London (overdubs) **Release:** October 1983, *Pipes of Peace*

The search for a lost identity and the regaining of a personal dimension among the masses were the themes most often dealt with in McCartney's songs.

After the melancholic character of "Another Day" (see sheet **17**) and the loneliness portrayed in "Lonely Old People" (see sheet **89**), in "Average Person" McCartney chose to describe ordinary people, with their struggle in standing out from mediocrity and from normality, when the latter condition is considered as monotonous and unsatisfying in its daily repetitive events. Precisely the same normality that Paul admits to seeking out for himself.

The grotesque gallery full of everyday people and their doings portrayed in the song, is a clear lashing out at society and the roles that define it. The list includes an engine driver who dreams of becoming a lion tamer, a waitress who wants to audition in Hollywood (but she loses the part to a boy!) and finally a frustrated boxer with a height complex.

Wisely, McCartney avoided any pathetic tones and opted for a cheerful, upbeat song. However, the direction that McCartney and Martin gave to the song was to no avail. The track's final arrangement came after several initial ideas were discarded.

Paul's demo (dating from August 1980) had been put through the sieve by Wings during the October rehearsals, which offer a peek at McCartney's meticulousness in the recording studio. Paul leads Denny and Linda's clumsy voices towards their correct pitch for the counter-melody and harmonies until finally achieving the desired results. The humorous tone of "Average Person" is better expressed in Paul's demo rather than in Wings' attempt: McCartney's first version has a certain freshness and a funny mood that were lost in the group's run-through.

Paul recorded "Average Person" twice: reportedly, the first take – unreleased to date – was taped in Montserrat on February 4th with Denny Laine and Dave Mattacks, but McCartney changed his mind about the arrangement, and the song was re-cut bringing in Ringo on drums. Some of that basic track may have been used in the final version but there is little information about this recording – the copyright assigned to MPL Communications Inc. is proof that the track was taped outside of the UK – and probably McCartney handled a lot of the instruments. Martin: "We thought of 'Average Person' as being a stagey sort of thing. It was Paul's idea, that theatrical aspect. We even tried having him doing the vocal like a stage. I lined up a lot of mikes and he actually did a funny walk on 'I say, I say' kind of thing…"[474]

Later – maybe during the March-December sessions or even during the *Pipes of Peace* recordings in 1982 or 1983 – McCartney and Martin added a galloping trumpet arrangement and an instrumental jazz intermezzo, thus burying the airy bass of the original demo.

"Average Person" was originally intended as the second track on *Tug of War*, instead of "Take it Away" but – in Paul's words – "it didn't work" and was not released until *Pipes of Peace*.

Musicians:

Paul McCartney vocals, backing vocals, piano, bass, acoustic and electric guitar (?) • **Linda McCartney, Eric Stewart** backing vocals • **Denny Laine** acoustic guitar (?), electric guitar (?) • **Ringo Starr** drums • **Unknown musicians** horns

On February 21st, Carl Perkins arrived in Montserrat: Carl and Paul spent their first day in the studio jamming and playing classics from Perkins' repertoire, like "Honey Don't" or "Lend Me Your Comb".

167 Get It (Paul McCartney)

Recording: February 24th, 1981 **Location:** AIR Studios, Montserrat **Release:** April 1982, *Tug of War*

Perkins' records were a must for many young musicians in the Sixties and McCartney was no exception. Perkins' rockabilly songs were regularly in The Beatles' repertoire and the group also recorded three of them ("Matchbox", "Honey Don't" and "Everybody's Trying to Be My Baby"). McCartney was a great admirer of the American rockabilly hero and he rose to the occasion, inviting Perkins to join him in Montserrat.

---

474 *Club Sandwich*, no.31, October 1983.

McCartney: "I rang him up, and he was in the States playing clubs (...) Anyone who was a legend in our formative years is still a legend. Carl is still the guy who wrote 'Blue Suede Shoes', and he can never do any wrong."[475]

For the occasion, Paul had written "Get It", a jumpy acoustic number that fits well with Perkins' characteristic style and in fact, he gave a spirited performance for this good-time duet.

There is a curious story about the recording of "Get It" that McCartney revealed in detail. At the end of the song one can hear a bellowing laugh from Perkins and this is how Paul tells it: "We were recording in Montserrat, and a musician friend was sailing around the world on a yacht, and he sailed into Montserrat and he invited us to his boat. Carl was really impressed with the buffet and the champagne, and the way it was all laid out. He came over to me and said, 'Paul, where I come from they call this shittin' in high cotton.' It's one of my favorite expressions. After that, we recorded 'Get It' and at the end both of us are laughing, and that's the joke we're laughing at. We had to cut it, because otherwise we'd have never gotten it played on the radio."[476]

The laughing-songs belonged to the humorous tradition of British music-hall: these songs – the most popular of which is "The Laughing Policeman", recorded in 1922 by Charles Penrose, also known as Charles Jolly – contained some melodies performed laughing.

You can be sure McCartney had left Perkins' laughing into the final recording intentionally, as a little tribute to that tradition. Paul: "I can always see Laurel & Hardy dancing to this track."[477]

This is a perfect example of the relaxed and friendly relationship established between Perkins and McCartney, who recalls: "I was just telling him about some of his old songs we loved, like 'Your True Love' or 'Lend Me Your Comb'. And then we'd sing together. Then we'd stop, and he'd say, 'Well, you know, Paul, I used to do this,' and he'd show me some fingerpicking things he used to do."[478]

Perkins stayed with McCartney for one week and the night before he left, he wrote a song that summed up his feelings about the visit.

Perkins' song, "My Old Friend", is an affectionate tribute to McCartney and was recorded the following day. Paul played guitar, bass, drums and added some harmony vocals to the track. It remained unreleased for fifteen years, until it was issued on Perkins' album *Go Cat Go!* (1996).

McCartney and Perkins would meet again many years later, backstage in Memphis, during Paul's American tour in 1993: they had some fun together, playing songs like "Get It", "Your True Love", "Lend Me Your Comb", "Movie Magg" and "Blue Suede Shoes".

[475] Tom Mulhern, *Guitar Player*, July 1990.
[476] *Ibid.*
[477] K. Badman, *The Beatles. The Dream Is Over, Off the Record 2*, 2002, p.303.
[478] *Ibid.*

Paul often takes the opportunity to perform Perkins' classics, especially during his soundchecks: a wild version of "Matchbox" is included in *Tripping the Live Fantastic*.[479] McCartney paid tribute to Carl's memory recording for his *Run Devil Run* album a touching rendition of "Movie Magg", the first single of Perkins' career. "Get It" is on *Tug of War* and was also used as the B-side to the "Tug of War" single.

Musicians:

Paul McCartney vocals, acoustic guitars, bass, percussion, synthesizer • **Carl Perkins** vocals, electric guitar

The Montserrat sessions ended with Stevie Wonder.

168 Ebony and Ivory (Paul McCartney)

Recording: February 27th-28th, March 30th (overdubs part 1) and October (overdubs part 2), 1981 **Location:** AIR Studios, Montserrat, AIR Studios, London (overdubs part 1) and Strawberry Studios South (overdubs part 2), Dorking **Release:** March 1982, single (from *Tug of War*)

It's a little known fact that "Ebony and Ivory" – one of McCartney's most popular and successful songs – was inspired by an argument with Linda.

McCartney: "I wrote 'Ebony & Ivory' after a little marital tiff with Linda: it was like, 'Why can't we get it together – our piano can.' You just grab any old idea to get yourself out of it?"[480]

In his Rude Studio, still in a bad mood ("I remember when I wrote it I wasn't feeling that brilliant"[481]) Paul sat down at his Rhodes piano: he had recently heard Spike Milligan talking about the notes on a piano and McCartney wondered what the keys were made of. And that's how the title came about.[482]

Paul found a chord sequence noodling around in E major and he recorded a demo at his Rude Studio at the beginning of 1980. This snippet (1:32), featuring double-tracked vocals and electric piano, had only the chorus part.

In its unfinished state, Paul brought "Ebony and Ivory" into the studio for Wings' rehearsals in October 1980. The recording is proof that McCartney had already thought of the song as a duet since he sang it with Denny Laine.

"Ebony and Ivory" slowly turned into a song about racial equality. The white and black keys were the perfect metaphor for an anti-racial statement.

While in Montserrat, Paul decided to contact Stevie Wonder and in the blink of an eye, he called him, spoke about the song and invited him to the session.

---

[479] Paul performed the song in his Tv show *Unplugged* but did not include it in the record.
[480] From *Record Collector*, June 1997.
[481] K. Badman, *cit*, p.301.
[482] George Martin, *Making Music*, 1983.

222

There in the Caribbean, McCartney and Wonder began sessions that Paul said have been the longest recordings that he ever dedicated to one of his songs.

During those days together Paul and Stevie had a lot of fun as it's clear listening to some outtakes (presented by Paul during his *Oobu Joobu* show) with the two improvising and joking. At first, they used a drum machine to help build the track.

McCartney: "We started off with a rhythm box, one of the first Lynn drum machines. (Stevie) brought it to Montserrat (…) After we put a track down with that, Stevie did the drums, and then we did the vocals."[483]

In the end, it resulted in a well-crafted production. One can hear Wonder's perfect drumming balanced out by a melodic bass part in typical McCartney fashion. Paul was portrayed with Wonder in the studio with his Yamaha bass.

McCartney: "I figured I had to put down a good bass part. I sat around and tried to work out something that would sympathize with the record; I was quite pleased with it."[484]

Mike Stavrou has a funny anecdote about Wonder: "I remember Stevie impressing everybody with his skills on the drum kit. When we miked up the kit one of the funniest things he said – we miked it up using expensive microphones – and before we started to play he made a joke, he said, 'You wouldn't believe how many UB87 (famous microphone label – author's note) I've smashed!' Everybody in the control room looked each other rather worried! Obviously he did not hit one!"[485]

Back in England, "Ebony and Ivory" was completed with several sessions dedicated to backing vocals, first at AIR in London and later at Strawberry Studios South in Dorking, where Paul also recorded vocals for his solo version. McCartney stated that they spent a lot of time cleaning-up and finishing the track.

The result of all that hard work is one of the most famous pop duets. "Ebony and Ivory" is a gleaming pop song: relying on his perfect melody, it features a brilliant arrangement with sparkling synthesizers and massive backing vocals. Even if the preachy lyrics rubbed some listeners the wrong way, "Ebony and Ivory" received much critical acclaim.

Released as a single, it went straight to #1 in the UK and in the US, sold over two million copies and got two Grammy Award nominations for Best Male Vocal Performance and Song Of The Year. The McCartney solo version was included in the "Ebony and Ivory" 12" single: the *Tug of War* version also appears on *All the Best!*

McCartney performed the song during the 1989/90 *Paul McCartney World Tour* and during the 1991 *Secret Gigs Tour*, singing it with Hamish Stuart. The version released on *Tripping the Live Fantastic!* is taken from the Rotterdam venue, on 8/11/1989.

---

[483] Tom Mulhern, *cit.*
[484] *Ibid.*
[485] Interview courtesy of Mike Stavrou, 08/01/2012.

The outstanding duet with Wonder at the Los Angeles Forum, on 27/11/1989 unfortunately remains unreleased. The song would be performed live again by McCartney and Wonder together many years later, for a unique event: the concert held at The White House, on June 2nd, 2010.

Musicians:

Paul McCartney vocals, backing vocals, bass, piano, synthesizer, vocoder, percussion, electric guitar • **Stevie Wonder** vocals, backing vocals, electric piano, synthesizer, percussion, drums • **Linda McCartney, Eric Stewart** backing vocals

169 What's That You're Doing (Paul McCartney-Stevie Wonder)

Recording: March 1st-2nd (basic track) and 30th (overdubs), 1981 **Location:** AIR Studios, Montserrat and AIR Studios, London (overdubs) **Release:** April 1982, *Tug of War*

The relaxed atmosphere of the "Ebony and Ivory" sessions drove McCartney and Wonder to carry on in the studio for two more days.

The idea for "What's That You're Doing?" began as a riff that Wonder found while messing around on his synth: while Stevie was creating one of his typical grooves, Paul played drums, adding his own input to the drum machine pattern.

McCartney admitted that he had a hard time playing drums: "He started jamming, so I jumped on the drums, thinking, 'Well he's playing a bass line on the keyboards so I won't go on bass and I'll get in his way'. So I started drumming and eventually he started cutting me back because I was doing too much on the drums. I was getting too busy and spoiling it, really. It ended up with me just doing bass drum and snare. When Stevie wasn't there I re-did the drums."[486]

Mike Stavrou confirmed that the track was born while Wonder was improvising in the studio: "Stevie came in and started jamming this song and maybe even writing the lyrics as he went along!"[487]

Once the basic track was completed, Paul overdubbed electric guitars and bass: then the two shared the vocal parts and came up with this electronic funky track, so typical of Wonder's style and a perfect counterpoint to "Ebony and Ivory"'s light pop.

Going on for over six minutes "What's That You're Doing" unravels a series of sexual double entendres over a jittery synth pad recognizably from the hand of Wonder. Unfortunately, the song's lightweight production is in clear contrast to its funky roots.

McCartney's vocal is quite a letdown as he chose not to use his black-tinged vocal style (ala "Why Don't We Do It in the Road?") and his "She Loves You" reference isn't enough to save the situation, either. During the overdub sessions Andy MacKay, Roxy Music's famous sax

---

[486] K. Badman, *The Beatles. The dream Is Over-Off the Record 2*, 2002, p.302.
[487] Interview courtesy of Mike Stavrou, 08/01/2012.

player, gave his contribution playing lyricon, the first electronic wind instrument, invented by Bill Bernardi. This song too is featured on *Tug of War*.

Musicians:

Paul McCartney vocals, backing vocals, bass, drums, electric guitars • **Stevie Wonder** vocals, synthesizer • **Andy MacKay** lyricon • **Linda McCartney, Eric Stewart** backing vocals

It's not clear why, but the Montserrat sessions were the last where Paul and Denny Laine would work together. Apparently while in the Carribean they had a fight: Denny had criticized the lyrics to "Somebody Who Cares" and Paul became furious and fired him.

However it went, Laine remained in Montserrat at least until Carl Perkins's arrival on the island, since he's portrayed in a picture with him and Paul.

Back in the UK, Denny decided to cut all his artistic ties with McCartney. Also as a result of the argument Paul, as suggested to him by Martin, began a solo career that no longer required a fixed backing band or the stress of touring. It wasn't long before Wings too, would break up. Paul didn't make an official announcement. A brief article appeared on *Club Sandwich* ("So Long Denny") after the departure of Laine, who in his own interview with ATV on April 27th explained his leaving "mainly because Paul is a studio person."

McCartney stated at the time: "I felt a bit limited working with the group and I just didn't fancy going in and making another group album (…) I hate the pressure of a group (…) With Wings, with so many changes in the line-up, it wasn't so easy. That often distracts you from the music and you start thinking a whole load of other things. You're thinking about the group image."[488]

As Linda McCartney perfectly recapped some years later: "Paul is such a good musician, and none of the Wings were good enough to play with him... Including me, for sure. They were good, not great."[489]

McCartney promptly resumed the sessions, with a long period of recordings between May and December at AIR Studios in London.

As usual, the sessions produced a large number of unreleased tracks, including "Blackpool", "Any Younger", "Stop, You Don't Know Where She Came From", "Peruvian Birdsong" and "Simon's Wigwam".

170 Here Today (Paul McCartney)

Recording: May-December, 1981 **Location**: AIR Studios, London **Release**: April 1982, *Tug of War*
Written "shortly after John died", "Here Today" is one of the most sincere and moving demonstrations of Paul's inner feelings for John Lennon.

---

[488] Ray Bonici, *Paul McCartney Wings It Alone*, in *Music Express*, April-May 1982, n.156.
[489] Joan Goodman, *Playboy* interview, December 1984.

McCartney: "I was kind of crying when I wrote it. It's like a dialog with John (...) The 'I love you' part was hard to say. A part of me said, 'Hold on. Wait a minute. Are you really going to do that?' I finally said, 'Yeah, I've got to.'"[490]

McCartney wrote the song "in the upstairs room of what is now my recording studio"[491], remembering something that really happened: "We were supposed to play a gig in Jacksonville, and we couldn't get in because there was some great hurricane. So we had to spend a night or two in Key West. And at that age, with that much time on our hands, we didn't really know what to do with it except get drunk. And so that was what we did. And we stayed up all night talking, talking, talking like it was going out of style. And at some point early in the morning, I think we must have touched on some points that were really emotional, and we ended up crying, which was very unusual for us, because we members of the band and young guys, we didn't do that kind of thing."[492]

The memories of that intimate moment pushed Paul to write a song that expressed how unique his relationship with Lennon was: the lyrics depict a very edgy John (he would always answer in some – apparently, at least – rude way to something gentle, probably laughing and saying the opposite thing), re-confirming his self-contained stance and his unconventional ways.

The reference to the "nights when we cried" is the most touching part of "Here Today", a gentle reenactment of the past perfectly counterpointed by a well-chosen instrumentation: Paul and his soft acoustic guitar are backed only by a toned-down string quartet, written by George Martin in the pure tradition of "Yesterday".

A strong cast of players was selected for the recording: Jack Rothstein (a well-known Polish-born violinist and conductor, which during World War II was invited to join the British Army playing for the troops. He also played violin in The Beatles' songs "I Am the Walrus" and "Within You, Without You"), Bernard Partridge, as well as Keith Harvey and Ian Jewel from the famous Gabrieli String Quartet.

Included in *Tug of War*, "Here Today" was performed live by McCartney for the first time on his 2002/03 *Drivin' Tour*.

Well-accepted by his audiences who empathized with the Lennon tribute, the song was difficult for McCartney to deal with, often causing him to well-up with emotion.

Taken from the 2002-03 *Drivin' Tour*, "Here Today" is included in the albums *Back in the US* and *Back in the World*.

The song was performed also during the tours between 2007 and 2014 and it was released in two other live versions. The first – taken from the 27/06/2007 concert – appears on *Live in Los Angeles*, the second is on *Good Evening New York City*.

---

[490] K. Badman, *The Beatles. The dream Is Over-Off the Record 2*, 2002, p.304.
[491] *Fresh Air*, April 2001.
[492] *Ibid.*

Musicians:

Paul McCartney vocals, backing vocals, acoustic guitar • **Jack Rothstein, Bernard Partridge** violin • **Ian Jewel** viola • **Keith Harvey** cello

171 Be What You See (Paul McCartney)

Recording: May-December, 1981 **Location:** AIR Studios, London **Release:** April 1982, *Tug of War*

During the sessions, McCartney couldn't resist a little experimentation and opted to use the most famous synthesizer – the vocoder – applying its effect to a 30-second segment of voice and acoustic guitar. The result was this brief, meditative bit included in *Tug of War*.

McCartney: "I wanted a few moments on the album where, like on a Pink Floyd album, you'll get a sound developing into another sound."[493]

McCartney sought for a counterbalance to the Perkins' belly laughing placed at the end of "Get It": "It was a genuine laughing but I wanted it to go into something more mystical. So I got on vocoder, which Herbie Hancock uses, where you play the actual notes with your mouth"[494].

McCartney expresses a sort of Eastern philosophy: with its mysterious pensive and cloister-like atmosphere – thanks to the vocoder – "Be What You See" underlines the possibility of a full personal affirmation.

Musicians:

Paul McCartney vocals, acoustic guitar, vocoder

172 Sweetest Little Show (Paul McCartney)

Recording: March-December, 1981 **Location:** AIR Studios, London **Release:** October 1983, *Pipes of Peace*

"Sweetest Little Show" jumped out from a jam during Wings' rehearsals in July 1980, and was built around a chord sequence "that was lying around for a while".

McCartney came back to this song the following month, recording a demo that was much slower than the released version. Other than that, the arrangement of "Sweetest Little Show" was very similar to the released version, including an agile bass part.

Initially, the song was part of a eight-minute long medley with the tracks "Any Younger" and "Unbelievable Experience" before the idea was discarded.

Probably handled by McCartney on his own – the use of the vocoder suggests that the song could have been recorded during the same session as "Be What You See" – the song was fine-tuned with the addition of a tasteful and classical-inspired acoustic guitar solo.

It was Paul's idea to add the guitar 'show': he was humorously applauded by all the engineers and studio assistants as can be heard in the final version.

---

[493] K. Badman, *The Beatles. The dream Is Over-Off the Record 2*, 2002, p.304.
[494] *Ibid.*

For good reason, McCartney didn't include it in *Tug of War* and when it was released on *Pipes of Peace*, it drew a lot of attention from the press.

Within the album's setting – dull sounding and lyrically trite – it seemed like a conscious effort to limit negative criticism. In some verses, Paul also seems to lay himself open to his critics: he's saying to himself that he's good and to answer with a smile to the critics.

It was a self-serving move, as if McCartney had run out of steam after years of receiving criticism.

Musicians:

Paul McCartney vocals, backing vocals, bass, acoustic and electric guitar, vocoder, piano (?), synthesizer (?), drums (?), castanets (?), shaker (?)

173 Say, Say, Say (Paul McCartney-Michael Jackson)

Recording: May 1981, April 1982 (overdubs part 1) and February 1983 (overdubs part 2) **Location:** AIR Studios, London (basic track and overdubs part 2), Hollywood Sound Studios and Cherokee Studios (overdubs part 1), Los Angeles **Release:** October 1983, single (from *Pipes of Peace*)

After their meeting in 1975 and the mutual tribute of "Girlfriend", Paul and Michael got back in touch on Christmas Day in 1980. Jackson called McCartney on the phone and they agreed to meet and try write something together.

McCartney: "Michael came over and we sat around upstairs on the top floor of our office in London and I just grabbed a guitar and 'Say, Say, Say' came out of it (…) Michael helped with a lot of the words. Michael's more just a vocalist than a writer."[495]

Although their songwriting partnership during those get-togethers may have been unconventional, they produced the most famous and highest selling song for McCartney in the Eighties.

It was also his last American number one. In the studio, "Say Say Say" immediately took an interesting turn: Paul wanted the song to be as commercial as possible. He knew he could really make it and secure new fame and a new target audience.

It's a funky tune that leans towards disco, sung as a duet – a remarkable piece in McCartney's discography. "Say Say Say" is another example of Paul's stylistic versatility, that found him completely at his ease, even though he found himself involved in a collaboration that clearly spanned both a generational gap and a different musical background.

After the first sessions in London, the track was put on the shelves for a while until it was resumed for further work in the Spring 1982 at the Cherokee Studios in Los Angeles.

Here, "Say, Say, Say" was worked on by Jackson's session-men and the track was completed with the addition of Jerry Hey's harmonica solo and a terrific horn arrangement, whose riff is one of the major hooks of the song. Gary Herbig played tenor sax.[496]

---

[495] *Paul McCartney World Tour booklet*, p.82.

Nathan Watts is credited for playing bass on the song and he tells how it went: "I did 'Say Say Say' with Michael Jackson at Hollywood Sound, and it was supposed to be a demo for Michael and Paul. Michael didn't really tell me what to play on it, I just played the feel and Michael said, 'I like that, do that!' And I thought that Paul McCartney was gonna overdub it, because he's Paul McCartney. But when it got to Paul, he said he liked the feel so much he was leaving it the way it was. Now *that* was a compliment!"[497]

The song's development is described by keyboard player, Bill Wolfer, famous for having come up with the celebrated intro to "Billy Jean".

Wolfer: "Michael came to me with a cassette of he and Paul singing the song with Paul playing acoustic guitar. We worked out a rhythm arrangement, and with a couple of keyboards, and a drum-machine, we recorded a 4-track demo for the musicians to hear to learn the song. We then went into the studio (Hollywood Sound, I think) to record it. We did the basic tracks, but the feel wasn't there. Michael was disappointed. I suggested we try again the next day with Nathan Watts on bass, and Ricky Lawson on drums. We did that, and it came out great." [498]

Then the track was completed and McCartney thought it was perfect: "Later that week, Michael called me back to do some synthesizer overdubs" – Wolfer says – "In the meantime, he had recorded the horns, guitar, and the harmonica solo. Michael had told me that he hoped that Paul would use his demo as the track for the album, and that's what happened. Michael took the 24-track tape to London, and Paul loved it, and wanted to use it as is. They just added their final vocals to it and mixed." [499]

The final touch consisted of some new overdubs done in England in February 1983 when Michael was invited by Paul at his farm. It was during that visit that Jackson spoke to McCartney about his wonderful idea to someday buy the Beatles' song catalogue.

Sometimes unfortunately, visions of the future – like good jokes – aren't understood with the immediacy they need and so Paul just laughed it off.

The single was a taster to the *Pipes of Peace* album, with exciting results: #1 in US (and two million copies sold) and #2 in the UK. The 12" includes a remix and an instrumental version.

A very elaborate video-clip for "Say Say Say" – directed by Bob Giraldi – was shot in California. Unfortunately, the success of the song would cost dearly to McCartney. The track was also included in *All the Best!*

Musicians:

Paul McCartney vocals, backing vocals, electric piano (?), electric guitar (?), percussion (?), synthesizer (?) • **Nathan Watts** bass • **Bill Wolfer** keyboards, synthesizer • **Linda McCartney, Eric Stewart** backing

---

[496] Interview courtesy of Gary Herbig, 25/01/2013.
[497] Interview by Rick Suchow, *in Nathan Watts: the Groove of Wonder*, in *Bass Player*, February 2011.
[498] Interview courtesy of Bill Wolfer, 25/07/2012.
[499] *Ibid.*

vocals • **Michael Jackson** vocals, backing vocals • **David Williams** electric guitar • **Chris Smith** harmonica • **Ricky Lawson** drums • **Jerry Hey, Ernie Watts, Gary E. Grant, Gary Herbig** horns

174 The Man (Paul McCartney-Michael Jackson)

Recording: May 1981, April 1982 (overdubs part 1)? and February 1983 (overdubs part 2) **Location:** AIR Studios, London (basic track and overdubs part 2) and Cherokee Studios, Los Angeles (overdubs part 1)?
Release: October 1983, *Pipes of Peace*

Paul played "The Man" to Jackson having only the intro. Reportedly, McCartney had recorded a demo titled "This Is the Man" at the beginning of 1980.

The two recorded a first demo: then Jackson had the idea of adding new lyrics and "The Man" was demoed again.

Jackson's voice dominates the scene. The arrangement features some ingenious orchestral ideas care of Martin as well as some lovely backing vocals. Jackson himself had insisted that Linda take part in the recording, and in the refrain Michael and Linda even share lead vocals.

The song contains a fuzz-toned electric guitar solo – probably by McCartney himself – as well as other brilliant instrumentation, like flutes and a mandolin part.

No further details have surfaced about this recording which, according to the copyright on *Pipes of Peace*, was not recorded in the United States, as was "Say Say Say".

Nevertheless, "The Man" began to get good rotation on radio, since the stations were looking for something new and fresh, having exhausted the "Say Say Say" wave.

This was also helped by the fact that EMI chose it as a single from *Pipes of Peace* in February 1984, backed by the unreleased song "Blackpool" on the B-side.

Paul's arrest for possession of cannabis in Barbados on January 16th, 1984 brought a halt to the commercial activity. McCartney didn't want to draw Michael into any negative publicity and so Paul missed out on obtaining another hit with Jackson…

Musicians:

Paul McCartney vocals, backing vocals, acoustic and electric guitar (?), bass (?), shaker (?) drums (?) • **Michael Jackson, Linda McCartney** vocals, backing vocals • **Eric Stewart** backing vocals • **Unknown musicians** strings, flutes, mandolin

1982

Expectation for the upcoming *Tug of War* was growing: Paul hadn't released an album in two years. When the album was launched on the market in April, it was immediately acclaimed: the critics considered McCartney's lyrics deep and meaningful and thought that his songs were inspired and equalled *Band on the Run*.

Tug of War was highly praised by *Rolling Stone*, who said that the album was "the masterpiece everyone has always known Paul McCartney could make". Its lavish production, reminiscent more of the sumptuous *Abbey Road* than of the stripped-back approach of the *McCartney* album, was particularly appreciated.

The album became an instant-classic, according to *Rolling Stone*'s critic Stephen Holden: "Together, McCartney and Martin had compiled a veritable encyclopedia of contemporary studio pop in the deluxe, high-tech tradition of Fleetwood Mac's *Rumours*, Michael Jackson's *Off the Wall* or Stevie Wonder's *Songs in the Key of Life*."

Tug of War went straight to #1 both in the UK and US charts – a never repeated feat – and got two Grammy Award nominations in the Best Album Of The Year and Best Sound Engineered Album categories.

In October, Paul got back into the studio to record some songs for the *Pipes of Peace* album. Possibly, McCartney worked again on some tracks in 1983, but no details about these sessions have surfaced.

Whereas some of the tracks on this album would be retrieved from the shelves of the *Tug of War* sessions or, like "Say, Say, Say" and "The Man" were part of a special project, the following songs – recorded at AIR – were intended specifically for the *Pipes of Peace* album, and included some of the best results of the whole LP. The recording of the "Radio One Jingle", a brief jingle written by Paul for BBC Radio One, could be from this period.

175 Pipes of Peace (Paul McCartney)

Recording: October, 1982 **Location:** AIR Studios, London **Release:** October 1983, *Pipes of Peace*

After *Tug of War*'s intense exploration both conceptually and lyrically, in the balance between war and peace or conflict and quiet, "Pipes of Peace" – that would become the title track of the following album – represents the landing place to McCartney's battle between good and evil. The racial harmony of "Ebony and Ivory" becomes a hopeful search for universal love. The danger in this case is how easily one can fall into the banal or obvious. But Paul succeeded in creating a memorable song that ideally re-connects with Lennon's pacifist anthems.

McCartney was inspired by the critic George Melly to write a song for children about peace in the world. Taking his cue from a line by the renowned Indian poet, Rabindranath Tagore ("In love all of life's contradictions dissolve and disappear"), McCartney developed his melodic ballad very cleverly, choosing various elements to create an original piece of work.

Opening with a curious horn intro mimicking the distant sound of bombs falling on a battlefield – the same effect would be used again in the *Liverpool Oratorio* in 1991 – "Pipes of Peace" is crowned with a couple of lilting verses. These serve as prologue and ending to the song, with Paul playing some suspended piano chords backed only by Adrian Brett's pan flute.[500] The song's title and the use of this instrument could once again be a McCartney tribute to music-hall, since "The Pipes of Pan" was a well-known song of this type of British theatrical entertainment, composed by Lionel Monckton at the beginning of the Twentieth Century.

A majestic key change (from E to C major) serves as a bridge to the heart of the song with its resplendent and singular blend of reggae-style piano and wide-open melody.

Thanks to the composer's tricks of the trade – the descending bass sequence on the D minor chord is pinched from "Michelle" – and a superb arrangement, featuring standout percussion like tabla and snare-drums and the Pestalozzi Children's Choir, "Pipes of Peace" was an immediate hit, thoroughly deserving its #1 position in the UK charts.

At first, McCartney had considered an ethnic arrangement that would have included various flutes from around the world as well as Indian instruments. It was impossible to find someone who knew how to play a shenhai[501], but for the tabla all it took was a phone call from George Martin to the Canadian percussionist James Kippen, an old friend and neighbor.

Kippen: "Paul gave me some idea of what he wanted for the first pattern. He used his hands on my drums to tap out a kind of rhythmic feel, and he was also speaking simple syllables (a bit like scat singing in jazz) in imitation of the drum syllables used by tabla players. I tried a few things and he seemed to like one particular pattern I played for him. It was that pattern, and variations or permutations of it, that I played over many takes."[502]

Shortly after, the recording began: "I tried something like 20-30 takes" – says Kippen – "The number of takes was dictated by George. What I played was similar each time, but not exactly the same. I was cued, I played, then stopped and waited for further instructions. There was a second section that I had to play too. Paul wanted some kind of fast drum roll. I showed him several. The one he liked was a cross-rhythmic pattern that grouped the strokes into 3+3+3+3+2+2, repeated."[503] It was more difficult to get an idea of the song: "The track was incomplete. There was only the click-track, Paul's piano and vocals. Paul, George and Geoff had a good idea about what they wanted, but I didn't!"[504]

---

[500] Interview courtesy of Adrian Brett, 26/09/2011.
[501] A sort of oboe from North of India.
[502] Interview courtesy of James Kippen, 23/10/2011.
[503] *Ibid.*
[504] *Ibid.*

Paul completed the recording adding a melodic bass part, some percussion (shaker, tambourine and knee-percussion – "we had some troubles doing it"[505] Paul admitted) on top of the drum-machine track and probably synthesizer. Finally, Martin completed the song with a rich orchestral arrangement.

"Pipes of Peace" is in a way a historical song: it is, to date, the last chart-topper for McCartney in the UK. Its accompanying video-clip deserves an honorable mention. Without a doubt the best clip in the vast series of McCartney's video repertoire; it is set during World War I in the trenches, with Paul playing both the part of a British and a German soldier who are divided by their rivalry but united by their common personal memories.

This sentimental dimension gives a deep meaning to the video. The clip also includes a re-enactment of an actual event: on Christmas day, 1914 the British and German soldiers momentarily put aside their harsh reality to socialize with each other and even exchange gifts. The track can also be found in *All the Best!* and *Wingspan*.

Musicians:

Paul McCartney vocals, backing vocals, piano, bass, synthesizer (?), shaker (?), tambourine (?), drums (?) • **Linda McCartney, Eric Stewart** backing vocals • **James Kippen** tabla • **Adrian Brett** Pan flute • **Pestalozzi's Children Choir** choir • **Unknown musicians** strings, horns

176 So Bad (Paul McCartney)

Recording: October, 1982 **Location**: AIR Studios, London **Release**: October 1983, *Pipes of Peace*

Paul had written "So Bad" the previous winter as a father might tell a fairytale to his kids. McCartney's reenactment is an intimate family moment: "I used to play *So Bad* around the house and I'd sing, 'Girl I love you so bad.' Suddenly, I thought of my son, James, who was feeling a little bit left out. So I started singing, 'Boy, I love you so bad.' He got all embarrassed…"[506]

Paul took that tender atmosphere and turned it into a delicate song that would divide the opinions of his audience: for McCartney's fans, "So Bad" is an example of refined songwriting – to his detractors it was the proverbial sugary-sweet vehicle. Either way, it would be unfair to not point out the qualities that make "So Bad" worthy of closer attention: McCartney's clean falsetto is really outstanding and his varied bass line is fluid, melodic and always interesting: it was probably played with the Rickenbacker, that Paul handled in the video-clip. A nice ARP synthesizer solo (Linda?) is also featured. McCartney, who had just invited Ringo Starr to act in his film *Give My Regards to Broad Street*, took advantage of his drumming on this track as well; as usual, Ringo's style is meticulous and clear.

[505] Video-interview by Russel Harty, *The Making of Pipes of Peace*, 1983. Paul and George Martin, together in the control room, let Harty hearing several tracks of the song, e.g. tabla, shaker and knee-percussion.
[506] Paul McCartney, *Give My Regards to Broad Street*, 1984, p.112.

Eric Stewart also appears on the track: "'So Bad' was nice. We did the backing track at AIR Studios with me on rhythm guitar. It felt really smooth, a gentle, flowing song that I loved."[507] Paul should have been particularly proud of this song, which was extracted as a single from *Pipes of Peace* in February 1984 for the US market – where "So Bad" reached #23 in the charts – and which was re-recorded in another version for *Broad Street* soon after.

This second version – even more polished than the original – includes some backing vocal embellishments with interesting modulation.

Musicians:

Paul McCartney vocals, backing vocals, piano (?), electric piano (?), synthesizer (?), bass • **Linda McCartney** backing vocals, synthesizer (?) • **Eric Stewart** backing vocals, electric guitar • **Ringo Starr** drums • **Unknown musicians** strings

177 Tug of Peace (Paul McCartney)

Recording: October, 1982 **Location**: AIR Studios, London **Release**: October 1983, *Pipes of Peace*

McCartney: "The songs I'm writing now don't come as easily. The least successful tracks turned out to be the ones that I multitracked myself."[508] Paul's admission explains the reason for this recording. "Tug of Peace" was probably born with some experimental aim. McCartney had recorded a first version of it, with a different set of lyrics and much longer.

Then – perhaps because he wasn't convinced – he shortened it and pasted on the lyrics almost word for word from "Tug of War". Even the title – a mix between "Tug of War" and "Pipes of Peace" – is further proof of the lack of originality: one gets an awful sense of *deja vu*. The song is built around a groove instead of a melody and is marked by tribal percussion hits.

The percussive strokes heard at the beginning were achieved by McCartney and Martin by hitting the studio floor with some real garden canes! The producer recalled: "I had the idea of having a kind of Zulu sound and I wanted to get the noise of thumping assegais on the ground. So we got a whole stack of garden canes, and Paul and I ended up with about 15 each, holding them and chomping them down, which is that tremendous sound you hear on the off-beat."[509] For everything else, it was very likely a solo recording by McCartney. It also features a drum-machine, used in some other tracks during these sessions. It was indeed Martin who urged McCartney to "make a slightly harder, a more funky album". His producer's usual quality control lacking, the song made it through and was included in *Pipes of Peace*.

Musicians:

Paul McCartney vocals, backing vocals, garden canes, bass (?), acoustic and electric guitar (?), keyboards (?), drums (?), shaker (?), tambourine (?) • **George Martin** garden canes

[507] Ken Sharp, *McCartney's 2nd "Second Banana". A Conversation with Eric Stewart*, in *Beatlefan*, n.140, p.18.
[508] *Capitol Radio interview with Paul McCartney*, broadcast on 24/12/1983.
[509] *Club Sandwich*, no.31, October 1983.

178 The Other Me (Paul McCartney)

Recording: October, 1982 **Location:** AIR Studios, London **Release:** October 1983, *Pipes of Peace*

Another run-of-the-mill track, "The Other Me" is a song about excuses – along the lines of "One More Kiss" – that deals with McCartney's dual personality.

McCartney: "This one is actually just a song about the other man in me, the other side of me that's lurking and waiting to get out (…). There's a side of me I don't like so much; there's a side that I prefer. The thing is to try and get a little more in contact with the side of myself that I prefer, and control myself, instead of just flying off the handle."[510]

It's a sweet song, stemming most likely from an argument with Linda. The sincere lyrics – notwithstanding the puzzling cockney slang ("I acted like a dustbin lid") – are the saving grace of an otherwise mediocre song, arranged with drum-machine and uninspired instrumentation, very likely added by McCartney (credited on piano, guitar and synth by *Club Sandwich* no.31).

He explained how Geoff Emerick achieved his particular voice quality: "I wanted that kind of sound where you can hear every breath. I think it's overcompressed. I like it."[511] Paul included it in *Pipes of Peace*, probably running out of ideas and lacking more solid songs.

Musicians:

Paul McCartney vocals, bass, electric guitar, piano, electric piano, synthesizer, tambourine, percussion

179 Through Our Love (Paul McCartney)

Recording: October, 1982 **Location:** AIR Studios, London **Release:** October 1983, *Pipes of Peace*

McCartney wrote "Through Our Love", a beautiful acoustic ballad, as a praise to the power of love, seen as a mysterious and unique experience.

McCartney: "I like the thought that people can use (the song) for their own things. Young married couples… That song fits perfectly for them… Looking at life."[512]

Perhaps it was the euphoria McCartney felt after writing "Through Our Love" that urged him to record it so quickly. Geoff Whitehorn, the future Procol Harum guitarist, guested on the recording. He recalled: "I only had a really cheap nasty acoustic guitar (…) So McCartney said, 'Well, better use this,' and he gave me this beautiful Gibson. It was a nice session (…) because Paul was actually playing bass, George Martin was playing electric piano and Dave Mattacks played drums and we knocked this song off in… An hour!"[513]

With the backing track completed, George Martin garnished the song with an odd idea: he took a bicycle wheel and turned it into an unusual percussion instrument. Then, with his customary aplomb, carried on with the orchestral arrangement.

---

[510] John Blaney, *Lennon and McCartney. Together Alone*, 2007, p.159.
[511] *Capitol Radio interview with Paul McCartney*, broadcast on 24/12/1983.
[512] Lesley Ash, *Interview with Paul McCartney*, broadcast on *The Tube*, 18/12/1983.
[513] www.procolharum.com/gb_beatle-2003.htm

Martin's score may be somewhat pompous: "Through Our Love" would have gained from a more acoustic treatment, but it is nevertheless suited to expressing the joy and enthusiasm of the lyrics. The resounding horns and the orchestral crescendo introduce a key change (from E to C major) and lift the song up to a spiritual and radiant dimension.

John Bradbury, violinist and orchestral conductor, took part in several recording sessions at AIR Studios between 1980 and 1983 with McCartney, Martin and Kenneth Sillitoe, acting often as leader. On one of those occasions – the track could be "Through Our Love", although Bradbury is not certain – a very strange accident occurred and he instead remembers it vividly: "The studio was booked for three hours, from 10 o'clock in the morning 'till 1 pm. Suddenly, the building was struck by lightning. Everything stopped, all the lights failed, we were there in total darkness! We didn't know but the whole building had been evacuated of all the office workers... All the lifts have been stopped... We were trapped in the roof! Fortunately, on the course of an hour we carried on and finished the session!"[514] Easily the best song on *Pipes of Peace* along with the title-track.

Musicians:

Paul McCartney vocals, backing vocals, bass, acoustic guitar (?), shaker (?) • **Dave Mattacks** drums • **Geoff Whitehorn** acoustic guitar • **Linda McCartney, Eric Stewart** backing vocals • **George Martin** piano, bicycle wheel • **Unknown musicians** strings, horns

180 Twice in a Lifetime (Paul McCartney)

Recording: October, 1982 **Location**: AIR Studios, London **Release**: August 1993, *Pipes of Peace (The Paul McCartney Collection* cd)

Around the beginning of the year, McCartney was contacted to write the title-track of the movie *Twice in a Lifetime*, starring Gene Hackman and Ann Margret. For what would have been his third soundtrack in three years, McCartney was requested once again a song about the subject of love's uniqueness.

McCartney harked back to the unreleased "Did We Meet Somewhere Before?" (and also to "Same Time, Next Year") – with which "Twice in a Lifetime" has a lot in common – and he probably recorded the song during the last sessions for *Pipes of Peace*.

The two tracks have a very similar feel, both in the moving melody and in the dreamy, celestial tone. In particular, the flowing sound of the saxophone echoes the clarinet used on the track heard on the Ramones' movie *Rock 'n 'Roll High School*.

Not too much information is available about the recording of this piano ballad, which could have been easily recorded almost by McCartney himself: piano, guitars and bass are typical of McCartney's style. Mellotron low-fi strings can be heard in the background. The sax part may

514 Interview courtesy of John Bradbury, 18/11/2011.

have been played by Andy MacKay, who is portrayed in the inner sleeve of *Pipes of Peace* as one of the guest-stars appearing on the album.

Lyrically, "Twice in a Lifetime" relies on how unrepeatable love is and manages to create an atmosphere that expresses one's personal sense of beatitude when in love.

This song had a similar fate to the previous two: while "Same Time Next Year" saw the light only twelve years after its recording and "Did We Meet Somewhere Before?" remained completely unreleased on vinyl, "Twice in a Lifetime" was included in the movie soundtrack in 1986 but it wasn't released on record until 1993, when it was added as a bonus-track to the remastered edition of *Pipes of Peace*.

There's a little anecdote about this track: the three-minute version was the result of a studio-edit, done by Richard Niles in 1986 when the producer was assigned by McCartney to work on some of his unreleased tracks.

Niles extended the original length of the track: "If Paul had had the time to release 'Twice in a Lifetime' as a single, I believe it would have been very successful. It had amazing lyrics, too. For the soundtrack, they asked him for a two-minute version, so we lengthened the track."[515] Finally, Niles embellished "Twice in a Lifetime" by a magnificent arrangement for strings, harps and horns that still lies unreleased.

Musicians:

Paul McCartney vocals, backing vocals, piano, bass, Mellotron, electric guitar (?), drums (?), percussion (?) • **Linda McCartney** backing vocals • **Eric Stewart** backing vocals, electric guitar (?) • **Unknown musician** sax

After finishing these recordings, McCartney started off one of the most catastrophic projects of his whole solo career, the movie *Give My Regards to Broad Street*. The title evoked the song "Give My Regards to Broadway", written by George M. Cohan for the play *Little Johnny Jones,* a musical first performed in a Broadway theatre in 1904. The recordings for the soundtrack and the film spanned a long period of time, between November 1982 and July 1984. New versions of many Beatles songs were recorded, including "Yesterday", "Here, There and Everywhere", "The Long and Winding Road", "Eleanor Rigby", "For No-One" and "Good Day Sunshine", all released on the album. Other three tracks – "Hey Jude", "Martha My Dear" (McCartney did not completed this remake, 'cause apparently he was not satisfied with his piano part) and "The Fool On the Hill" – were left out of the soundtrack. McCartney's post-Beatles repertoire was also revisited, with remakes of "Band On the Run" (not used), "Silly Love Songs", "Wanderlust", "Ballroom Dancing" and "So Bad".

---

[515] Interview courtesy of Richard Niles, 7/10/2011.

1983

In January, McCartney worked with classical guitarist John Williams. The two prepared a couple of demos of a new Paul's composition, that would be used as the main theme for the movie soundtrack of *The Honorary Consul*. This beautiful Latin-American tinged melody for classical guitar was released in October as a single by John Williams.

Give My Regards to Broad Street went along with shootings and recordings of two songs, that probably were cut during (or shortly before) the filming of the band rehearsing in the old warehouse called E. Austin & Son, in London, between March 8th-11th.

During the sessions, the musicians found themselves with some time to kill and they launched into old rock'n'roll songs. Chris Spedding recalls: "We went through all these rock'n'roll classics. No Beatles tunes. The multitrack was there and I remember thinking, 'Why aren't the tapes running? This is gold!' What a shame...I wish I had a tape of that!"[516]

181 Not Such a Bad Boy (Paul McCartney)

Recording: March (?), 1983 **Location**: AIR Studios, London **Release**: October 1984, *Give My Regards to Broad Street*

This nitty-gritty, hard-rocking track is one of the most enjoyable moments of the *Broad Street* soundtrack. Paul had taped a demo of "Not Such a Bad Boy" at the beginning of the year at AIR Studios. Later the track was recorded live at the Austin & Son warehouse, as the result is surprisingly straightforward. The track was laid down with a basic line-up: McCartney on Rickenbacker bass, Dave Edmunds and Chris Spedding on guitars, Linda on keyboards, Ringo on drums and Jody Lindscott on percussion. In the movie, "Not Such a Bad Boy" is presented as a rehearsal of the band in a crumbling hangar. This energetic take – probably included without overdubs in *Give My Regards to Broad Street* – features a raging vocal performance by Paul. The Fifties' teddy boy mood is recreated by the biting skiffle-style electric guitars.

Musicians:

Paul McCartney vocals, bass • **Linda McCartney** backing vocals, keyboards • **Dave Edmunds, Chris Spedding** backing vocals, electric guitars • **Jody Lindscott** percussion, tambourine • **Ringo Starr** drums

182 No Values (Paul McCartney)

Recording: March (?), 1983 **Location**: AIR Studios, London **Release**: October 1984, *Give My Regards to Broad Street*

McCartney has always credited the genesis of his songs to a sort of mystery. "Yesterday" is the most famous example of this 'unconscious' songwriting process, having been envisioned while sleeping. "No Values" also saw the light of day thanks to one of Paul's dreams.

---

[516] Interview courtesy of Chris Spedding, 12/08/2014.

The song was from the late Seventies. One night, McCartney had this dream of the Rolling Stones performing it. Paul did not recall any similar Stones's song ("I won't tell Mick Jagger… He'll probably claim the copyright!"[517]) and soon ran into his studio, laying down a demo of the track, that was rehearsed by Wings in October 1980.

The song was already well-structured, with almost completed lyrics and a laid-back feeling, missing from the official recording: "No Values" could have been a perfect stage number for Wings' repertoire. Paul took up work again on it some months later, recording another version of the song in Montserrat during the *Tug of War* sessions, right after the "Hey, Hey" jam with Stanley Clarke and Steve Gadd (see sheet **164**), but also this attempt remained unissued.

A minor-key rocking track, "No Values" appears on the *Broad Street* soundtrack in a very tight performance, complete with an ending jam, featuring Spedding and Edmunds interchanging electric guitar solos. Chris Spedding: "That was my idea. Paul wanted me to play lead but I thought, 'Why am I standing here with the great Dave Edmunds and he's not playing lead? So I played a few bars then I turned to him and he started doing his bit. It wasn't discussed before!"[518] The song ends abruptly with a "fake" error by Paul.[519]

Musicians:

Paul McCartney vocals, bass • **Linda McCartney** backing vocals, tambourine • **Dave Edmunds, Chris Spedding** backing vocals, electric guitars • **Jody Lindscott** percussion • **Ringo Starr** drums

In August, McCartney recorded some more demos, including "I Remember Days" (in R'n'B style), "Freckles" (a reggae song) and "Make it to Victoria" (an ethnic/African flavored track). Probably around this time, he also taped "On the Wings of a Nightingale", a song penned for the Everly Brothers, who were reunited after their breakup in 1973. Issued on 45 in 1984, it reached #50 in the US. The new album, *Pipes of Peace* was finally issued on October 31st. It was received wearily by the critics, who considered it as a not so successful follow-up to *Tug of War*. Parke Putherbaugh of *Rolling Stone* gave it a two-star review and wrote: "Underneath all the elaborate arrangements and high-sheen production on *Pipes of Peace*, is a humble man who retains affection – fascination even – with the lot of common folk. But most of the time he tries so hard to be an average man, that he winds up making below-average music. Confusing slightness and simplicity, *Pipes of Peace* is, by and large, mediocre McCartney."

The sales were also unsatisfying: *Pipes of Peace* was a failure, reaching #4 in the UK and only #15 in America, selling under expectations there, although it remained 24 weeks on the charts.

---

[517] Paul McCartney, *Give My Regards to Broad Street*, MPL, 1984.

[518] Interview courtesy of Chris Spedding, 12/08/2014.

[519] The version appearing in the movie is the complete take, lasting one minute more than the one featured on the album soundtrack. McCartney's comment, "Sorry, it's my fault!" was left in also in the album soundtrack version.

183 Corridor Music (Paul McCartney)

Recording: November-December, 1983 **Location**: AIR Studios, London **Release**: October 1984, *Give My Regards to Broad Street*

Towards the end of the year, McCartney and Martin went back to AIR Studios to record some background (or "incidental") music to be used for *Give My Regards to Broad Street*.

During these sessions, filmed and broadcast on the *South Bank Show* in October 1984, Paul got the idea for "Corridor Music". In the movie, this instrumental can be heard in a scene that occurs in a corridor of the record company's office: hence the title "Corridor Music". The track is no less than a riff variation on "Mumbo" (see sheet **40**), included in *Wild Life* in 1971.

Musicians:

Paul McCartney electric guitar

184 Goodnight Princess (Paul McCartney)

Recording: December 11th, 1983 **Location**: AIR Studios, London **Release**: October 1984, *Give My Regards to Broad Street* (cd version)

Although a bit boring, the movie *Give My Regards to Broad Street* featured a lot of autobiographical connections.

One of the most touching moments of the film is the final sequence. Paul visits old Jim – a character whose name obviously recalls Paul's father – who affably invites him to go into his old apartment. In the background, one could hear an old-fashioned song, in the style of the Thirties, the age in which Jim McCartney played his jazz repertoire with the Jim Mac's Jazz Band. The song is "Goodnight Princess", whose title comes from a sentence that Paul says to the little monkey standing on Jim's shoulder, just before leaving the house.

It's a warm tribute to Paul's father: the song recalls "Walking in the Park With Eloise" – see **1974** – and reminds of the old "Midnight, the Stars and You" (1934).

The song was completely arranged for a jazz orchestra: one could imagine being in an old smoky American club from the Twenties or the Thirties. With a light nostalgic overtone, Paul brings to life a part of his youth, when he was sitting in the living room of his house, listening to his father, who was playing some classics like "After You've Gone" or "Stairway to Paradise" on the piano. The track appears on the cd editions of *Give My Regards to Broad Street* in an instrumental version, although McCartney also recorded a vocal take, still unreleased.

Musicians:

Paul McCartney narration • **Eric Ford** electric guitar • **Russ Stableford** double-bass • **Gerry Butler** piano • **Ronnie Hughes, Bobby Haughey** trumpet • **Chris Smith** trombone • **Derek Grossmith** alto sax, clarinet • **Eddie Mordue** tenor sax, clarinet • **Vic Ash** tenor sax • **Pat Halling, Laurie Lewis, Raymond Keenlyside, Tony Gilbert** violin • **John Dean** drums, percussion

1984

After a short vacation in February, in the following months – no exact dates are available – McCartney continued shooting his movie and put the finishing touches to the soundtrack. During the sessions, McCartney also recorded the unreleased song "Kiss Me Now", that would be later overdubbed with an orchestra in 2013.[520]

185 No More Lonely Nights (Ballad) (Paul McCartney)

Recording: June-July (?) 1984 **Location:** Elstree Film Studios, London **Release:** September 1984, single (from *Give My Regards to Broad Street*)

Broad Street had just been completed when reviewing the footage in post-production – before vocals are added – Paul realized that it needed another song: "I was trying to write a song called 'Give My Regards to Broad Street' but I gave up before I started... I don't think it was an easy title to write!" [521]

At that point, McCartney wrote the song, starting from a heavy-echoed bass riff that he came up with while improvising in the recording studio. In some footage on the *South Bank Show* tv program, Paul is seen on his Yamaha bass working on the track with Martin helping on piano.

Thus, "No More Lonely Nights" was born; a piano ballad that is among the most remarkable examples of McCartney's melodic style. Paul expressed his self-confidence about it: "It's a nice track. I think maybe it's good as the old (Beatles') songs."[522]

McCartney was able to deliver a sure hit to Twentieth Century Fox. The song's sweet melody – which features a poignant chorus in a minor key – won over the public and brought McCartney his last single to chart simultaneously in both the US and UK top ten: #6 in the USA and #2 in the UK. The song was nominated both for a Golden Globe and a BAFTA for Best Original Song.

The recording of the track was enhanced by two old acquaintances of Paul: Herbie Flowers on bass[523] and David Gilmour on guitar. "No More Lonely Nights" was recorded over a three-hour session live in the studio, as David Gilmour recalled: "I found it quite amazing doing 'No More Lonely Nights' with Paul McCartney. In one three-hour session with a band we learnt it and put it down, and Paul played piano and sang the lead vocal live, and I put the guitar solo down, bang."[524] Gilmour's participation could help date the session, although the exact recording date remains unclear. In 1990 Gilmour told Jim Ladd in an interview that the track was the last thing recorded by McCartney for the soundtrack.

---

[520] http://webpages.charter.net/ram71/mrs.htm
[521] *Paul McCartney 1984 Interview*, http://www.mygoldmusic.co.uk/article.asp?id=587762
[522] *Ibid.*
[523] Flowers played during the *Thrillington* sessions in June 1971.
[524] David Gilmour interview, in *Q Magazine*, 1986.

Paul's statement – about the composition of the song near the end of the *Broad Street* completion – would indicate that the track did in fact get recorded during the summer, shortly before or even during the David Foster sessions with Gilmour in September. Probably after these recordings, Paul decided to take advantage of Gilmour's sound for this song, too. The song appears on *Broad Street*, *All the Best!* and *Wingspan*.

Musicians:

Paul McCartney vocals, backing vocals, piano • **Herbie Flowers** bass • **Stuart Elliott** drums • **David Gilmour** electric guitar • **Ann Dudley** synthesizer • **Linda McCartney, Eric Stewart** backing vocals

186 No More Lonely Nights (Playout Version) (Paul McCartney)

Recording: July (?) or September (?), 1984 **Location:** AIR Studios, London **Release:** September 1984, "No More Lonely Nights" single B-side (from *Give My Regards to Broad Street*)

The final touch to the *Broad Street* soundtrack was a song meant for the end credits. To appease the film production company's request, Paul decided not to obsess too much about it and quickly came up with a dance re-make of "No More Lonely Nights".

The process was quite simple: McCartney speeded-up the tempo, adapted some of the verses to the new beat and the song was ready in record time.

Since he was in a hurry, Paul played all instruments, except for the horn section, for which he hired some special guests, including jazz sax player Stan Sulzmann. He recalls an anecdote: "The horn arrangement was ready. Paul liked playing around with a trumpet and had a flugelhorn with him, and then he 'sat in' and played along with the professionals!"[525]

Unfortunately, it wasn't exactly a masterpiece, even though not out of place in the current dance scene of that period. McCartney released it as a 12" single from *Broad Street* and the track was also promoted in 1985 with a video-clip. One hair-raising fact about this song was the plethora of remixes that was released. Not counting the differences between the CD, LP and single versions (the last two are simply edits of the first and complete version), there are five more versions:

1. *Extended Version*, appears on the first 12" of "No More Lonely Nights" (included as a bonus-track in the *Broad Street* re-mastered version, track 16).

2. *Special Dance Mix:* appears on the second 12" of "No More Lonely Nights".

3. *Special Dance Edit:* could be found on the 12" American promo, and appears as a bonus-track in the *Broad Street* re-mastered version, track 17). It's not a derivation from the previous one.

4. *Mole Mix:* mixed by Arthur Baker, included in a limited edition, one-sided promo.

5. *Extended Edit* by Warren Sanford: issued only for disc-jockeys on the album *Hot Tracks - Series 3, Issue 8*.

---

[525] Interview courtesy of Stan Sulzmann, 19/08/2011.

The track is also on *Wingspan*, which uses the same version as *Broad Street*, editing the electric guitar intro.

Musicians:

Paul McCartney vocals, backing vocals, electric and acoustic guitar, bass, drums, keyboards • **Linda McCartney, Eric Stewart** backing vocals • **Derek Watkins, John Barclay, Chris Pyne, Stan Sultzmann, Dan Willis** horns

McCartney got back into the studio between September 25th and October 2nd, with David Foster producing. Dave Mattacks and David Gilmour appear on these sessions.

187 We Got Married (Paul McCartney)

Recording: September 25th-October 2nd, 1984 and June-July (overdubs), 1988 **Location:** Hog Hill Studio, Icklesham **Release:** June 1989, *Flowers in the Dirt*

According to David Foster, "We Got Married" was the weakest of the three tracks recorded during the sessions, which also included the unreleased "Lindiana".

McCartney: "I wrote the first couple of verses and recorded with Gilmour and Mattacks the main backing but I left it empty."[526] The original recording was very similar to the version issued in 1989 on *Flowers in the Dirt*: Gilmour's section was some bars longer, the bass was more prominent, while the track was lacking the trumpet solo in the coda, added in June 1988 along with other overdubs. Furthermore, the track had a full ending.

With its simple harmonic structure – based mostly around three chords in the key of C – the track is built with the gradual addition of various instruments. Inspired by McCartney's marriage to Linda, the song ideally depicts the upward arc of their love.

The almost-whispered beginning of the song, accompanied by Paul's Mexican guitar, contains one of the most striking lines to come from McCartney's (as solo artist) pen, celebrating the euphoria of a couple madly in love: "Going fast, coming soon/We made love in the afternoon" One single couplet that manages to encompass all the uniqueness of love in its early phases, both frenetic and unstoppable. McCartney: "The first verse is very John and Cyn: 'Going fast, coming soon, we made love in the afternoon', 'cos they were like art students and it was the first time I'd ever heard of anyone making love in the afternoon. I was about 16, and fairly 'Whaaat! In the afternoon? Whoo! It's like a French film!' It was fairly naïve."[527]

"We Got Married" proceeds until the magnificent explosion of Gilmour's chords: a sumptuous performance, typical of his both majestic and simple style.

[526] *The Paul McCartney World Tour Booklet*, p.78.
[527] Paul Du Noyer, *Maybe I'm Amazed*, 1989.

The final section – featuring Guy Barker on trumpet – epitomizes the meaning of the song and perfectly expresses McCartney's world view: a world where man creates his own destiny and is in charge of the events of his existence, with love indisputably at the center.

"We Got Married" would become one of the most effective numbers of the 1989/90 *Paul McCartney World Tour*, lengthened with a long keyboard solo by Wix in the coda. The live version appears on *Tripping the Live Fantastic!*

Musicians:

Paul McCartney vocals, vocal harmonies, Mexican guitar, bass, percussion, tom • **David Gilmour** electric guitar • **Dave Mattacks** drums • **David Foster** keyboards • **Robbie McIntosh** acoustic guitar • **Hamish Stuart** vocal harmonies • **Guy Barker** trumpet • **Chris Whitten** percussion

188 I Love This House (Paul McCartney)

Recording: September 25th-October 2nd, 1984 and March, 1985 (overdubs) **Location:** Hog Hill Studio, Icklesham **Release:** April 1997, "Young Boy" cd-single 1

"I Love This House" was inspired to McCartney by his farm in Sussex. As he did in "Fixing a Hole", Paul reveals his 'homebody/do-it-yourself' side, in an ode to his house. Some pleasantly auto-ironic lyrics depict the cracks and holes in all the rooms, making the house seem more suitable to animals than to people.

The main riff – whose irregular rhythm drives the song – is the work of McCartney and Gilmour on electric guitars: their skittish solos in fact give the song a certain character. After recording the basic track, McCartney fixed it during the *Press to Play* sessions, but left it unused for thirteen years: the song would be issued only in April 1997, on the first "Young Boy" cd-single.

Musicians:

Paul McCartney vocals, electric guitar, bass • **David Foster** keyboards • **David Gilmour** electric guitar • **Dave Mattacks** drums

Give My Regards to Broad Street (movie and soundtrack album) was released in October and was critically panned: it remains one of McCartney's least fortunate moment.

The poor reception was reflected in harsh reviews. The *Columbus Dispatch* wrote: "McCartney's first foray into feature filmmaking as a non-Beatle is an embarrassing disaster. His skeletal screenplay is humorless and redundant."

While the movie was a total failure and was withdrawn from distribution after two weeks, the soundtrack did better, reaching #1 in the UK charts. In America, the record was a real dud, only reaching #21 on the *Billboard* charts.

1985

In March, McCartney began the sessions for *Press to Play* in his own new studio. They would be among the most challenging and difficult recordings that he would face during his entire career. Looking for a new sonic approach, McCartney hired young Hugh Padgham as a producer. In fact, it was Padgham who pushed McCartney in a different direction, both creatively and technically.

The album's experimental flavor made it one of the boldest McCartney's solo efforts so far; surprising and confusing critics and fans alike.

McCartney also sought out fresh inspiration in his songwriting, collaborating on ten of the seventeen recorded songs with 10cc guitarist, Eric Stewart, whom he had known since *Back to the Egg*. One of these songs was the acoustic ballad, "Yvonne" that 10cc would record in 1995.

The group of musicians involved in laying down the basic tracks was very stripped-down: along with Paul were Eric Stewart (guitar or keyboards) and drummer Jerry Marotta, a trusted Peter Gabriel session-man who had been suggested to McCartney by Hugh Padgham. It was a return to a band situation for McCartney after several years. The trio taped twelve very raw and hard-sounding backing tracks. The initial recordings saw Martin Chambers (The Pretenders) on drums and John Kelly (The Clash) producing, but those songs were never used.

Later on, Carlos Alomar (David Bowie's guitarist) was brought in "when we realized that there were certain types of guitar that neither Eric (Stewart) nor myself could play", as Paul put it. Alomar personally chose the songs he wanted to play on.

The sessions weren't very satisfying and had some tense moments. Eric Stewart – who initially believed that he would produce the record himself – was quite stunned when Paul enrolled Padgham to the task.

Hugh Padgham, twenty-eight at the time, was the go-to producer of the moment. He had produced The Police's *Synchronicity* and Phil Collins' *No Jacket Required.*

When McCartney contacted him, Padgham was blown away: "He couriered to me a cassette to the studio when I was working with Phil Collins (…) I went home incredibly excited to listen to a cassette of those demos that he had recorded with Eric Stewart."[528]

Padgham could tell something wasn't right and although he had many misgivings, he convinced himself that he should accept the job: "I can honestly tell you now that I was underwhelmed when I heard those songs. I thought, well, hang on, who am I to know, as a little 28 year old guy, that Paul McCartney has given me these songs that are not very

---

[528]   *Gary   James   Interview   with   Record   Producer   Hugh   Padgham,*   in
http://www.classicbands.com/HughPadghamInterview.html

impressive? It must be me not being able to sort of see these songs that are effectively them sitting around a campfire with a couple of acoustic guitars."[529]

Under these circumstances, it wasn't long before troubles arose in the studio. Padgham: "Paul McCartney became quite annoying as far as I'm concerned (…) After sort of a year of every day in the studio, he's not on the same pedestal as when you started (…) I don't think he was in an era of writing good songs."[530]

The mood only worsened. One day Paul asked Padgham for his opinion on a song that Stewart had said needed perfecting: "I don't think it's good enough, Paul", the producer confirmed.[531] McCartney reacted badly: "Hugh, when did you write your last number one?"[532]

Padgham also recalled that McCartney seemed not confident about his bass playing and at some point he even thought to hire some other bassist. In the end, Paul played bass in all the tracks, using his Yamaha, but burying it under overproduction and load of effects.

189 Stranglehold (Paul McCartney-Eric Stewart)

Recording: March-May and October 1st-December 6th (overdubs), 1985 **Location:** Hog Hill Studio, Icklesham **Release:** August 1986, *Press to Play*

In keeping with lessons learned from George Martin, Paul knew that it was best practice to kick-off an album with a powerful track. He chose "Stranglehold", a rocker written with Eric Stewart as the opener for *Press to Play*. It was also the first song recorded during the sessions.

McCartney: "We started off with this track, putting rhythmic words in, using lyrics like a bongo, accenting the words. We enjoyed the experience, then went on to write."[533]

As heard on the rough mix, the vocals and instrumentation were originally drier – a quality that "Stranglehold" lost as it reached completion.

Eric Stewart: "The song sounded great with just Paul on bass, me on electrified acoustic guitar and Jerry on kit. I went home feeling very very happy and got a call, which my wife Gloria answered. It was Paul and he said, 'Tell that bloke of yours that is bloody good and I'm really looking forward to tomorrow!'"[534]

After the backing track was completed, guitars and backing vocals were overdubbed, adding as many tracks as possible. It doesn't sound like a typical McCartney recording and although Marotta's drumming is remarkably crisp, the initial idea was compromised. Paul thought he could beef-up "Stranglehold" by adding horns, most likely played by Gary Barnacle and Dick Morrissey – they were Paul's most often-used session men and according to Richard Niles,

[529] *Ibid.*
[530] *Ibid.*
[531] Howard Sounes, *Fab. An Intimate Life of Paul McCartney*, 2010, p.399.
[532] *Ibid.*
[533] *Club Sandwich*, n.42, Autumn 1986, p.3.
[534] K. Sharp, *cit.*, p.19.

Morrissey was actually Paul's favorite sax player – since this is one of the few tracks on the album to feature horns and both players are credited in the *Press to Play* liner notes.

Unfortunately, horns didn't fit in with the arrangement. "Stranglehold" seems to suffer from a sterile imbalance of too many instruments struggling to make a point, the real Achilles' heel of *Press to Play*. Clearly dissatisfied, Paul opted for yet more overdubs and remixes as he would do with most of the tracks on the LP.

Thus "Stranglehold" – chosen as the second single for the US market (using the album version and not the re-mix, which was available only on the 12" single) – was one of the least successful releases in McCartney's career, barely reaching #81 on *Billboard* in November 1986.

Musicians:

Paul McCartney vocals, backing vocals, acoustic and electric guitar, bass • **Eric Stewart** backing vocals, acoustic and electric guitar • **Jerry Marotta** drums • **Gary Barnacle (?)**, **Dick Morrisey (?)** horns

190 Good Times Coming/Feel the Sun (Paul McCartney)

Recording: March-May and October 1ˢᵗ-December 6ᵗʰ (overdubs), 1985 **Location**: Hog Hill Studio, Icklesham **Release**: August 1986, *Press to Play*

One of McCartney's many talents consists in creating medleys out of tunes that apparently have nothing in common: a clever way to get the most from unfinished songs. "Good Times Coming/Feel the Sun" is a perfect example of this kind of studio work. In all probability, neither song would have seen the light of day on their own, McCartney relied on the medley formula, as both songs had a summery feel along the lines of "Good Day Sunshine".

McCartney: "There's a nostalgic air about summers… It's pretty a strong feeling, even for people who are only seventeen: they can remember a summer when they were ten."[535]

From the rough mix, you can get an idea of how the song was conceived. This unreleased version – lasting 7:08 – is one of greatest regrets in McCartney's catalogue.

The first of the two songs was "Good Times Coming" that begins with a vocal fade-in. Jerry Marotta: "We went outside the studio with one of the maintenance guys and we were playing guitar and singing along like around a fire."[536]

It's a reggae tune whose basic track consisted of drums, electric guitars and bass; later, it was dragged down by many electronic parts added during autumn, including some quirky-effected guitars (named "eddies" guitars on one of Paul's stereo drawings printed on *Press to Play*).

McCartney sang lead in falsetto and added a great bass part on his Yamaha – recorded on the studio roof! – that shifts between his melodic style and syncopated Jamaican phrasing.

Paul revealed: "In the first verse, I don't really play notes on the bass. It's something I suddenly got off as I was making the track. So I was quite chuffed with the originality of that."[537]

---

[535] Bill Harry, *The Paul McCartney Encyclopedia*, 2002, p.382.
[536] Interview courtesy of Jerry Marotta, 22/10/2011.

The second half of the medley was "Feel the Sun", a sunny tune in D major with one of those hooks that sticks in your head. The early take had different verses, a nice bridge in a minor key and a warm feel created by the electric guitars and Hammond organ.

For some reason Paul decided to re-record it, reducing the "Feel The Sun" section to just a taste of what it was before. This has made the early version a collector's item among McCartney's fans. The song appears on *Press to Play*.

Musicians:

Paul McCartney vocals, backing vocals, bass, electric guitar, electric piano (?), shaker (?), keyboards (?) • **Carlos Alomar** electric guitar • **Jerry Marotta** drums • **Eric Stewart** electric guitar • **Ruby James, Kate Robbins** backing vocals

191 Footprints (Paul McCartney-Eric Stewart)

Recording: March-May and October 1st-December 6th (overdubs), 1985 **Location:** Hog Hill Studio, Icklesham **Release:** August 1986, *Press to Play*

Co-written with Eric Stewart, "Footprints" was an intimate song recorded without frills. An early version gives a glimpse of the potential of this delicate acoustic song before it was buried in overdubs. "Footprints" was a wintry, melancholy guitar ballad.

Eric Stewart: "I got to Peasmarsh in the snow. I said, 'It's beautiful outside...' He (Paul) said, 'That's great, OK' and he started singing. And we wrote the whole song within minutes."[538]

The first idea was about a magpie looking for food, but Paul didn't like it: "It seemed like a nature program. So it became just a lonely fella, a bit like the character in 'Eleanor Rigby'."[539]

"Footprints" was added to *Press to Play* at the last minute. Jerry Marotta: "It was the last thing we recorded. Paul came in one day and he started playing it on acoustic guitar. What I did was programming a pattern with a LinnDrum. It became clear to Paul and Hugh Padgham that this song really needed to be on the record! We did percussion overdubs, mainly tom-toms."[540]

Later, the song underwent some heavy over-production with redundant instrumentation. The ending result is cold, with loads of electric guitars, various percussion (including woodblocks), a spinet, a Pan flute solo played through a synthesizer and Stewart and McCartney's acoustic guitars buried in the mix. Thankfully, the track features a terrific Paul's Spanish guitar solo.

Musicians:

Paul McCartney vocals, acoustic and Spanish guitar, bass, keyboards, spinet • **Eric Stewart** acoustic guitar, electric guitar (?), synthesizer (?) • **Jerry Marotta** LinnDrum programming, percussion

---

[537] *Capitol Radio interview with Paul McCartney*, broadcast on 12/10/1986.
[538] *Paul McCartney. Rock 'n' roll Legend*, MTV, 1986.
[539] John Blaney, *cit.*, p.177.
[540] Interview courtesy of Jerry Marotta, 22/10/2011.

192 Press (Paul McCartney)

Recording: March-May and October 1st-December 6th (overdubs), 1985 **Location:** Hog Hill Studio, Icklesham **Release:** July 1986, single (from *Press to Play*)

"Press" was another song stacked with overdubs in order to make it more commercial for its release as a single.

The first version taped by the McCartney-Stewart-Marotta trio was quite different from the final master. The basic track had a stripped-down instrumentation: a few electric guitars – including a nice solo by McCartney that made it to the final version – bass, drums and keyboards with a little bit of electronic percussion thrown in.

During the overdub sessions, Carlos Alomar made his contribution: "I went to Sussex and when I arrived I spoke with Paul for two hours. Then he asked me if I wanted to play on some tracks that I find interesting. 'Press' was the first track I heard. I was so anxious to please him immediately, and this was the most enjoyable song I played. It had some guitar parts that he had put down but it wasn't finished. He told me to play, so I did and he went crazy… He thought it was fantastic! What you hear on the record it's my second take!"[541]

McCartney had probably written the song off the cuff and later made it one of the most blatantly dance-influenced tracks of his career – keeping in line with the typical commercial trends of the 80s that saw an abundance of electronics, drum machines and sequencers.

Later, Paul would play it down describing "Press" as a "depressing" piece. The lyrics had already left everyone baffled: some lines seemed strange and unrelated.

McCartney tried to explain: "*Oklahoma was never like this* can mean whatever you want it to mean. To me, when you're writing songs, you often get a line you assume you're going to edit later (…) But every time I came to that line I couldn't sing anything but that; it was just the scanning…"[542] As John Blaney pointed out in his book, *Together Alone*, Paul might have been referencing the Rodgers & Hammerstein musical *Oklahoma!* (1931) but he never confirmed it.

Some other lyrics had subtle sexual innuendos. The verse "Right there, that's it, yes" was lifted word for word from Gary Glitter's song "Do You Want to Touch Me" but no-one noticed the real meaning. "Press" did have a catchy melody and when it was released as the first single from *Press to Play*, it did pretty well on the charts, reaching #25 in the UK and #21 in the US.

There are three version/mixes available:

1. Available on LP, 12" and CD (Remastered version)
2. Available on 45 and CD (first issue, 1987): drier sounding, distinguished by Carlos Alomar's long electric guitar arpeggio at the end.
3. *Dubmix* (on the 12" single): mostly instrumental.

---

[541] Interview courtesy of Carlos Alomar, 22/08/2011.
[542] John Blaney, *cit.*, p.174.

Musicians:

Paul McCartney vocals, backing vocals, electric guitar, keyboards, synthesizer (?) • **Eric Stewart** backing vocals, electric guitar (?), synthesizer (?) • **Jerry Marotta** drums • **Carlos Alomar** electric guitar • **Linda McCartney** backing vocals

193 Pretty Little Head (Paul McCartney-Eric Stewart)

Recording: March-May and October 1st-December 6th (overdubs), 1985 **Location:** Hog Hill Studio, Icklesham **Release:** August 1986, *Press to Play*

McCartney: "I don't like to trying really be *very* commercial. I think it would be all 'Eurovisioned' if every single track was a snappy catchy hit. So, on some of the tracks we've definitely gone anti-commercial."[543]

"Pretty Little Head" was the most experimental idea of the *Press to Play* sessions. It started off as a jam, with an unusual line-up featuring McCartney on drums, Stewart on keyboards and Marotta on vibraphone. Eric Stewart: "It actually wasn't a previously written song. And because everything we played in the studio, even the jams, was recorded religiously, we suddenly had a backing track that sounded very interesting!"[544]

"Pretty Little Head" – originally called "Back To Pepperland" – is a heavy experimental track: dark moods interspersed with electronic studio trickery. Over a percussion groove featuring keyboards and ambient guitars, McCartney later added a vocal helped by Eric Stewart, who came up with the chorus melody "Ursa Major/Ursa Minor".

Paul's faraway and almost unrecognizable voice tells of the ways and customs of the hillmen, human subspecies who live in the hills, similar to "Bogey Music" (see sheet **149**).

During the autumn sessions, "Pretty Little Head" was partly re-recorded and re-mixed by John Potoker. A disco groove was added, and McCartney overdubbed new vocals, more percussion and some slap-bass: enough to contradict his anti-commercial theory.

In fact, this remake of "Pretty Little Head" became the second European single from the album in November 1986! The video for the song contained scenes of a girl arguing with her parents and running away from home, using a snippet of "She's Leaving Home" in the intro: nevertheless, the song went unnoticed and didn't chart in the UK.

There are three versions of "Pretty Little Head": as well as the version on *Press to Play*, the remake appears on the 7" single and in an extended version (6:56) on the 12" single.

Musicians:

Paul McCartney vocals, backing vocals, bass, electric guitar, drums, piano (?), keyboards (?) • **Linda McCartney** backing vocals • **Eric Stewart** backing vocals, keyboards, electric guitar (?), piano (?) • **Jerry Marotta** vibraphone, percussion

---

[543] *The Paul McCartney Special*, MPL Home video, 1986
[544] K. Sharp, *cit.*, p.20.

194 Move Over Busker (Paul McCartney-Eric Stewart)

Recording: March-May and October 1st-December 6th (overdubs), 1985 **Location:** Hog Hill Studio, Icklesham **Release:** August 1986, *Press to Play*

"Move Over Busker" can be considered one of McCartney's filler tracks. A basic rock standard that Paul sometimes puts on his records to fill them out.

As a rock'n'roll kind of track, recording it should have been fun for Paul and his musicians. It was captured live in the studio: the basic track consisted of drums, guitar, a very punchy bass – probably added later by Paul – and an Elton John-ish honky-tonk piano.

The original rough-mix sounds clearer and more aggressive, if compared to the version released on *Press to Play*. "Move Over Busker" was further enriched during the overdub sessions by Carlos Alomar's guitar solo, even though not specified in the liner notes.[545]

The most exciting part of the song is during the bridge, the only moment where one feels the energy and urgency that is essential to good old rock'n'roll. But generally the song doesn't work and McCartney's vocal performance – looser on earlier takes – isn't convincing.

Lirically, the surreal, ironic and humorous verses referring to movie icons like Mae West and Errol Flynn, were almost incomprehensible: as McCartney explained, the "Mae West, sweaty vest" reference was an inside joke among the Beatles, so no-one else got it.

Musicians:

Paul McCartney vocals, backing vocals, bass, piano, electric guitar (?), cow-bell (?), maracas (?) • **Eric Stewart** backing vocals, electric guitar • **Jerry Marotta** drums, cow-bell (?), maracas (?) • **Carlos Alomar** electric guitar • **Kate Robbins, Ruby James** backing vocals

195 However Absurd (Paul McCartney-Eric Stewart)

Recording: March-May and October 1st-December 6th (overdubs), 1985 **Location:** Hog Hill Studio, Icklesham and Abbey Road Studios (overdubs), London **Release:** August 1986, *Press to Play*

Closing an album with a majestic song was another rule that Paul learned from George Martin. On *Press to Play*, "However Absurd" is a perfect example of the use of this Beatles technique. The track deserves an honorable mention if only for its surrealistic lyrics, inspired by poet W.H.Auden.

The basic track consisted of piano (McCartney), electric guitar (Eric Stewart) and drums (Jerry Marotta). The drummer says: "It was kind of an *avant-garde* song, very reminiscent of *Sgt. Pepper's*. To me, that song is very Lennon… It was a bit of a tribute to him. It was not a typical McCartney-song, but kind of funky, strange but very interesting."[546]

---

[545] Interview courtesy of Carlos Alomar, 22/08/2011.
[546] Interview courtesy of Jerry Marotta, 22/10/2011.

"However Absurd" is a weird track, not typical of McCartney's style. The insistent opening piano chords announce a powerful song to come. The chorus is underscored by some strong drum hits and heavily distorted electric guitars.

Anne Dudley arranged the orchestral parts. These were recorded in the autumn using both a real orchestra and synthesizer and gave a kind of majestic feeling to "However Absurd". She worked on a Beatle-esque ending reminiscent of "A Day in the Life" – featuring a wild orchestral and horn outro – which closes the track. She recalled: "(Paul) asked me to arrange a couple of tracks on *Press to Play*. I was very nervous (…) On one song, 'However Absurd', at Abbey Road the lyrics were very peculiar and the point of the string arrangement was to sound surrealistic – so what happens is the orchestra bursts out and plays a little symphony at the end for no apparent reason. Some of the orchestra had worked on Abbey Road and *Sgt. Pepper's* so they'd done the chaotic bit on 'A Day In the Life'."[547]

McCartney's heavy-flanged voice is almost unrecognizable: it's as if Paul wanted to wear a clown's mask to mock and surprise his audience.

During the harmonious bridge, McCartney's lyrics deal with the theme of loss: the unique quality of love is replaced by the feeling of a broken dream, that is impossible to express with words. Lyrics are full of bitterness and delusion, something unusual in McCartney's songs.

Musicians:

Paul McCartney vocals, backing vocals, piano, bass, acoustic and electric guitar, keyboards (?) • **Eric Stewart** electric guitar, acoustic guitar (?) • **Jerry Marotta** drums • **Unknown musicians** strings, horns • **Ann Dudley (?)** synthesizer (?)

196 It's Not True (Paul McCartney)

Recording: March-May and October 1st-December 6th (overdubs), 1985 **Location:** Hog Hill Studio, Icklesham **Release:** July 1986, "Press" single B-side

This sweet ballad was inspired by Linda. The lyrics seem to be clearly in defense of Linda and her supporting role. The arrangement is sparse: McCartney uses a few suspended chords of electric piano backed by a drum-machine, while the chorus is held up by Marotta's powerful drumming. Lenny Pickett took care of the sax solo and Carlos Alomar added an electric guitar arpeggio. It was released as the B-side to "Press" and appears on the *Press to Play* cd in a longer version (by about a minute and a half). The best version is the 7" single edit, which removes the electric guitar intro and features less intrusive vocal parts by LaBouche.

Musicians:

Paul McCartney vocals, backing vocals, electric piano, bass, keyboards (?) • **Eric Stewart** electric guitar, keyboards (?) • **Jerry Marotta** drums • **Carlos Alomar** electric guitar • **LaBouche** backing vocals • **Lenny Pickett** sax

---

547 Phil Sutcliffe, *Anne Dudley on arrangement*, in *Q Magazine*.

197 Write Away (Paul McCartney-Eric Stewart)

Recording: March-May and October 1st-December, 6th (overdubs), 1985 **Location:** Hog Hill Studio, Icklesham **Release:** October 1986, "Pretty Little Head" single B-side

"Write Away" brought a touch of jazz to *Press to Play*. The song was the result of a jam: while Paul was playing electric piano his foot-tappping kept the beat.

This bizarre but ingenious sound was blended in with Marotta's percussion work in the final mix. Stewart: "This track was a weird one (…) It features Paul on Fender Rhodes and his feet recorded while he danced while playing."[548]

From the early version one can tell that Paul was still working on the melody, lyrics and instrumentation, as is noticeable from the rough-sketched guitar solo. During the overdub sessions, this section was filled with the addition of Carlos Alomar's guitar.

He recalls how the session went: "I remember I put down three different solo sections on that song. But at the end of the day, Paul and the engineer had the ability to flesh them together and to create new solos. When I asked if I could listen to it, some of the solos that I heard were not the same solo… I know that they have taken a little bit from one solo and another bit from another solo! And it worked fine for me!"[549]

During another session, an extraordinary piano solo was added by Eddie Rayner from New Zealand band Split Enz. Paul overdubbed a synth bass, while a sax track by Lennie Pickett – although credited in the liner notes – was removed at the last minute: if you listen closely you can still hear a faint trace of it. It was one of the best recordings of the sessions but ended up only as the B-side to "Pretty Little Head" and appears on the cd version of *Press to Play*.

Musicians:

Paul McCartney vocals, backing vocals, electric piano, synth-bass • **Eric Stewart** backing vocals, electric guitar • **Linda McCartney** backing vocals • **Jerry Marotta** percussion, drums • **Eddie Rayner** keyboards • **Carlos Alomar** electric guitar • **Lenny Pickett** sax

198 Tough on a Tightrope (Paul McCartney-Eric Stewart)

Recording: March-May and October 1st-December 6th (overdubs), 1985 **Location:** Hog Hill Studio, Icklesham and Abbey Road Studios? (overdubs), London **Release:** December 1986, "Only Love Remains" single B-side

McCartney and Stewart were probably inspired by "Fool on the Hill" while writing and recording this soft piano ballad.

The opening chord (D major 6th) and some of the instrumentation used (e.g. the recorder) seem to hint at this *Magical Mystery Tour* tune. Thanks to its crystalline melody, "Tough on a Tightrope" is one of the best results of McCartney and Stewart's partnership.

---

[548] K. Sharp, *cit.*, p.20.
[549] Interview courtesy of Carlos Alomar, 22/08/2011.

The simple arrangement heard on the rough mix was later overdubbed with Carlos Alomar's brilliant electric guitar solo and an orchestra, probably arranged again by Anne Dudley.

Again, the production work weakened the song. When Padgham got his hands on it, he buried McCartney's voice under a wash of reverb, while the bass sound was flattened using a Moog pedal. Fortunately, the acoustic guitars were given a crispy treatment.

From a lyrical point of view, the airy middle eight gives a rare peek into the relationship between Paul and Linda, with some unusually bitter lyrics that seem to underline some troubles within the couple at the time. One has to wonder why this track was excluded from the *Press to Play* LP and only appears on the cd. Maybe McCartney thought it didn't fit with the experimental direction of the album: too bad, because the song had qualities to spare.

Issued as the B-side of "Only Love Remains", the song appears on the 12" of the single in an extended version (7:36) with an acoustic intro, some extra strings and a cello in the finale.

Musicians:

Paul McCartney vocals, backing vocals, piano, bass, acoustic and electric guitar, synthesizer (?) • **Linda McCartney** backing vocals • **Eric Stewart** backing vocals, acoustic and electric guitar • **Jerry Marotta** drums, congas (?) • **Carlos Alomar** electric guitar • **Unknown musicians** strings

After the nightmare performance at *Live Aid* in Wembley on July 13th – where Paul sang the entire first minute of "Let It Be" with his mike not on – McCartney rushed back into the studio to record "Angry" in a special session with Phil Collins and Pete Townshend.

199 Angry (Paul McCartney-Eric Stewart)

Recording: July and October 1st-December 6th (overdubs), 1985 **Location:** Hog Hill Studio, Icklesham
Release: August 1986, *Press to Play*

As is the case with many of his songs, Paul had started writing "Angry" several years earlier. It was during a Wings rehearsal in 1980 at Finchden Manor that they came up with this punk-ish guitar riff that might have been a tribute to the Sex Pistol's "Holiday in The Sun".

That improvised guitar lick later turned into a real song that ended up on *Press to Play*. The first studio attempt was recorded with Stewart and Marotta, but McCartney wasn't satisfied and erased the recording. Then, he thought to have some special guests on the track, inviting drummer Phil Collins and Pete Townsend to play guitar.

McCartney: "Every time I played it I felt like Pete. There was plenty of these windmill arms when I played it, and I'd always imagined him doing it."[550]

"Angry" is one of the best songs on *Press to Play*. It's a relentless heavy rock track, recorded in a two-hour session – that took place in the days immediately after *Live Aid* – with Paul on Yamaha bass (as seen on photographs taken from the *Press to Play* presskit), Phil Collins on

[550] J. Blaney, *cit.*, p.178.

drums and Townshend on electric guitar. Paul delivers a punchy vocals and underscores the song with a fast bass, borrowed from "Soily". McCartney also contributed percussion.

McCartney didn't pull any punches in his lyrics, probably lashing out at the press for all the years of harassment. The opening verse, "What the hell gives you the right to tell me what to do in my life?" was something Paul had said and Eric Stewart suggested to use it in the song.

It seems to express McCartney's bitterness towards those who criticized not just his music, but also his lifestyle. McCartney also gave a wider – and unlikely – interpretation of the lyrics: "What makes me angry" – said Paul – "Are things like Thatcher's attitude to the blacks in South Africa and Reagan calling it South America."[551]

A few months later, the track was remixed by Larry Alexander. This version highlights the bass and vocals and features a horn section, arranged by Dave Matthews. It turned out to be one of McCartney's most powerful productions and was released as the B-side to the "Pretty Little Head" 12" single (UK) and to the "Stranglehold" 7" single (US) in October 1986.

Matthews: "I was contacted by Phil Ramone to work on this track. I imagined an arrangement and thought of a powerful horn section, doing the main riff and some other touches during the song. It was recorded at A&R Studios: two trumpets (Jon Faddis and Lew Soloff), a tenor sax (George Young) and a baritone sax (Ronnie Cuber). It was very quick, not bad, uh?"[552]

Musicians:

Paul McCartney vocals, backing vocals, electric guitar, bass, drums • **Linda McCartney** backing vocals • **Eric Stewart (?)** backing vocals • **Pete Townshend** backing vocals, electric guitar • **Phil Collins** drums • **Lenny Pickett (?)** sax • **Ray Cooper** tambourine

200 Spies Like Us (Paul McCartney)

Recording: September 1985 **Location:** Hog Hill Studio, Icklesham **Release:** November 1985, single

McCartney himself probably would find it hard remembering this song, but it should be burned into his memory since it was his last single to date to have entered the US top ten.

The song was recorded as the title-track for the John Landis film starring Dan Akroyd and Chevy Chase. The film was fairly successful at the box office and it proved how strong a promotional vehicle movies can be for songs. Paul had been requested specifically by Landis, who felt that his film had a lot in common with The Beatles' movies: this drove him straight to McCartney. Paul: "He said he wanted an up-tempo rock'n'rolly thing. I thought I might have done a Bondy song – the 75-piece orchestra, more melodic, with maybe an Eastern touch… One of the fun things of what I'm doing now is varying those things a bit."[553]

[551] *Club Sandwich*, n.42, Autumn 1986, p.6.
[552] Interview courtesy of Dave Matthews, 05/09/2012.
[553] Bill Harry, *cit.*, p.804.

McCartney accepted and began working on the song. Starting with a drum groove, Paul recorded two demos which he completed in as little as four sessions. The first demo had a more prominent bass and more aggressive guitar playing, while synthesizer and the final chorus were still missing. A lot of the demo parts did end-up on the official record.

Eddie Klein assisted Paul in the studio: "I was very tense over possible equipment failures" – recalled the engineer – "In view of the deadline!"[554]

After adding-on the vocals – including a catchy chorus in the coda – and a brilliantly played guitar solo, McCartney called Eddie Rayner to add synthesizer.

Searching for a different and modern sound, Paul produced a disco-oriented track, with the help of Phil Ramone and Hugh Padgham. The single did very well, reaching #7 on the US charts and #13 in the UK. Inexplicably, Paul excluded the song from his *All The Best!* album in 1987. The 12" contains two remixes: the first by John Potoker and the second by Art Of Noise. The complete version (5:37 as opposed to the 3:58 of the 12") was released in 2012 by Art Of Noise on the album *The Art of the 12" Vol.Two*.

Musicians:

Paul McCartney vocals, backing vocals, electric guitar, bass, drums, percussion, keyboards, tambourine • **Eddie Rayner** synthesizer • **Linda McCartney, Eric Stewart, Ruby James, Kate Robbins** backing vocals

Recording sessions for *Press to Play* resumed in October. At some point, several weeks after McCartney and Padgham's argument, Eric Stewart decided he'd had enough and left.

Stewart: "The backing tracks were wonderful. But when you start putting a production like Hugh Padgham, it loses any credibility for me."[555] The recordings were completed with three brand new songs and with vocal and instrumental overdubs, including horns and orchestra.

During an interview with Japanese tv shot at MPL office in Soho Square in November, McCartney talked about the album in the making, saying: "We recorded about 20 tracks. I think it will be released next spring. It's harder and rockier than my usual ones. I like it."

201 Talk More Talk (Paul McCartney)

Recording: October 1st-December 6th, 1985 **Location:** Hog Hill Studio, Icklesham **Release:** August 1986, *Press to Play*

According to Paul, "Talk More Talk" was written in the studio and the song was "finished in a single day". The track became one of the most elaborate on *Press to Play* – full of drum-machines and various electronic instruments.

---

554 *Club Sandwich*, n.40, 1986, p.2
555 Interview with Eric Stewart, 1992. See https://www.youtube.com/watch?v=ZrM3Xd-bxCs

The starting point for the song was rhythmic improvisation. After a gloomy intro drawn from some spacey keyboards and vocals by Linda, Paul's son James, Eddie Klein and studio assistants John Hammel, Matt Howe and Steve Jackson, "Talk More Talk" heads into a heated gospel direction. The entire track features a double-tracked vocal part by Paul, whose lyrics were inspired by a Tom Waits interview. Although not typical McCartney's output, the song's experimental quality makes it interesting. In particular, the 12-string guitar arpeggios heard throughout the song are among the most original ideas on *Press to Play*.

Paul must have been pleased with "Talk More Talk" because he prepared a three-minute edit and planned to release it as a single in October 1986. McCartney then opted for "Pretty Little Head". A re-mix was made and is available on the 12" of "Only Love Remains".

Musicians:

Paul McCartney vocals, acoustic and 12-string electric guitar, bass, keyboards, drums • **Linda McCartney, James McCartney, John Hammel, Matt Howe, Steve Jackson** vocals

202 Hanglide (Paul McCartney-Eric Stewart)

Recording: October 1st-December 6th, 1985 **Location**: Hog Hill Studio, Icklesham **Release**: July 1986, "Press" 12" single

One of the most experimental tracks written by Paul and Eric Stewart, this song is a result of jamming. Clocking-in at over five minutes, "Hanglide" is an instrumental that borders on ambient music. Built entirely on a drum machine and a bass groove – with keyboards and percussion weaving in and out – this could have been the soundtrack to a rainforests documentary and it soon becomes boring. "Hanglide" was released on the "Press" 12".

Musicians:

Paul McCartney bass, electric guitar, keyboards (?) • **Eric Stewart** electric guitar (?), keyboards (?)

203 Only Love Remains (Paul McCartney)

Recording: October 1st-December 6th, 1985 **Location**: Hog Hill Studio, Icklesham **Release**: August 1986, *Press to Play*

McCartney endend the sessions with one last throw of the dice by moving away from the experimental and back to his trusted ballads with a love song dedicated to Linda. "Only Love Remains" is the real *Press to Play* classic.

On this occasion, Paul decided to do something special by recording the song live with an entire orchestra. "Only Love Remains" was taped at Hog Hill Studio – as seen in some footage stills appeared on the internet – with John Bradbury leading the orchestra.[556]

Tony Visconti: "In the early summer of 1985, I was pleased to hear Paul's voice on the phone. He was enquiring if I'd like to arrange a song for his new album. I drove down to his

---

[556] Interview courtesy of John Bradbury, 18/11/2011.

outrageously beautiful recording studio on the Sussex (...) Paul played me (this) gorgeous ballad. He said he wanted to record it live with a small orchestra of strings, woodwind instruments and a rhythm section."[557]

"The plan was to try and record a rhythm track in the morning, to be safe, and overdub the orchestral instruments in the afternoon" – Visconti adds – "Once that was achieved we had a go recording the entire ensemble with Paul singing and play live (...) I stood next to him as he played piano and sang, while I conducted the orchestra: it was like having my own private McCartney concert (...) He never made a mistake and each take was a *keeper*."[558]

The basic recording was a three-way affair, with Simon Chamberlain and Graham Ward, who recalls: "We were invited by Tony Visconti. When we got into Paul's studio, he played us a demo, so to get a rough idea of the song. I remember it was very simple, only with piano, vocals and click-track or a metronome for the tempo."[559]

Then recording began. Ward: "We started to throw in some ideas... Rehearsing different rhythms and different tempos. Paul showed something with his bass that Simon played through a synthesizer. Probably Paul wanted him to play synth bass only as a guide, but then he liked it and he kept it in the final recording."[560]

Later on, the song was completed with more instruments; some marimba played by Ray Cooper and some classical guitar overdubbed by McCartney.[561] "Only Love Remains" is a carefully produced example of McCartney's classic melodic style with its sumptuous orchestra and fluid piano parts.

For its release as a single the song was overdubbed – adding a sax part and keyboards – and re-mixed by Jim Boyer. The track reached a disappointing #34 in the UK, when it was released in December 1986 and it wasn't the Christmas hit McCartney was expecting.

It was performed on the TV program The Tube on December 11th, 1986 with a bare arrangement: Paul on piano, Linda and Tessa Niles on vocals and an unidentified sax player.

Musicians:

Paul McCartney vocals, backing vocals, piano, classical guitar, synthesizer (?) • **Linda McCartney, Kate Robbins, Ruby James** backing vocals • **Eric Stewart** backing vocals, acoustic guitar (?) • **Graham Ward** drums • **Simon Chamberlain** synth bass • **Ray Cooper** marimba, tambourine (?), shaker (?) • **John Bradbury** violin • **Unknown musicians** strings

---

557 T. Visconti, *Bowie, Bolan and the Brooklyn Boy*, 2007, pp.326-327.
558 *Ibid*, p.327.
559 Interview courtesy of Graham Ward, 05/11/2011.
560 *Ibid.*
561 Hugh Padgham, in *Club Sandwich*, n.44, Spring 1987, p.2.

1986

The year began with McCartney recording some other material for *Press to Play*.

204 Simple as That (Paul McCartney)

Recording: February 1986 **Location:** Abbey Road Studios, London **Release:** November 1986, *The Anti-Heroin Project- It's a Live in World*

The Phoenix House Charity, an association overseeing the Anti-heroin Project, asked McCartney to contribute a song to an album intended to collect some funds in aid of young drug abusers. Paul gave them "Simple as That", a relaxed reggae probably written some years earlier: a demo with the same title dates back to August, 1980.

The song is a stand against drugs, while also praising the joy to live. Not much information has emerged about the recording other than that it was a family affair with Linda, Mary, Stella and James singing harmony vocals. Paul probably handled most of the instruments. The electric guitar does sound like Carlos Alomar's style, but he didn't confirm his involvement.

This track, initially released in November 1986 on the double album *It's a Live-In World* (Various Artists), was next included in 1993 in the *Pipes of Peace* remastered edition.

Musicians:

Paul McCartney vocals, backing vocals, bass, keyboards (?), electric guitar (?), drums (?) • **Linda McCartney, Mary McCartney, Stella McCartney, James McCartney** backing vocals **Carlos Alomar** (?) electric guitar (?)

On June 20th, McCartney appeared at the *Prince's Trust* concert at Wembley and was enthusiastically welcomed. Paul wooed the crowd and fellow artists on stage, performing mega renditions of "Get Back", "I Saw Her Standing There" and "Long Tall Sally": the Beatles' legacy was no longer to be seen as such embarrassing.

That summer, Paul invited Peter Gabriel to his studio and they co-wrote the song "The Politics of Love", recorded in October and still unreleased. It is said that Gabriel played it during the Japanese leg of his *So* Tour, in December: but no evidence of that performance has surfaced.

Gabriel shed some light about the collaboration with Paul: "It was fantastic – I'm an old Beatles fan… So hanging out, generating ideas with Paul was a real treat. It sort of fizzled out a bit, so we never got it finished. I think that was largely my fault (…) The lyrics weren't quite getting nailed, but there were some lovely melodic ideas and a beautiful burst that Paul had generated. So it would be great if it saw the light of day in some form."[562]

While McCartney was in New York doing some promotion for the upcoming *Press to Play*, he told a strange story, perhaps sensing a failure: "When we started working on the record, Hugh

---

[562] http://www.wmmr.com/music/news/Story.aspx?ID=1546798

came in one day and said he dreamed he woke up one morning and he had made this really bad, sirupy album with me…that it had blown his own career. We took that as a little warning." He also booked a couple of days at Power Station Studio with producer Phil Ramone, recording two tracks, "Loveliest Thing" and "Beautiful Night" (see sheet 282).

Dave O'Donnell, who worked as an assistant engineer to Steve Rinkoff, recalls: "The session was at Studio C at Power Station. We set up and recorded like we always did in the studio. It was still the days of analogue, so we recorded on 24 tracks 2" tape."[563]

205 Loveliest Thing (Paul McCartney)

Recording: August 21st, 1986 and June-July, 1988 (overdubs) **Location:** Power Station Studio, New York and Hog Hill Studio (overdubs), Icklesham **Release:** November 1989, "Figure of Eight" cd-single

"Loveliest Thing" was the first track to be taped in N.Y.C.: McCartney combined two of his demos together, "Loveliest Thing" and "Without Permission" and recorded this ballad live in the studio playing piano, accompanied by Neil Jason on bass, David Brown on electric guitar, Liberty Devitto on drums and David Lebolt on synthesizer.

Dave O'Donnell: "Paul sent a tape ahead of time, or a lead sheet, because he was delayed to the session and the musicians had time to learn the song before he got there (…) When he arrived they played the first song. They did one take, which was great, and Paul said something like, 'Well I guess we might as well do another take.' He played the piano and sang live with the band. The second day he overdubbed vocals."[564]

The group's performance is flawless. McCartney added an excellent vocal and Phil Ramone's production is clean. The song ends majestically, thanks to the use of the final Picardy third, the same trick used in "And I Love Her". It was released in November 1989 on the "Figure of Eight" limited edition cd-single and on the Japanese *Flowers in the Dirt* double cd (1990).

Musicians:

Paul McCartney vocals, piano • **Neil Jason** bass • **David Brown** electric guitar • **Liberty Devitto** drums • **David Lebolt** synthesizer

Press to Play was released on September 4th. McCartney started a heavy promotional campaign, with a large number of interviews. In his typical fashion, Paul surrounded the album with great expectations. McCartney: "I'm not very good in comparing my albums. If I just made an album, I find it very difficult to step back and be objective on it. I don't know how it compares to the others. Some people have said it's my best since *Band on the Run* so… I don't know if that's true… I like it!" Some critics spoke favorably about the album, thanks to the experimental flavor of many songs. But generally, the response was unenthusiastic.

---

[563] Interview courtesy of Dave O'Donnell, 07/12/2012.
[564] *Ibid.*

The album reached only #30 in *Billboard* and #8 on the UK charts and then sank without trace in a few weeks. At that point, McCartney changed his initial plans to go on tour.

And yet, *Rolling Stone* wrote a quite positive review. If McCartney wanted to sound modern, he hit the target according to critic Anthony DeCurtis, who said: "*Press to Play* plants firmly McCartney in the present. Padgham supplies the album with an electronically dense contemporary sound and Stewart pushes McCartney in some new directions."

In September, Paul got back to his *Cold Cuts* project. He brought in producer Richard Niles, who recalls: "I got a call from my contractor and he was booking orchestras for McCartney. He said that Paul really liked what I did for 'Slave to the Rhythm' with Grace Jones and he really like you to work with him on this project. McCartney has sent me a copy of his album *Press to Play*, and the first question he asked was what I thought of that. I said, 'It sounds like an experimental kind of album. Some of these songs are quite successful, others less.' He said, 'I'm really glad you said that to me because is exactly what the case is. This is not typical McCartney. I'm not happy with it. Everybody around me tell me it's great. I don't think so'."[565] Niles spent two weeks with McCartney and one day Paul unexpectedly asked for his opinion: "I came into the studio one day and Paul sat at the piano. He played me this beautiful song with beautiful chords. He said, 'I've got this song but I have a problem. I want to play it for you and ask you a question.' It was called 'Your School' (the song is still unreleased but Paul played a portion of it on his *Oobu Joobu* Radio Show in 1995 – author's note). I noticed that when he got to a certain part the song was modulated, in the middle section, he hit a new key. He said, 'Now I don't know what to do, because I want to go back to the original key and I can't, 'cause it sounds terrible!' So I said, 'That's not a problem... On the last chord of the middle section, hold that last chord for two more beats and then go back to the song. He said, 'That sounds great! How's it possible?' I explained to him that by letting the chord hang there, the ear relaxes. Psychologically, the ear hears a new beginning. He said, 'I'm so happy about that, thank you! That means I'll get dinner tonight... I've been struggling with this song for the last two weeks, every night, playing it over and over again and Linda is completely sick of it and said to me, 'Today if I didn't finished the song I wasn't going to get dinner!'"[566] In December, McCartney went to his Sussex studio to record the instrumental "Squid".

206 Squid (Paul McCartney)

Recording: December 12th, 1986 **Location:** Hog Hill Studio, Icklesham **Release:** July 1997, "The World Tonight" cd-single

A solo recording by McCartney, who probably was flirting with this riff from some time and decided to commit it to tape. Originally titled "Be Vegetarian", "Squid" is a long instrumental

---

[565] Interview courtesy of Richard Niles, 07/10/2011.
[566] *Ibid.*

track entirely based upon ringing acoustic guitars. The song is orchestrated in a typical McCartney style, layering different instrumental variations and counter-melodies on top of the main theme. The song was included in "The World Tonight" cd-single (1997).

Musicians:

Paul McCartney acoustic and electric guitars, bass, keyboards, synthesizer, piano

Earlier, Niles witnessed one of the most intimate and secret sessions in McCartney's career. On the occasion of Linda's 45th birthday, Paul wanted to give her a special gift by recording a cover of the famous song "Linda" written by Jack Lawrence in 1942 which specifically uses the name of little Linda Eastman, the daughter of his lawyer, Lee Eastman. Paul had Niles write an arrangement in record time and Niles worked day and night in order to bring the finished piece into the studio. Niles: "Paul said, 'I want to do a present for Linda's birthday. We're going to make a recording for her. A vinyl single. We will record it on Monday morning, I've already booked the studio!' I said that we should record the song in the style of the Forties, with my band Bandzilla. But I didn't even know which key the song was in, so Paul sat down at the piano and played it…It was an A flat. For the B-side, which he didn't even think of, I said, 'Why don't we do the same song in a completely different style? A Latin-salsa kind of?' And he said, 'Great, see you!' He left without giving me further instruction… He told me that he trusted me completely! Since it was Thursday night, I realized I had a lot of writing to do, since I have to write it down and then give copies to the musicians for the different parts… Seventeen parts! I worked all the weekend… In the studio it went extremely well… Paul joked around with the band, he picked up one of the trumpets, just chatting to everyone, putting them at their ease. I think it was a deliberate action from his part."[567]

Young trombone player Pete Beachill was one of the hired musicians whom Paul had asked to keep his song secret. But when Pete went home for Christmas, he couldn't resist telling his family and his mother in turn, told a reporter. Beachill: "I think there were 2 or 3 trombones, 2 or 3 trumpets, 4 saxes and a rhythm section. Guy Barker was on trumpet, Phil Todd on sax and Mitch Dalton on guitar. I remember us all thinking, 'Great to be working for Paul McCartney but how sad that nobody will get to hear what we're recording, because it was a special personal recording…They said they were only going to press one copy!"[568]

[567] Ibid.
[568] Interview courtesy of Pete Beachill, 29/01/2013.

1987

Since McCartney was favorably impressed by Ramone's work during the previous summer in New York, he invited the American producer to his Sussex studio.

The McCartney-Ramone sessions produced ten tracks; but this project – probably inspired by the *Sgt.Pepper's Lonely Hearts Club Band* twentieth anniversary – never came to light.

Following this idea, Paul recorded a new version of "Sgt. Pepper's…" as well as another track titled "Return to Pepperland": both are still unissued. In February, before starting sessions at Hog Hill, at the Audio International Studios he also added his vocals to "P.S. Love Me Do", a dreadful medley of "Love Me Do" and "P.S. I Love You".

Other tracks recorded during the sessions and still unreleased included an early version of "This One" (see sheet **223**), the instrumental "Christian Bop" – whose melody would be reworked by Paul for his *Liverpool Oratorio*'s Third Movement, "Crypt" (see **1991**) – and "Big Day", a never-ending chant. The sessions were not successful: McCartney and Phil Ramone did not share the same approach to the songs and eventually Ramone left.

Steve Lyon assisted Jon Jacobs engineering the sessions and confirms: "I don't think Paul got on very well with Phil Ramone. There were musical discussions and the situation was a little bit sticky… And Phil left the sessions. Paul wanted a different kind of sound and Phil Ramone, who had a very successful history with Billy Joel, was really into song-playing…But not that much into electronic sounds and drum-machines. They were stumbling around trying to find something…We tried some drum-machines and Phil was not at ease with those things."[569]

Lyon also noticed: "When the band was there, it was brilliant… Really a lot of fun. When it was just Paul, Phil, Jon and myself, it really changed the atmosphere…"[570]

207 Back on My Feet (Paul McCartney-Elvis Costello)

Recording: March 9th, 1987 **Location:** Hog Hill Studio, Icklesham **Release:** November 1987, "Once Upon a Long Ago…" single B-side

Early in the year, Paul got in touch with Elvis Costello. Having burst on the scene in 1977, Costello was one of most original and talented artists from the punk era, whose music was a combination of Beatles' flavors and New-Age anger.

A new partnership had begun, and was highly praised by the musical press at the time; Costello's strong personality could positively influence McCartney's music. Costello and Lennon were compared to each other by many critics. McCartney played his part, perfectly conscious that the media would be attracted by anything connected to The Beatles' legacy.

---

[569] Interview courtesy of Steve Lyon, 11/09/2012.
[570] *Ibid.*

McCartney: "When we came together, there were similarities between Elvis and John. They've both got specs… I think people with glasses can be a little more introverted and a bit more aggressive on the outside. We sat down and we enjoyed each other's skills (…) He helped me with words particularly, which he's full of. He's very wordy! Normally I encourage people to tell me if (a song) it's rubbish, but there was no problem with that with Elvis… He's going to tell you! He's got a very opinionated attitude!"[571]

The first song completed by McCartney with the help of Costello was in fact "Back on My Feet". Issued as the B-side to the single "Once Upon a Long Ago…" (see sheet **209**), was also the first released song of their partnership.

In some interviews, Paul said that the song was mostly finished but needed some work on the words. Elvis was a great help: the track's lyrical richness – a Costello trademark – depicts this surreal story with effectiveness, thanks to a movie camera imagery technique.

Harmonically, the track is uncharacteristic by McCartney's standards: the chord sequence is particularly interesting and the chorus – towards the end of the song – sounds like a tongue-twister.

The track was the first to be recorded during the Ramone sessions. Steve Lyon recalls that Paul presented the songs directly in the studio to the band. Lyon: "Paul sat down saying, 'This is how the song goes!' From the very simple presentation that Paul had done on piano or on guitar, the band started jamming around and created his arrangements."[572]

McCartney recorded the basic track playing piano, accompanied by Tim Renwick on guitar, Nick Glennie-Smith on keyboards and Charlie Morgan on drums. Paul later overdubbed an excellent bass part in his distinctive style, with plenty of melodic phrases and hooks. Excellent electric guitars stand out, along with Paul's crystalline vocals. The track was also included in the 1993 remastered version of *Flowers in the Dirt*.

Musicians:

Paul McCartney vocals, backing vocals, bass, piano, electric guitar • **Tim Renwick** electric guitar • **Nick Glennie-Smith** keyboards • **Charlie Morgan** drums • **Linda McCartney** backing vocals

208 Love Come Tumbling Down (Paul McCartney)

Recording: March 10th, 1987 **Location:** Hog Hill Studio, Icklesham **Release:** November 1997, "Beautiful Night" single B-side

After the unsatisfying collaboration with Hugh Padgham, Paul approached Phil Ramone with a clear mind: the production work should have highlighted his catchy pop songs. Exactly what the audience was expecting from him.

---

[571] Home video *Put It There*, 1989.
[572] Interview courtesy of Steve Lyon, 11/09/2012.

McCartney worked with Ramone on several pop-oriented tracks and "Love Come Tumbling Down" was one of those: it came out as the best result of these sessions along with "Once Upon a Long Ago…"

The track caught Ramone's attention: "What Paul had was a mostly unfinished (song) or snippets of songs that he was working on" – Ramone recalled – "'Love Come Tumbling Down' was one of those songs that he played for me. I heard it and I said, 'Boy, sure sounds like one you want to develop.'"[573]

The production isn't particularly original as the track would not have been out of place on *Pipes of Peace*. Nevertheless, "Love Come Tumbling Down" is marked by a crystal clear melody with both a basic yet clever arrangement.

For this recording, McCartney was accompanied again by Charlie Morgan (drums), Nick Glennie-Smith (keyboards) and Tim Renwick (electric guitar) and added a well-developed bass part[574] which stands out, agile and continuously underlining the track. Furthermore, Paul filled the song with several melodies layered on top of each other. The harmonic structure of the song, with the use of two intertwining choruses, is so typical of McCartney's counterpoint skill and makes "Love Come Tumbling Down" a really brilliant pop song.

The track was left in the vaults for many years; it would be released in 1997 as the B-side to the single "Beautiful Night".

Musicians:

Paul McCartney vocals, backing vocals, bass, electric guitar (?), keyboards (?) • **Tim Renwick** electric guitar • **Nick Glennie-Smith** keyboards • **Charlie Morgan** drums

209 Once Upon a Long Ago… (Paul McCartney)

Recording: March 11th-12th and July 1st (overdubs), 1987 **Location:** Hog Hill Studio, Icklesham and Abbey Road Studios (overdubs), London **Release:** November 1987, single

"Once Upon a Long Ago…" was among the brand-new tracks that Paul presented to Phil Ramone: in an interview to a German radio he said that he wrote it around autumn 1986. McCartney had composed the verses probably taking as a starting point a variation on two piano chords – C and F major seventh – with bass alternating between C and B flat.

To the verses, with their nonsense lyrics – typical of McCartney's songwriting (each one finishing with the question "What does it mean?", as if Paul makes it clear he's conscious of it) – Paul added a chorus in a minor key, probably borrowed from another unfinished song.

---

[573] *Phil Ramone-In the Studio with McCartney, Starr and Lennon (Julian, That Is)* in *Beatlefan*, n.119, July- August 1999, p.20.
[574] Not credited on the liner notes, as other instrumentation on the track. Very likely Paul overdubbed a lot of other things later.

Again, the two stitched-together bits worked well: "Once Upon a Long Ago…" could be considered one of the best McCartney songs from the Eighties. Reportedly, it was composed for the film *The Princess Bride* but director Rob Reiner rejected it.

Musically and harmonically, "Once Upon a Long Ago…" is amazingly rich. After the basic track was completed (Paul on piano, Tim Renwick on acoustic guitar, Henry Spinetti on drums and Nick Glennie-Smith on keyboards), McCartney himself overdubbed a lot of other instruments (bass, acoustic guitars, the electric guitar solo).

In the following months, "Once Upon a Long Ago…" was refined and completed with Stan Sulzmann on sax, Nigel Kennedy on electric violin and an orchestral arrangement by George Martin: these overdubs were added in a special session at Abbey Road.

Stan Sulzmann has a clear memory of that session: "I went into the studio for my sax part. I remember that Paul really just liked solos to stick fairly closely to the tune so I did a soft variation. We tried lots of things but it always came back to the tune. Paul didn't really like improvised solos, he just wanted what he had in his head."[575] The sax-player's memories are confirmed by a somewhat curious detail: listening closely to the isolated tracks on the 5.1 mix – that can be found on the dvd *The McCartney Years* (2007) – one can catch McCartney off-mike, humming a carbon copy of the sax solo that would be overdubbed!

Adrian Brett too was invited in the studio to play recorder, buried in the mix or even removed later: "I remember we recorded in Abbey Road Studio One with quite a big orchestra. There was a separate booth for the three 'soloists' (myself on recorder, Nigel Kennedy on violin and Stan Sulzmann on tenor sax). I recall Paul joking with me because I had been playing an opera at Glyndebourne in Sussex that afternoon and came back to London for his session!"[576]

A perfectly bright production does justice to this ballad's instrumental and vocal blending. The closing minute and a half is a gem: first, an *a cappella* interlude with different vocal harmonies (along the lines of "Daytime Nighttime Suffering"), next two scintillating solos – electric guitar and violin – following one another. A really unforgettable instrumental sequence.

"Once Upon a Long Ago…" hit the mark: it reached #10 in the UK charts, thus making it the last McCartney to do so in his homeland to date.

"Once Upon a Long Ago…" was released in November 1987, and it was a huge success all over Europe – in Italy the single reached #2 and entered Top 30 in fifteen countries, selling around two and a half millions copies[577] – thanks to a massive promotional campaign done by Paul, with several tv appearances, including the Sanremo Festival, Italy, in February 1988. Furthermore, the song had a charming clip, which combined spectacular footage of McCartney

575 Interview courtesy of Stan Sulzmann, 19/08/2011.
576 Interview courtesy of Adrian Brett, 26/09/2011.
577 *Club Sandwich*, n.47- 48, Spring 1988, p.2.

and his musicians playing on the edge of a cliff in the Valley of the Rocks, Devon and some nice cartoons, showing the magic of a snowy Christmas.

In all, four different versions of the song were issued. The only difference between the first (included in *All the Best!*) and the second (released on the 7" single) is the closing section: a fade-out on the album version, and a full ending – with the chorus reprise – on the single.

Two others versions were released: the *Long Version* – which lasts 4:34 and is featured on the pink covered 12" single. It has more of Paul's vocals and a full ending – and the *Extended Version*, which lasts 6:06 and is on the blue covered 12" single. Here, the closing electric guitar solo – with Paul's vocals on top – is longer and is followed by a synth coda.

Musicians:

Paul McCartney vocals, backing vocals, bass, acoustic and electric guitar, piano, synthesizer • **Linda McCartney** backing vocals, tambourine • **Nick Glennie-Smith** keyboards • **Tim Renwick** acoustic guitar • **Henry Spinetti** drums • **Nigel Kennedy** violin • **Stan Sulzmann** sax • **Adrian Brett** flute • **Unknown musicians** strings, horns

210 Atlantic Ocean (Paul McCartney)

Recording: March 20th, 1987 **Location**: Hog Hill Studio, Icklesham **Release:** April 1997, "Young Boy" cd-single 2

Perhaps wanting something different and more contemporary-sounding, Paul asked Phil Ramone to produce this sort of experimental rap song. Precisely the kind of things that the producer didn't like.

Phil Ramone recalled that the track was born in the studio: "It was one of those things we were messing around with percussion loops and started with just straight backbeat from an old drum-machine and then (Paul) started playing shakers and didn't play the bass part until the end."[578]

With its percussive sounds, "Atlantic Ocean" is somewhat similar to "Pretty Little Head" (see sheet 193). A really unconventional track: the whole thing is spoken rather than sung. The lyrics deal with the African slave trade and go back to some Beatles' memories, mentioning Penny Lane. A less than memorable song, which over the course of the following years would be heavily overdubbed by several musicians, including Jethro Tull guitarist Martin Barre.

Aired by McCartney during the *Oobu Joobu* radio show – although in a slightly different mix – "Atlantic Ocean" would be released on the second "Young Boy" cd-single in April 1997.

Musicians:

Paul McCartney vocals, keyboards, bass, electric guitar, maracas, percussion • **Phil Picket** keyboards • **Louis Jardim** percussion • **Stuart Elliott** drums • **Martin Barre** electric guitar

---

[578] *Beatlefan*, n.119, July- August 1999, p.20.

211 Love Mix (Paul McCartney)

Recording: April 24th, 1987 and September-November, 1988? (overdubs) **Location:** Hog Hill Studio, Icklesham and Olympic Studios? (overdubs), London **Release:** December 1997, "Beautiful Night" cd-single

Paul – whose songs at times could lie unused for half-decades – had composed this catchy chorus at the piano in the early Seventies, taping a demo called "Waiting for the Sun to Shine". When the moment arose, Paul added some verses, tailoring this light and simple catchy pop-song in the studio. "Love Mix" was probably recorded alone by McCartney, although the piano – so typical of McCartney's style and maybe used as a guide-instrument for the basic track – and drums are not credited on the sleeve notes. He also employed Yamaha DX-7 synth – one of the most used in Eighties pop songs – to get the punchy bass sound.

Very likely, the track was perfected after Phil Ramone left. One day, young engineer Steve Lyon (22 years old at the time) found himself alone in the studio with McCartney. He recalls: "He was jamming around while I was working on the desk and he said to me, 'What's your favorite Beatles song?' and I said, 'Fool on the Hill'. He played it at the piano for me!"[579]

The song could have been a summer hit, but Paul immediately discarded it: the track was overdubbed with some guitar by Robbie McIntosh – probably added during the *Flowers in the Dirt* sessions in 1988-89 – but the thing was put on hold.

"Love Mix", though, was not completed for years: still in 1995, Paul introduced it on *Oobu Joobu*, as an unfinished song. The track would find the right spot only in December 1997, when it was issued on the "Beautiful Night" cd-single.

Musicians:

Paul McCartney vocals, backing vocals, synth-bass, keyboards, piano (?), drums (?) • **Robbie McIntosh** electric guitar

The Ramone sessions were another flop for McCartney. So bored after many years in the studio, trying to craft songs filled more with instruments rather than ideas, McCartney decided to shake-up his career. Paul got back to his rock'n'roll roots, gathering some young musicians in his own studio for July 20th-21st. A two-day session of Fifties standards: "Kansas City", "Twenty-Flight Rock", "Lawdy Miss Clawdy", "Lucille", "Summertime", "Crackin'Up", "Ain't That a Shame", "Just Because", "I'm Gonna Be a Wheel Someday", "Midnight Special", "Bring It on Home to Me", "I'm In Love Again", "That's All Right (Mama)", "Don't Get Around Much Anymore". Fun was the name of the game: McCartney quickly introduced the tracks to his musicians only giving them the key and where to break for the solo.

The sessions, although not intended for release, went down so well that they resulted in the album *Back in the USSR*, a.k.a. "The Russian album" because of its exclusive destination to the

579 Interview courtesy of Steve Lyon, 11/09/2012.

Soviet Union market. An unspecified number of tracks was recorded, many of which still unreleased: among them, a new version of "I Saw Her Standing There" and other recordings done with Smiths' guitarist Johnny Marr, including "No Other Baby" (re-recorded in 1999 for *Run Devil Run*), "Poor Boy" (an Elvis song), "Cut Across Shorty" (Eddie Cochrane), "Lend Me Your Comb" (Carl Perkins) and "Take This Hammer" (Lonnie Donegan).

Marr recalled: "I didn't do a recording session with him as such, but we did get together for a good long eight-or-nine-hour day, and just played and played and played very intensely, really loudly. Which was pretty great, obviously. He was pretty good! We played 'I Saw Her Standing There', 'Twenty Flight Rock', 'Tutti Frutti'. I got him to play 'Things We Said Today', and I think we played some Wings stuff. 'C Moon', I remember. That was fun. He and I were singing harmonies on 'I Saw Her Standing There' – that was a pretty good moment, too."

The record would be released in 1988: it reached #63 in UK and #109 in the US.

212 I Wanna Cry (Paul McCartney)

Recording: July 21st, 1987 **Location:** Hog Hill Studio, Icklesham **Release:** July 1989, "This One" 12" single

As the *Choba B CCCP* sessions were intended only for jamming and playing rock'n'roll oldies, Paul made only a couple of exceptions to the rule, basically to please his musicians who were often asking if they could have played some McCartney originals. The first being The Beatles' classic "I Saw Her Standing There", the other was "I Wanna Cry", a laid-back blues in the vein of "Summertime". The track was probably recorded as a jam during a break on the second day in the studio. McCartney took up his electric, leaving the bass to Nick Garvey, and started improvising some guitar phrases. Unfortunately, "I Wanna Cry" fails to capture the freshness and the excitement that surely should have been breathing during these sessions. McCartney's blues attempt is a complete flop, with uninspired vocals and ad-libbed lyrics. Not included in *Back in the USSR*, the track was released in July 1989 on the "This One" cd-mix.

Musicians:

Paul McCartney vocals, electric guitar • **Nick Garvey** bass • **Henry Spinetti** drums • **Mick Gallagher** piano

During the autumn, McCartney went into his MPL Studio with Elvis Costello. They taped demos for nine tracks, helping each other to finish songs and writing some new ones. Among the tunes, "My Brave Face", "The Lovers That Never Were", "Don't Be Careless Love" and "You Want Her Too". Two other tracks, "Twenty Fine Fingers" and "Tommy's Coming Home" are still unissued: the latter has been played live by Costello on June 25th, 2014.

Just before Christmas, McCartney got together with George Martin to record "Tropic Island Hum", a song intended for an animated film written by Paul himself.

213 Tropic Island Hum (Paul McCartney)

Recording: December 1st and 14th-19th, 1987 and September, 1994 (overdubs) **Location:** Hog Hill Studio, Icklesham and AIR Studios (overdubs), London **Release:** September 2004, single

McCartney's fondness for animation did not stop with Rupert the Bear. Paul's idea was to put up an original story, based on some of his drawings.

McCartney sketched a script, that was a combination of old and new ideas: the tropical island and the *Froggo* character take the cue from the songs "Sunshine, Sometime" and "We All Stand Together", while *Wirral the Squirrel* was a lovely squirrel newly invented by Paul.

Paul immediately wrote a tune and he gave to George Martin "Tropic Island Hum", an infectious ode to happiness and lightheartedness: McCartney set to music the animal village's celebration producing one of his most joyful and cheerful songs.

McCartney hams it up and displays the lively bunch of animals, playing and voicing almost all the characters. Vocal contributions featured Marion Montgomery (1934-2002), a well-known jazz singer from the Forties and the London Gospel Community Choir, led by Bazel Meade.

Lance Phillips, who worked as an assistant engineer to Peter Henderson, recalls: "They flew in Marion Montgomery from the US. She was very charming and absolutely lovely. She did her bits and she left... Peter and I were absolutely paranoid that we might lose or erase the recording somehow! So we made about 15 safety copies of her vocal!"[580]

With its feisty arrangement, "Tropic Island Hum" is a rich and lively recording: the song ranges from vaudeville to jazz, blended together by exotic and tribal rhythms. McCartney acts like a comedian, doing hundreds of funny voices; the song is compelling and can be fully appreciated within the context of the cartoon. No further details have surfaced about this recording: but very likely, McCartney employed some jazz musicians for the majority of the instrumental parts. Drums could have been handled by Chris Whitten, employed during the *Choba B CCCP* sessions: "I got a call to do one of his animation projects. There was me on drums, Paul on bass and a couple of brass players with Geoff Emerick recording and George Martin doing the arrangements. I thought, 'I can't believe I am sitting here.'"[581]

In September 2004 "Tropic Island Hum" was issued as a single and got a good chart placement in the UK (#21). The complete version (5:50) can only be found on the dvd, while the single version is edited down to 3:15.

Musicians:

Paul McCartney vocals, piano (?), double-bass (?), percussion (?) • **Marion Montgomery** vocals • **The London Gospel Community Choir** vocals • **Chris Whitten (?)** drums (?) **Unknown musicians** mandolin, percussion, horns, double-bass (?), acoustic guitar, electric guitar

---

580 Interview courtesy of Lance Phillips, 29/08/2012.
581 Greg Phillips, 10/09/2007, http://www.australianmusician.com.au/chris-whitten-world-party-paul-mccartney/

Searching for a different path, McCartney commenced new recordings calling producers Steve Lipson and Trevor Horn, a duo made famous by its work with Frankie Goes To Hollywood. In his studio, he started a quick four-day session in December, resuming work in January 1988. An intensive plan of recordings that would generate four tracks for the future *Flowers in the Dirt*.

214 Rough Ride (Paul McCartney)

Recording: December 21st-24th, 1987 and January 2nd-21st, 1988 (overdubs) **Location:** Hog Hill Studio, Icklesham **Release:** June 1989, *Flowers in the Dirt*

While noodling with an E minor chord on his acoustic guitar, Paul found a little riff: and "Rough Ride" was born. The actual inspiration came from the blues: "It's me trying to be Big Bill Broonzy" – McCartney said – "I'd seen a blues program and I thought, well these guys do a song and it's all one chord, two verses and a little guitar riff!"[582]

Once in the studio, McCartney worked hard with producers Steve Lipson and Trevor Horn, and put them in the corner. Paul: "I'd heard (that they could take) even three months to make a single, and I didn't fancy getting involved in a single that takes three months! So I said, 'Do you fancy trying doing something over two days?'"[583]

The result was this modern sounding track, based on funky guitar riffs and synth horns. "Rough Ride" sounds unusual for McCartney's standards, and it features syncopated rhythm, a deep bass, computers and drum-programming. McCartney handled a lot of instruments and was helped by the producer duo, acting also as musicians.

Lipson: "I had a Yamaha RX5 drum machine and I'd pre-programmed a bunch of rhythms and Trevor commented about one of them saying, 'We could do something with that.' When we got to Paul's place and Trevor heard him play 'Rough Ride', he thought he'd found the perfect home for it. We played Macca the rhythm and he said, 'Yeah, allright, we'll use that.' I came up with this extraordinary bass sound – it came from a Yamaha TX802 and a Roland MKS-70. When Macca heard it, he said, 'I like that, you play that and I'll play guitar.'"[584]

But the session didn't went off smoothly: "We had an issue with the middle eight. I thought it was crap at one point I said so. Paul said, 'If you think it's crap, what do you think we should do instead?' I said, 'I haven't got a clue, that's your department. My job is to tell you what I think.' Then, to my tremendous relief, he said, 'Right, I'll go re-write it then!'"[585] The version released on the "Figure of Eight" cd-single – from the *Paul McCartney World Tour* rehearsals

---

[582] B. Harry, *cit*, p.762.
[583] Home video *Put It There*, 1989. In the video, Paul plays a few bars of the song on acoustic guitar, as it was originally conceived: the track is somewhat similar to "Bip Bop" (1971) and vaguely recalls Big Bill Broonzy's guitar style.
[584] Howard Massey, *Stephen Lipson*, in *Performing Songwriter*, Jan-Feb 2009, p.73.
[585] *Ibid.*, p.74.

(February-April 1989) – sounds much looser than the original. A live version of "Rough Ride" is on *Tripping the Live Fantastic!*

Musicians:

Paul McCartney vocals, synthesizer, electric guitar, drums, percussion • **Linda McCartney** backing vocals **Steve Lipson** bass, drums and computer programming, electric guitar • **Trevor Horn** keyboards

215 Figure of Eight (Paul McCartney)

Recording: December 21st-24th, 1987 and January 2nd-21st, 1988 (overdubs) **Location:** Hog Hill Studio, Icklesham **Release:** June 1989, *Flowers in the Dirt*

McCartney: "I did 'Figure of Eight' with Steve Lipson and Trevor Horn and again it was a two-day thing. The tune was fair sort of lowish, but because I was leading the drummer playing bass I decided to take it up a little bit, I started to busk it up higher."[586]

Paul launched himself into "Figure of Eight" trying to capture a take-one performance: therefore, McCartney recorded the basic track singing and playing his bass live in the studio, accompanied only by Chris Whitten on drums.

Paul was satisfied with the results and his bass part was later refined: "We didn't fix the take but for the bass, that was nicked 'cause I was doing that sort of silly singing."[587] The following January, "Figure of Eight" was overdubbed with more guitars and keyboards. The track, originally lasting 5:09, was later edited down to 3:15: despite a strangely sloppy ending.

The recording came out as fresh and spontaneous as it was intended: a fast rocker, typical of McCartney's style – in the vein of "Get Back!" or "Junior's Farm".

When Paul drew up the 1989/90 *Paul McCartney Word Tour* concert setlist, he chose "Figure of Eight" as an opener: a great chance to start the evening with a new song.

During the tour rehearsals, McCartney developed the song arrangement with his band. In September 1989, before the *Paul McCartney World Tour* kick-off, the track would partly be re-recorded for its release as a single. Results were disappointing: #42 in the UK and #92 in the US. A live version from Rotterdam (October 1989) is included in *Tripping the Live Fantastic!*

Musicians:

Paul McCartney vocals, backing vocals, handclaps, bass, celeste, acoustic and electric guitar, tambourine • **Linda McCartney** mini Moog, handclaps • **Chris Whitten** drums, handclaps • **Steve Lipson** computer programming, electric guitar • **Trevor Horn** keyboards, handclaps

All the Best! – a compilation containing hits both by Wings and McCartney as a solo artist – was released in November: in the UK the album went straight to #2 and stayed in the US *Billboard* charts for seventeen weeks, reaching #62. To date, it has sold over five million copies worldwide and was certified double platinum in the US.

---

[586] Home video *Put It There.*
[587] *Ibid.*

1988

216 How Many People? (Paul McCartney)

Recording: January 2nd-21st and September-November (overdubs?), 1988 **Location:** Hog Hill Studio, Icklesham and Olympic Studios (overdubs?), London **Release:** June 1989, *Flowers in the Dirt*

As part of the enormous promo campaign that surrounded *Flowers in the Dirt*, McCartney emphasized a tribute song that lay therein. "How Many People?" was dedicated to the memory of Chico Mendes (1944-88), a Brazilian trade union leader and environmentalist who fought for the Amazon rain forest and was assassinated on December 22nd, 1988.

McCartney: "That got the dedication after I've written the song. There's a line that says 'How many people have died? One too many right now for me'. I've heard about Chico's fight for the rainforest (…) He got shot… And I thought the least I can do is mention him somewhere (…) It seemed to fit…"[588]

"How Many People?" was another reggae tune that Paul wrote while in Jamaica. He suggested the song to Lipson and Horn and both producers assisted him – playing respectively electric guitar and keyboards – along with Whitten on electronic drums.

Numerous overdubs were later added, including percussion played by Jamaican musician Jab Bunny of the Cimmarrons, whom Paul had produced a few years back.

Unfortunately, the song is not so inspired and the two producers did little to help, other than to bury the track under a wash of echo.

Producer Neil Dorfsman, who worked with McCartney on the *Flowers in the Dirt* sessions starting from late 1988, recalls: "I did not choose this track to be on the album. I didn't think it was as strong as the other tunes that he had given me. But Paul loved the song he did with Horn and Lipson and I don't think I added much to that one, maybe we did a new vocal and we overdubbed a guitar with Robbie McIntosh."[589] Dorfsman jokingly says: "I thought that the idea of the song was great, but I always worry when American and English people do reggae!"[590]

Paul and his band rehearsed it for the 1989/90 *Paul McCartney World Tour* but after several TV appearances the song was excluded from the setlist. In particular, the track wasn't played in Rio de Janeiro, where it may have risked causing controversy in the press. "How Many People?" is included in *Flowers in the Dirt*.

Musicians:

Paul McCartney vocals, backing vocals, bass, piano, electric guitar, Mellotron, tambourine, flugelhorn • **Linda McCartney** backing vocals • **Chris Whitten** drums synth, cymbals, backing vocals • **Steve Lipson**

---

[588] *Ibid.*
[589] Interview courtesy of Neil Dorfsman, 07/09/2012.
[590] *Ibid.*

drum programming, electric guitar • **Trevor Horn** keyboards, backing vocals • **Hamish Stuart** vocals • **Jab Bunny** percussion

217 Où Est Le Soleil? (Paul McCartney)

Recording: January 2nd-21st and September-November (overdubs), 1988 **Location:** Hog Hill Studio, Icklesham **Release:** June 1989, *Flowers in the Dirt* (cd version)

The last track of the Lipson-Horn sessions was the most unusual. Most likely it was the only way to give form to a song that Paul had written as a lullaby for his children.

In 1969, while on holiday with Linda near St. Raphael on the French riviera, Paul had heard the expression "Où Est Le Soleil?"

In 1975 McCartney recorded a home demo, later aired during the *Oobu Joobu* radio program in 1995. He decided to record this lullaby as a dance track. He also re-worked the original "Valley Road" recording that had completely different lyrics and added it to this weird snippet.

The song turned into a mega production, full of keyboards, synthesizers and all kinds of programmed effects and grooves. McCartney even played a washboard, in the fashion of young bands of the late Fifties in Liverpool who couldn't afford real drums. "Où Est Le Soleil?" was added at the last minute to the cd version of *Flowers in the Dirt* and it's probably one of McCartney's most annoying songs.

The reason for its recording was revealed by Neil Dorfsman: "Paul was playing a lot of the material for his kids, and he kept on saying, 'My kids really like it, my kids really like it' and it's hard to vote against somebody's kids!"[591] Although the producer is not credited for any contribution on the track, this could mean that more work has been done during Autumn.

The song's hammering bass groove was at least appreciated in some dance clubs. It was released separately as a 12" (different from the cd version) and underwent various re-mixes:

1. *Extended Remix*: included in the second 12" of "Figure of Eight"
2. *Tub Dub Mix*: appears on the 12" and on the second 12" of "Figure of Eight"
3. *Instrumental Mix*: appears on the 12" and on the third 12" of "Figure of Eight"
4. *7" Mix*: B-side to the "Figure of Eight" single

Musicians:

Paul McCartney vocals, backing vocals, percussion, electric guitar, drums, keyboards, washboard • **Chris Whitten** tom • **Steve Lipson** computer and drum programming, bass, keyboards • **Trevor Horn** keyboards, computered drums • **Eddie Klein** computer programming • **Hamish Stuart** electric guitar

Paul planned a new batch of recordings in Sussex dedicated to songs he wrote with Elvis Costello. Eight tracks were taped: "My Brave Face", "You Want Her Too", "Don't Be Careless Love", "That Day Is Done", "The Lovers That Never Were", "Wish You Were Mine", "So

---

591 *Ibid.*

Like Candy" and "I Don't Want to Confess". The band in the studio besides McCartney and Costello included Hamish Stuart (famed ex-member of the Average White Band) on guitar and vocals, Chris Witten on drums and Kevin Armstrong (guitar), whom Paul had contacted after the previous November's TV appearance for *The Last Resort*.

Here and there a few other session-men such as Nicky Hopkins and Steve Nieve (The Attractions' pianist) also played but something went wrong and McCartney wasn't satisfied with the sessions. Three of the songs got re-worked and another one was re-recorded with Mitchell Froom the following Autumn.

Armstrong recalls: "The sessions were started with Paul or Elvis showing to me, Hamish and Chris the songs, by singing them with a couple of guitars and then we would lay down live tracks all together (...) I only played on some backing tracks and did a few overdubs. I recall one of the songs was 'So Like Candy'."[592]

The songs were developed without a clear plan: "There wasn't much discussion about an overall approach" – says Armstrong – "We just followed what Elvis and Paul wanted on a particular day. But all the instruments from The Beatles' past at Abbey Road were laying around for use at Hog Hill... The Mellotron from 'Strawberry Fields Forever', the upright bass used by Bill Black with Elvis Presley..."[593]

Armstrong had the privilege of seeing McCartney and Costello working together, although just for a few weeks: "The recordings were at an early stage when I left the project. My impression was that Elvis was trying to be more retro/Beatle-esque with the approach than Paul wanted to be. He even had Chris Whitten banging on cardboard boxes at one point trying to get that dull Ringo sound!"[594]

Following Costello's advice, McCartney dusted off his old Hofner bass for several songs during the sessions ("My Brave Face", see sheet **230**).

218 You Want Her Too (Paul McCartney- Declan MacManus)

Recording: January-February, September-November (overdubs part 1) and October, 31st (overdubs part 2), 1988 **Location:** Hog Hill Studio, Icklesham, Olympic Studios (overdubs part 1), London and Sunset Sound Factory (overdubs part 2), Los Angeles **Release:** June 1989, *Flowers in the Dirt*

Paul is first to admit that he and Elvis Costello wrote "You Want Her Too" attempting to follow the same writing process that Lennon and McCartney had used for their first compositions together; shooting melodic and sharp lines back and forth at each other. Nevertheless Paul had his doubts: "I really resisted at first. I said to Elvis, 'Look, this is really getting like me and John, this is dangerous!' So I tried singing both, just trying to do a harder

---

592 Interview courtesy of Kevin Armstrong, 10/09/2012.
593 *Ibid.*
594 *Ibid.*

voice for Elvis' part… But it never worked. The guy who was mixing it said it worked great with Elvis, so we put the fader up again!"[595] It was a good decision. The song is about a young person's self-questioning concerning his feelings for a girl and the single voice would have been unnatural. This process is emphasized in the duet version released on *Flowers in the Dirt*. But Paul and Elvis' 1987 acoustic demo really captures the essence of the song, with the two harmonizing in The Beatles' style. It was a faster and simpler version, without frills.

The actual recording of the song wasn't easy. According to some sources, McCartney got stuck when he had to cancel the first two takes because of Chris Whittten's drumming. McCartney recorded the basic track with a very heartfelt live vocal but – according to the engineers there at the time – he had to discard those takes.

At that point, the whole song was re-recorded with Froom during the Autumn sessions, keeping only Costello's vocals and the carnevalesque intro in 3/4 time, quite reminiscent of "Being For the Benefit of Mr. Kite!" Played by Costello on keyboards, this melody also reappears just prior to the Hollywood-style orchestral finale.

Chris Davis played sax: "The whole section was played in a single track, everything was done live, with no overdubs. We were twelve, maybe fifteen elements. That's what Paul wanted for the session… A big band track."[596]

Richard Niles worked on that arrangement: "I wrote a piece of music, but I thought it was going to be something significant, to go on for a minute and a half. But in fact they only used fifteen seconds of it. Paul was working with the producer Mitchell Froom and probably he changed his mind."[597] The final result is a polished production that tones down Costello's vibrant and explosive ideas.

Musicians:

Paul McCartney vocals, backing vocals, 12-string acoustic guitar, electric guitar, bass, tambourine • **Elvis Costello** vocals, keyboards (intro) • **Hamish Stuart** backing vocals, electric guitar • **Robbie McIntosh** electric guitar • **Chris Whitten** drums, percussion • **Mitchell Froom** keyboards • **Chris Davis** sax • **Unknown musicians** horns

219 Don't Be Careless Love (Paul McCartney-Declan Mac Manus)

Recording: January-February, September-November (overdubs part 1) and October 28th-29th (overdubs part 2), 1988 **Location:** Hog Hill Studio, Icklesham, PWL Studios ? (overdubs part 1), London and Sunset Sound Factory Studios (overdubs part 2), Los Angeles **Release:** June 1989, *Flowers in the Dirt*

Many believe this song to be the weakest of the McCartney-Costello co-writes on *Flowers in the Dirt*. Also in this case, the pair had recorded a simple acoustic guitar demo. After the song was

---

[595] *Beatlefan*, June-July 1989.
[596] Interview courtesy of Chris Davis, 21/09/2011.
[597] Interview courtesy of Richard Niles, 07/10/2011.

attempted with Costello during the January sessions, McCartney was not satisfied and he reworked it from scratch later with Mitchell Froom producing.

"Don't Be Careless Love" – which opens with a gospel-like *a cappella* intro – is influenced by Elvis Costello (whose original keyboard part was retained in the final version), specially in the swirling choruses. The song was completed with some overdubs done in L.A. in the Autumn, including a Jerry Marotta drum part that was later dropped. The result is mediocre at best.

Musicians:

Paul McCartney vocals, backing vocals, bass, acoustic guitar, tambourine, finger snaps • **Hamish Stuart** backing vocals, electric guitar, tambourine • **Chris Whitten** backing vocals, drums • **Elvis Costello** backing vocals, keyboards • **Mitchell Froom** keyboards

220 That Day Is Done (Paul McCartney- Declan Mac Manus)

Recording: January-February and September-November (overdubs), 1988 **Location:** Hog Hill Studio, Icklesham and Olympic Studios (overdubs), London **Release:** June 1989, *Flowers in the Dirt*

"That Day Is Done", another McCartney-Costello collaboration released on *Flowers in the Dirt*, stands out on the album for its colourful and original styling. R&B and soul music reign in this gospel-tinged piano piece.

McCartney: "We kept the piano and vocal and added some Hovis brass to give it a silver band/New Orleans marching band feel... I said to Elvis, 'Oh yeah, I get it, New Orleans funeral music.'"[598]

For the recording, Paul left the piano to Nicky Hopkins and put forth an amazing vocal that did perfect justice to Costello's lyrics on the subject of death.

Costello: "I had a fair opening statement and all these images. It was from a real thing, my grandmother's funeral (…) Paul said, 'It needs something like this' and he just sat down and played the chorus. It was sort of like a moment, like 'Let It Be', the creation of a semi-secular gospel song. It was shocking when he did that bit."[599]

Neil Dorfsman commented on the brass section: "It sounds like a New Orleans thing but it was actually a tip of the hat to an English factory band (brass bands formed in England and sponsored by factories – author's note). Richard Thompson, the Fairporth Convention guitarist, introduced Froom to that particular thing that was from the turn of the century and he did it again on a Paul record."[600]

MacManus's influence is obvious in the choice of 3/4 timing. The backing vocals are memorable thanks to the stylistic and harmonic blending between Paul, Hamish Stuart and Elvis Costello. Also for this song, McCartney chose a very polished production style.

---

[598] *Club Sandwich*, n.52, Summer 1989, p.5
[599] Elvis Costello, *Mojo!*, August 2011, p.83.
[600] Interview courtesy of Neil Dorfsman, 07/09/2012.

Costello: "Paul sort of gave (the songs) a more highly polished sound which obviously was what he heard in them."[601] Nevertheless, the song works – and is in pleasant contrast to the "be here now" theme of most of the tracks on *Flowers in the Dirt*.

McCartney rehearsed the song for the 1989/90 *Paul McCartney World Tour*, but the track was never performed live.

Musicians:

Paul McCartney vocals, backing vocals, bass • **Hamish Stuart** backing vocals, electric guitar • **Robbie McIntosh** electric guitar • **Chris Whitten** drums, tambourine • **Elvis Costello** backing vocals • **Nicky Hopkins** piano • **Mitchell Froom** keyboards • **John Taylor, Tony Goddard** horn • **Ian Peters** euphonium • **Ian Harper** trumpet (tenor)

On February, 27th Paul went to Italy and attended the Sanremo's Festival, with two mimed performances of "Once Upon a Long Ago…" and "Listen to What the Man Said". In April, McCartney carried on the *Flowers in the Dirt* sessions, this time with Geoff Emerick engineering. It could be during this period that McCartney spent five days recording with David Clayton of Simply Red on keyboards, who remembers: "I was recommended by Chris Whitten, the drummer at the time. I went to the windmill studio for 5 days and did jamming with the band… Paul, Chris, Hamish Stuart and Linda. I was doing overdubs on the tracks... Very dance-oriented style, as I was doing a lot of House music productions at the time. I think this session was also an audition for the band of some sort... But I think my style was too Jazz style, and I did not know any Beatle tunes, as suprisingly I was never a fan! I am now, many years later…"[602]

Clayton: "I remember doing work on around 4 tracks… I did drum programming and bass synth as well as piano on a few tracks…. I was under the impression that Paul wanted a 'Modern Approach/Club' style, almost a remix approach to the tunes. I never heard any finished product…I heard from someone that he re-did the album, as he changed the direction and style…"[603]

Based on the descriptions of the songs provided by Clayton, one can only guess which tracks he worked on: "Good Sign" and the remix version of "This One" both have a dance-flavor but no specific credits are available. "Où Est Le Soleil?" is another example of a dance track that could have featured him: Clayton's name appeared on a *Club Sandwich* issue about the *Flowers in the Dirt* album (credited on playing keyboards on the track "Motor of Love", see sheet 231), but – maybe due to some mistake or to the fact that his contribution was erased at the last moment – he is not officially credited for playing in this song or any other.

601 Graeme Thomson, *Complicated Shadows. The Life and Music of Elvis Costello*, 2004, p.255.
602 Interview courtesy of David Clayton, 24/07/2012.
603 *Ibid.*

221 Distractions (Paul McCartney)

Recording: April-July and November 1st (overdubs), 1988 **Location:** Hog Hill Studio, Icklesham and Mad Hatter Studio (overdubs), Los Feliz **Release:** June 1989, *Flowers in the Dirt*

McCartney composed the melody for "Distractions" in August 1987 at the piano, instinctively – as is clear by the smooth flowing notes on the D minor natural scale – and rushed to Rude Studio to tape a demo.

He decided on an acoustic recording with a string arrangement. The basic track was completed at Hog Hill Studio with just Paul on bass (judging from the deep sound, McCartney could have used his Wal 5 string), Hamish Stuart on acoustic guitar and Chris Whitten on drums: some percussion and a lovely acoustic guitar solo by McCartney were later added.

In November, McCartney travelled to California for the string overdub. Paul recalled: "I heard an album a few years ago by someone off Prince's label, Paisley Park, called the Family... And there were some string arrangements on it that were really interesting... I thought, 'Wow, great. I wonder who this is?' It said Clare Fischer. So I said to Linda, 'These arrangements are incredible and it's this Clare Fischer... Some LA chick, I think...' And while she thought it was this kind of great, blonde LA lady she didn't like them. We found out, actually, it's this guy who's about 50 years old, who's got a grey beard and he's a great fellow... So then Linda was saying, 'I love these arrangements, I love this guy's work!' That's wives, you know!"[604]

Brent Fischer, son of the famous composer and arranger Clare Fischer (1928-2012), reveals: "The first thing my father had to do was the transcription of the recording tracks that Paul sent us. The cassette tape had McCartney's band playing and his vocals. He always preferred to have the song already well-defined so he could have a clear picture. The process of creating an orchestral arrangement is like putting the pieces of a puzzle together. The string arrangement on 'Distractions' is classic Clare Fischer. Paul only gave some general instructions, 'cause he recognized the virtuosity of Clare Fischer's work and his talent. For the recording, we carefully selected the players of the orchestra. The session was easy and went smoothly. I remember we recorded two or three different takes, so not to have any unwelcome surprise."[605]

The outcome was this sweet song with a full Hollywood-style orchestra (14 violins, 4 violas, 2 violoncellos, 1 acoustic bass) that swoops and swirls in typical 1940's fashion, emphasizing the melancholic and nostalgic nature of the piece. A dreamy clarinet intro opens this evocative and melodious song that is further enriched by McCartney's vocal whispers and sighs. Lyrically, "Distractions" is a manifesto of Paul's world view: again, his universe is at home, the only

---

[604] *Club Sandwich*, no.52, Summer 1989, p.4.
[605] Interview courtesy of Brent Fischer, 24/10/2011.

possible dimension.[606] Life's 'distractions' are to be avoided in this utopian world where there is only room for dreams, and especially the greatest dream of love.

A clip was prepared and is included in the *Put It There* video: it features a different mix with more acoustic guitar parts. "Distractions" was planned as the third single from *Flowers in the Dirt* backed by "Lindiana" on the flipside. In the end, it was replaced by "Figure of Eight".

Musicians:

Paul McCartney vocals, backing vocals, bass, percussion, acoustic guitar • **Linda McCartney** backing vocals • **Hamish Stuart** acoustic guitar, backing vocals • **Chris Whitten** drums, percussion • **Unknown musicians** strings

222 Put It There (Paul McCartney)

Recording: April-July (basic track) and September-November (overdubs part 1 and 2), 1988 **Location:** Hog Hill Studio, Icklesham (basic track and overdubs part 1) and AIR Studios? (overdubs part 2), London **Release:** June 1989, *Flowers in the Dirt*

Paul's childhood memories of his dad were of a typical reliable father, ready to give advice, always there for him in difficult times. "Put It There" is an affectionate tribute to his father Jim, inspired by a phrase Paul and his brother Mike often heard him say.

McCartney: "My dad used to say when we were kids, 'Put it there, if it weights a ton'. And when we're asking, 'Why we have to do this?' He said also, 'Because there's no hair on seagull's chest'. It's the kind of thing you'd say to your own son (…) You can either say that is really simplistic, but to me that's really deep… It's something that's a bit of a choker to me, that line."[607]

The worldly wisdom of those words inspired a delicate acoustic song that Paul wrote during the winter of 1987 on the balcony of his chalet in Zermatt, Switzerland.[608]

McCartney: "The song was done very quickly when I was on holiday (…) We were on this skiing holiday in Zermatt. In the evening after you've been skiing all day, you take those big heavy boots off and sit on the balcony with a drink, cooling out. I'd get my guitar and just sit out the balcony. It was a very simple song."[609]

For "Put It There" Paul flushed out his usual studio tricks. He wanted to preserve the acoustic feel of the song by not weighing it down with too many instruments; the only exception being a brief orchestral passage, care of George Martin and probably added at AIR.

At Hog Hill Studio, McCartney recorded the basic track playing his acoustic, supported only by Hamish Stuart on bass and Whitten on drums and percussion. Paul then decided to add some

---

606 See also "Waterfalls".
607 Home video *Put It There*.
608 Here, Paul also composed "For No-One".
609 *The Paul McCartney World Tour Booklet*, p.78.

other percussion that was simple yet effective. Macca simply sat on a stool and did a bit of knee-slapping with his hands, warning that "they have to be very dry".[610]

Lance Phillips, who worked as assistant to Geoff Emerick on that session, recalls: "When I went to Sussex most of the tracks had been recorded. This was the only song that had not been recorded at all prior to sessions I've worked on. It was not a complicated song, and I think Paul recorded acoustic guitar and vocal live and he added the knee percussion later. He just sat down in the middle of the room and we recorded."[611]

According to Neil Dorfsman, more work on the track have been done later: "The knee percussion was Mitchell Froom's idea. Paul did everything in one day, vocals, guitar and percussion."[612] It was an old gimmick of Buddy Holly and the Crickets (e.g. "Everyday") that McCartney fell back on in many songs.

This gentle piece could be easily considered the best song on *Flowers in the Dirt*: a little McCartney jewel. Built around a simple D major scale, the song recalls "Blackbird" in its opening sequence. The alternate bass playing give the song its lullaby feel that mixes a compelling sense of nostalgia with childhood memories.

McCartney succeeds in expressing the feeling of security that a child finds in his father's words. The holding of hands, the friendship and trust that the young Paul placed in his father Jim, are the sentiments that run through this song. McCartney expresses the idea of a conversation between a father and a son by alternating falsetto and the bass tones of his vocal range.

"Put It There" was issued in February 1990 as a single, reaching #32 on the UK charts. A live version is available on *Tripping the Live Fantastic!* and also became the B-side to the single "All My Trials" in the UK and "The Long and Winding Road" in the US in November 1990.

Musicians:

Paul McCartney vocals, backing vocals, acoustic guitar, percussion • **Hamish Stuart** bass, percussion • **Chris Whitten** drums, percussion • **Peter Henderson** computer programming • **Unknown musicians** strings

223 This One (Paul McCartney)

Recording: April-July and September-November (overdubs), 1988 **Location:** Hog Hill Studio, Icklesham and Olympic Studios (overdubs), London **Release:** June 1989, *Flowers in the Dirt*

"'This One' is about regrets" – Paul said explaining the meaning of the song – "You're always off in some other moment, either the past or dreaming of the future. Now is never very important to much people, but it's all you've got. It's really all we live in."[613]

---

[610] Home video *Put It There*.
[611] Interview courtesy of Lance Phillips, 29/08/2012.
[612] Interview courtesy of Neil Dorfsman, 07/09/2012.
[613] Home video *Put It There*.

Just how autobiographical "This One" is, is hard to say. Clearly, "This One" offers an array of day to day stories that are often left on the sidelines. McCartney: "You have an argument, for instance... You think, 'If I'd only been smart I just could have said, 'You're right' (...) or 'If I'd only sent her some flowers...'"[614]

The poignant theme of regret is here entrusted to a happy up-tempo pop song with a catchy hook: to some degree, a way to redirecting emotions.

The definitive arrangement of "This One" came about as an afterthought: the original version was completely different.

Work in the studio on "This One" began with an idea that McCartney had come up with on the piano. On March 18th-19th, 1987 (other sources report Feb 2nd at the Audio International Studios), Paul recorded an early take of "This One" as a sweet ballad with a nostalgic tone.

When McCartney came back to the song during the *Flowers in the Dirt* sessions, he re-modelled "This One" as a Beatle-esque pop gem. He built a lively arrangement around the simple melody, fine-tuning the song and enriching the sound with an abundance of instruments. Paul added a bouncing bass and filled the intro with every instrument he could get his hands on, including a sitar, a harmonium and even some wine glasses.

Lance Phillips: "This song had a very long intro, with sort of strange noises. McCartney wanted to put in some wine glasses, so we tuned them by putting the right amount of water in each glass. The problem was that he wanted three notes and it's just not possible to play three wine glasses at the same time! So he asked for someone from the control room to come in to help him... I was standing near to McCartney playing one wine glass, as he was playing the other two!"[615]

From a technical point of view, some risks were taken and there was also a little problem that needed solving.

Phillips: "All the album was recorded on a 24-tracks. Because 'This One' was a dense track, and there wasn't so much space left to add new stuff on, so all of the noises in the introduction were recorded on the same track! But when we were doing these overdubs, it was really important that I could hear the four beat count before the main track guitar came in... So I was able to punch the machine out and record. This worked brilliantly all the time that Geoff remembered to leave the count so I could hear it. Unfortunately on one overdub he didn't! And I chopped the beginning of the guitar track! It didn't go down very well at all... There was a very frosty silence... But my mistake was forgiven eventually!"[616]

Finally, other vocals were added, including Hamish Stuart's contribution. Dorfsman handled the backing vocal overdubs: "We worked on backing vocals with Paul and Hamish and we

---

[614] *Ibid.*
[615] Interview courtesy of Lance Phillips, 29/08/2012.
[616] *Ibid.*

even got some background vocals female singers on a couple of songs, one of which was Tessa Niles."[617]

It turned out to be a catchy pop song with a sunny mood similar to "Hello Goodbye": another example of McCartney's pop style. "This One" became an obvious choice as a single. It was released in August 1989 as the second single off *Flowers in the Dirt* and reached #18 on the UK charts. In the US its release went mostly unnoticed.[618]

In Europe "This One" got lots of airplay and was an audience favourite during the following *Paul McCartney World Tour*, also thanks to a cool video-clip that recalled all The Beatles' themes of the Sixties – peace, love and the Orient. An unusual re-mix called 'Club Lovejoys Mix' is on the flipside of the "Figure of Eight" 12" while *Tripping the Live Fantastic!* includes a live version from the Detroit show (1/2/1990).

Musicians:

Paul McCartney vocals, backing vocals, acoustic and electric guitar, bass, keyboards, harmonium, tambourine, sitar, glasses • **Linda McCartney** backing vocals • **Hamish Stuart** vocals, backing vocals, acoustic and electric guitar • **Robbie McIntosh** acoustic guitar, electric guitar • **Chris Whitten** drums, percussion • **Judd Lander** harmonica • **Lance Phillips** glasses • **Tessa Niles (?)** backing vocals

224 The First Stone (Paul McCartney-Hamish Stuart)

Recording: April-July, 1988 **Location:** Hog Hill Studio, Icklesham **Release:** July 1989, "This One" single B-side

This was the first official McCartney-Stuart collaboration. "The First Stone" was mostly written by McCartney with a little help from Hamish on some of the lyrics.

They were inspired to write the song by watching some television evangelists and all their moralizing and censorship. Once in the studio, they came up with an unusual and somewhat heavy tune. The basic track was recorded by McCartney, Stuart, Hopkins and Whitten, with McCartney's heavily effected lead vocal added in a later session. The song opens with a jazzy intro – probably Hamish's idea – and is mostly carried along by the hard distorted guitar parts. The track was issued as the B-side to the single "This One".

Musicians:

Paul McCartney vocals, backing vocals, bass (?), electric guitar (?) • **Linda McCartney** backing vocals • **Hamish Stuart** backing vocals, electric guitar • **Chris Whitten** drums • **Nicky Hopkins** keyboards

---

[617] Interview courtesy of Neil Dorfsman, 07/09/2012. Tessa Niles, said to be one of the best English backing singers, isn't credited in any of the songs on *Flowers in the Dirt*. In 1986 she sang backing vocals on "Only Love Remains" during McCartney's TV appearance on The Tube.
[618] The single only reached no.94 in Billboard, a sure sign of McCartney's commercial decline in that period. There is an anecdote about a conversation between an American radio dj and McCartney's publicist Geoff Baker. The dj asks Baker: "How about the next single? 'This One' could be a great choice!" An embarrassed Baker replied that the single had already been out for a month.

225 Flying to My Home (Paul McCartney)

Recording: April-July and September-December (overdubs), 1988 **Location:** Hog Hill Studio, Icklesham and Olympic Studios (overdubs), London **Release:** May 1989,"My Brave Face" single B-side

"Flying to My Home" was one of the most original songs McCartney came up with during the sessions and he treated this brilliant pop song specially. For the recording of this infectious track, Paul acted mostly as a one-man band even taking over on drums[619], relegating Chris Whitten to a small synthesizer part.

"Flying to My Home" was built around a bed of electric and acoustic guitar tracks over a straightforward rhythm section. An autoharp was also used: it's a little string instrument, a sort of chorded zither[620] that was given to Linda by Johnny Cash during the sessions held on May 9th for the recording of "New Moon over Jamaica", a song that McCartney had demoed in a reggae version at the beginning of the year.

Paul worked on the vocal parts with many overdubs: after laying down his lead vocal (later sped up), "Flying to My Home" was further embellished by an a cappella intro – achieved by overdubbing Paul's many vocal tracks – and by some fine backing vocals by the whole group. The track also includes a slide guitar solo handled by Hamish. Released in May 1988 as the flip-side to "My Brave Face", this song ranks as one of the best B-sides in McCartney's career.

Musicians:

Paul McCartney vocals, backing vocals, bass, drums, acoustic and electric guitar, autoharp • **Linda McCartney** backing vocals • **Hamish Stuart** backing vocals, acoustic guitar and slide guitar • **Chris Whitten** backing vocals, synthesizer

226 Same Love (Paul McCartney)

Recording: June 1st, 1988 **Location:** Hog Hill Studio, Icklesham **Release:** December 1997, "Beautiful Night" cd-single

One of McCartney's most explored themes is the unique quality of love.[621] Lyrically, "Same Love" looks at the special alchemy that keeps love alive.

McCartney recorded this thoughtful ballad with Hamish Stuart and Nicky Hopkins. Hopkins created the majestic opening of "Same Love" with a heart-rending piano solo that clocks in at 50 seconds, making it one of the longest instrumental intros in a McCartney song. Paul's soulful vocal performance is faultless, while Hamish's signature rhythm guitar has a funk feel, in perfect Average White Band style. Whitten might have contributed the drumming, but no-one is credited on the sleeve notes and the sound is suspiciously close to a drum-machine.

The song was released in 1997 on the second cd-single of "Beautiful Night".

---

[619] M. Easter-C. Madinger, *cit*, p.305. Although Whitten is credited in the *Flowers in the Dirt* cd liner notes as playing percussion on the track, Mitchell Froom recalled that it was Paul instead.
[620] McCartney played it also in "Hope of Deliverance" and "Too Much Rain".
[621] "Same Time, Next Year", "Did We Meet Somewhere Before?", "Twice in a Lifetime".

Musicians:

Paul McCartney vocals, backing vocals, bass, keyboards (?) • **Linda McCartney** backing vocals • **Hamish Stuart** backing vocals (?), electric guitar • **Nicky Hopkins** piano

227 Don't Break the Promise (Paul McCartney-Eric Stewart)

Recording: June 9th, 1988 **Location:** Hog Hill Studio, Icklesham **Release:** July 1997, "The World Tonight" cd-single

Paul's ongoing passion for reggae music finds another example in this track. In this case, Paul took a song that Eric Stewart had written some years before and demoed it with the help of Hamish Stuart on guitar. McCartney played everything else; bass, electric guitar, a harmonium and probably drums, although the latter are not credited. The recording was playful – with Paul's falsetto at the forefront – but "Don't Break the Promise" remained unused. The song was finally released with a pop arrangement by 10cc on their 1992 album, *Meanwhile*. Paul's version appears on the second European single of "The World Tonight" (1997).

Musicians:

Paul McCartney vocals, bass, electric guitar, harmonium, drums (?) • **Hamish Stuart** backing vocals, electric guitar

228 Good Sign (Paul McCartney)

Recording: July, September-November (overdubs part 1) and December 8th (overdubs part 2), 1988 **Location:** Hog Hill Studio, Icklesham, Olympic Studios (overdubs part 1), London and Mad Hatter Studios (overdubs part 2), Los Angeles **Release:** July 1989, "This One" 12"single

It's easy to presume that "Good Sign" must have been inspired by the bass riff that it is built around. For one of his earliest sessions with McCartney, Robbie McIntosh borrowed Hamish Stuart's brand-new Steinberg guitar to record his intricate solos.

With a chorus added by McCartney and some funky riffing from Stuart, the song sounds somewhat similar to "Coming Up". The track was completed with the addition of some piano and synth. McCartney was pleased with the results and passed "Good Sign" on to Clare Fischer in L.A. for the overdubs. A horn section was added (three saxes, three trumpets and two trombones) as well as some ethnic percussion care of Alex Acuña, famed member of the jazz-fusion group Weather Report. McCartney was going to include this number on *Flowers in the Dirt* then decided otherwise: "Goog Sign" can be found on the second 12" of "This One".

Musicians:

Paul McCartney vocals, backing vocals, bass, piano (?), synthesizer (?) • **Linda McCartney** backing vocals • **Hamish Stuart** electric guitar • **Robbie McIntosh** electric guitar • **Wix (?)** synthesizer • **Chris Whitten** drums • **Alex Acuña** percussion • **David Clayton (?)** piano (?), synthesizer (?) • **Unknown musicians** horns

229 In Liverpool (Paul McCartney)

Recording: April-July, 1988 **Location:** Liverpool Institute of Performing Arts, Liverpool **Release:** February 2005, *Liverpool Oratorio* DVD

"In Liverpool" evokes Paul's nostalgic and sentimental ties to his native city. Not a well-known song, "In Liverpool" only appears on the 2005 DVD *The Liverpool Oratorio*, but the song deserves mentioning in this context. McCartney recorded it live with just his acoustic guitar during a performance at the Liverpool Institute of Performing Arts when he was in town in the summer of 1988 and visited his old school.

The institute had been closed for many years and – as seen in the *Ghosts from the Past* documentary – was in a state of deterioration.

In the halls of this old Victorian building, Paul touchingly and amusingly revisits the memory of his schooldays. The film ends with the performance of "In Liverpool".

The song touches on a gallery of characters straight off the streets of Liverpool. It's a moving song, with minor chords underlining this depiction of a post-war, working class Liverpool: an unusual track in McCartney's discography. Another version was recorded during the *Off the Ground* sessions in 1992 but it was never released. McCartney played the song during his gig at the *Liverpool Sound Concert* in June 2008, arranged for acoustic guitar and accordion.

Musicians:

Paul McCartney vocals, acoustic guitar

The *Flowers in the Dirt* sessions resumed, with Mitchell Froom producing and Robbie McIntosh on guitar. Earlier on, Paul had recorded a handful of demos: "Motor of Love", "D Backing Track" (studio notes say "beautiful melody") and "Come Back" (described as "fuzz-rock").

230 My Brave Face (Paul McCartney-Declan MacManus)

Recording: September-October, 1988 **Location:** Olympic Studios, London **Release:** May 1989, single (from *Flowers in the Dirt*)

"My Brave Face" holds an important place for McCartney and his relationship with The Beatles' legacy, as conceived by Paul towards the end of the Eighties.

After "Coming Up" Paul took a break from that role which was beginning to verge on self-irony. But with "My Brave Face" things changed. The Beatles were not just a musical legacy but an emotional one as well.

McCartney and Costello laid down a demo of this song in 1987. Their writing method is interesting in more ways than one. Costello came up with the main melody in his typical rough style (an excerpt can be heard in the *Put It There* video) was later replaced by McCartney's melodic approach. McCartney softened Costello's original version, relying on his clear vocals and his fluid bass playing, the winning hook of the song.

McCartney: "Elvis said, 'What about your Hofner bass? I love the sound of it!' (I thought) It's not a very expensive instrument and not very good keeping in tune (…) I'd given up recording with it… But Elvis said, 'Go on and try!' We recorded it great, it's got lovely tones for a little bass… That's how that riff arrived."[622]

The challenging task of creating a more Beatle-esque sound was up to Neil Dorfsman: "I remember one day, we were overdubbing bass on something and I got really frustrated because I could not get sounding like The Beatles! Same instrument, same player, same everything… That Hofner bass is not considered a very punchy and powerful one, but in The Beatles it is like that! I remember asking Geoff Emerick how he recorded it and he didn't want to tell me!"[623] The bridge was probably added by McCartney, and features the same descending bass scale over minor chords used in "Michelle".

Then he worked with Elvis on the chord structure of the chorus: "There's a line, 'Take me to that place' that is really like me and John."[624]

Recording didn't go smoothly. McCartney wasn't satisfied with the first version committed to tape during the January sessions with Costello, finding it too slow. The song was entirely re-recorded at Olympic Studios by McCartney, Hamish Stuart, Froom and Chris Whitten.

Neil Dorfsman: "When Mitchell Froom and I arrived in London, we heard what was basically a demo of the song that Paul had cut earlier. We both thought that it had to be re-recorded and slightly re-arranged. I do remember that demo was slightly different. The first day, when we got into the studio we did multiple takes of the song with the band. We wanted to make a slightly more edgier and pop-sounding, because we all thought it was a single. It was easy to record and all the four songs that I worked on with Froom were recorded fairly quickly, I think in just two or three days."[625] Dorfsman talks about the different approach that McCartney wanted for the sessions: "We cut that song as a quartet, with Paul playing bass and singing at the same time. He approached the song like the old school, performing it… All the takes he was performing and singing live! Most of that vocal is a live vocal. We tried to overdub some bass on some track but most of his parts were done live with the backing track."[626]

The song was then finished with overdubs; backing vocals, an EBow guitar by David Rhodes, some almost inaudible saxophones and lots of acoustic guitars thus obtaining a beautiful and clear sonic blend. Dorfsman again: "We brought in David Rhodes, just to make it more

[622] Home video *Put It There*.
[623] Interview courtesy of Neil Dorfsman, 07/09/2012.
[624] Home video *Put It There*.
[625] Interview courtesy of Neil Dorfsman, 07/09/2012.
[626] *Ibid.*

modern-styled. David style is almost like a painter, he doesn't play *normal* guitars… He played it with an EBow, that's a device that makes it sound more liquid."[627]

Rhodes: "It was at Olympic Studios. I arrived in the morning and I was introduced to Paul from Mitchell Froom. He thought I could add something to a couple of songs. Paul made some work with Gabriel a couple of years before and we spoke a little bit about it. Mitchell said he just wanted an ebow part on the track. It didn't take so long. Then we got to lunch. We ordered sandwiches and as I started working on another track, Paul came back and saw Mitchell eating a chicken sandwich…"[628]

Paul also added a tambourine which – according to Dorfsman – it's not an easy instrument to play: "We tried tambourine with somebody else and eventually Paul just picked it up and played… It was amazing!"[629] The result was this sincere and moving song: a McCartney classic. The song tells the tale of a man dealing with harsh realities, who realizes there is always room to dream and find that place to make it happen. If happiness resides in memories, the nostalgic reference to the past was obvious to fans.

With his story in place, Paul was ready to act on it: "My Brave Face" was released in May 1989, preceding *Flowers in the Dirt* and was accompanied by a promo video showing the adventures of a Japanese collector of Beatles memorabilia.

Footage of the band rehearsing in the studio was mixed with shots of vintage Beatles references such as a *Sgt. Pepper's* jacket and a Hofner bass. The song was the biggest hit delivered by *Flowers in the Dirt*, thanks to a heavy radio campaign. Surprisingly though, the song only reached #18 in the UK and #25 in the US. "My Brave Face" became a well-acclaimed number in McCartney's repertoire during the 1989/90 *Paul McCartney World Tour*.

A live version, recorded in Wembley on 19/01/1990, has been issued on *Tripping the Live Fantastic!* The track was also part of the 1991 *Secret Gigs Tour*.

Musicians:

Paul McCartney vocals, backing vocals, 12-string acoustic guitar, bass, tambourine • **Hamish Stuart** backing vocals, electric and acoustic guitar • **Robbie McIntosh** electric and acoustic guitar • **Chris Whitten** drums • **Mitchell Froom** keyboards • **David Rhodes** electric guitar (with EBow) • **Chris Davis, Chris White, Dave Bishop** sax

---

[627] *Ibid.* The EBow was invented in 1976 by Greg Heet, who says: "I do remember sending Paul an EBow (unsolicited) but I never talked to him. I'm very honored that David Rhodes used my invention on one of Paul's recordings." Interview courtesy of Greg Heet, 07/02/2014.
[628] Interview courtesy of David Rhodes, 30/04/2013.
[629] Interview courtesy of Neil Dorfsman, 07/09/2012.

1989

McCartney put the finishing touches to *Flowers In The Dirt*, recording another track and finishing mixing the album between January 30th and February 4th.

231 Motor of Love (Paul McCartney)

Recording: January, 1989 **Location:** Hog Hill Studio, Icklesham **Release:** June 1989, *Flowers in the Dirt*

Among the *Flowers in the Dirt* songs, "Motor of Love" had the most complicated development in the studio. McCartney had recorded a demo in early 1988: it was an intimate little idea with Paul playing electric piano along with an unusual percussive pattern, similar to a heartbeat.

McCartney brought the song into the studio during the September-October sessions (maybe with the involvement of David Clayton, credited on keyboards by *Club Sandwich* but not mentioned in the official booklet) but things got complicated and he decided not to use that version. The song however, was one of Paul's favorites and he wanted it to be on the album.

Thus, he came up with the idea of putting "Motor Of Love" into the hands of Chris Hughes and Ross Cullum, two producers who had previously worked with Tears For Fears. Giving the song to outsiders would allow McCartney to have a different perspective. The Hughes-Cullum approach to production was very high-tech – more than any other song on the album. They dressed this ballad in massive quantities of synthesizers and computers.

Greg Hawkes, ex-Cars' keyboard player and multi-talented instrumentalist (his 2008 album, *The Beatles Uke*, revisits some Beatles' classics arranged for ukulele only), recalls how it went: "Chris Hughes was the one that got me involved. He told me if I was interested to do a session for a Paul McCartney song, knowing that I'm a huge Beatles fan! Paul had played him a demo and told him that he wanted it to sound a little like *Drive* by the Cars! As I went into the studio – Paul was not there – we worked on the song using a Fairlight computer… Sort of putting the form of the song into it and putting the basic chords. We had like a rhythm track (…) In the middle of the afternoon, Paul came into the studio and he said, 'I think the song needs a bit of writing, it needs a bridge…' He came at the piano and in about 15 minutes he had the bridge! He said, 'Ok, this is what the bridge is going to be, I have to work on the lyrics…' After a couple of days in London we moved to his windmill studio in Sussex. Paul would come in every 2-3 days. At the time, he was still working on some songs with Mitchell Froom and in a third studio with an engineer mixing other tracks…"[630]

In the meantime, the song changed considerably: "In the middle of the second week, when it was time for Paul to do his vocals, it was funny because he still hadn't written the lyrics to that bridge! He said, 'Ok, wait a minute!' and 15 minutes later he got the words written… It was so

---

[630] Interview courtesy of Greg Hawkes, 17/07/2012.

much fun seeing him doing it. There's sort of a 'b-section' on the song, 'I won't steal anything from you…' which on the demo went on kind of a shuffle groove… It was kind of an Eddie Cochrane thing… And we thought it was better to have a more pop feel. Paul also played piano, bass and electric guitar, the Epiphone Casino, I think…"[631]

The overall effect – maybe purposely – is cold and ethereal: the song seems to express McCartney's faith in God. The expression "Heavenly father" calls up a blend of paternal figure ("It's like *Mother Mary* in 'Let It Be'", Paul said) and Creator, looking down protectively from above. His greatest gift is love, like a joyous light, that has the power to lift one's inner spirit. "Motor Of Love" sums up McCartney's philosophy of life; to always wear a smile. The image of God's Constant Motor runs throughout the song – an expression of gratitude and ecstasy. The guitar arpeggio in the coda with its looping effect, seems to suggest an eternal, never-changing divine place.

Musicians:

Paul McCartney vocals, backing vocals, bass, electric guitar, piano • **Hamish Stuart** electric guitar, backing vocals • **Greg Hawkes** keyboards • **David Clayton (?)** keyboards **Chris Hughes** computer programming, drums

A special session dedicated to an old song written by Paul, who recorded "Oobu Joobu" completely on his own.

232 Oobu Joobu (Paul McCartney)

Recording: February 2nd, 1989 **Location**: Hog Hill Studio, Icklesham **Release**: April 1997, "Young Boy" cd-single

The title of this song – that in 1995 would have worked as a jingle to his radio program with the same name – came to Paul from *Monsieur Ubu*, a character by playwright Alfred Jarry, inventor of Pataphysics, a subject previously referenced by McCartney in his song "Maxwell's Silver Hammer" from The Beatles' *Abbey Road* (1969).

McCartney shut himself in the studio and most likely recorded all the instruments: it resulted in an hilarious number, a catchy jingle that would work perfectly on the *Oobu Joobu* radio show.

The song reproduces some typical noises heard in the American cartoon series: the comic effect is achieved combining the infectious chorus and a lot of Mellotron effects.

The tune can be found as the opening to all three cd-singles released by McCartney in 1997 ("Young Boy", "The World Tonight", "Beautiful Night"), clockin' in at just under a minute.

Musicians:

Paul McCartney vocals, backing vocals, bass, drums, electric guitar, keyboards, Mellotron

---

631 *Ibid.*

In February, McCartney began a series of rehearsals for his World Tour set to kick-off in September. These rehearsals took place at the Barn Studio, a hall just a few steps from Paul's studio in Sussex. Over sixty songs were rehearsed as possible tracks in the setlist.

233 Party, Party (Paul McCartney-Linda McCartney-Hamish Stuart-Robbie McIntosh-Paul Wickens-Chris Whitten)

Recording: April 26th-28th, 1989 **Location:** The Barn Studio, Icklesham **Release:** November 1989, cd-single

"Party Party" went to tape while McCartney and his band were improvising in the studio. The freewheeling feeling of the song is captured in the *Put It There* video where "Party Party" can be heard in its raw form, with no overdubs. This funky-rap *scherzo* was released as a limited edition mini-cd single in September 1989.

Musicians:

Paul McCartney vocals, electric guitar (?) • **Hamish Stuart** bass • **Robbie McIntosh** electric guitar • **Linda McCartney** keyboards • **Wix** keyboards • **Chris Whitten** drums

Flowers in the Dirt was released on June 5th. Reviews were quite positive. Anthony DeCurtis from *Rolling Stone* wrote: "McCartney set out to hone his edge on *Flowers in the Dirt*, and he succeeds to a significant degree. Part of the effort involved writing songs with punk veteran Elvis Costello, four of which turn up on this record. The McCartney-Costello partnership works best on the brashly assertive 'My Brave Face' (…) But the virtues of *Flowers in the Dirt* are not at all limited to Costello's contributions (…) *Flowers in the Dirt*, however, is hardly an unmitigated triumph. The Paulie ballads 'Distractions' and 'Motor of Love' meander, together, for nearly eleven minutes to no purposeful end. Those soft spots weaken but fail to undermine *Flowers in the Dirt*'s essential force. McCartney comes alive on this album, and if he hits the road, as rumored, this fall, he will have a half dozen or so new tunes that can ably hold their own alongside his standing repertoire. In the case of one of the finest songwriters in the history of rock, that's no mean accomplishment."

The *Chicago Tribune* titled his review "Paul is Back. Well, Almost" saying that the album had some weak points but summing up: "*Flowers in the Dirt* is a welcome, if not wholly fantastic, return from the 'fabbest' of the Fab Four."

McCartney began setting-up a massive promo plan which involved a world tour to launch the record and to once and for all, create an indissoluble tie between himself and The Beatles.

Heralded by "My Brave Face", the album went to #1 in the UK charts, while it was a little less successful than expected in the US, only reaching #21.

Nevertheless – thanks to the simultaneous long-running American tour (November 1989–July 1990) – it was one of the longest charting albums in McCartney's career, with forty-nine weeks.

The reason the record took so long to come into being was basically due to the sonic approach and to the production style. Initially, McCartney had thought to co-produce it with Elvis Costello but their stylistic differences drove them apart.

Paul recalled the argument: "I said to Elvis, 'Look man, we're trying to make scintillating fab hit records that are gonna make people go, Wow!' I kept bringing all these happening hits, and Elvis was bringing in Eskimo drum music and the Bulgarian All Stars!"[632]

McCartney saw himself making a comeback in style, with a classy pop album; Costello, on the other hand, wanted to change Paul's happy-go-lucky image. Considering the end results, they were both right. *Flowers in the Dirt* does contain some fine pop material but not consistently. Some of the songs are second rate and Costello's input would have given more color to a record that was unfortunately awash in too much reverb and over-production.

In any case, McCartney's audience wouldn't have accepted another experimental album after *Press to Play* and Paul needed to go on tour with a hit record. In August, Paul took advantage of a quiet break to record some demos: "Get a Hold on Yourself Tonight", "Rhodes Piece", "Acoustic Guitar Instrumental", "Inside" and "Akai Lynn Drum Demos".

In September, the *Paul McCartney World Tour* got off to a low-key start with some dates in Scandinavia – far away from the buzz of the UK or America. Those dates helped McCartney hone his show into one of the best in rock history. The European tour covered Germany, France, Italy, Spain, Switzerland and – after the US leg in November and December – finally culminated in a great crescendo of enthusiasm during eleven sold-out dates at Wembley, UK in January 1990. The setlist was mostly the same for the whole tour:

"Figure of Eight" – "Jet" – "Rough Ride" – "Got to Get You into My Life" – "Band on the Run" – "Ebony and Ivory" – "We Got Married" – "Maybe I'm Amazed" (replaced by "Let 'em In" from March 1990) – "The Long and Winding Road" – "The Fool on the Hill" – "Sgt. Pepper's…" – "Good Day Sunshine" – "Can't Buy Me Love" – "Put it There" – "All My Trials" (only in Milan, 27/10/89) – "Things We Said Today" – "Eleanor Rigby" – "This One" – "My Brave Face" – "Back in the USSR" – "I Saw Her Standing There" – "Twenty Flight Rock" – "Coming Up" – "Let it Be" – "Ain't That a Shame" – "Live and Let Die" – "Hey Jude" – "Yesterday" – "Get Back!" – "Golden Slumbers/Carry That Weight/The End". Among other songs performed over the tour, the medley "P.S. Love Me Do" (Rio de Janeiro, 20-21/04/90), "Mull of Kintyre" (Glasgow, 23/6/90), the Lennon tribute "Strawberry Fields Forever/Help!/Give Peace a Chance" (starting from Liverpool, 28/06/90 and until the end of the tour, except for the Washington venue, 04/07/90) and "Birthday" (premiered at the Knebworth concert, 30/06/90).

---

[632] J. Blaney, *cit.*, p.189.

234 Together (Paul McCartney-Linda McCartney-Hamish Stuart-Robbie McIntosh-Paul Wickens-Chris Whitten)

Recording: December 5th, 1989 **Location:** Rosemont Horizon Stadium, Chicago **Release:** November 1990, *Tripping the Live Fantastic!*

Recorded in Rosemont, "Together" resulted from one of the jams that Paul and the band enjoyed during soundchecks. In this case, the song was a little bit more structured than their usual lengthy blues improvisations. McCartney's ad-libbed vocal sits on top of a relaxed, reggae track credited to the whole group. "Together" is included in *Tripping the Live Fantastic!* (see **1990**)

Musicians:

Paul McCartney vocals, bass (?), electric guitar (?) • **Hamish Stuart** backing vocals, electric guitar (?), bass (?) • **Robbie McIntosh** backing vocals, electric guitar • **Linda McCartney** backing vocals, tambourine • **Wix** backing vocals, keyboards • **Chris Whitten** drums

From December 18th to the 24th, McCartney organized some sessions at Hog Hill Studios to record the soundtrack for the animated film, *A Daumier's Law*.

The film was presented at the 1992 Cannes Film Festival and contained twenty minutes of instrumental music divided in six acts: "Act One (Right)", "Act Two (Wrong)", "Act Three (Justice)", "Act Four (Punishment)", "Act Five (Payment)", "Act Six (Release)".

1990

The *Paul McCartney World Tour* resumed with seventeen dates in the UK, including six concerts in Birmingham.

235 **Inner City Madness** (Paul McCartney-Linda McCartney-Hamish Stuart-Robbie McIntosh-Paul Wickens-Chris Whitten)
Recording: January 2nd, 1990 **Location:** National Exhibition Centre, Birmingham **Release:** November 1990, *Tripping the Live Fantastic!*
McCartney always says that improvisations are the funniest and most genuine moments for musicians. One cannot deny that, hearing this short instrumental recorded during a soundcheck in Birmingham and which would be included in *Tripping the Live Fantastic!*
"Inner City Madness" – whose title recalls the well-known Marvin Gaye's song "Inner City Blues" – shows the carefree side of McCartney and his band: swirling heavy guitars, counterpointed by Wix's synthesizer for one minute of true industrial-rock.
Musicians:
Paul McCartney bass (?), electric guitar (?) • **Linda McCartney** keyboards (?) • **Hamish Stuart** electric guitar (?), bass (?) • **Robbie McIntosh** electric guitar • **Wix** synthesizer • **Chris Whitten** drums

The *Paul McCartney World Tour* continued in America, broke only by some historical concerts: in Tokyo – where McCartney played for the first time after The Beatles' tour in 1966 – and in Rio de Janeiro. The venue of April 21st was held before 184.000 people, the largest paying audience of all times: McCartney entered the *Guinness Book of Records*.
After the completion of the US Tour, McCartney got back in the UK in June, with three shows to be remembered by the next generations: on the 23rd in Glasgow, on the 28th in Liverpool where Paul had prepared a tribute to John Lennon, a medley with "Strawberry Fields Forever/Help!/Give Peace a Chance" – the crowd pushed McCartney to restart singing John's anthem – and on the 30th at Knebworth, where Paul performed with a cast featuring Pink Floyd, Genesis, Mark Knopfler and Eric Clapton before an audience of 100.000 people.
The last part of the tour happened in July again in the US, finishing on the 29th at the Chicago Soldier Field. The tour resulted in a mammoth triple album, called *Tripping the Live Fantastic!* and issued in November. It contained the complete show from the *Paul McCartney World Tour*, with some nice additions from various soundchecks. The album reached #26 in the US and #17 in the UK. Immediately afterward, it was issued on an edited version (a single LP with seventeen tracks, including "All My Trials", a traditional song released simultaneously as 45 rpm in the UK) called *Tripping the Live Fantastic – Highlights!* Despite its mediocre placement in the *Billboard* charts (#141), it was certified platinum for one million copies sold in the US.

1991

Paul started off the year with the recording of the acoustic TV show *Unplugged*. McCartney reunited the band (in the meantime, Blair Cunningham replaced Chris Whitten on drums) in January for some rehearsals during which some seventy songs were auditioned, including: "Put It There" – "Heart of the Country" – "Mrs. Vandebilt" – "My Love" – "She's My Baby" – "C Moon" – "Rough Ride" – "Figure of Eight" – "Her Majesty" – "Rocky Raccoon" – "Michelle" – "And I Love Her" – "Mother Nature's Son" – "All My Trials" – "What's Goin' On" – "True Love" – "Summertime" – "It Won't Be Long" – "Heartbreak Hotel" – "No Other Baby" – "Lend Me Your Comb" – "Twenty Flight Rock" – "Good Rockin' Tonight" – "Lucille" – "We're Gonna Move" – "Hi-Heel Sneakers" – "Shake, Rattle and Roll" – "Blue Suede Shoes" – "You Are My Sunshine" – "Listen to Me". The concert was held at Limehouse Television Studios, London, on January 25th and it went as follows: "Mean Woman Blues", "Matchbox", "Midnight Special", "I Lost My Little Girl", "Here, There and Everywhere", "San Francisco Bay Blues", "We Can Work It Out", "Blue Moon of Kentucky", "I've Just Seen a Face", "Every Night", "Be-Bop-a-Lula", "She's a Woman", "And I Love Her", "The Fool", "Things We Said Today", That Would Be Something", "Blackbird", "High-Heel Sneakers", "Good Rockin' Tonight", "Junk", "Ain't No Sunshine", "Singing the Blues".

The show was done with no amplification: the microphones were placed right close to the instruments. During the twenty-two-song show Paul debuted "I Lost My Little Girl".

236 I Lost My Little Girl (Paul McCartney)

Recording: January 25th, 1991 **Location:** Limehouse Television Studios, London **Release:** May 1991, *Unplugged*

"I Lost My Little Girl" is a capital song. It's the first song McCartney ever wrote. The story is well-known: shortly after losing his mother in 1956, Paul developed an obsessive interest in the guitar, playing it everywhere, even in the bathroom.

Basically, this is what sparked his songwriting imagination: thus, "I Lost My Little Girl" was born – an innocuous ditty based on three chords (G, G7 and C) with obvious Buddy Holly influences. From then on, the song remained unused. Paul often described in interviews how the song came to life, in some cases performing a snippet of it. "I Lost My Little Girl" was attempted during the *Get Back!* sessions, with Lennon on vocal. Clearly, the song – which Paul played to him on their first encounter on July 6th, 1957 – made a strong impression on John.

This live rendition included in *Unplugged – The Official Bootleg* (Paul added a newly written bridge), finally gave the public a chance to hear the very first effort to ever come from the pen of one of the most important composers of contemporary music. McCartney performed the song in Liverpool, during the 2003 *Back in the World Tour*.

Musicians:

Paul McCartney vocals, acoustic guitar • **Linda McCartney** backing vocals • **Hamish Stuart** backing vocals, acoustic bass • **Robbie McIntosh** acoustic guitar • **Wix** shaker • **Blair Cunningham** drums

The success of *Unplugged* pushed McCartney to play some venues. A summer tour that would also help promote the simultaneous release of the album from the TV show was organized. Paul took the same idea that had inspired his *Wings' University Tour* back in 1972; in May and June he did a series of small and almost unannounced concerts across Europe.

McCartney: "The thrills of doing the small gigs are kind of getting back to your roots. You got your audience right there, you can see them, how many there are… It's quite exciting. If you make a mistake you can kind of stop and say, 'It's Friday night, we'll start this one again!'"[633]

The 1991 *Secret Gigs Tour* setlist was split in two different sets, the acoustic one mirroring the TV show while the electric part collected some of the finest moments from the 1989/90 *Paul McCartney World Tour*.

Acoustic set: "Mean Woman Blues" – "Be Bop a Lula" – "We Can Work It Out" – "San Francisco Bay Blues" – "Every Night" – "Here, There and Everywhere" – "That Would Be Something" – "Down to the River" – "And I Love Her" – "She's a Woman" – "I Lost My Little Girl" – "Ain't No Sunshine" – "Hi-Heel Sneakers" – "I've Just Seen a Face" – "Good Rockin' Tonight" - Electric set: "My Brave Face" (or "Twenty Flight Rock") – "Band on the Run" – "Ebony and Ivory" – "I Saw Her Standing There" – "Coming Up" – "Get Back!" – "The Long and Winding Road" – "Ain't That a Shame" – "Let It Be" – "Can't Buy Me Love" – "Sgt. Pepper's…"

Unplugged – The Official Bootleg was released on May 8th, 1991 and contained most of the songs performed that January during the show, with the exception of "Mean Woman Blues", "Matchbox", "The Fool", "Midnight Special" and "Things We Said Today" (the latter two would be released on the "Biker Like an Icon" cd-single in 1994). Critics and audience alike declared it a success. *Unplugged* reached #7 on the UK charts and #14 in the US: it was McCartney's highest position in America between *Tug of War* and *Flaming Pie*.

The following month was dedicated to the *Liverpool Oratorio*. On June 28th and 29th, the Liverpool Anglican Cathedral hosted the world premiere of the *Liverpool Oratorio*, the first classical opera ever composed by McCartney – helped by the conductor Carl Davis – commissioned in honor of the 150th anniversary of the Royal Liverpool Philharmonic Society. McCartney worked in a traditional manner together with Davis, writing the melodies at the piano or on guitar. But he had never written for baritones or tenors before.

Davis: "My first meeting with Paul was at his home and I was very nervous. Minutes after I met him, he asked me which Beatles songs I liked. My mind went blank and I named one – I think it was 'A Hard Day's Night' – that he hadn't written. He seemed rather perturbed (…) The work evolved over a long time because Paul was touring. Throughout our meetings he was curious about the process, but I felt to some extent he pretended he didn't know as much as he did. As for singers, he said, 'Who is the best soprano in the world? Get the best you can.' So we cast Dame Kiri Te Kanawa."[634]

The opera, divided into eight movements ("War", "School", "Crypt", "Father", "Wedding", "Work", "Crisis", "Peace") wasn't very original but it did contain some important autobiographical passages. Through his lyrics, McCartney called-up past episodes in his life, some extremely painful and dramatic, such as his father's passing or Mary Dee, a character who, as well as in name, is clearly a reference to Paul's mother.

Carl Davis: "The idea of using only classical instruments was Paul's idea. We talked about the combination of classical and pop instruments, but Paul wanted it to be very pure. We met and discussed what we might do and the results were pretty quick. The title *Liverpool Oratorio* was his. At first, we thought of *Liverpool Requiem*. My father had died recently and Paul had a strong attachment to his father, but then he came up with this idea and that was the title." [635]

Carl was amazed at Paul's composing method and at his creative flow: "The process was like this: he began talking about his life. And I was thinking to myself, 'Oh, that would be a great movement!' By the end of the meeting I had eight or nine ideas written down… Five of the movement in the *Liverpool Oratorio* were based on that first meeting. Then came the big challenge…how we were going to work on this. Would he be able to dictate it to me, would he be able to play it to me. Obviously we were working in a very old fashioned way, 'cause I was going to write it down. That took a while. Every meeting we had was productive. It was very focused on what it was about, it was led by the subject, by what are we trying to say. The musical content was mainly by Paul in terms of the melody, harmony, rhythm etcetera and I would try to interpret what he did and make suggestions. We've been slow for some time, but it was very light, a lot of fun, I think we were both very productive with each other. Some time he would come up with a melody, other times I would play and he would sing, or I would say, 'C'mon give a bass line here, what would you play on your guitar…' (It was like) a long two-year conversation. 'The Drinking Song' was beautiful. That was achieved in one hour. I would say this about Paul, that is fascinating for me: words and music come at the same time. Maybe the lyrics wouldn't be absolutely complete, but the concept for the vocal line was there together, it was conceived at the same time. And I thought this is fantastic, this is what popular

[634] Georgia Dehn, *Carl Davis Recalls Collaborating With Paul McCartney in Liverpool Oratorio 1991*, in *The Telegraph*, 11/08/2011.
[635] Interview courtesy of Carl Davis, 27/08/2012.

songs is about, very different from a classical idea where a composer would say, 'I need to have a song and I will look in a book of poetry or I'll look in the Bible, or I'll look for a source...' The 'McCartney way', which is the way in which pop music works, it thinks a come together at the same time. This is what I was exposed to for the first time and it was just terrific."[636]

The double album – released at the end of October – met with the public's good favor, enjoying an amazing amount of success in the classical charts and selling over 250.000 copies.

In November, McCartney and the band began recording *Off The Ground*. Paul chose a different approach from his previous albums, recording live in the studio to give the album more freshness. In the months to come, McCartney and his band worked under lock and key: Monday to Friday from 2 to 8 p.m. The sessions produced enough material for a double album with the usual handful of unreleased songs, such as "Is It Raining in London?", "Cello in the Ruins" (later recorded with Liam Gallagher and Paul Weller), "On a Pedestal", "Simple Song", "Magic Lamp" and "If You Say So".

The November warm-up, meant only as a rehearsal, also produced two songs that would end up on the *Off the Ground* album.

237 Biker Like an Icon (Paul McCartney)

Recording: November 25th, 1991 **Location:** Hog Hill Studio, Icklesham **Release:** February 1993, *Off the Ground*

For his first album with a band since Wings – and his first studio album since *Flowers in the Dirt* – McCartney brought in his musicians and had them listen to very acerbic, undeveloped recordings, compelling them to create their own ideas and arrangements.

McCartney: "I didn't do serious demos. I just sang the songs with guitar or piano on to a Sony Walkman. The point was to leave room for ideas for the band and the co-producer, Julian Mendelsohn."[637] Paul presented 23 songs to the group. Blair Cunningham said: "One day, late in 1991, Paul came into the studio and said, 'Okay, here are the songs.' He played them through for us acoustically, on guitar or piano (...) We just sat around, he gave us the lyrics to read as well, and we listened."[638]

According to Wix, McCartney did nothing but said, "this is a rock'n'roll one, this is a band bash." Hamish Stuart remembers: "As soon as he played the songs to us I got the feeling there were some serious contenders there. You can get all kind of sophisticated demos, but I think the way he did it was the best way to encourage input from the band."[639]

Paul wanted to rehearse immediately, without worrying too much about the arrangement and in the case of "Biker Like an Icon", as Blair Cunningham recalls, "it just worked straight from

---

[636] *Ibid.*
[637] *The New World Tour Booklet*, 1993, p.65.
[638] *Ibid.*
[639] *Ibid.*

demo to track the same as he'd presented it to us (…) He started up and we were after it, four-on-the floor for that one."[640]

Recorded on November 25th, 1991 "Biker Like an Icon" launched the *Off the Ground* sessions. That day had been meant for rehearsals only but it went so well that the band learned the structure of the song in fifteen minutes before recording it. Two weeks later back in the studio, Paul and the others listened back to the tape and decided that they had nailed it in one shot. In fact, the recording of "Biker Like an Icon" exudes all the immediacy of a first take. This syncopated, dark and mysterious rocker in E minor, led by McCartney's acoustic guitar, is one of the best cuts on the album. The rhythm section works perfectly thanks to Stuart's bass groove and Cunningham's fast drumming. McIntosh contributed an edgy slide guitar. One can forgive the lyrics that see "biker" rhyming with "like her" and "met her" with "let her" and just enjoy the song for what it is.

Paul recalled: "Linda was talking about cameras and she said, 'I like a Leica, I like a Nikon.' I started messing with that and it became a biker who had a girl who loved him like an icon. BIKER LIKE AN ICON. I like confusing titles."[641]

During concerts, "Biker Like an Icon" received some very effective scenography – with Byzantine-styled Madonna and Child icons wearing leather motorcycle jackets and helmets. It became a highlight of the 1993 *New World Tour* and can be best appreciated on *Paul Is Live!*

Issued as a single in April 1994 (the cd-single includes the live version, whereas an alternate studio take can be found on the video-clip), "Biker Like an Icon" unfortunately did not chart.

Musicians:

Paul McCartney vocals, backing vocals, acoustic guitar, percussion • **Linda McCartney** keyboards • **Hamish Stuart** backing vocals, bass • **Robbie McIntosh** slide guitar • **Wix** piano, keyboards • **Blair Cunningham** drums

238 Peace in the Neighbourhood (Paul McCartney)

Recording: November 25th-December 6th, 1991 and December 9th, 1991-June 1992 (overdubs) **Location:** Hog Hill Studio, Icklesham **Release:** February 1993, *Off the Ground*

After "Biker Like an Icon" the group dived into "Peace In The Neighbourhood", a R&B style song.

The recording of "Peace in the Neighbourhood" was one of the most exciting moments during the *Off the Ground* sessions, as McCartney recalled: "The take on the album is a rehearsal. That take had such a good feel that we couldn't improve on it, a beautiful slapping sound on the drums, real R&B."[642]

---

[640] *Ibid.*, p.66.
[641] *Ibid.*, p.69.
[642] *Ibid.*

And it was a very special moment for Robbie McIntosh: "That was a good one for me, that guitar outro. We were rehearsing, so I wasn't thinking, 'Woo, I've got the chance to show off now!' It was aimless in a way and yet it ended up sounding quite nice."[643]

Producer Julian Mendelsohn pointed out that the song worked as it was. McCartney and his band were in the studio ready to record the song, when Mendelsohn announced that it wouldn't be necessary – he then played them the recording of the rehearsal. In the following months, Paul and the band added only a few touches to the original take. Its live energy can be appreciated not only in the solid sound but also in the little imperfections and band ad-libs not omitted from the final version.[644]

Musically speaking, the song is rather ingenious with its bluesy sixth chords and McCartney's lead singing supported by some fine backing vocals. Paul played electric guitar leaving the bass to Hamish – all in a lovely relaxed groove. However, the lyrics to "Peace in the Neighborhood" were among the most criticized on *Off the Ground*. The scenes depicted in "Peace In The Neighbourhood" are full of stereotypes and banal optimism. Universal peace and social harmony find their safe haven inside the nuclear family, a shrinking horizon when compared to the utopian values of the Sixties, which McCartney himself in many ways embodied.

Premiered during the *Ed Sullivan Theatre* concerts on December 10th and 11th, 1992 "Peace in the Neighbourhood" did not miss a show on the 1993 *New World Tour*. There is a cool rendition on *Paul Is Live!* although it is shorter than the version included in *Off the Ground*

Musicians:

Paul McCartney vocals, backing vocals, electric guitar, congas • **Linda McCartney** backing vocals, percussion • **Hamish Stuart** backing vocals, bass • **Robbie McIntosh** backing vocals, electric and acoustic guitar • **Wix** backing vocals, piano • **Blair Cunningham** drums, percussion • **Keith Smith, Eddie Klein** conversation

---

643 *Ibid.*
644 In the coda one can overhear bits of conversation between two studio assistants as well as Robbie rehearsing his solo from "Hope of Deliverance".

1992

239 Off the Ground (Paul McCartney)

Recording: December 9th, 1991-July, 1992 **Location:** Hog Hill Studio, Icklesham **Release:** February 1993, *Off the Ground*

During the *Off the Ground* sessions, keyboard player Wix suggested that McCartney try doing a computer-based song.

Paul had already written the title track of the upcoming album. McCartney: "I had this song, rather *folksy*, doodle-doodle-doodle-da-dum-cha... Wix had said to me if I ever wanted to try computer recording as an alternative he'd come in one day and we could goof around. So I said to everyone else, have a day off."[645]

Wix: "You should have heard the demo. It's nothing like the album version. I thought, 'How am I going to do this?' And he wanted to build it entirely on the computer. We put some drum loops in and the feel changed totally. We added some of Robbie's guitar and it worked out brilliantly. Got it done in a day, basically."[646]

McCartney added drums and some percussion, leaving the rest up to Wix. The other band members chimed in on some lovely backing vocals and more percussion. The final version of "Off the Ground" – that was added to the album at the last minute – is a Wings-like pop-rock song with an electronic beat, a catchy verse/chorus sequence and McIntosh's slide-guitar work. On the other hand McCartney and Mendhelsohn's production buried the vocals under too much reverb: maybe realizing this, McCartney issued two different mixes of "Off the Ground" where the vocal is clearer. The first – and best – was remixed by Bob Clearmountain, the second by Keith Cohen: this version starts with a fade-in of the chorus.

McCartney revealed how the song became the album title track: "I happened to be speaking to my daughter and she said, 'What did you do today, dad?' and I said, 'We did this song. It's called 'Off the Ground'. She said, 'Oh, that's a great album title!'"[647]

"Off The Ground" was released as a single in the US during the 1993 American tour with the idea of helping the album sales that – three months after its release – were just hovering above 600.000 copies in the US. It didn't sell at all nor did it make it onto the charts, thus signaling the commercial lowest point of McCartney's career. Although Paul performed it live during the 1993 *New World Tour*, the song didn't make it onto *Paul Is Live!*

These live versions – due to their slightly off-key vocals – just weren't convincing enough to justify another release.

Musicians:

---

[645] *The New World Tour Booklet*, p.69.
[646] *Ibid.*
[647] K. Badman, *The Beatles. The Dream Is Over, Off the Record 2*, p.431.

Paul McCartney vocals, backing vocals, drums, percussion • Linda McCartney backing vocals • Hamish Stuart backing vocals, percussion • Robbie McIntosh electric guitar, percussion • Wix backing vocals, keyboards, computer programming, piano, synth-bass

240 Looking for Changes (Paul McCartney)

Recording: December 9th, 1991-July, 1992 Location: Hog Hill Studio, Icklesham Release: February 1993, *Off the Ground*

McCartney: "When Linda and I met, we discovered that we'd both been nature lovers as kids, and still were. Then we became vegetarians, which makes you even more aware of animals and their right and makes you want to explain to other people."[648]

"Looking for Changes" marks the first time Paul directly approaches the theme of animal rights. The song is one of McCartney's most aggressive. He said: "Protest songs are quite hard to do. Love songs come easier, at least to someone like me, but in this case I'd been looking through magazines like *The Animal's Voice* and *Animal Agenda*, that show some of the experimentation that goes on in the name of cosmetics and started to write the song after I saw a picture of a cat with a machine implanted in its head (…) I came up with the line 'I saw a cat with a machine in his brain' and just made it up from there (…) I think it's 'change or die' time for this planet."[649]

Over the quickly assembled verses, McCartney urgently wrote a hard kicking rocker that perfectly expresses his anger and disgust towards these vile practices. Paul's explicit invective is something unusual for him: the word 'bastard' was suggested by poet Adrian Mitchell, who helped McCartney with some lyrics in *Off the Ground*.[650]

This concise and biting song is a good example of a certain lyrical harshness on the whole *Off the Ground* album. In 2 minutes and 43 seconds, Paul delivers a pure rock performance, shouting out against the injustices taking places in laboratories.

This recording was not overdubbed too much and has a spontaneous live feel: Paul's raw vocals are supported by the angry guitar riffs performed by McIntosh, Hamish and McCartney himself. "Looking for Changes" was a great live track as shown during the 1993 *New World Tour*. An even rowdier version appears on *Paul Is Live!*

Musicians:

Paul McCartney vocals, backing vocals, bass, electric guitar • Linda McCartney backing vocals • Hamish Stuart backing vocals, acoustic and electric guitar • Robbie McIntosh backing vocals, acoustic and electric guitar • Wix backing vocals, clavinet • Blair Cunningham backing vocals, drums

---

[648] *Club Sandwich*, n.65, Spring 1993, p.5.
[649] *Ibid.*
[650] *The New World Tour Booklet*, p.65.

241 Hope of Deliverance (Paul McCartney)

Recording: December 9th, 1991-July, 1992 and July 17th, 1992 (overdubs) **Location:** Hog Hill Studio, Icklesham **Release:** December 1992, single (from *Off the Ground*)

McCartney: "I went up into the attic of our house, just to get away from everyone. There's a trap door, you go up a little ladder and then close it and no one can get at you, so then you know you've got a couple of hours to yourself."[651]

Up there, Paul quickly threw together "Hope of Deliverance": "I took with me a Martin 12-string guitar and just for a bit of fun, I put a capo on it" – McCartney said – "That very jingly sound remind(ed) me of Cathedrals and Christmas. So that led me into the field of hope, of deliverance, and then I added about the darkness that surrounds us."[652] After a mere two hours Paul came out of the attic with the finished song. It's also possible that McCartney re-worked some earlier ideas: judging from the title, a demo – called "Spanish Hop" and taped at Rude Studio in August 1986 – could easily be the first attempt to the song.

In the studio, Paul worked with Robbie McIntosh to get that full acoustic guitar sound, that is so distinctive of "Hope of Deliverance".

The rest of the group helped give the song its flavor by trial and error. Cunningham: "That was a try-this, try-that track, until one sunny day I said, 'It sound Caribbean, calypsoey'."[653]

"Hope and Deliverance" took on a Latin flavor, thanks to its percussion bed and its flamenco-ish guitar solo. Even Linda joined in, playing chords on autoharp. McCartney enjoyed singing this bouncy pop song, overdubbing giggles and shouts in a sort of Spanish *gramelot*.[654]

Maurizio Ravalico, an Italian percussionist residing and working in London at the time, remembers his overdub session on July 17th, 1992: "I was contacted through Paul's booker Graham Perkins, who was assigned to hire three percussion players, since they wanted to add some Latin-American flavor to one song. Graham came to see me playing with Davide Giovannini during a Picante's concert and he talked about the session. We brought in the third percussionist, our friend and colleague Dave Pattman."[655]

Once together in the studio the percussion trio was given free reign: "A few days later" – Ravalico says – "We were invited to McCartney's private studio in Sussex. They had us to hear the track, that was already completed and mixed, giving some generic instructions. We only learned that they wanted a Latin flavor on the song and so we brought to the studio a van full of instruments! We presented a couple of rhythmic patterns to Paul and Julian Mendelsohn

---

[651] *Club Sandwich*, n.65, Spring 1993, p.3.
[652] *Ibid.*
[653] *Ibid.*
[654] During the instrumental break you can hear McCartney shouting "tres conejos". Paul had recently composed a song of the same title that appears on Movement II on the Liverpool Oratorio.
[655] Interview courtesy of Maurizio Ravalico, 02/09/2011.

and we opted for a sort of Cuban Songo. I played congas, Dave played bongos and Davide put together a hi-hat, a little 10" tom – I think – and a Cha Cha Cha cow-bell."[656]

The overdubs only took a couple of hours. Ravalico: "We were in the studio for half a day. Everything went smoothly and quickly, but without any pressure. Both McCartney and Mendelsohn were wide-open to our suggestions and they did not give any indication about our instruments or the playing style. They hired us exactly because they were seeking for a creative input from the outside."[657]

"Hope Of Deliverance" was released ahead of the album *Off the Ground* in December 1992. It became a worldwide success selling over 4 million copies – it was a massive hit in Germany – even though it only reached #18 in the UK charts and a disastrous #83 in the US. "Hope Of Deliverance" also gained popularity thanks to McCartney's 1993 *New World Tour* where the song was always a showstopper. Audience response was particularly amazing in Latin America where the song was elevated to anthem status by the fans. A cool live version with Wix adding more acoustic guitar is available on *Paul Is Live!*

The song was included in some Latin-American dates during the 2012 *On the Run Tour* and the 2013 *Out There! Tour*.

Musicians:

Paul McCartney vocals, backing vocals, acoustic and electric guitar, Spanish guitar, bass • **Linda McCartney** backing vocals, autoharp • **Hamish Stuart** backing vocals • **Robbie McIntosh** backing vocals, acoustic and Spanish guitar, electric guitar • **Wix** backing vocals, piano, drums programming, Lynn drum, percussion • **Blair Cunningham** backing vocals, percussion, drums • **Davide Giovannini, Dave Pattman, Maurizio Ravalico** percussion

242 Mistress and Maid (Paul McCartney-Elvis Costello)

Recording: December 9th, 1991-July, 1992 **Location**: Hog Hill Studio, Icklesham and Whitfield (Hit Factory) Studios (overdubs), London **Release**: February 1993, *Off the Ground*

Co-written with Elvis Costello, "Mistress and Maid" is one of the most harmonically complex and lyrically sophisticated songs on *Off the Ground*.

In typical Costello 3/4 time, the track features some biting lyrics attacking male chauvinism: the whole song proceeds step-by-step with precision as if in a scene from a play. The story builds dramatically from the wife's loving care for her man as he returns home, to his indifference (he simply seats and starts dreaming, while looking at girls in magazines), finally concluding with her being overcome with anxiety and fear. A very theatrical song.

The scene recalls an episode from the *Liverpool Oratorio*, when an argument between Mary Dee and Shanty ruins their relationship. In this case, one is struck by the woman's inability to

---

[656] *Ibid.*
[657] *Ibid.*

unleash her anger: her shouts are merely an unexpressed need. The basic track was recorded with few instruments (bass, acoustic and electric guitar, keyboards, tambourine and drums): Wix's keyboards shine through, in the style of "Being for the Benefit of Mr. Kite".

A fifteen-piece orchestra was later added. Paul asked Carl Davis for an orchestral arrangement, having already worked with him on the *Liverpool Oratorio*.

Hamish Stuart: "Paul and Carl took tapes of my guitar and Robbie's guitar and wrote horn arrangements around the lines we were playing."[658]

Carl Davis: "This was really reversing our relationship, because Paul had a very clear idea of what he wanted, the song was already written and recorded. For me it was simply a job. He said to me, 'I would like to have this brass ensemble and I'll tell you exactly what I want it to be.' He came not to me as a composer." [659]

David Juritz, who was among the violinists in the orchestra, recalls: "I think we recorded it at Whitfield Studios. I remember recording a string track that consisted mainly of long held 'A's... McCartney came out to say hello, but I was a pretty junior member of the orchestra so didn't actually get to speak to him!"[660]

Stephen Wick played tuba: "All the information that I had about the session was the time and place. I arrived at the studio an hour before the session was due to begin and to my embarrassment I arrived at the front door at exactly the same moment as Paul, who had just got out of a chauffeur-driven car. 'You must be here to play for my album', Paul said. Of course, I had no idea who I was playing for – there was more than one studio at Whitfield Street Studios and I didn't know if was working for Paul or not. Not wanting to appear unfriendly or stand-offish I said, 'I guess I am!'"[661]

Once underway, the recording became a perfect example of the crossing over of different musical cultures. Wick: "Paul found it hard to explain exactly what he wanted, but had boundless energy and really wanted us to put everything into the music. His instructions, to be honest, were a little confusing for us. 'I want it a little bit ragtime, but with a baroque feel' was one of his directions. Studio musicians usually like to have slightly more specific instructions, such as, 'Please play this more *marcato*' or 'Play the eighth notes shorter.' Paul communicated what he wanted through Carl Davis, the arranger, and was very happy with the result!"[662]

The song could have conveyed more pathos if only it had benefitted from a simpler arrangement. "Mistress and Maid" did get a simpler treatment in a live version performed by McCartney and Costello at St. James Palace in London March 23rd, 1995 only using acoustic

[658] *The New World Tour Booklet*, p.65.
[659] Interview courtesy of Carl Davis, 27/08/2012.
[660] Interview courtesy of David Juritz, 24/11/2011.
[661] Interview courtesy of Stephen Wick, 15/01/2012.
[662] *Ibid.*

guitars. Here, the blend of their voices expresses the heartfelt mood that was missing from the *Off the Ground* version.

Musicians:

Paul McCartney vocals, backing vocals, bass, tambourine • **Linda McCartney** tambourine • **Hamish Stuart** backing vocals, electric guitar • **Robbie McIntosh** acoustic guitar • **Wix** keyboards • **Blair Cunningham** drums • **Gordon Hunt** oboe • **Susan Milan** flute • **Frank Lloyd** horn • **Colin Sheen** trombone • **Paul Stringsbald, Richard Martin** trumpet • **Stephen Wick** tuba • **Belinda Bunt, Jonathan Evans-Jones, Roger Garland, Roy Gillard, David Juritz, Pauline Lowbury, Brendan O'Reilly, Maciej Rakowski** violin

243 I Owe It All to You (Paul McCartney)

Recording: December 9th, 1991-July, 1992 **Location:** Hog Hill Studio, Icklesham **Release:** February 1993, *Off the Ground*

Paul explains how the inspiration for "I Owe It All to You" came about: "I'd been to a place in South of France – the kids took us there for Linda's birthday. I drove past this sign which said *Cathedrale des Images*. It turned out to be this huge place carved out of the rock. They have dozen of projectors and they throw images on the walls – suddenly it's an Egyptian temple, next thing it's all stained glass and so on. It's a trip!"[663]

Inspired by that visions, McCartney proceeded to write down the first verses, simply describing the big screen with all the evocative images and enchanting landscapes appearing on it.

He brought into the studio a dreamy and delicate acoustic song, with the whole band putting a lot of hard work into it. The song is dedicated to Linda, who plays the opening celeste sequence that leads into the soft acoustic guitar arpeggio.

Hamish Stuart recalls the session well: "I felt very involved in that song, played a lot and sang and it came out very straightforwardly."[664] Robbie McIntosh contributed a fine slide-guitar part.

"I Owe It All to You" was performed at the Ed Sullivan Theatre (December 10th-11th, 1992) but was not in the tracklist for the 1993 *New World Tour*, making some appearances during soundchecks. The track appears on *Off the Ground*.

Musicians:

Paul McCartney vocals, acoustic guitar, Mellotron, tambourine, vocal percussion • **Linda McCartney** backing vocals, celeste, clavinet • **Hamish Stuart** backing vocals, bass • **Robbie McIntosh** electric slide guitar • **Wix** piano, percussion • **Blair Cunningham** drums, percussion

663 *The New World Tour Booklet*, p.65.
664 *Ibid.*

244 Golden Earth Girl (Paul McCartney)

Recording: December 9th, 1991-May, 1992 and May 18th, 1992 (overdubs) **Location:** Hog Hill Studio, Icklesham and Withfield (Hit Factory) Studios (overdubs), London **Release:** February 1993, *Off the Ground*

Right after he composed "Golden Earth Girl", Paul thought to record it with a full orchestra but then – as Hamish Stuart recalls – "the song became a band number."

"Golden Earth Girl" is a piano ballad in the purest McCartney melodic tradition. The lyrics mix nature with liturgical imagery. The line "in eggshell seas" – a play on words of the Latin *in excelsis* – is part of the delicate, pure and celestial atmosphere created throughout the song. Paul depicts an alternate world (the personification of the elements and fauna vaguely recall the franciscan "Cantico delle Creature") where man can find his true dimension in touch with nature. Unfortunately, here McCartney lacks a real inspiration. The opening chord sequence gives a feeling of *deja vu* and recalls "Maybe I'm Amazed" and "Warm and Beautiful".

Nevertheless, the arrangement succeeds in emphasizing the dreamy quality of the song and the band instrumentation is augmented in the middle section by an oboe and flute solo.

Carl Davis arranged the track. He recalls: "Paul said, 'I want to add a flute here and there and this is what I want them to play.' The score was done by me, but very dictated by Paul." [665]

Gordon Hunt played oboe on the track. He recalls: "I was contacted by Paul Wing, Carl Davis' agent, for an afternoon session at Hit Factory Studios, in Whitfield St. in London and it was on May 18th, 1992. The music was all written down. Carl was in the studio when I got there. Paul came out from the recording box and talked to us, me and Susan Milan on flute. The way he was asking us to play was not the way we were used to being asked. He didn't have that sort of professional language, but he was always charming. He knew exactly where he wanted it to go… He got a very clear idea about the solo: how it should be phrased, how it should be sounding. I was very impressed by that…"[666]

However, they didn't get it on the first take. Hunt adds: "Our parts for flute and oboe were played together at the same time. It was a very simple part but we recorded it a lot of times. As we did it more and more we understood it more and more what he was asking for. And so we got closer to his idea…"[667]. "Golden Earth Girl" is on *Off the Ground* and an orchestral version appears on *Working Classical*.

Musicians:

Paul McCartney vocals, backing vocals, piano • **Linda McCartney** backing vocals, harmonium • **Hamish Stuart** backing vocals, bass • **Robbie McIntosh** acoustic and electric guitar • **Wix** keyboards, percussion • **Blair Cunningham** drums • **Gordon Hunt** oboe • **Susan Milan** flute

---

[665] Interview courtesy of Carl Davis, 27/08/2012.
[666] Interview courtesy of Gordon Hunt, 05/11/2011 and 14/11/2011.
[667] *Ibid.*

245 The Lovers That Never Were (Paul McCartney-Declan Mac Manus)

Recording: December 9th, 1991-July, 1992 **Location:** Hog Hill Studio, Icklesham **Release:** February 1993, *Off the Ground*

"The Lovers that Never Were" was the first song written from scratch by Paul and Elvis Costello (again credited as Declan MacManus). McCartney: "Elvis and I got together to see if we could write a few songs. First of all, I fixed one of his songs up, then he fixed up one of mine. That led us to find that it was quite easy, so one day we decided to write one from scratch. The question then was, where do we start? We had the whole musical universe to choose from – a rock'n'roll song, a love song – so I said, 'Well let's start with Smokey Robinson and The Miracles, let's think of them and (this song) came out."[668]

The demo they recorded was very rough and basic: just guitar and piano with a very heartfelt, R&B-ish vocal by Paul.

Costello: "The demo is one of the great vocal performances of his solo career. He's standing up playing a 12-string guitar and, weirdly enough, I'm playing piano, just thinking, 'Don't fuck up, he's really singing this!' He's singing a ballad in the voice of 'I'm Down'. I had never heard him doing that before."[669]

Problems arose when McCartney decided to record the song during the *Flowers in the Dirt* sessions. Something went wrong and Paul put it aside. He tried it again during the *Off the Ground* sessions.

Blair Cunningham: "It was a waltz and not working until Paul said, 'How about putting a 4/4 on top of this thing?' I said, 'Just give me five minutes.' A real head twister, but it was such a groove. Made the song happen."[670]

With its driving beat (the whole group played percussion, according to the credits for the *Off the Ground* tracks taken from the *Club Sandwich* magazine no.65) "The Lovers That Never Were" is one of McCartney's best love songs, thanks to its uplifting poetic lyrics – in which Costello surely had a hand – that contrast eternal sentiment with the transience of the material world. The track is on *Off the Ground*.

Musicians:

Paul McCartney vocals, backing vocals, bass, percussion • **Linda McCartney** backing vocals, percussion • **Hamish Stuart** backing vocals, acoustic guitar, percussion • **Robbie McIntosh** backing vocals, mandolin, acoustic guitar, percussion • **Wix** piano, Hammond organ, percussion • **Blair Cunningham** drums, percussion

---

668 *Club Sandwich*, n.72, Winter 1994, p.5.
669 *Mojo!, cit.*, p.83.
670 *The New World Tour Booklet*, p.69.

246 Get Out of My Way (Paul McCartney)

Recording: December 9th, 1991-July, 1992 **Location:** Hog Hill Studio, Icklesham **Release:** February 1993, *Off the Ground*

McCartney: "'Get Out of My Way' was really an attempt at writing a straightforward rock'n'roll song. A lot of people will tell you that they're often the hardest songs to write, even though they sound very simple. To get them to sound authentic is difficult."[671]

Paul went into the studio to produce a spontaneous and fresh sounding recording: the result being "Get Out of My Way", later included in *Off the Ground*.

Robbie McIntosh: "The big thing about the album for me was that nearly everything I did was done live on the backing track – and the band wouldn't let me change it! On 'Get Out of My Way' I did a guitar solo when we were bashing through it which I thought was only all right, so I had another couple of cracks at it and they all said, 'Naah, leave it'. So it's the original on the record."[672]

Wix amusingly recalls: "Me, I was locked in the box for that one, playing rock'n'roll on the 'Magic Piano' (a multi-colored piano that Paul played during the *New World Tour* – author's note). They built an acoustic box round me to stop sound spill."[673]

McIntosh and Wix's solos take the lion's share on this McCartney road song. It's hard to listen to it without picturing oneself driving across the US in a fast set of wheels. A fat horn arrangement (played by the Midnight Horns quintet) does not succeed in making "Get Out of My Way" a gritty rock'n'roll number: the sound is too polished. "Get Out of My Way" was performed live at the pre-tour *Up Close* gigs in December 1992 and during the first half of the 1993 *New World Tour*. It was later replaced by "Looking for Changes".

Musicians:

Paul McCartney vocals, bass • **Linda McCartney** harmonium, percussion • **Hamish Stuart** electric guitar • **Robbie McIntosh** electric guitar • **Wix** piano • **Blair Cunningham** drums • The Midnight Horns: **Frank Mead** alto sax • **Nick Payn** baritone sax • **Andy Hamilton, Nick Pentelow** tenor sax • **Martin Drover** trumpet

247 Winedark Open Sea (Paul McCartney)

Recording: December 9th, 1991-July, 1992 **Location:** Hog Hill Studio, Icklesham **Release:** February 1993, *Off the Ground*

Always searching for new inspiration, McCartney taps into the imaginary on this title. "Winedark Open Sea" once again confirms Paul's fascination with the sea. In this case, the references to the wide open spaces of the immense oceans serve as the pretext to yet another love song, considered by many to be the weakest on *Off the Ground*.

---

[671] *Club Sandwich*, n.65, Spring 1993, p.5.
[672] *The New World Tour Booklet*, p.69.
[673] *Ibid.*

Paul had written it in August 1991 and demoed it a month later with the title "Sailing on the Winedark Open Sea". In the studio, he went for a simple arrangement. McCartney accompanied himself on a Wurlitzer piano – and probably added an acoustic guitar that was not officially credited – backed only by Wix's synth bass, Cunningham's drums and McIntosh and Stuart's electric guitars.

Stuart liked its sparse instrumentation: "I know I would have added more to it" – said Hamish – "But it's a case of magic's in there and you've got to leave it alone."[674]

"Winedark Open Sea" is almost six minutes long, featuring a long coda – a typical cliché in McCartney's repertoire. Judging from a long jam aired on his *Oobu Joobu* radio show, maybe McCartney considered the song for the 1993 *New World Tour*. But since Paul quickly started jamming, he must have realized that "Winedark Open Sea" wasn't suitable for live gigs.

Musicians:

Paul McCartney vocals, backing vocals, electric piano, acoustic guitar (?) • **Linda McCartney** harmonium • **Hamish Stuart** backing vocals, electric guitar • **Robbie McIntosh** electric guitar • **Wix** bass synth, percussion • **Blair Cunningham** drums

248 C'mon People (Paul McCartney)

Recording: December 9th, 1991-June, 1992 and June 30th, 1992 (overdubs) **Location:** Hog Hill Studio, Icklesham and Abbey Road Studios (overdubs), London **Release:** February 1993, *Off the Ground*

Paul was on holiday in Jamaica in 1991 when he wrote "C'mon People". McCartney: "I love people there, it's very laid back and I feel very musical when I'm there. So I always try to get a piano or something in case I want to write. Often, in the afternoon, I sat around and see if I fancy writing a song and one day I just started chugging on this little riff and 'C'mon People' came out."[675]

Based on the four variations in C major that accompany the chorus, "C'mon People" quickly turned into a Beatle-esque song.

Paul had intended it to be as a very up-lifting song, a call to change and renewal with a Sixties vibe. The lyrics took a more decisive turn, thanks to poet Adrian Mitchell, as Paul explains: "For instance, I'd written, 'We've got a future and it's coming in', but Adrian said, 'Do you want to be a little bit stronger here?' So I said 'rushing' the first time and the second time I made it 'charging'."[676]

Although the lyrics may be generic, the music itself is McCartney at his best. "C'mon People" is an enticing piano piece in four parts. To the first part – the verse, a sort of spoken introduction – and to the second – the chorus with Paul's exhortation – McCartney put beside

674 *Ibid.*
675 *Club Sandwich*, n.65, Spring 1993, p.4.
676 *The New World Tour Booklet*, p.64.

a magnificent middle section sustained by a majestic orchestral passage. An explosive coda – with a catchy whistled melody – closes the song. A perfect ending to an album.

Blair Cunningham: "I remember playing it on this Friday, lovely, sunny day (…) Paul said, 'We'll just bash through this one, tape it, come back on Monday and do it properly' One take, that's all we did. Julian Mendelsohn, the producer, got on the intercom and said, 'Come and have a listen to this'. We're all looking at one another grinning, and I'm thinking, I'll never be able to play it like that again, no way."[677]

Nevertheless, Paul thought that something was still missing: "(I) thought (I)'d like to have an arrangement on it. It was one of the only songs on the album that felt like it could take an orchestra, to make it a bit more of an anthem. So I called George Martin, and he said, 'Are you sure you want to use me?' because he (wa)s almost trying to retire. 'Of course I want to use you. It would be brilliant. We'll work the same way we always did – sit down together and decide what to do, then you'll write and conduct it.'"[678]

The orchestral overdub session was held at Abbey Road, on June 30th, 1992: "Halfway through the session" – Paul recalls – "George leaned over me and said, 'Super song, Paul.' Later Wix noticed that on the score George had written 'C'mon People', arranged by Paul McCartney and George Martin, 30 June 1962', which he'd then crossed out and changed to 1992! It was like a Freudian slip, he went right back…"[679]

Issued on March 1993 as a single from *Off the Ground*, "C'mon People" had poor sales. In the UK the song reached #41 in the charts, while in America failed to enter the *Billboard* Hot 100. "C'mon People" was part of the 1993 *New World Tour*. A killer version is on *Paul is Live!*

Musicians:

Paul McCartney vocals, backing vocals, piano, electric guitar, celeste, whistle • **Linda McCartney** backing vocals, Moog • **Hamish Stuart** backing vocals, bass • **Robbie McIntosh** acoustic and electric guitar • **Wix** synthesizer, congas • **Blair Cunningham** drums, congas • **Irvine Arditti, Alan Brind, Benedict Cruft, Miranda Fulleylove, Roger Garland, Roy Gillard, Pauline Lowbury, Rita Manning, David Ogden, Bernard Partridge, Jonathan Rees, Michael Rennie, Celia Sheen, Galina Solodchin, Barry Wilde, Donald Weekes, Jeremy Williams, David Woodcock** violin • **Roger Chase, Ken Essex, Andrew Parker, George Robertson, Graeme Scott, John Underwood** viola • **Robert Bailey, Paul Kegg, Ben Kennard, Anthony Pleeth, Roger Smith, Jonathan Williams** cello • **Paul Cullington, Chris Laurence** bass • **Skaila Kanga** harp • **Nicholas Busch, Frank Lloyd** horn • **Josephine Lively, Richard Morgan** oboe • **Martin Parry, Jane Pickles** flute • **Guy Barker, Derek Watkins** trumpet • **Tristan Fry, Terence Emery** percussion

---

[677] *Ibid.*
[678] *Club Sandwich*, n.65, Spring 1993, p.4.
[679] *Ibid.*

249 Cosmically Conscious (Paul McCartney)

Recording: December 9th, 1991-July, 1992 **Location:** Hog Hill Studio, Icklesham **Release:** February 1993, *Off the Ground*

McCartney's 1993 *New World Tour* was once again about getting back to the Sixties. Beatles material took over the stage with 18 out of 32 songs. The press was ready to go with the hype and so including a song on the record that was somehow connected to the Fab Four, could have been a good marketing move. In fact, McCartney had written "Cosmically Conscious" in Rishikesh in 1968 (or at least that's what he said)!

Thus Paul decided to dig out "Cosmically Conscious" for the *Off the Ground* sessions. At Hog Hill studio McCartney and the band worked on a psychedelic arrangement, full of vintage instruments such as harmonium and sitar.

With its powerful rhythm, the song captures the excitement and enjoyment of this unique recording. With its looped circus-like hook, the swirling bass and endless sound effects, "Cosmically Conscious" is a fun Beatles extravaganza. The *Off the Ground* album only features a snippet of the track – about one minute and a half – while the full version (4:39) appears on the "Off the Ground" cd-single.

McCartney played "Cosmically Conscious" live for the first time on April 4th, 2009 during the David Lynch Foundation benefit concert with Ringo Starr guesting on drums.

Musicians:

Paul McCartney vocals, acoustic guitar, sitar, ocarina • **Linda McCartney** backing vocals, harmonium • **Hamish Stuart** backing vocals, bass • **Robbie McIntosh** mandolin • **Wix** piano • **Blair Cunningham** drums

250 Big Boys Bickering (Paul McCartney)

Recording: December 9th, 1991-July, 1992 **Location:** Hog Hill Studio, Icklesham **Release:** December 1992, "Hope of Deliverance" cd-single

In March 1990 Paul and his band arrived in Tokyo, where they performed six concerts. It was Paul's first time back in Japan since his arrest there in January 1980. It wasn't easy re-visiting Tokyo after such an experience.

McCartney: "It was kind of exorcism (…) The first few nights we had strange dreams and screaming headaches."[680]

During that visit Paul wrote "Big Boys Bickering", his first protest song since "Give Ireland Back to the Irish": "Since then" – Paul said – "I've avoided them. You have to be very incensed to find the inspiration to do it right."[681]

---

[680] *Ibid*, p.69.
[681] *Ibid*.

The first chance to record the track came with the *Off the Ground* sessions. From listening to it, the track was probably recorded live in the studio with Paul on acoustic, Hamish on bass, Blair on drums, McIntosh on slide-guitar and Wix on accordion. A simply arranged country/folk song.

"Big Boys Bickering" deserves an honourable mention for its lyrics: Paul harshly attacks the corrupt political establishment and its pilfering ways. He even resorts to invective: the line "fuck it up for everyone" from the closing chorus owes a lot to Lennon, according to Paul.

McCartney: "I think there's a bit of John Lennon inspiration in this one. It's Lennonesque to my mind anyway. John wouldn't have thought twice about saying 'fuck' in a song."[682]

The song was immediately censored in the US where it was being promoted with a video. Included in the "Hope Of Deliverance" 12" single, the song deserved better exposure, but it was not included in the *Off the Ground* tracklist. During the concerts at the Ed Sullivan Theatre in December 1992 – only a month and a half before the album release – Paul had introduced "Big Boys Bickering" as a track taken from the new album.[683]

The track didn't make it onto the 1993 *New World Tour*, either. In *Paul Is Live!* just before playing "Biker Like an Icon", Wix hints at the song on his accordion but Paul jokingly says: "Not tonight!"

Musicians:

Paul McCartney vocals, acoustic guitar • **Linda McCartney** backing vocals, tambourine • **Hamish Stuart** backing vocals, bass • **Robbie McIntosh** backing vocals, slide guitar • **Wix** backing vocals, accordion • **Blair Cunningham** drums

251 Long Leather Coat (Paul and Linda McCartney)

Recording: December 9th, 1991-July, 1992 **Location:** Hog Hill Studio, Icklesham **Release:** December 1992, "Hope of Deliverance" single B-side

In the Spring of 1990, while on tour in the US, Paul commented to the press that he had composed several new songs, including one with Linda, after many years.

The song McCartney was probably referring to was "Long Leather Coat", a track whose outspoken animal rights lyrics surely suggest that Linda had a hand in writing them.

In the studio, Paul put together a hard-hitting anti-fur rocker. Over a pounding rhythm, the track is filled with many electric guitars grinding their teeth in a vast explosion of sonic distortion.

"Long Leather Coat" features a strong vocal performance by McCartney – treated with a limiter in the acappella intro – backed by some well-executed backing vocals, where Linda's voice can be heard clearly. The raw-edged lyrics depict man's cruel treatment of animals.

---

[682] *Ibid.*
[683] This could simply be an error of McCartney's who often forgets the contents of his albums or maybe the track was removed at the last minute from *Off the Ground.*

"Long Leather Coat" was relegated to the "Hope of Deliverance" cd-single and to the B-side of the 45. It would have been a nice addition to the 1993 *New World Tour* setlist.

Musicians:

Paul McCartney vocals, backing vocals, bass (?), electric guitar (?) • **Linda McCartney** backing vocals, tambourine (?) • **Hamish Stuart** backing vocals, electric guitar • **Robbie McIntosh** backing vocals, electric guitar • **Wix** keyboards, synthesizer • **Blair Cunningham** drums

252 Kicked Around No More (Paul McCartney)

Recording: December 9th, 1991-July, 1992 **Location**: Hog Hill Studio, Icklesham **Release**: December 1992, "Hope of Deliverance" cd-single

"Kicked Around No More" is another McCartney ballad, this time unusually featuring lyrics that exude disappointment.

The arrangement is very original. McCartney's piano chords, held up by a deep bass, give the song its unrelenting cadence and a cool-jazz mood.

Original sound textures are built around the minor 9th chords, while the syncopated rhythm guitars and McIntosh's solos give the song a jazzy feel. All this is tied together with a continuous drum-machine groove.

"Kicked Around No More" could have been a nice addition to *Off The Ground*: unfortunately, it ended up only as a filler track on the "Hope Of Deliverance" cd-single.

Musicians:

Paul McCartney vocals, backing vocals, piano, bass (?) • **Linda McCartney** backing vocals, keyboards (?) • **Hamish Stuart** backing vocals, bass (?), electric guitar (?) • **Robbie McIntosh** backing vocals, electric guitar • **Wix** keyboards • **Blair Cunningham** drums

253 Keep Coming Back to Love (Paul McCartney-Hamish Stuart)

Recording: December 9th, 1991-July, 1992 **Location**: Hog Hill Studio, Icklesham **Release**: February 1993, "C'Mon People" cd-single

McCartney: "Hamish Stuart is a really good soul singer and because he's in the group and he's a writer it was a natural thing to suggest, 'Why don't we try to write together?'"[684]

Although McCartney and Stuart had previously co-written some material (see "The First Stone" sheet 244), during the *Off the Ground* sessions their songwriting partnership became closer. McCartney: "We wrote a couple (together). I think our voices blend amazingly well together when we sing harmonies."[685]

The first of these two compositions was "Is It Raining In London?", an atmospheric ballad recorded at Abbey Road Studios with a grandiose orchestral arrangement by Angelo

---

[684] Home Video *Movin' On*, 1993.
[685] *Ibid.*

314

Badalamenti, unbelievably still unreleased.[686] A snippet of the sessions is included in the *Movin' On* documentary in 1993.

Badalamenti: "I got a call from his office saying that Paul wanted me to come to Abbey Road and work with him, doing an orchestral arrangement on one of his songs. It was just me and Paul with an orchestra… As we were rehearsing he stopped the orchestra and said, 'I must tell you the story'. He said, 'I was asked by the Queen to perform 35 minutes of my music to help celebrate her birthday at Buckingham Palace. Here comes the night and I'm about to go on. The Queen walks by and I said, 'I'm so glad that you invited me to perform!' She said, 'Oh, Mr. McCartney, I'm so sorry but I can't stay… Don't you see? It's five minutes to eight and I must go upstairs and watch "Twin Peaks"!' Paul turned around and punched me right on my arm… 'Because of your show, I could not perform for the Queen!"[687]

The second McCartney-Stuart song was "Keep Coming Back To Love". Paul explained that he had inadvertantly suggested the title to Hamish, when Stuart called him one day while driving in the car. Hamish said he lacked inspiration and Paul suggested to 'keep coming back to love'.

In the studio, the song was recorded as a duet and in fact, the blend of Paul and Hamish's soulful voice works perfectly. Hamish probably contributed some very R&B/funky sounding chords and riffs. The keyboard intro in particular recalls Ray Charles' "What'd I Say". Not included in *Off the Ground*, the song was released on the "C'mon People" cd-single.

Musicians:

Paul McCartney vocals, backing vocals, bass, electric piano (?) • **Linda McCartney** tambourine (?) • **Hamish Stuart** vocals, electric guitar • **Robbie McIntosh** electric guitar • **Wix** keyboards, piano (?) • **Blair Cunningham** drums

254 I Can't Imagine (Paul McCartney)

Recording: December 9th, 1991-July, 1992 **Location:** Hog Hill Studio, Icklesham **Release:** February 1993, "C'Mon People" single B-side

During the prolific *Off the Ground* sessions Paul also presented "I Can't Imagine", a melancholic love song arranged with a myriad of instruments.

The band worked admirably on this McCartney acoustic ballad. Most notable are McIntosh's Spanish guitar playing and Hamish Stuart's harmony vocals. Multiple echo effects were added to this Latin-tinged arrangement, making "I Can't Imagine" one of the finest tracks of the sessions. The song includes a psychedelic ending with percussion and electric guitar, an excerpt from a four minute instrumental called "On a Pedestal" (still unreleased), written in France during the same sojourn that inspired "I Owe It All To You".

---

[686] A note from MPL from 1992 gives the release of the song as a single at a later time (1996) and it was considered for inclusion on a solo album of Hamish Stuart.
[687] *Angelo Badalamenti Interview*, from the DVD *Secrets From Another Place*.

The song, released as the B-side to the "C'mon People" single and its 12", is yet another great McCartney flipside.

Musicians:

Paul McCartney vocals, backing vocals, bass, acoustic guitar (?), tambourine (?) • **Linda McCartney** backing vocals, tambourine (?) • **Hamish Stuart** backing vocals, electric guitar (?) • **Robbie McIntosh** backing vocals, electric guitar, Spanish Guitar • **Wix** keyboards, synthesizer • **Blair Cunningham** drums, percussion (?)

255 Down to the River (Paul McCartney)

Recording: December 9th, 1991-July, 1992 **Location**: Hog Hill Studio, Icklesham **Release**: February 1993, "C'Mon People" cd-single

McCartney's stylistic versatility would drive the band to crossover into many different genres during the sessions. They moved to Country and Western with "Down to the River", that had been played during the *Secret Gigs Tour* the previous summer. Probably McCartney himself had fun playing harmonica and the band – especially thanks to McIntosh's guitar and Wix's accordion – managed to give a care-free feel to the song. "Down to the River" was issued on the "Off the Ground" cd-mix.

Musicians:

Paul McCartney vocals, backing vocals, acoustic guitar, harmonica • **Linda McCartney** tambourine • **Hamish Stuart** backing vocals, bass • **Robbie McIntosh** acoustic and electric guitar • **Wix** accordion, piano (?) • **Blair Cunningham** drums

256 Style, Style (Paul McCartney)

Recording: December 9th, 1991-July, 1992 **Location**: Hog Hill Studio, Icklesham **Release** (US only): April 1993, "Off the Ground" cd-single

Within McCartney's body of work during the *Off the Ground* sessions, he and his band found room for "Style, Style" a lengthy, sort of modern-rock track with an ethereal chorus. It was probably inspired by Linda ("She's got an American accent/From head to the toes") and lyrically speaking, should have received more care than it did: the main character could have been named, something McCartney in his long solo career often neglected to do.

"Style Style" was carefully arranged and was crowded with instruments; McIntosh recorded several guitar parts – with some aggressive solos "played backwards"[688] and a variety of riffs – and Cunningham contributed some strong drumming. The song appears on the "Off the Ground" cd-mix.

Musicians:

---

[688] Robbie McIntosh, in *PaulMcCartney.fm*, March 2002, n.2, p.26.

Paul McCartney vocals, backing vocals, acoustic guitar (?), bass • **Linda McCartney** backing vocals, tambourine (?) • **Hamish Stuart** backing vocals, electric guitar (?) • **Robbie McIntosh** backing vocals, acoustic and electric guitar • **Wix** backing vocals, keyboards, piano (?) • **Blair Cunningham** drums

257 Sweet, Sweet Memories (Paul McCartney)

Recording: December 9th, 1991-July, 1992 **Location:** Hog Hill Studio, Icklesham **Release** (US only): April 1993, "Off the Ground" cd-single

"Sweet Sweet Memories" once again confirms the self-confident approach of McCartney and his band to different musical styles. For this recording – in the purest Beatles tradition – McCartney came up with a shifting, melodic bass part.

The track is full of references to all the typical Beatles' trademarks, from the whole band's vocals – that recall the fade-out of "You Never Give Me Your Money" – to the psychedelic-flavored guitars and keyboards. The song found its place on the "Off the Ground" cd single.

Musicians:

Paul McCartney vocals, backing vocals, bass • **Linda McCartney** backing vocals, tambourine • **Hamish Stuart** backing vocals, electric guitar • **Robbie McIntosh** backing vocals, electric guitar • **Wix** backing vocals, keyboards • **Blair Cunningham** drums

258 Soggy Noodle (Paul McCartney)

Recording: December 9th, 1991-July, 1992 **Location:** Hog Hill Studio, Icklesham **Release** (US only): April 1993, "Off the Ground" cd-single

This brief vamp released on the "Off the Ground" cd-single is basically McCartney messing about on electric guitar for a few seconds, with a hint at "I Owe It All to You". This snippet is also the opening to the *Off the Ground* video-clip.

Musicians:

Paul McCartney electric guitar

On his own in his home studio, McCartney had George Martin produce two of his best acoustic tracks. A third, "When Winter Comes" has never been released.

259 Calico Skies (Paul McCartney)

Recording: September 3rd, 1992 **Location:** Hog Hill Studio, Icklesham **Release:** May 1997, *Flaming Pie*

During their annual trip to visit family relatives in Arizona in August 1991, the McCartneys ran into Hurricane Bob. They had a total blackout at their house.

McCartney: "The hurricane knocked out all the power; it was all candle-light, cooking on a woodfire..."[689]

---

[689] *Flaming Pie* booklet.

This intimate and primal situation inspired Paul to write "Calico Skies", a delicate acoustic watercolour of celestial hues. "Calico Skies" is a simple folk song – featuring the typical McCartney's finger-picking style –recorded and produced in a single session.

This love song ("that became a sixties protest song", in McCartney's words) depicts Paul's unchanging love for Linda as something inevitable that marks you forever, a solid many-faceted love that can resist everything. McCartney describes his destiny of loving Linda with very touching words.

The song was released several years later on *Flaming Pie* (1997). McCartney thought to include the track in his 2002 *Drivin' USA Tour* but as happens "in rehearsals certain numbers just oust others."[690] Thus, "Calico Skies" was performed only during soundchecks but starting from the Japanese dates in November 2002 the song was added to the setlist. It was then included in the live album *Back in the World*, in a folksy arrangement featuring acoustic guitars, acoustic bass, accordion and drums.

"Calico Skies" has been played live during the 2007 *Memory Almost Full Promo Tour* (the song was performed on October 25th, 2007 at the Roundhouse in London with a real string section) and in 2008-09 shows. A version recorded at Citi Field in New York on July 17th, 2009 is included in *Good Evening New York City*. A version for orchestra is on *Working Classical*.

Musicians:

Paul McCartney vocals, acoustic guitar, percussion

260 Great Day (Paul McCartney)

Recording: September 3rd, 1992 **Location:** Hog Hill Studio, Icklesham **Release:** May 1997, *Flaming Pie*

On that dark night on Long Island hugging his acoustic guitar, Paul's memory took him back twenty years. "Great Day" dates back to the *RAM* period (see **1970**) and was one of those little ditties that McCartney sang occasionally while "sitting around the kitchen or when the children were dancing", as he put it.

Another simple finger-picking acoustic track, "Great Day" was recorded without any bells or whistles. Lead vocal, acoustic guitar and some knee percussion was all it took. The song popped up again five years later when McCartney was looking for something short and simple to close *Flaming Pie*. A possible source of inspiration for this song was provided to McCartney by the well-known song "(It's Gonna Be a) Great Day" – performed among others by American singer and entertainer Frances Langford in 1948 – since the melody vaguely recalls this tune. A sort of ghost track, naked and basic. To McCartney's attentive fans, the similarity of melody to "Big Barn Bed" did not go unnoticed. McCartney performed it in September 2003 in Los Angeles, at the annual charity concert for the *Adopt a Minefield* campaign.

---

[690] *Interview with Jody Denberg*, 2002.

Musicians:

Paul McCartney vocals, acoustic guitar, percussion • **Linda McCartney** vocals

Shortly thereafter, McCartney began work on a very eccentric and unusual project that he released under the pseudonym of the Fireman, easliy unmasked. In a four-day session in early October, McCartney worked with Martin Glover, ex-bass player of Killing Joke (he too, used a pseudonym, Youth) to create broken down, dance re-mixes of the *Off the Ground* tracks. Chris Potter engineered the project and Matt Austin was programmer. McCartney also took part playing bass, banjo and flute on some tracks The resulting *Strawberries Oceans Ships Forest* was made into nine re-mixes all from the same single track!

261-262-263-264-265-266-267-268-269 Transpiritual Stomp, Trans Lunar Rising, Transcrystaline, Pure Trance, Arizona Light, Celtic Stomp, Strawberries Oceans Ships Forest, 444, Sunrise Mix (The Fireman)

Recording: October 7th-10th, 1992 **Location**: Hog Hill Studio, Icklesham **Release**: November 1993, *Strawberries Oceans Ships Forest*

The *Strawberries Oceans Ships Forest* project was the strangest McCartney had ever put together. Youth pushed him in that direction: Paul wanted some remixes of the *Off the Ground* tracks but Glover had the idea to work a little bit on them, building something completely new.[691] McCartney accepted the plan, excited by the idea of going back to his roots: after all, in the Beatles days, he was the first who tried experimenting with tape-loops and different sounds. Paul had a lot of fun during the sessions and managed to record some of the parts.

Glover: "Then we'd start jamming. Paul playing most of it and I'd occasionally get on the bass (…). He's got an amazing studio (…) He's got Mellotron. He's got Bill Black double-bass. So we'd just go, 'Let's put some of that on and let's do some of this.'"[692]

In the end they came up with a fair amount of techno-dance, full of odd bits, including samples of "Reception" or "Broadcast" – both from *Back to the Egg* – and even "Boys, Boys, Boys" by Italian singer Sabrina. All the tracks were released on The Fireman's double-LP *Strawberries Oceans Ships Forest*.

Musicians:

Paul McCartney banjo, flute, double-bass • **Martin Glover** bass

---

[691] I. Peel, *cit.*, p.131.
[692] *Ibid.*

1993

In January, Paul reunited the band in his Sussex studio, where they rehearsed for the *New World Tour* that would start in February.

By then, McCartney's band was working like clockwork, and Paul prepared an almost entirely new show, that would have included some other Beatles' classics not performed in the 1989/90 *Paul McCartney World Tour* ("Michelle" and "Penny Lane" to name but two) as well as new songs.

A taster of the upcoming show took place on December 10th and 11th, 1992 at the Ed Sullivan Theatre for a program called *Up Close*. During one of his best live performances, McCartney launched into twenty songs, half of which were taken from the unreleased (at the time) *Off the Ground*. Paul recalled that it was curious to see the audience's reaction to new songs they had never heard before.

At the end of January, it was *Off the Ground*'s turn. The album was previewed by the single "Hope of Deliverance" and was heavily promoted by McCartney.

Billboard gave the album a three and a half star rating: "*Off the Ground* contains some fine songs and sustains a guardedly optimistic mood that conveys a faith in the future (…) It's a tad undercooked – a soufflé that doesn't quite rise to the grand heights its creator envisioned." Despite favorable critics and reviews, the album did not enter the Top Ten in the US, stopping at #17. It was in any case the best chart position for McCartney since 1983, except for *Unplugged*.

In the UK, the album reached #3, but critics were not so favorably disposed. McCartney was considered as "out of this world": a somewhat strange reaction to an album that contained some of the most raging and biting lyrics of Paul's career. The tour that followed was launched on March 5th in Perth, Australia – after some warm-up European dates in Milan on February 18th-19th and Frankfurt on 22nd-23rd – and seemed to be a scaled-down version of the previous *Paul McCartney World Tour*. The tour was shorter, with 79 venues instead of 102 and the show was mainly a tribute to The Beatles' splendor, rather than offering new music.

The show was surely above average, although McCartney's new material was surprisingly limited to a very few numbers. Paul played no more than six tracks from *Off the Ground* each night, whereas he performed nine at the Ed Sullivan concerts – the soundchecks were more appealing and offered alternate setlists – and the concert was almost entirely missing Wings songs. Paul was determined to recover The Beatles' legacy.

Anyway, the show was welcomed with great enthusiasm everywhere. Here's the setlist-matrix:

"Drive My Car" – "Coming Up" – "Get out of My Way" – "Another Day" – "All My Loving" – "Let Me Roll It" – "Peace in the Neighbourhood" – "Off the Ground" – "I Wanna Be Your

Man" – "Robbie's Bit" (a guitar instrumental by McIntosh) – "Good Rockin' Tonight" – "We Can Work It Out" – "And I Love Her" – "Every Night" – "Hope of Deliverance" – "Michelle" – "Biker Like an Icon" – "Here, There and Everywhere" – "Yesterday" – "My Love" – "Lady Madonna" – "Live and Let Die" – "Let It Be" – "Magical Mystery Tour" – "The Long and Winding Road" – "C'mon People" – "Paperback Writer" – "Fixing a Hole" – "Penny Lane" – "Sgt. Pepper's…" – "Band on the Run" – "I Saw Her Standing There" – "Hey Jude".

Very few changes were made to this set. From March 20th "Can't Buy Me Love" replaced "I Wanna Be Your Man"; from April 14th "Get Out of My Way" was substituted with "Looking for Changes" and special songs were played at some venues ("Mull of Kintyre" in Australia and Canada, "Mother Nature's Son" at the Hollywood Bowl, "O' Sole Mio" in Florence). Some slight variations were introduced from September 3rd: "Jet", "I Lost My Little Girl", "Ain't No Sunshine" and "Back in the USSR" replaced "Another Day", "And I Love Her", "Every Night" and "Fixing a Hole".

While the tour was coming to an end with the South-American venues, in November another live album was released, the third over a period of four years.

It came as no surprise that the double LP, called *Paul Is Live!* – on whose cover McCartney was photographed on the famous Abbey Road zebra-crossing along with his dog Arrow – would chalk up one little negative record after another: #34 in the UK charts and #78 in the US meant respectively the first time out of the UK Top Ten in Paul's solo career and his lowest-ever chart position on *Billboard*.

In America, the album sold poorly, with only 250.000 copies in its first six months: a real disappointment, that could certainly not be softened by the clever marketing gimmick used for the cover artwork, a hint at the *Abbey Road* one and at the *Paul Is Dead* hoax.

Furthermore, the album was professionally out of any context. The LP sounded perfect but was nevertheless redundant, and left all McCartney's fans with a bitter taste. Due to the double – instead of triple – LP format, the original setlist was shuffled and heavily cut. Tracks like "Another Day", "Off the Ground" or "Get Out of My Way" were left off the album, thus making it not very desirable to Paul's solo career fans.

270 Hotel in Benidorm (Paul McCartney)

Recording: May 26th, 1993 **Location:** Folsom Field, Boulder **Release:** November 1993, *Paul Is Live!*

As usual during soundchecks, Paul and the band enjoyed launching into jams – often lengthy instrumentals – as a warm-up.

Sometimes, starting from a rough idea, jams could turn into real songs. "Hotel in Benidorm" is one of them.

Recorded during the Boulder soundcheck (and later released on *Paul Is Live!*) the song – inspired by Paul's holiday there in 1972 – came out while the band was toying with the acoustic instrumentation. It was conceived as a Latin-flavored track, with nice acoustic guitar solos by McIntosh, while McCartney sang some made-on-the-spot lyrics, inspired by an unfinished hotel in Benidorm, the well-known holiday resort.

Musicians:

Paul McCartney vocals, acoustic guitar • **Linda McCartney** tambourine • **Hamish Stuart** bass • **Robbie McIntosh** acoustic guitar • **Wix** accordion • **Blair Cunningham** drums

271 A Fine Day (Paul McCartney)

Recording: June 11th, 1993 **Location:** Giants Stadium, East Rutherford **Release:** November 1993, *Paul Is Live!*

The second track taken from a *New World Tour* soundcheck to be included in *Paul Is Live!* "A Fine Day" is another improvisation that shows how Paul's good ideas could be preserved in their best shape as long as they weren't brooded over too much.

"A Fine Day" is a spontaneous rock track, built only on two chords and with some great slide-guitar work by Robbie McIntosh throughout: some slight studio work, a bit of overdubbing and the addition of a middle eight, would have made it worthy of inclusion in an album in a more conventional form.

Musicians:

Paul McCartney vocals, bass (?), electric guitar (?) • **Linda McCartney** keyboards • **Hamish Stuart** bass (?), electric guitar (?) • **Robbie McIntosh** slide guitar • **Wix** piano • **Blair Cunningham** drums

Simultaneously to *Paul Is Live!* McCartney released the album *Strawberries Oceans Ships Forest*, under the pseudonym The Fireman. Within a few weeks, the real identity of the artist was discovered by hard-core fans, who were among the small group that bought the few copies of the double LP…

1994

Paul gave himself a break during this year, except for some demo recordings ("Higgy Baggers Guitar Course" and "Someone Rockin' My..."). Also, he started writing *Standing Stone*, his second classical work. Based on a poem written by Paul himself, it was commissioned to McCartney for the EMI 100th Anniversary, to be celebrated in 1997.

Highlights of the year were indeed the new recordings with George Harrison and Ringo Starr. To launch The Beatles' *Anthology* project – a collection of unreleased recordings from the group's whole career – in February the 'Threetles' (as they were renamed) went back in studio together to complete some unfinished songs by John Lennon.

Over John's demos, Paul, Ringo and George overdubbed their instruments and vocals. Two of these recordings, "Free as a Bird" and "Real Love" were issued as singles respectively in November 1995 and in March 1996.

McCartney: "We just started listening to the cassette, which was just a mono cassette with John's voice and his piano locked in. Anyone who knows anything about recording knows that, for a mix, you try to isolate the voice and the piano on separate tracks to give yourself a bit of control. But we had a fixed tape. First of all, George and I tried to put some acoustics on, and play along with it as it stood, because we wanted to be as faithful as possible to the original. But because he was doing a demo John went out of time a bit."

Jeff Lynne worked on the demo, putting it in time and cleaning it up. Paul: "Once that had been done we were able to play with it because John was now perfectly in time and there were just little gaps where he'd sped up or gone out a bit. After that we did acoustic guitars and I learned John's piano part. I'd been studying it a little bit the week before we did the session, and Jeff Lynne had studied it very hard and showed me one or two interesting little variations that John had put in there, that I hadn't picked up (...) Then I put the bass on, which I kept very, very simple: I didn't want to do any of my trademark swoops or get it too melodic, I just wanted to anchor the piece. I did one or two little tricks but they're very subtle, like I used my five-string bass, which has got a very low string on it, and saved the low string till the tune does a big key change in the solo, and it really lifts off there. So instead of doing the same bass note I went right down to my second lowest note on the instrument." The following McCartney's statement sums up the experience: "The only recording session I've ever written about was 'Free as a Bird'. It was an exciting week and shortly afterwards I went on holiday to America. On the plane I wrote down what had gone on at the session. Just to remember the facts really, before they were forgotten."

1995

After "Free as a Bird", Paul and Yoko Ono seemed to get closer. In January, McCartney invited Yoko and Sean Lennon to Sussex and all together with Paul's family they even recorded a track called "Hiroshima Sky Is Always Blue", in memory of the event of the atomic bombs fifty years before.

Just after he finished "Real Love", McCartney got together again with Steve Miller, blues guitarist and Steve Miller Band leader, for the first time after 25 years. On May 9th 1969, the two had recorded the track "My Dark Hour" at Olympic Studios when Paul walked into the studio after a Beatles' mixing session had ended abruptly due to an argument: McCartney refused to sign a contract to appoint Allen Klein as Apple's financial manager.

The first McCartney-Miller sessions were held in February in the US, both in Miller's personal studio and then in Seattle; in May, recordings resumed at Paul's home studio in Sussex. Six tracks were recorded and two of them, "Soul Boy" and "(Sweet Home) Country Girl", still remain unreleased.

272 Young Boy (Paul McCartney)

Recording: February 22nd and March 21st-22nd (overdubs), 1995 **Location:** Steve Miller Studio, Sun Valley and Hog Hill Studio (overdubs), Icklesham **Release:** April 1997, single (from *Flaming Pie*)

McCartney composed "Young Boy" on August 18th, 1994: "That was another written against the clock. I wrote it in the time it took Linda to cook a lunch for a feature in *The New York Times*. I had taken my guitar and was sitting around in a nearby room when a song came up... It started to be, 'It's just a poor boy, looking for a way to find love...' But it reminded me of an old Elvis song (...) So I thought 'Young Boy'. I liked the words better. I started making up this song just thinking about all the young people I know who are starting off on a romance (...) I remember well enough myself... 'Is there somebody out for me? How am I ever going to meet her?' I was perplexed at that age! I called up Steve Miller and said, 'I've got a song and I think we could do it great!' Working with Steve again was like falling back into an old habit."[693]

As soon as he arrived with Geoff Emerick at Miller's studio in Idaho, Paul presented "Young Boy", an acoustic track in C major with simple chords. The basic track was laid down with Paul on drums and Steve on guitar.

Frank Farrell, an American sound engineer that conducted the session in Steve Miller's studio, recalls: "It was unique the way we did it (actually, it's the way McCartney records his drum parts – author's note). We had a drum-machine there and Paul laid down a pattern that I

---

[693] *Flaming Pie* booklet.

recorded. That was the basic groove pattern. Then Paul did cymbal crashes and all the sweetening, like tom rolls. It was a combination of those two parts." [694]

Overdubs would follow: McCartney added his Wal bass and a Hammond organ, Miller recorded the electric guitar solos and together the two laid down a bed of acoustic guitars.

The recording went as quickly as possible for a very particular reason: "Steve was anxious to have Paul come in" – Farrell reveals – "He was a bit nervous and he wanted everything to go absolutely perfect... Steve's idea was to sing and play for Paul and then he was hoping there would be time to have Paul play and sing one of his songs... After one session, when Paul and Linda went out to their cottage, Steve said, 'We're going to stay up all night and we're going to finish that so we can move up to my stuff.' We had recorded from nine to five and Steve worked until four in the morning putting down the solo! We built that up adding six guitar parts, and lots of harmony parts. We also did all the vocal harmonies that night! But Paul wanted to concentrate on his own stuff."[695]

Farrell reveals also how Paul wanted to get the acoustic guitar sound: "Steve's studio has got a top part, sort of an open control room and downstairs all the different rooms for the recordings, that I set up for the session. The way you can get down to the basement is either a stairway or a cesar lift. Paul said, 'I love this room!' and we recorded the guitars in the control room where that cesar lift was... In that room there was no cabling, so I had to quickly grab the two mikes that I set up and put them in there and we recorded it, just like that!" [696]

Definitely one of McCartney's catchiest songs, "Young Boy" – although a less refined production than others – is nonetheless spontaneous and in the moment. It turned out to be a lovely, rustic folk single with Miller's guitar solo (in typical McCartney style!) drawing in the listener and a mid-tempo finale where the organ part pays homage to the classic "A Whiter Shade of Pale" by Procol Harum. "Young Boy" was released in April 1997 as the lead single from *Flaming Pie*: it was McCartney's first new record since January 1993.

After a four-year wait, most critics found the song too lightweight but "Young Boy" can be best appreciated in the context of *Flaming Pie*: its comforting chords introduce a positive mood in stark contrast to the dramatic "Somedays". Sales were not sensational but the track got good airplay and it achieved the best chart position in the UK since "My Brave Face", reaching #19.

McCartney played the song with his guitar on the rooftop of the MPL building at 1 Soho Square, London on April, 1997. When told that there was a crowd on the streets listening to him, Paul replied: "I know, I've done it before."

Musicians:

---

[694] Interview courtesy of Frank Farrell, 01/08/2012.
[695] *Ibid.*
[696] *Ibid.*

Paul McCartney vocals, drums, bass, acoustic guitar, Hammond organ • Steve Miller backing vocals, electric and acoustic guitar

273 Broomstick (Paul McCartney)

Recording: May 4th, 1995 **Location:** Hog Hill Studio, Icklesham **Release:** April 1997, "Young Boy" cd-single 2

In the studio, McCartney and Miller got more familiar with each other through some classic blues with two tracks: "Used to Be Bad" – recorded the next day, see sheet 274 – and "Broomstick", an acoustic blues number in the vein of Harrison's "For You Blue". Once again, Miller's guitar work – this time in a country style – stands out, played over a bed of instruments mostly handled by McCartney which included his drumming – full of breaks and syncopation. A funny track, released on the second cd-single of "Young Boy".

Musicians:

Paul McCartney vocals, backing vocals, drums, acoustic bass, acoustic guitar, organ, piano, percussion, sound effects • Steve Miller electric and acoustic guitar

274 Used to Be Bad (Paul McCartney-Steve Miller)

Recording: May 5th, 1995 **Location:** Hog Hill Studio, Icklesham **Release:** May 1997, *Flaming Pie*

The following day at Hog Hill Steve Miller suggested some real blues to Paul. So he got into the studio, bringing a load of guitar riffs, as McCartney reveals: "Steve whacked out these blues riffs, I got on the drums and we just went for it. We did the vocal in one take."[697]

That jam turned into a song when Miller started singing some typical blues lines into his mike. Paul and Steve were sharing the same microphone and recorded the vocal.

McCartney was amused when he looked at Miller's technique for his vocals before the recording: "He's got a vocal warm-up technique! We'd make fun of him (…) I'll tell you who I saw doing that once: Jagger! That really gave the game away for me – Jagger doing vocal warm-ups! Anyway…"[698]

With bass (Paul used Fender Jazz this time) and rhythm guitar overdubs done, the song became the closest thing to a 'dirty blues' in all of McCartney's discography, but mostly thanks to Miller's wailing voice. McCartney is no bluesman and this foray into this less familiar musical style confirms it. This duet appears on *Flaming Pie* and also appears as the B-side to the single "The World Tonight" (UK).

Musicians:

Paul McCartney vocals, drums, bass • Steve Miller vocals, electric guitar

---

[697] *Flaming Pie* booklet.
[698] *Meet the New Paul McCartney*, in *Q Magazine*, 1997.

275 If You Wanna (Paul McCartney)

Recording: May 11th, 1995 **Location:** Hog Hill Studio, Icklesham **Release:** May 1997, *Flaming Pie*

Paul wrote "If You Wanna" when he was in Minneapolis during the American Tour in 1993. On a day-off – that would put the composition of the song somewhere between May 24th and 26th, 1993 – stuck in a skyscraper for hours, on end McCartney fought-off his boredom by directing his creative energies towards a new composition.

"I wanted to write something that would reflect America" – Paul said – "For when you're driving across the desert on that big road with the flat horizon."[699] McCartney came up with a typical 'driving across America' kind-of song and the version recorded with Miller nails it. McCartney grabbed his 12-string while Miller sumptuously accompanied him with some Knopfler-esque guitar playing, to produce a perfect West Coast sound. McCartney also played drums, Ernie Ball Axis electric guitar and Wal bass. "If You Wanna" is as unstoppable as the Cadillac in the narrative and is highlighted by some beautiful vocal harmonies from Miller. A curious detail: listening carefully, you can hear some strange "beep" that pop up throughout the song (precisely at 0:16, 0:23, 1:09, 1:16, 3:43 and 3:50). The track is included in *Flaming Pie*.

Musicians:

Paul McCartney vocals, drums, bass, electric guitar, 12-string acoustic guitar • **Steve Miller** vocal harmonies, electric and acoustic guitar

While in the midst of the recordings with Steve Miller, McCartney was active on many fronts. First, on March 23rd with his appearance at St. James Palace in London (a benefit concert for the Royal College of Music) and then with his radio show *Oobu Joobu* airing weekly for two months on Radio Westwood One. The London concert was another special night for Paul. In front of the Prince of Wales Charles, he premiered his newly written classical piano piece, "A Leaf" – performed by young Russian pianist Anya Alexeyev – and performed some tracks with Elvis Costello ("One After 909", "Mistress and Maid") or accompanied by the Brodsky Quartet ("For No-One" –"Eleanor Rigby" – "Yesterday" – "Lady Madonna").

The *Oobu Joobu* project dates to the Seventies when Paul had the idea to do a radio show based on a character by Alfred Jarry[700], "Monsieur Ubu". The show was conceived as a musical container including unreleased tracks, new songs either played live or taken from soundchecks along with selections of Paul's favorite music. Special guests like Chet Atkins or Carl Perkins appeared in various episodes all hosted by McCartney and including all kinds of weird goings-on that kept it all very exciting: the "Oobu Joobu" jingle itself was a real hit, done in at least half a dozen different versions.

---

[699] *Flaming Pie* booklet.
[700] Alfred Jarry is the inventor of pataphysics. Paul mentioned him in "Maxwell's Silver Hammer" (1969, *Abbey Road*).

Meanwhile, on May 1st McCartney recorded the instrumental track "Stella May Day", that he composed as a background to a fashion show of his daughter Stella; after that – first with a session on May 18th, then with two more working days in the studio, on November 18th and 19th – he committed to tape the song "Whole Life" along with Dave Stewart (Eurythmics). The track would see the light of day in 2003, though as a new recording.

In November, McCartney returned to more conventional projects and in his studio in Sussex he taped the song "Somedays". After a few days, he started a new batch of sessions for *Flaming Pie* with the help of Jeff Lynne.

Two years earlier when Harrison insisted on using Jeff Lynne to produce "Free as a Bird", McCartney had bristled, only to change his mind after the recording was completed. The collaboration was successful, and McCartney scheduled the Electric Light Orchestra ex-leader for some new recordings. Between November 1995 and February 1996 McCartney and Lynne worked hard, producing and recording together five tracks that would later be issued on *Flaming Pie*.

276 Somedays (Paul McCartney)

Recording: November 1st-3rd, 1995 and June 10th (overdubs), 1996 **Location:** Hog Hill Studio, Icklesham and AIR Lyndhusrt Studio (overdubs), London **Release:** May 1997, *Flaming Pie*

On March 18th 1994, having accompanied Linda to a photo session for one of her cookbooks, Paul found himself with time to kill and a guitar at hand. It took him a couple of hours (until Linda's return) to write one of the most amazing songs in his career. McCartney: "When she'd finished and would say: 'Did you get bored? What did you do?' I said, 'Oh, I wrote this song. Wanna hear it?'"[701]

"Somedays" is the most outstanding song on *Flaming Pie*; and manages to capture the sense of how Paul's love for Linda was predestined. The lyrics would soon seem like a terrible premonition when a few months later, McCartney's wife would be diagnosed with breast cancer; a fact that would cast a shadow of hopelessness and anguish over them.

Paul's lyrics deal with the magic of love and the poignancy of nostalgia for one's youth that escapes into the distance leaving only a bittersweet yet healing smile on your lips.

McCartney's performance – only with vocals and acoustic guitar – was captured in a single take. During the overdubs, McCartney himself added his 5-string Wal bass and a short solo on Spanish guitar (McCartney had bought it in Australia on suggestion by guitarist John Williams) playing call-and-response notes that sound like falling tears. The word "mine" as sung during the last verse is one of the most touching moments in McCartney's career.

---

701 *Flaming Pie* booklet.

"Somedays" was embellished with something special: McCartney got George Martin to hear the song, asking him for an orchestral arrangement.

Martin was enthusiastic about it: "You haven't lost your touch!" He then prepared a magnificent orchestral score in a eighteenth-century fashion, reminiscent of The Beatles' "For No-One" – an harpsichord part is not credited in the booklet but was played by Paul according to *Club Sandwich* – that exquisitely enhances a real McCartney classic. In particular, the relentless march of a military drum is suggestive of our implacable destiny and its inescapable occurrences.

The orchestra was conducted by David Snell and that percussion part was played by Gary Kettel. He recalls: "George Martin contacted me. Over the years I had done a few things with him and Paul... I had previously played tympani on 'We All Stand Together'. McCartney in a way was in awe of George Martin but Paul always knew what he wanted. He made suggestions like 'more crescendo' even though he's not an academically trained musician. He would let the musicians have their say and was very open to suggestions. I played a military drum together with a small chamber orchestra. I remember that it came out really nice... We played some nice music which, as free-lance players, is not always the case!"[702]

Kettel has a good story to tell about McCartney: "I was walking out from Abbey Road Studios after a recording and I was waiting to cross. A car stopped to let me go and the passenger window in the front went down and a voice said, 'What are you doing on my crossing?' It was Paul!"[703] A rough-mix of "Somedays", containing an extra verse, was included in a *Flaming Pie* promotional tape, circulated on January 30th, 1997. The track is on *Flaming Pie*, while *Working Classical* features a version for strings only.

Musicians:

Paul McCartney vocals, acoustic guitar, Spanish guitar, bass, harpsichord • **Keith Pascoe, Jackie Hartley, Rita Manning, Peter Manning** violin • **Christian Kampen, Martin Loveday** cello • **Peter Lale, Levine Andrade** viola • **Andy Findon** alto flute • **Martin Parry, Michael Cox** flute • **Gary Kettel** percussion • **Skaila Kanga** harp • **Roy Carter** oboe, english horn

277 The Song We Were Singing (Paul McCartney)

Recording: November 6th-10th, 1995 **Location:** Hog Hill Studio, Icklesham **Release:** May 1997, *Flaming Pie*

Paul composed "The Song We Were Singing" during his holiday in Jamaica in January 1995, the same that would produce "Souvenir" (see sheet 280). This time, the track was inspired by the memories that – more than anything else – linked Paul to John: songs.

---

702 Interview courtesy of Gary Kettel, 11/12/2011.
703 *Ibid.*

McCartney: "I was remembering the Sixties; sitting around late at night, dossing, smoking pipes, drinking wine, talking about the cosmic solution."[704]

"The Song We Were Singing" was built entirely on acoustic instruments – there's no drums – and Paul played Bill Black's Kay double bass. Many Lennon's references are scattered throughout the song, from the guitar sound to the oriental-style modulations of McCartney's vocals.

The basic track was recorded by McCartney in a gentle mood: only his almost whispered singing and a soft acoustic guitar arpeggio. Paul sings the powerful chorus with passionate strength. The song is the *Flaming Pie* opening track.

Musicians:

Paul McCartney vocals, vocal harmonies, acoustic guitar, bass, double-bass, electric guitar, harmonium • **Jeff Lynne** vocal harmonies, acoustic and electric guitar, keyboards

278 The World Tonight (Paul McCartney)

Recording: November 13th-17th, 1995 **Location:** Hog Hill Studio, Icklesham **Release:** May 1997, *Flaming Pie*

McCartney wrote "The World Tonight" while on holiday in America in August 1995. As usual, it all happened by chance: "The lyrics were just gathering thoughts" – McCartney said – "Like 'I go back so far/I'm in front of me'. I don't know where that came from, but if I'd been writing with John, he would have gone, 'Ok, leave that one.'"[705]

The song contained references to the stressful life of a superstar, a social status that McCartney always refused. Paul gave to Jeff Lynne an entirely acoustic demo. Lynne took it from there to add layers of instrumentation turning "The World Tonight" into a Travelling Wilburys-style song. To the main guitar riff – which has echoes of songs like "Letting Go" or even "Let Me Roll It" – Lynne added his typical production feel: a 12-string guitar bed and some heavy drums. The result was a melodic rock track, particularly suitable for the US market and radios. For the occasion, McCartney employed his Hofner bass.

In an attempt to climb the American charts with the kind of modern rock song that was being programmed on radio at the time, "The World Tonight" was chosen as the first single from *Flaming Pie* as opposed to the more lightweight "Young Boy", launched as an opener in the rest of the world. The song got some excellent airplay, but chart results were unremarkable: in the US, "The World Tonight" reached only #64. Maybe Paul was hoping for a Top Forty, since the track was included in the soundtrack of the movie *A Father's Day*. In the UK, where it was launched as the second single, the track reached #23.

---

[704] *Flaming Pie* booklet.
[705] *Ibid.*

A Father's Day's soundtrack includes an alternate mix of "The World Tonight" that cannot be found anywhere else.

Musicians:

Paul McCartney vocals, vocal harmonies, acoustic guitar, bass, piano, drums, electric guitar, percussion • **Jeff Lynne** vocal harmonies, acoustic guitar, electric guitar, keyboards

279 Little Willow (Paul McCartney)

Recording: November 21st, 1995 **Location:** Hog Hill Studio, Icklesham **Release:** May 1997, *Flaming Pie*

Composed by McCartney in February, after he learnt of the death of Maureen Cox (ex-wife of Ringo Starr) , "Little Willow" is a song whose hopeful lyrics try to eschew the pain.

Paul did not intend to celebrate the sadness of that loss but to express something positive: "I wanted to somehow convey how much I thought of her. For her and her kids."[706]

McCartney brought into the studio a gentle, acoustic song and the subject of death is expressed in "Little Willow" by way of a very effective arrangement.

McCartney and Lynne combined vocals, harpsichords and even an electric spinet to portray an angelic choir, which surrounds Paul's clean vocals, set in a cobweb of acoustic guitar arpeggios.

The song is included in *Flaming Pie* and it was later donated to the charity album *Diana: Princess of Wales* released as tribute to Princess Diana, who tragically passed away in August 1997.

Musicians:

Paul McCartney vocals, backing vocals, acoustic guitar, Spanish guitar, bass, piano, electric guitar, harmonium, harpsichord, Mellotron, percussion • **Jeff Lynne** backing vocals, electric spinet, harpsichord

---

[706] *Ibid.*

1996

280 **Souvenir** (Paul McCartney)

Recording: February 19th, 1996 **Location:** Hog Hill Studio, Icklesham **Release:** May 1997, *Flaming Pie*

In the case of "Souvenir", McCartney's muse once again inspired him during a vacation in Jamaica in January 1995.

Paul played the original demo for Jeff Lynne with the intention of preserving its atmosphere which "carried the additional sounds of a ringing telephone and a tropical downpour."[707]

And so the cassette demo was utilized as a guide track for the recording. McCartney and Lynne's collaboration resulted in one of the best songs on *Flaming Pie*. This is the most accomplished R&B song ever written by McCartney. A "Wilson Pickett number" – with shades of Al Green, thanks to the song's similarity to "How Can You Mend A Broken Heart?" – where the looped electric guitar riff sustains a heartfelt vocal performance.

Jeff Lynne: "It was one of those little acoustic demos, done in Jamaica or somewhere. It was much more bluesy. I wanted to go for an R&B kind of thing, and so did Paul. I think it came off as that."[708] McCartney played both Hofner and Wal bass guitars in the song.

"Souvenir" was filled with a strong horn arrangement, overdubbed later. Chris "Snake" Davis played sax: "That was a very exciting session, done at Paul's studio in Sussex. It was also a lot of fun… Paul joked with me and called me 'Lizard' all the time! It was just the three of us, me, Dave Bishop and Kevin Robinson and I'm pretty sure that the arrangement was our effort, as there wasn't written music, in combination with some of Paul's ideas. It took about three hours."[709] The song ends with an original flair: the curious scratchy sound of McCartney's voice as if on an old dusty 78 rpm record, played on a gramophone.

Musicians:

Paul McCartney vocals, backing vocals, acoustic guitar, bass, piano, drums, electric guitar, harpsichord • **Jeff Lynne** backing vocals, acoustic guitar, electric guitar, keyboards • **Kevin Robinson** trumpet • **Chris "Snake" Davis** sax • **Dave Bishop** baritone sax

281 **Flaming Pie** (Paul McCartney)

Recording: February 27th, 1996 **Location:** Hog Hill Studio, Icklesham **Release:** May 1997, *Flaming Pie*

The allusion to the Beatles' myth inspired McCartney to record "Flaming Pie" in a Sixties manner, that is, very quickly. The result was a driving, straightforward rocker led by McCartney's bedeviled piano. Paul sings this witty tongue-twister all in one breath. The lyrics are half way between the visionary and the imaginary with some of his typical nonsense also

---

[707] *Ibid.*
[708] Gary Graff, *The Last Beatle.*
[709] Interview courtesy of Chris Davis, 21/09/2011.

thrown in. The title *Flaming Pie* is a reference to a story John Lennon told in *Mersey Beat* in 1961 about the origin of The Beatles' name.

A tempo change introduces a brief coda with Paul playing piano in typical barrelhouse fashion. The song – which became the title-track of the album – has been performed during the 2004 *Summer Tour* and 2005 *US Tour*, being played frequently also in McCartney's concerts from 2007 to 2009 and during soundchecks. A live version is included in *Good Evening New York City*.

Musicians:

Paul McCartney vocals, backing vocals, bass, piano, drums, electric guitar • **Jeff Lynne** vocal harmonies, electric guitar

The May recordings also saw Ringo Starr in the studio. He hadn't recorded with Paul since the *Broad Street* days.

282 Beautiful Night (Paul McCartney)

Recording: May 13th-14th, 1996 and February 14th, 1997 (overdubs) **Location:** Hog Hill Studio, Icklesham and Abbey Road Studios (overdubs), London **Release:** May 1997, *Flaming Pie*

Bibliographies and music critics never gave much weight to an essential aspect of evaluating McCartney's creative flow: the time gap between the writing, the recording and the release of his songs. This leitmotif of his solo career should be taken into consideration in order to better analyze McCartney's shape as a songwriter.

Whether this can be attributed to Paul's prolific output – inhibiting his timely releases – or to his inability to correctly evaluate his material, is another question. What is clear is that many analysises about the quality of his career should be reviewed. In the case of "Beautiful Night", the song was recorded three times in three different versions before Paul finally decided to release it on *Flaming Pie* after well-over eleven years.

"Beautiful Night" was first recorded on August 21st, 1986 in New York City with Phil Ramone producing (this version was issued in 1997 on the "Beautiful Night" cd-single). Paul (vocals and piano) was accompanied by Liberty Devitto on drums, Neil Jason on bass, David Brown on electric guitar and David Lebolt on synthesizer.

The structure of the song was similar to the one released on *Flaming Pie* but somewhat inconsistent, with the bridge coming right after the verses and before the chorus: the recording seems unfinished, with Paul's vocals ad-libbing in the coda and Devitto's drumming of such epic force clearly out of place.

McCartney returned to the song in July 1987 with George Martin working on orchestral overdubs but Paul wasn't satisfied and the song didn't get released. Reportedly, Paul re-recorded it in November 1990, but this version too remained unreleased.

McCartney dusted off "Beautiful Night" during the *Flaming Pie* sessions, when Ringo was there. McCartney recalled: "For years I'd been saying to Ringo we'd never done so much work outside The Beatles (...) I realized that we hadn't done for so long, but it was very comfortable."[710]

Paul changed some lyrics and added an up-tempo finale to this ballad. The result was an intense love song – limpid and harmonious in its chord progression leading to a dramatic and very Latin-influenced refrain. In the coda Paul pulls out some of his best rock guitar playing while also leaving room for Ringo's vocals that recall "Carry That Weight". Paul brought in George Martin to work on a sumptuous orchestral arrangement. Footage of the session – that took place on February 14th, 1997 from 2.30 to 5.30 pm[711] – reveals that the two had kept on good terms: Paul gives instructions to Martin and the orchestra about the horn arrangement, making suggestions and joking with everyone.

Michael Thompson played horn: "Even if the final result is a full orchestra, very often the instruments are recorded in separate groups and then mixed together. I think in this particular case we played at the same time with the other instruments. There's a funny story I remember... We were at Abbey Road Studios and Paul said that he'd walked down that morning from his house near there. I asked him, 'Did you walk over the crossing?' Were there a lot of people taking photographs?' He said, 'Yes of course' and I said, 'Did any of those kind of recognize you?' He answered, 'No, of course not!'"[712]

Issued as the third single from *Flaming Pie* in December 1997, "Beautiful Night" was better known for the controversy around the video clip – containing a naked female – than for its commercial success. In fact, the video was immediately censored by the BBC and the song stalled at #25 on the UK charts.

Musicians:

Paul McCartney vocals, backing vocals, bass, acoustic and electric guitar, piano, electric piano, Hammond organ, percussion • **Linda McCartney** backing vocals • **Jeff Lynne** backing vocals, acoustic and electric guitar • **Ringo Starr** vocals, drums, percussion • **John Barclay, Andrew Crowley, Mark Bennett** trumpet • **Richard Edwards, Andy Fawbert** trombone • **Michael Thompson, Richard Watkins, Nigel Black** horn • **Marcia Crayford, Adrian Levine, Belinda Bunt, Bernard Partridge, Jackie Hartley, Keith Pascoe, David Woodcock, Roger Garland, Julian Tear, Briony Shaw, Rita Manning, Jeremy Williams, David Ogden, Bogustav Kostecki, Maciej Rakowski, Jonathan Reeves** violin • **Robert Smissen, Stephen Thees, Levine Andrade, Philip Dukes, Ivo Van Der Werff, Graeme Scott** viola • **Anthony Pleeth, Stephen Orton, Martin Loveday, Robert Bailey** cello • **Chris Laurence, Robin McGee** double-bass • **Susan Milan** flute • **David Theodore** oboe

[710] *Flaming Pie* radio special, 1997.
[711] Mark Lewisohn, *A Beautiful Day's Night. Mark Lewisohn witnesses the final session for Flaming Pie,* in *Club Sandwich,* n.82, 1997, p.13.
[712] Interview courtesy of Michael Thompson, 17/12/2011.

283 Really Love You (Paul McCartney-Richard Starkey)

Recording: May 14th, 1996 **Location:** Hog Hill Studio, Icklesham **Release:** May 1997, *Flaming Pie*

Following the recording of "Beautiful Night", McCartney was jamming with Ringo and enjoying it like in the old days. What resulted from this impromptu session was "Really Love You", the only song to ever be released written together by McCartney and Starkey: "Doing 'Beautiful Night' with Ringo wasn't enough" – Paul said – "I wanted more fun. So we jammed. The actor's worst dream is being on stage not knowing what play he's in – doing this vocal was like that, you can go anywhere."[713]

Paul grabbed his Hofner bass and with Ringo backing him up on drums and Jeff Lynne on guitar, went on to jam for half an hour searching for the right groove.

Ringo: "Paul had a few ideas for a jam, playing his bass. We were jamming, he was shouting these words, and it turned into a song. Jeff Lynne was playing a little funky guitar. It was just the three of us. It's organic… It grows!"[714]

Jeff Lynne: "We did two jams, one of which was called 'Really Love You'. We ke(pt) it as a trio and we did a bit of overdub, just one guitar. So the rest of the track is totally as it was recorded."[715] McCartney and Lynne took this basic blues (with Paul's improvised vocals mimicking Michael Jackson) and added piano and some edgy descending electric guitar phrases – the most original idea in the song. "Really Love You" is on *Flaming Pie*.

Musicians:

Paul McCartney vocals, backing vocals, bass, piano, electric guitar • **Jeff Lynne** backing vocals, electric guitar • **Ringo Starr** drums

284 Looking for You (Paul McCartney)

Recording: May 14th, 1996 **Location:** Hog Hill Studio, Icklesham **Release:** April 1997, "Young Boy" single B-side

"Looking for You" was generated from the same session as "Really Love You"; a blues-rock number that was left mostly untouched in order to best preserve the live-in-the-studio sound of the performance. Born from a jam, "Looking for You" is more an improvisation than a real song, as is exemplified in the sparse lyrics and vocal dropped in to the backing track. The production recalls the atmosphere of *McCartney II* thanks to its loud echo on the vocal and its hypnotic Hammond organ. The track was issued as the B-side to the single "Young Boy".

Musicians:

Paul McCartney vocals, backing vocals, bass, Hammond organ • **Jeff Lynne** backing vocals, electric guitars • **Ringo Starr** drums, congas

---

713 *Flaming Pie* booklet 1997, p.19.
714 *Flaming Pie* radio special, 1997.
715 *Ibid.*

285 Heaven on a Sunday (Paul McCartney)

Recording: September 16th and October? (overdubs), 1996 **Location:** Hog Hill Studio, Icklesham and Abbey Road Studios (overdubs), London **Release:** May 1997, *Flaming Pie*

McCartney wrote "Heaven on a Sunday" in August, 1996 while relaxing on a boat off the US coast: "Just me, the sail, the wind. Peaceful, like *Heaven on a Sunday*."[716]

He was inspired to write this laid back acoustic ballad, drifting along peacefully like a ship on the ocean. Paul committed it to tape as soon as he got back to England. It became another of his family recordings. This time along with Linda on backing vocals, Paul brought in his son, the aspiring guitarist James. This would be the second time he appeared on his father's records: or the third, if one includes his whimpering, captured seventeen years before on "Daytime Nighttime Suffering"! Paul: "James is getting really good on guitar (...) I thought it'd be nice to play with James, so we traded phrases. I played the acoustic stuff and let the *Young Turk* to play the electric stuff. Lovely to do."[717]

The song's middle bars – where McCartney and McCartney perform their duet – are the perfect example of the passing of the baton: the intertwined guitar riffs are influenced by the blues (Paul's acoustic) and by classic Seventies rockers (James' stinging electric *à la* David Gilmour), resulting in a well-crafted piece.

Later on – the exact date is unknown but very likely in October – a French horn quartet was added, but unfortunately this contribution was buried in the final mix. Michael Thompson was one of the four French horn players at Abbey Road, where the overdub was recorded: "I already knew McCartney, because we spent about a week recording a few tracks for the *Broad Street* soundtrack, and one of them was 'Wanderlust'. The French horn arrangement was very much a Paul's idea. The recording was done at Abbey Road Studio 1 and very quickly. Paul was very friendly with everyone. He likes the relationship with musicians either rock'n'roll or classical trained. All the music was written down on sheets and we recorded overdubs for other two tracks."[718] Lyrically, this melancholy song is all about love seen as an inevitable choice and as a nameless reality that can quickly turn into a dream. The track is on *Flaming Pie*.

Musicians:

Paul McCartney vocals, backing vocals, drums, bass, acoustic and electric guitar, harpsichord, electric piano, vibraphone, percussion • **Linda McCartney** backing vocals • **James McCartney** electric guitar • **Jeff Lynne** backing vocals, acoustic guitar • **Michael Thompson, Richard Bissill, Richard Watkins, John Pineguy** French horn

---

[716] *Flaming Pie* booklet, 1997, p.19.
[717] *Ibid.*
[718] Interview courtesy of Michael Thompson, 17/12/2011.

1997

Flaming Pie was released in May, and was almost unanimously acclaimed by critics (*Rolling Stone* wrote a three-star review). McCartney – who now could be addressed as Sir Paul, since he was knighted on March 11th – was celebrated as a composer and as a multi-instrumentalist. The album was a great commercial success, and went straight to #2 in the US charts (the highest debut position in McCartney's solo career) and in the UK. In America, *Flaming Pie* went gold with 500.000 units sold in its first week. McCartney did not tour to promote it, and only made a few tv appearances. Paul said to *Billboard* that he didn't want to do mega campaigns for *Flaming Pie*. "I wanted to make an album for the kid in the bedroom. The Beatles, we all wanted to make records for the kid in the bedroom somewhere, because we had recently been that kid in a bedroom." *Flaming Pie* got a Grammy Award nomination in the Best Record Of The Year category, but it was beaten by Bob Dylan's *Time Out of Mind*.

In September, it was followed by *Standing Stone*, the second classical work by McCartney. It was a success: the record held #1 on *Billboard* classical charts for an incredible ten weeks run.

McCartney chose a particular composing method, taking advantage of his computer (using the software *Cubase*) and with some help from arranger David Matthews (who corrected Paul's notation), saxophonist John Harle (who helped him develop some melodies) and the famous composer Richard Rodney Bennett, who supervised the entire work, giving suggestions and even criticizing McCartney's ideas in his brusque manner.

McCartney: "I would often fax a section of music from my computer to him. I'd sent him one, thinking it was pretty good. A few minutes later I got a fax back with the word FEEBLE scribbled across it. I phoned him straight back and said, 'Richard, that's what my teacher wrote on essays. You're a sensitive artist. If you don't like something, could you please write: 'That's a little below par.'"[719]

Speaking about classical music in a press conference for *Standing Stone*, McCartney said: "The thing about writing orchestral music for me is I'm lucky because I don't really know much classical music. I never heard much. I used to listen to Bach, and more recently I listened to Monteverdi. I didn't actually listen to anyone when I was making this piece, except to see what I shouldn't do, because they've done it already. I listened to Beethoven just to see what he did. My favorite at the moment is Monteverdi, I think he has a lot in common with the early Beatles' music. I'm lucky… When I sit down there's nothing… It's quite good, 'cause everything I write is possibly more original. It's an advantage to not know much… Ignorance is bliss in my case…"

---

[719] John Blaney, *Lennon and McCartney. Together Alone*, 2007, p.229.

1998

McCartney started the new year with some recordings for another experimental project: he brought back to life his alter ego "The Fireman" for chapter two. The sessions lasted only one week and in the studio Paul was joined again by Youth. Eight of these ten ambient-tinged mainly instrumental tracks would be included in the album *Rushes*, released in September. Two of them, "Plum Jam" and "Through the Marshes" are unissued to date.

286 Watercolour Guitars (The Fireman)

Recording: February, 1998 **Location:** Hog Hill Studio, Icklesham **Release:** September 1998, *Rushes*

McCartney chose this "Watercolour Guitars" as the main theme of the whole Fireman project. It was a little instrumental idea that Paul decided to extend with the help of Youth.

The whole track is based upon a dreamy and hypnotic acoustic guitar arpeggio, very reminiscent of Pink Floyd's style. Step by step, the piece is enriched and colored by different effects, which transform and modify synthesizer, keyboards and electric guitars into a liquid and mysterious sound texture. This is the opening track on *Rushes*.

Musicians:

Paul McCartney acoustic and electric guitars, synthesizer, keyboards

287 Palo Verde (The Fireman)

Recording: February, 1998 **Location:** Hog Hill Studio, Icklesham **Release:** September 1998, *Rushes*

"Palo Verde" – the second song on *Rushes* – is a lengthy track, whose harmonic structure is similar to "Watercolour Guitars". It is also a sort of tribute to Linda, as in the opening of the song some horses' pawing and neighing can be heard.

The track features an haiku recited by Linda (she and Paul were both keen on this poetry form), with the meaningful verse "So amazing that you think you're on drugs". Over the acoustic guitar bed, McCartney added the rhythm section – bass, drums and synthesizer – and later embroidered the track with some weird and warped electric guitar phrases.

Halfway through the song, Paul threw in a brief vocal part, an excerpt from his 1995 unreleased composition "Let Me Love You Always". Beside his vocal, transfigured and disintegrated by thousands of effects and treatments, McCartney added other odd sounds and noises, including a piano piece (a sample?), reminiscent of "Revolution n.9".

Musicians:

Paul McCartney vocals, acoustic and electric guitars, bass, synthesizer, keyboards, vibraphone (?), piano (?), drums • **Linda McCartney** vocals

288 Auraveda (The Fireman)

Recording: February, 1998 **Location:** Hog Hill Studio, Icklesham **Release:** September 1998, *Rushes*

The Beatle-esque references on *Rushes* were not limited only to heavily experimental sound effects but also involved the use of Sixties-style instrumentation.

"Auraveda" is indeed a sort of affectionate tribute to Harrison's Indian music. To re-create the Eastern texture, Paul recorded the track playing a long sitar solo, accompanied by tabla and various percussion. He then finished it with the addition of dissonant electric guitars, synthesizer and various effects. Lasting over 12 minutes, it is the longest track on *Rushes*.

Musicians:

Paul McCartney vocals, electric guitar, synthesizer, keyboards, sitar, percussion, shaker, tabla, harmonium, flute, tambourine, bells

289 Fluid (The Fireman)

Recording: February 1998 **Location:** Hog Hill Studio, Icklesham **Release:** September 1998, *Rushes*

The catchiest track included in *Rushes*, "Fluid" is an instrumental in the pure ambient-music tradition. Opening with an ethereal piano arpeggio, the song leaves room for the imagination to relax and wander as the ocean waves roll in the background. It is then followed by a very trippy electric guitar that outlines the main riff. A woman's erotic moaning gives the song – and the whole album – its most risqué moment.

It's rumored that McCartney and Youth had called a hot-line, sampling the whispers and voices that they heard. This was consistently denied by various press releases.

Towards the end, the track includes a gloomy drum-machine pattern and a guitar riff, based on two recurring notes. It was released both as a 12" single and on a promo-cd containing three remixes by Nithin Sawhney, British Indian musician/producer who would work again with McCartney in 2008 on the song "My Soul", released on Sawhney's album *London Undersound*.

Musicians:

Paul McCartney piano, bass, electric guitar, synthesizer, keyboards, percussion, drums

290 Appletree Cinnabar Amber (The Fireman)

Recording: February 1998 **Location:** Hog Hill Studio, Icklesham **Release:** September 1998, *Rushes*

For "Appletree Cinnabar Amber", probably one of the best moments on *Rushes*, McCartney thought to do something really unusual. He began drumming, working on a sort of hip-hop groove and built this acid-jazz flavored track, which develops the melody of the previous "Fluid". Then McCartney overdubbed a harpsichord, which helped increase the tense and almost *noir* atmosphere of the track, punctuated over and over by mysterious female voices.

Musicians:

Paul McCartney electric guitar, bass, synthesizer, keyboards, piano, percussion, harpsichord, drums

291 Bison (The Fireman)

Recording: February, 1998 **Location:** Hog Hill Studio, Icklesham **Release:** September 1998, *Rushes*

The heavy basic track of "Bison" was recorded together by McCartney and Youth, who played a very distorted bass part while Paul was working on his drum groove. Glover recalls: "That was a jam. McCartney's a good drummer, so we said, 'Ok, let's have a jam and I'll play bass.' We did a live take to get the drums and then Paul said, 'Go on, have another go at doing your bass as an overdub' and I went through all that."[720]

Youth's bass was given some strong distortion, which fits in very well with Paul's drum track. When he came to overdub, McCartney placed a dissonant guitar riff as well as evocative keyboards and Mellotron phrases. The most aggressive track on *Rushes*.

Musicians:

Paul McCartney drums, percussion, acoustic and electric guitar, keyboards, synthesizer, Mellotron • **Martin Glover** bass

292 7am (The Fireman)

Recording: February, 1998 **Location:** Hog Hill Studio, Icklesham **Release:** September 1998, *Rushes*

An hypnotic track, "7am" is a sort of long interlude, based on an almost electronic synthesizer riff. McCartney later added some chords on keyboards and Mellotron, producing an eerie sound texture. Some backwards effects completed the track, perhaps the least interesting of the *Rushes* project, except for the fact that it contains another vocal guest appearance – a sort of self-cameo – of McCartney, who sings some verses taken from a demo of his unreleased composition from 1995, "Hey Now (What Are You Looking at Me For?)".

Musicians:

Paul McCartney vocals, bass, drums, percussion, electric guitar, keyboards, synthesizer, Mellotron

293 Watercolour Rush (The Fireman)

Recording: February, 1998 **Location:** Hog Hill Studio, Icklesham **Release:** September 1998, *Rushes*

As always, fascinated by sonic themes and concepts, McCartney thought of an ending in the *Band on the Run* fashion. "Watercolour Rush" is a condensed version (1:45) of the opening track, with the same ethereal atmosphere. This brief instrumental closes *Rushes*.

Musicians:

Paul McCartney acoustic and electric guitar, keyboards, synthesizer

After the completion of *Rushes*, Paul got back into the studio to put the finishing touches on a solo album by Linda. He completed *Wide Praire*, that was released in October. Earlier in the year, on April 17th Linda had lost her battle against cancer.

---

720 I. Peel, *cit.*, p.166.

1999

In March, Paul came out from his seclusion and, at Abbey Road Studio 2, reunited one of the most incredible bands of his career, to work on a rock'n'roll covers' album: it was his second attempt, twelve years after *Choba B CCCP*. Paul was joined by David Gilmour (electric guitar), Ian Paice (drums), Mick Green (electric guitar), Pete Wingfield (keyboards); drummer Dave Mattacks and pianist Geraint Watkins also played in some tracks.

A breath of fresh air for McCartney who went back to his musical roots, trying to come to terms with Linda's death; she was the driving force that pushed Paul to make the *Run Devil Run* album. Paul: "It's something that Lin and I were talking about and she was very keen on the idea. She loved that rock'n'roll. So she loved the idea of me doing some of these songs that I never did with the Beatles."

McCartney's song selection was totally different than in 1987. He chose lesser known tracks, introducing them to the band directly in the studio. Paul explained the approach: "Anybody knows 'No Other Baby'? No? Here's how it goes... And as we were doing it, I thought, 'God, I haven't done this since I was 14. And I got the same feeling back.'"

The sessions started off as jams, not intended for an album, but they turned out so good that Paul immediately thought to release them. McCartney and friends plunged into solid covers of "Blue Jean Bop", "She Said Yeah", "All Shook Up", "No Other Baby", "Lonesome Town", "Movie Magg", "Brown-Eyed Handsome Man", "Coquette", "I Got Stung" (originally planned as a single), "Honey Hush", "Shake a Hand", "Party", "Fabulous" (issued only as the B-side to the single "Brown-Eyed Handsome Man"), "There's a Leak", "Ready Teddy", "Rip it Up" (these last three remained unreleased), as well as three McCartney originals.

294 Run Devil Run (Paul McCartney)

Recording: March 3rd, 1999 **Location:** Abbey Road Studios, London **Release:** October 1999, *Run Devil Run*

Paul was in Atlanta with his son James, when he came across a crazy shop "like one of these sort of voodoo shops, where you get cures for everything."

McCartney: "I was looking in the shop window and saw this bottle of bath salts called *Run Devil Run*. I thought that was a good title for a song."[721]

Later on, while on holiday, McCartney thought of some words that could fit with his idea: "I was actually out sailing when I did the verses" – Paul recalled – "'Run devil run, the angels havin' fun' and it came quite easy."[722]

---

[721] *Run Devil Run* interview disc, 1999.
[722] *Ibid.*

In the studio, McCartney offered Gilmour and the others this fast, dirty and rough sounding rocker in Fifties style, one of the most authentic standards ever written by Paul.

A rapturous track, where McCartney's idea to record original songs in the same vein as rock'n'roll standards came close to perfection. A great vocal performance by Paul, backed by the group in this really burning take. The track is on *Run Devil Run*.

Musicians:

Paul McCartney vocals, bass • **David Gilmour** electric guitar, lap steel guitar • **Mick Green** electric guitar • **Pete Wingfield** piano • **Ian Paice** drums

295 What It Is (Paul McCartney)

Recording: March 4th, 1999 **Location:** Abbey Road Studios, London **Release:** October 1999, *Run Devil Run*

The inclusion of "What it Is" in *Run Devil Run* was a tribute to Linda. The song came to McCartney one day, "when I was playing bluesy riffs on the piano."[723] Linda was there with Paul and he liked the fact that she was beside him, "for the feedback she gave."[724]

"What It Is" was another track arranged in the Fifties style of the whole record: a tight and powerful blues-rock, with strong vocals by McCartney, like in the old days.

Musicians:

Paul McCartney vocals, bass, electric guitar • **David Gilmour** electric guitar • **Mick Green** electric guitar • **Pete Wingfield** piano • **Ian Paice** drums

296 Try Not to Cry (Paul McCartney)

Recording: May 5th, 1999 **Location:** Abbey Road Studios, London **Release:** October 1999, *Run Devil Run*

After Linda died, Paul went through a long period of depression: "I had a year of doing nothing" – McCartney said – "Everyone told me, 'You must keep busy'. I said, 'No, that's like denial'. I refused to get busy. I had a whole year of letting any emotion come sweeping over me. And it did."[725] McCartney again: "For about a year, I found myself crying – in all situations, around anyone I met. Anyone who came over, the minute we talked about Linda, I'd say, 'I'm sorry about this. I've got to cry.'"

"Try Not to Cry": the title of the song is embarrassingly clear. Significantly, Paul expresses the vital importance of crying, preferring to go with a compelling track rather than a mournful one. As McCartney had shown during the promo interview for *Run Devil Run*, "Try Not to Cry" was composed on the piano, originating from one single upbeat chord.

Skillfully, in the studio Paul turned the song into a vigorous stomper, that fits like a glove into the roaring mood of the album. In stark contrast to the melody, the lyrics of "Try Not to Cry"

---

[723] *Ibid.*
[724] *Ibid.*
[725] *Ibid.*

are a bold confession of a man's emotional crisis and who's trying to recover and get back to the real meaning of life: this makes the song possibly the best on *Run Devil Run*. A rare example of the difficult emotional period that McCartney had been through in the previous months.

Musicians:

Paul McCartney vocals, bass, percussion • **David Gilmour** electric guitar • **Mick Green** electric guitar • **Geraint Watkins** piano • **Dave Mattacks** drums, percussion

On September 16th, McCartney booked Capitol Tower Studios in Los Angeles to record a cover of Buddy Holly's "Maybe Baby", assisted by Jeff Lynne. The song would be included in 2000 in the sountrack album of the film *Maybe Baby* by Ben Elton.

Run Devil Run was released in October. Although it contained very few songs composed by McCartney, the record was quite successful: #12 in UK – gold disc for 100.000 copies sold – and #27 in the US. The double A-side single "No Other Baby"/"Brown-Eyed Handsome Man" reached only #42. McCartney did some heavy promotion, supporting the record with two historical performances: on December 2nd appearing on the Michael Parkinson Show – Paul fulfilled a promise made to Parkinson years earlier, when the talk-show host appeared on the *Band on the Run* cover – and on December 14th holding a special concert at the Cavern Club, the well-known Liverpool club, which hosted over 300 Beatles concerts in the early days. The gig was a media event: McCartney was ideally saying farewell to the Century. Paul took advantage of the new mass media power. Mass hysteria scenes took place during the ticket sales and someone even offered sex to get one! The show was aired live on the Web, with over 50 million people trying to connect worldwide. In the end, six millions lucky fans succeeded in seeing it. The show brought *Run Devil Run* back in the charts and included the following set: "Honey Hush" – "Blue Jean Bop" – "Brown-Eyed Handsome Man" – "Fabulous" (with false start) – "What It Is" – "Lonesome Town" – "Twenty-Flight Rock" – "No Other Baby" – "Try Not to Cry" – "Shake a Hand" – "All Shook Up" – "I Saw Her Standing There" – "Party"

Pete Wingfield: "To be honest, I didn't enjoy the gig itself very much. I was honored to be part of the event, but from a strictly practical point of view, it wasn't a great gig. The small stage was covered with lighting and camera equipment. Everything was way too loud and I hardly heard anything I played throughout the set."[726]

Working Classical, a selection of old and new McCartney compositions arranged for orchestra and chamber music, was simultaneously released

It was premiered at the Liverpool Philharmonic Hall on October 16th, 1999. It took over from *Standing Stone*, dominating the US classical charts during the winter.

---

[726] *Interview with Pete Wingfield*, in *Let It Rock*, April 2003. http://dmme.net/interviews/wingfield.html

2000

Another relatively relaxed year, with no musical releases, except for another one of McCartney's side-projects, which gained immediate publicity in late August. Paul unexpectedly came up with *Liverpool Sound Collage*, a bizarre collection of experimental sounds, gathered by McCartney himself.

He had presented his avant-garde project – mainly based upon fragments taken from Beatles' sessions and interviews he recorded with passers-by and shoppers in Liverpool, as well as chats with students at The Liverpool Institute for Performing Arts – some months earlier as a musical background for a Peter Blake exhibition about Pop Art at the Tate Gallery in London.

Later on, he went to Abbey Road Studios, where he remixed some tracks with the help of the Welsh group Super Furry Animals and Youth.

Speaking about it, Paul said: "I compiled sounds and made the basic collage… I asked Cian Ciarán of Super Furry Animals to mix something from it, which he kindly did, and my mate Youth used his talents to add a final touch."[727]

These five tracks were all in an experimental vein. One of them, called "Free Now", was sent to radio stations as a promo and got some good airplay, but it was not officially issued as a single. The album received a nomination for a Grammy Award in the Best Experimental Album category, but the award went to *Kid A* by Radiohead.

On December 8th – the Twentieth anniversary of John's death – McCartney entered Abbey Road for more conventional recordings. Paul cut three new tracks with a big orchestra, in a perfect Nat King Cole style (as they say) as well as a complete version of "Mist Over Central Park", a song that was premiered the previous year on the Michael Parkinson Show. These recordings have not yet surfaced.

---

[727] www.paulmccartney.com

2001

In February, Paul went to Henson Studios in Los Angeles, where over three weeks he recorded most of his future album *Driving Rain*. Instinctively, he chose to record the album in a sort of "voyage into the unknown."[728]

Bill Porricelli, MPL promoter from NYC, submitted to Paul a list of potential producers. McCartney chose David Kahne ("I liked his approach, he's very musical, but modern"[729]), with whom he had never worked before.

He didn't even know the musicians (keyboard player Gabe Dixon, guitarist Rusty Anderson and drummer Abe Laboriel Jr.) and with them McCartney approached the sessions "the old way we used to record with The Beatles around the time of the early albums. I realized that George, Ringo, George Martin and our engineer Geoff Emerick all didn't know what song we were going to do until John and I brought it in."[730]

After he presented the songs to the band, they soon started to record, so as to get as much of a live feel as possible, with little room for overdubs or post-production.

McCartney: "I did it on *Run Devil Run* – the band for that album had said to me, 'Can we learn up what songs we're going to do, like a week before we go into the studio?' And I'd said, 'No, no homework.' So we did it the same way with this new album, following the same technique (…) I've mainly been the bass player in the band. Which again is a good feeling; it's my place to be the bass player… I sing and I play bass."[731]

According to the *Driving Rain* liner notes, McCartney used his Hofner bass in all the songs, except for the track "Spinning on an Axis" (see sheet **305**), where he played Rickenbacker.

Three tracks from the sessions remain unreleased: "You Are Still Here", a moving ballad written for Linda, "Always Be There" and "If This Is Wrong".

297 About You (Paul McCartney)

Recording: February 16th, 2001 **Location:** Henson Studios, Los Angeles **Release:** November 2001, *Driving Rain*

The first song recorded during this day at Henson Studios, was composed by McCartney in Goa, India: "One afternoon I wrote 'About You' on a little travel guitar I've got which has its own amp in it. I picked some words out for the song after seeing a copy of *The India Times* which was lying around."[732]

---

[728] *The Driving Rain Interview*, www.paulmccartney.com, November 2001.
[729] *Ibid.*
[730] *Ibid.*
[731] *Ibid.*
[732] *Ibid.*

So impatient to unleash his newly found exuberance, for this rocking track McCartney dabbled in playing electric guitar – leaving the bass to Rusty Anderson – and sang a powerful live vocal, accompanied by Gabe Dixon on piano and Laboriel Jr. on drums.

After the basic track was recorded, more overdubs were added. Paul sang other vocal parts, Rusty played a 12-string electric guitar, Abe a tambourine and Dixon an organ. The result is a solid and vigorous recording, with its funky guitar riffs and its beautiful Hammond organ.

McCartney seems to underline a sense of liberation and regeneration from his previous discomforted state due to his losing Linda.

Paul definitely wanted to celebrate his new path with Heather (his new girlfriend) as exemplified in some of the most explicit lyrics of *Driving Rain*.

Paul swore that he took inspiration from a simple word ("power") in composing the track. But the positive energy of the song's lyrics seems to be the typical outcome of a subconscious flow: McCartney sings of light and power as opposed to darkness and death. The track is on *Driving Rain*.

Musicians:

Paul McCartney vocals, electric guitar • **Rusty Anderson** 12-string electric guitar, bass • **Gabe Dixon** electric piano, Hammond organ • **Abe Laboriel Jr.** drums, tambourine

298 Lonely Road (Paul McCartney)

Recording: February 16th, 2001 **Location:** Henson Studios, Los Angeles **Release:** November 2001, *Driving Rain*

On *Driving Rain* McCartney had "mainly been the bass player in the band", as he put it. Paul had found new enthusiasm for his bass playing and on this album he gave the instrument a more significant and prominent role than in the recent past.

This is undeniable hearing "Lonely Road", the second song recorded in Los Angeles and which would also become the opening track on the new album.

"Lonely Road" has got the most basic intro in all of McCartney's discography: alone for the first eight bars, Paul's deep and dark bass sets the tone to the track.

Its sound recalls a beating heart, thus to convey the deep emotional meaning of the song: "It's symbolic for anyone who's been through any sort of problems. It's a defiant song against loneliness"[733], Paul said.

Although the lyrics don't contain any specific personal references, some verses deal with the subject of loneliness and clearly reflect McCartney's pain and frustration in the two years that followed Linda's death.

Paul had written "Lonely Road" in January, while he was on vacation in Goa[734], where he started the new year with Heather. It was the first time that he visited India since the Sixties.

---

[733] *Ibid.*

McCartney: "I was enjoying the beach and the sea (…) I had a few moments in the afternoon, which is always a good time for me, to go off and fondle my guitar. The song basically wrote itself in about an hour (…) in a hotel room."[735]

This tight rocker in E minor was recorded live in the studio. McCartney's raspy vocal performance was recorded live along with the bass and kept – for the most part – in the final version. This croaky sound on Paul's vocals was only partly intentional: McCartney revealed that he entered the studio just one week after having completely lost his voice

"Lonely Road" was later completed with overdubs: an organ by David Kahne, a couple of acoustic guitars and many contributions by Anderson on electric guitars, including a pedal steel guitar. The result was a very strong and punchy track, one of the best included in *Driving Rain*.

McCartney performed the song on October 20th, 2001 during the *Concert for NYC* at Madison Square Garden and later on his 2002-03 *Drivin' Tour*. Hence the inclusion of the track both in the *Back in the US* and *Back in the World* live albums.

A remixed version – lowered by a semitone, featuring more reverb on Paul's vocal and with some newly recorded guitar parts – was used as a promo-single sent to American radio stations in March 2002.

Musicians:

Paul McCartney vocals, bass, acoustic and electric guitar • **Rusty Anderson** acoustic and electric guitar, pedal steel guitar • **Gabe Dixon** electric piano • **Abe Laboriel Jr.** drums, tambourine • **David Kahne** organ

299 Riding into Jaipur (Paul McCartney)

Recording: February 16th, 2001 **Location:** Henson Studios, Los Angeles **Release:** October 2001, "From a Lover to a Friend" single B-side (from *Driving Rain*)

The first day at Henson ended in an unusual way with the recording of this Indian pastiche, titled "Riding into Jaipur". It was a track that Paul put together in two different moments, first finding the melody on his travel-guitar while on holiday to the Maldives with Linda.

McCartney: "(It) seems to have a bit of a sound on certain frets, like a sitar and because I was in the middle of the Indian Ocean, the two came together in that song."[736]

McCartney had completed the song in January in India, adding to the melody some words that came to him while he was travelling on a train to Jaipur ("It was a very exotic overnight journey" in Paul's words).

Apart from "Auraveda" (see sheet 288) from *Rushes*, this is the first McCartney song done completely in an Eastern style. With the help of his Martin simil-sitar acoustic guitar, some real

---

[734] The verse "I tried to go somewhere old" is a reference to India.
[735] *The Driving Rain Interview*, www.paulmccartney.com, November 2001.
[736] *Ibid.*

Indian instruments (tampura) and David Kahne's synthesizer, McCartney had a good time recording this Harrison-style sort of tribute, building the whole track around the most typical Indian harmonic shape: the drone. "Riding into Jaipur" is included in *Driving Rain*.

Musicians:

Paul McCartney vocals, acoustic guitar, bass, electric guitar • **Rusty Anderson** tampura, 12-string electric guitar • **Gabe Dixon** piano • **Abe Laboriel Jr.** electronic percussion • **David Kahne** synthesizer

300 She's Given Up Talking (Paul McCartney)

Recording: February 17th, 2001 **Location:** Henson Studios, Los Angeles **Release:** November 2001, *Driving Rain*

Paul said that he was inspired by some recording techniques used by The Beatles for *Driving Rain*. "She's Given Up Talking" it's a *Revolver*-influenced track, mainly for its experimental flavor, that makes it one of the most original songs in McCartney's discography.

The track opens with some backwards tapes, in the best *Revolver* tradition. David Kahne: "We were recording on tape when I heard the backwards sound. I thought it was cool because I remembered a lot of sessions where I would be hearing that half the time. Paul said we should use it somewhere so I just recorded it on DAT and spun it into the top of it."[737]

McCartney had composed the song a couple of years earlier, in Jamaica, inspired by his friend's daughter, who never talked at school: "I remembered this story of this girl who wouldn't talk to the teachers" – Paul said – "And his idea of her giving up talking seemed like a good title to me."[738]

With his typical laziness, Paul left the song unfinished and put together the middle section ("but when she comes home…") just "ten minutes before the session."

The track opens with McCartney's Martin acoustic guitar: a sort of intro, that is soon followed by a heavy layering of instrumentation – mostly overdubbed – in a dark and gloomy atmosphere, crammed full of effects and treatments, with many superimposed hard-sounding guitars and McCartney's fuzz-bass.

With its hypnotic pace, the song marches slowly and heavily, thanks to a drum part by Paul himself – perhaps the tape was slowed down with Varispeed, so to get the drum deep sound heard in the track – and to a great job on Rusty Anderson guitars, that range from hard-rock, to experimental and electronic sounds. Abe Laboriel Jr. contributed some electronic percussion and even David Kahne was involved, playing an electric guitar track.

"She's Given Up Talking" is a unprecedented recording for McCartney, where the instrumental part is the real core of the track.

---

[737] Claudio Dirani, *An exclusive Interview with David Kahne*, November 2001.
[738] *The Driving Rain Interview*, www.paulmccartney.com, November 2001.

It was also a very spontaneous and immediate recording, even though extensively overdubbed. The fragment of dialogue between Paul and Rusty that can be heard just before the first guitar solo was captured accidentally by David Kahne: "We didn't know we'd be keeping the take" – Kahne reveals – "I just left the yell in, and Paul said OK."[739]

Musicians:

Paul McCartney vocals, acoustic guitar, bass, drums • **Rusty Anderson** electric guitars, Leslie pedal • **Gabe Dixon** Hammond organ • **Abe Laboriel Jr.** electronic percussion • **David Kahne** electric guitar

301 I Do (Paul McCartney)

Recording: February 17th, 2001 **Location:** Henson Studios, Los Angeles **Release:** November 2001, *Driving Rain*

"I Do" – the third *Driving Rain* song composed by Paul in India – is one of the most poignant tracks on the album. The song is a love declaration for Heather, but at the same time evokes a golden past. McCartney: "It was one of those 'If you only knew' songs, like just talking to someone; 'If you only knew, that it's OK from my side'. It's like a communicative statement to someone – 'Whatever you think at any given time, remember this, I do.'"[740]

The basic track of "I Do" was recorded with this simple quartet: McCartney on acoustic guitar, Rusty Anderson on electric, Gabe Dixon on piano and Laboriel Jr. on the drum kit.

During the overdubs, the track was enriched by some orchestral samples by David Kahne and Paul's moving vocal part. McCartney recalled how, during the recording, he changed his mind about his singing: "I started singing it low" – Paul recalls – "But then, as a vocal trick to kick the song along in the second verse, I found I could actually easily lift it an octave and a nice little moment happened that I like on this song, when I'm catching my breath in order to go up the octave. It's a little signature thing that happened which I didn't mean to happen, but it's good that there are those little accidents..."[741]

Later, McCartney graced the track with a fluent bass. It's hard to say to which woman (Heather or Linda) the song is aimed at: it feels like both were coexisting in Paul's heart, suspended between past and present. The nostalgic tone of the song refers to the meaning of an eternal love, free from all mundane ties, but in the middle-eight McCartney also expresses the bitter feeling about the transience of our lives: days are passing quickly and life "is never easy" even in the best moments. In this middle section it's not coincidental to hear what sounds like a joyful ringing of a nuptial church bell, halfway between the happy thought of the past with Linda and the future wedding with Heather, that would be celebrated only some months later.

Musicians:

---

[739] C. Dirani, *An exclusive Interview with David Kahne*, November 2001.
[740] *The Driving Rain Interview*, www.paulmccartney.com, November 2001.
[741] *Ibid.*

Paul McCartney vocals, acoustic guitar, bass • **Rusty Anderson** electric guitar • **Gabe Dixon** piano • **Abe Laboriel Jr.** drums, tambourine • **David Kahne** orchestral samples

302 Your Way (Paul McCartney)

Recording: February 18th, 2001 **Location:** Henson Studios, Los Angeles **Release:** November 2001, *Driving Rain*

McCartney: "I haven't sweated the lyrics on this album. I've just sort of let it all come out very naturally (…) I just trusted to my instincts."[742]

And McCartney was surely thinking about "Your Way", a song whose lyrics are full of his typical love-rhymes, nonsense and wordplays. "Your Way" was another track that McCartney wrote during the Jamaican holiday that also inspired "She's Given Up Talking": but when it came into the studio, the track was arranged with a country flavor.

McCartney: "It (wa)s the first song with which we tried harmonies with the guys in the band and the nice thing about the guys is they can all sing."[743]

McCartney leads the band in this catchy and lighthearted song, perfected with his usual studio tricks, e.g. the knee-percussion, used earlier on "Pipes of Peace" or "Put It There". The song is marked by the deep bass (some phrases seem to recall "Bip Bop", see sheet 41) – that McCartney let Anderson play – and by a flawless vocals by Paul, which alternate between two different octaves, "a bit like two sides of a personality singing to each other, like a man and a woman."[744]

Musicians:

Paul McCartney vocals, electric guitar, drums, percussion • **Rusty Anderson** bass, pedal steel guitar, backing vocals • **Gabe Dixon** Hammond organ, backing vocals • **Abe Laboriel Jr.** drums, electronic drums, backing vocals

303 Rinse the Raindrops (Paul McCartney)

Recording: February 19th, 2001 **Location:** Henson Studios, Los Angeles **Release:** November 2001, *Driving Rain*

McCartney: "When I was in India some carpet salesman ripped me off with a purchase that I made. He told me that this carpet was like the rarest thing ever; but then I got to the next town and found about twenty of them. So I rang him up and I was telling him that he was a rip-off. And as I was doing it, that and probably the weather, I started to lose my voice. The following day my voice really went, I couldn't talk. It took a while to clear and I was thinking, 'It's only a week to the recording sessions.'"[745]

---

[742] *Ibid.*
[743] *Ibid.*
[744] *Ibid.*
[745] *Ibid.*

Nevertheless, McCartney chose to go on with the planned sessions. And McCartney took maximum advantage of his hoarse vocal shape on "Rinse the Raindrops", a monster-track whose length (10:08) is surpassed only by a few tracks in McCartney's discography.

Derived from a thirty-minute "free-for-all" kind of session, "Rinse the Raindrops" it's an erratic jam. But its inclusion in *Driving Rain* would not have taken McCartney's hard-core fans by surprise, as used as they are to hearing this kind of improvisation during soundchecks.

Built on a very simple harmonic and lyrical structure (a single verse – a haiku – sung by Paul in a thousand different rip-roaring ways), "Rinse the Raindrops" is nevertheless interesting. With all its twist and turns, its quirky sounds and experimental oddities, the track is a perfect example of the *Driving Rain* recordings that – according to producer David Kahne – were approached "with very few rehearsals". In fact, Paul wrote the song directly in the studio! McCartney: "I've only ever written a couple of songs where the lyrics came first. 'All My Loving' with The Beatles was the first one of those. This was a similar thing, I was sailing and some words came to me that I wasn't sure whether they were a poem or a song."[746]

McCartney arrived at the session only with a couple of verses and "a rough melody in my head", thinking to turn it into something crazy.

So, he played the song to the band on acoustic guitar and he made up an instrumental bridge on the spot; then, Paul took his bass and led the group through a mammoth jam that lasted over thirty minutes, singing the verses "about 48 times"!

Next, Paul gave "Rinse the Raindrops" to David Kahne, hoping he could make something of it: "We left him to stay up until four in the morning to work on it."[747]

Kahne's editing was a cut-and-paste of the best bits of the performance. Paul revealed: "David said, 'I couldn't get it down any shorter than this', he'd collaged together all the bits he liked, and it's like a ten-minute song. It reminds me of festivals in summer, hippies and bands jamming. There's a good energy to it."[748]

Musicians:

Paul McCartney vocals, bass, Spanish guitar • **Rusty Anderson** electric guitar • **Gabe Dixon** piano, electric piano, Hammond organ • **Abe Laboriel Jr.** drums, accordion

304 From a Lover to a Friend (Paul McCartney)

Recording: February 20th, 2001 **Location:** Henson Studios, Los Angeles **Release:** October 2001, single (from *Driving Rain*)

One night at his home studio Paul recorded a demo for "From a Lover to a Friend": soon he noticed that his mind was travelling down a crucial psychological path.

---

[746] *Ibid.*
[747] *Ibid.*
[748] *Ibid.*

Again – according to McCartney – the songwriting happened accidentally, starting with the music. To Paul's acknowledgement, the track was no other than "a patchwork of a couple of bits I'd had, which I liked but I didn't think I'd finished up the songs."[749]

In his home studio with the assistance of Eddie Klein, Paul found the nighttime perfect for the song's feel and noticed that the different bits – although not conceived to coexist – could work well together.

McCartney: "It had a very intimate quality in the voice and so I tried to keep that and not clean up the record so much that I'd lose that lazy late-nightness."[750]

When Paul presented the demo to the band for the recording, the response was enthusiastic. McCartney: "Instead of it all being 4:4, it was like 5:4 in places or 2:4, which was something I like. And when I played the demo to the band and to the producer, everyone was all very keen on faithfully following all those little 5:4 bars, just to give it a different musical structure. They loved those little odd-bars."[751]

If the music took shape almost unconsciously, the same happened with the lyrics that – in a typical Freudian slip – are among the most revealing of McCartney's inner self, although also in this case, McCartney admitted that he included in the demo some random words: "I really didn't find words for… And a couple of bits didn't make sense, like *Despite too easy ride to see.*"[752]

Paul was inspired to put in the song some meaningless verses and words by a visit to *Cirque du Soleil* with Heather, George Harrison and Olivia, while he learnt from one of the circus' singers that "we want like everyone to get it – so it's no language": as a matter of fact the song took on a deeper meaning and became a vehicle to express his need for love.

"I'm in a dilemma": Paul is uncertain and doesn't even dare to start off. It seems that McCartney tries to dispel his doubts through his weakness' consciousness and the verse "Let me love again", is really Paul asking Linda's permission to get back to life. It's no coincidence that the track closes on these words, followed by the sound of a death toll, a sort of tribute to Linda's memory.

First, McCartney recorded his piano part – doubled by Dixon – with its looping-like chords: the opening bars recall the hypnotic atmosphere of "Free as a Bird".

Later, he overdubbed his heart-felt lead vocals and a bass line very reminiscent of "Come Together": "From a Lover to a Friend" is the classic song on *Driving Rain*.

Chosen as the first single from the album – Paul revealed that Ringo suggested it – the song was unfortunately one of the biggest commercial failures of McCartney's solo career.

---

749 *Ibid.*
750 *Ibid.*
751 *Ibid.*
752 *Ibid.*

352

Paul had supported the families of the fallen firemen during the September 11th rescue operations in New York with a charity release of the single.

For unknown reasons, he cancelled the US 45 "From a Lover to a Friend" at the last minute, replacing it with "Freedom". In the UK the track only reached #45 in the charts.

The cd-single features two remix versions by David Kahne. Both have an experimental flavor, where the song is broken into different parts by isolating the tracks (vocals, guitars, bass) and is enriched by some orchestral samples, in the same *Rushes* style.

Paul presented the track at the *Concert for NYC* on October 20th, 2001, but did not perform it during the following world tour.[753]

Musicians:

Paul McCartney vocals, piano, bass • **Rusty Anderson** 12-string electric guitar • **Gabe Dixon** piano • **Abe Laboriel Jr.** drums

305 Spinning on an Axis (Paul McCartney-James McCartney)

Recording: February 21st, 2001 **Location**: Henson Studios, Los Angeles **Release**: November 2001, *Driving Rain*

First of the two *Driving Rain* songs written together by Paul and his son James, "Spinning on an Axis" came out when the McCartneys were in New Hampshire visiting some relatives.

McCartney: "The sun was going down and me and James, my son, were talking about how the sun actually isn't going down, we're turning around away from it… We had a little keyboard thing there and James was playing a little riff on it and I was doing a parody rap thing just goofing off with no real melody, on those thoughts of spinning on an axis."[754]

Paul soon captured that jam on his little tape recorder and later brought the track into the studio: unfortunately, "Spinning on an Axis" – mainly built around the hypnotic guitar riff – is probably the least successful track on *Driving Rain*.

The basic track was recorded with McCartney on Rickenbacker bass, Laboriel Jr. on drums and Anderson on electric guitar; then they dedicated a lot of time to overdubs, including percussion (which were played by everyone, even by James), acoustic and electric guitars. An unconvincing McCartney excursion into the rap arena, "Spinning on an Axis" clearly unveils his improvised nature and hardly stands up in the album context. Nevertheless, the track has an intriguing groove and some interesting slide guitar sound in the bridge.

Musicians:

Paul McCartney vocals, bass, acoustic and electric guitar, percussion • **Rusty Anderson** acoustic and electric guitar, percussion • **Gabe Dixon** percussion • **Abe Laboriel Jr.** drums, percussion • **David Kahne** piano • **James McCartney** percussion

---

[753] The performance was not very good: McCartney is a bit out of tune and the whole band seems to struggle keeping time.
[754] *The Driving Rain Interview*, www.paulmccartney.com, November 2001.

306 Tiny Bubble (Paul McCartney)

Recording: February 25th, 2001 **Location:** Henson Studios, Los Angeles **Release:** November 2001, *Driving Rain*

Paul got the idea for "Tiny Bubble" during a visit to Kintyre. McCartney: "I have always found inspiration in the calm beauty of Scotland and again it proved the place where I found inspiration."[755] As soon as he wrote the song (August 2000), Paul ran into his Rude Studio to cut a demo. He was very pleased with it, and some parts of it were kept in the recording later issued on *Driving Rain*: "It started a bit more ballady" – Paul recalled – "But as happened with a a few of the songs when you bring them to a band - with a drummer - they hip up a bit."[756]

Therefore, the final recording – in which some studio noises were left in to preserve the atmosphere – turned into something unusual. "Tiny Bubble" is a pop song full of all McCartney's trademarks – including a very melodic and prominent bass part – but with a relaxed blues feel "towards Al Green or something", perfectly expressed by McCartney's Rhodes piano, Gabe Dixon's Hammond organ and call and response vocals.

A refrain borrowed from Harrison's song "Piggies" brings the curtain down on this song, that seems to be another confession of Paul's difficult moment, with some lyrics referencing to "what I've been going through". In McCartney's words the track wraps up his naïf world view, where angst is resolved in a sort of fairy tale: "It was just a stream of consciousness, saying all the world's a tiny bubble."[757]

Musicians:

Paul McCartney vocals, piano, bass, electric guitar • **Rusty Anderson** electric guitar • **Gabe Dixon** Hammond organ • **Abe Laboriel Jr.** drums

307 Magic (Paul McCartney)

Recording: February 25th, 2001 **Location:** Henson Studios, Los Angeles **Release:** November 2001, *Driving Rain*

Losing Linda was a nightmare for McCartney. His frustrated state led him to think that he would no longer be able to write songs or endure his pain.

Step by step, Paul found restoration in music and after composing some "very sad" songs, he succeeded in conveying something positive in a track.

McCartney: "Towards the end of the year that Linda died, I wrote a song called 'Magic', about the night I first met her I realized I had turned a corner with that song, because I suddenly thought, 'I'm really proud to have known someone as beautiful as Linda for 30 years."[758]

---

[755] *The Scottish Daily Record*, 11th November 2001.
[756] *Ibid.*
[757] *Ibid.*
[758] *The Daily Mail*, 10th November 2001.

Due to its positive nature, McCartney chose this song for the album, after he had discarded other tracks he had composed dealing with Linda's memories.

McCartney: "This is about meeting Linda, at *Bag O' Nails*. I always thought years after, particularly after she died, that if I hadn't stood up that night in a club we might never have met again. It was something I never normally did; I wouldn't normally stand up as someone was about to leave and say, 'Er, excuse me, hello....' I didn't do that. It was a bit embarrassing for a young guy to do that. I didn't normally do that but it was just one of those things that I felt I just had to do that night – 'Hi, um, I'm Paul, who are you?' And she sort of smiled and said, 'Linda'. I said, 'Er, we're going onto another club. Are you going home? Shall we meet up at this other club?' It must have been some sort of magic that made me do that."[759]

For the recording, Paul opted for an intense but straightforward arrangement: McCartney and Anderson went on electric guitars, accompanied by Laboriel on drums and Dixon on piano.

Then Paul overdubbed his lead vocal – treated with much reverb – and his bass, which underscores the whole song by exploiting scales, ascending-descending lines, octave jumps and all the melodic shapes so characteristic of McCartney's playing.

"Magic" goes on without drawing breath, almost as going fast as memory when one travels once again through the most important things in our lives.

For the ending, McCartney chose a lighthearted approach and the song closes weirdly with a triple false-ending – with some powerful guitar breaks, in the same fashion of rock bands trying to extend the song before the crowd's roar and applause – which leads to the lively reprise, where Kahne's synthesizers reproduce a string quartet.

A charming and funny sequence – which recalls the Beatles' "I'm So Tired" – where Laboriel's vigorous drumming act as a counterbalance to the graceful strings. "Magic" appears on *Driving Rain*.

Musicians:

Paul McCartney vocals, bass, acoustic and electric guitar • **Rusty Anderson** acoustic and electric guitar • **Gabe Dixon** piano • **Abe Laboriel Jr.** drums • **David Kahne** synthesizer

308 Driving Rain (Paul McCartney)

Recording: February 27th, 2001 **Location:** Henson Studios, Los Angeles **Release:** November 2001, *Driving Rain*

When McCartney went back to Los Angeles in June to finish the *Driving Rain* recordings, he played this still unissued track at the Greek Theatre on June 14th, 2001.

Very likely, Paul had thought of "Driving Rain" as a lead-off single, but – like in the case of "Off the Ground" (see sheet 239) – the song would become the title-track of the album (whose early title was *Blue Skies*) only at the last minute.

---

[759] *The Driving Rain Interview*, www.paulmccartney.com, November 2001.

Indeed, Paul had composed the song just a couple of days before its recording: it was one of the most spontaneous sessions held in Los Angeles.

McCartney: "'Driving Rain' was written out here in Los Angeles – there was a lot of rain out here in February and so on our day off we went off for a drive in this little Corvette that I hired, we drove off up the Pacific Coast Highway and went on up to Malibu (…) In the evening, feeling great after a nice day out, I was sitting around at the piano and I just started writing something half-based on the day out."[760]

"Driving Rain" is another perfect example of McCartney's talent to take a cue from anything and convey it into music. McCartney: "The funny thing about the song 'Driving Rain' was that the alarm system in the house we were renting in Los Angeles was always on. There was a little electrical LED box on the wall and it always said, 'Something's Open'. I thought what the fuck good is that? And no matter if you shut every window and door in the whole bloody place, this alarm always said, 'Something's Open'. Not very reassuring, but in the end I thought, 'Fuck it' – and I took the words into a song (…) I just used them as an opening line of 'Driving Rain'."[761]

The song started off as a ballad, but Paul changed his mind and tried to speed it up. The track was recorded live in the studio, just with a few overdubs: McCartney led the band with his throbbing bass through this upbeat song.

"Driving Rain" is one of the most pleasant tracks on the album and – despite its childish rhyme, that brings to mind The Beatles' song "All Together Now" – is flawlessly produced.

From its opening riff, "Driving Rain" slips away with its genuine enthusiasm, thanks to a particularly catchy refrain.

One of the few tracks from the *Driving Rain* album to be played live during the 2002-03 *Drivin' Tour*, it was included both in *Back in the US* and *Back in the World*.

"Driving Rain" was never released as a single, although McCartney also prepared a remix version in a rap style.

Musicians:

Paul McCartney vocals, bass, acoustic guitar • **Rusty Anderson** electric guitar and 12-string electric guitar • **Gabe Dixon** electric piano • **Abe Laboriel Jr.** drums • **David Kahne** synthesizer

309 Back in the Sunshine Again (Paul McCartney-James McCartney)

Recording: February 28th, 2001 **Location:** Henson Studios, Los Angeles **Release:** November 2001, *Driving Rain*

McCartney's artistic vein is clearly aroused by exotic and sunny places: "Back in the Sunshine Again" is another example. The song's title came while Paul was on holiday in Arizona in 1996.

---

760 *Ibid.*
761 *Ibid.*

McCartney: "The idea of getting out of the English winter and into the Arizona sun was very appealing, so I started writing it."[762]

Paul was helped by his son James, who composed the main riff and the bridge. The song is a sort of ode to joy, that perfectly expresses McCartney's mood: "It's about leaving behind all our troubles" – said Paul – "And moving forward into the sunshine…"[763]

McCartney completed the song in California, just before starting the sessions and James also guests on the recording, although in a less characteristic performance than on "Heaven on a Sunday".

"Back in the Sunshine Again", a laid-back blues in a minor key reminiscent of the well-known "Summertime", reflects in its peaceful tone and its lazy lyrics – randomly gathered but very fitting to McCartney's inner mood – Paul's awareness for his newly found self-confidence and peace of mind.

The bridge, mainly built around James' guitar riff, adds a nostalgic feel to the song – unusual for McCartney – which emphasizes the fleeting nature of worldly events ("Life's too short to spend it lonely…": the verse recalls Lennon's lines on "We Can Work It Out"). The track is on *Driving Rain*.

Musicians:

Paul McCartney vocals, bass, electric guitar • **Rusty Anderson** electric guitar • **Gabe Dixon** piano • **Abe Laboriel Jr.** drums • **James McCartney** electric guitar

310 Heather (Paul McCartney)

Recording: March 2nd, 2001 **Location:** Henson Studios, Los Angeles **Release:** November 2001, *Driving Rain*

McCartney: "When you are married and have a family, it's completely different starting a relationship and Heather and I had to be really sensitive to their feelings. I talked to the kids and said, 'How would you feel if I started getting feelings for another woman?' At first it was difficult. They were used to seeing me driving up in a car with my wife – their mum – and now I was with another woman."[764]

When Paul and Heather Mills' engagement became public, many rumors begun floating around: his kids were concerned and started to oppose their relationship and Paul admitted that the *Driving Rain* songs he wrote for Heather were difficult for him to play for his children, saying, "It was like, 'Oh my God, I can't play this to the kids.'"[765]

One of those was called "Heather", just a little piano improvisation that came out accidentally: "It actually came about early one morning" – McCartney says – "I'd got up and was just

---

[762] *Ibid.*
[763] *Ibid.*
[764] *The Daily Mail*, 10 November 2001.
[765] *Ibid.*

jamming on the piano and Heather, who doesn't know all of The Beatles songs because she's young, said, 'That's great – which Beatles song is that?' I said, 'It's not, I'm just making it up'. And she's like, 'What? Now? Making it up now?' Yeah. Suddenly she's saying, 'Get it down! You've got to get that down, get it on a tape, now!' I'm saying, 'No, it's OK, I'm just noodling', but she's insisting, 'Get it down!' so we found a little Dictaphone and played it into that."[766]

McCartney brought his demo into the studio and again opted for a very simple arrangement: the piano demo was used as a basic track for the recording that was almost entirely a one-man-band performance. Paul handled electric guitars, acoustic guitars and bass, while the band supported him on vocal harmonies.

The final result makes "Heather" one of the most infectious instrumental tracks within McCartney's body of work; the song's inspiration is nothing more than a doodling upon the E major chord, but its catchy melody (played by piano, violin and sampled strings), the guitar breaks – backed by Laboriel's solid drum-rolls – and the dreamy tone of the vocal harmonies, they all give to the track both graceful elegance and strength.

The lyrics – that maybe were not needed – seem to express Paul's continuous search for peace, finding him in his usual Epicurean mood. "Heather" is on *Driving Rain*.

Musicians:

Paul McCartney vocals, backing vocals, piano, bass, electric and acoustic guitar • **Rusty Anderson** backing vocals • **Gabe Dixon** backing vocals • **Abe Laboriel Jr.** drums • **David Kahne** strings sampling • **Ralph Morrison** violin

In May, after many years of video and audio archival research, McCartney launched his *Wingspan* project, a retrospective on the Wings' period from 1971 to 1980, also containing some extra-Wings tracks. A double-cd in two parts: *Hits*, containing all the singles and *History*, a selection of McCartney's favorites. A TV documentary was also produced, based on an interview with Paul conducted by his daughter Mary with a lot of unseen footage from the Wings' days.

On the wave of *One*'s big success – this Beatles' compilation was released around Christmas and sold over 20 million copies worldwide – *Wingspan-Hits and History* became the fastest selling album of McCartney's entire career.

McCartney did a heavy promotion, launching his new Website, www.paulmccartney.com, granting a large number of interviews and making important public appearances.

The album debuted at #2 on *Billboard* (and it reached #5 in the UK) and soon went double-platinum in America. In June, after some European promotion for *Wingspan* (Berlin, Milan, Cannes), McCartney went back to Los Angeles to finish *Driving Rain*. These sessions produced

---

766 *The Driving Rain Interview*, www.paulmccartney.com, November 2001.

the still unreleased track called "Washington", a "blue-grass style song" as David Kahne revealed.

On June 14th, Paul made a surprise appearance in Los Angeles, at the Greek Theatre. Backed by his new band, he performed "Driving Rain", and The Beatles' classics "Yesterday", "Let It Be", "The Long and Winding Road" – in the latter two McCartney played bass and not piano – and "I've Just Seen a Face", in a duet with Paul Simon.

311 Your Loving Flame (Paul McCartney)

Recording: June 19th, 2001 **Location:** Henson Studios, Los Angeles **Release:** November 2001, *Driving Rain*

Although recorded later in the game, "Your Loving Flame" ironically was the earliest of the compositions that made it onto *Driving Rain*.

As McCartney told Michael Parkinson during the show on December 2nd, 1999 – where Paul premiered the song playing it at the piano with a cameo by David Gilmour on guitar – the song was born a few weeks before: "I went to New York and they put me in the Carlisle Hotel" – McCartney recalled – "I went to the lift at the 31st floor and I went to look at the room they gave me. It overlooked Central Park with a big plate glass window and to the right there was a little baby grand piano! So it was, 'Wow! What am I going to do it with that set up?' If you're a songwriter the only thing to do it's write a song. The next day I sat at the piano… And this one came to me in about one hour."[767] Paul added: "I thought I was walking into a Cole Porter movie!"[768]

With this gentle ballad, Paul revealed to the world his new love Heather Mills: "Your Loving Flame" witnesses a moment in which Paul still had to solve many doubts. McCartney says that he wants to discover what's in Heather's mind and heart.

McCartney recalled that this was the "first song I wrote for her": the track, "that has got three notes" kind of wrote itself. Right after finishing it, Paul, phoned Heather and had her listen to the song.

McCartney had told Parkinson that the song was unfinished but in comparison to the final recording, only a few changes were made: except for being completed with the group instrumentation and lengthened a little bit, "Your Loving Flame" would maintain the same structure.

At Henson Studios, the track was recorded with the full band instrumentation – bass, guitars, drums, organ – and later enriched by a string arrangement, achieved combining David Kahne's samplers and a real string quartet, the latter kept very low in the mix.

---

[767] *Michael Parkinson Show*, 02/12/1999.
[768] *The Driving Rain Interview*, www.paulmccartney.com, November 2001.

McCartney presented the track in a mimed performance in Oslo during the Nobel Prize evening (December 12th, 2001) and dedicated the song to George Harrison's memory. "Your Loving Flame" was included in his 2002-03 *Drivin' Tour*. A live version is featured on *Back in the US* and *Back in the World*. "Your Loving Flame" appears in a remix version on the radio promo cd-single (March 2002): strings are mixed higher than in the *Driving Rain* version.

Musicians:

Paul McCartney vocals, backing vocals, piano, bass, tambourine • **Rusty Anderson** backing vocals, electric and acoustic guitar • **Gabe Dixon** backing vocals, Hammond organ • **Abe Laboriel Jr.** backing vocals, drums • **David Kahne** string samples • **David Campbell, Matt Funes** viola • **Joel Derouin** violin • **Larry Corbett** cello

312 Vanilla Sky (Paul McCartney)

Recording: June, 2001 **Location:** Henson Studios, Los Angeles **Release:** December 2001 (US) – February 2002 (UK), *Vanilla Sky Soundtrack*

According to David Kahne, "Vanilla Sky" is not an outtake from *Driving Rain*, although it was recorded during these sessions. It was intended specifically as the soundtrack and the title-track for the movie.

According to the film writer and director, Cameron Crowe: "Music always establishes the tone of something before I ever write or make it… (At that time) I was listening to folk songs a lot. I thought Alejandro Amenabar's movie was like a folk song – a simple tale that's a fable."[769]

Crowe's mind went to no other than McCartney: in Los Angeles Paul invited him to the studio, and he offered him a chance to listen to a couple of songs from his new album.

Crowe was not completely satisfied and in a brave move asked Paul for a folksier song. McCartney accepted and within a few days he came back to Crowe with a new tune.

For the occasion, McCartney came out with one of his typical acoustic ditties, maybe too typical in this case: "Vanilla Sky", in fact, opens with the same chords and even with the same melody line as "Biker Like an Icon" (see sheet **237**)! It's a little example of subconscious auto-plagiarism (unless Paul asks himself for royalties…): apart from that, the song has a completely different atmosphere from the *Off the Ground* track's mysterious solemnity.

The inspiration came from a waiter in a restaurant. McCartney: "Before the first course, he brought something we hadn't ordered. He said, 'Here's an *amuse-bouche*.' With my limited knowledge of French, I worked out that he meant a sort of palate-pleaser… That became the first line of the song…'The chef prepares a special menu.'"[770]

---

[769] *Writing Vanilla Sky*, 14/12/2001, http://mcbeatle.de
[770] *ET interview about Vanilla Sky*, 18/01/2002. http://www.youtube.com/watch?v=F0JHiIqTqO4

"Vanilla Sky" is a pleasant little song, as simple as all of McCartney's acoustic compositions: with its infectious refrain, the track is marked by a Latin-flavored flute solo. The recording is very basic and may have been completed by McCartney almost entirely by himself.

Thus, McCartney was surprised when the song – that he wrote in ten minutes in the kitchen – got no less than an Oscar Nomination, twenty-nine years after "Live and Let Die"!

For this one – and to date, only – Oscar performance, held on March 24th, 2002 McCartney presented the song in a specially-recorded version, ad-libbing it on stage with Rusty Anderson (guitar) and Jim Walker (flute). Galvanized by the event, Paul included the track during his 2002 *Drivin' USA Tour* and in the live album *Back in the US*.

The crowning achievement of the song's critical acclaim was its nomination at the 2003 Grammy Award in the Best Original Soundtrack category. The track can be found on the *Vanilla Sky* soundtrack album.

Musicians:

Paul McCartney vocals, acoustic guitar, percussion (?), keyboards (?), electric guitar (?) • **Rusty Anderson** (?) acoustic guitar (?), electric guitar (?) • **Gabe Dixon (?)** keyboards (?) • **Abe Laboriel Jr. (?)** percussion (?) • **Unknown musician** flute (?)

On October 20th, McCartney was the closing act in NYC at the Madison Square Garden concert, that he organized to support victims of the September 11th attack.

Paul and the band played the following set: "I'm Down", "Lonely Road", "From a Lover to a Friend", "Freedom", "Yesterday", "Let it Be", "Freedom" (encore).

313 Freedom (Paul McCartney)

Recording: October 20th and 23rd (overdubs), 2001 **Location:** Madison Square Garden and Quad Studios (overdubs), New York **Release:** November 2001, *Driving Rain*

McCartney was actually in New York on September 11th, 2001, the day of the Twin Towers attack and he witnessed that epoch-making event. McCartney: "I was in New York when it was attacked. Immediately after the disaster I wrote this song which is about our right to live in freedom against any who would attack that right."[771]

Heather Mills: "I watched it with Paul. We were about to take off from JFK Airport when the captain put the brakes on and I saw smoke coming out of tower one."[772]

McCartney was stuck at the airport for hours. This dramatic event prompted Paul to take out his guitar. According to his version, within a few minutes he had composed "Freedom" on the spot, although reportedly a demo called "Give Me the Right to Freedom" was sitting in

---

[771] *Heroes Inspire a New Song-Freedom*, 19/10/2001, http://mcbeatle.de
[772] *Thoughts On Afghanistan*, 1/11/2001, http://mcbeatle.de

McCartney's vaults from 1992. The song was his desperate cry in support of one of the fundamental rights of human kind.

McCartney was hit hard by the disaster, and soon he made a plan to organize a benefit concert, to raise funds for the victims. *The Concert for New York City* was held on October 20th at Madison Square Garden.

McCartney strongly supported America not only by organizing the concert. After the USA decision to send troops to Afghanistan, he made some very resolute statements, partly distancing himself from the Sixties pacifism, which he confessed he never was a fan of.

McCartney: "Normally you're a pacifist and you don't want any kind of war at all, but occasionally something so atrocious happens there's gotta be some kind of response. I'd like to see the bombing stop but what are you gonna do, turn the other cheek? After the New York attack, my attitude was like, screw you man, just screw you. I've got kids living in London. Are you gonna do a bombing campaign? How dare you? If you want to take my kids out – well, screw you!"[773]

The Madison Square Garden concert was the perfect occasion to present this new composition. "Freedom" could be considered the most political song of McCartney's entire career: its aggressive mood overtaking even "Give Ireland Back to the Irish" (see sheet 🔲).

But it was really an overly simplistic move: the word "freedom" was enough for Paul to build around some basic themes, and for the first time in a McCartney song God is named.

Paul gives the impression to use God's name as a way of expressing his non-pacifist feelings. The word "fight" seems to be not necessarily used in a metaphorical sense: an angry mood rarely expressed in McCartney's music.

In New York, the song was performed with Eric Clapton on guitar, making his first appearance with McCartney. Probably, McCartney made his decision on the spot, in the wake of the night's emotion: footage from *The Love We Make* DVD (2011) – a documentary about McCartney's journey in New York in the aftermath of the September 11th attacks – shows Paul and Clapton discussing about the track.

One could forgive the inconsistency of the song, no more than a chant built around a very basic harmonic structure: nevertheless, the song was acclaimed at the MSG – Paul played it twice, first with his band and as an encore with everyone on stage – and for McCartney this was enough to go into the studio and complete the track for its release.

In the days following the concert, Paul went to Quad Studios in New York to refine it: he fixed his vocals and he recorded the first guitar solo and a bass part, doubling or maybe replacing the previously recorded track by Will Lee. The song was rush-released and included in *Driving Rain* in a version called *Studio Mix*.

---

[773] Gavin Martin, *Normally, He's a Pacifist*, The Independent, 15/11/2001.

An instant-marketing plan that didn't succeed. Released in the US as a single – replacing "From a Lover to Friend" – "Freedom" only reached #97 on the *Billboard* charts.

The version without overdubs appears on *The Concert for New York City*. The track was performed by McCartney in 2002 during the SuperBowl and in his *Drivin' USA Tour*.

A radio edit (lasting 2:37) appears on the promo-cd, and the song was issued in a third version (!) on the live album *Back in the US*.

Musicians:

Paul McCartney vocals, acoustic and electric guitar, bass • **Rusty Anderson** electric guitar • **Gabe Dixon** electric piano • **Abe Laboriel Jr.** drums • **Eric Clapton** electric guitar • **Will Lee** bass

Driving Rain, Paul's first album of new material after four and a half years, was released on November 13th. The record gained good reviews, all focused on its sound freshness and its spontaneous feeling, as well as for the experimental flavor on some tracks.

Rolling Stone wrote: "Paul McCartney is one kick-ass bass player. A listener could live inside the voluptuous notes he effortlessly threads through *Driving Rain* (…) The album exploits this virtue to the fullest with fuss-free arrangements that magnify the interplay of a decent little four piece rock & roll band comprising three relatively unknowns and one living legend."

Everything seemed to foresee a great success. In truth, the album was one of the biggest commercial failures of McCartney's career: in the US the album entered the charts at #26 – selling only 66.000 copies in its first week – and left the Top 100 within a month, while in the UK *Driving Rain* stopped at #46, the lowest ever chart position for McCartney in his own country.

On November 29th George Harrison died. Paul said: "He was my little baby brother".

2002

McCartney started the year playing at the SuperBowl, where he performed "Freedom" and then announced his new American tour, with 27 dates between April and May, hoping to help the *Driving Rain* poor sales: only 320.000 copies in America four months after its release. The marketing plan was huge: the *Drivin' USA Tour* was promoted through a dedicated website and the *Driving Rain* album was re-issued with a different cover.

McCartney was backed by a new band: Rusty Anderson on guitar, Abe Laboriel Jr. on drums, Brian Ray (guitar and bass) and his old pal Wix on keyboards.

Once more, the concert was full of Beatles' songs: a heated debate about the setlist took place on McCartney's official forum. Many fans complained about the choice to limit Wings and solo material to a few numbers.

Initially, Paul thought to open the show with "Honey Hush", but in the end he changed his mind. He was also open to suggestions from band members, choosing to include in the setlist songs like "Getting Better" following Rusty Anderson's advice.

The setlist included a surprising tribute to Harrison, with Paul playing "Something" only with a ukulele:

"Hello, Goodbye" – "Jet" – "All My Loving" – "Getting Better" – "Coming Up" – "Let Me Roll It" – "Lonely Road" – "Driving Rain" – "Your Loving Flame" – "Blackbird" – "Every Night" – "We Can Work It Out" – "Mother Nature's Son" – "Vanilla Sky" – "You Never Give Me Your Money/Carry That Weight" – "The Fool on the Hill" – "Here Today" – "Something" – "Eleanor Rigby" – "Here, There and Everywhere" – "Band on the Run" – "Back in the USSR" – "Maybe I'm Amazed" – "C Moon" – "My Love" – "Can't Buy Me Love" – "Freedom" – "Live and Let Die" – "Let It Be" – "Hey Jude" – "The Long and Winding Road" – "Lady Madonna" – "I Saw Her Standing There" – "Yesterday" – "Sgt. Pepper's…/The End". Among the few variations McCartney played "Mull of Kintyre" in Toronto, Canada.

The success of the tour helped the *Driving Rain* sales, and at the end of April the album was certified gold by the R.I.A.A. for 500.000 units sold in the US.

Once the tour ended in Fort Lauderdale on May 18th, McCartney was one of the guests for the Buckingham Palace concert on June 3rd: a special night to celebrate Queen Elizabeth 50th Anniversary.

McCartney closed the evening with a special set: "Her Majesty" ("I had to do it!" Paul shouted) – "Blackbird" – "While My Guitar Gently Weeps (with Clapton on lead vocals, McCartney on piano and vocal harmonies) – "Sgt. Pepper's…/The End" – "All You Need Is Love" (with everyone joining in on stage) – "Hey Jude" – "I Saw Her Standing There"

The marriage between McCartney and Heather Mills, on June 17th did not stop Paul's projects. On September 21st a new tour called *Back in the US Tour* started in America with 23 dates, then went to Mexico (November 2nd-3rd) and finally to Japan (five dates, Tokyo and Osaka, November 11th-18th).

Again, a few changes occurred to the setlist. Only three new songs were added: "Michelle", "Let'em In" and "She's Leaving Home", the latter never played before live. Some surprise-tracks were played here and there: "Midnight Special" in Houston and "Calico Skies" in Osaka.

On November 29th McCartney performed at the Royal Albert Hall in London for the *Concert for George*, a tribute to Harrison's memory, playing "Something", "For You Blue" and "All Things Must Pass". Simultaneously, *Back in the US – Live 2002* was issued as a double cd and DVD, containing the show taken from the US tour.

The DVD was announced as a fascinating "behind the curtains" musical journey: three hours of music and footage, and a special access to the Paul McCartney website, with an exclusive *Secret Show* to be aired on December 16th.

Reaction was great: the album climbed the *Billboard* charts at #8 – with over 225.000 copies sold in its first week – whereas the DVD broke a record as the fast-selling in history with 67.000 copies. *Back in the US* remained in the US charts for 16 weeks.

The *Secret Show* was an interesting idea: McCartney offered through a web access footage from the soundcheck held in New Orleans on October 12th.

The setlist was somewhat unusual: Paul opened with a lively version of "Honey Hush", followed by a brief jam – based on the Hendrix "Foxy Lady" guitar riff – then switched to acoustic guitar, playing a very unique "Blackbird" – fast version, in barrelhouse-style – and "Calico Skies", with a folk-Cajun arrangement. Then, the show went on with "Matchbox", "Celebration" aka "Sea Melody" (the track from *Rupert the Bear*, performed by Paul on piano), "Welcome to the Secret Show" (a sort of jam, nothing more than a chance to introduce band's members), "India" (an unreleased song) and "Lady Madonna" (featuring Howie Casey on sax).

2003

McCartney was in for some good news and surprises right from the start of the year. First came the R.I.A.A. certification for 2 million copies of *Back in the US* sold in the United States and triple platinum results for its related DVD (300.000 copies). Then came the Grammy Award nomination for "Vanilla Sky" in the Best Soundtrack Category. McCartney also announced his upcoming 30-date European tour. To promote it, he released *Back in the World,* a modified version of *Back in the US* with some changes and substitutions: Paul replaced "C Moon", "Vanilla Sky" and "Freedom" with "She's Leaving Home", "Let'em In", "Michelle" and "Calico Skies", and included a different version of "Hey Jude". "Birthday" was also on the concert tracklist but didn't appear on the album. The public response was massive; on-line ticket sales broke all records with the London gigs selling out in only nine minutes!

Back in the World also entered the UK charts (reaching #5) and during his tour, McCartney engaged in some of the most significant events of his career, performing in major historic and artistic venues such as the Coliseum in Rome (May 11th) and Red Square in Moscow (May 24th). An inconvenient bout of laryngitis caused Paul to have to cancel one gig in Sheffield on April 6th and in order to give his vocal cords a break, McCartney replaced some of the hardest songs in the repertoire (e.g. "Maybe I'm Amazed") with softer acoustic Beatles' material ("Things We Said Today", "I've Just Seen a Face" and "Two of Us").

As the tour came to a close, McCartney started recording his new album. For the new batch of sessions, he once again called in David Kahne as producer and the band. At Abbey Road Studio 2, McCartney recorded nine demos.

After only a few recordings, McCartney asked George Martin for some other producer and he came up with Nigel Godrich's name. Paul began talking to Nigel Godrich about a completely new project.

As soon as the sessions began, Godrich had convinced McCartney to change direction. Paul broke the news to the group: "(It was) very embarrassing, I had to say to the guys, 'Look, he wants to go in this other direction and he's the producer so I can't really say, 'No, you've got to work with my band.' I said, 'How do you feel about it?' and they were really cool."

Up until then they had only recorded one song, "Follow Me" that would end up on *Chaos and Creation in the Backyard* in 2005.

314 Follow Me (Paul McCartney)

Recording: September 2003 and April 2005 (overdubs) **Location:** RAK Studios and AIR Studios (overdubs), London **Release:** September 2005, *Chaos and Creation in the Backyard*

McCartney: "When we started to do the album that two weeks at RAK Studios, Nigel Godrich said, 'I'd like to take you out of your safety zone. You know these guys and you know what you're doing with them…"[774] And so Paul had the unenviable task of firing the band after only a few recordings. One of these was "Follow Me", an acoustic song that pretty much "wrote itself" and was the only one to make it onto *Chaos and Creation in the Backyard* in 2005.

McCartney was thinking of "Let It Be" and had the idea of a song that was "quasi religious, very uplifting."[775] He began strumming away in the key of C major ("a very sort of open key") and the lyrics followed easily: the song became a sort of mini-anthem.

The intimate atmosphere of "Follow Me" is further enhanced by its simple arrangement. Paul, Rusty and Brian recorded a bed of three acoustic guitars. McCartney also double-tracked Laboriel's percussion and tambourine as well as recording (or re-recording) the drum track. Paul then added an electric guitar and a very heartfelt vocal. Later on, some strings were overdubbed onto the track.

Premiered during the 2004 *Summer Tour* at the Glastonbury concert, "Follow Me" was included in the show *Chaos and Creation at Abbey Road* (August 24th, 2005) and in the *US Tour* 2005.

Musicians:

Paul McCartney vocals, acoustic and electric guitar, bass, drums, percussion, tambourine • **Rusty Anderson** acoustic guitar • **Brian Ray** acoustic guitar • **Abe Laboriel Jr.** percussion, tambourine • **Millennia Ensemble** strings

McCartney resumed the sessions working alone.

315 This Never Happened Before (Paul McCartney)

Recording: September, 2003 and April, 2005 (overdubs) **Location:** RAK Studios, London **Release:** September 2005, *Chaos and Creation in the Backyard*

"This Never Happened Before" is another McCartney song which celebrates love's uniqueness. The track had no specific inspirational references, as Paul said: "It's always a big help if you get a nice little chord sequence and the opening chords to the verse of that go a nice place, so they settle you down with your melody and you feel like you're going somewhere…"[776]

After writing the song, McCartney immediately began working on it with Godrich. In fact, the song nails it: it's a romantic ballad infused with an unusual glow. Paul recorded it with piano and a drum-machine, that was kept in the final recording. Later on, McCartney beefed it up with some electric guitar parts and an orchestral arrangement care of Joby Talbot.

Talbot recalls: "I was brought on board through Nigel Godrich. He thinks about strings in a different way than I would think about an orchestral arrangement… He thinks of them occupying a small space in songs (…) I remember I was sitting home looking after my young

---

[774] *Gary Crowley Interview*, July 2005.
[775] *Ibid.*
[776] *Ibid.*

son, who was two years old at the time. The phone rang and it was Paul. He said, 'Could you come out to the studio?' So I went to RAK Studios to hear the song 'This Never Happened Before'. We recorded the orchestra twice: at AIR Studios the first time, but then we re-did it at RAK, because Nigel wasn't happy with the sound of the song at AIR, it seemed very bright and modern and he preferred doing it at RAK, the studios where he grew up."[777]

Paul had a funny anecdote to share: "I was in America and I was actually getting a massage and I happened to play it and the girl who was doing the massage said, 'Oh, I love that song, it's magnificent.' She happened to tell me she was getting married (…) I sent her a little letter saying, 'Look, if you love it that much, why don't you play this at your wedding?' So I said, 'But this is highly bootleggable,' I said, 'So just play it and send it me back. You can't keep it, but,' I said, 'I'll send you the proper record when we're done with it.' She wrote me a letter, thanks and told me about the wedding and she just put this one little line, 'You know we had a great time. We laughed. We cried.' And I thought that sums up that song for me."[778]

The song appears on *Chaos and Creation in the Backyard* and McCartney also planned a single release in February 2006. Unfortunately, it was withdrawn at the last minute for unknown reasons. It would have included three other songs as well; "A Modern Dance", "Perfect Lover" and "Watching My Fish Drown". If it hadn't been cancelled the track would have obtained lots of media exposure, as it was featured on the soundtrack for *Lake House*. This soundtrack contains an edited version without the instrumental intro.

Musicians:

Paul McCartney vocals, piano, bass, electric guitar, drums • **Millennia Ensemble** strings

316 Comfort of Love (Paul McCartney)

Recording: September, 2003 **Location**: RAK Studios, London **Release**: August 2005, "Fine Line" single B-side

When "Comfort of Love" was rehearsed in September with the band for the upcoming annual gala benefit, *Adopt A Minefield*, the song was already well-structured. Paul recorded it in one of the earliest sessions for *Chaos and Creation*. The song was one of the less original taped during the sessions – with its light handed Jeff Lynne production style. Even though it has its moments – such as the metronome intro, the use of a spinet (a smaller harpsichord) or the pulsating piano hook – it still remains a modest effort. "Comfort of Love" is on the cd-single of "Fine Line".

Musicians:

Paul McCartney vocals, piano, electric piano, bass, acoustic and electric guitar, drums, spinet, tambourine, metronome, shakers, bells

777 Interview courtesy of Joby Talbot, 21/09/2012.
778 *Gary Crowley Interview*, July 2005.

McCartney was still unsure about Godrich's work. So, he started some new recordings with David Kahne and the band at Abbey Road Studios. During the sessions, McCartney and his band recorded "Whole Life", a song written by Paul with Dave Stewart that was given to the anti-Aids charity project called 46664.

317 Whole Life (Paul McCartney-Dave Stewart)

Recording: October 22nd-23rd, 2003 **Location:** Abbey Road Studios, London **Release:** November 2003, iTunes (digital download); January 2005, *46664: 1 Year On* (EP)

"Whole Life" dates back to mid-Nineties. McCartney had written it with Dave Stewart during the *Flaming Pie* sessions but never used it. The song came in handy for another project; an anti-AIDS benefit album.

Paul arrived at the studio and offhandedly told the band that he wanted to do this song and that Dave Stewart was on his way over.

A video of the session – uploaded during the benefit campaign – shows Paul and Rusty Anderson on electric guitars, Stewart on acoustic and Brian Ray on bass, while recording the basic track. Anderson recalled: "I wasn't sure if – I thought Dave Stewart plays guitar – I won't even be part of this (…) But then we all got together and we all sort of did it live (…) Dave Stewart played acoustic and Paul and I played electric and Brian played bass and Abe played drums. It was really fun actually (…) We really quickly g(ot) the song together. Then we all got around the mike, I guess the four of us, Paul, Abe, Brian and I... And did all the background vocals."[779]

Notwithstanding the spontaneity of the recording, "Whole Life" remains an uninspired rock track built on some guitar riffs recycled from other songs such as "Letting Go" and "The World Tonight". McCartney's vocal is also less than brilliant.

The song can only be found on the limited edition EP *46664* released in Spain (6000 copies) and as a download on iTunes.

Musicians:

Paul McCartney vocals, electric guitar • **Rusty Anderson** electric guitar • **Dave Stewart** acoustic guitar • **Abe Laboriel Jr.** drums • **Wix** electric piano, organ • **Brian Ray** bass

---

[779] www.macca-central.com/macca-musicians/rustyanderson/rusty_interview_12-15-03.cfm

2004

In February, McCartney proceeded with the recordings with Kahne at Abbey Road. Several tracks were recorded, seven of which were not resumed until 2007 for the *Memory Almost Full* album.

318 Only Mama Knows (Paul McCartney)

Recording: February, 2004 and January-February, 2007 (overdubs) **Location:** Abbey Road Studios, London and Hog Hill Studio (overdubs), Icklesham **Release:** June 2007, *Memory Almost Full*

"Only Mama Knows" was a made-up story. McCartney: "I'm not always writing from a personal perspective. So it's kind of nice because you get more into your imagination. Writing about 'Eleanor Rigby': I don't know a woman who picks up rice in a church, nor do I know anyone who was stranded in the transit lounge of an airport, as in 'Only Mama Knows'..."[780]

The musical setting was a driving rocker in a minor key. The track was recorded live in the studio, as Kahne reveals: "You can hear the Abbey Road room sound... A big room with a close feel."[781]

Later, it was given some treatment, adding that heavy reverb on vocals and instruments, especially on Laboriel Jr.'s drums. McCartney played bass, Anderson and Brian Ray electric guitars.[782]

The final touches were some strings played by both a real orchestra and synthesizer, used as an intro and for the ending: "We had an idea and put it on there, to hear the theme in a different setting" – Kahne revealed – "It fitted very well, the results were great."[783]

In the song, McCartney tells a story of family abandonment much like in "She's Leaving Home" but in this case, it's the girl who finds herself alone. The desperation and soul searching are undeniable in the break: "Hold on/I've got to hold on".

It's easy to assume that Paul is making references – at least subconsciously – to his own personal dramas. Relinquishing one's mother or possibly never seeing one's father again are topics that could have a psychoanalytic interpretation.

"Only Mama Knows" was performed in the *Memory Almost Full Promo Tour* (June-July 2007). This version has been released on the *Amoeba's Secret* EP and on *Live in Los Angeles* while a different live version – taken from the 2009 Tour – appears on *Good Evening New York City*.

The track, included in *Memory Almost Full*, got a Grammy Award nomination in 2008 in the Best Solo Rock Vocal Performance category.

---

[780] www.memoryalmostfull.com
[781] C. Dirani, *Interview with David Kahne*, May 2007.
[782] Michael Wright, *The Gibson Interview: Paul McCartney Guitarist Brain Ray (Part Two)*, 08/09/2010 in www.gibson.com/en-us/Lifestyle/Features/brian-ray-0809/
[783] C. Dirani, *Interview with David Kahne*, May 2007.

Musicians:

Paul McCartney vocals, backing vocals, bass, Mellotron, electric guitar (?) • **Rusty Anderson** backing vocals, electric guitar • **Abe Laboriel junior** backing vocals, drums • **Wix** backing vocals, piano, keyboards, synthesizer • **Brian Ray** backing vocals, electric guitar • **Unknown musicians** strings

319 You Tell Me (Paul McCartney)

Recording: February, 2004 and March-April, 2006 (overdubs) **Location**: Abbey Road Studios, London and Hog Hill Studio, Icklesham or AIR Studios, London or RAK Studios, London or See Squared Studios, New York (overdubs) **Release**: June 2007, *Memory Almost Full*

McCartney wrote "You Tell Me" during a summer visit in Long Island: "I started off just remembering summers (…) For a lot of people your memories, particularly childhood memories, they seem so golden. 'Did it really never rain all summer or am I just imagining the sunny bits?"[784]

How time helps fade unwanted memories is the main theme of this song, a heart-rending ballad built around McCartney's acoustic guitar arpeggio and reminiscent of "Winter Rose".

Paul recalls an incident: "I was just looking at a red cardinal. For someone English it's magical, seeing a bright red bird coming out of a tree, so he appeared in the lyric."[785]

Unlike his usual cheerful approach to his summery songs, such as "Good Times Coming/Feel the Sun", Paul went for a nostalgic minor key track with a psychedelic organ intro played backwards.

The sparse arrangement is highlighted by Laboriel's drum-pad and samples and by Anderson's stinging electric guitar that underlines the melancholy mood of the song.

McCartney recorded his vocals – in a very high key, maybe *too* high – in one take accompanied by some lovely backing vocals from the band. The song appears on *Memory Almost Full*.

Musicians:

Paul McCartney vocals, acoustic guitar, bass • **Rusty Anderson** backing vocals, electric guitar • **Abe Laboriel Jr.** backing vocals, drums • **Wix** backing vocals, electric piano • **Brian Ray** backing vocals

320 Vintage Clothes (Paul McCartney)

Recording: February, 2004 and March-April, 2006 (overdubs) **Location**: Abbey Road Studios, London and Hog Hill Studio, Icklesham or AIR Studios, London or RAK Studios, London or See Squared Studios, New York (overdubs) **Release**: June 2007, *Memory Almost Full*

McCartney: "'Vintage Clothes' is about my clothes from the '60s. I meet quite a few guys in young bands and a question they always ask is, 'Did you keep the clothes?' As a matter of fact I have!"[786]

---

[784] www.memoryalmostfull.com
[785] *Ibid.*
[786] *Ibid.*

McCartney didn't intend it to be a nostalgic song. On the contrary, it was more about looking forward and the message is clear from the start: the past is something not to rely on and life is something that runs fast. "Vintage Clothes" do not represent anything, except for something that could bring up good memories.

On the other hand, the arrangement makes clear references to the past: the piano intro opens a window onto a colorful, almost psychedelic musical space, while the Mellotron produces a kaleidoscope of sounds that further enhances the song's spirited and exciting hook.

McCartney played both piano and acoustic guitar – and, according to Brain Ray, he overdubbed the bass part that Ray himself had played during the basic track – leaving Rusty Anderson to play electric guitar.

David Kahne's eyes popped out when he heard that guitar: "I like some of the electric guitar sounds because it's evocative of some of the sounds they achieved at Abbey Road like on the *Sgt. Pepper's* reprise…"[787]

McCartney chose "Vintage Clothes" as the opening track to his *Memory Almost Full* 'pseudo' medley. It's actually a sequence of crossfaded songs with no recurring themes or different melodies put on top of each other as on *Abbey Road* or *Red Rose Speedway* but only linked by the subject of life's memories.

Musicians:

Paul McCartney vocals, acoustic guitar, piano, Mellotron, bass • **Rusty Anderson** electric guitar • **Abe Laboriel junior** drums • **Wix** keyboards

321 That Was Me (Paul McCartney)

Recording: February 2004 and March-April, 2006 (overdubs) **Location**: Abbey Road Studios, London and Hog Hill Studio, Icklesham or AIR Studios, London or RAK Studios, London or See Squared Studios, New York (overdubs) **Release**: June 2007, *Memory Almost Full*

McCartney chose "That Was Me", a rollicking, rockabilly number, as the vehicle to go through various episodes and flashbacks from his life. Paul wrote the lyrics as a kind of photograph of the day to day goings-on that apparently without rhyme or reason make up a person's life.

McCartney relives some of his own life experiences such as his scout camp days, his unexpected fame, his marriage and much more.

Most likely, the band recorded this track live in the studio. Musically, the song is flat and uninspired: McCartney plays a few repetitive acoustic guitar chords, giving the song a Fifties feel, similar in atmosphere to "Summer of '59" (see sheet 341) that Paul would record during the following *Chaos and Creation in the Backyard* sessions. Maybe, sensing that the track was a bit boring, McCartney suggested bringing in some variations. Kahne: "We were talking about

[787] Matt Hurwitz, *Memory Track by Track*, www.mixonline.com, 01/10/2007.

needing a lift for the third verse, after the vocal/guitar solo riffs. Paul said maybe he'd sing it up an octave. What's on the track is the second take. My hair was standing on end."[788]

Another interesting moment came from the piano riffs that Wix chanced upon. Kahne: "Wix was goofing around on the piano and he hit that chord and I thought it sounded great because it's so dissonant. Paul liked it, so we put it in."[789] And finally Paul wrapped it up with one of his walking octave-jumping bass parts.[790]

"That Was Me" is on *Memory Almost Full*. McCartney performed the track on his 2007 *Memory Almost Full Promo Tour*. The live version is included in the *Amoeba's Secret* EP and in the album *Live in Los Angeles* and in 2009 got a Grammy Award nomination in the Best Male Pop Vocal Performance category.

Musicians:

Paul McCartney vocals, acoustic guitar, bass, electric guitar (?) • **Rusty Anderson** electric guitar • **Abe Laboriel Jr** drums • **Wix** piano • **Brian Ray** acoustic guitar (?)

322 Feet in the Clouds (Paul McCartney)

Recording: February, 2004 and January-February, 2007 (overdubs) **Location:** Abbey Road Studios, London and RAK Studios (overdubs), London **Release:** June 2007, *Memory Almost Full*

Paul's memories of his years at the Liverpool Institute of Performing Arts were always with him. In the *Liverpool Oratorio* DVD, Paul can be seen strolling through the halls of this grand institute, that at the time of filming (1988) was not in use. Paul, taking the situation to heart, decided to re-establish it. "Feet in the Clouds" is Paul's musical tribute to his schooldays.

McCartney: "Some of my teachers were complete maniacs (…) School was very dark and gloomy, the building itself wasn't the lightest of buildings, it was an 1825 building. This seemed to affect the attitude of the teachers…"[791]

The arrangement for "Feet in the Clouds" was highly unconventional and the Oriental influenced intro – with its very Lennon-like sixth chord – had been well thought-out.

Kahne: "We worked quite a while to get that particular acoustic sound. There's no drums for a while, so size was important (…) I wanted it to feel like it was holding the voice in his hand, to make it extremely close and personal because of lyric in the chorus."[792]

The original recording of this simple song was mostly re-made. With the exception of the backing vocals and Anderson's electric guitar, Paul re-recorded everything. For the ending of the track, he wanted to do something more bizarre, so he put together a very intricate choral coda – an obvious tribute to Brian Wilson.

---

[788] C. Dirani, *Interview with David Kahne*, May 2007.
[789] *Ibid.*
[790] Andre Gardner, *Radio Interview with David Kahne*, in *Breakfast with the Beatles*, 09/05/2007.
[791] www.memoryalmostfull.com
[792] C. Dirani, *Interview with David Kahne*, May 2007.

McCartney: "I wanted to go robotic on some harmonies, to do a vocoder type thing because it's kind of a nostalgic sound and yet it's robotic. It could be from the future but in fact it's from the past. I liked it."[793]

Kahne admitted that the recording was "really fun (and very painstaking) to work on."[794] McCartney's vocals were recorded through a vocoder: accompanied only by synthesizer and tambourine, they create a very suggestive, intensely moving harmonic effect: one of the best moments on *Memory Almost Full*.

Musicians:

Paul McCartney vocals, backing vocals, acoustic guitar, vocoder, tambourine, drums, piano, synthesizer, bass, shaker, spinetta (?) • **Rusty Anderson** backing vocals, electric guitar • **Abe Laboriel Jr., Wix, Brian Ray** backing vocals

323 House of Wax (Paul McCartney)

Recording: February, 2004 and March-April, 2006 (overdubs) **Location:** Abbey Road Studios, London and Hog Hill Studio, Icklesham or AIR Studios, London or RAK Studios, London or See Squared Studios, New York (overdubs) **Release:** June 2007, *Memory Almost Full*

On "House of Wax" McCartney dusted off his poetic yearnings. After fiddling around with a couple of chords ("not so complex", as Paul admitted) he was inspired enough to write some very surreal lyrics.

The opening verses introduce the dark and mysterious mood of the song. Being so involved with his lyrics may have caused Paul to pay little attention to the melody, which seems a little bit weak. Nevertheless, he made room for a powerful and strong arrangement: "There's three drum kits" – David Kahne unveiled – "One of them slowed down to half speed."[795] In fact, it is Laboriel Jr.'s drum kit that sets the solemn tone for "House of Wax" with its thunderous toms in the introduction. After the backing track was recorded, McCartney took a breather and left a few bars of the song empty until further inspiration came his way. Kahne suggested that Paul try playing some guitar solos, "maybe changing each solo feel-wise to build the song". McCartney jumped at the chance and had the part done in half an hour: first a slow and melodious solo, then a second almost hysterical one as a perfect contrast to it. Unfortunately, heavy distortion is noticeable particularly during the guitar solos (See **2007** about the "Loudness War").

"House of Wax" was performed during the *Memory Almost Full Promo Tour* and a live version appears on the EP *Live at ICA, London, July 5th 2007* (available on iTunes). "House of Wax" is included in a different live version as the B-side to the single "Ever Present Past". The track is on *Memory Almost Full*.

---

[793] www.memoryalmostfull.com
[794] C. Dirani, *Interview with David Kahne*, May 2007.
[795] *Ibid.*

Musicians:

Paul McCartney vocals, piano, electric guitar, bass (?), tambourine (?) • **Rusty Anderson** electric guitar • **Abe Laboriel Jr** drums, tambourine (?) • **Wix** keyboards, synthesizer • **Brian Ray** bass (?)

324 The End of the End (Paul McCartney)

Recording: February, 2004 **Location:** Abbey Road Studios, London **Release:** June 2007, *Memory Almost Full*

"The End of the End" can be considered a sort of watershed song for McCartney. It's the moment in time when he tries to understand his place and legacy in the world.

Paul used to think that death was an audacious topic to write about but changed his mind after something happened to him.

McCartney: "An Irish woman wished me well by saying, 'I wish you a good death,' and I was like, 'Say what!?' And then I thought, well I like the Irish approach of a wake, where it's celebratory."[796]

And so he wrote the song: "I thought (to my funeral), 'Well, what would I like?'" – Paul said – "Jokes, wake, music, rather than everyone sitting around glum saying, 'He was a great guy,' So that led into the verse, 'On the day that I die/I'd like jokes to be told/And stories of old to be rolled out like carpets.'"[797]

When Paul played the song for his kids things got very emotional: "It's a strange combination, because you're talking about a very serious subject. But I'm dealing with it lightly."[798]

The one thing to avoid in these cases is rhetoric. McCartney preferred a clean approach, with a minimal arrangement; vocal, piano, some synthesizers and a small string section with two string quartets.

Kahne remembers the brief session: "On 'The End of the End' Paul was singing and playing live, and he had on headphones. After a few takes, he stopped and said he didn't need the headphones (…) About three takes later, he did the take you hear on the album."[799]

Paul gave one knock on the hoop and another on the barrel: his performance is crystal clear but not too polished. The piano (the 'Mrs.Mills' upright one used on "Lady Madonna") is treated with a sort of metallic timbre and Paul's whistling carries him off to the hereafter.

Issued on *Memory Almost Full*, this is one of McCartney's most moving solo songs.

Musicians:

Paul McCartney vocals, piano, synthesizer • **Unknown musicians** strings

---

[796] www.memoryalmostfull.com
[797] *Ibid.*
[798] *Ibid.*
[799] C. Dirani, *Interview with David Kahne*, May 2007.

During summer, Paul made his final decision about the producer of his new album: Nigel Godrich, who persuaded McCartney to record the album almost entirely solo, with him playing the majority of instruments, including Hofner bass. So Paul moved to Los Angeles for the most important and intense batch of recordings for *Chaos and Creation in the Backyard*.

That said, Godrich didn't leave McCartney alone. First, he got in touch with Jason Falkner, then a 36 year-old multi-instrumentalist and producer (a few years earlier Paul had liked his reinterpretations of some Lennon-McCartney classics in an album titled *Bedtime with The Beatles*) and then recruited drummer Jason Gadson, one of the most famous and ubiquitous R&B studio musicians. Having put together the trio, they recorded three songs, and Gadson and Falkner contributed separately to three other tracks.

Falkner recalls: "(Godrich) called me one day and was like, 'Hey Jay, would you be interested in working with Paul McCartney?' I got the call and I was just like, 'Uh…' [Nigel Godrich] was like, 'I need an ally. I need people in my corner, because he's got so many yes men around him (…) So I'd like to put together my own guys and I'm thinking just you and James Gadson on drums.' He basically just wanted me to be there to kind of play on the skeletal tracks and then he was gonna really work at getting Paul to go back and redo most of that stuff himself so he would do another record where he's playing almost everything like his first solo album." [800]

325 A Certain Softness (Paul McCartney)

Recording: April, 2004 **Location:** Ocean Way Recording Studios, Los Angeles **Release:** September 2005, *Chaos and Creation in the Backyard*

Once again, for "A Certain Softness", the relaxing moments during a holiday provided his inspiration. McCartney was on a boat trip in Greece when a sort of "latiny moment" came upon him. He found some nice chords and built the lyrics around the words "a certain softness/a certain sadness".

The song – which according to McCartney is something "sexy, very romantic" – was recorded in a very informal session with Jason Falkner and Joey Waronker.

McCartney: "I like very much the way we recorded it, which was very simple. It was just me playing guitar, and we just decided to have a go at it. And this was in LA and the bongo player, Joey, was just sitting on the floor, and the guitar player was just sort of sitting there, and I had a guitar, so it was just two guitars and bongos (…) But we just got a good little take on it and then we built it up from there." [801]

Falkner: "I remember we were recording on the first day, and Paul and I were both on acoustic guitars. And I was like playing this very simple song, and I was looking around the studio and I forget every once in a while where I was, because I was just kind of lost in the song. And I

[800] http://transatlanticmodern.com/2013/03/11/interview-jason-falkner/
[801] *Gary Crowley Interview*, July 2005.

look up at Paul and he's trying to get my attention, and he mouths, 'Where are we?' – meaning in the arrangement. Like, what's coming up? Is it the second chorus or the third? What's happening? And I knew exactly where I was until he asked me. And just because he was like "Where are we?" I was like 'I-I don't know! Fuck!' We just collapsed. Hilarious!"[802]

"A Certain Softness" – an exotic-flavored song halfway between "Bluebird" and "And I Love Her" – has the typical kindness and melodic sense of McCartney's best acoustic ballads. He revealed a tasty anecdote on the recording: while seeking a particular sound, Paul eyed a gong in the studio next door. With brilliant timing, he borrowed it, got his sound out of it and gave it back to the musicians in time for their next session. The song is on *Chaos and Creation in the Backyard*.

Musicians:

Paul McCartney vocals, piano, bass, classical guitar, gong, triangle, cymbals, harmonium • **Jason Falkner** classical guitar • **Joey Waronker** percussion, bongos, shakers

326 Growing Up, Falling Down (Paul McCartney)

Recording: April and October, 25th (overdubs) 2004 **Location:** Ocean Way Recording Studios, Los Angeles **Release:** August 2005, "Fine Line" cd-single

The next song recorded with Jason Falkner – and this time with James Gadson on drums – was "Growing Up, Falling Down".

During the overdub sessions in October, McCartney decided to use wind instruments to give a *World Music* touch to this oriental-style composition with an experimental flavour, adding a dark and mysterious instrumental part. So he decided to bring in Pedro Eustache, who had just recorded a duduk track in "Jenny Wren" (see sheet 333).

During the session (held on October 25th, according to Eustache's diary) he also added a didgeridoo, an ancient "natural" instrument (in fact, its interior is hollowed out by termites) from Australia, that makes a hypnotic sound.

For Eustache, the studio experience with McCartney was "absolutely amazing (...) What struck me the most was Sir Paul's genuine, down-to-earth humility, as well as the depth of his musical sensibility."[803]

Eustache tells the story: "The idea that Paul and the producer had was to create a symphony with a group of ethnic wind instruments. Just before starting the recording I asked for God's help praying, 'Lord, help me... This is Paul McCartney!' I played the duduk, the didgeridoo, and many more, at least fifteen instruments. We finished it all in about one hour."[804] Obviously not all of Eustache's contributions were used, but for sure "Growing Up, Falling Down" is one of

---

[802] http://transatlanticmodern.com/2013/03/11/interview-jason-falkner/
[803] www.pedroflute.com/page8_2005.html
[804] Interview courtesy of Pedro Eustache, 16/10/2011.

McCartney's most unique recordings ever. The song was released as the B-side to the "Fine Line" single.

Musicians:

Paul McCartney vocals, piano, classical and electric guitar, bass • **James Gadson** drums • **Jason Falkner** classical guitar, piano • **Pedro Eustache** duduk, didgeridoo

327 At the Mercy (Paul McCartney)

Recording: April and September (overdubs), 2004 **Location:** Ocean Way Recording Studios, Los Angeles and AIR Studios (overdubs), London **Release:** September 2005, *Chaos and Creation in the Backyard*

McCartney wrote "At the Mercy" during a week-end off in L.A: "Sometimes when you get into recording an album, you start to sort of get a feel of what you and the producer are going for and what kind of a new song might fit with what you've already recorded. So this one was just made up like on the Sunday when I was having the weekend off. We'd worked all week. So on the Sunday I just sort of thought, 'Oh I'd like to take this in tomorrow' and have a new completely new thing that he hadn't heard and that I hadn't heard. So I was just sort of messing around on the piano and I just got a couple of chords that I liked, slightly darker chords than I might normally have..."[805]

The title of the song came when McCartney started chanting a kind of mantra while seeking inspiration: "And this phrase just kept sort of coming. A lot of people do this, when they're writing, they just let anything happen, so that it can be 'Scrambled Eggs, Baby o var, Baby's legs Oh no ver, Man of here, Man of Fire' (…) and with me it just came 'At the Mercy, At the Mercy of a busy road.' I didn't really attach any significance to it but one of the things that I like about my songs when I've written them is you can attach very specific significances to them..."[806]

The shadowy expression was reflected in a Lennon-style song, with a gloomy and anguishing atmosphere: it's not McCartney's way to declare himself at the mercy of events. Here instead, Paul seems psychologically disarmed and preoccupied with escaping from responsibility.

The lyrics create a backdrop to a dense and intense arrangement, with dark tones. For the basic track, McCartney was accompanied once again by Gadson on drums and Falkner on electric guitar, overdubbing everything else himself. The chord sequence break is quivering but the most intense part is when the deep violoncello (a *first* for Paul) comes in to play.[807] The bow seems to emerge from the underground and stick right into the listener's heart, making it one of the most dramatic passages of "At the Mercy": Paul said in an interview to BBC: "There was a cello part that we were trying to get. No-one could understand so I actually took it".

---

[805] *Gary Crowley Interview*, July 2005.

[806] *Ibid.*

[807] Talbot said that the cello "was already recorded when we came in to do the overdubs". Interview courtesy of Joby Talbot, 21/09/2012.

Paul seems to sum up a sentimental situation halfway through a happy but distant past and a stormy present, of which he says he is disappointed. His separation from Heather Mills in 2006 (and later his divorce) will just confirm those suspicions. For this reason, "At the Mercy" must be considered one of the most important and representative songs of the emotional fragility of the mature McCartney. The track is on *Chaos and Creation in the Backyard*.

Musicians:

Paul McCartney vocals, piano, bass, electric guitar, cello, tambourine, organ, vibrachimes • **James Gadson** drums • **Jason Falkner** electric guitar • **Millennia Ensemble** strings

328 I Want You to Fly (Paul McCartney)

Recording: April, 2004 **Location:** Ocean Way Recording Studios, Los Angeles **Release:** November 2005, "Jenny Wren" cd-single

Inspiration arising from the new partnership with Godrich were soon to be seen, and awakened McCartney's experimental and eccentric side.

For "I Want You to Fly" Paul thought of a sinuous blues with a laid back beat, featuring electric piano and sung in falsetto. Then in the studio McCartney got other ideas, or added a snippet of another track that he had left unfinished. He presented the song to Falkner and Gadson – whose drum part was then doubled by Paul – according to the official credits.

The tempo suddenly accelerates as the chorus fades out – the change is clear at 3:15 – leading into an almost improvised coda, a container of bizzare elements full of references to the Sixties and Seventies. McCartney tacked a strong chorus and a variety of instrumentation and vocal effects onto the "Monkberry Moon Delight"-style piano *insistendo*, ending the song with a comical-experimental flavor. The song is a bit like a second-hand dealer's store: the results are interesting, but not totally understandable. "I Want You to Fly" is on the "Jenny Wren" CD-single.

Musicians:

Paul McCartney vocals, piano, bass, acoustic and electric guitar, electric piano, drums, synthesizer • **Jason Falkner** electric guitar • **James Gadson** drums

329 Riding to Vanity Fair (Paul McCartney)

Recording: April (basic track and overdubs part 1) and January (overdubs part 2), 2005 **Location:** Ocean Way Recording Studios (basic track and overdubs part 2), Los Angeles and Record One Studios (overdubs part 1), Sherman Oaks **Release:** September 2005, *Chaos and Creation in the Backyard*

Picking Nigel Godrich as producer faced McCartney with a challenge he had never had before: having to hear the truth. During the recording sessions, Godrich spared no criticism and doubts on the quality of some of Paul's songs and the two even had violent arguments. At some point, the producer approached McCartney while he was busy overdubbing a bass part:

"You know that song we were doing the other day? I think it's crap!"[808] said Godrich. McCartney was upset by such openness (and timing), but decided to swallow it: he had realized that Godrich's criticism would help him create a high quality record.

When McCartney introduced "Riding to Vanity Fair" in the studio, the song had a faster tempo and a completely different melody. As it was, Godrich didn't like it: so McCartney decided to modify the track, slowing it down and rewriting some melodic passages right there and then in the studio, overcoming moments of understandable embarrassment.

Added to *Chaos and Creation...* only at the last moment, the piece garnered a lot of attention from critics, mainly due to its lyrics, a very open confession full of bitterness towards misplaced trust. Paul declares that he's open to "friendship" but on the other hand there is no-one available to share his feeling.

The song seemed to be addressed to Geoff Baker, McCartney's spokesman, with whom Paul had broken in 2003 after a dispute started in London, when a swarm of journalists had surrounded Paul. McCartney accused Baker of being behind the ambush and fired him immediately.

According to others, Paul was accusing none other than his wife, Heather – a far more plausible theory, especially after their divorce – but McCartney had denied that the song was addressed to anyone in particular.

But there is little room for doubt that "Riding to Vanity Fair" – too full of emotion and resentfulness – is autobiographical: Godrich's excellent production, with a strong echo on vocals, makes it a dark song with a hypnotic pace, that McCartney recorded all by himself, except for Gadson on drums.

Its main riff played on a tinkling toy-glockenspiel – a kind of little xylophone already used in "Junk" – blends into its intense orchestral passages: McCartney's singing finds an emotional continuation in the brief conversation between the electric guitar and a harp. This contribution – recorded at Record One Studios in Sherman Oaks, California – went uncredited but was performed by Stephanie Bennett[809], which revealed that "only a little part of my original contribution was included in the recording."[810] For its sincerity and atmosphere, this song closely resembles the famous "Dear Friend" (see sheet **39**).

Musicians:

Paul McCartney vocals, electric piano, bass, acoustic and electric guitar, toy glockenspiel • **James Gadson** drums • **The Los Angeles Music Players** strings • **Stephanie Bennett** harp

---

808 The song was "Perfect Lover", the first version of "Ever Present Past".
809 www.harpworld.com/index.html
810 Interview courtesy of Stephanie Bennet, 20/09/2011.

330 This Loving Game (Paul McCartney)

Recording: April, 2004 **Location:** Ocean Way Recording Studios, Los Angeles **Release:** November 2005, "Jenny Wren" cd-single

McCartney probably wrote this song in a psychological condition of extreme disappointment and bitterness for his emotional plight with Heather, as is seems clear in the lyrics.

His dissatisfaction resulted in a sad ballad that Paul recorded with only the company of James Gadson on drums. Then, in line with the rest of the sessions done with Godrich, "This Loving Game" was entrusted to a basic and straightforward arrangement, its only distinctive sign of quality.

Unfortunately, after an interesting piano and bass intro, neither the melody nor McCartney's interpretation redeem the mediocrity of the song, in which only a few passages on electric guitar stand out, during the middle-eight modulation to a minor key.

The second song included in the "Jenny Wren" CD single, "This Loving Game" is one of the least convincing results of the *Chaos and Creation in the Backyard* recording sessions.

Musicians:

Paul McCartney vocals, piano, bass, acoustic, classical and electric guitar, tambourine, harmonium, shakers • **James Gadson** drums

Between May and June, McCartney launched his 2004 *Summer Tour* with a series of fourteen performances. This is the setlist of his concert in Madrid on May, 30th:

"Jet" – "Got to Get You Into My Life" – "Flaming Pie" – "All My Loving" – "Let Me Roll It/Foxy Lady" – "You Won't See Me" – "She's a Woman" – "Maybe I'm Amazed" – "The Long and Winding Road" – "In Spite of All the Danger" – "Blackbird" – "We Can Work It Out" – "Here Today" – "All Things Must Pass" – "I'll Follow the Sun" – "For No-One" – "Calico Skies" – "I've Just Seen a Face" – "Eleanor Rigby" – "Drive My Car" – "Penny Lane" – "Get Back!" – "Band on the Run" – "Back in the USSR" – "Live and Let Die" – "I've Got a Feeling" – "Lady Madonna" – "Hey Jude" – "Yesterday" – "Let It Be" – "I Saw Her Standing There" – "Helter Skelter" – "Sgt.Pepper's.../The End"

The *Chaos and Creation in the Backyard* sessions were resumed in September in London, with the recording of five songs. Three tracks went unissued: "Watching My Fish Drown", "A Modern Dance" and "Perfect Lover". The latter would be re-recorded by McCartney in 2006 as "Ever Present Past" (see sheet 342).

331 Fine Line (Paul McCartney)

Recording: September 2004 **Location:** AIR Studios, London **Release:** August 2005, single (from *Chaos and Creation in the Backyard*)

"Fine Line" was based on one phrase ("There is a fine line between recklessness and courage") that had been buzzing in Paul's head for some time: "I just sat down at the piano and started that kind of chuggy thing, keeping it very simple and then the little hook, 'Fine line, it's a fine line' came so I brought it into the studio in Los Angeles…"[811]

Paul went into the studio with the song and while still searching to complete it, something unexpected happened: "I was working it out and on that little bit there's a little riff that goes around the 'Fine Line' bit and when I was playing that I made a mistake and I went to a wrong bass note and Nigel goes, 'That's great. That's it.' I went, 'Actually it's a wrong note.' He said, 'No, no, check it out. Listen to it.' 'Ooh, I see what you mean.' It just didn't go where you expected it. It was supposed to be like an F# and it went to an F!"[812]

Thanks to a great studio work, "Fine Line" is a pop-song to be considered among McCartney's finest. Driven by McCartney's continuous piano, "Fine Line" is simple and straightforward, filled with an infectious chorus: the melody resembles the famous Peggy Lee hit from 1947, "It's a Good Day". A compelling pop-production, featuring a brilliant arrangement that relies on acoustic guitars and orchestra.

Joby Talbot reveals: "That strings were sort of a tribute to George Martin's arrangements on some of the more up-tempo Beatles songs."[813]

In the lyrics, McCartney is like a master beckoning to his following to get back on the straight and narrow road. Something that seems to recall the famous Parable of the Prodigal Son, from the Gospel of Luke.

McCartney was ambiguous about the true meaning of the song, denying any political content like some critics pointed out: "It was first inspired just by the idea that some people will jump off a cliff or drive a car off a cliff and think they're courageous. When someone like me will think it's actually just reckless. But I must say I was listening to it a couple of weeks ago and it suddenly struck me that it did have quite a political message. I suddenly realized you could apply it to troops serving abroad. 'C'mon brother, all is forgiven/ We all cried when you were driven away.' It's strange. I hadn't meant that, but that's one of the things I think is very interesting about writing songs. Because you can write one way with one meaning, and suddenly they can become applicable in other ways."[814]

---

[811] *Gary Crowley Interview*, July 2005.
[812] *Ibid.*
[813] Interview courtesy of Joby Talbot, 21/09/2012.
[814] Kevin O'Hare, *Yesterday and Today. Rock's Renaissance Man Is Back,* in *The Republican*, 25/09/2005.

The track was issued as a single ahead of *Chaos and Creation in the Backyard*. Despite its not so successful charts position – it reached #20 in the UK – "Fine Line" was praised by critics and got a 2006 Grammy Award nomination in the Best Male Pop Vocal Performance category. "Fine Line" was performed during *Chaos and Creation at Abbey Road* , in the 2005 *US Tour* and again in 2008.

Musicians:

Paul McCartney vocals, bass, acoustic and electric guitar, piano, drums, tambourine, shakers, spinetta •
Millennia Ensemble strings

332 Too Much Rain (Paul McCartney)

Recording: September, 2004 **Location:** AIR Studios, London **Release:** September 2005, *Chaos and Creation in the Backyard*

Pensive, musing and dark are the adjectives that best describe the mood of *Chaos and Creation...* And "Too Much Rain" is a prime example of this atmosphere. This song was also dedicated to Heather Mills. The melancholy mood of "Too Much Rain" can't disguise McCartney's praise for optimism and fortitude. Writing the song, Paul was inspired by Charlie Chaplin: "The actual inspiration for 'Too Much Rain' is Charlie Chaplin's song 'Smile'... He wrote it for a film, *Modern Times*. It's a great song ... 'Smile even though you heart is breaking...' When you're really down this song could get you up."[815]

Paul says he thought about Heather and all her trials: the chorus seems to be a call to arms against the injustices that can occur in people's life. But a different reading of the lyrics might reveal something more autobiographical. Perhaps after yet another argument with his wife, Paul was reminded of losing Linda and used this song to exorcise his present unhappy situation.

In the studio with Godrich, Paul envisioned "Too Much Rain" as an acoustic ballad in the current Brit pop style. Rich acoustic guitar and piano chords sustain the sweet melody and the arrangement is one of McCartney and Godrich's best. The deep and melodic bass is very clever: "I'll always go up the octave and just vroom, vroom, slur into high notes for a few little runs, and then come back down and nail the bass part ... a sort of signature of mine! The slides and slurs are, as we said, from playing guitar (...) I love the sub-hook. It's something I'm very proud of."[816] For the drum part, McCartney decided to pare it down: "I reminded Nigel – and myself – that on Beatles records you'd have a tambourine for a verse, then it would stop and a snare or something would take over (...) I was thinking of that when we were working on 'Too Much Rain'. I said, 'When I was writing this on solo acoustic, where the lyrics are like

815 *Ibid.*
816 Chris Jisi, *Meet the Beatle. Paul McCartney Records a Unique Solo Album, Without Help From His Friends. He Can Work It Out*, in *Bass Player*, October 2005.

It's not right, in one life, too much rain, that meant something. And now we've got boom, bing, bang, going over it. It doesn't mean as much, so we can knock that out and build that up again?'"[817]

The brief electric guitar solo halfway through the song seems to represent a sort of breathing space for Paul's voice and thoughts. McCartney's vocal performance is subtle as it meanders and rises from his soul in an attempt to hold on to what is left of hope. The track was included in the *Chaos and Creation at Abbey Road* show.

Musicians:

Paul McCartney vocals, bass, acoustic and electric guitar, 12-string acoustic guitar, piano, drums, maracas, autoharp

After a pause, the McCartney-Godrich team returned to the studio in late October.

333 Jenny Wren (Paul McCartney)

Recording: October (overdubs on 25th), 2004 **Location:** Ocean Way Recording Studios, Los Angeles
Release: September 2005, *Chaos and Creation in the Backyard*

Critics acclaimed "Jenny Wren" almost triumphantly, when the song was released on *Chaos and Creation in the Backyard*: the positive reviews for this piece are reflected in one of McCartney's most poignant acoustic ballads.

Obviously inspired by the harmonic structure of "Blackbird", the song lacks the originality of The Beatles' well-known classic: nevertheless, its melodic elaborate fingerpicking is the most impacting element of "Jenny Wren".

McCartney wrote the song in the vastness of a canyon near Los Angeles: "I wanted to go and play my guitar in the great outdoor, getting away from all the traffic and everything…"[818]

Once on site, McCartney sat down and wrote the basis of the piece, and finished it up at home while dinner was getting made.

For the name of the song's character Paul was inspired by a Dickens novel, *Our Mutual Friend*, which he had read some time before, but had completely forgotten: "Jenny Wren is a really cool little girl who's sort of magical, who sees the good in things (…) A wren is one of my favourite birds, little English bird (…) to me it was just something to do with 'Blackbird'."[819]

Godrich's ability as a producer opened McCartney's eyes. Paul was amazed by the quality of his voice: the vocal richness inspired him a different idea for a solo.

[817] Robert L. Doerschuck, *Paul McCartney: The Beatles' Other Drummer*, in *Drum! Magazine*, October 2005. http://www.drummagazine.com/features/post/paul-mccartney-the-beatles-other-drummer/
[818] *Gary Crowley Interview*, July 2005.
[819] *Ibid.*

In November 2003, during the Harrison tribute at the Royal Albert Hall, McCartney was impressed by one of the players of Ravi Shankar's band, playing his duduk, the traditional Armenian woodwind instrument similar to a large pipe and made of apricot wood.

The renowned Venezuelan musician Pedro Eustache was invited in the studio and tried several instruments with McCartney: in the end, the evocative sound of the duduk seemed to fit perfectly with "Jenny Wren"'s soft atmosphere. McCartney and Godrich even had to convince Eustache not to add reverb on the instrument, preferring to preserve its natural sound.

The instrumental duduk interlude – one of the rare examples of ethnic fusion in McCartney's solo recordings – is the most moving part of this folk acoustic ballad full of twilight melancholy.

Eustache has an unforgettable memory of that session: "After having finished 'Growing Up, Falling Down' we all went up to the roof of the studio for a lunch break. When we came back in, Paul picked up his acoustic guitar and played 'Jenny Wren' for me. After a few minutes I had learned its structure and understood its key. Soon Nigel Godrich told us to record as soon as possible, then he played the basic track and I recorded my solo. Just one take. When I went into the control room to listen to it, I said to Paul, 'I can't wait to hear the song with the rest of the instruments, bass, keyboards...' He told me that it was already complete: he wanted it to sound like two friends playing together in a pub."[820]

Recorded as a single in Great Britain, "Jenny Wren" reached #22 on the charts. The song was performed live in *Chaos and Creation at Abbey Road* and during the 2005 *US Tour*.

"Jenny Wren" got a Grammy Award nomination in 2007 in the Best Male Vocal Interpretation category.

Musicians:

Paul McCartney vocals, acoustic guitar, tom • **Pedro Eustache** duduk

334 English Tea (Paul McCartney)

Recording: November, 2004 and April, 2005 (overdubs) **Location:** Ocean Way Recording Studios, Los Angeles and AIR Studios (overdubs), London **Release:** September 2005, *Chaos and Creation in the Backyard*

With good reason one of the most acclaimed tracks of *Chaos and Creation in the Backyard*, "English Tea" is one of the prettiest watercolors ever composed by McCartney. The song was started in Lisbon during the European Tour.

Paul got the idea for this self-ironic portrait of the British aristocracy's salons starting from observation of the English stereotype that is most widespread in the world, that of tea.

McCartney: "I was on holiday, and if you want a cup of tea, you don't do what you do in England, say, 'A cup of tea please', They always say, 'What kind of tea?' You know like in

---

[820] Interview courtesy of Pedro Eustache, 16/10/2011.

England nobody would ever say, 'What kind of tea?' Well they actually would these days (…) and you have to say, 'English Breakfast tea' and then they go, 'Oh, OK' and you get it you know you get an ordinary cup of tea!"[821]

To draw this Victorian-flavoured painting, McCartney also used some old fashioned expressions that recreated the so typical British atmosphere: "There's one particular older English person I'm thinking of who instead of saying, 'Do you want a cup of tea?' might say, 'Would you care for a cup of tea?' It's just the way they say it, and I love that (…) And so I really went to town on that whole fruity way of talking.[822]

McCartney was inspired by other expressions found in literature, in particular again from Dickens: "I read Dickens quite a bit (…) I thought there is a word 'peradventure' (…) And I thought, 'I do hope I'm right cos I've put it in the song.' 'Do you know the game croquet … Peradventure we might play'… You know I thought, 'Oh, I hope this is right.' I looked it up in the dictionary, 'Peradventure perhaps, maybe' 'Yes!' I' (m) very proud of (it)."[823]

Filled with lexical archaisms and charming floral images, "Engish Tea" smells of the English countryside and lawn, with its sophisticated pastimes and its gentlemen, exchanging one another invitations for endless croquet games.

In the studio, McCartney turned these feeling into music, sitting at his piano and adding little else – but making the song distinctive with tubular bells and a bucolic-flavored flute solo – before a delicious string quartet was added by the Millennia Ensemble.

Arranger Joby Talbot recalls: "On that one, Paul was very specific about what he wanted. He was talking about how he worked with George Martin, saying that George was always very interested in the way the chords were spaced when he played them on guitar. Often guitar chords are spread out in a very strange way for a keyboard player like me and like George. But Paul was very keen to show me exactly how all the different notes are laid out in the chords. He wanted that string quartet for that kind of *genteele* English feeling for the introduction."[824]

The catchy melodic texture is enriched with a purposely affected arrangement, in the style of famous English actor and composer Noel Coward (1899-1973) "He's who I was thinking of when I wrote the song"[825] Paul revealed.

Together with the playful tone of the song, this makes it an unforgettable *pastiche*. "English Tea" was premiered during *Chaos and Creation at Abbey Road* and played in the *US Tour 2005*.

Musicians:

---

[821] *Gary Crowley Interview*, July 2005.
[822] *Ibid*.
[823] *Ibid*.
[824] Interview courtesy of Joby Talbot, 21/09/2012.
[825] Brent Day, *Paul McCartney Walks the Fine Line Between Chaos and Creation*, 26/10/2005, http://www.pastemagazine.com/articles/2005/10/paul-mccartney.html. McCartney covered Coward's song "A Room With a View" , released on the album "20th Century Blues. The songs of Noel Coward" (Various Artists) in 1998.

Paul McCartney vocals, piano, bass, flute, percussion, tubular bells • **Millennia Ensemble** strings

335 Promise to You Girl (Paul McCartney)

Recording: November, 2004 **Location:** Ocean Way Recording Studios, Los Angeles **Release:** September 2005, *Chaos and Creation in the Backyard*

McCartney had started composing "Promise to You Girl" from a simple piano riff. As he recalled: "It's a little two part piano thing. The right hand is doing the melody and the bass has got a definite part instead of just vamping away so it was just like a little mathematical problem trying to work out how I could do this…"[826]

At that point, Paul was thinking about a Motowny song, with tambourines and all the typical black music elements: "I could hear the Funk Brothers putting a backing track to that (…) Originally that was slightly less positive… I can't remember what it was, but it wasn't 'We know how to save the world.'"[827]

McCartney added a second part to it, the nostalgic line "Looking through the backyard of my life/Time to sweep the fallen leaves away", that he put as an intro to the track and that ends it as well. Having stitched the two bits together, McCartney faced the challenge of making his solo recording sound like a band: encouraged by Godrich, Paul layered on multiple electric guitar licks and a lot of great vocal tracks. The song is on *Chaos and Creation in the Backyard*.

Musicians:

Paul McCartney vocals, piano, bass, electric guitar, drums, tambourine, Moog, triangle, shakers, flute (?)

336 Anyway (Paul McCartney)

Recording: November, 2004 and April, 2005 (overdubs) **Location:** Ocean Way Recording Studios, Los Angeles and AIR Studios (overdubs), London **Release:** September 2005, *Chaos and Creation in the Backyard*

Rumors say that while at the Ocean Way Studios in Los Angeles, Paul waited for hours for a call from Heather that never came. That seems to be what inspired "Anyway", something of an almost desperate invocation to find a solution.

If that's how things went, you can imagine how McCartney must have felt the urge to write something. And that would explain why Paul used a familiar chord sequence, in no way hiding the similarity of its piano riff with "People Get Ready", the famous song by the Impressions: "I was getting this feeling as if it was the deep south of America, like Charlestown, Savannah, something about the chords, I think. There was just something reminding me, almost sort of Randy Newman kind of thing."[828]

Then, McCartney added a bridge and a chorus. In these two parts the song wonderfully blends words and music. The bridge, with its descending chord sequence, introduces a mood of

---

[826] *Gary Crowley Interview*, July 2005.
[827] *Ibid.*
[828] *Ibid.*

anxiety with the awareness of a worrying slide towards the worst (the sense of falling). The refrain – introduced by a passage reminiscent of "Little Willow" from *Flaming Pie* – expresses a feeling of wait, where McCartney seems to leave the door open for a second chance.

Once the basic track was recorded, McCartney left the orchestral arrangement to David Campbell and Joby Talbot. The overdubbing, in line with the sobriety of the production of *Chaos and Creation...* makes "Anyway" one of the best tracks of the album: rich, intense and worthy to being issued on a 45: unfortunately, it never happened. McCartney performed "Anyway" live during *Chaos and Creation at Abbey Road.*

Musicians:

Paul McCartney vocals, piano, bass, acoustic and electric guitar, drums, harmonium, Moog • **Millennia Ensemble** strings, horns

337 She Is So Beautiful (Paul McCartney)

Recording: November, 2004 and April, 2005 (overdubs) **Location:** Ocean Way Recording Studios, Los Angeles and AIR Studios (overdubs), London **Release:** September 2005, *Chaos and Creation in the Backyard* (Japanese Edition)

Within the turbulent love affair between Paul and Heather, full of ups and downs, "She Is So Beautiful" – at least according to unofficial sources – expresses a time of enchantment by McCartney for his young bride.

It seems that McCartney wrote the song one morning on a boat, seized by state of grace. Paul set to music this ode that sings the beauty of Heather, referred to as a deity.

The ballad expresses the magic and his everyday amazement with a masterful recording of bare simplicity. Paul find some very bright images (the smiling of a person) so to convey his ecstatic feeling.

Here McCartney – probably acting again as one man band – did not fill the song with too many overdubs. Its balanced arrangement added to vocals and piano just some percussion, a few acoustic guitar strumming and a light brass contribution.

It's probably one of McCartney's best ballads and one of the most difficult to find: "She Is So Beautiful" is only on the Japanese version of *Chaos and Creation in the Backyard.*

Musicians:

Paul McCartney vocals, piano, bass, acoustic guitar, percussion, dingers • **Millennia Ensemble** brass

2005

338 **How Kind of You** (Paul McCartney)

Recording: April, 2005 **Location:** AIR Studios, London **Release:** September 2005, *Chaos and Creation in the Backyard*

McCartney went into the studio with "How Kind of You" still unfinished. In fact, most of the ideas of the final recording had been worked out while experimenting with Godrich. McCartney changed the original idea for the song, in particular slowing its rhythm: "(We) put like a harmonium thing in there so it became (…) like a limbo land, like an Indian piece."[829]

The idea for the title came when McCartney noticed the typical upper class way of talking of some of his acquaintances: "I've got a couple of sort of older posh English friends who instead of saying, 'That's very nice of you,' or 'Thanks a lot,' where I come from – they might say, 'How kind of you,' and, you know, so I just started with that phrase and this whole idea."[830]

This song is surely one of the bleakest in McCartney's career. McCartney got Godrich involved to produce some loop-effects and the whole song turned into a classic Beatles-like experimentation. "How Kind of You" utilizes the same layering technique that is often seen in McCartney's work.

The whole instrumentation with a deep bass, heavy piano and a skeletal acoustic guitar gives the song its dark atmosphere. It seems a dramatic confession of human frailty, dealing with solitude of the kind Paul was familiar with after Linda's death: maybe he was recalling the terrible moments of his last night beside Linda and expresses a sense of loneliness, anguish and fear.

McCartney opened the *Chaos and Creation at Abbey Road* TV show with this song. A soundcheck performance taken from the US Tour 2005 appears on the DVD *The Space Within US*. The song is on *Chaos and Creation in the Backyard*.

Musicians:

Paul McCartney vocals, bass, acoustic and electric guitar, piano, drums, flugelhorn, shakers, guerrero, tape loops, harmonium • **Nigel Godrich** tape loops

339 **Friends to Go** (Paul McCartney)

Recording: April, 2005 **Location:** AIR Studios, London **Release:** September 2005, *Chaos and Creation in the Backyard*

McCartney confessed that he wrote "Friends to Go" as a sort of tribute to George Harrison: "I had just sat down to write and the feeling of George came over me and I just kept writing it

---

[829] *Gary Crowley Interview*, July 2005.
[830] *Ibid.*

thinking, 'George could have written this.' It was nice. It was like a sort of friendly song to write."[831]

With its dry humour, oddly fitting chords, and that certain sense of melody, it's almost like listening to a Harrison cover. The essential arrangement of "Friends To Go" – somewhat parodic – makes it one of the most self-ironic songs on *Chaos and Creation...* The growling electric guitar and the flugelhorn add spice to a track that recalls some Harrison productions from the Seventies.

"Friends To Go" was also included in *Chaos and Creation at Abbey Road* and in the 2005 *US Tour* soundchecks: one of these versions is on the DVD *The Space Within Us.*

Musicians:

Paul McCartney vocals, bass, acoustic and electric guitar, piano, drums, flugelhorn, shakers, melodica

340 I've Got Only Two Hands (Paul McCartney)

Recording: April, 2005 **Location**: AIR Studios, London **Release**: September 2005, *Chaos and Creation in the Backyard*

McCartney chose to wrap up the *Chaos and Creation...* album with this hidden track, a really unconventional one. A three-part instrumental piece, that from the get-go, sets out to celebrate McCartney's musicianship as a one-man band.

Godrich liked the idea and suggested that Paul knock-off a few improvised tracks: "'O.K. I'll do three just to show him" – McCartney recalled – "So I came to the piano."[832]

First to be recorded was a melodic piano arpeggio that was then placed as a bridge between the opening section – that was filled with rough and distorted guitars – and the final segment that McCartney built from a simple drum groove. After his hard-hitting drum performance, Paul added some fuzzy noise and sound effects, including what sounds like an old car horn. The whole thing was done in an hour and as they say 'waste not want not': so, "instead of choosing one of them for the beginning we stuck three of them all together and put them at the end."[833]

There is a rough take on the *Chaos and Creation in the Backyard* DVD.

Musicians:

Paul McCartney bass, acoustic and electric guitar, piano, keyboards, drums

341 Summer of '59 (Paul McCartney)

Recording: April, 2005 **Location**: AIR Studios, London **Release**: November 2005, "Jenny Wren" single B-side

"Summer of '59", a fast-paced rockabilly number seems to come straight out of a Buddy Holly record. The simple three-chord progression probably allowed McCartney to easily find the

---

831 *Ibid.*
832 *Gary Crowley Interview*, July 2005.
833 *Ibid.*

right take, recording acoustic guitar, electric guitar and bass, later overdubbing harmonized vocals. The song is a nostalgic bow to the music of the Fifties and a faithful replica of that atmosphere. Oddly issued only on vinyl, "Summer of '59" was the B-side to the single "Jenny Wren".

Musicians:

Paul McCartney vocals, bass, acoustic and electric guitar

In June Paul presented *Twin Freaks*, another experimental project. It consisted of re-mixes by DJ Freelance Hellraiser (Roy Kerr) who took 12 songs from McCartney's solo repertoire.

In the months leading up to *Chaos and Creation in the Backyard*'s release, McCartney created a buzz of anticipation and expectation. *Time* magazine declared *Chaos and Creation in the Backyard* to be McCartney's first album that matters since the Beatles broke up and *Rolling Stone* gave it a four-star rating. The onslaught of promotional activity saw McCartney taking part in several radio programs performing cuts from the new album. This culminated in the BBC *Chaos and Creation at Abbey Road* special with McCartney doing solo versions of his new and old songs in Studio 2 at Abbey Road. The album was a commercial success: *Chaos and Creation...* went to #10 in the UK and #6 in the USA, where it sold almost 400.000 copies in the first weeks. Appreciated by both critics and fans, the record immediately became a classic. The album – mellow, delicate, evocative and dramatic in places – has a twilight atmosphere. It received three Grammy nominations. With all the critical success of *Chaos and Creation in the Backyard*, McCartney was encouraged to do another tour of 39 dates across Canada and the US.

Here's the concert standard setlist:

"Magical Mystery Tour" – "Flaming Pie" – "Jet" – "All My Loving" – "I'll Get You" – "Drive My Car" – "Let Me Roll It" – "Got to Get You Into My Life" – "Fine Line" – "Maybe I'm Amazed" – "The Long and Winding Road" – "In Spite of All the Danger" – "I Will" – "Jenny Wren" – "For No-One" – "Fixing a Hole" – "English Tea" – "I'll Follow the Sun" – "Follow Me" – "Blackbird" – "Eleanor Rigby" – "Too Many People" – "She Came in Through the Bathroom Window" – "Good Day Sunshine" – "Band on the Run" – "Penny Lane" – "I've Got a Feeling" – "Back in the U.S.S.R." – "Hey Jude" – "Live and Let Die" – "Yesterday" – "Get Back!" – "Helter Skelter" – "Please, Please Me" – "Let It Be" – "Sgt. Pepper's Lonely Hearts Club Band"

2006

In February, McCartney played live at the Grammy Award for the first time ever. *Chaos and Creation in the Backyard* – despite three nominations – went home empty handed. After months of endless rumors, on May 17th, Paul and Heather Mills officially separated, thus ending a relationship rife with arguments and misunderstanding. In March, Paul returned to his studio to record five songs. According to engineer Eddie Klein and producer David Kahne, four of these were taped in one six-hour session.

342 Ever Present Past (Paul McCartney)

Recording: March, 2006 **Location:** Hog Hill Studio, Icklesham **Release:** May 2007 (US), single (from *Memory Almost Full*); June 2007 (UK), *Memory Almost Full*

McCartney composed "Ever Present Past" on acoustic guitar. The song had been recorded during the *Chaos and Creation...* sessions as "Perfect Lover". McCartney and Godrich had opted for a folksy arrangement but the producer then had second thoughts and decided to ax it against the wishes of McCartney, who pushed for a release until the single "This Never Happened Before" got cancelled.

Paul suggested the song to David Kahne, developing a brand new arrangement once in the studio: "Sometimes I just sit down and try and write a pop song. Something catchy that might be attractive. It starts off, 'I've got too much on my plate'. The way I write I just follow that thought and think, 'What did I mean by that? Explain yourself'. After I'd got the verse, this idea of my past came about."[834]

Therefore, McCartney took another shot at it during the *Memory Almost Full* sessions: "Paul showed it to me on piano" – says Kahne – "And then we started recording."[835]

Recording went quickly as David Kahne recalls: "We recorded an electric guitar track to a loop, Paul went and played the drums, then more guitar, then bass, then sang it (...) The mystery is not where or what Paul was referencing; the mystery to me is where his ideas flow from inside himself..."[836]

Unfortunately, this time McCartney left his fingerprints on the scene of the crime: the opening bars are lifted from the well-known "Don't Get Around Much Anymore" by Duke Ellington – Paul had covered it for *Choba B CCCP* (see **1988**) – and some of the instrumentation is very reminiscent of The Beatles, such as the harpsichord from "For No-One" or the clavioline (?) from "Baby You're a Rich Man".

---

[834] www.memoryalmostfull.com
[835] M. Hurwitz, *Memory Track by Track*, www.mixonline.com, 01/10/2007.
[836] C. Dirani, *Interview with David Kahne*, May 2007.

At first, this tight, electro-pop song was only available digitally for the US market. Then it did come out as a 45 and cd single in England, where it reached #85. "Ever Present Past" is on *Memory Almost Full*.

Musicians:

Paul McCartney vocals, bass, electric guitar, harpsichord, keyboards, drums, clavioline (?), flugelhorn, tambourine

343 Mr.Bellamy (Paul McCartney)

Recording: March, 2006 **Location:** Hog Hill Studio, Icklesham **Release:** June 2007, *Memory Almost Full*

With "Mr.Bellamy", McCartney offers a song based on a specific character after many years. This time, he went further and built an entire story around him, populated by people from the streets and based on that character's contemplation to commit suicide by jumping off a ledge.

McCartney: "I had a little piano riff (...). I wanted some lyrics that would poke in and poke out of this piano riff. "I'm not coming down/No matter what you say/I like it up here"... I got a picture of a guy sitting on top of a skyscraper and all the people in the street, the rescue team, the psychiatrist, the man with the megaphone shouting, 'Don't jump'... So I fished around for a name and came up with 'Bellamy', which sounded like someone who might want to jump."[837] Interestingly, "Mr.Bellamy" is also the title of a 1961 pop art painting by Roy Lichtenstein (1923-1997).

Interpretations of "Mr.Bellamy" saw him as a misunderstood outcast or maybe Paul himself dealing with depression in the aftermath of his divorce. McCartney once again, played dumb: "Who is Mr. Bellamy? I never know who these people are. Who are Chuck and Dave, Eleanor Rigby, Desmond and Molly... I don't know, I make them up. I like giving characters names."[838]

To make this mini-drama more enjoyable, McCartney took on the various roles utilizing his vast repertoire of voices. Paul in turn gives voice to the suicidal man, the passersby and first responders – all giving advice and suggestions. An unusual performance, somewhat suggestive of Peter Gabriel's style. In fact "Mr.Bellamy" may owe much to "Harold the Barrel" from *Nursery Cryme* by Genesis (1971).[839]

Truly a work of genius, enhanced with the addition of a harmony part by McCartney. Kahne: "We had the song there, and Paul wrote a counter melody. His melodies are always strong, and the two melodies worked together the way some classical pieces do, so we put them together."[840]

---

[837] www.memoryalmostfull.com
[838] *Ibid.*
[839] The song tells the story of a restaurant owner who after serving his customers his own toes, threatens to jump off a balcony.
[840] Claudio Dirani, *Interview with David Kahne*, May 2007.

For the basic track, McCartney played all the instruments, beginning with the ingenious piano riff that rushes up and down the keyboard. Paul invited Thom Yorke of Radiohead to play that part, but he turned down the offer, revealing: "I listened to the tune and really liked it (…) but the piano playing involve two hands doing things separately. I don't have that skill available. I said to him, 'I strum piano, that's it.'"[841]

With Yorke out of the picture, McCartney resorted to bass, keyboards, synthesizer and finally added some grinding guitars.

The amazing ending, with its delicate and dreamy piano notes, sums up the story. McCartney: "There he is, little Bellamy sitting on the ledge, enjoying it up in the clouds…"[842]

"Mr.Bellamy" was enriched by a full orchestral arrangement both in the intro and in the finale.

On a final note, if one listens closely – at 16 seconds into the song – a camera shutter can be heard ("We were recording, and there was a guy there doing a photo shoot, taking some pictures. You can actually hear his shutter snap on the song, which I left in the intro because the guy in the song is sort of in that situation, which fits"[843]). Without a doubt, as far as inventiveness and originality are concerned this is the best track on *Memory Almost Full*.

Musicians:

Paul McCartney vocals, backing vocals, bass, piano, acoustic and electric guitar, keyboards, synthesizer, drums • **Unknown musicians** strings, horns

344 Gratitude (Paul McCartney)

Recording: March, 2006 **Location:** Hog Hill Studio, Icklesham **Release:** June 2007, *Memory Almost Full*

According to rumors that came out on the eve of the release of *Memory Almost Full*, there were to be numerous references to the recent McCartney-Mills divorce scattered on the album. This wasn't the case. Paul had already addressed it on *Chaos and Creation* but no one had noticed. "Gratitude" is however the one occasion where McCartney revisits the bitter experience, albeit in the form of self-parody.

This is the only key to interpreting this song. Paul went for a gospel approach – transforming praise for the Lord into a sarcastic praise for an ex, with lyrics expressing a sense of gratitude, although without any specific reference.

McCartney avoided the question by simply saying: "I've always had a couple of voices (…) My ballad voice I think was based on Elvis and the screaming voice was me trying to be Little Richard (…) That sort of gritty soul-y voice. So on this track I was just thinking of how much

[841] Scott Tolothan, *Thom Yorke Reveals Reason Behind Paul McCartney Snub on the Song Mr. Bellamy*, 10/12/2007. See http://www.gigwise.com/news/39327/thom-yorke-reveals-reason-behind-paul-mccartney-snub
[842] www.memoryalmostfull.com
[843] M. Hurwitz, *Memory Track by Track*, www.mixonline.com, 01/10/2007.

there is to be grateful for in life and I wanted to put that into song and use this voice to do it with."[844]

He worked quite hard on the vocals in the studio with Kahne: "As we worked on the vocals more and more" – Kahne says – "Paul took more and more chances, and it kept getting better and better. It was like watching a flower bloom, actually."[845]

Paul overdubbed a notably rich and creative bass part and the song was completed by adding strings and horns: these contributions are not credited in the album liner notes and they were recorded at unspecified dates. "Gratitude" is on *Memory Almost Full*.

Musicians:

Paul McCartney vocals, backing vocals, bass, piano, electric guitar, keyboards, organ, drums • **Unknown musicians** strings, horns

345 Nod Your Head (Paul McCartney)

Recording: March, 2006 **Location:** Hog Hill Studio, Icklesham **Release:** June 2007, *Memory Almost Full*

McCartney: "'The End of the End' was going to be the last track on the album, but then we thought we can't leave everyone going, 'Oh, God, I'm not going to listen to that again.' So we had a little stompy rocker called 'Nod Your Head', and we thought, 'We've just got to let them off the hook.'"[846]

As he did on *Chaos and Creation in the Backyard* McCartney opted for an out-of-the-ordinary ending to the album. Kahne: "There was some talk of this being an instrumental. When Paul finally put a vocal on it, I was stunned."[847]

While Kahne was searching for the best vocal sound, the takes followed one another: "The take wasn't coming together, and we redid it, and did it, and did it, and it wasn't working" – Kahne says – "It got a little tense, and then the next take Paul got it. But he started goofing around, and he started yelling while he was playing, and that yelling is still a really cool part of the song."[848]

McCartney recorded the basic track on piano overdubbing the rest of the instrumentation.[849] It was definitely a rather improvised recording, arranged and put together quickly without too much thought going into it. A terrible song: McCartney's gritty but unconvincing vocals are not supported by a decent backing track.

Performed on the *Memory Almost Full Promo Tour*, "Nod Your Head" appears in a live version on the EP *Live at ICA, London, July 5th 2007*. A remix version is included in the "Dance Tonight" cd-single.

---

[844] www.memoryalmostfull.com
[845] C. Dirani, *Interview with David Kahne*, May 2007.
[846] www.memoryalmostfull.com
[847] C. Dirani, *Interview with David Kahne*, May 2007.
[848] M. Hurwitz, *Memory Track by Track*, www.mixonline.com, 01/10/2007.
[849] A. Gardner, *cit.*

Musicians:

Paul McCartney vocals, bass, piano, electric guitar, keyboards, drums, synthesizer • **Unknown musician** sax

346 In Private (Paul McCartney)

Recording: March, 2006 **Location:** Hog Hill Studio, Icklesham **Release:** June 2007, *Memory Almost Full* (2-cd Edition)

Some say that McCartney's instrumentals aren't very interesting because they are missing the key element, his vocals.

There are only a few exceptions to this rule: "In Private" is a good one. Most likely the song came about from Paul's tapping on the body of his acoustic guitar – ingeniously used at the beginning of the song. McCartney then developed the song along the lines of "Heather" (see sheet 310): an arpeggio – acting as the main melody – followed by some chord stabs.

McCartney wrapped the song's core in an effective arrangement: first, he added some acoustic guitars, then he brought in his Epiphone Casino to record some fuzz-laden tracks – so to reinforce the main riff – and finally he overdubbed an harpsichord.[850] "In Private" was included as a bonus-track in the *Memory Almost Full* 2-CD Edition.

Musicians:

Paul McCartney bass, piano, acoustic and electric guitar, keyboards, drums, harpsichord

McCartney proceeded with the *Memory Almost Full* sessions, recording two other tracks.

347 See Your Sunshine (Paul McCartney)

Recording: April-July, 2006 **Location:** Hog Hill Studio, Icklesham **Release:** June 2007, *Memory Almost Full*

McCartney acknowledged that Heather Mills was the inspiration behind the song "See Your Sunshine": "A lot of the album was done before, during and after our separation" – said McCartney – "That one was written during a good time with Heather. I don't want to deny those times. I didn't go back and take out any songs to do with her."[851] This was another song rejected by Godrich during the *Chaos and Creation in the Backyard* sessions. McCartney wasn't fazed and presented the song to Kahne as an Eighties-style pop song with jazz overtones (the ninth chords). The recording was then worked by Kahne, who added some strong effects to McCartney's vocals. Seeing that the overall instrumentation was minimal, Paul – by chance or necessity – dedicated some time to overdub a very busy bass part: and it is indeed the bass that leads the way in "See Your Sunshine".

---

[850] M. Hurwitz, *Memory Track by Track*, www.mixonline.com, 01/10/2007.
[851] Ryan Parry, *Song for Heather*, 22/06/2007.

McCartney: "I'd already recorded most of the song, but when it came to put the bass on it. I did it fairly straightforward. Then just for my own pleasure I started goofing around, playing way too much, going over the top and I joked with the producer at the end of the take, 'Whoa, that was way over the top!' He said, 'No that's great, do another take like that. I think that's exactly what the song needs'. I think I only did two takes."[852]

McCartney wisely took Kahne's advice and his virtuoso bass playing works 'cause it sits in contrast to the rest of the piece. To complete the recording, McCartney laid down the drum track with much sweat and tears. David Kahne: "We just kept doing more and more drums and loops, just getting the groove right and the tempo. We gave it several tempo changes!"[853] "See Your Sunshine" appears on *Memory Almost Full*.

Musicians:

Paul McCartney vocals, bass, electric guitar, keyboards, piano, drums, tambourine, xylophone, harpsichord

348 Why So Blue? (Paul McCartney)

Recording: April-July 2006 **Location:** Hog Hill Studio, Icklesham **Release:** June 2007, *Memory Almost Full* (2-cd Edition)

McCartney has always been inclined to scatter wonderful songs here and there throughout his catalogue (B-sides,12", bonus tracks, etc.): in this case, it was the turn of "Why So Blue?" to be excluded from an album. This beautiful acoustic ballad would have gone on to win awards for best song on *Memory Almost Full* along with "Mr. Bellamy": but Paul dropped it by the time he had completed the tracklist of the album.

Nevertheless, McCartney had invested heavily in the song, considering that this take was alleged to be a re-make of the first version, a faster version recorded in October 2003 at Abbey Road with the band, before Godrich came in. Several months later, Paul took another shot at it alone with Godrich but that version was also dropped after only one take. Finally, McCartney recorded "Why So Blue?" from scratch with Kahne producing. Most likely the basic track was recorded on acoustic guitar with various overdubs following: a simple and well-executed arrangement, including a harpsichord part and overdubbed strings. The song's minor key underlines its pensive mood, that would have well-suited to the general atmosphere of *Chaos and Creation...* Harmonically, the song has some McCartney's typical melodious verses but the chorus takes off in a surprisingly new direction both in key and rhythm. The song gets more intense with piano and keyboards sustaining a flowing *quasi*-experimental refrain. McCartney then delivers a great bridge that maybe was added later (a result of Godrich's doubts about the

[852] www.memoryalmostfull.com
[853] M. Hurwitz, *Memory Track by Track*, www.mixonline.con, 01/10/2007.

song?) A poignant coda ends the track. "Why So Blue?" appears as a bonus tracks on the special edition of *Memory Almost Full*.

Musicians:

Paul McCartney vocals, acoustic guitar, piano, keyboards, drums, percussion, tambourine, electric guitar, harpsichord • **Unknown musicians** strings

The year came to an end with the release of *Ecce Cor Meum*, McCartney's fourth classical work. The project had been commissioned to Paul in 1997 by Anthony Smith during Paul and Linda's visit to the Magdalen College of Oxford. After attempting to compose an Oratorio in four parts, Paul found the right inspiration at the Church of Saint Ignatius of Loyola, New York where he saw the phrase 'Ecce Cor Meum' written under a statue. Linda's death put the project on hold. At a certain point, McCartney felt it was time to express his grief. He composed one of the most moving pieces in his repertoire, "Interlude (Lament)", written as the expression of his mourning. An early version of *Ecce Cor Meum* was performed in 2001 but Paul went back to re-work some of the passages that weren't suitable for the voices of the young members of the chorus. The final version was recorded at Abbey Road, between March 13th and 17th, 2006.

The album was a huge success on the classical charts, reaching #2 both in America and in the UK, although reviews were mixed.

Michael Church of *The Independent* wrote: "Once or twice a melody surfaced, before being swallowed up in the easy-listening soup (…) The President of Madgalen hoped this piece 'could be sung by young people the world over – something equivalent to Handel's *Messiah*.' No surprise that *Ecce Cor Meum* should fail to match the greatest choral work ever written: since McCartney is still a beginner at this game."

Geoffrey Norris of *The Telegraph* noted that "the musical substance is just not strong enough to support the piece's expanse" while Adam Clayson on *Record Collector* found that the music had a "nice reposeful daintiness."

Right after Christmas, Paul got back into the studio to record a couple of brand new tracks, among which the recently composed "Dance Tonight".

2007

349 **222** (Paul McCartney)

Recording: January-February 2007 **Location:** Hog Hill Studio, Icklesham **Release:** June 2007, *Memory Almost Full* (2-cd Edition)

During the *Memory Almost Full* sessions, McCartney also brought some experimental ideas into the studio, wanting to explore different music styles and fields. "222" is an odd semi-instrumental track in a jazzy mood. Paul built the whole song on his bass riff and created a track with a vaguely ambient atmosphere, reducing his vocals to a whisper.

McCartney used some curious instrumentation: stinging guitars, organ and a xylophone. He even played a flugelhorn solo in the fluid section in an odd 6/8 time. During a later session, a clarinet part was overdubbed, probably employing the same musician who brought his talents to "Mr. Bellamy". "222" was issued as a bonus-track on the special edition of *Memory Almost Full*.

Musicians:

Paul McCartney vocals, bass, piano, electric guitar, keyboards, drums, xylophone, vibraphone, organ, celeste, flugelhorn • **Unknown musician** clarinet

350 **Dance Tonight** (Paul McCartney)

Recording: January-February, 2007 **Location:** RAK Studios, London **Release:** June 2007, *Memory Almost Full*

"Dance Tonight" was added to *Memory Almost Full* at the last minute. McCartney was in a musical instrument shop when the shopkeeper caught his attention: "I was in London and I was on my way into a meeting, but before I actually got there, I had a bit of a walk to experience life for a minute. There's a guitar shop that I always drop in on, and I was chatting to the guy in there. He mentioned that he had a left-handed mandolin that he wanted to show me. The great thing about it was that I didn't know how to play. It's tuned like a violin, so I had no idea what the chords were."[854]

Paul brought the mandolin home for Christmas and began strumming away. The rest was done by little Beatrice. McCartney: "I started stomping in the kitchen, just enjoying myself, trying to find chords. I start singing, 'Everybody gonna dance tonight.' Every time, my little girl would come running in and start dancing. The song kind of wrote itself."[855]

McCartney decided to keep things simple in the studio as well, and opted for a basic arrangement for what was to become the last track recorded for *Memory Almost Full*: "I ran into

---

[854] www.memoryalmostfull.com
[855] *Ibid.*

the studio to record "Dance Tonight", and I stuck it on the album. It seemed like a good atmospheric opening."[856]

The song has a rustic sing-along feel: three chords and a melody that goes on forever. Paul keeps the time with his foot ("It's actually Paul stomping on a piece of wood with his foot"[857] Kahne revealed) adding to the mandolin just a few skillful touches: an autoharp to reinforce and sustain the chords, a fuzz-bass and, as a final touch, some electric guitars and keyboards on the instrumental bridge.

McCartney reveals how they managed to achieve a grinding sound on the record: "On this track actually we used the air conditioning grids... So we got a bit of metal, pulled up all the grids and stuck it on the box." [858]

An odd choice for a single, but with respectable results: "Dance Tonight" climbed to #26 in the UK charts and to #69 in Billboard's Hot 100.

The song was included in the *Memory Almost Full Promo Tour* (this version is on *Live in Los Angeles*) and in several concert dates in 2008, 2009, 2010, 2011 and 2012. Another live version, taken from the New York performance in 2009, is included in *Good Evening New York City*.

Musicians:

Paul McCartney vocals, mandolin, electric guitar, bass, keyboards, drums, percussion, autoharp

Memory Almost Full was issued in June, right after the announcement of a new contract signed by Paul with Hear Music, a label owned by Starbucks, the well-known American coffee-shop chain.

McCartney had left EMI due to differences concerning their antiquated approach to the record business and marketing. Paul believed in the new digital music formats and different distribution models. Thus, the album was distributed at 10.000 Starbuck shops along with traditional retail outlets. A winning strategy, at least at first: *Memory Almost Full* nearly entered the US charts directly at #1, reaching #3 with over 161.000 copies sold in the first week. Moreover, it remained on the Top Ten for one month, for the first time since *Tug of War*. The record was well-received in England as well (#5), here too selling better than previous McCartney releases.

McCartney revealed that the title came to his mind from a message displayed on his mobile phone, but back in 1994, speaking about his memory, had said to Mark Lewisohn: "You cannot remember everything. I liken the human mind to a computer, where a message will appear saying, 'You have used 99 per cent of the available memory, I cannot proceed unless you wipe something'." The album was a sort of pleasant interval – it became unusual for

[856] *Ibid.*
[857] M. Hurwitz, *Memory Track by Track*, www.mixonline.com, 01/10/2007.
[858] Paul McCartney, in *On the Set of "Dance Tonight"*.

McCartney to release an album within two years of the last one – in stark contrast with the darker mood of 2005's *Chaos and Creation...* that had been more pensive and disillusioned. Paul now seemed free of burden, as his memory took him back to his carefree youth.

Maybe the upbeat feeling helped the album get good reviews from the musical critics and press: Daryl Easlea of the *BBC* said that the album "sounds very much of the now (...) what we have is clean, clear, upbeat McCartney", while Robert Cristgau of *Rolling Stone* wrote a three-star review, piercingly noting that "what's most remarkable about McCartney's inaugural album for Starbucks' Hear Music imprint is its cross-promotional hoo-ha."

In December, *Memory Almost Full* got a Grammy Award nomination in the Best Male Vocal Performance category. World sales were around two million copies.

On the other hand, the quality of the album's mastering caused a harsh debate between McCartney's fans over various forums and Websites. The heavily compressed sound of *Memory Almost Full* was considered by many as part of the infamous "Loudness War", an expression used to indicate the fact that record manufacturers were distorting sounds to make them seem louder, affecting sound quality.

At some point, some fans asked directly Bob Ludwig, who was responsible for the album's mastering. He said: "The final CD is exactly the way Paul and the producer wanted, every note."

During the summer, Paul launched a little promotional tour for the album and in Autumn held two special concerts, in Paris and at the London Roundhouse.

These were the tracks played on June 7th at the Electric Ballroom in London: "Drive My Car" – "Only Mama Knows" – "Dance Tonight" – "C Moon" – "The Long and Winding Road" – "I'll Follow the Sun" – "Calico Skies" – "That Was Me" – "Blackbird" – "Here Today" – "Back in the USSR" – "Nod Your Head" – "House of Wax" – "I've Got a Feeling" – "Matchbox" – "Get Back!" – "Hey Jude" – "Let It Be" – "Lady Madonna" – "I Saw Her Standing There"

Furthermore, Paul had started working on another project. This time it was something very challenging for him: a concerto for classical guitar and orchestra. To develop it, McCartney had invited to his studio no less than Carlos Bonell, one of the greatest classical guitarists in the world.

The sessions with Bonell commenced in May 2006, but they were not born under a lucky star: the very same day, McCartney announced his separation from Heather Mills.

After a one year hiatus, the two got together again in the studio. Bonell's role was to transcribe on a musical score the notes or the portions of the concerto that Paul had played and composed on guitar or on his computer: "Paul establishes a theme and knows how to develop it; he completely understands classical composition. Which is incredible in its way, because he can't read or write music."[859]

McCartney and Bonell worked together on several pieces of the concerto: two of them were titled "Romance" and "Farmboy".[860] Footage of the two working together was aired at the time through McCartney's official website.

Bonell shed some light on this project, still unissued: "We started in 2006 and we worked hard until about 2009 and then he put it on hold but with the intention of going back to it. It's a very important work, a very interesting combination of guitar and orchestra: the concerto contains a mixture of styles, there's definitely an aspect of the Beatles, in the music and in the lyrical inspiration and there's also a Spanish quality because of his fascination for the Spanish culture and because of the association with the classical and Spanish guitar."[861]

McCartney composed relentlessly: "Paul has written so much music, probably enough for two concertos" – Bonell confirms – "The unifying concept was a work for classical guitar and orchestra, a simple collection of tunes. We have worked in different ways. In some occasion, McCartney already had the idea quite clearly and my job was simply to help him releasing the classical guitar and to notate the music. On the other hand, he sat with me and actually improvised in front of me and I wrote down his ideas. In some cases the idea was already formed, in some others the idea was made up while we were together."[862]

Towards the end of the year, McCartney began new recordings for a project that would become *Electric Arguments*, the third act of the "Fireman" saga. For the brand new episode of his alter ego, Paul got together again with Youth.

[859] John Colapinto, *When I'm Sixty-Four*, in *New Yorker*, 04/06/2007.
[860] *Ibid.*
[861] Interview courtesy of Carlos Bonell, 09/08/2012.
[862] *Ibid.*

2008

Without any definite direction, McCartney cut thirteen tracks in as many days in the studio, basically ad-libbing them. After that, he started to lay down some vocals, just to see if something interesting would come out. As usual, he played all the instruments, while Youth gave his contribution on guitar on one unspecified track.

351 Travelling Light (Paul McCartney)

Recording: December, 2007-June, 2008 **Location:** Hog Hill Studio, Icklesham **Release:** November 2008, *Electric Arguments*

The first song recorded in the studio during the *Electric Arguments* sessions with Youth was "Travelling Light".

McCartney: "I'd been listening to a CD of sea shanties, and Youth runs a folk label called *Butterfly*. They put out these compilations called *What The Folk*, so he'd sent me them."[863]

"Travelling Light" is the result of these influences; a dark ballad in a medieval-folk vein that McCartney sang in a deep voice, very likely pitched-down. McCartney arranged the song for piano, guitar and flute, adding a tempo change-up in the coda – that hardly fits the mood of the song – and some vocal improvisations. "Travelling Light" is on *Electric Arguments*.

Musicians:

Paul McCartney vocals, acoustic and electric guitar, bass, drums, keyboards, Mellotron, piano, percussion, flute, dingers

352 Nothing Too Much Just Out of Sight (Paul McCartney)

Recording: December, 2007-June, 2008 **Location:** Hog Hill Studio, Icklesham **Release:** November 2008, *Electric Arguments*

McCartney: "In the Sixties, I used to hang out with a black singer called Jimmy Scott, the guy who said, 'Obladì-Obladà/Life goes on.' He also used to say, 'Nothing too much just outta sight.' Youth said it was a good start for a song."[864]

Paul started improvising in the studio, screaming into his mike in the same vein of "Helter Skelter" and adding raging words that, according to some critics, contained references to Heather and to the divorce experience. This is how McCartney explains the lyrics' writing process during the sessions: "I'd get out poetry books and just kind of scour them and find

[863] Andy Welch, *Paul McCartney's Looking Forward to Some Time Off-But Has No Intention of Stopping*, Liverpool Daily Post, http://www.liverpooldailypost.co.uk/liverpool-life-features/liverpool-arts/2009/01/03/paul-mccartney-s-looking-forward-to-some-time-off-but-has-no-intention-of-stopping-64375-22596789/ , 03/01/2009.
[864] Simon Cosyns, *McCartney Loves Birds*, in *The Sun*, www.thesun.co.uk/sol/homepage/showbiz/sftw/article1980204.ece, 28/11/2008.

phrases, then stick them to a phrase from another book."[865] Using his familiar recording process – drums, bass (here with a fuzzing effect) then guitars and vocals – "Nothing Too Much Just Out Of Sight" came out of it. The song – that would become the opening track of *Electric Arguments* – was enhanced with some raw harmonica playing that brings a genuine bluesy touch to it.

Musicians:

Paul McCartney vocals, bass, electric and slide guitar, drums, harmonica

353 Two Magpies (Paul McCartney)

Recording: December, 2007-June, 2008 **Location:** Hog Hill Studio, Icklesham **Release:** November 2008, *Electric Arguments*

"I've always liked birds. It's a theme of mine" – Paul explained – "I think they're symbolic of freedom, of flying away."[866] There's no doubt that this delicate tune about two magpies came during some "Blackbird"-inspired strumming. In the first few seconds, McCartney can be heard at home with his voice recorder, capturing the first ideas for the song. His little Beatrice can be heard in the background, laughing and squealing. Paul brought this bit in the studio and worked on it some more, adding vocals, acoustic guitar, double-bass and drums, played with brushes.

McCartney probably didn't take long finishing this fingerpicking-style song. Some of the lyrics quote the old nursery rhyme "One for sorrow, two for joy, three for a girl, four for a boy". "Two Magpies" is on *Electric Arguments*.

Musicians:

Paul McCartney vocals, acoustic guitar, drums, double-bass

354 Sing the Changes (Paul McCartney)

Recording: December, 2007-June, 2008 **Location:** Hog Hill Studio, Icklesham **Release:** November 2008, *Electric Arguments*

Although *Electric Arguments* was basically an experimental album, there was still room on it for McCartney's more traditional pop songs: the euphoric "Sing the Changes" is a perfect example. This catchy and energetic song – surely a hit, if only it had been issued in the Seventies – is the most commercial track on *Electric Arguments*.

McCartney wouldn't need to do too much in the studio to wrap up this gem of a song. The joyous melody line is upheld with bursts of acoustic guitars and further enhanced with a stadium-like chant, treated with much reverb. An unmissable singalong: McCartney put it out

[865] Neil McCormick, *Sir Paul McCartney's Electric Arguments*, in *Daily Telegraph*, www.accessinterviews.com/interviews/detail/electric-arguments/7487, 10/10/2008.
[866] S. Cosyns, *cit.*

as a single and he did shoot a video-clip that certainly helped the third Fireman album to achieve very good sales results.

The track was performed during the 2009 tour, the 2010 *Up & Coming Tour* and the 2011-12 *On the Run Tour*. A live version appears on *Good Evening New York City*.

Musicians:

Paul McCartney vocals, backing vocals, acoustic and electric guitar, mandolin, bass, drums, keyboards, tambourine

355 Highway (Paul McCartney)

Recording: December, 2007-June, 2008 **Location:** Hog Hill Studio, Icklesham **Release:** November 2008, *Electric Arguments*

McCartney had intended for *Electric Arguments* to be recorded quickly, without giving in to the temptation to over produce it. Some straight rock'n'roll would have been perfect. So, during the sessions he recorded "Highway", an up-tempo track in the vein of road-songs. After recording a solid backing track, Paul continued with a very aggressive arrangement, adding electric guitars, piano and harmonica, and completed the recording with a gritty vocal and a strong chorus.

The breakdowns and various guitar riffs made it one of the best songs on the album. Clearly, "Highway" would have been a strong stage number. In fact, it was included in the set list in McCartney's concerts in 2009 and 2010. The live version is on *Good Evening New York City*.

Musicians:

Paul McCartney vocals, backing vocals, acoustic and electric guitar, bass, drums, piano, harmonica, tambourine

356 Light from Your Lighthouse (Trad. Arr. Paul McCartney)

Recording: December, 2007-June, 2008 **Location:** Hog Hill Studio, Icklesham **Release:** November 2008, *Electric Arguments*

After *Electric Arguments* was released, rumors began flying around in the music press: someone accused McCartney of plagiarism, stating that his track "Light From Your Lighthouse" had copied the old song, "Let Your Light Shine on Me" by the African-American Blind Willy Johnson (1897-1945). McCartney denied any liability, stating that he had credited Johnson's song in his liner notes as his inspiration and that he had not infringed on the copyright. He and Youth had simply covered a traditional song that was in the public domain. McCartney's lighthearted version of this spiritual invocation was arranged with mandolin and some Varispeed-treated vocals. The result is an enjoyable track that fits in well with the spontaneous mood of these sessions.

Musicians:

Paul McCartney vocals, backing vocals, double-bass, drums, acoustic guitar, mandolin, percussion, harmonium

357 Sun Is Shining (Paul McCartney)

Recording: December, 2007-June, 2008 **Location:** Hog Hill Studio, Icklesham **Release:** November 2008, *Electric Arguments*

McCartney was slowly beginning to recover from the stress and depression brought on by his separation from Heather. In fact, by the time of the *Electric Arguments* recordings, Paul had pretty much regained his physical and psychological strength. It was therefore natural for him to go into the studio with sunny and joyful songs that extolled his return to happiness: the music of tracks like "Sun Is Shining" and "Sing The Changes" (see sheet **354**) perfectly matches the positive mood of McCartney.

In the studio, Paul wrought out a pop song *à la* "Good Day Sunshine". Based on acoustic guitars, "Sun Is Shining" would later receive many overdubs: Paul added one of his typical melodic bass lines, some experimental electric guitars, and a killer chorus. One of the best tracks on *Electric Arguments*. The song has been performed during soundchecks for the *Up & Coming Tour* 2010.

Musicians:

Paul McCartney vocals, backing vocals, acoustic and electric guitar, bass, drums, keyboards

358 Dance 'Till We're High (Paul McCartney)

Recording: December, 2007-June, 2008 **Location:** Hog Hill Studio, Icklesham **Release:** November 2008, *Electric Arguments*

McCartney's high-spirited approach to the recordings of *Electric Arguments* is clearly expressed in several songs that are brimming with new enthusiasm.

During the recording sessions, he created a lively and grandiose arrangement for "Dance 'Till We're High", a song built on a strong crescendo. The ringing Christmas-like bells that open the track give this song a festive touch – very likely a celebration of the new-found love between Paul and Nancy Shevell.

Paul then added a full piano part and his irresistible vocals, double-tracked and layered with reverb. "Dance Till We're High" is another spontaneous, but, at the same time, well-constructed song of *Electric Arguments*.

A remix version called "(Xmas Mix)" has been issued on the *Electric Arguments* Deluxe Edition.

Musicians:

Paul McCartney vocals, backing vocals, acoustic and electric guitar, bass, drums, keyboards, piano, tambourine, tubular bells

359 Lifelong Passion (Paul McCartney)

Recording: December, 2007-June, 2008 **Location:** Hog Hill Studio, Icklesham **Release:** November 2008, *Electric Arguments*

During the sessions, McCartney delved into Indian rhythms, a favorite of his since The Beatles' days. "Lifelong Passion" is one of the most peculiar songs of *Electric Arguments*. After creating this dirge built entirely around one chord, McCartney added textural layers of electric piano, synthesizer, guitars and bass. He then recorded his strongly-echoed vocals to create an ethereal effect. To achieve the typical Eastern-influenced sound, he relied on instruments he had used in previous experimental recordings such as the harmonium (as in "How Kind of You") and what sounds like a clavioline, memorable for its appearance in "Baby You're a Rich Man".

Musicians:

Paul McCartney vocals, acoustic and electric guitar, bass, drums, keyboards, synthesizer, electric piano, percussion, harmonium, harmonica, clavioline (?)

360 Is This Love? (Paul McCartney)

Recording: December, 2007-June, 2008 **Location:** Hog Hill Studio, Icklesham **Release:** November 2008, *Electric Arguments*

The experimental flavor of most of the songs on *Electric Arguments* was balanced with McCartney's typical melodic vein, especially if compared to earlier Fireman releases. "Is This Love?" was a foray into ambient music. Once again, McCartney went into the studio and recorded the backing track with drums, percussion, tambourine, guitars and bass, which features some of his typical modulation. He then had fun recording a long, bucolic flute solo that dominates the song. For his vocals – keeping in line with the spirit of the project – Paul quickly recorded a repetitive mantra-like vocal, so typical of the airy and spacious atmosphere of the whole album.

Musicians:

Paul McCartney vocals, acoustic and electric guitar, bass, drums, keyboards, percussion, piano, flute, tambourine, vibraphone

361 Lovers in a Dream (Paul McCartney)

Recording: December, 2007-June, 2008 **Location:** Hog Hill Studio, Icklesham **Release:** November 2008, *Electric Arguments*

With nothing inhibiting him, McCartney was able to take the *Electric Arguments* sessions to new and different directions, producing some very unconventional sounding music. The inspiration for "Lovers in a Dream" probably grew out of a studio jam. Basically, the song consists in one single repeated verse accompanied by a disco groove. The dark mood of the recording is enhanced by the use of horror movie effects like the gloomy violoncello, the icy organ riff. Paul's vocals were treated with striking effects: the distant echo on his lead part is combined with shadowy backing vocals, enveloping the song in a very claustrophobic atmosphere. The track is included in *Electric Arguments*

Musicians:

Paul McCartney vocals, electric guitar, bass, drums, electric piano, keyboards, percussion, organ, cello, vibraphone, synthesizer

362 Universal Here, Everlasting Now (Paul McCartney)

Recording: December, 2007-June, 2008 **Location:** Hog Hill Studio, Icklesham **Release:** November 2008, *Electric Arguments*

"Universal Here, Everlasting Now" was the most experimental recording of the *Electric Arguments* sessions. In this case, McCartney and Youth looked back to their previous *Rushes* album style and recorded an almost entirely instrumental track.

The track starts with a quite piano intro, surrounded by some disturbing effects: barking dogs, mumbled words and whispers. The rest of the song moves along over an electronic drumbeat with some strange and heavily distorted electric guitars and ambient riffs. It finally concludes as it began, on the notes of the piano.

Musicians:

Paul McCartney vocals, electric guitar, acoustic guitar, bass, drums, keyboards, percussion, piano

363 Don't Stop Running (Paul McCartney)

Recording: December, 2007-June, 2008 **Location:** Hog Hill Studio, Icklesham **Release:** November 2008, *Electric Arguments*

Recording a song per day meant that most of McCartney's studio tracks were born of improvisation. After recording the basic track – Paul might start hitting his drum kit, playing guitar or piano – he would add vocals following his instincts and according to his mood that day. "Don't Stop Running" is a classic example of this approach. Once he had completed the backing track, he began freely tossing out words ("silent lovers", "angels smiling") thus obtaining another jam. The recording was filled-out with more instrumentation, overdubbing a somber harpsichord, a flute and a mandolin. "Don't Stop Running" is on *Electric Arguments*.

Musicians:

Paul McCartney vocals, acoustic and electric guitar, bass, drums, keyboards, percussion, harpsichord, mandolin, flute, synthesizer

364 Road Trip (Paul McCartney)

Recording: December, 2007-June, 2008 **Location:** Hog Hill Studio, Icklesham **Release:** November 2008, *Electric Arguments*

On an album as esoteric as *Electric Arguments* there had to be a ghost track. "Road Trip" closes the album with what amounts to a long sustained chord played on synthesizer and keyboards, over which McCartney layers some mysterious effects and backwards vocals, in the most typical Beatles fashion.

Musicians:

Paul McCartney vocals, synthesizer, keyboards

During the second half of the year, McCartney went back on tour, with several noteworthy performances. On June 1st, he was in Liverpool for the Liverpool Sound concert, on the occasion of Liverpool's nomination as a European Capital of Culture, 2008. The concert was the occasion to present some songs for the first time: "Hippy Hippy Shake" – as the opening song – "In Liverpool" and the epic "A Day in the Life", that was unfortunately spoiled, as Paul struggled to remember the lyrics to his very own middle section. Then came the gig in Kiev on June 14th to celebrate the anniversary of Ukrainian independence: the highlight of the show was the performance of "Mrs.Vandebilt" to an erupting crowd. More concerts followed in Quebec City (July 20th) and Tel Aviv (September)

This setlist was played in Kiev: "Drive My Car" – "Jet" – "All My Loving" – "Only Mama Knows" – "Got to Get You Into My Life" – "Let Me Roll It" – "C Moon" – "My Love" – "Let'Em In" – "The Long and Winding Road" – "Dance Tonight" – "Blackbird" – "Calico Skies" – "I'll Follow the Sun" – "Mrs. Vandebilt" – "Eleanor Rigby" – "Something" – "Good Day Sunshine" – "Penny Lane" – "Band on the Run" – "Birthday" – "Back in the USSR" – "I've Got a Feeling" – "Live and Let Die" – "Let It Be" – "Hey Jude" – "A Day in the Life/Give Peace a Chance" – "Lady Madonna" – "Get Back!" – "I Saw Her Standing There" – "Yesterday" – "Sgt. Pepper's Lonely Hearts Club Band/The End"

In November, *Electric Arguments* revealed for the first time the true identity of The Fireman. McCartney promoted the record doing interviews, making videos and through his website, finally re-issuing the record with a bright red cover that stated 'Paul McCartney is the Fireman'. Commercial success was soon to come. For the first time, a Fireman album made it onto the charts reaching #69 in Billboard and remained on the charts for a good ten weeks.

Musically, *Electric Arguments* benefits from being an instinctively improvised work. It can be considered McCartney's most successful experimental work under the Fireman pseudonym. The critics were very positive. "Rolling Stone" gave it a 4 star review.

2009

Around Summer, McCartney came back into the studio with Geoff Emerick engineering, recording twenty new songs. One of them, "(I Want to) Come Home", was commissioned for a movie soundtrack.

365 (I Want to) Come Home (Paul McCartney)

Recording: June and July, 6th (overdubs), 2009 **Location:** Hog Hill Studio, Icklesham and AIR Studios (overdubs), London **Release:** March 2010, single

When McCartney was contacted by director Kirk Jones to write a song for the movie *Everybody's Fine* (starring Robert De Niro), he immediately accepted.

Paul: "When I was shown the film originally, it was in a little viewing theater in Soho. And I was kind of on my own. And so I was just watching the film enjoying it and thinking, 'Well, if I'm gonna do a song, what might it be?' I was not really getting ideas, but an atmosphere. And they laid in 'Let It Be' unbeknownst to me sung by Aretha Franklin. 'Ah, ok, this'd be really easy. I can write another 'Let It Be' and I can sing like Aretha Franklin. Thank you, director, throwing me such a curveball!'"[867]

McCartney went home depressed, thinking that he'd better give up, when the very same night, "I got a little idea."[868]

Step by step, the song took shape. McCartney: "The original song was a little bit different. But I found a little bit in the middle of it which was sort of... *For too long, I was out on my own.'* And so that sounded like the start of a song then. So I started to work it around that."[869]

McCartney sent a demo to Jones (originally titled "Come Home") and they met to work on it: "I remember going over in the cab" – said Jones – "And saying the only way I could do justice to him and the film was to be honest."[870]

Jones didn't stop to think and suggested some changes to McCartney: he requested an instrumental intro and said to Paul to switch the verses sequence and change some lyrics.

McCartney accepted Jones' suggestions and ran to his studio to record "(I Want to) Come Home", a beautiful piano ballad. To the piano track, Paul added a slight amount of instrumentation: drums, a touch of bass and a bit of acoustic guitar. Finally, he found room for a tuneful electric guitar solo.

Next, McCartney got in touch with Dario Marianelli, the film's orchestral score composer, to work on a string arrangement. It was overdubbed in July at AIR Studios in London with a thirty-seven piece orchestra, that was conducted by Marianelli himself.

---

[867] http://www.baltimoresun.com/entertainment/news/paul-mccartney-song
[868] *Ibid.*
[869] *Ibid.*
[870] David Bauder, *McCartney Pens Song for DeNiro Film About Widower, The Associated Press*, 03/12/2009.

McCartney promoted the song during his European Tour in December 2009 and also included it in some dates of his 2010 *Up & Coming Tour*.

Highly praised by critics, the song got a *Golden Globe* nomination, winning the *Critics' Choice Award*. "(I Want) to Come Home" was released in March 2010 as a digital single through the iTunes platform. It did not chart at all.

Musicians:

Paul McCartney vocals, backing vocals, piano, bass, acoustic guitar, electric guitar, drums, tambourine • **Unknown musicians** strings, horns

In the Autumn, McCartney recorded a new track called "Meat Free Monday". Paul had improvised this little tune on his guitar to launch a new vegetarian campaign. Later, he entered the studio overdubbing bass, drums, electric guitar and piano. The track was offered as a free download through McCartney's official website. A new tour had started in the summer. The American leg – nine dates – was introduced by three concerts at the Citi Field in New York. The setlist:

"Drive My Car" – "Jet" – "Only Mama Knows" – "Flaming Pie" – "Got to Get You Into My Life" – "Let Me Roll It/Foxy Lady" – "Highway" – "The Long and Winding Road" – "My Love" – "Blackbird" – "Here Today" – "Dance Tonight" – "Calico Skies" – "Mrs. Vandebilt" – "Eleanor Rigby" – "Sing the Changes" – "Band on the Run" – "Back in the USSR" – "I'm Down" – "Something" – "I've Got a Feeling" – "Paperback Writer" – "A Day in the Life/Give Peace a Chance" – "Let It Be" – "Live and Let Die" – "Hey Jude" – "Day Tripper" – "Lady Madonna" – "I Saw Her Standing There" – "Yesterday" – "Helter Skelter" – "Get Back!" – "Sgt. Pepper's Lonely Hearts Club Band"

The recording of the Citi Field concert from July 16th was officially released in November on the album *Good Evening New York City*. The album reached #16 in the US charts and #28 in the UK.

The *Good Evening Europe Tour* (eight venues), included some nice surprises. In some dates, McCartney performed "(I Want to) Come Home", "Wonderful Christmastime" and "Mull of Kintyre", including "Obladì-Obladà" for the first time in his live repertoire.

2010

McCartney spent 2010 mainly touring. In May, he announced the *Up & Coming Tour*. The tour started off in Phoenix on March 28th and lasted until August, with 25 dates. The concerts took place in the United States, Puerto Rico, Mexico, UK and again in North America.

McCartney retrieved some Wings' classics, that had been missing from his concerts for many years. Here's the setlist, taken from the Job Arena performance in Phoenix:

"Venus and Mars/Rock Show" – "Jet" – "All My Loving" – "Got to Get You into My Life" – "Highway" – "Let Me Roll It/Foxy Lady" – "The Long and Winding Road" – "1985" – "(I Want to) Come Home" – "My Love" – "I'm Looking Through You" – "Every Night" – "Two of Us" – "Blackbird" – "Here Today" – "Dance Tonight" – "Mrs.Vandebilt" – "Eleanor Ribgy" – "Something" – "Letting Go" – "Sing the Changes" – "Band on the Run" – "Obladi-Obladà" – "Back in the USSR" – "I've Got a Feeling" – "Paperback Writer" – "A Day in the Life/Give Peace a Chance" – "Let it Be" – "Live and Let Die" – "Hey Jude" – "Day Tripper" – "Lady Madonna" – "Get Back" – "Yesterday" – "Helter Skelter" – "Sgt.Pepper's/The End"

Sometime during the year, Paul also got in touch with composer Marty O'Donnell on Bungie's videogame *Destiny*. O'Donnell – who scored the highly acclaimed Bungies' *Halo* titles – recalls that the collaboration took shape when a friend reached out to McCartney on his behalf: "I never in a million years thought I'd be able to just call him 'Paul!'"[871]

Their partnership started in 2011: "Paul's one of these guys who just never seems to want to stop developing and moving, so we had a great meeting and started collaborating. And for two years we traded music back-and-forth, met at several studios. We did this session at Abbey Road. I'm really looking forward to getting that out for people to hear because it has... it's the 50-minute suite that tells its own story that's within the story of the Destiny universe. It's written by Mike Salvatori, me and Paul McCartney. He seemed excited about it. He's played *Halo* with his grandkids and was... I can't speak for Paul, but I think he's pretty excited that he's stretching into an area he hasn't stretched before."[872]

The tour resumed on November 7th with five dates in South America. The setlist included a few small changes: "Bluebird" was played in Buenos Aires. Approaching the end of the year, Paul held some special concerts: on December 13th at Harlem Apollo in New York, on the 17th at 100 Club and on 18th at Hammersmith Apollo in London, finishing at the Academy in Liverpool on 20th. In some dates McCartney performed "Wonderful Christmastime". Some time this year, Paul recorded a special message about *Children's Miracle Network* hospitals. The clip features some guitar background, probably written and taped by McCartney.

---

871 Paul McCartney's videogame *Destiny* – Bungie's Martin O'Donnell on working with a music legend, in http://m.edge-online.com/features/paul-mccartneys-videogame-destiny/, 01/08/2013.
872 *Ibid.*

2011

The last part of the *Up and Coming Tour* was dedicated to five special concerts: May 9th in Lima, 11th in Santiago, 22nd-23rd in Rio de Janeiro and June 10th in Las Vegas. Back in April, McCartney had started recording again for a new album. This time, it was his tribute to the music of the Twenties and Thirties, an album of jazz standards: "Home", "Always", "The Inch Worm", "My One and Only Love", "It's Only a Paper Moon", "Bye Bye Blackbird", "The Glory of Love", "Get Yourself Another Fool", "We Three (My Echo, My Shadow and Me)", "More I Cannot Wish You", "My Very Good Friend the Milkman" and "Ac-Cent-Tchu-Ate the Positive". Producer Tommy Lipuma was called: "I was introduced to Paul by a woman whom used to work with at Elektra, Nancy Jeffries (…) She told me that Paul wanted to do a standards-type album."[873] Paul and Tommy's first meeting was in March 2010. Lipuma: "I went to East Sussex and spent about four or five days with him, just went through songs (…) I brought a piano player with me, Tamir Hendelman, an L.A. session guy."[874]

For the recording of the future *Kisses on the Bottom*, the producer gathered an outstanding cast of musicians at Columbia Studios in Los Angeles, including Diana Krall and her band. John Clayton, a jazz bassist, composer and arranger, recalls: "I was contacted by Tommy Lipuma and Diana Krall, telling me that it was for Paul's project. But we didn't find out what the project was about until we got in the studio. He wanted to keep it a bit of a secret."[875]

The recording process was very simple and relaxed, as usual for McCartney. Clayton: "We looked at the songs that had dropped and came up with the arrangements on the spot. Paul was very open to input from everyone involved, from the bass, to drums, to the piano. Of course, Paul had the last word, but he was very easy, very open. On 'The Glory of Love' we did a couple of versions and we were satisfied but Diana said, 'Could we just try one more time in another way only with Paul and John together?' The band join in the middle but the opening and the end it's only Paul's voice and the bass."[876] All the tracks were recorded live in the studio: "We had a lot of fun, especially on the track 'My Very Good Friend the Milkman'. We did not do too many takes, because we wanted to keep the magic. McCartney sang live along with the band."[877] Along with this dozen covers, Paul also recorded new versions of "Baby's Request" (included in the Deluxe Edition of the album) and "Goodnight Princess" plus two still unreleased originals, "If I Take You Home Tonight" and a second one whose title is

---

[873] Howie Edelson, *Q&A: Tommy Lipuma, Making McCartney's Kisses Album*, in *Beatlefan*, n.196, May-June 2012, p.18.
[874] *Ibid.*
[875] Interview courtesy of John Clayton, 29/12/2011.
[876] *Ibid.*
[877] *Ibid.*

unknown. Speaking of "If I Take You Home Tonight", Elvis Costello said: "It's a lovely melody, almost like a little Elizabethan tune or something."

366 My Valentine (Paul McCartney)

Recording: April-May (?) and October 5th or 6th (overdubs), 2011 **Location:** Avatar Studios, New York and Abbey Road Studios (overdubs), London **Release:** February 2012, *Kisses on the Bottom*

Dedicated to Nancy Shevell by Paul on the occasion of their marriage on October 9th, 2011 "My Valentine" is a pure declaration of love in music. The title – which brings to mind the classic "My Funny Valentine" (1937) by Rodgers and Hart – in this case means 'my lover' or 'my Valentine's Day gift'. Paul wrote the song while on holiday in Morocco with Nancy, on a rainy Valentine's Day afternoon. Recorded during the *Kisses on the Bottom* sessions, it's a very romantic song, so typical of Paul's style but enriched by a jazz arrangement, in the same vein of the whole album.

Tommy Lipuma had encouraged McCartney to compose some original tracks to be included in the album: "(I said to Paul) You should write some things and if they fit within the realm of what we're doing, it would be nice to have original things by you. And a few months before we went in, he sent me a demo of 'My Valentine', with just him and piano."[878]

"My Valentine" is a languid, dreamy and melodic song. Upon close listening, some typical clichés can be heard; the lithe core of the melody for instance, is a callback to "Love of the Loved", one of the earliest Lennon & McCartney songs.

This was the first time that Paul, while in the studio, did not play any of the instruments. McCartney concentrated on his vocals, leaving the band to create a sweet, understated underscore. But the final version was a remake: "I didn't like the way it came out" – Lipuma unveils – "It was a little too lush and there was a sort of break in the song with a flute playing. It felt forced (…) About a month later, we recorded at Avatar in New York and it worked, there was no question."[879] This version, arranged by John Mandel, was released through iTunes in November 2012 on *Complete Kisses*, a special version of *Kisses on the Bottom*.

With the backing track arrangement finally in place, there could only be room for one overdub – and that would have to be a very special guest: Eric Clapton came to Abbey Road to add some acoustic guitar solos in his unmistakeable style, overwriting the phrases that McCartney had done as guide tracks. The finishing touch was given again in London, with the overdub of an orchestra, conducted and arranged by Alan Broadbent, an old friend of Lipuma since Natalie Cole's "Unforgettable". Broadbent recalls: "I was given a demo of the finished recording prior to the overdub session. Paul and Tommy had another recording of the song

---

[878] Howie Edelson, *Q&A: Tommy Lipuma, Making McCartney's Kisses Album*, in *Beatlefan*, n.196, May-June 2012, p.19.

[879] *Ibid.*, pp.19-20.

but the previous arrangement was more involved than they wanted. They were looking for a more intimate approach."[880]

The entire arrangement was left to Broadbent: "I discussed with Tommy the various entrances for the strings, but other than that it was up to my personal taste to make a contribution according to how I was moved when listening to the overall take."[881]

The recording took place in October 5th or 6th (Broadbent is unsure about the correct date). A quite large orchestra was used and everything went for the best.

Broadbent: "There were ten 1st violins, eight 2nd violins, six violas and six cellos. Because they play together all the time there was an uniformity of tone that was very moving to conduct. And even though the chart was relatively quiet and simple, they played it with interest and without condescension."[882]

Some ideas were thrown around with McCartney contributing: "Paul was hearing a rising set of chords in the introduction, which I wrote, but it seemed to distract from the setting of the mood, so it was taken out. But he definitely wanted to add a harp part and as luck would have it, a player was working in the studio next door, so we hired him on his lunch break and I wrote his part at that time too!"[883]

Broadbent won out over Paul concerning the finale: "He did question what he calls an 'ooblie' in my last chord… It simply means a dissonance, in this case a suspended second. But I convinced him that the major 3rd would be too final, and I wanted the feeling of something that would not end."[884] The track is on *Kisses on the Bottom*. A special version, starring actor Johnny Depp on acoustic guitar, was prepared for the song clip. Paul played a piano solo version of "My Valentine" during an interview with David Frost in November 2012. The track was performed during the 2012 *On The Run Tour* and the 2013/14 *Out There! Tour*.

Musicians:

Paul McCartney vocals • **Eric Clapton** acoustic guitar • **Diana Krall** piano • **Karriem Riggins** drums • **Robert Hurst** bass • **John Pizzarelli** electric guitar • **The London Symphony Orchestra** strings

367 Only Our Hearts (Paul McCartney)

Recording: April-May (?) 2011 **Location:** Columbia Studios, Los Angeles **Release:** February 2012, *Kisses on the Bottom*

"Only Our Hearts" was the second McCartney original song recorded for *Kisses on the Bottom*: he had presented it to Lipuma during their first meeting, back in March 2010.

---

[880] Interview courtesy of Alan Broadbent, 26/09/2012.
[881] *Ibid.*
[882] *Ibid.*
[883] *Ibid.*
[884] *Ibid.*

"He played me this song and I loved it, I thought it was great"[885] said the producer. McCartney took this opportunity to regroup some earlier melodic ideas that he had stockpiled. Some passages recall the intro to "Suicide" – in its complete never released version – while other parts seem to hail back to another unreleased track called "Your School". All in all, "Only Our Hearts" is a lovely song with a fine harmonica solo from Stevie Wonder – who was last heard on a McCartney record thirty years before.

McCartney recalled: "Stevie came along to the studio in LA and he listened to the track for about ten minutes and he totally got it. He just went to the mic and within 20 minutes had nailed this dynamite solo!"[886] The song was finally crowned with a beautiful orchestral arrangement by John Mandel. The track appears on *Kisses on the Bottom*.

Musicians:

Paul McCartney vocals • **Stevie Wonder** harmonica • **Tamir Hendelmann** piano • **Vinnie Colaiuta** drums • **Chuck Berghoffer** bass • **John Chiodini** electric guitar • **Unknown musicians** strings

In June, four tracks for a new project, the ballet *Ocean's Kingdom*, were recorded. Actually, McCartney used one track that he had composed for the soundtrack of Disney's film *Oceans* but that went unissued.

In July, McCartney announced his new *On the Run Tour*, starting with eight venues in America. Here's the setlist played at the Yankee Stadium's concert in New York, on July 15th: "Hello, Goodbye" – "Junior's Farm" – "All My Loving" – "Jet" – "Drive My Car" – "Sing the Changes" – "The Night Before" – "Let Me Roll It/Foxy Lady" – "Paperback Writer" – "The Long and Winding Road" – "1985" – "Let'Em In" – "Maybe I'm Amazed" – "I've Just Seen a Face" – "I Will" – "Blackbird" – "Here Today" – "Dance Tonight" – "Mrs.Vandebilt" – "Eleanor Rigby" – "Something" – "Band on the Run" – "Obladì-Obladà" – "Back in the USSR" – "I've Got a Feeling" – "A Day in the Life/Give Peace a Chance" – "Let It Be" – "Live and Let Die" – "Hey Jude" – "Lady Madonna" – "Day Tripper" – "Get Back!" – "Yesterday" – "Helter Skelter" – "Golden Slumbers/Carry That Weight/The End"

Right after the launch of *Ocean's Kingdom* – that went to #1 on the US classical charts, despite some unfavourable reviews (*The Guardian* said that the work failed because of the "lack of memorable or arresting melody") – on October 9th, McCartney married Nancy Shevell at the Marylebone Register Office in London. After a break for the honeymoon, another eleven live dates between November and December for the *On the Run Tour* were announced.

McCartney added some new songs to the setlist: "Come and Get It", "I Will" and "The Word/All You Need Is Love".

---

[885] Howie Edelson, *Q&A: Tommy Lipuma, Making McCartney's Kisses Album*, in *Beatlefan*, n.196, May-June 2012, p.19

[886] www.paulmccartney.com

2012

In January, McCartney got back into the studio, holding sessions with different producers. He came up with the idea to have different inputs from them: so he looked for young producers on the scene. Throughout 2012 and 2013 McCartney worked with Ethan Johns (son of producer Glyn Johns), Mark Ronson (Amy Winehouse producer), Paul Epworth and Giles Martin, son of The Beatles' producer. Giles acted as a supervisor of the whole project.

McCartney: "All the hot producers seem to be the age of the sons of my contemporaries, but with those two, like their dads, they're great guys who are serious about they do; they had a lot to live up to – but they all proved themselves." [887]

Instead of choosing one, McCartney preferred to go for a multi-producer album. Paul: "It turned out I got on with all of them! We made something really different with each producer, so I couldn't choose and ended up working with all four. I ended up falling for them all. We just had a good time in different ways. Ethan was a bit more acoustic-leaning, Mark would be a little more R&B...they each had a different approach but were all great in their own field." [888]

According to Giles Martin, 22 songs were recorded for the upcoming *New* album and McCartney played Hofner bass, using Rickenbacker on one unspecified track. The first producer that was called by McCartney was Paul Epworth. Although McCartney presented 20 new songs to him, Epworth decided to do something different, jamming in the studio with Paul to see if some exciting music would come out. The two recorded at Epworth's small studio, Wolf Tone, in London, moving later to Hog Hill and AIR. Epworth says: "I feel like I thrive as a producer from getting in a room with somebody, and making music from scratch. He came down for a meeting, to sit down and have a chat, and within an hour we were in the live room with him on bass and me on drums – that was definitely a pinch yourself moment! – and within 20 minutes we had this riff together, which became the first song on the record." [889]

368 Save Us (Paul McCartney-Paul Epworth)

Recording: January 2012, March (overdubs part 1), May? (overdubs part 2) and ? (overdubs part 3), 2013 **Location:** Wolf Tone, Queen's Park and AIR Studios (overdubs part 1), London, Henson Studios (overdubs part 2), Los Angeles and Hog Hill Studio (overdubs part 3), Icklesham **Release:** October 2013, *New*

Epworth: "We worked out a basic vibe for 'Save Us' with the bass and the drums. Then I said, 'Why don't we try it on the piano?' So McCartney sat down on the piano and moved between these chords and gave it a sort of pounding rhythm. I watched him playing that piano and

---

[887] *Producing Macca. The Four Studio Wizards on Working with Paul on "New"* in NME, November 2013.
[888] *Ibid.*
[889] *Ibid.*

taking the chords I'd been playing, shifting the fingering around a bit and suddenly it sounded like a McCartney song. I was pretty astonished – it was like a big reveal!"[890]

The two laid down the track with some fuzzy guitars, and Epworth suggested Paul try a vocal. McCartney was surprised: "How can I try?" – Paul asked – "There's no song!"[891]

After some moments, he decided to delve into it. McCartney: "I gave a disclaimer to the engineers, 'This is maybe 100% crap! Please excuse me if it's rubbish!'"[892] The result was a fast track, with a frenetic guitar riff, that was chosen as the opening number on *New*.

It was premiered in Las Vegas at iHeart Radio Music Festival on September 22nd, 2013 and performed during the *Out There!* Tour in 2013 (Japanese leg) and 2014.

Musicians:

Paul McCartney vocals, backing vocals, electric guitar, bass, piano, tambourine (?) • **Paul Epworth** drums

369 Queenie Eye (Paul McCartney-Paul Epworth)

Recording: January 2012, March? (overdubs part 1) and May? (overdubs part 2), 2013 **Location:** Hog Hill Studio, Icklesham, AIR Studios (overdubs part 1), London and Henson Studios (overdubs part 2), Los Angeles **Release:** October 2013, *New*

McCartney composed "Queenie Eye" taking inspiration from the name of the game he used to play with his friends as a kid: "This song 'Queenie Eye', is based on a game we used to play when I was kids. You got to remember that's a long time ago and basically in kind of a poor area I was from. What you did you entertain yourself was go out in the street and play street games. There wasn't that much traffic, so you were pretty safe. One of the games was called 'Queenie Eye'. What used to happen is one person would turn away from us and throw a ball over his head which one of us would catch. And then we would say, 'Queenie Eye, Queenie Eye, who's got the ball? I haven't got it. It isn't in my pocket. O-U-T spells out.' And when we said, 'Out', he could turn around ...or she could turn around and look at us and try to work out which one of us had caught the ball, which, of course, we all pretended to have behind our backs. I just liked the rhythm. I ended up in the studio and we made into this next song."

The recording process was very spontaneous, as Epworth recalls: "I think that something like 'Queenie Eye' developed into something that it wasn't before [because of that]. It had a slow genesis but I don't think we would have been able to get to the result we got in the end without having done it that way. The way 'Queenie Eye' started was very raw: two of us in the room, two amplifiers. It was maybe a little bit Death From Above 1979 in the drums and

890 *Ibid.*
891 *The Living Room Tour. Paul McCartney Q&A with Bang & Olufsen*, 15/10/2013.
892 *Ibid.*

keyboard sounds."[893] The basic track was very likely recorded at Hog Hill, with Epworth on drums and McCartney on piano, Mellotron and Moog. Then "Queenie Eye" was overdubbed by Paul with other instrumentation, both at AIR and Henson Studios: the rhythm and the chorus seem to recall the typical shouting of kids playing in the streets. An odd, ethereal and quite bridge breaks the song in two parts. A tough track, with some powerful drumming by Epworth, "Queenie Eye" is reminiscent of The Clash's, "Sound of the Sinners" (1980). As revealed by Giles Martin, the song was to be the opening number of *New*, but it was later replaced by "Save Us".

It was released as the second single from *New*, on October 8th, 2013. "Queenie Eye" was premiered live on October 10th in New York, during an impromptu gig in Times Square and performed during the *Out There!* Tour in 2013 (Japanese leg) and 2014.

Musicians:

Paul McCartney vocals, backing vocals, piano, Mellotron, bass, electric guitar, lap steel guitar, synthesizer, tambourine, Moog • **Paul Epworth** drums

370 Road (Paul McCartney-Paul Epworth)

Recording: January 2012, March? (overdubs part 1) and May? (overdubs part 2), 2013 **Location:** Hog Hill Studio, Icklesham, AIR Studios (overdubs part 1), London and Henson Studios (overdubs part 2), Los Angeles **Release:** October 2013, *New*

Also "Road" came up from some impromptu session between McCartney and Epworth, with the two starting jamming on their instruments: drums (Epworth) and Moog (McCartney).

Epworth: "I guess with that one we were aiming for something that was a little more esoteric and musically complex than the others I'd worked on. It's like a journey. That actually started out with me on drums and him on Moog and it sounded like something by The Fall or Can."[894] The result was a dark track, which closes *New*: over Epworth drums, McCartney filled it with xylophone, celeste, piano, keyboards, adding a nice bass. An epic closer for the album.

Musicians:

Paul McCartney vocals, piano, keyboards, celeste, percussion, bass, xylophone (?), harmonica (?), Moog, acoustic guitar (?) • **Paul Epworth** drums

371 Struggle (Paul McCartney-Paul Epworth)

Recording: January? 2012 and May? (overdubs) 2013 **Location:** AIR Studios, London and Henson Studios (overdubs), Los Angeles **Release:** October 2013, *New* (Japanese Edition)

Included only in the Japanese edition of *New*, "Struggle" is the most experimental result of the McCartney-Epworth collaboration.

---

[893] *Producing Macca. The Four Studio Wizards on Working with Paul on "New"* in NME, November 2013.
[894] *Ibid.*

This time, it was a McCartney solo effort. He laid down a texture of gritty guitars and piano, building an incessant rhythm. The vocal part was probably added on the spot, with some spoken verses. The whole track recalls some of the heaviest improvisations of *McCartney II*.

Musicians:

Paul McCartney vocals, electric guitar, drums, celeste, synthesizer, bass, tape-loops, Mellotron

Then came Ethan Johns. After two days together at AIR Studios, Johns and McCartney continued working at Abbey Road Studios. They recorded a total of four new songs over one month. Johns says: "There was no plan. It was, 'Let's just go into the studio for a few days and see what happens.' It was a complete blank canvas."[895]

372 Hosanna (Paul McCartney)

Recording: February-March (basic track and overdubs part 1), 2012 and May? 2013 (overdubs part 2)
Location: AIR Studios (basic track) and Abbey Road Studios (overdubs part 1), London and Henson Studios (overdubs part 2) **Release:** October 2013, *New*

The first *New* track taped at AIR Studios by McCartney and Johns was "Hosanna", a sleepy-paced acoustic song. Ethan Johns said of it: "There's a song on the record called 'Hosanna' which is absolutely heartbreaking – just Paul and an acoustic guitar. It's gorgeous."[896]

Back in March 2012, *Rolling Stone* depicted the song as "an acoustic ballad that would have been not out of place on his first solo album *McCartney*."

Johns: "He walked in with this incredible song, we threw up a couple of microphones and within four hours, we had this great track. I think we did an edit between the first two takes. It had an incredible feel – a really evocative piece of music, a very interesting lyric, and the performance was great."[897]

The song was something new that McCartney wanted to record on the spur of the moment. Johns recalls: "He had a CD, which had a number of titles on it. But then he said, 'I've got this song called 'Hosanna', and played it through on acoustic guitar. And the feeling of it was... I mean, I just lit up like the sun when I heard it, because I could feel the inspiration, the connection, the musicality of it. It wasn't trying to be something it wasn't, it just was. It was right. So it was simple."[898]

The track was recorded to analog tape and was enriched by some experimental sounds, using tape loops and strange effects. Johns: "Then we started to experiment with it, and I put a bunch of psychedelic strangeness on it. You have fun. 'Oh, try this! Do that!' It's just very

895 *Ibid.*
896 http://www.guardian.co.uk/music/2012/oct/19/paul-mccartney-speculation-two-new-albums
897 Simon Vozick-Levinson, in *Rolling Stone*, 29/08/2013.
898 *Producing Macca. The Four Studio Wizards on Working with Paul on "New"* in NME, November 2013.

inspiring to be around."[899] The result is a very unique track: besides McCartney's vocals and acoustic guitar, a bed of effects (tape-loops by McCartney and tambora app coming from Johns' iPad) underlines the whole song, which conveys a sense of melancholy and yearning. McCartney also added drums and a great bass part that floats across the songs.

Musicians:

Paul McCartney vocals, acoustic and electric guitar, bass, drums, tape-loops • **Ethan Johns** iPad Tambora app

373 Early Days (Paul McCartney)

Recording: February-March, 2012 and May? 2013 (overdubs) **Location:** Hog Hill Studio, Icklesham and Henson Studios, Los Angeles (overdubs) **Release:** October 2013, *New*

McCartney: "'Early Days' is a song based on my reminiscences of formative times with John before the Beatles, when we were first starting out."

The musical background to those recollections is a simple folk song, with a country feel, in the vein of American popular ballads *à la* Neil Young. The track was recorded at Hog Hill Studio, with McCartney playing acoustic guitar and Ethan Johns on drums and percussion. Paul himself added Bill Black's double-bass and harmonium. The song was later overdubbed with an effective instrumentation, featuring Brian Ray on dulcimer, Rusty Anderson on slide guitar and McCartney on percussion: according to Giles Martin, he miked Paul's trousers to obtain the percussion effect. Many have noted the croaky quality of McCartney's voice, surely left on purpose on the recording: it conveys an emotional feeling to the song and its story.

Ethan Johns convinced Paul to keep his first vocal take on the song: "It's vulnerable. But it's you." "Early Days" is included in *New*. A video has been released in July 2014.

Musicians:

Paul McCartney vocals, acoustic guitar, double-bass, harmonium, knee-percussion • **Ethan Johns** drums, percussion • **Brian Ray** dulcimer • **Rusty Anderson** acoustic or electric guitar • **Abe Laboriel Jr.** backing vocals

374 Turned Out (Paul McCartney)

Recording: February-March, 2012 (basic track and overdubs part 1) and May? 2013 (overdubs part 2) **Location:** Abbey Road Studios, London, Hog Hill Studio, Icklesham (overdubs part 1) and Henson Studios, Los Angeles (overdubs part 2) **Release:** October 2013, *New* (Deluxe Edition)

The third composition worked during the sessions with Johns was "Turned Out", a catchy pop tune. To lay down the track, this time it was McCartney's turn on drums: to record the basic track, he probably sat on his kit with Johns playing acoustic guitar.

---

899   http://www.rollingstone.com/music/news/paul-mccartney-producer-previews-revelatory-new-album-20130814#ixzz2c6yN0j6V

Later, the song was enriched with more guitars by Ray and Anderson – who probably added some nice slide-guitar work, in perfect Harrison style – and Laboriel on drums and backing vocals. A calm bridge comes in, with piano and tubular bells by McCartney himself. "Turned out" is included as a bonus-track in the *New* Deluxe Edition.

Musicians:

Paul McCartney vocals, acoustic guitar, bass, drums, keyboards, synthesizer, tubular bells, percussion, piano (?) • **Ethan Johns** acoustic guitar • **Brian Ray** electric guitar • **Rusty Anderson** electric guitar • **Abe Laboriel Jr.** backing vocals, drums

The album *Kisses on the Bottom* was released in February. The record was well-acclaimed by the majority of critics and it met with good success, reaching #5 in the US charts.

Rolling Stone wrote a three-star review: "McCartney is better transforming influences than mirroring them. But it's fun, and touching, to hear him crooning his way through the great American songbook." Patrick Humpries (*BBC*) described it as "a pleasurable set of less-than-common covers". Other reviewers were less thrilled: *The Independent* said it was "a misstep. The Achilles' Heel is McCartney's delivery, with a wheedling edge betraying the strain of singing in too a register", and *The Guardian* noted that McCartney's vocal were "a little papery".

The record got a Grammy Award in 2013 in the Best Traditional Pop Vocal Album category. To promote it, McCartney held a special concert at Capitol Studios aired on February 14th. Paul was accompanied by the cast of all–star musicians who had joined him on the record, performing nearly the whole album. This performance would be included on the iTunes release *Kisses on the Bottom – Complete Kisses* and in the DVD *Live Kisses*, which in 2014 won two Grammy Award in the Best Surround Sound Album and Best Music Film categories.

Between March and May, McCartney resumed his *On The Run Tour*, with 13 concerts across Europe (Switzerland, Holland and Belgium, plus a special venue in London for the "Teenage Cancer Trust") and South America (Uruguay Paraguay, Colombia, Brazil and Mexico).

In May, the album *RAM* was released in a remastered edition, featuring a Deluxe version: a box full of photos, interviews and outtakes from the sessions. It re-entered the US charts at #24 and was nominated for two Grammy Award, in the Best Historical Album and Best Boxed or Special Limited Edition Package categories.

In November, McCartney played other 5 concerts in the US and Canada for the final leg of the tour. Live gigs would not stop in 2013, with a new tour called *Out There!* Paul included in the set list five Beatles' songs never played before: "Being for the Benefit of Mr.Kite!", "Eight Days a Week", "Your Mother Should Know", "All Together Now" and "Lovely Rita".

Another noteworthy collaboration for McCartney was with young producer Mark Ronson. As Paul puts it, "he DJed at mine and Nancy's wedding, and kept us dancing till 3am. So I knew I liked his taste."[900] Ronson recalled that McCartney phoned him a couple of months after the wedding, meaning that their first meeting (at Hog Hill Studio) probably happened in early 2012, with work resuming in July and during 2013. The sessions produced three tracks, including a new version of "Heart of the Country". Ronson: "I don't know if (our stuff) is revolutionary, but they're brilliant songs. I just tried to give him a sound he was looking for."[901]

375 New (Paul McCartney)

Recording: January? and July (overdubs part 1), 2012, March? (overdubs part 2) and May? (overdubs part 3), 2013 **Location:** Hog Hill Studio, Icklesham, Avatar Studios (overdubs part 1), New York, AIR Studios (overdubs part 2), London, and Henson Studios (overdubs part 3), Los Angeles **Release:** August 2013, single (from *New*)

Working with Ronson pushed Paul to present some very commercial tracks, trying to take advantage of the producer's sound. One of them was called "New". McCartney: "It's catchy, it's summery... It's basically a love song, but it says, 'Don't look at me, 'cause I haven't got any answers, I don't know how it happens, but it's good!'"

McCartney: "It was late night and I was at home in London, playing my dad's old piano... I just came up with 'New'. It kind of wrote itself."[902]

Ronson was excited when he heard the song: "It was just such an instant classic. I said, 'I would love to work on that song with you!' And that's how it started... It was a masterclass in learning how to put together a f---ing incredible song – just watching his mind work."[903]

McCartney recalled: "We had a lot of fun together. What he brought to the table? Expertise, energy, enthusiasm." They came up with "New", an energetic song driven by harpsichord and with a very upbeat mood. The arrangement features hand-claps, a horn section (probably added at AIR Studios in London) and powerful guitars.

A coda with Paul and the band's vocals backed by horns – an almost acappella caroling with a Baroque feel – ends the song on a light note. "New" stands out as pure McCartney pop. Filled with little hooks and catchy choruses, it's a short track (2:56) with Paul playing the majority of instruments. The whole track seems to be a sort of McCartney's self-tribute; the melody hints at songs like "Got to Get You Into My Life", "A Love For You" and "Too Much Rain". If this *pastiche* is intentional or due instead to lack of inspiration, we can't know...

"New" – the title-track of the album – was released as a digital single in August, 2013 and has been played live at the iHeart Radio Music Festival on September 22nd, 2013 and during the *Out There!* Tour 2013 (Japanese leg) and 2014.

[900] *Producing Macca. The Four Studio Wizards on Working with Paul on "New"* in NME, November 2013.

[901] *Mark Ronson and Paul McCartney Collaborates on Three Songs*, in *Billboard*, 22/03/2103.

[902] *The Living Room Tour. Paul McCartney Q&A with Bang & Olufsen*, 15/10/2013.

[903] Brenna Ehrlich, *Mark Ronson Almost Missed a Career-Changing Phone Call From Paul McCartney. Ronson Lends His Producing Talents to Tracks "New" and "Alligator" Off of McCartney's Upcoming Record*, in www.mtv.com, 30/08/2013.

Musicians:

Paul McCartney vocals, backing vocals, piano, harpsichord, Mellotron, Wurlitzer electric piano, bass, conga, maracas, bouzuki with pencils • **Rusty Anderson** backing vocals, electric guitar, bouzuki with pencils • **Brian Ray** backing vocals, electric guitar • **Abe Laboriel Jr.** drums, backing vocals • **Wix** backing vocals • **Steve Sidwell** trumpet • **Jamie Talbot** tenor saxophone • **Dave Bishop** baritone saxophone

376 Alligator (Paul McCartney)

Recording: January? and July (overdubs part 1), 2012; March? (overdubs part 2) and May? (overdubs part 3), 2013 **Location:** Hog Hill Studio, Icklesham, Avatar Studios (overdubs part 1), New York, AIR Studios (overdubs part 2), London, and Henson Studios (overdubs part 3), Los Angeles **Release:** August 2013, single (from *New*)

The second song produced by Mark Ronson was another special recording: "Alligator" was taped relying on the original four-track recorder that was used on the *McCartney* album.

Ronson called the song "brooding": "That was one where we experimented a lot" – Ronson explained – "Because his music is just so all around us now, we forget that Paul, with The Beatles and solo, was always on the cutting edge of technology. So it makes sense that he would want to try out all these new pieces of equipment. We used a TC Helicon for the vocals, which is what Kanye uses a lot on his stuff, so there's some really interesting things going on with the vocals in the bridges of that song."[904]

According to McCartney, "Alligator" is the oldest song written for the album. It came out one day, when Paul found himself with a couple of free hours, waiting to pick up Beatrice from school: "On that particular day, I was trying to find a chord I didn't know. I was just messing around with my guitar and…" [905] The song starts with Paul mumbling 'Okay' and with the sound of his small portable recording device, probably containing the original demo.

Like a child, McCartney throws his toys all over the floor: he plays glockenspiel and even a "play-me-a-song" book, both contributing to the sinister riff. Some stinging guitar licks enrich the song, giving it its marshy atmosphere. Easily the best track on *New*.

"Alligator" has been played during soundchecks in Tokyo on November 19th and 21st, 2013.

Musicians:

Paul McCartney vocals, backing vocals, acoustic guitar, bass, glockenspiel, electric guitar, synthesizer, celeste, percussion, "play-me-a-song" book • **Rusty Anderson** electric guitar • **Brian Ray** acoustic or electric guitar • **Wix** keyboards • **Abe Laboriel Jr** drums

The last producer was Giles Martin: "I was first approached last December (2012 – author's note). We did this video game called *Destiny*, by the guy who made *Halo* and after that he phoned me up and said, 'Shall we try and do other some tracks?' I just said, 'Let's do stuff but

[904] *Producing Macca. The Four Studio Wizards on Working with Paul on "New"* in NME, November 2013.
[905] *The Living Room Tour. Paul McCartney Q&A with Bang & Olufsen*, 15/10/2013.

let's do it in a way where we work really quickly and if we don't like something we'll just redo it, as opposed to spending hours and hours remixing and re-recording stuff."[906]

The music for the *Destiny* video game, titled *Music of the Spheres* – composed by McCartney, Marty O'Donnell and Michael Salvatori (see **2010**) – was recorded at Abbey Road during a four day session (November 20th-23rd), with the London boys choir LIBERA and a big orchestra, with Giles Martin producing.

A symphonic and choral suite in eight movements: "Path", "Union", "Ruin", "Tribulation", "Rose", "Ectasy", "Prison" and "Hope", the latter also being the title of the theme song specifically written by Paul.

Attracted by the idea to contribute a song to the project, McCartney came up with a big ballad dealing with the theme of hope: reportedly, the bridge section was taken from the unreleased song "Kiss Me Now" (see **1984**). Probably he taped an intial track for the song at Hog Hill Studio around May.

According to Marty O'Donnell[907], the first session for the song took place on September 20th, at Avatar Studios in New York, with McCartney on piano and acoustic guitar, accompanied by his touring band and Toby Pitman on programming and additional keyboard. The last touch was a bombastic string arrangement, with a 120-piece orchestra – conducted by Ben Foster – added in Abbey Road during the aforementioned dates in late November.

The song appears on the end credits of the videogame and is planned for release as a single. The sessions with Martin would go on throughout 2013, producing seven tracks later released on *New*. Two more titles, "Demons Dance" and "Hell to Pay" were also recorded.

---

[906] *Producing Macca. The Four Studio Wizards on Working with Paul on 'New'* in NME, November 2013.
[907] Interview courtesy of Marty O'Donnell, 11/09/2014.

2013

377 On My Way to Work (Paul McCartney)

Recording: March, May? (overdubs part 1), July? (overdubs part 2) and ? (overdubs part 3), 2013
Location: AIR Studios, Henson Studios (overdubs part 1), Los Angeles, Abbey Road Studios (overdubs part 2), London and Hog Hill Studio (overdubs part 3), Icklesham **Release:** October 2013, *New*

"On My Way to Work" brings up personal memories from Paul's childhood. McCartney: "That's all remembrances from Liverpool. The bus, top deck, me going to work… The specific work I was thinking of was my first job, as a second man on a lorry. The second man helps the driver unload when you get to the destination; the driver is the first man. He was very nice, because I was always knackered, and he would let me sleep. I would help load up the lorry, then get in and just sleep until we got half an hour from the destination, when he'd wake me up: 'Oi, look lively!' I was also a coil winder in a factory. But there was always the bus involved to get there. Big green buses, always the upper deck, for a ciggie, getting to work, clocking on…"[908] The title came from a picture in a catalogue by British artist Damien Hirst called 'On My Way to Work'.[909] McCartney went for a simple arrangement: he played acoustic, accompanied by his group on guitars. Then McCartney overdubbed piano, drums, bass and the cigar box guitar he played during the *12.12.12* concert in New York. A 11-piece orchestra was engaged to add strings during the instrumental break, which has an Oriental feel to it. The song has been played during soundchecks in Japan in 2013 and during the *Out There! Tour* in 2014.

Musicians:

Paul McCartney vocals, acoustic guitar, ciguitar, bass, piano, drums • **Rusty Anderson** electric guitar • **Brian Ray** acoustic or electric guitar • **Wix** acoustic guitar, piano, accordion • **Abe Laboriel Jr** drums • **Cathy Thompson, Laura Melhuish, Patrick Kiernan, Nina Foster** violin • **Peter Lale, Rachel Robson** viola • **Caroline Dale, Katherine Jenkinson, Chris Worsey** cello • **Richard Pryce, Steve McManus** bass

378 Everybody Out There (Paul McCartney)

Recording: March, May? (overdubs part 1), July? (overdubs part 2) and ? (overdubs part 3), 2013
Location: AIR Studios, Henson Studios (overdubs part 1), Los Angeles, Abbey Road Studios (overdubs part 2), London and Hog Hill Studio (overdubs part 3), Icklesham **Release:** October 2013, *New*

Giles Martin: "When we did 'Everybody Out There', we'd basically done the whole song in six hours, from start to finish. And Paul looked at me at the end and went, 'Wow, that was like

---

[908] Miranda Sawyer, *Paul McCartney at 71: Still Here, There and Everywhere*, The Observer, 13/10/2013, http://www.theguardian.com/music/2013/oct/13/paul-mccartney-new-liverpool-nancy?CMP=twt_fd. Lennon (1971): "His dad told him to get a job, he fucking dropped the group and started working on the fucking lorries. So I told him on the phone 'Either come or you're out.'"
[909] *Paul McCartney: World Café Interview*, 19/10/2013.

Beatles pace!"[910] This anthem-like tune was tapedd with Paul on bass, Anderson and Ray on guitars and Laboriel on drums. An orchestra was added at Abbey Road and the whole McCartney family contribute to the chorus. It was played during the *Out There!* Tour 2013/14.

Musicians:

Paul McCartney vocals, acoustic guitar, bass, piano electric guitar (?), Mellotron • **Rusty Anderson** electric guitar • **Brian Ray** acoustic or electric guitar • **Abe Laboriel Jr** drums • **Giles Martin** foot stamp • **Cathy Thompson, Laura Melhuish, Patrick Kiernan, Nina Foster** violin • **Peter Lale, Rachel Robson** viola • **Caroline Dale, Katherine Jenkinson, Chris Worsey** cello • **Richard Pryce, Steve McManus** bass • **Eliza Marshall, Anna Noakes** alto flute

379 I Can Bet (Paul McCartney)

Recording: March, April? (overdubs part 1) and May? (overdubs part 2), 2013 **Location:** AIR Studios, London, Hog Hill Studio (overdubs part 1), Icklesham and Henson Studios (overdubs part 2), Los Angeles **Release:** October 2013, *New*

Rumors say that at a certain point during 2012, McCartney suffered from some serious throat problems and a surgical operation was needed: that would be the reason behind the cancellation of two shows planned in June in Denmark. It has also been rumored that Paul was not satisfied with his vocal parts on the album and he had to re-record them. One thing is sure hearing many songs on *New*: vocals are heavily filtered and "I Can Bet" is no exception.

This pop song was laid down almost entirely by McCartney, who played acoustic guitar, bass, drums and percussion, helped by Anderson on electric guitar and Wix on Hammond organ. Then – probably at Hog Hill Studio – he added some vintage instruments, such as the Wurlitzer electric piano and a Moog solo. The final touch was the addition of some tape loops, that can be heard near the end, where also some piano notes come in.

Musicians:

Paul McCartney vocals, acoustic guitar, bass, Wurlitzer electric piano, Moog, drums, percussion, piano (?) tape loops • **Rusty Anderson** electric guitar • **Wix** Hammond organ • **Toby Pitman** programming

380 Get Me Out of Here (Paul McCartney)

Recording: March and May? (overdubs), 2013 **Location:** AIR Studios, London and Henson Studios (overdubs), Los Angeles **Release:** October 2013, *New* (Deluxe Edition)

"Get Me Out of Here" (used as a bonus on the *New* Deluxe Edition) is a tribute to early acoustic blues numbers. The recording has a vintage atmosphere, with McCartney playing acoustic guitar and a skiffle-era washboard (with thimbles on his fingers, according to the credits). The rest of the instrumentation is a combination of ethnic instruments and various objects: Paul used a ngoni (an African string instrument), while Laboriel contributed djembe drum (a rope-tuned skin-covered African drum), Ray congas and Anderson a water bottle.

---

[910] *Producing Macca. The Four Studio Wizards on Working with Paul on "New"* in NME, November 2013.

Musicians:

Paul McCartney vocals, acoustic guitar, ngoni, washboard and thimbles • **Rusty Anderson** water bottle • **Brian Ray** congas, backing vocals • **Abe Laboriel Jr** djembe drum, bass drum, backing vocals

381 Looking at Her (Paul McCartney)

Recording: April? and May? (overdubs) 2013 **Location:** Hog Hill Studios, Icklesham and Henson Studios (overdubs), Los Angeles **Release:** October 2013, *New*

It was probably at Hog Hill Studio that Martin recorded "Looking at Her" a nice ballad with a slight exotic flavor on his iPhone.[911] Later at Henson, McCartney chose a modern arrangement, putting some drum programming on the background: the production style has a Eighties vibe. Paul played guitar, bass, and drums, probably leaving the sweet guitar solo to Anderson. McCartney finished the track, overdubbing noises with Moog and Mellotron.

Musicians:

Paul McCartney vocals, bass, electric guitar, Mellotron, Moog, drums, percussion • **Rusty Anderson** electric guitar • **Toby Pitman** programming, keyboards

382 Appreciate (Paul McCartney)

Recording: May? and ? (overdubs), 2013 **Location:** Henson Studios, Los Angeles and Hog Hill Studios (overdubs), Icklesham **Release:** October 2013, *New*

Searching for modern textures, while overdubbing at Henson Studios in Los Angeles, McCartney came up with 'Appreciate', in the end making it an almost hip hop track.

Martin: "We had all these tape loop sounds that he'd brought in, and guitar loop sounds. And we started chopping it all together into this big collage, and I remember saying to him, 'We should try and make this into a song', and he gave me this look, like, 'You're so boring!'. Then we found this chorus that he'd done previously, over something completely different, and we spliced that together and it all just worked."[912] Some heavy drumming (both McCartney and Laboriel Jr. are credited as drummers) drives the song, with Paul relying on his falsetto register. Anderson played bouzouki and more guitar parts with Ray. McCartney added the fuzz-guitar closing solo on his cigar box guitar: he said it was one of the memorable moments of *New*.

Musicians:

Paul McCartney vocals, ciguitar, keyboards, drums • **Rusty Anderson** electric guitar, bouzouki, backing vocals • **Brian Ray** electric guitar, baritone guitar, backing vocals • **Abe Laboriel Jr** drums, backing vocals • **Toby Pitman** programming

---

[911] *Giles Martin: Meet the Producer.* Interview at the Apple Store in Regent Street, London, October 2013.
[912] *Producing Macca. The Four Studio Wizards on Working with Paul on 'New'* in NME, November 2013.
428

383 Scared (Paul McCartney)

Recording: ? 2013 **Location:** Hog Hill Studio (?), Icklesham **Release:** October 2013, *New*

When asked if he finds it hard to write new songs, McCartney confessed: "Yeah, a bit. Only because I've done so much. You've gotta do something different after having done 5,000 things. How can you be different? I follow clues."[913]

That's probably why only a few tracks on *New* are typical Paul's ballads, considered by many the main course of McCartney's restaurant. And that's probably why one could hear a few too many melodic clichés in "Scared", a somber song placed as a hidden track on *New*. And yet, "Scared" is a remarkable song: a poignant confession of fragility, that McCartney recorded with just vocals and piano, using gloomy chords. Martin: "We tried various arrangements, but to me this had to be just him on his own. Funnily enough, I was talking to Ethan about a thing his dad had said to him, which was 'When the hairs on the back of your neck stand up, you should just step back'. 'Scared' is one of those. It's a great end to the album."[914]

The song's atmosphere is dark: it expresses the uncertainty of McCartney: "I was newly in love with Nancy, and I was finding it a little difficult to say, 'I love you.' Number one, I'm a guy, and that's a *big* excuse, but it is a bit true to form… That song is about she and I, and the middle eight is about when we met. And we did exactly as I say in the song, we welled up."[915]

Musicians:

Paul McCartney vocals, piano, double-bass (?), keyboards

New was released in October 14th. It reached #3 both in the UK and US charts. Reviews were particularly favourable. *Rolling Stone* gave it a four-star rating: "*New* feels energized and full of joyous rock and roll invention. More than a sentimental journey, it's an album that wants to be part of the 21-st century pop dialogue." *The Daily Telegraph* was enthusiastic: "In calling his 16th solo album *New*, Paul McCartney is celebrating his fresh attitude rather than a change of musical direction. These 12 songs are vintage Macca. This album proves his talent is timeless."

[913] *Ibid.*

[914] *Ibid.*

[915] Miranda Sawyer, *Paul McCartney at 71: Still Here, There and Everywhere*, *The Observer*, 13/10/2013.

BIOGRAPHIES

Carlos Alomar: Puerto Rican guitarist and composer, best know for his work with David Bowie. He appears on album like *Young Americans* (1975), *Station to Station* (1976) and *Heroes* (1977).

Kevin Armstrong: English guitarist, producer and songwriter. Kevin joined Prefab Sprout for the *Steve McQueen* album and tour. This led on to a ten year working relationship with Bowie (*Absolute Beginners*, *Tin Machine*). In 2007 he toured with Sinéad O'Connor.

Pete Beachill: English trombone player, composer and arranger. As a sessions musician, he has worked with Joni Mitchell, Peter Gabriel, Pink Floyd, Grace Jones, Eric Clapton, Gloria Gaynor, Diana Ross, Dusty Springfield, Swing Out Sister, Pete Townsend, Style Council, Herbie Hancock and Wayne Shorter. He has arranged brass for *Jesus Christ Superstar* for Sir Andrew Lloyd Webber.

Stephanie Bennet: American harpist, composer, arranger and vocalist. Bennett plays harp on soundtracks for movies and television.

Mark Berry: American sound engineer and producer. After graduating from IAR, Mark arrived at AIR Studios, owned by Sir George Martin. One of his first assignements was Carly Simon's *No Secrets* album. At AIR, Mark worked with engineers/producers such as Bill Price, Geoff Emerick, Chris Thomas, Jeff Lynne and Tony Visconti. In the 70's, he began freelancing around New York. In the 80's he moved into the area of 7" radio and 12" mixing and re-mixing (David Bowie, Duran Duran, Yes, Billy Idol).

Robin Black: English engineer and producer. He worked with Jethro Tull (*Aqualung*, *Thick as a Brick*), Black Sabbath and Alice Cooper.

Brian Blood: He has worked as a professional recorder player on film, TV, radio, recordings and concerts with the Dolmetsch Consort. Dr. Blood is a governor of the Dolmetsch Foundation Inc.

Carlos Bonell: classical guitarist. Born in London of Spanish parents, he started to play at the age of five. After Carlos' New York début in 1978, The *New York Times* described him as an artist of 'superb poetic gifts'. His album *Magical Mystery Guitar Tour* (2012) is dedicated to the music of The Beatles in his own arrangements for solo guitar. It went to n.1 on the iTunes classical charts in May 2012.

John Bradbury: British violinist. He was Leader of the Brighton Philharmonic Orchestra and of the BBC Concert Orchestra. As a free-lance, his work included leading for all the James Bond movie sound tracks since 1998. He has toured for Shirley Bassey, Lesley Garrett, Russell Watson and Andrea Bocelli.

Geoffrey Brand: English conductor and arranger. He made his career as a professional trumpet player with the Royal Philharmonic, Philharmonia and Covent Garden orchestras. He worked with brass and military bands as a BBC Producer (1955-68). He assumed leadership of the Black Dyke Mills Band in 1967.

Adrian Brett: British flute player. He played for a two year period with the Royal Philharmonic Orchestra. In 1974 he was appointed principal flute with the BBC Radio Orchestra. Adrian Brett has played on over 2000 film and TV scores. He can be heard on some James Bond movie tracks and the Pink Panther movies. In 1979 his solo album *Echoes of Gold* was the first solo instrumental album to reach the top 20.

Alan Broadbent: New Zealand pianist, composer and arranger. He has worked with Diana Krall, Natalie Cole. Kirk Silsbee of *The Los Angeles Times* called Broadbent "one of the greatest living jazz pianists".

John Lang Brown: Scottish piper. He played in the Campbeltown Pipe Band.

Ron Carter: American jazz double-bassist. His appearances on over 2,500 albums make him one of the most-recorded bassists in jazz history. He has recorded with Gil Evans, Bill Evans, B.B. King, Dexter Gordon, Wes Montgomery. He was a member of the Miles Davis Quintet (1963-68). He was named Outstanding Bassist of the Decade by the Detroit News, Jazz Bassist of the Year by Downbeat magazine, and Most Valuable Player by the National Academy of Recording Arts and Sciences. In 1993 Ron Carter earned a Grammy award for Best Jazz Instrumental Performance for *A Tribute to Miles* and another Grammy in 1998 for "Call Sheet Blues", from the film *Round Midnight*.

David Clayton: British keyboard player and record producer. He has recorded or played with, among others, Simply Red, Depeche Mode, U2, Bob Marley, Sinéad O'Connor, George Michael, Elton John.

John Clayton: American jazz bassist, composer and conductor. He served as the Artistic Director of Jazz for the Los Angeles Philharmonic from 1999 through 2001. John has written and arranged music for Diana Krall, DeeDee Bridgewater (including her Grammy Award winning CD *Dear Ella*), Natalie Cole, Quincy Jones, George Benson, Dr. John, Gladys Knight, Regina Carter, Queen Latifah and many others.

Tony Clark: sound engineer and producer, was born in London on April 2nd, 1946. He started his career at Abbey Road Studios in 1964 as a tea-boy, and becoming tape operator, mastering operator, assistant engineer and finally reaching Senior Engineer and producer for the studios. As an engineer/producer, he worked on a wide range of musical genres. With The Beatles he worked on the *Abbey Road* album. He was involved in several Sir Paul McCartney's projects (*Thrillington*, *Wild Life*, *Wings at the Speed of Sound*, *Press to Play*, "Give Ireland Back to the Irish"). Throughout his career he worked with many prestigious artists and he calls it "an incredible journey through music": Badfinger ("Come and Get It", written and produced by Paul McCartney), John Lennon ("Cold Turkey", *Live Peace in Toronto*), Sir Cliff Richard, Sky (winners of an Ampex Golden Reel Award), Olivia Newton John, the Shadows, Hurricane Smith, Stevie Wonder, Stan Getz, Art Garfunkel, Fela Kuti, Everly Brothers, Yehudi Menuhin and Stephen Grappelli, Babe Ruth. He also worked on many soundtracks and live albums. In 1977 he won a "NME Award to Music Industry" for Sir Cliff Richard's single "Devil Woman" ("Best Engineered Rock Record"). He collaborated with BRIT School (British Record Industry Trust School for the Performing Arts) - which supported artists like Amy Winehouse, Adele, Kooks - managing the recording studios, radio studios, TV studios and performances theatre. He's a trustee of Hackney Music Development Trust. Hackney Music won two Royal Philharmonic Awards (2004-2008). *The Times* said it's "one of the very few idealistic organizations.... Which advocates the use of music in human development. Genuine Heroes".

Tony Coe: English jazz musician, clarinet ans tenor saxophone player. He was invited to join the Count Basie band and was featured in the bands of Humphrey Lyttleton, John Dankworth, Kenny Clarke/Francy Boland, Stan Tracey and Henry Mancini (playing the tenor saxophone theme in most of the Pink Panther films), working and recording with musicians including Stan Getz, Dizzy Gillespie, Sarah Vaughan.

Jerry Conway: English folk and rock drummer/percussionist. He performed with the backing band for Cat Stevens in the 1970s, Jethro Tull during the 1980s: currently he's a member of Fairport Convention.

Carl Davis: CBE, is an American-born conductor and composer. Davis is a conductor with the London Philharmonic Orchestra, and regularly conducts the Royal Liverpool Philharmonic Orchestra. He has written music for more than 100 television programs, but is best known for creating music to accompany silent films. In the 1970's, Jeremy Isaacs commissioned him The World at War TV Series and the BBC scores for classic serials, including *The Snow Goose*, *Our Mutual Friend* and *The Mayor of Casterbridge*. He has written a number of film scores including *The French Lieutenant's Woman* (1981), for which Davis won the BAFTA Award for Best Film Music.

Chris "Snake" Davis: English sax and flute player. As a sessions musician, he has played with Lisa Stansfield, Ray Charles, Tom Jones, Culture Club, George Michael, Tina Turner, Take That, Cher, Swing Out Sister, Dave Stewart, Paul Young, Pet-Shop Boys, Robert Palmer, Motorhead.

Richard Davis: American jazz bassist. Among his most famous contributions to the albums of others are Eric Dolphy's 1964 Blue Note LP *Out to Lunch!*, Andrew Hill's *Point of Departure* and Van Morrison's *Astral Weeks*, of which critic Greil Marcus wrote, "Richard Davis provided the greatest bass ever heard on a rock album". Downbeat International Critics Poll named him Best Bassist from 1967-74. He has recorded a dozen albums as a leader and 3000 recordings/jingles as a sideman. Some of his performance/recording credits include Bruce Springsteen, Frank Sinatra, Barbra Streisand, Miles Davis. In the field of classical music, he has played under the batons of George Szell, Igor Stravinsky and Leonard Bernstein.

Neil Dorfsman: American producer and sound engineer. He produced albums like Dire Straits' *Brothers in Arms* and *Love Over Gold*, Sting's *Nothing Like the Sun* and recorded Bruce Springsteen's *The River*, Bob Dylan's *Infidels* and Weather Report's *Weather Report*.

Pedro Eustache: a Venezuelan-born flautist-"World-Music" woodwinds-reeds-synthesist-composer. He did a large number of sessions for movies as a flute/woodwinds instrumentalist, playind duduk, reed and flute in Mel Gibson's *The Passion of the Christ*, Spielberg's *Munich*.

Frank Farrell: American recording and mixing engineer. He has worked with The Who, U2, Steve Miller, Dave Matthews Band, Phil Vasser, Beach Boys.

Brent Fischer: American composer, arranger, bandleader, bass guitarist and percussionist. The son of noted composer, arranger, and Clare Fischer. Brent has produced all of his father's albums. *¡Ritmo!*, the first to be released after Dr. Fischer's death, won the 2013 Grammy Award for Best Latin Jazz Album.

Clare Fischer: American keyboardist, composer, arranger, and bandleader. Consistently cited by jazz pianist and composer Herbie Hancock as a major influence ("I wouldn't be me without Clare Fischer"), he was nominated for eleven Grammy Awards during his lifetime, winning for his album, *Clare Fischer & Salsa Picante Present "2+2"* (1981). In the early 1970s, Fischer became a much sought after arranger, providing orchestral 'sweeteners' for artists such as Prince, Michael Jackson, Celine Dion.

Martyn Ford: arranger, conductor and record producer, has worked with some of the World's greatest rock artists including The Rolling Stones, Elton John, Phil Collins, Bryan Ferry, Cliff Richard, The Who, Lou Reed, Bob Marley, Kate Bush, Led Zeppelin, Toto, Harry Nilsson, The Grateful Dead, Johnny Nash, Barclay and with Lord Andrew Lloyd Webber and Sir Tim Rice on the original *Jesus Christ Superstar* album.

Greg Hawkes: American keyboard player, composer and co-founder of The Cars. His signature sounds include the Prophet-5 "touch sync" sound heard on "Let's Go" and "Hello Again".

Gary Herbig: American sax player. He has played on hundreds of movies, TV shows and more than 1,000 records. His albums, *Gary Herbig* and *Friends to Lovers* reached the top ten on the Billboard contemporary jazz charts. He's toured with Tower of Power, the Percy Faith Orchestra and Elvis Presley. He has played on chart toppers such as Olivia Newton John's "Physical" and Donna Summer's "Bad Girl".

Richard Hewson: English producer, arranger, conductor and multi-instrumentalist. As an arranger he worked with The Beatles ("The Long and Winding Road"), James Taylor ("Carolina in My Mind"), Carly Simon, Art Garfunkel, Supertramp, Herbie Hancock. In 1977 he founded the RAH Band.

Steve Holley: English drummer. At age eleven, Steve formed his first group, The Formula. He recorded Elton John's *A Single Man* album. In the Eighties, he worked on many prestigious recordings including Julian Lennon's debut. His new career culminated with a three year stint in the Joe Cocker band.

Gordon Hunt: English oboist. He was principal oboist of the Philharmonia Orchestra. Hunt has held principal positions at the London Philharmonic and the London Chamber Orchestra. He has played as Guest Principal with the Berlin Philharmonic. He appears regularly as soloist with international orchestras.

Laurence Juber: English guitarist and composer. Since Wings, he has established himself as world-renowned guitar virtuoso, composer and arranger. He has released 22 solo albums. *LJ Plays The Beatles*, was voted one of Acoustic Guitar Magazine's all-time Top Ten albums. Juber's solo arrangement of "The Pink Panther Theme" earned him a second Grammy Award after "Rockestra Theme".

David Juritz: British violinist. He is one of the most versatile violinists currently working in the UK, working as guest leader with many of Britain's finest orchestras and leading his own group, the London Tango Quintet. He has directed the Royal Philharmonic as well as many other ensembles.

Brian Kay: is an English radio presenter, conductor and singer. He is well known as the bass in the King's Singers during the group's formative years from 1968 until 1982, and as such is to be heard on many of their 1970s LP recordings. He was also the voice of Papageno in the film *Amadeus*.

Gary Kettel: British percussionist. He became co-principal percussionist of the BBC Symphony Orchestra at the age of 20. Since then has become one of Britain's most sought after percussionists. Gary has worked with artists as Jerry Goldsmith, Henry Mancini, John Williams, Michael Kamen.

James Kippen: Born in London, he is a teacher and tabla player. He teaches ethnomusicology at the University of Toronto.

John Leach: cimbalom player born in London with an English father and Austro-Hungarian mother. He has recorded with the Vienna Philharmonic and most of the Symphony orchestras of Europe.

John Leckie: British sound engineer/producer. He started as an Abbey Road tape-op in 1970, working under Phil Spector on George Harrison's *All Things Must Pass* and John Lennon's *Plastic Ono Band* albums. As an engineer, he worked on Pink Floyd's *Dark Side Of The Moon* and *Wish You Were Here*.

Steve Lyon: English engineer/producer. He has worked with Depeche Mode, The Cure, Suzanne Vega.

Wil Malone: English arranger and producer. He has worked with artists including Black Sabbath, Iron Maiden, Todd Rundgren, The Verve, Massive Attack and Depeche Mode.

Jerry Marotta: American drummer. He has worked with Peter Gabriel, Joan Armatrading, Tears for Fears, Hall and Oates, Suzanne Vega. He now carries his experience into his own career as a producer.

Dave Mattacks: English drummer. Best known for his work with Fairport Convention, Mattacks has also worked with artists like Chris Rea, Jethro Tull, Brian Eno, Cat Stevens, Gary Brooker, Spyro Gyra.

Dave Matthews: American keyboardist, pianist, and arranger. He is the leader of the Manhattan Jazz Quintet. In 1970, he began working as both an arranger and bandleader for James Brown. David was the musical director for the original Simon and Garfunkel Reunion Concert in Central Park. He also arranged Julian Lennon's *Valotte*, Frank Sinatra, *L.A. Is My Lady* and Billy Joel's *An Innocent Man*.

Bazil Meade: Born in Montserrat, he is the founder and principal of the London Community Gospel Choir. Under his direction and tuition some of the finest gospel and R'n'B singers have found successful careers.

Richard Niles: American composer, producer, songwriter, arranger, conductor, and musical director. He was born in a Holywood family. His father, Tony Romano, worked with Cole Porter.

Leo Nocentelli: Born in New Orleans, Louisiana is one of the founding members of the New Orleans funk band, The Meters. Lead guitarist, composer, songwriter and musical originator of the syncopated funk-style that won international acclaim for him and the Meters. He recorded with artists like Stevie Wonder, The Temptations, Dr.John, Sting, Peter Gabriel, Etta James, Robbie Robertson.

Dave O'Donnell: American producer, mixer and engineer. He has recorded and mixed with many top artists, including James Taylor, Eric Clapton, BeeGees, Rod Stewart, Joss Stone, Morrissey and Ray Charles. Recordings Dave has worked on have been nominated for 18 Grammys and won 9 times.

Alan O'Duffy: Irish producer, sound engineer/mixer. He engineered album like *Jesus Christ Superstar* (Lloyd Webber-Tim Rice), *Blind Faith* (Eric Clapton-Steve Winwood), *Let It Bleed* (Rolling Stones).

Lance Phillips: English lawyer. Chief Recording Engineer at AIR Studios (1987-93). After twelve years in the music industry he qualifyied as a solicitor, working across music, media and interactive departments.

David Pogson: British cornet player. He has been for over 20 years a member of Black Dyke Mills Band.

George Porter jr.: American musician best known as the bassist and singer of The Meters. Along with Art Neville, Porter formed the group in the mid 1960s and came to be recognized as one of the progenitors of funk. He has been performing and recording with wide range of artists including Dr. John, Robbie Robertson, Willy DeVille, Patti Labelle, David Byrne.

Maurizio Ravalico: Italian percussionist. Between 1989 and 1991 he went through an intensive period of study of Congas and Afro Cuban Percussion. He was the percussionist of Jamiroquai and of the James Taylor Quartet (1994-98). With drummer Davide Giovannini he co-founded the duo Afroshock.

David Rhodes: English guitarist. He has played with Joan Armatrading, T-Bone Burnett. He is most well known for his longtime collaboration with Peter Gabriel (*Peter Gabriel III, Peter Gabriel IV, So, Us*).

Denny Seiwell: American drummer and percussionist. He worked on records by Art Garfunkel, James Brown, Astrud Gilberto, Janis Joplin's posthumus *Farewell Song* album, Billy Joel's *Cold Spring Harbor*. Other Highlights of his career include work with Joe Cocker, Donovan, and The Who with the London Symphony Orchestra in their ground breaking version of the Rock Opera *Tommy*.

Kenneth Sillito: British violinist, he is internationally recognised as one of Britain's most distinguished musicians. He is renowned as a chamber musician. In 1967 he founded the Gabrieli String Quartet.

Marvin Stamm: American trumpet player, he was in the Thad Jones and Mel Lewis Orchestra (1966-1972, and with Benny Goodman (1974-75). In the 1970s he began a career as a session musician. He has recorded with the Average White Band, Bill Evans, Quincy Jones, Freddie Hubbard and George Benson.

Mike Stavrou: Australian recording and sound balance engineer. He has worked with Queen, Stevie Wonder, Elton John, America, Cat Stevens, David Bowie, Diana Ross, Jeff Beck and John Williams. He won a Grammy in the "Best Instrumental of the Year" category for "The Spy Who Loved Me".

Stan Sulzmann: English jazz saxophonist and composer, Sulzmann's career stretches back to the 60's, when he played with Graham Collier, John Taylor, Kenny Wheeler, Gordon Beck, as well as leading many groups of his own. Since then Stan has been at the forefront of European contemporary jazz: his talents have been sought by a host of discerning musicians, including Gil Evans and Mike Gibbs.

Tim Summerhayes: English sound engineer/producer. He began his career at Mickie Most's RAK Studios, becoming an engineer for the studios and for the RAK mobile truck, one of the first mobiles in the UK. Tim became an expert in live sound recording. Among his credits: Police, Metallica, Pavarotti.

Joby Talbot: British composer and arranger. Talbot has composed widely for major orchestras, soloists and vocal groups (the madrigal *The Wishing Tree* for The King's Singers; *Sneaker Wave* for the BBC National Orchestra of Wales; and an arrangement of Purcell's *Chacony* in G Minor for the BBC Symphony Orchestra). Talbot scored silent films and wrote the themes for British comedy series.

Michael Thompson: British horn player. Thompson was appointed Principal Horn with the BBC Scottish Symphony Orchestra aged just 18 years. By the age of 21 he was offered positions as Principal Horn with both the Philharmonia and Royal Philharmonic Orchestras. He is a member of the London Sinfonietta.

Fiachra Trench: Irish arranger, composer and musician. He has worked with artists like Van Morrison, Elvis Costello, Art Garfunkel, Sinéad O'Connor and The Chieftains. He has composed, orchestrated and directed the scores to the feature films *Bogwoman*, *Moondance*, *A Love Divided* and the *Boys from County Clare*. He has composed the music for commercials (Woolwich, American Express and Renault).

Mike Vickers: British arranger and musician who came to prominence as guitarist, flautist and saxophonist with the 1960s band, Manfred Mann. One of his most familiar TV compositions is "Jet Set," the theme music first for the NBC game show, *Jackpot* in 1974-75.

Graham Ward: American drummer, composer and producer. He has worked with Tom Jones, Jimmy Page, Donna Summer, Mark Knopfler, Ray Charles, Dionne Warwick, Bee Gees, Ben E. King or classical artists as José Carreras, Placido Domingo, Kiri Te Kanawa. He has performed with the Royal Philharmonic Orchestra, London Symphony Orchestra, the London Philharmonia and the Royal Philharmonic Orchestra.

Stephen Wick: tuba player, conductor, arranger and teacher. He's director of Denis Wick Products, firm of mouthpiece and mute makers. He has played for Pink Floyd, Frank Zappa, Led Zeppelin, Roger Waters, all the great London orchestras and on soundtracks like *Star Wars*, *Alien*, *James Bond* and *Pink Panther*.

Ernie Winfrey: American sound engineer. He worked in Nashville with some of the best-known musicians in the world: Paul Simon, Dolly Parton, Willie Nelson, Wlson Pickett, Otis Blackwell, Joan Baez.

Bill Wolfer: American keyboard player. He worked on Michael Jackson's *Thriller*. He has been responsible for the intro on "Billie Jean".

SONG BY SONG INDEX